THE LONDON FRIENDS' MEETINGS.

*For Olive Yarrow
whose book this is*

with many thanks

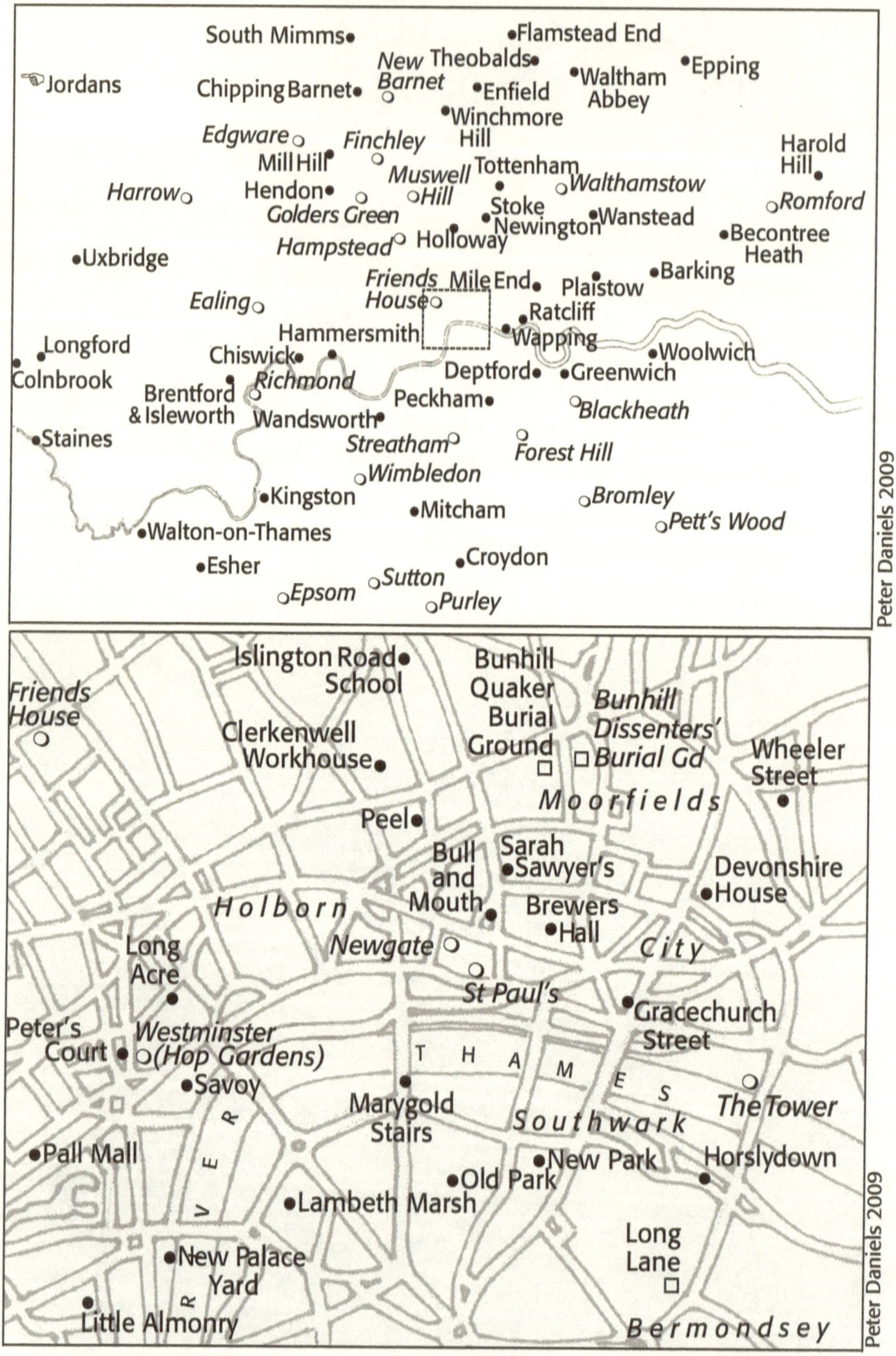

Modern London, with approximate locations of historic meetings
• Quaker meetings   □ Burial grounds   ○ Modern meetings or non-Quaker sites

THE LONDON FRIENDS' MEETINGS:

SHOWING THE RISE OF

THE SOCIETY OF FRIENDS

IN LONDON;

ITS PROGRESS, AND THE DEVELOPMENT OF ITS DISCIPLINE;

WITH ACCOUNTS OF THE VARIOUS

Meeting-Houses and Burial-Grounds,

THEIR HISTORY AND GENERAL ASSOCIATIONS.

Compiled from Original Records and other Sources,

BY

WILLIAM BECK AND T. FREDERICK BALL.

LONDON:
F. BOWYER KITTO, 5, BISHOPSGATE STREET WITHOUT.
1869.

Facsimile reprint, with a new introduction by
Simon Dixon & Peter Daniels; illustrations; and index
London: Pronoun Press, 2009

Pronoun Press is an imprint of Peter Daniels Publisher Services
35 Benthal Road, London N16 7AR, UK

www.pronounpress.co.uk

The London Friends' Meetings by William Beck and T. Frederick Ball was first published by F. Bowyer Kitto, 1869.
This edition © Pronoun Press 2009

ISBN
978-0-9556183-4-5 (hardback)
978-0-9556183-5-2 (paperback)

Introduction copyright © Simon Dixon and Peter Daniels 2009
Index copyright © Peter Daniels 2009

The moral rights of the authors are asserted in accordance with the Copyright, Designs and Patents Act 1988. All rights reserved. No part of this book may be reproduced or utilised, in any form or by any means, electronic or mechanical, without permission in writing. For permissions please contact the publisher. Reviewers may quote brief passages.

For full acknowledgement of illustrations, see pp.xxxiii–xxxvi.

Illustrations copyright © Library of the Religious Society of Friends, London; © City of London, London Metropolitan Archives; © City of London, Guildhall Library; © Christ's Hospital; © Hackney Archives Department; © Peter Daniels

CONTENTS.

Preface to the original edition	ix
Introduction by Simon Dixon and Peter Daniels	xii
Illustrations	...xxxiii

Original text of *The London Friends' Meetings*:

CHAPTER I.
INTRODUCTORY.

	PAGE
Introductory Remarks	1

CHAPTER II.
LONDON.

London in the Days of Cromwell	3

CHAPTER III.
STATE OF RELIGIOUS PARTIES.

Sketch of the State of Religious Parties in London at the time of the Rise of "Friends" there in 1684 [sic]	8

CHAPTER IV.
NOTES ON THE HISTORY OF FRIENDS IN LONDON 1654—1666,

Including an account of Meetings held in Private Houses previous to the Establishment of the six London Monthly Meetings ...	18

CHAPTER V.
ORIGIN OF THE DISCIPLINE.

Sketch of the Origin of the Discipline up to the Establishment of the Six-Weeks Meeting, including some Notes on the Yearly Meeting	41

CHAPTER VI.

PENAL LAWS.

General Sketch of the Penal Laws which affected Friends' Meetings ... 60

CHAPTER VII.

LONDON AND MIDDLESEX QUARTERLY MEETING.

The Quarterly Meeting—Care of the Churches—Church Arrangements—Appeals—Miscellaneous ... 69

CHAPTER VIII.

THE TWO-WEEKS MEETING—THE SIX-WEEKS MEETING—AND MEETING OF TWELVE.

The Two-Weeks Meeting—Comparative Tables of Marriages—The Six-Weeks Meeting—George Fox's Papers—The Meeting of Twelve—Care of the Churches—Delinquency—Table of Disownments—Meetings for Worship and Discipline—Friends in the Ministry, and Care of their Horses—Marriages—Care of the Poor, &c.—Education—Miscellaneous ... 85

CHAPTER IX.

GRACECHURCH STREET MONTHLY MEETING.

Bull and Mouth, or City, or London Meeting—Gracechurch Street, or White Hart Court—Historical Associations—Funerals connected with White Hart Court—The Second Stoke Newington Meeting—Appendix: William Dewsbery's last Sermon—Destruction of Gracechurch Street Meeting-house—Closing Minute of Gracechurch Street Monthly Meeting ... 134

CHAPTER X.

DEVONSHIRE HOUSE MONTHLY MEETING.

Wheeler Street—Devonshire House—Boundaries of the Monthly Meetings — Numerical Condition — Persecutions — George Whitehead and other Worthies—Meetings for Worship—Meetings for Discipline—Marriages—Care of the Poor—Finance — Removals — The Quarterly Monthly Meeting — Religious and Moral Condition—Appendix: Testimonies of Denial—A Paper of Condemnation ... 162

CHAPTER XI.

PEEL MONTHLY MEETING.

The Peel Meeting-house—Sarah Sawyer's Meeting-house—Boundaries—Peel Worthies—Size of Peel Meeting—Meetings for

Worship — Times of holding Meetings — The Monthly Meeting—Care of the Poor—Delinquency—The Library, &c. —Funerals—History of the Monthly Meeting—The First Stoke Newington Meeting 192

CHAPTER XII.

SOUTHWARK MONTHLY MEETING.

Southwark—Horslydown—The Old Park Meeting-house—New Park Meeting-house—Long Lane, Bermondsey—Deptford—Woolwich — Peckham — Population, &c. of the Monthly Meetings—Meetings for Worship—Meetings for Discipline—Troublesome Characters—Marriages—Delinquency—Prisoners—Poor—Miscellaneous—Appendix: Report by the Surveyor to the Six-Weeks Meeting—Peter the Great and Friends ... 214

CHAPTER XIII.

WESTMINSTER MONTHLY MEETING.

Little Almonry—Peter's Court, or Hemming's Row—Savoy—Long Acre — Meeting Arrangements — Boundaries — Numbers—Ministers—Sufferings—Discipline—Poor—Library—Hammersmith—Holloway—Appendix: Emperor of Russia's Visit ... 240

CHAPTER XIV.

RATCLIFF MONTHLY MEETING.

The Meeting at Captain Brock's House—Ratcliff Meeting-house—Wapping — The Ratcliff Burial-ground — Ratcliff Monthly Meeting 266

CHAPTER XV.

BARKING MONTHLY MEETING.

Barking—Wanstead—Plaistow—Harold's Hill, or Harold's Wood —The Monthly Meeting 274

CHAPTER XVI.

LONGFORD MONTHLY MEETING.

Longford — Colnbrook — Staines — Uxbridge — Brentford — The Monthly Meeting and the Discipline — General Monthly Meeting—Appointed Meetings—Care of the Young, &c.—Sufferings—Marriages—Care of the Poor—Ministers 282

CHAPTER XVII.

TOTTENHAM MONTHLY MEETING.

Waltham Abbey—Epping—Flamstead End—Chipping Barnet—South Mimms—Kit's End—Winchmore Hill—Enfield—Tottenham—General Survey—Meetings for Discipline ... 295

CHAPTER XVIII.

HENDON MONTHLY MEETING.

Hendon—Mill Hill 308

CHAPTER XIX.

KINGSTON MONTHLY MEETING.

Kingston—Esher—Kingston Monthly Meeting—Wandsworth—Croydon—Croydon Monthly Meeting—Appendix 311

CHAPTER XX.

BURIAL GROUNDS.

Bunhill Fields and Whitechapel Burial-Grounds 329

CHAPTER XXI.

MORNING MEETING OF MINISTERS AND ELDERS.

Records—Report—Extracts from Minutes 336

CHAPTER XXII.

WOMEN'S MEETINGS.

Including their Quarterly, Monthly, and Two-Weeks Meetings, as also the Box Meeting for the Care of the Poor 343

CHAPTER XXIII.

JORDANS MEETING.

Old Associations—The Annual Gathering—Appendix 355

CHAPTER XXIV.

SCHOOLS, ETC. IN THE QUARTERLY MEETING.

Clerkenwell Workhouse—Plaistow Home for Ancient Friends—Islington Road School—Croydon School 360

General Appendix 381

General Observations 392

Bibliography (2009 edition) 397

Index (2009 edition) 419

PREFACE.

This work had its origin in a Lecture given at the Friends' Institute, London, some years since (in 1856)[*] by W. Beck, entitled "The London Friends' Meeting-houses and their Associations." Since then much time has been spent in consulting the records and papers of the various London Meetings, to which free access has in all cases been kindly permitted.

The former part of the work is the original Lecture, but rewritten and greatly expanded by its Author; the other portion has been prepared by Thomas Frederick Ball, so as to give in an epitomised form the history of each of the London Monthly and other meetings, drawn from the great amount of documents, minute-books, and papers they possess.

To some readers a knowledge that the work has been so largely founded on original records, may cause anticipations of interest not realised in its perusal. The prominent features of the Society are already well known, and its minuter details, where given, may not be thought of much importance; so that some will say, We find in this book none "such things as we supposed," no doctrine nor high Christian counsel, but only minor details regarding things of everyday life.

[*] Evidently a misprint for 1865

Such must, at the outset, be made aware that Monthly Meetings in the Society have had more to do with Christian practice than abstract doctrine. Hence this search into their records will show more of care over the things of outward and daily life than spiritual questions—the latter must be learnt from other sources, for they came not within the compass of Monthly Meetings until long after their first establishment.

With this preliminary caution the book may be left to speak for itself, its authors are conscious of their imperfections in seizing the pith and marrow of voluminous documents; they may be found in error by some acquainted with special points of detail, if so, they would feel obliged by being informed of any such, and will accept with pleasure any additional information Friends may incline to send, as there may be an opportunity of using it on a future occasion; any such could be sent to W. Beck, 33, Finsbury Circus.

The kindness shown in all cases from those Friends and meetings having care of the various records, must be again acknowledged. The authors would also allude to the valuable assistance derived (especially in the account of the Six-Weeks Meeting) from a paper and notes that had been prepared by Charles Hoyland, of which free use has been permitted to be made; also of some general information furnished by Thomas Wise, jun.

It must be borne in mind that the work, though so largely drawn from " Records," is not to be regarded as in any way officially recognised by any one or other of the meetings whose history it describes; and the authors are themselves alone responsible for the sentiments expressed, or the accuracy of the extracts and quotations. They feel how difficult it has been, from amid some 300 volumes of minutes, &c., to give in a condensed form any adequate picture. What is given will be found to illustrate somewhat three periods of the Society; its rise—its middle age—its renewed life in 1760, &c.; but of these most will be found as to its rise—the facts of the other periods being so much better known, as to seem less calling for development in a work where brevity had to be studied.

Imperfect as it confessedly is, it may yet prove of some interest to the members of the Society, and stimulate further inquiry. If it should come before those not so connected with us, it may assist towards a more correct view being formed of our founders, their task, and the way they were helped through.

To subscribers and purchasers, the authors can say that, if any want of adequate fulness be apparent, the work has even in its present state incurred an amount of expenditure beyond what any expected sale would warrant, if pecuniary profit had been their object.

Fifth Month, 1869.

Devonshire House Yard: from *Yearly Meeting 1860: From original pen and ink sketches*, by J.J. Willson (Headley Bros, 1906). "The two figures in the foreground are exact representations of two ancient Friends (the brothers Bratt) who continued to wear the old Quaker costume of their father's day, and were notable figures at Yearly Meetings."

Peter Daniels

Introduction

The influence of this book and the authors' method

FIRST PUBLISHED in 1869, William Beck and T. Frederick Ball's *The London Friends' Meetings* has remained the standard history of Quakerism in London for the ensuing 140 years. The book's undoubted value as a work of reference is reflected by the continued willingness of successive generations of historians to cite from it in their work: for instance David Butler's two volume *The Quaker Meeting Houses of Britain* (1999) makes extensive use of Beck and Ball in sketching the history of the individual meeting houses in London. We rely on the book for a general overview of the development of Quakerism in London during its first two centuries, largely because until recently no new attempts had been made to address the subject in any great detail. It is not just Quaker historians who have continued to use Beck and Ball as the authority on Friends in London. In the last two decades the book has been cited in works on such diverse subjects as women and pamphlet culture in mid-seventeenth century England, crime in eighteenth century London, and the life of the prophet and visionary TheaurauJohn Tany.[1]

Indeed, the book's authority has been somewhat taken for granted. Certain established "facts" about early Quakerism in London can be traced back to *The London Friends' Meetings*, such as their population figure (see below, p.xix). But in assessing the value of Beck and Ball's study to the modern researcher, it would be wrong to judge their work entirely by the standards of current scholarship. While the period in which they were writing was beginning to see the emergence of history as a professional academic discipline, their work is firmly rooted in an amateur tradition of antiquarianism.

This was becoming a Victorian cultural phenomenon, with the enjoyment of finding curiosities for their own sake, and occasionally the kind of romantic imaginings typified by William Frederick Yeames's painting "And When Did You Last See Your Father?"[2], and Quakers were developing their own version of it. Beck and Ball can become flowery in their language, and (for Quakers)

---

[1] Marcus Nevitt (2006), pp.174-5, 197; Peter Linebaugh (2003), pp.13, 69, 464; Ariel Hessayon (2007), p.314. For full details of works cited, see Bibliography, p.397.
[2] http://www.liverpoolmuseums.org.uk/walker/collections/lastseefather/ (accessed July 2009) for this 1878 painting in the Walker Art Gallery, Liverpool.

noticeably starstruck about royalty and aristocratic connections, as with Peter the Great (pp.223–24): "It is well known that this wonderful man, whom Macaulay has daguerrotyped in eloquent picture-language..." But Macaulay also provided a role-model as a professional historian, notwithstanding Quaker annoyance at the unflattering portraits of William Penn and George Fox in his *History of England* (1849), remarked upon by Thomas Hamm[3].

This was a time when the Society of Friends was undergoing a renewal in gathering and disseminating information about itself, and writing history was part of this. Thomas Hamm identifies the 1860s and 1870s as "the transitional period of Quaker historiography" that laid the foundations for the scholarly work of William Braithwaite and Rufus Jones in the early twentieth century[4]. Publication of *The London Friends' Meetings* followed a flurry of books relating to the early Quaker movement. Maria Webb's popular works on *The Fells of Swarthmore Hall* (1865) and *The Penns and Peningtons of the Seventeenth Century* (1867) were followed in 1868 by the evangelical London Friend William Tallack's *George Fox, the Friends, and the Early Baptists*. Joseph Smith's bibliography of Quaker books (1867) is an essential resource for appreciating what had been published over 200 years, and awareness of current Quaker deliberations was furthered by the printing of London Yearly Meeting's proceedings, starting in 1857[5]. By the end of the 1860s another evangelical British Friend, Robert Barclay (1833-1876) had begun the research that would result in the most important contribution to Quaker history of the period, *The Inner Life of the Religious Societies of the Commonwealth* (1876)[6]. The heart of Beck and Ball's project is its attempt to turn the wealth of Quaker meeting records into a combined narrative and reference history, showing where Quaker meetings were held, who was prominent in them, and how they were run.

Across the nonconformist denominations there was also a substantial corpus of historical literature on which they could draw. Among the authors cited in the course of the book are the eighteenth century Independent minister Daniel Neal (on p.140), the nineteenth century Congregationalist John Stoughton (p.7), and the General Baptist Adam Taylor (pp.13–14). Further evidence that Beck and Ball were up to date with the historical literature available to them is provided by reference (p.68) to Herbert Skeats's *History of the Free Churches of England*, the first part of which appeared in 1868. From the Quaker perspective, they were naturally familiar with William Sewell's *The History of the Rise, Increase and Progress of the Christian People Called Quakers* (1712), Joseph Besse's *Sufferings* (1753) and Thomas Clarkson's *Portraiture of Quakerism* (1806). They also show a sound knowledge of the printed spiritual autobiographies and journals of early London Friends such as William Crouch, Gilbert Latey, George White-

---

[3] Thomas Hamm (2004), p.12. [4] ibid. [5] Thomas Kennedy (2001), p.42.
[6] Thomas Hamm (2004), p.13–17

Manuscript volumes in the strong room, Devonshire House: photo by Walter Benington, 1925. At the top are the Great Books of Sufferings; minute books below them; the A.R. Barclay manuscripts are in a box on a lower shelf [LSF].

head, and Benjamin Bangs while A. R. Barclay's edition of *Letters &c. of Early Friends* (1841) is cited regularly throughout.

So it is evident that Beck and Ball were well versed in a wide range of published literature available to them at the time, relating both to the history of Quakerism and the wider history of English nonconformity. William Beck also associated himself with other Friends concerned with the history of the movement. William Tallack acknowledged his assistance "for collecting proofs of the Baptist origin of the chief portion of the constitution of Quakerism" [7].

While the list of printed sources available to Beck and Ball firmly locates their work within the intellectual context of the late 1860s, it is their extensive use of a wide range of manuscript sources that has ensured its enduring value. In their preface, the authors state that the history of each of the London meetings is "drawn from the great amount of documents, minute-books, and papers they possess" (p.ix). Subsequent historians who have attempted to research and write about London Quaker history can sympathise with the complaint of "how difficult it has been, from amid some 300 volumes of minutes, &c., to give in a condensed form any adequate picture" (p.xi). Frequent references to the manuscript records, and extensive quotations from them, help to make *The London*

[7] William Tallack (1868), p.vi.

Friends' Meetings a useful resource for researchers. Naturally, anyone seeking to write the history of London Quakerism or of a local meeting today needs to consult the original records at Friends House Library, but the book offers a valuable introduction to the available records as a starting point for further research. Although the modern academic apparatus is generally lacking, the organisation of the book mostly follows the administrative structure of Quakerism in London, assisting with the location of the original records.

This in itself is a convincing reason why it is worth reprinting after 140 years. From Chapter VII onwards we have essentially a series of administrative histories of the various meetings that constitute the Quaker organisation in London. This institutional approach is no longer fashionable among historians seeking to chart the history of Quakerism in different parts of the country: modern authors tend to favour a thematic approach that can leave the institutional context remaining obscure. The administrative structure of London Quakerism was particularly complex, with a serious of administrative bodies spanning the whole of the London and Middlesex area in addition to the normal quarterly and monthly meeting (MM) structure. Beck and Ball's history helps the researcher to negotiate through a labyrinth of meetings that includes such bodies as the Two Weeks Meeting, Six Weeks Meeting, Meeting of Twelve, Morning Meeting of Ministers, and the different women's meetings that covered the capital.

The Quaker 1860s, and the historical outlook

READERS OF Beck and Ball today should remain conscious of the context within which their work was undertaken, and the debates taking place within the Society of Friends during the Victorian period.

The London Friends' Meetings appears in the first decade of the period identified in the subtitle of Thomas Kennedy's 2001 book *British Quakerism 1860–1920* as "the transformation of a religious community", the time when John Stephenson Rowntree's prize essay *Quakerism, Past and Present* (1859) on the state of the Society of Friends set the tone for Quakers to understand more about themselves and how they had reached this situation. Results of concern about the inward-turning Society and its offputting rules were the Marriage (Society of Friends) Act 1860, allowing "marrying out" without disownment, and a revision of the Discipline in 1861, in which such aspects as admonishments about plain dress and vain sports were reduced.

The early to mid-nineteenth century had seen tensions developing between conservative Friends on the one hand, and evangelical Quakers on the other, while a liberal strand related to the Hicksite point of view in America was also developing in Britain. Compared with their conservative and Hicksite contemporaries, evangelical Quakers placed greater emphasis on the authority of scripture and on a belief in atonement as the path to salvation; and they expressed concern about the lack of active ministry among Friends[8]. William Beck shows clear evangelical sympathies, while T. Frederick Ball was employed by the Bedford Institute, a practical project of the evangelical Quakers among the poor and under-educated people of Spitalfields.

The authors display a preoccupation with the missionary zeal exhibited by the early Friends, and are interested in the 1760s "revival of the discipline" with approving reference made to the work of Samuel Fothergill (p.393). Where an account is given from Fox's *Journal* of a meeting held at Waltham Abbey the fact that Fox "went forth, *Bible in hand*" is emphasised with italics, with a footnote commenting that this was ordinary practice for Fox, Burrough and others (p.296). They refer somewhat impatiently to conservative reliance on spontaneous promptings of the Spirit when in 1703 "Richard Claridge ... and John Farrand are appointed 'to *prepare papers of advice* suitable to the occasion.' It appears that our ancestors had not always that dread of a prepared document which influences some of us at the present day" (p.280).

In the account of London and Middlesex Quarterly Meeting the case of Hannah Barnard, a travelling American minister who was censured by the Morning Meeting for her unsound views on the authority of the scriptures, is described with clear disapproval of her (pp.82–83): at the Yearly Meeting hearing Joseph Gurney Bevan and her opponents "tracked her subtle intellect through all its devious windings" before approving the decision to recommend that she refrain from ministering[9].

A desire to connect the theological position of nineteenth-century evangelical Quakers with the views of early Friends would also appear to be behind the extensive extracts from William Dewsbury's final sermon appended to Chapter IX. The doctrine espoused by Dewsbury reflects views of salvation and atonement found in the writings of nineteenth-century evangelical Friends (pp.159–161)[10]. An evangelical agenda is also presented in the "General Observations" that close the volume, with contrasts drawn between the "Latin and the Greek churches ... the missionary, propaganding spirit of the former and its increase – the absence of it in the latter, and its dull, stationary character" (p.395).

The nineteenth-century context within which Beck and Ball were researching and writing is reflected in their interpretation of particular historical episodes and themes. The depiction of James Nayler's entrance into Bristol in 1656 describes Nayler's followers as "fanatical, if not crazy people" whose conduct would in Beck and Ball's day "have issued in the confinement of the

---

[8] See Thomas Kennedy (2001) pp.12–46.   [9] On Hannah Barnard, see Thomas Kennedy (2001), pp.19–20.   [10] Thomas Kennedy (2001), p.34.

actors in some asylum" (pp.29-30). This interpretation forms part of a long historiographical tradition that has portrayed Nayler and his followers as mad or demented. Whereas modern writers[11] have attempted to understand and explain the actions of Nayler and those around him, Beck and Ball's emphasis is on his subsequent repentance, "so touching as to draw tears from those who heard him" (p.30). The comment that "James Naylor's [sic] case no doubt served as a warning to many others, to make more careful use of scriptural terms" (p.30) can also be read in the context of evangelical Quakerism, and echoes similar sentiments expressed by William Tallack in his work on Fox[12]. In documenting the sufferings of London Friends, Beck and Ball's approach adopts a similar hagiographical tone to that found in Joseph Besse's monumental work on the subject. The "cruel persecution" perpetrated by individuals in authority such as Alderman Richard Brown and Lieutenant of the Tower Sir John Robinson are emphasised (pp.34-35), as are the "Christian zeal" (p.67) and "meekness" (p.268) of the suffering Quakers. The account of Longford Monthly Meeting attributes the persecution of Friends to "harsh laws", "bigoted priests", "unprincipled informers" and "prejudiced and intolerant judges" (p.292). In explaining their motivation for giving prominence to accounts of sufferings Beck and Ball state that "it is done not so much to reproach the persecutors as to exhibit the strength and power of those convictions which could support men amid sufferings of forty years' duration" (p.392). Recent accounts of religious conflict in seventeenth-century London[13] have developed a more nuanced and complex picture of metropolitan society, where tensions existed over the existence of Quakers, Baptists, Presbyterians and Independents as a significant minority within the London population. The fault lines of religious difference can been seen throughout society, including the grass roots level of the parish or precinct. Where religious dissent divided local communities, tensions were not simply between nonconformists and Anglicans. Rather, they tended to be between dissenters, or those unwilling to prosecute dissent, and those less prepared to countenance religious tolerance [14].

The London Friends' Meetings deals with some significant episodes in the history of London Quakerism in rather cursory fashion. The case of Solomon Eccles, who processed naked through Bartholomew Fair with a pan of fire and brimstone on his head, is referred to fleetingly, and with some embarrassment, in one brief sentence and a footnote (p.142). More surprisingly, the celebrated

---

[11] For example Leo Damrosch (1996), pp.6–8; Erin Bell (2008), pp.426–27; Kate Peters (2005) pp.233–51. [12] Hamm (2004), p.12; Tallack (1868), pp.117–18. [13] For example, see Tim Harris (1987) on *London Crowds in the Reign of Charles II*; Gary de Krey (2005) on *London and the Restoration*; Mark Goldie (1998) on "The Hilton gang and the purge of London in the 1680s", and Simon Dixon (2007) on "Quakers and the London Parish 1670-1720" [14] Tim Harris (1987), p.62.

trial of William Penn and William Mead at the Old Bailey in 1670 is passed over with the comment that the "character and incidents of this trial are too well known... to require further note here" (p.153). The case of Hannah Lightfoot, supposed first wife of George III, is alluded to with extracts from the Westminster Monthly Meeting records referring to her disownment, but with no explanation of what the controversial marriage was supposed to have been. Instead they note that the minute "may be of some interest, as the case has excited of late public attention, but they do not cast much light on the disputed points in the controversy"[15].

There are inevitably some areas of uncertainty which readers should be aware of. Beck and Ball's assertion that "in 1678, Friends numbered 10,000 in London alone" (p.32) has become the basis for subsequent attempts to estimate the size of the London Quaker population during the later seventeenth century. Barry Reay included a modified version of this figure in his 1985 work on *The Quakers and the English Revolution*, allowing several successive historians to note that London Quakers "numbered almost 10,000"[16]. Beck and Ball's estimate is based on the number of deaths recorded in a single year (1678), multiplied up according to the death rate among Friends in London and Middlesex during the first decade of the nineteenth century, then revised downwards "to allow for supposed higher death-rate in early times" (p.32n). Further work is needed to establish more accurate estimates of the London Quaker population during the later seventeenth and eighteenth centuries. However, recent research has suggested that Quaker numbers in the capital never exceeded 7,000–8,000 during the seventeenth century, and by the second decade of the eighteenth century the figure may have been closer to 5,000[17].

In preparing this new edition some errors in references have emerged: one is for the Islington Road School engraving, which is not on p.412 of any of the four volumes of James Peller Malcolm's *Londinium Redivivum* but p.412 of Thomas Cromwell's *History and Description of the Parish of Clerkenwell* of 1828[18].

There is a sensational feeling to the story of Wheeler Street, where Sir John Robinson the constable of the Tower is particularly harsh with the Quakers (p.164): this derives from Gilbert Latey's own narrative[19], although not explicitly referenced. It is converted into quite a dramatic dialogue, which stands out as historically unprofessional these days: perhaps this was from use as educational material for the adult school students at the Bedford Institute, whose premises were in Wheeler Street opposite the site of the old meeting house.

[15] See Matthew Kilburn, "Lightfoot, Hannah (b. 1730, d. in or after 1758)", *Oxford Dictionary of National Biography* (2004). [16] Barry Reay (1985) pp.26–30; John Coffey (2000), p.151; David Scott (1991), p.3. [17] Simon Neil Dixon (2005 thesis) p.7. [18] Identified from the 2008 *Survey of London* on Clerkenwell, thanks to Jeremy Smith at Guildhall Library. [19] Gilbert Latey (1707) pp.75–76.

Another item about Wheeler Street is given a slight but significant improvement. The meeting house suffered in the great storm of 1703 (much worse than the hurricane of 1987) and was evidently not much of a building in the first place; the meeting was discontinued in 1742, and in 1745 Six Weeks Meeting enquired about the state of the property. According to the book (p.166), Devonshire House MM replied, "Wheeler St meeting house has tumbled down". In fact the minutes of both Devonshire House and Six Weeks Meeting say it "is fallen down", which is a little less eye-catching, while meaning the same.

This dramatisation seems a by-product of the enthusiastic and celebratory kind of history familiar in the present-day love of anniversaries as a way of connecting with the past. Beck and Ball identify the 1760s "revival of the discipline" as the kind of reform that their contemporaries were continuing in their own way a hundred years on, and there was evidently some awareness that the 1850s just past would have been an opportunity for celebrating the bicentenary of Quakerism in a manner that Quakers would officially have eschewed. One notable passage is on p.355, taking the opportunity to write about Jordans. This was not within London & Middlesex Quarterly Meeting, but at this period was open once a year for a session of that quarterly meeting, evidently much attended by Friends from London as a day out.

> It has been remarked, in the course of this work, how little attachment Friends as a body have shown to the outward relics of a former time, even taking care, as in some instances, to destroy anything which a too reverential regard for the past might invest with distinction. In like manner the Society observing no times or seasons as of any value in themselves; commemorating no occasions as special festivals; keeping no jubilees or centenary or bicentenary celebrations, have shown themselves content with the regular unvaried periodic round of

Minute of Devonshire House MM, 3rd 3mo. 1749, responding to Six Weeks Meeting's enquiry, that Wheeler Street meeting house "is fallen down" [LSF]

monthly and quarterly gatherings, culminating to the general annual one in London at Whitsuntide.

Quakers had certainly been attached to past practices, and the traditionalists had been much on the defensive about change in marriage regulations, plain dress etc. The reference to Whitsun may be an oblique reflection on the inconsistency of not observing times and seasons except for the one that, if acknowledged, would relate the Quakers gathering in the Spirit with the apostles at Pentecost. This unspoken evocation of the New Testament has the tone of an evangelical agenda being followed with some tact: it seems the authors' historical interests mean that, even if not fully in sympathy, they understand the conservative Quaker view on the past; at least they concur with the sentimental manifestations of it at such occasions as the annual trip to Jordans. This building developed a status that can only be called "iconic" and came to represent the classic meeting house, featuring in paintings by J. Walter West and Doyle Penrose[20]. At least such a celebratory relationship with the past keeps the public interested, as professional historians will concede.

The value of their work today

As we noted above, Beck and Ball do display an admirable familiarity with the historical literature of their day. However, the modern reader approaching their work enters a world before W.C. Braithwaite or Rufus Jones had devoted a significant proportion of their lives to rewriting the history of Quakerism. History as a professional discipline was only beginning to emerge in the 1860s, and the founding of the Friends Historical Society was still over thirty years away. Like all good historians, Beck and Ball freely admitted that their work would not stand as the final word on its subject. In the preface to the book they expressed the hope that "Imperfect as it confessedly is, it may yet prove of some interest to members of the Society, and stimulate further inquiry" (p.xi). Surprisingly, given the importance of London to the early history of Quakerism, and the continued wide interest in Quaker history, the call for "further inquiry" appears to have gone largely unheeded and many aspects of London Quaker history still await their historian.

Naturally, London Friends and their meetings figure prominently in all of the general histories of early Quakerism, from Braithwaite in the early twentieth century with *The Beginnings of Quakerism* (1912) and *The Second Period of Quakerism* (1919) to Rosemary Moore at the start of the twenty-first with *The*

---

[20] James Doyle Penrose (1862–1932), "The Presence in the Midst", 1916; J. Walter West (1860–1933), "The Promise", circa 1928

Light in their Consciences: the early Quakers in Britain 1646–1666 (2001). Studies focusing on specific themes within Quaker history also have much to tell us about the role of London within the wider movement and the experiences of London Friends. Craig Horle's unsurpassed account of *The Quakers and the English Legal System, 1660-1688* (1988) reflects on the role of London Friends as leaders of the national movement and also contains a valuable statistical analysis of the records of sufferings of London and Middlesex Friends. Kate Peters' *Print Culture and the Early Quakers* (2005) discusses the role of London as the centre of early Quaker publishing activities.

Just as historians of Quakerism often have much of interest to tell us about London, so a number of historians of London have shed valuable light on Quaker history. Tim Harris's study *London Crowds in the Reign of Charles II* (1987) ,and the doctoral thesis on which it is based, analyse the records of religious persecution found in the court records for London and Middlesex, within which Quakers naturally feature prominently. The position of Friends within the wider politics of religion in seventeenth and early eighteenth century London can be viewed through Gary de Krey's books *A Fractured Society: The Politics of London in the First Age of Party 1688-1715* (1985) and *London and the Restoration, 1659-1683* (2005). Accounts of religious intolerance during the Restoration period inevitably include discussions of Quakerism. The role of George Whitehead and other London Friends in the eventual defeat of the Hilton Gang of informers is covered expertly by Mark Goldie (1998). In a rather different area of research, the richness of Quaker records of births, marriages and burials has led to their exploitation as a source for the study of historical demography. John Landers' *Death and the Metropolis: studies in the demographic history of London, 1670-1830* (1993) uses Quaker records to supplement findings from the Bills of Mortality to demonstrate changes in mortality and fertility rates in London over an extended period. Doreen Evenden found the Quaker practice of recording the names of all of those present at the birth of a child of value in her study of *The Midwives of Seventeenth-Century London* (2000).

Between these twin currents of Quaker history and London history, a renewed interest is emerging in the history of London Friends, in which we ourselves take part. Simon Dixon's recent doctoral thesis on "Quaker Communities in London, 1667–c.1714" (2005) fits within a wider context of current work on Quakerism in the British localities[21]; he has also contributed articles and essays[22] on the London Friend Peter Briggins, the relationship between Quakers and the London parish and the "Battle for Gracechurch Street Meeting House", the latter episode having been first noted by Beck and Ball

---

[21] Including Adrian Davies (2000) on Essex, Nicholas Morgan (1993) on Lancashire, and Richard C. Allen (2007) on Wales.

[22] See bibliography for details of these publications.

(pp.153-54). The story of Quakers in Stoke Newington has been told in articles by Peter Daniels (2002 and 2008). Meanwhile, Jordan Landes' forthcoming doctoral thesis at the Centre for Metropolitan History in London will explore the role of London in the creation of a transatlantic Quaker community in the late seventeenth and early eighteenth centuries. Women's Meetings in London are covered in Chapter XXII of *The London Friends' Meetings*, but a more recent account can be found in a doctoral thesis by Michele Denise Ryan, " 'In my hands for lending': Quaker women's meetings in London, 1659–1700" (University of California, PhD thesis, 2003).

Despite a growing interest in the history of London Quakerism, a number of areas remain where further work is needed. Whilst research by Simon Dixon and Jordan Landes ventures into the early 1700s, much of the eighteenth century remains unstudied. An exception is Jacob M. Price, "The great Quaker business families of 18th century London: the rise and fall of a sectarian patriciate"[23]. The rise and decline of one of the most important London meetings, that at Gracechurch Street, would benefit from further research – restricted of course in comparison with others by the destruction of its records in the fire of 1821. Too little is known about William Penn's co-defendant in the 1670 conspiracy trial, William Mead, while there is no satisfactory biography of arguably the most important early London Friend, George Whitehead. A full modern evaluation of his life and work would be welcomed for John Bellers, although we do have George Clarke (ed.), *John Bellers: his life, times and writings* (1987), and for the Clerkenwell workhouse we can refer to *Richard Hutton's Complaints Book: the notebook of the steward of the Quaker workhouse at Clerkenwell, 1711–1737*, edited by Tim Hitchcock (1987). Further work is needed on the developing relationship between Quakers and a number of areas of London society during the later seventeenth and eighteenth centuries. After the Affirmation Act (1696) Quakers became increasingly involved with the running of the London livery companies, but the extent to which this continued throughout the eighteenth century is unknown.

For the local historian, Winifred White's tercentenary history of Six Weeks Meeting (1971) has been a useful stopgap, and is the only London overview post-1869; there have been useful local meeting histories, some published as pamphlets by the meetings themselves. There is much more to be investigated, and we hope that the re-publication of Beck and Ball's history will awaken an interest among Friends in London in the history of their own meetings.

---

[23] Jacob M. Price, (1986), pp.363–99

Left: William Beck: from an album of portraits of the Friends War Victims Relief Committee, 1870–71. Right: T. Frederick Ball: carte de visite by C.A. Gandy of Bishopsgate Without, London, date unknown [LSF]

The authors

WILLIAM BECK was born in 1823, the oldest of five brothers and four sisters surviving to adulthood. The Becks were part of an influential network of Quakers in Stoke Newington, where many of the families of Gracechurch Street meeting had been migrating since the late eighteenth century. Their father Richard Low Beck (1792-1854) was a chemist, and combined scientific interests and trade in a way characteristic of early nineteenth-century Quakers: he followed his uncle Joseph Jackson Lister in a wine business that supported a sideline in optics (Joseph Jackson developed the microscope into a fully practical scientific instrument, enabling his son Joseph Lister to pioneer microbiology and antiseptics). William became an architect, while his brothers Richard and Joseph continued in the optical business, and Ernest stayed with the wine trade. Richard died in 1866, and his widow in 1870: William returned from urban bachelorhood in Finsbury Circus to Stoke Newington so that he could look after their orphaned children. He never married.

In the testimony of the monthly meeting on his death in 1907, he is said to have instigated the printing of members' lists[24], the first being his own Devon-

---

[24] Testimony of Devonshire House MM in London Yearly Meeting *Proceedings*, 1908 p.221.

shire House MM in 1863, soon taken up by other monthly meetings: another case of the Society taking an interest in information about itself (and very useful now to the researcher). The testimony also acknowledges that "It was largely his enthusiastic energy that founded the Bedford Institute and Friends' mission work in London and guided the Institution's extending work later." He designed the first Bedford Institute building. The historical project that became this book is of course connected with his interest in premises as an architect, and as an officer of Six Weeks Meeting: in present-day charity rules he would have been in a conflict of interest, as not only was he a member of Six Weeks Meeting and therefore a trustee, but he was employed from 1849 as rent-collector, receiving a five percent commission on the rents paid[25], and soon became their surveyor, which he remained until 1874 [26].

William Beck's evangelical Quakerism was strongly held and active, but his historical perspective and sense of a broad Quaker readership for the book may have kept him from the evangelical triumphalism of a J.B. Braithwaite [27]; there was also a family reason for some tenderness, as his youngest brother Ernest left the Society while continuing the family wine business. William subscribed to the evangelical keenness on temperance, and was trustee of a temperance pub, the "British Workman" in Stoke Newington, run by the Devonshire House Young Men's Committee from 1872 to 1875 [28]. References to inns and alcohol in *The London Friends' Meetings* tend to take a puzzled tone, rather than one of shock: for instance on pp.126–27, on stabling for travelling ministers, "it is curious to observe, in connection with these horses, notices of Friends as innkeepers in the days of primitive Quakerism" – yet such practical functions for inns in the local community would have been still familiar in William's own day, and no more curious for a Quaker's occupation than his own father's wine business, except of course for some class assumptions.

Not long after the publication of *The London Friends' Meetings*, William and his brothers took an active part in the Friends War Victims Relief Committee for the Franco-Prussian war (1870–71), mostly as the "home" organisation, although they did travel to France. His portrait opposite is from an album of members of the FWVRC.

In the Library at Friends House there is a copy of *The London Friends' Meetings* which contains his annotations, with correspondence and further notes bound in (continued by other hands well beyond his death in 1907, mostly by members of the Library staff). In the Preface, William had solicited further

---

[25] He was a member of Six Weeks Meeting from 27th 11mo. 1848; arrangements for the collector, Six Weeks Meeting minutes, 10th 12 mo. 1849. [26] Winifred White (1971), pp.64–65, notes that he was replaced by two people. [27] See Thomas Kennedy (2001) on "JBB". [28] Devonshire House MM Young Men's Committee minutes 1872-1888, with separate sequence at back of volume for British Workman business.

historical information "as there may be an opportunity of using it on a future occasion" (p.x), but the annotated copy is largely disappointing as a further mine of material for London Quaker history, apart from a few factual clarifications such as full names of some people mentioned[29]. Confirming the effect of disownments for "marrying out", there is a table[30] of marriages, admissions, disownments and resignations for Devonshire House 1802–1853, noting "In 50 years the MM has disowned 3 times as many as it has admitted. The Regular marriages have been 166. Those occasioning disownment 120" – other disownments were "54 moral, 31 bankruptcy, 48 non-att[endan]ce" and "26 resigned". There is some correspondence from other history enthusiasts including J.J. Green, mostly pursuing various hobby-horses; notes of comparison about other denominations and their habits of standing in prayer, or exceptions to the removal of hats in the presence of royalty; news cuttings whose relevance is often obscure; and some amusing anecdotes, such as a story about Dr Robert Pope and a highwayman. He tells the highwayman in surprise that he has lost his watch, as it is not in his pocket; he later discovers that it has slipped through the lining, and intends to go back to give it to the highwayman, but is persuaded by his companion (Elizabeth Beck, William's grandmother) that he was truthful at the time in sincerely believing it lost. William continued compiling these family stories (and some useful hard facts) in the privately published *Family Fragments* of 1897.

William Beck published a number of other works, the most germane to this one being *Six Lectures on George Fox and his Times* (1877); the *Biographical Catalogue* compiled for the Friends' Institute, 1888; *The Friends: Who they are, what they have done* (1893); a version of George Whitehead's autobiography (1901); and *Devonshire House: historical account of the acquisition by the Society of Friends...* (1903, revised edition 1908). He continued as a major figure in Stoke Newington meeting, but retired from Quaker committees, through deafness according to the monthly meeting's testimony; he also retired early from practice as an architect. He died in 1907 and was buried at Stoke Newington. His notes on local history were published posthumously as the pamphlet *A Description of Church Street, Stoke Newington* (1927).

---

[29] Only the brief factual annotations have been included in this edition.
[30] Annotated copy (MS Vol S 453), bound in at p.178, chapter on Devonshire House MM.

THOMAS FREDERICK BALL was born in 1836 and grew up in Devonshire House, where in 1843 his father Thomas (1790–1866) became "doorkeeper". Six Weeks Meeting set out the doorkeeper's duties in detail as to cleaning etc in the building, noting "the whole of their time should be given up to the above service"[31]. This caretaking post of doorkeeper needs to be distinguished from the role of minimising the disturbance to the stillness of a meeting from latecomers (although this also formed part of Thomas Ball's duties). The Ball family's position draws attention to a class element in nineteenth-century Quaker society; they were not at all of the professional class of intermarrying Quaker families such as the Becks, Listers and Allens of Stoke Newington. There is a very helpful entry for T.F. Ball in the "Dictionary of Quaker Biography" files (DQB) at Friends House Library, from which the following is mostly taken.

He attended the Friends' School in Croydon, which had moved there from Islington Road and previously Clerkenwell: by then it had lost the associations of its original function as a workhouse, but T.F. Ball's education would have been paid for by the monthly meeting, in the way that they had always supported young people under the provision for their "poor". He stayed at Croydon as a teacher, and then spent time from 1858 to 1860 at Carrick on Suir in Tipperary. He returned to London, and at Devonshire House in 1861 married Ellen Hayes Withers, daughter of a boarding-house keeper; in the register he is described as an accountant. Only three of their eight children survived infancy.

T.F. Ball published his *Poems* in 1865, and *Anecdotes of Aborigines: or, Illustrations of the coloured races being "Men and Brethren"* appeared in 1868, by which time must have been working on the research for *The London Friends' Meetings*. He had been appointed in 1867 as secretary of the Bedford Institute First-Day School and Home Mission Association, and from 1873 was also on the committee of the Friends' Institute. Unfortunately, things went badly wrong. The following summary of events recounted in the Devonshire House MM minutes is taken directly from the "DQB".

> On 12 March 1874 Devonshire House MM noted that a report had been received from one of the overseers that "the conduct of Thomas Frederick Ball, one of our members, with reference to justice in dealing, has been such as to claim the attention of this Meeting", and a committee of three Friends was appointed to visit him. They made their report on 16 April 1874; they had seen him, and had to say "with much pain, that during the year 1871, and for some short time before Thos. Fredk. Ball had misappropriated money paid into his hands for

---

[31] Six Weeks Meeting minutes 25th 9mo. 1843.

> *Monthly Meeting 14th of 5th Month, 1874.*
>
> *charges brought against him; confirmed the same and, under a feeling of deep sorrow, feels bound to issue a testimony of disunity. — and hereby disowns Thomas Frederick Ball as a member of our religious Society.*
>
> *It nevertheless desires, in Christian love, to record its sympathy with his wife and family under such trying circumstances: and to express the hope that, although thus separated from us in membership, Tho! Fred.k Ball may be led to seek forgiveness of God through Christ Jesus, who can abundantly pardon; and that sincere repentance and consistent future conduct may enable him, if so inclined, to again become a member of our religious society.*
>
> *In conclusion, this Meeting tenderly warns Tho! Fred.k Ball of the danger, both to himself and others, of attempting religious instruction whilst so unfit to give effect to his words by example and conduct; — and would earnestly impress upon him the importance of a circumspect walk and continual watchfulness unto prayer.*
>
> *Signed in and on behalf of the Meeting.*
>
> *Will.m Beck   Clerk.*

Devonshire House MM fair copy minutes, 14th 5mo. 1874: the minute of disownment is signed as by William Beck, but not in his hand. [LSF]

specific purposes by the Committee of the Bedford Institute and Shoreditch Schools, to the extent of £140. 6. 6., having further incurred debts to the amount of £10. 8. 0., together £150. 14. 6., all of which was liquidated by the kind contributions of several friends. They find that, subsequent to this discovery and payment, Thos. Fredk. Ball was reinstated to his position as secretary to the Bedford Institute with an increased salary.

"In 2nd mo. 1874 Thos. Fredk. Ball was dismissed from his post on the disclosure of further defalcation, – which the Committee find amounts to £86. 11. 2. – extending over the year 1872–3; besides further debts which he had no means of paying, amounting to nearly £100.

"The Committee also learn with much regret that, during the time these misappropriations were going on, Thos. Fredk. Ball was taking an active part in religious services, thereby bringing down additional reproach upon the Institutions and upon the Society of which he is a member". The visitors asked to be excused from suggesting any further course to be taken in the matter; the meeting saw no other possibility than issuing a testimony of disownment against T.F. Ball. The notice of disownment was brought in on 14 May 1874; it expressed sympathy with his wife and family, and the hope that, by repentance and amendment, he might be enabled to rejoin the Society, and in conclusion warned him of "the dangers, both to himself and others, of attempting religious instruction whilst so unfit to give effect to his words by example and conduct" [32].

The minute of disownment was duly signed by the clerk of Devonshire House Monthly Meeting, who at the time happened to be William Beck.

We do not have this actual signature, as the rough minutes (held at Guildhall Library, not Friends House) contain the necessary preambles in his hand but not a signature on the minute of disownment itself. There would of course have been a signed separate sheet to be delivered to T.F. Ball. In the fair-copy minute book at Friends House the full text is written out in the clear hand of William Frederic Wells, who took over as clerk following William Beck's unusually short tenure of one year (this was also the year that he gave up being the surveyor to Six Weeks Meeting).

T.F. Ball never did rejoin the Society, but his family continued in membership. He worked as a journalist and writer, publishing *Queen Victoria: Scenes and Incidents of Her Life and Reign* in 1886, in time for her jubilee (and successful enough for a second edition). He died aged 57 on 16 May 1894, some fourteen months after his wife, and was buried at Tottenham Quaker burial ground.

How the book was written and published

In *The Friend* for First Month 1861, under "Notes and Queries", appears a lengthy item headed "Materials towards a history of Friends of London", in which the author notes "Our late and much-esteemed friend, William Forster, was very anxious to see such a history of London Friends. Through the kind permission of James Bowden and Charles Hoyland [recording clerks] I have gleaned many biographical facts from the MS registers". There is an extensive

---

[32] Summary and extracts from minutes taken from the "DQB" with the permission of the Library of theReligious Society of Friends.

list of topics to be covered. This is unsigned, but in the next month's issue there is a shorter continuation listing early London preachers which is signed "W."

The authors' description of their method in the Preface is reiterated in *The Friend* of May 1869:

> Most of our readers are probably aware that it originated in a lecture given at the Friends' Institute, London, in 1865, by our friend William Beck.
> That lecture, revised and augmented, occupies mainly the earlier chapters in the work, the remaining chapters being chiefly the result of a laborious investigation, by our friend T.F. Ball, into all the records which are under the care of the Monthly Meetings, forming the Quarterly Meeting of London and Middlesex.

This clearly corrects the unlikely date of 1856 given in the preface. The division of the work between the authors seems quite clear-cut from this; although the 1861 "Notes and Queries" show that William Beck had already been searching manuscript sources, this is called "gleaning" rather than systematic "laborious investigation". There is only one note on the subject in the annotated copy, on Chapter XX: "This chapter was written by T.F. Ball with the exception of the portion relating to the funeral of George Fox."[33]

The project arose from the Friends' Institute, effectively a Quaker club, rather than more structurally official Quaker channels, but the authors had access to all the minute books, and therefore the implicit co-operation of the meetings concerned, despite it being "not to be regarded as in any way officially recognised by any one or other of the meetings whose history it describes" (Preface, p.x–xi). It is noticeable that while delicate on subjects like Hannah Lightfoot's marriage, they do not gloss over matters like disputes between meetings.

William Beck and T.F. Ball were both on the Friends' Institute committee at various times. Unfortunately no Friends' Institute minutes survive before 1900, but there are annual reports. William's lecture "Our London Meeting Houses and their associations" is listed in the report for 1865–66, but there is nothing in the accounts about subsidy for a publication. The publisher F. Bowyer Kitto is also the editor and publisher of *The Friend* at this time. The main finance appears to be by subscription: the Preface (p.xi) refers to "subscribers and purchasers", and the 1893 Supplement to Joseph Smith's 1867 bibliography lists, under W. Beck, *Circular and Table of Contents of the Origin, History, and Circumstances of the London Meetings, which it is proposed to publish 4to.* [1869] and *Lithographed circular-letter to the Clerks of Monthly Meetings, soliciting subscriptions for the above work for the Meeting-House Libraries* (dated 14. 6mo. 1869, which is in fact the same month as its publication is announced in *The Friend*). Neither of these apparently survive in the Library at Friends House.

---

[33] Annotated copy, MS vol S 453, p.329

The print run may have been kept to the number of subscribers. Notices appear to have been limited to the Quaker periodicals, and of those *The Friend* was effectively its publisher. The conservative *British Friend* [34] remarked:

> It surprises us that so much important historical matter in connection with the Society and its first meetings in the metropolis has so long been allowed to remain in obscurity; so that the compilers have rendered an acceptable service to Friends by this publication, and we quite expect it will find many purchasers. The insight thus afforded respecting the way in which our early Friends were concerned for the welfare of the Society is valuable and instructive.[35]

The notice in the *Friends Quarterly Examiner*, which Kennedy describes as "middle-of-the-road" [36], recruited Quaker history to make a point in the drama of the "Manchester Difficulty" unfolding at Yearly Meeting[37]. The reviewer was impressed by how "it brings out in strong relief the humanity and patience of George Fox towards fellow-professors who strove bitterly against him"; and quoting Edward Burrough's advice (on p.43) "... hearing and determining every matter coming before you in the love, coolness, gentleness and dear unity...", asked "Can we tender better counsel than this for the guidance of our coming Yearly Meeting?" [38]

We do know that the book went over length and over budget – *The Friend* noted on publication in June 1869 that "pages number some 150 more than were originally intended" [39]. Although William Beck must have had considerable means and may have subsidised it, he was evidently not providing unlimited finance, and was businesslike about payment: bound into the annotated copy is a note from him to a purchaser that prompt payment "will be esteemed a favour for in a desire to make the work compendious it has become increased whilst passing through the press – in a manner which a regard for pecuniary remuneration would have checked".

The authors' professional relationship is not clear, although William Beck is the one whose lecture began the project, and who solicits further information in the Preface. Did he pay T.F. Ball for his work? Was F. Bowyer Kitto as publisher in a position to pay? It seems likely that T.F. Ball was an enthusiast in his own right, from growing up at Devonshire House, but he had a family to support. His identification as a journalist might lead us to assume that he went for the more sensational stories, but with his acknowledged archival work he may well have been the more sober historian. William Beck certainly had a taste for

---

[34] See Thomas Kennedy (2001) p.53 on the *British Friend*. [35] *British Friend* 5mo. 1869, p.125. [36] Thomas Kennedy (2001) p.56. [37] The events of the 1869 Yearly Meeting are covered by Thomas Kennedy (2001) pp.65-67. [38] *Friends Quarterly Examiner*, 1869, p.311. [39] *The Friend*, 1869, p.149.

anecdote and despite his evangelical views was a collector of the kind of miscellaneous information that admittedly shows "more of care over the things of outward and daily life than spiritual questions" (Preface, p.x).

Between them they set out to show something of who the Quakers were. Outward and daily life does tend to be what interests the twenty-first century rather more, but the history of Quaker spirituality has not been neglected recently. What the book tells us about the inner life of Quakers in the early period is inevitably filtered through nineteenth-century minds, but as a nineteenth-century document the book itself reveals something of the authors' own attitudes to spiritual questions in a way that would merit further study.

Simon Dixon and Peter Daniels
London, July 2009

SIMON DIXON completed his PhD thesis on "Quaker Communities in London, 1667–c.1714" in 2005, and is currently revising it for publication. He has published several essays on London Quaker history, and presented his work at conferences in Britain, Ireland and America. He is a postdoctoral research fellow at Queen Mary, University of London, where he is researching the history of the dissenting academies in the British Isles, 1660–1860. He lives in the London Borough of Sutton.

PETER DANIELS worked as an assistant librarian at Friends House for more than eighteen years, and has also been listings editor of *Poetry London*. From 2003 to 2007 he was publications manager for Britain Yearly Meeting of Quakers, and is now a freelance editor and publisher. He has researched and written on the history of Stoke Newington Quaker meeting, where he is a member.

Acknowledgements

The book is scanned from a copy generously made available by Olive Yarrow of Bunhill Fields meeting. Her bookbinding skills have made it open freely, which has facilitated good reproduction. We could not have produced our edition without her kind help, and cannot adequately express our thanks.

The staff of the Library at Friends House have been helpful as ever, especially Joanna Clark, Pictures Librarian; likewise the staff of Guildhall Library, and Jeremy Smith in particular.

Finally, thanks to James Grant and Margaret Dowling for their help and facilities in the late stages.

Illustrations

Because there is a limited choice of pictures contemporary with or older than the 1869 book, later illustrations have been included, as much as possible from the period up to the death of William Beck in 1907. There are also items from the Hubert Lidbetter collection that continue into the 1940s: they are often not easy to date, but are rarely different from how they would have appeared to the authors, apart from electric lighting.

Most of the illustrations are from the Library of the Religious Society of Friends, Friends House, London [LSF]; several are from the London Metropolitan Archives, City of London, where the former Guildhall Library picture collection has migrated during the course of publication.

Modern London showing locations of historic sites [PD] ii
Devonshire House Yard: from *Yearly Meeting 1860: From original pen and ink sketches*, by J.J. Willson, published 1906 [PD] xi
Devonshire House: manuscript volumes in the strong room, photo by Walter Benington, 1925 [LSF] xvii
Devonshire House MM minutes, 3rd 3mo. [May] 1749 [LSF] xx
William Beck: from album of portraits of the Friends War Victims Relief Committee, 1870–71 [LSF] xxiv
T. Frederick Ball: carte de visite by C.A. Gandy, date unknown [LSF] xxiv
Devonshire House MM minutes, 14th 5mo. 1874 [LSF] xxviii
William Beck in later life: photo from obituary, *The Friend*, 1907 [LSF] ..xxxvi
Meetings in London 1863: from Devonshire House MM members list [LSF] ....facing p.2
London meetings in the 17th and 18th centuries [PD] ....facing p.3
Bull and Mouth: inn courtyard, from a 19th century print [LSF] ..facing p.24
Bull and Mouth: detail of Sands' plan, 1717 [City of London, London Metropolitan Archives, by permission of Christ's Hospital] ....facing p.24
"The Quakers meeting": late 17th century engraving from painting by Egbert van Heemskerk; "M[arcel] Lauron pinx" [LSF] ....facing p.25
"The Quakers Synod", from Francis Bugg, *Pilgrim's Progress from Quakerism to Christianity*, 1698 [LSF] ....facing p.54

White Hart Court: print taken from a steel engraving in Picart's folio
Cérémonies et coutumes religieuses (1723–43), in *Quaker Pictures – second series*
(1897) [LSF] ....facing p.55

London & Middlesex Quarterly Meeting: paper on plainness issued to the
monthly meetings in London and Middlesex, 1717 [LSF] ....facing p.78

"The London Quaker": engraving, probably late 17th century
[LSF] ....facing p.79

The Testimony of the Lord Concerning London, by Edward Burrough, 1657:
title page [LSF] ....facing p.88

Peel Monthly Meeting condemnations book: extract, 1705 [LSF] ..facing p.89

Gracechurch Street: meeting for worship, Isaac Sharples ministering;
anonymous oil painting circa 1770 [LSF]....................................facing p.156

Stoke Newington, exterior: front view, 1907 [LSF] ....facing p.157

Stoke Newington, interior: photo by H.W. Sale, 1940s
[LSF, Lidbetter] ....facing p.157

Bedford Institute, Wheeler Street: "William Beck, Arch^{t}"[LSF] ....facing p.166

Devonshire House courtyard: etching and aquatint by Sylvia Smee
(1886–1969) [LSF] ....facing p.167

Devonshire House courtyard: at Yearly Meeting 1865, from a series of
stereoscopic photographs [LSF] ....facing p.170

Devonshire House: the Institute reading room, photo by Walter Benington
1925, before the Society's offices moved to Euston [LSF] ....facing p.170

Devonshire House, Bishopsgate entrance: ink drawing by
Henry S. Newman 1845 [LSF] ....facing p.171

Devonshire House, Bishopsgate entrance: photo c.1900 [LSF] ....facing p.171

Peel courtyard: drawing by A.S. Hartrick, 1905 [LSF] ....facing p.210

Peel: from St John Street, undated photo [LSF] ....facing p.210

Stoke Newington: the building used by the first meeting, drawing 1825
[Hackney Archives Dept] ....facing p.211

Horslydown (in use as Cambrian Chapel): Engraving with watercolour by G.
Yates, 1825 [City of London, London Metropolitan Archives]..facing p.220

New Park meeting house, exterior: Engraving with watercolour by G. Yates,
1825 [City of London, London Metropolitan Archives] ....facing p.220

New Park meeting house, women's monthly meeting room (first floor):
Engraving with watercolour by G. Yates, 1825 [City of London, London
Metropolitan Archives] ....facing p.221

New Park meeting house, interior: engraving with watercolour by G. Yates,
    1825 [City of London, London Metropolitan Archives] ....facing p.221
Deptford: undated reproduction from a watercolour [LSF] ....facing p.224
Deptford: photo 1907, soon before demolition [LSF].....................facing p.224
Peckham, undated lithograph by Howard Dudley [LSF] ....facing p.225
Westminster, entrance: pencil sketch by Henry S. Newman,
    probably 1846 [LSF]..facing p.260
Hammersmith, interior: photo by Oliver Dell; first half of 20th
    century [LSF, Lidbetter] ....facing p.261
Hammermith, exterior: photo from *Home of the Ealing Free Library*,
    1902 [LSF]...facing p.261
Holloway: group photo at foundation stone laying, 1864 [LSF]....facing p.264
Holloway, interior: undated photo before 1938 [LSF, Lidbetter] ..facing p.264
Westminster: "The Quakers Meeting", etching with watercolour,
    by Thomas Rowlandson and A.C. Pugin, 1808 [LSF] ....facing p.265
Westminster, interior: pencil and pastel by Hubert Lidbetter, "from an old
    water-colour painting" (before 1880) [LSF, Lidbetter] ....facing p.265
Ratcliff, view from street: undated watercolour by William Edward Fox
    (1872–1948) [LSF] ....facing p.276
Ratcliff, interior: photo 1901, from Clement Y. Sturge, *Leaves from the
    Past*, 1905 [LSF] ....facing p.276
Barking: 1758 building, undated photo (before 1908) [LSF]........facing p.277
Plaistow, exterior: undated photo (before 1923) [LSF, Lidbetter] facing p.277
Plaistow, interior: undated photo (before 1923)[LSF, Lidbetter] p.281
Longford: undated photograph [LSF] ....facing p.286
Staines, exterior: photo H.W. Sale, before 1935 [LSF, Lidbetter]..facing p.286
Uxbridge, exterior: undated photo, H.W. Sale [LSF, Lidbetter]....facing p.287
Uxbridge, interior: undated photo, probably H.W. Sale
    [LSF, Lidbetter] ....facing p.287
Brentford & Isleworth, exterior: undated sketch [LSF]..................facing p.287
Staines, interior: photo H.W. Sale? before 1935 [LSF, Lidbetter] p.294
Winchmore Hill, exterior: photo 1940s? [LSF, Lidbetter].............facing p.300
Tottenham, exterior: photo, 1905 [LSF]...facing p.301
Tottenham burial ground: plan from Six Weeks Meeting records
    [LSF] ....facing p.301

Kingston: undated ink drawing formerly owned by Thomas Chalk of Kingston [LSF] ....facing p. 316

Esher, interior: photo H.W. Sale?, 1942 [LSF, Lidbetter] ....facing p.316

Wandsworth, exterior: photo H.W. Sale, 1940s? [LSF, Lidbetter]..facing p.317

Wandsworth, interior: photo probably H.W. Sale, 1940s? [LSF, Lidbetter] ....facing p.317

Bunhill Fields: Memorial Buildings 1881, publicity drawing [LSF] ....facing p.334

Bunhill Fields: indenture for the original purchase of the land, 1661, and the same document folded [LSF] ....facing p.334

Whitechapel burial ground: undated photo after it had become a recreation ground [LSF]...facing p.335

Women's Yearly Meeting at Devonshire House: from *The Illustrated London News*, June 1843 [LSF] ....facing p.354

Jordans: etching by Schnebbelie of a drawing by H. de Cort, 1798, published by C.J. Smith, London, 1835 [LSF] ....facing p.355

Islington Road Schools: engraving by J. & H.S. Storer, in Thomas Kitson Cromwell, *History & Description of the Parish of Clerkenwell*, 1828 [City of London, Guildhall Library, printed books collection] ....facing p.378

Croydon School: photo 1874, from an album of Croydon and Saffron Walden Schools [LSF] ....facing p.379

William Beck in later life: this photo was used for his obituary in *The Friend*, 1907 [LSF]

THE LONDON MEETINGS
AND THEIR ASSOCIATIONS.

CHAPTER I.

INTRODUCTORY REMARKS.

"Not forsaking the assembling of yourselves together."—HEB. x. 25.

For men to meet together on subjects affecting their common interest is a tendency so natural and so strong as to amount in its force to the power of an instinct; which Christianity, by offering to the human race an object of the highest importance and universal interest, has so developed as to make the assembling together of its professors conspicuous from their earliest history. This Pliny noticed at a time when Christians were but a sect in the Roman Empire. "They meet," says his letter to the Emperor, "at the dawn of day"; and now, when Christianity has become a world-spread and dominant religion, the infinite variety of its assemblies and the buildings these have called forth render the same congregating tendency of its faith yet more apparent. Wherever the eye ranges over a Christian land, whether amid the throng of the city or the seclusion of the village, no buildings are more conspicuous than those devoted to the purpose of Christian assembly—none are more varied in their form, though similar in their purpose, ranging through every gradation of age, of size, of richness, and of art—from the cathedral, hoary with ages and rich in products of human genius, to the modern chapel, or more humble meeting-house —each so different from the other, and yet all in their way and measure bearing the same testimony to the congregating influence of the Christian faith.

It may seem strange that, amid this universally-developed feature, any one sect among Christians should become at all conspicuous for meeting together, yet the Society of Friends has from the time of its origin been somewhat distinguished in this respect. It commenced its meetings in unsettled days, when to assemble in numbers was a prelude to arrest on suspicion of plotting or insurrection; it maintained them when Royal Proclamations and Acts of Parliament enacted the sharpest penalties on their attendance. No opposition was availing to check them; persecution failed in its efforts for their dispersion; laws were enforced to the extreme, and even beyond their letter or spirit; yet the Friend persevered in holding his meeting: and even as at Reading, when at one time all the parents were in prison, their children met and kept up the meeting by themselves. Such pertinacity made the maintenance of a Friends' meeting conspicuous in the early day; and now, amid the wise and liberal spirit of toleration which prevails, its maintenance seems scarcely less remarkable because none of those external means are employed which others adopt to attract a congregation. There is in a "Friends' meeting" so little of outward inducement, no prescribed order of service, no song or chant, no organ to swell the anthem of praise, not even an appointed minister or the certainty of hearing any discourse, that to most it must still seem strange Friends should "not forsake the assembling of themselves together."

Thus "the Meeting"—originated amid persecution, and maintained during two centuries of varied experience—is a conspicuous feature in Friends' arrangements. To show how these Meetings arose in the Metropolis—the form they took —their numbers and general history—will be the object of the following work, in which, it is hoped, various subjects of interest connected with them may become developed.

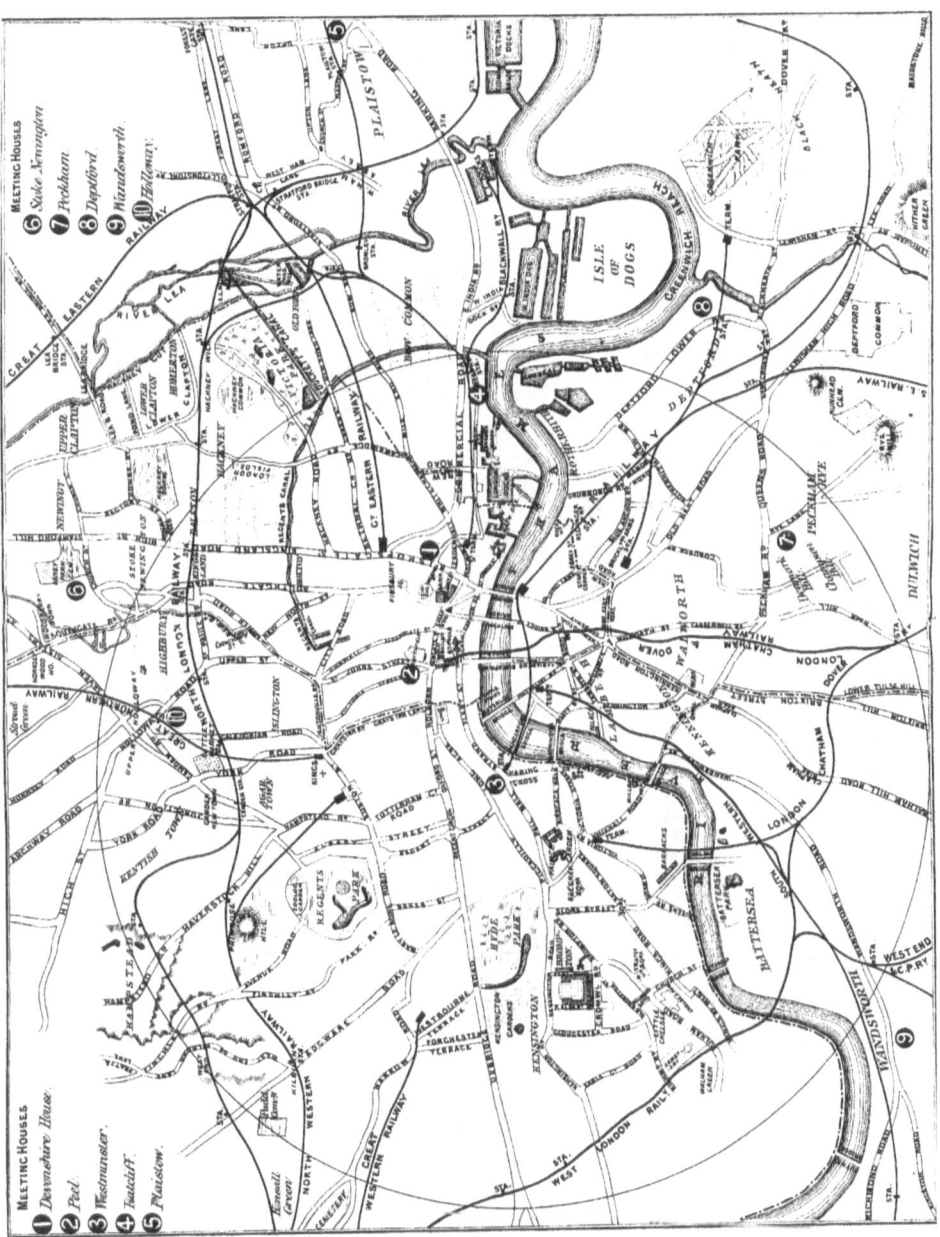

Quaker London at the time this book was published: this map of meetings in London is from the 1863 Devonshire House Monthly Meeting printed members list, which was a new venture instigated by William Beck. Reduced to 60% of original size. [LSF]

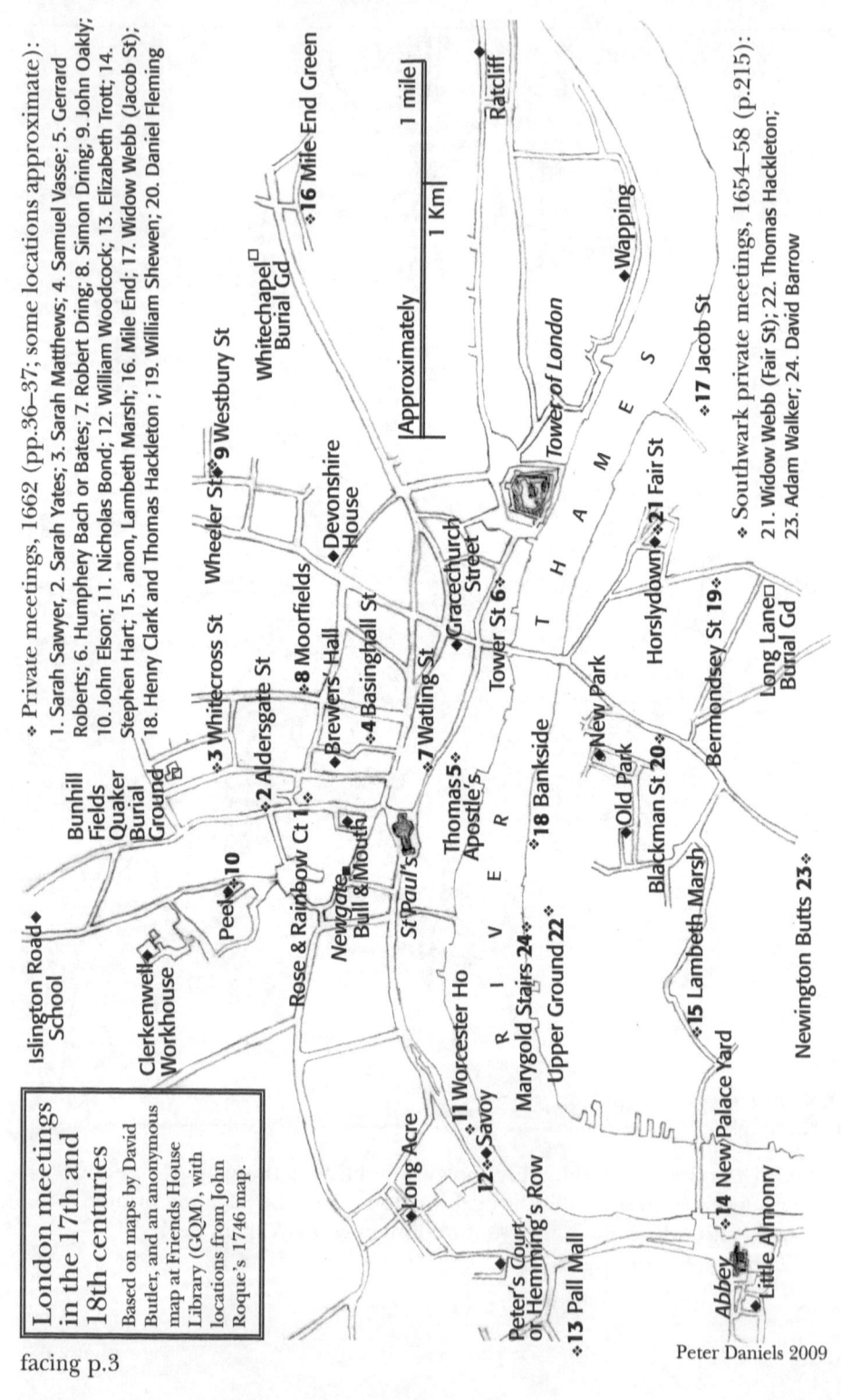

CHAPTER II.

LONDON IN THE DAYS OF CROMWELL.

BEFORE proceeding to narrate the particulars of the establishment of Friends' meetings in London and its suburbs, a brief sketch may well be allowed of the external and social aspects of the city in the days of the Protector, so as to understand the scene amid which the early Friends were called to labour.

London, in 1654, was a quaint mediæval city, not a tenth the size of the present metropolis, but within its confined area densely populated. Surrounded by walls whose foundations had existed from the times of the Romans, its only entrances were through embattled gateways, jealously guarded by a local militia; within these it was a labyrinth of narrow lanes and winding streets, amid which one or two main thoroughfares — such as Cheapside or Cornhill — were conspicuous. There were some signs of the modern commercial life being developed in the Royal Exchange and houses of rich merchants; but the general aspect was unchanged and mediæval, for buildings of that age gave the character to its streets. Even its great cathedral, though it had lost a spire (once the highest in Europe), and had become fronted with a Corinthian portico from the hands of Inigo Jones, was yet a Gothic work, and churches reared in the days of Plantagenet or the Edwards were thickly planted within the city wards; there, too, monastic buildings of great extent, with quadrangle and chapel, though changed in use, occupied large space amid her streets. Still was the citizen dwelling in those carved timber houses we now see only in prints, where story overhangs story, so that the narrow street below was like a covered way, and acquaintances shook hands across it from their casements. Few of our modern comforts were then known. The pavements, where any, were so rough that no carriages could go over them save at a footpace. Most of the sewers were open brooks that in storms rushed brawling in torrents to the Thames. There was no lighting of the streets at night, each one who ventured out after dark having to carry his own torch or lanthorn, and his own weapon of defence, for, except the trainbands or local militia, there were no watchmen. The tradespeople kept shop in open places unprotected by glass, and closed at night by doors or shutters. The citizens lived with but few of our social appliances; they fetched their own water either from the conduit or the public pump, finding too often that the one was dry or the other infected from surrounding graves; happily, they always had the great river, on which waterworks were early established; and the conduits, though but feeble precursors of the torrents of water now supplied by our water companies, really brought the citizens good running streams from the surrounding country, and being mostly the gift of private munificence (like our modern drinking fountains) the water they gave was free, which was an advantage our companies do not realise.

Looking beyond his city's walls, the Londoner of 1654 found strong lines of distinction between what he knew as the city and those surrounding places now indefinitely merged within it. To him Islington, Hoxton, Homerton, Clerkenwell, Stepney, Shadwell, meant villages separated from his city wall and ditch by pleasant fields, as free then from dwellings as our parks alone are now. Westminster was a distinct city—the Strand its connecting link, having mansions and gardens of noblemen and bishops on either side, extending from Temple Bar to Charing Cross. Southwark was a separate borough, and the whole southern side now so intimately connected with bridges, was inaccessible to the citizen except by boat or barge, or by one narrow bridge encumbered with lofty houses. To him, as he walked out of Moorgate he really came on to moorland, and found Finsbury (or Fensbury) was much of it a fen in fact as well as in name; his cows still fed at Cow Cross and on Clerkenwell Green; Smithfield was still a field; Long Acre a pasture, and Spitalfields as free from houses as it is now full of them; where, on a spot yet known as Artillery Lane, he met to practise his crossbows, arquebusses and other light artillery.

Such was London as a city in the days of Cromwell—venerable in its external aspect—strangely different in all such particulars from the modern metropolis, and yet containing within it the germs of those social forces which in their expansion were to promote the greatness both it and the country have since realised.

Her citizens, largely engaging in commerce, and offering a home to all, were (during the Protectorate) beginning to emancipate both themselves and their trade from cumbrous restrictions and fetters which City companies had imposed. The Jew—proscribed for three centuries—was again permitted to reside there, and through him, and the Friends just then arising, an increased commercial power in the fructifying use of money was to become developed. In Education, the numerous foundation schools established by King Edward had borne fruit; a knowledge of Greek and Latin had emancipated the learned from the trammels of monkish literature, and they had exchanged the dry and musty atmosphere of the missal or the legend to breathe the freer air of the Greek philosopher or historian. Shakespeare's works were beginning to be generally understood, a Milton was moulding the vernacular into classic English; and above all, the Bible had become a popular book. Many of the ministers of religion were learned, eloquent divines. Men of cultivated manners were becoming accomplished in arts learnt in foreign Courts, and were modelling the language of English compliment to imitate the politeness of continental neighbours—the old Saxon *thou* was giving place to the more courtly *you*; and the head, seldom uncovered except in sign of reverence or obeisance, was now bared in compliment by any one who wished to be thought fashionable or polite.

In Natural Science, though little *outward* progress had been made, the foundations were being laid of that system of inductive inquiry which was so soon to bear fruit through the labours of men then in their youth—a fruit destined in after time to ripen, until those marvellous discoveries of the hidden forces of nature should appear, which, in their application to social life, have realised to man more power and wealth than ever the alchemist searched for, or the philosopher dared to imagine.

Cromwell's era was like a spring-time as to some of these things, and showed its action in many ways. The coinage, grievously debased, was rearranged by him, and such pieces struck, under the management of Simon (whom he appointed over the Mint), as not even Wyon, of our day, can excel. The carriage (introduced a century before, but still cumbrous) was being mounted on springs to lessen its joltings; and the stage coach, long so highly prized, dated the commencement of its career from this period. At this time, also, the

Post Office system took its rise. And more important, perhaps, than all, the daily newspaper was introduced, appearing amid a flood of broadsheets, squibs, and pamphlets of that controversial age; and as the eye looks back on that day of unrest and striving, it sees with interest that such was the period when the foundation was first laid of that free and independent journalism which has now become a fourth estate in the realm.

Nevertheless, amid all these signs of life, the national fabric had been rudely shaken, and nothing (at the time when our Friends arose) was yet re-established. Royalty, the bishops, the House of Lords, had been swept away; all the ancient pillars had fallen in the torrent of civil and religious strife, and men's minds surged to and fro, not knowing what next to look for—a king, or a republic, or a Cromwell stronger than either.

In the events which produced this agitation, London had taken an important share; her citizens had contributed much of the gold that gave sinew to the parliamentary force; her ministers, from their pulpits, had developed the doctrines that made liberty precious; her train-bands had shielded the five members when a king searched for them in vain; in her prisons had lain a prime minister and an archbishop, under sentence of death, and on her Tower Hill they had come out to suffer; so also the king himself, from a "window of his own palace" (as Walpole says), came out on to the scaffold to die, ending at Whitehall (so near to the city) that strange and chequered career. Such scenes, with all the intrigues and factions of which they were the result, agitated the minds of the London citizens into a ferment on all *political* questions; and on *religious* subjects (which really lay at the root of much of the political changes), their minds were especially unsettled. Here, all order and authority seemed uprooted as if for ever. The Mass-book of the Pope and the Prayer-book of the Bishop were alike deprived of all State authority, the whole Episcopal bench had lost their sees, and, amid the confusions and distractions that prevailed, sects and parties, strangely intermingled, strove with one another for power or religious influence.

Religion was, during the early Protectorate, a prominent topic of the day. "Divinity as a Science" (*see* "Lady Hutchinson," Introduction, p. xvi.) "was a study then in vogue." It seems to have tinctured the conversation and writings of the greater part of society. Election and reprobation were then popular themes. Men discussed Articles and creeds in every social circle, as well as the varieties and points of a doctrine with the keen zest evinced in after years on the state of markets or the prices of the funds; they assembled in crowds to hear sermons, where they stood for three or four hours at a time to listen to the words of some gifted preacher. In a work called "The Ministers' Morning Exercises," it is recorded of Howe, one of these eminent preachers, that "on public fast-days he would commence the service about 9 in the morning, with prayer for about a quarter of an hour, and afterwards read and expound a chapter, in which he would spend about three quarters of an hour; then pray for about an hour; preach for another hour, and pray for about half an hour. After this [12.30], he would retire and take some little refreshment for about a quarter of an hour, the people singing all the while; and then he would come again into the pulpit and pray for another hour; preach another sermon, of about an hour's length; then spend about half an hour more in prayer, and conclude the service about 4 in the afternoon, i.e. after seven hours of preaching." *

The relative merits of infant or adult baptism were questions often transferred from the teachings of a pulpit to the stormier arena of public debate, where men (unbred in colleges, but grown experienced in the art of controversy) contended for hours before excited audiences.

A stern necessity seemed laid on every man (the result of prolonged party strife) for him to determine for himself in all things, religious as well as political, what was Truth; and in the violent controversies this teaching engendered through the land, London seemed as a centre in the strife; and during its height was it that Friends' views first became known there.

---

* Of William Bates, another Nonconformist of those days, the following portrait is given:—" Comely in person, with bold features, and richly curling locks; graceful, with the action of a finished orator; of superior natural endowments, and considerable literary culture; possessing a memory of extraordinary retentiveness, and a voice so sweetly musical that he won the name of the silver-tongued; with large stores of theological knowledge, and also gifted with a Nestor-like eloquence, which fell in gentle flakes—this extraordinary pulpit orator was in high repute among the upper classes, and indeed, amongst people of all grades."—*Stoughton's Ecclesiastical History*, vol. ii. p. 185.

CHAPTER III.

SKETCH OF THE STATE OF RELIGIOUS PARTIES IN LONDON AT THE TIME OF THE RISE OF "FRIENDS" THERE IN 1654.

The year 1654 was the time when Friends' religious views were first publicly preached in London. Oliver Cromwell had but shortly before been installed as Protector, viz. December, 1653, whereby the heat of men's minds on *political* subjects was somewhat allayed; but they still engaged with much ardour in debate on questions respecting religion, into which free inquiry was for a time permitted. His rule thus became marked as a time when the ferment long existing on these subjects in the nation grew into yet fuller development, and in London the excitement and debate it occasioned seemed concentred as in a focus.

Great was "the shattering" which this spirit of free inquiry produced among the sects already existing, and very numerous were the new ones to which it gave birth, to last, in most cases, but for the day in which they arose.*

It seems due, in describing the meetings of one of these bodies—now known as The Society of Friends, and yet remaining in full operation—to pass cursorily in review the struggle of religious thought which had prevailed in England for centuries, and was the cause of those differences which produced " sects."

This struggle had commenced earlier than the Tudors, but was notably developed under their rule, when the names of Catholic and Protestant distinguished the contending principles, and each side suffered or inflicted cruelties according as they were in or out of power.†

On Protestantism gaining the political ascendancy in

---

* The early Friends' letters speak of " many societies ;" and names of Seekers, Levellers, Ranters, Fifth-Monarchists, Waiters, Manifesterians, and others, occur frequently in the works of early Friends—besides the older and established sects of Presbyterian, Independent, and Baptist. Ephraim Pagitt, in his " Heresiography " (1654), gives a list of about forty sects as then existing in England.

† Much of the harshness of conduct in these early days seems owing to an undue prominence having been given by them to the teachings of the Old Testament.

England, by the King assuming the function of Head of the Church, signs were not wanting to show that men, content to strive in union against Papal supremacy, would be impelled, by differing views on the question of Church government, to contend strongly among themselves so soon as partial success had crowned their efforts against a foreign spiritual yoke.

Not only in England, but on the Continent generally, these differences rapidly developed, and, embracing a great variety of subjects, became grouped along two very distinct lines of thought, known respectively by the great men who had suggested them as Lutheran and Calvinistic.

In our country the ruling party attempted a middle course that should *embrace* all, rather than *decide* between these parties; and founded a Church of which it has been said the liturgy is Popish, the articles Calvinistic, and the creed Lutheran.

In this Anglican Church, as by law established amongst us, prominence is given in its government to an order of clergy, small in number, but claiming to inherit, under the name of bishops, those powers with which our Lord had endowed his apostles; and it was in a denial of these claims that some of the earliest oppositions were first developed by a sect known as the Presbyterians. These objected to any "spiritual Lords"—and not only regarded all the clergy as brethen of equal power, but admitted an admixture of pious laymen to a share in the internal government of the Church. To this system Scotland early pronounced its adhesion, under the influence of John Knox; and its claims were so strongly enforced in England as to be brought to a solemn decision under James the First—whose verdict, in favour of Episcopacy, was expressed in the oft-repeated words "No Bishop—No King." He had known, as King of Scotland, how a Presbytery could annoy, if not control him; and he saw in the dependence of a bishop on the Crown more prospect of a quiet rule in ecclesiastical affairs than if a larger and less controllable body were placed at the head of the Church. Presbyter, said the King, is nothing, but "Priest writ large." Disappointed as he certainly was in his hope of thus reducing all to uniformity, or else "harrying them (as he called it) out of the kingdom," he nevertheless found (as his predecessors had experienced) that bishops were a loyal order—and as such they have ever been popular with governing powers, remaining so even now when the Royal prerogative has ceased to be personally exercised, but is practically directed by ministers of state.

The reason of this is obvious, for the source through which alone a member of the clergy can under this system become invested with high and so-called "apostolic" power, rests in the nation itself—acting formerly by the decision of its king, and now by the minister who may happen through the will of the Parliament to be in power. Great as are considered to be the gifts and grace-bestowing power of a bishop—magical as is the asserted result of his touch—all these lie dormant, or are guided towards any particular individual of the clerical order by the selection of the nation acting through its representative on the throne, or on the bench of the Treasury. Hence its popularity with all the ruling powers, and those who affect rank, fashion, and position. Hence, also, the deep-seated objections felt from the period of its establishment in the minds of those unable to believe that a clergyman can be developed into a so-called apostle just when a king or a minister may give a *congè d'elire*.

No spirit of comprehension in Elizabeth, or coercion under James her successor, could make all Englishmen so think and believe alike on this question, as to realise a one undivided Church throughout the land.

Those who dissented became known as the great Puritan party, who, for peace' sake, preferred to quit the land, emigrating to America, hopeless of freedom here, but they appear to have left behind such a legacy of religious inquiry as multiplied, rather than diminished, the differences that arose.

For some time two distinct lines of thought had been observable in the men thus opposing Episcopacy, which are those generally known as the Presbyterian and Independent sects, of whose points of difference some explanation should be offered. The former preferred Church Government by Synods of clergy of equal rank and laity intermixed; they objected also to a common form of Prayer, preferring "a Directory" instead, and they denounced the use of those garments and ceremonies the bishops had retained. As a body the Presbyterians were wealthy and influential. Composed of men of education and station, they were numerous in the cities and especially so in the City of London. The Independents went much further, and believed that all power in Church government rested in the members of every individual Church; and according to their views, a company of believers (however small) was a Church, if by mutual covenant they had come together. Such could and were at liberty to govern themselves as they thought best, and select any one whom they deemed gifted to be their minister, whose office as it arose from, so also was it dependent upon, their pleasure. These Independent doctrines found great favour in England before the Civil war commenced, especially amongst tradesmen in towns, and the sturdy yeomen and smaller farmers of the country; they suited the spirit of enterprise in the one, and the love of freedom in the other; they elevated, whilst they emancipated, their thought—for becoming consciously members in a Church older than the Church of Rome, and deeming themselves inheritors of all the promises of God. They viewed questions of Church and State on a truly independent basis, in which, by opening the ranks of the ministry to all powerful and gifted minds, they became so directed as to prove a most formidable opponent to any principles not based on free liberty of conscience in Divine worship. By their influence, so soon as the " great Independent " (Cromwell) arose to concentrate the individual power of their Churches, a king lost both his throne and his life.

Here, however, their power in the State ended, for (wanting a common cause) so soon as the king who threatened all Nonconformists alike was gone, this great proportion of the nation, ranking for a time as Independents, and as such joining heart and hand with Presbyterians against Episcopacy, became greatly dispersed by the natural development of those very religious views their system promoted.

Such consequences must arise in times of great national excitement, like those succeeding the civil wars; men had learned to think on all subjects, and, more than all, to decide on them, for life or death had been the issue; every man had had more or less his property and even existence dependent on the terrible arbitrament of the sword or the bullet, leading him to search deep before his decision, but to *act* upon his convictions when once formed.

Such "searchings of heart" in these (so-called) times of confusion, had a marked effect on the great Independent party in separating from them a set of men even yet more strict than they were in their observance of Scriptural injunctions, especially on the subject of water baptism. Men who required the ordinance to be confined to the believer when of full age—who considered it a rite of admission, not of regeneration, and obtained for themselves, in consequence of their views, the name of Baptists or Anabaptists.

Resulting as this sect did from inquiry and deep searching

of Scripture, it is peculiar to no country, but has arisen in all parts of the world whenever such inquiring times as these were have prevailed. Happily, in England the movement was free from the fanaticism and excitement which the Baptists showed in the days of Luther, although the English Baptist thought himself (like the German Anabaptist) "a saint that could not be lost." Such views, whilst nerving the pikemen in their stubborn resistance to Rupert's impetuous charges, or firing the zeal of the invincible "Ironsides," never led to scenes of lawless violence or bloodshed, such as happened at Munster, in Germany.

Bishop Burnet, vol. i. 79, gives the following testimony to the good conduct of the troops:—"I remember well three regiments coming to Aberdeen. There was an order and discipline and a face of gravity and piety among them that amazed all people. Most of them were Independents and Anabaptists. They were all gifted men and preached as they were moved. But they never disturbed the public assemblies in the churches but once. They came and reproached the preachers for laying things to their charge that were false. I was then present. The debate grew very fierce. At last they drew their swords, but there was no hurt done, yet Cromwell displaced the governor for not punishing this."

From this sect of Baptists, Friends, when they arose, drew so large a proportion of their members as to make it desirable to dwell more particularly on their views, in order to understand how far these converts might have been brought in the development of religious inquiry previous to joining our Society.

The members of this sect, besides their peculiar views on the rite of baptism, insisted more strongly that the Independents on the inviolability of a man's conscience, and have never sanctioned persecution on account of religion. They were also more strict in their observance of the exact letter of Scripture than the latter, which led many among them to use the plain language, to avoid compliments, to dress simply, to reject vain swearing, and to call the days of the week and the months of the year by numbers rather than by names. They were strong in the denunciation of priestly power, and in maintaining that Christ was Head over his Church. That He alone could qualify his ministers, of the fitness of whom the Churches might judge and recognise, but could not create. Those having gifts in the ministry mostly exercised them gratuitously or without stipend, mere hirelings being denounced. The minister received only gifts, and often

supported himself wholly by some trade or handicraft.*
Their meetings for worship were frequent, to which were
added those for controversy or debate, where any who chose
might speak; and through these last they often discovered latent
talents, which became developed by fostering care into ministerial gifts. They recognised but two orders in the Church, the
Elder and the Deacon; the latter attended to the more
secular arrangements, such as care of the poor, &c. The
former was the term under which their ministers were known,
being adopted as more scriptural and less assumptive of
priestly power.† To these two were added in some Baptist
Churches a third and superior order, known as "the
Messenger," a name derived from a passage in one of Paul's
Epistles. In constitution each Church was in principle, like
those of the Independents, separate, but a district union of
these several Churches was often made, and numerous distinct
Churches, would, by appointed deputies, confer at general
meetings like those of the Friends' Yearly Meeting. Much
care was devoted to maintain propriety of conduct among the
members, and the authorities in the Churches possessed and
exercised summary powers in cutting off offenders; but the
authority rested rather with the officers than the body of the
Church. Such a band of earnest Christians like these Baptists,
becoming widely diffused as they were throughout the land,
could not but exert great influence in training up men to lead
good Christian lives, and leavening society for good. Their
ministers were sometimes those risen from the ranks, like
Bunyan, and of no education, but more often ejected churchmen, like Knollys, or learned laymen like Edwards and
Powell, who freely gave up themselves and often their substance to the cause. Some of the best of the Parliamentarians,
such as Fleetwood and Hutchinson, were members of their
Churches, and from their pulpits came one, who, by his inimit-
able "dream," has alike charmed, instructed, guided, and
consoled, wherever the English tongue is known.

As a Church the Baptists never realised in effective power
what their actual numbers would have given them had
they been united together by a more perfect organisation;
but, deriving from Independency the principle of isola-
tion of their separate communities, they became further

---

* See *Taylor's General Baptists*, and *Crosby's Baptists*.
† Our Friends were like them in applying the term Elder to Ministering Friends.

divided among themselves by the differences which their great desire to follow the letter of Scripture produced. On many subjects these several Churches thus disagreed: some being for sprinkling in administering baptism, others insisting on a total immersion; some were for allowing it to be done in private or in a building, others considered that nothing less public than a river or some running water would suffice. The rite of the Lord's Supper occasioned also differences among them as among other bodies of Christians: some maintaining that it should be taken fasting, others after a meal; some that the recipients must kneel in receiving it, others that they must stand; others, again, permitting it to be received sitting—each mode having its earnest advocates. The observance of the Sabbath was another difficulty; some, keeping more strictly to the letter of Scripture, insisted on the claims of the Seventh over the First day of the week, and became thereby known as Sabbatarian Baptists; and the strictness or otherwise of omitting all work of any kind during it was much canvassed. Much diversity also existed in the mode of appointing ministers, such as whether the imposition of hands were needful or unnecessary; whole Churches dividing on this one question alone. " During the civil wars" (see Taylor, in vol. i. p. 431, of " General Baptists ") " they seem to have had stated public exercises for the discussion of religious subjects, in which any one was at liberty to propose and defend his own opinion," when these views so tenaciously held were warmly discussed—until meetings held for conference and adjustment, became sometimes the scene of violent difference—which was often, it would appear, the case among the numerous Baptist communities when Friends first arose.

The peace of the Baptist Churches was also being disturbed on those cardinal points of doctrine, as to Election and Free Grace, which had separated the Reformation party into Lutherans and Calvinists a century before, and were a century later to divide the Methodist societies in England under Wesley and Whitfield. Among the Baptists these questions excited great commotion; and Friends arising at this time, their early preachers found much acceptance among those inclined to the doctrine of Free Grace, of which the Baptist records themselves contain full evidence—see Taylor's " History of the General Baptists," from which are taken the following extracts:

Vol. i. p. 147 (1651. Streatham, Cambridgeshire).—" About

this period the Quakers, Ranters, and other enthusiasts, were very active in spreading their extravagant notions, and too successful in making proselytes. Many members of this Church fell into their errors, and, pretending to have superior manifestations of the Holy Spirit within, despised the Scriptures and neglected the means of grace."

Vol. i. p. 154 (neighbourhood of Fenstanton).—" Indeed the strange and impious tenets which were then propagated by many wild enthusiasts, rendered such a watchful jealousy highly necessary. The Quakers especially were very busy in those parts, and several Baptists were led away by them."

Vol. i. p. 157 (Warboys).—" In the years 1648 and 1649, the hearers increased, and several were added to the Church, but in the following year the Quakers, Ranters, and Levellers seduced so many of the members, that the remainder were discouraged, and the regular meetings of the congregation were much neglected. For a short season indeed they appear to have been nearly discontinued." *

Those adhering to the *Calvinistic* views as to Election and Reprobation were not, it appears, so much shaken—these became known as the Particular Baptists, with which section especially those violent controversies were maintained which marked the early annals of the " Friends." The other section, known as the General or Arminian Baptists, were so much reduced, that, from being at first the more numerous body of the two, they have, since the rise of Friends, so declined in numbers as to become much smaller than the Particular or Calvinistic Baptists. Thus, to any student of these times, it will be evident that there was a shattering amid all the sects going forward, accompanied with much fermentation in men's minds. And surveying this, as we can now do, in the calmness imposed by a distance of two centuries, we see a preparation favourable to the entrance of that new sect which was about to make its appearance on the troubled scene.

Apostolic tradition, custom, practice of the Fathers, ordinances, and priesthood, had been worked out to what they thought a sure, safe, and comprehensive basis by the Episcopalians. The Presbyterians, rejecting tradition and accepting Holy Scripture alone as their guide, claimed for their system a safer and surer basis, free from the superstitions, as they

---

* The early Baptist records are difficult to meet with, but there seems no reason why these from the Eastern Counties should not be taken to fairly represent the state of matters in their Churches elsewhere.

considered them, which the Episcopal Church retained. Following on in this course, the Independents professed, in the light of Scripture and by a blessing on its study, to have been led into a yet more excellent way—which the Baptist societies maintained had become yet more thoroughly perfected by their doctrine and practice, through taking the word of Scripture as their still more exclusive and literal rule of Faith. Is it difficult to realise what would result, when these religious bodies, earnestly seeking the right way as discerned in the page of Holy Scripture, guiding themselves and all they did by its words and its histories, and the light, which by study, by prayer, and fasting, might be shed upon them, should hear, as they did hear, that not alone had narratives been preserved of prophets in days of old, but that prophets had arisen among them, and were proclaiming their message to wondering thousands? So that not alone in a former and far-distant time, on the sacred soil of Syria, but even then in England, on the moors of Yorkshire, and in the streets of London, all over the country, and in every town, the words "Thus saith the Lord" were freely spoken, and a like authority claimed for the utterance of their inspirations as if the messenger were a prophet among the Hebrews.*

Such a phenomenon was to the men of the Cromwell Era, so intensely engaged on religious subjects, as startling as the discovery to us would be of another continent, or a new power (such as electricity and steam), and, as such, the new doctrine encountered the extremes of joyful recognition or indignant denial.

The men who embraced these new views and admitted the

---

* What Robertson, in "Lectures on the Corinthians," p. 89, says of the Hebrew Prophet may, in some measure, be applied to the early Friends:—"They developed another kind of deliverance founded on no prescriptive authority, but on the authority of Truth. They stood up against King and Priest. They witnessed against Kingcraft and Priestcraft, against false social maxims, against superstitions, against all that was enslaving the Jewish soul. And how did they effect this deliverance? They proclaimed God as he is. Their invariable preface was, 'Thus saith the Lord.' They fell back on deep first principles. They said that 'to do justice, to love mercy, to walk humbly with God,' was better than praying and fasting and sacrifices. They revealed and declared the true character of God, which had become incredible to the people through the false glosses it had received. And so the prophet also was the deliverer of his people, loosing them from not slavery, nor political oppression, but a worse bondage, the bondage which comes from ecclesiastical and civil institutions when they have ceased to be real."

prophetic claim, became placed in antagonism with the other gathered Churches. All denominations denounced them, and, unfortunately for both sides, railing was at times returned for railing. The Baptist charged the Friend, when he exalted the Light within, as depreciating the one great and all-availing outward sacrifice made by our Lord himself. The Independent ridiculed this inward monitor, as nothing but natural conscience; the Presbyterian abhorred it as blasphemy when the Friend said Christ dwelt in him; the Episcopalian denounced Quaker scruples as a crime against society and Holy Church: all had their special points of difference and debate with the Friend, all had their grounds of union one with another in denouncing him, and yet, under this separate and combined opposition, the new views spread, and the Friend, like Israel of old, " grew and multiplied."

Such were some of the troubles and opposition the Society encountered when its doctrines were first promulgated among the sects by the early preachers, when its claim to a prophetic power was most strongly enforced, and the words " Thus saith the Lord " were most freely used. Highly aggressive and strongly assumptive, the Society had in it germs which, in the intense excitement of the Cromwell period, threatened to become developed into a fanaticism, which the episode of James Naylor happily both illustrated and restrained. It is a high testimony to the humility and judgment of its leaders and their dependence on Divine guidance that they should have brought, as they did, a newly-formed society through such a period, and were enabled, as the national mind became more settled, to consolidate the body and keep it intact during the time that succeeded, when it was not only opposed by tongue and pen, but also by the power of the State and Acts of Parliament.

This wisdom and prudence were early shown, even in the fervour of its youth, in the arrangements for the outward welfare of the congregations—such as the establishment of regular meetings; securing places in which they could assemble, both for the multitudes who came to listen, and in more retired places for the members themselves.

It is chiefly in illustration of this feature of the Society of Friends in London and its neighbourhood that the following accounts are given.

CHAPTER IV.

NOTES ON THE HISTORY OF FRIENDS IN LONDON, 1654—1666.

INCLUDING AN ACCOUNT OF THE MEETINGS HELD IN PRIVATE HOUSES PREVIOUS TO THE ESTABLISHMENT OF THE SIX LONDON MONTHLY MEETINGS.

THE rise of the Society of Friends in London did not occur until some years after its development in the Midland counties, and some two or three years later than in Yorkshire and other northern districts, nor was its commencement due as in those parts to the personal labours of George Fox, who found on his arrival in London, in 1654, a work in convincement already begun by the Gospel services of other ministers of the Society.

George Fox had previously been in London as early as 1644; but was then undergoing his season of trial and conflict, and found nothing there to comfort him.* Yet, he mentions an uncle as a "pious man," also "some tender people," who would have had him stay among them.

At the close of the year 1653, Gervase Benson (a North country gentleman, a friend of Judge Fell, himself a Justice of the Peace, and lately become a Friend), was in London, where he found, however, but little at that time to encourage him. "Here is," writes Gervase [see Letters, p. 2], "nothing I can have any fellowship with, only the Lord is raising up a light in many (both priests and people) that discovers the carnal actings, both of magistrates and ministers—so called, and they are carried forth publicly to declare against them." He visited some of these meetings, but took an unfavourable view of them, as "spending their time in

---

* "I was under great misery and trouble there. For I looked upon the great Professors of the City of London, and I saw all was dark and under the chain of darkness, and I had an uncle there, one Pickering, a Baptist (and they were tender then) yet I could not impart my mind to him nor join with them. For I saw all young and old where they were, some tender people would have had me stayed, but I was fearful and returned homewards."—*G. F.'s Journal.*

putting questions one to another, and jangling about things they could not witness." In a P.S. to the same letter, he notes that "there are many hereaway inquiring after Friends in the North, and the truth made manifest in you, and much writing for and against the priests."

It was early in 1654, and therefore shortly after this visit of Gervase Benson, that Isabel Buttery, and another woman Friend, coming up together from the North, undertook to distribute in London a paper lately issued by George Fox, on the subject of the Kingdom of Heaven. This document is printed first in his collected epistles, and by its title alone, framed according to the manner of that day, some idea of its contents may be formed : " To all that would know the way to the Kingdom, whether they be in Forms, without Forms, or got above all Forms, a direction to turn your minds within, where the voice of God is to be heard, whom you ignorantly worship as afar off; and to wait upon Him for true wisdom. That you may know Truth from Error, the Word from the Letter, the Power from the Form, and the true Prophets from the False, given forth by one of those whom the World in scorn calls Quakers." Among those who received and assisted Isabel Buttery and her companion, were two brothers, Simon and Robert Dring, one having a house in Watling Street, and the other in Moorgate, each of whom opened their dwellings for the meeting of those who inclined to assemble after this new way; these were the *first meetings* of Friends held in London, and were mostly seasons of *silent waiting*, except that now and then (as W. Crouch* says), "Isabel did speak a few words." Amos Stoddart (formerly a captain in the Parliamentary forces) was also a frequenter of these early gatherings at the brothers Dring, as well as Ruth Brown, who became the wife of William Crouch, also Anne Downer, afterwards married to George Whitehead. Of these some further mention will have to be made, as they became subsequently prominent members of the London Friends' Society.

Such were the small beginnings of our Society in the great city, confined at first mainly to the distribution of papers, and leading only to the gatherings of a few kindred spirits to wait

---

* A well-known London Friend, some of whose papers were published after his decease, under the title of " Posthuma Christiana," from which many of the particulars given here of the early meetings are taken.

together in a reverential, but seldom broken silence, in one or two private houses. Yet even in this its earliest and most quiet stage, some opposition was experienced; for Isabel, whilst distributing her papers one First-day evening, in St. Paul's Churchyard, was arrested, and with Robert Dring's maid (her companion) carried before the Lord Mayor, who committed them both to Bridewell for the offence of Sabbath breaking—thus showing both the fanatical spirit of the times and of those in authority, when the distribution of religious books, which is now considered meritorious, was then so great an offence to these rigid Sabbatarians then in office, as to lodge two maidens in a common gaol, where women only of the lowest character were put.* Such sentences, though slight as to duration of the punishment, served to indicate the feeling that would be aroused if a larger development of the Society were to occur, and prepare us to expect what was now at hand.

George Fox, in his Journal, under date of the beginning of 1654, when he himself was in the North, says, "About this time did the Lord move upon the spirits of many whom He had raised up .... to travel Southward .... in the service of the Gospel. .... As Francis Howgill and Edward Burrough to London, John Camm and John Audland to Bristol, through the countries; Richard Hubberthorne and George Whitehead to Norwich; Thomas Holmes into Wales; and others otherways, for above sixty ministers had the Lord raised up and did now send abroad out of the North Country." These "more than sixty ministers," mostly young men, or those who were in "manhood's prime," seem, like the Seventy of Old, to have journeyed two and two together to their various fields of service, and in all directions great results followed from their Gospel labours—those in London, the scene of Francis Howgill and Edward Burrough's ministry not being the least. These two ministers, though from time to time associated with others, were prominent in the beginning of the work here, and were both so eminently qualified for the service and blessed in their labours, as to leave their names inseparably connected with the rapid rise and increase of the Society in London.

---

* Maitland's *History of London*, vol ii. p. 937 :—" For the third degree they provided Bridewell, where the vagabonds and idle strumpets are chastised and compelled to labour to the overthrow of the vicious life of idleness."

Both came from the Yorkshire Dales, and though Francis Howgill was much the elder of the two, yet he was only thirty-six, his companion being as to years but a youth of eighteen. They had embraced the views of Friends about two years before, having each previously undergone long-continued periods of varied and deep religious experience, of which their writings bear evident trace. Francis Howgill had been led, as he describes in his " Dawnings of the Gospel Day," to unite himself with various sects in succession, searching therein for truth, and had been held in such esteem as to become himself a teacher among them, and was able (as he says) to "glory in it." He was a man of some literary acquirements; had married a wife with a small competence, and was occupying a somewhat conspicuous position among the professors in the district around Sedbergh at the time of George Fox's visit. He was much impressed with the ministry of that remarkable man; and on first hearing him in public exclaimed (when a colonel sought to oppose),— " He preaches as one having authority and not as the scribes." A subsequent interview at the chapel where Francis Howgill himself was accustomed to preach confirmed this impression, and embracing at once the views of Gospel truth as set forth by George Fox, he became himself one of its most effective and zealous promulgators, closing a ministry of sixteen eventful years by suffering for the cause unto death in the prison of Appleby Castle.

Even yet more remarkable and prominent in the work was his youthful companion, Edward Burrough, who at the time of their first visit in London was only eighteen years of age, and yet had passed through so many and varied religious experiences as to have become a man of deep knowledge in the school of Christ.* Like Francis Howgill he had been led, in his search after truth, to unite himself with various sects in succession, but without finding that full peace for which his soul yearned. Awakened by the ministry of George Fox to a more excellent way, he embraced what he felt was to him the truth, and submitting to the reproach of his parents

---

* " He was a very understanding boy in his youth . . . he had the spirit of a man when he was but a child, and I may say grey hair was upon him when he was but a youth, for he was clothed with wisdom in his infancy. . . . His whole delight was always among good people, and to be conferring and reading the Scriptures . . . His very strength was bended after God."—*F. Howgill's Testimony.*

and relations, who cast him off as mad, he threw the whole energy of his ardent soul into the promulgation of those views which had brought him such abundant peace. Leaving the Dales of Yorkshire, he travelled with Francis Howgill and J. Camm to London, which became the chief scene of his Gospel labours, and there he also laid down his life a prisoner for conscience' sake, after a brief but eventful ministry of ten years, and at the early age of twenty-eight. He was eminently fitted for this sphere of labour, being possessed of a natural eloquence that attracted the multitude, and combining with it considerable talent in debate which enabled him to stand his ground with opposers. Gifted with great physical power of voice he could command attention from a noisy crowd, and whilst so vehement in denunciation and invective as to be styled a Son of Thunder, he was withal so loving to the tender-hearted that they felt him as a Son of Consolation,— thus filled both with power and love he gave himself up to spend and be spent. Bold, as Thomas Ellwood says, in his Master's quarrel, yet open and free to every thirsty lamb, he was in life the stay of his friends, and even by his death encouraged them in the maintenance of that form of faith for which he died as a martyr.

It was in the summer of 1654 that these two earnest evangelists came up from their native Dales to London, and assembled for worship with the little companies of Friends before mentioned; but these small and silent gatherings were far from suited to absorb or develop their latent powers, and they at once sought a more public field for the exercise of their gifts.

The times, as before shown, were those of great controversy on religious subjects, for all was unsettled, and the public (especially the citizens of London) showed such an intense interest in these questions as to hold frequent meetings for argument and debate in churches or elsewhere. To these any who had an opinion were free to come and express it,*

---

* As an instance where the message, though given in a church, was well received, an extract from the Letters, p. 42, is given. "The last First-day my dear yokefellow and I went in the forenoon to two of the highest notionists and the greatest deceivers in the city, at two steeple-houses, where the wise of the city come, and I had great liberty and spoke towards an hour; all were silent, and some confessed they never heard so much truth in power delivered. Many would have had me to their houses, but we lay hands on none hastily."

only at the peril of much personal abuse if what was said were disapproved.

Of such occasions Francis Howgill and Edward Burrough were quick to avail themselves, and brief as are the accounts remaining of their movements we can trace them in (the Letters) going from one gathering to another; visiting all sorts of sects, then very numerous, and in some obtaining a full and fair hearing, amid others encountering a storm of opposition, and, in some, receiving personal abuse.

At first discouragement was experienced by them when they found how "subtle was the spirit" of the London congregations; very different from those they had left in the Yorkshire Dales, and earnest desire arose for wisdom and guidance in an experience so new to them. This was granted, and in such full measure that the tone of discouragement is soon found to be exchanged for one of joy, for they were able to say "hundreds are convinced, and thousands wait to see the issue; very many societies we have visited, and are now able to stand."

No doubt the London citizen, accustomed to the pulpit eloquence of learned divines, or the practised perorations of the teachers and expounders of those days, regarded at first these simple dalesmen with their provincial dialect as but the "setters forth of some new notions" (see Letters) among the many such then prevailing; and, holding their "persons in contempt," thought but little of the message. Yet this prejudice soon gave way before the wisdom and fervid zeal with which they spoke, whereby the doctrine rose into dominion; "for," as they wrote (see Letters, p. 16), "to that we speak which brings us in remembrance when they see us not."

Thus in a spirit and power like martyrs (which they both became), and borne up through a strength not their own, they successfully encountered "the high-flown wisdom and notions" (as they termed it) of the "subtle Londoners," and keeping them from "disputing and questioning," they "raised up a witness in their consciences," which made the hundreds and thousands thus reached perceive how far short their previous experience had been of "possessing that which they professed."

The success of this ministry became so quickly apparent, that a few weeks produced this result; and, after three months of service, they had gathered in so many from the other societies as to have meetings of their own—as many as three or four a week—very different in size from those early ones at the houses of the brothers Dring, being now become larger (as the Letters, pp. 16 and 19, say) than any place we can get will contain, so that we are much put to it.

Difficulties now arose of another kind, which seriously impeded and threatened to imperil the continuance of the success, for no separation could be obtained for Friends, and crowds of noisy and rude persons so poured into the large meeting-places, that unless one gifted like Edward Burrough were present to tame these "lions and savage apprentices," the scene became one of uproar and confusion. "Our burden" (writes F. Howgill, see Letters, p. 27), " is great—we cannot get any separation for the multitude, and so Friends do not much know one another, and we cannot conveniently get any place to meet in, that Friends may sit down."

To meet these difficulties, a large meeting-place, known as the Bull and Mouth, which would hold 1,000, it is said, was obtained, and the meetings so arranged as to devote it to service among all who chose to attend, whilst those already convinced were in future to be gathered with Friends in smaller private meetings, for which purpose some thirty Friends now offered their houses—this was within six months of the coming of Francis Howgill and Edward Burrough. (See account of Bull and Mouth.)

The wisdom of this arrangement soon became apparent, both in the increase of converts gathered in out of the " multitude " frequenting the general meeting-place, and the building up of those already *reached* into union and fellowship one with another, through the influences exerted by the numerous smaller and more retired gatherings: it offered, also, a fuller scope for the exercise of individual gifts, allowing many to minister in these meetings, at the dwelling-houses, whose power was lost in scenes such as the large meeting-place presented. Thus, Friends came really to know one another, and a foundation was laid for that union of Friend with Friend, which has characterised the body during its continuance until the present day.

The system of having these two kinds of meetings, some public and others private, prevailed among the London Friends for some years after their rise—indeed, as long as the work

Bull and Mouth:

Left: the inn yard, from a nineteenth-century print [LSF]

Below: detail of Sands' plan, 1717, showing the meeting house in relation to the inn. North is at the bottom. [City of London, London Metropolitan Archives, by permission of Christ's Hospital]

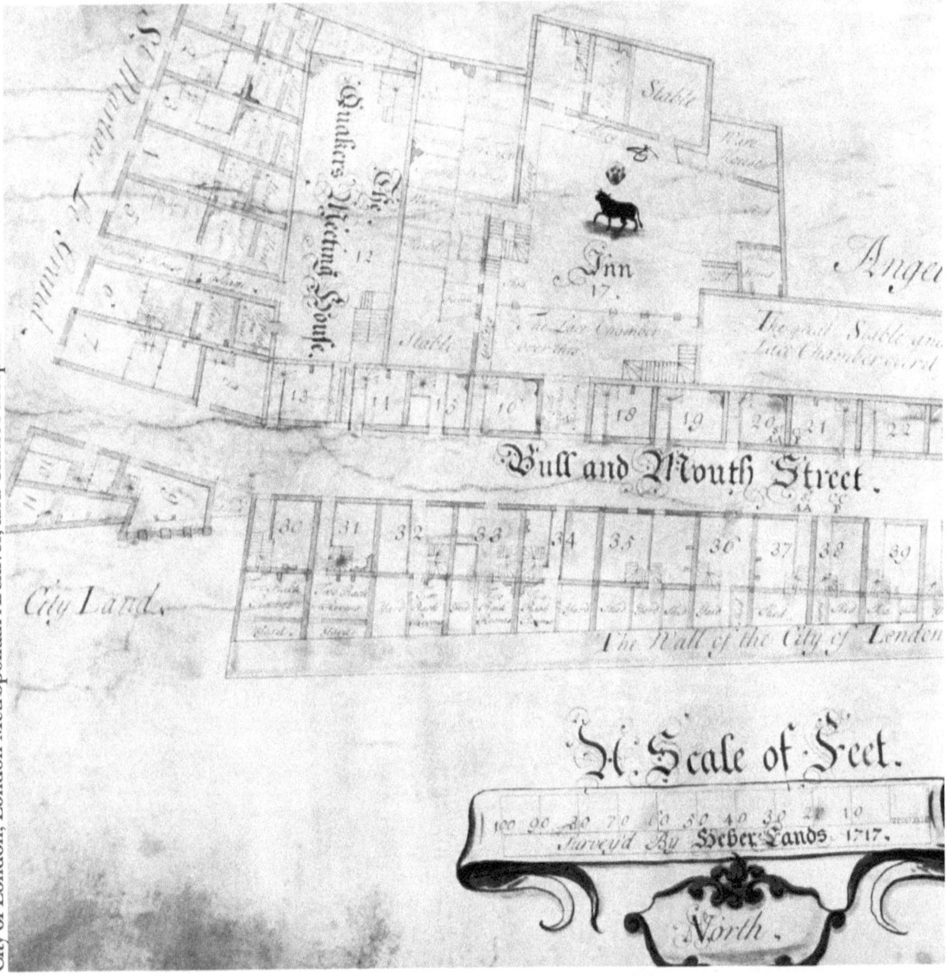

facing p.24

"The Quakers meeting": late seventeenth-century engraving from a painting by Egbert van Heemskerk; "M[arcel] Lauron pinx" [LSF]

facing p.25

of general evangelisation among the populace continued—and the ministry in these, and the building-up of the gathered Church, were recognised as distinct spheres of Gospel service, continuing until the care arising from the great numbers of convinced appears to have slackened the efforts for evangelisation among the masses.

Francis Howgill and Edward Burrough were zealous evangelists, and shrank not from any encounter with the London populace, so that they could but win souls for Christ. It needed men of special power to successfully meet such gatherings. "We have great giants (say the Letters, p. 19) to encounter with; . . . the devil rules, and is head in all sorts;" great numbers of ranters, and "rude people," and "savage apprentices," are frequently mentioned, and as often "that the power of the Lord rose above all, and chained the mouths of Lions."

Amid such scenes, where even a man like George Fox found his voice and outward man (see Letters, p. 27) "almost spent," Edward Burrough was accustomed to labour; "threshing," as he called it, among the multitude, to the admiration of his friends. Then truly the power that wrought in him rose into dominion over all opposition. Thus writes W. Crouch, p. 26, " I have beheld him filled with power, by the Spirit of the Lord, for instance, at the Bull and Mouth, when the room, which was very large, hath been filled with people, many of whom have been in uproar contending one with another, some exclaiming against the Quakers, accusing and charging them with heresy, blasphemy, sedition, and what not; that they were deceivers and deluded the people; that they denied the Holy Scriptures and the Resurrection: others endeavouring to vindicate them, and speaking of them more favourably. In the midst of all which noise and contention, this servant of the Lord hath stood upon a bench, with a Bible in his hands (for he generally carried one about with him), speaking to the people with great authority . . . . and so suitable to the present debate amongst them, that the whole multitude was overcome thereby, and became exceeding calm and attentive, and departed peaceably, and with seeming satisfaction." Such was the power of this zealous evangelist as described to us by an eye-witness; and in the more quiet gatherings, his presence was as much valued to comfort and sustain, as his power of "threshing" amidst the multitude, also his self-denying conduct, in giving up all that he might preach Christ, nerved his friends by example to endure as he endured.

Of Edward Burrough's power over excited crowds, one further instance, as witnessed also by William Crouch, may be given in nearly his words. It was an occasion when Edward Burrough happened, whilst in Moorfields, to come upon a mob of London journeymen and rude apprentices, gathered in an excited state around a ring, within which sports of wrestling were going forward. The moment was a critical one in the sport, for a " lusty young fellow who had thrown several antagonists in succession," was moving defiantly about the ring, calling out for some one to try a fall with him—a challenge which none who had seen his powers, inclined to accept. Edward Burrough, however, stepped forward into the midst of the circle, and looking " austerely and gracefully upon him," in some few well-spoken words, " checks his fury and fortitude, so that his courage and strength are vanquished." Then turning himself to the bystanders, and suiting his discourse to the occasion, he called upon them in deeply earnest tones, to forsake vanities, and to fight the true fight—the fight of faith, whose prize was not a wrestler's honour, but a crown of life immortal. Touched by the young man's persuasive eloquence, the sports ceased, and with the close of the sermon, the crowd dispersed, many, it is said, owning afterwards, that their first impressions for good had been received in that discourse—the first, and possibly the last, ever preached by a Friend within a ring formed for the practice of "manly sports."

The system of having at this particular time two distinct kinds of meetings, though not directly traceable to the influence of George Fox, may very possibly have been in a measure due to his judgment and influence, for it is evident he was in London at the time it was adopted *—having been sent there by Col. Hacker, and having been liberated with words of commendation from Oliver—and was freely moving about among

---

* That such arrangements were in accordance with his views may be seen by an extract from an epistle of his so early as 1652. Vide *G. F.'s Epistles*, vol. ii. p. 13 : "And when there are any *Meetings* in unbroken *Places*, ye that go to Minister to the World take not the *whole meeting* of Friends with you thither, to suffer with and by the world's spirit ; but let Friends keep together, and wait *in their own Meeting Place*, so will the Life (in the Truth) be preserved and grow. And let *Three* or *Four* or *Six* that are grown up and are strong (in the Truth) go to such unbroken *Places* and thresh the *Heathenish Nature*, and there is true service for the Lord."

the Friends who at this time, writes Alexander Parker, "do not know much of George, and he is not very free, but of this they take notice that, in any company where George is present the rest for the most part are silent" (such was the influence possessed by this remarkable man over his brethren, and at a time when he himself was barely thirty-two); it can scarcely be doubted his advice was sought in the emergency that had arisen, and that the same judgment which became so apparent in directing the later affairs of the Society is to be traced in these arrangements of its early stage—to him even the most gifted of the preachers ever looked up as a son to a father. "Dearly salute us"* (says F. Howgill and E. Burrough a few months later in this same year to G. F.); "one hour with him would be great joy to us;" but whether the name of George Fox may be associated with these arrangements or not, it is interesting for those who in this day find it so desirable to make arrangements as to meetings according to the different condition of those invited, to observe that the Society, when in its earlier force, did recognise such diversity of operations, and that under this freedom and adaptation to circumstance a blessing of great increase resulted. Thus they had meetings to thresh in public—meetings for Friends only in private houses—also more select gatherings, afterwards known as "retired meetings,"—as will be seen in our accounts of the various meetings. The doctrine promulgated by these early preachers may be understood by their numerous pamphlets and treatises which still remain to us. In nearly all is observable a claim to somewhat of prophetic inspiration; their paragraphs contain a frequent use of the words "Thus saith the Lord." But how far such a claim can now be maintained for them, and their works be exalted into a rank parallel with Hebrew prophets, need not be discussed; if they ever had such a position it was temporary, whilst that of the Hebrew Scripture is permanent. Faith has been rekindled since then in thousands and thousands by the utterance of an Isaiah, whose words the Holy Spirit continues to bring home to the seeking soul with power, whilst

---

* We can see how G. F. saluted them, see his *Epistles*, vol. ii. p. 107, "Stir abroad whilst the Door is open and the Light shineth . . . the Lord give you an understanding in all things and his arm go along with you that ye may be to his glory. Dear Francis and Edward, In the Life of God wait, that ye may with it be led . . . that as good *Plow-men* and good Thresher-men ye may be to bring out the wheat."

the redundant periods of a Howgill, or a Burrough, excite now but little energising influence save to warm our hearts at the zeal of their authors.*

The subject matter of these Treatises, some hundreds in number, and extending over twelve years, ranges through a great variety of doctrinal questions; but the key-note to the whole may be found in the paper of George Fox that Isabel Buttery distributed. It was said by William Penn of this gifted man "that his words were a theme on which many a fair discourse was founded, and as abruptly and brokenly as sometimes his sentences would fall from him about divine things, it is well known they were often as texts to many fairer declarations" (W. Penn's Preface to G. F.'s Journal, p. xxvii.); and the same may be said of his Epistles, for they contain the germs of which the treatises and pamphlets of his early followers are to some extent an expansion.

It was the work of another to combine the germ and its expansive growth into those syllogistic sentences whereby a Barclay, in his Apology, has given to Quaker Doctrine the terseness and logical cohesion of a more definite creed.

Nevertheless, though at first but unsystematic and receiving varied developments according to the nature of the individual preacher, there is observable throughout a prevailing idea which, like a central cord, is found penetrating and connecting the whole—even the precious truth that Christ is in you.† It was the realisation of this truth inwardly revealed, that brought peace to the troubled soul of George Fox. This same truth proclaimed by him and brought home by the Spirit's power, gave peace also to Howgill, Burrough, Naylor, and Farnsworth, Hubberthorne, and Caton, and all of that early band who have left us their experiences on record. This was

---

* See Ellis Hookes' title to his edition of Edward Burrough's works, viz :— "The Memorable Works of a Son of Thunder and Consolation, namely, that *True Prophet* and Faithful Servant of God and Sufferer for the testimony of Jesus, Edward Burrough."

† "And whereas it hath been said by them without, you must come and hear Christ preached : the answer is from the *Possessor* of him, I have examined myself, and proved myself, and have found *Christ Jesus* in me, and he rules in my heart by Faith ; and I am in him and he is in me, and *behold all things is become new.*"—*G. F. Epistles*, vol. ii. p. 333.

G. F. was also full on the subject of our Redemption. " It cost him his *Blood*, his Life, and he doth not leave us in the state as Adam and Eve was in before they fell, but sets them down in himself who never fell, a safer state than Adam was in before he fell."—*Epistles*, vol. ii. p. 192.

the sun and centre of their doctrine—the kingdom of God is nigh, Christ is in you; this was what the hundreds and thousands rejoiced over, even that He whom they had worshipped as far off, was nigh them and in them, and working through them. The same truth was it that a century before had emancipated Luther from Rome—the same that under a Whitfield and a Wesley awoke an ignorant populace to rejoice in God's free salvation; the same that, in our own day, gives such power to the modern evangelist, when he calls on all to a personal, conscious, loving union through God's free grace with Christ our Saviour.

Taking such to be a fair inference from the general tenor of the doctrine as promulgated by George Fox and the early preachers, it remains to show that whilst these views received through the zealous men a development that contributed to their success, there was one of the number who by grievous misconduct afforded a painful illustration that a truth pushed to extremes becomes the deepest error.

No one of the early preachers was more remarkable in his day than James Naylor, for he attracted great numbers to his ministry, and the indwelling of Christ in man was a prominent topic of his discourse. This preacher, gifted with a persuasive eloquence which finds expression (unlike most of his co-workers) in his *writings*, was valued not so much for his power in debate, or for subduing crowds to order like Edward Burrough, but for his capacity of giving a full and melodious utterance to the deepest truths, with which his hearers were charmed, and to which even rank and fashion came to listen (see Letters). Continuing, though in London, to dress in the plain garb of a Yorkshire yeoman, and thus appearing in the meetings just as he used to do when at plough on his own lands, he the more astonished the polished Londoner when such eloquence and grand discourse flowed forth from one apparently "unacquainted with letters" (see Ellwood); the impression of his wonderful voice was heightened by possessing a presence thought to be like the type of countenance used for representing the Saviour, to which he added by allowing his "brown hair to fall below the cheeks." Thus gifted, and preaching with power the doctrine of the indwelling of Christ in the renewed man, he suffered the popularity he awakened to darken his mind, and giving heed to the blasphemous flattery of some followers, especially of a few women, he was led into grievous error. These fanatical, if not crazy people, believed that James himself would become a further manifestation of the Lord Jesus, whom he had thus so powerfully preached—as such they extolled him above other preachers—causing thereby a division in the camp and carrying their proceedings so far as to perform worship to him; saying, amongst other attributes, that "He was fairest among ten thousand." They and some few men proceeded to enact in the streets of Bristol, despite a drenching rain, a parody of the triumphal entry; leading James Naylor, on horseback, into the city, amidst their "buzzing" songs.

In our day such a scene would have issued in the confinement of the actors in some asylum, but in those times Quakerism was dreaded by the authorities, and the conduct of this bewildered man was thought sufficient in importance to engage the attention of Parliament itself. James Naylor underwent before its Committee a long examination. Parliament, after frequent considerations of the Committee's report, sentenced him to a punishment that was cruel even in that rough age. The whole matter excited much attention at the time, and can be so easily read in narratives that remain, as to need no further mention here, beyond observing that James Naylor bore his sufferings with patience, showed no malice, but embraced the executioner who had pierced his tongue and branded his forehead. Ultimately he recovered his bodily strength, though brought down near unto death by grievous scourgings, and spent the short remainder of his days in fellowship and unity with his friends, having experienced deep repentance, and made confession of his error, so touching as to draw tears from those who heard him.

James Naylor's case no doubt served as a warning to many others, to make more careful use of scriptural terms, lest even truth by false enthusiasm should develop into error; and the persecution maintained against the Society during the Commonwealth may also have assisted by limiting its members to those who could endure suffering; and their utterances to only the essential truths.

The reason of all this suffering seems difficult to understand in connection with Oliver Cromwell's professed desire to give liberty of conscience to all; but under his rule the ministers of the various sects had great power with the magistrates, and they were as a body jealous of the Society, for through its aggressive power they lose, writes F. Howgill in his Letters, "their members so fast they know not what to do." Hence the desire to suppress this increase of the Friends, by handing them over to the civil power. They charged them with blasphemy (never proved); denial of the Scriptures (shown to be false); non-observing the Sabbath (that is, in their Puritan fashion); not paying tithes, &c.—all of which and many more the magistrate proved ready to recognise as grounds of commitment, until more than a thousand Friends were in prison throughout the kingdom, at a time when liberty of conscience was *professed* as the law of the land.

This was the treatment Friends received when Presbyterians and Independents were in power; such was the use they made of laws intended for evil-doers, and passed to secure the peace of those unsettled times; but, not content with these, and professing to be alarmed at the "Great Meetings of the Quakers," they passed a separate act apparently against vagrants, but so worded as to be specially applied to the restraint of Friends from meetings, and under this act, which committed offenders at once and without trial, to the martial law under which Cromwell ruled the kingdom, many of the Friends at this period suffered their imprisonment. In London there was but little suffering at this time. Some of the Protector's Court were favourable, if not in profession with Friends,* and from this cause persecutions may have been held in check in a place where the court resided. But, though exempted themselves at this time, the London Friends were earnest in endeavours for the relief of their brethren elsewhere, and spent much time and labour on their account.

Cromwell himself was often applied to by them, but his interference could not be secured; and as he grew older, a moroseness of disposition made him less inclined to promote rights of conscience than to secure his own authority, then much endangered by plots and conspiracies. In vain did some of the more eminent ministers among the Friends plead with him; he neither yielded to their entreaties nor regarded their denunciations, though one went so far as to tear his cap in the Protector's presence, as a sign "that the Lord would tear the kingdom from him." George Fox, who, in the early days of the Protectorate, found favour with Cromwell, now experienced no access to his heart: "I will be as high as thou art," said he, and went away in a light manner (see Journal); and

---

* The name of "Ellin Claipoole" occurs in the List of Friends in the Six-Weeks Meeting.

when at the last G. F. met the Protector in Hampton Court Park, and boldly rode alongside his horse, the yielding, if any there was, came too late, for the next day the Protector's death-sickness had commenced, and so nothing was done by him towards the relief of Friends.

Meanwhile the numbers of the London Friends continued greatly to increase, and the priests confessed there was such a power among them (see Letters, p. 61) that none who came to them can escape. Edward Burrough, writing at this time (Letters, p. 59), says the meetings are always large, quiet, and precious; Truth spreads and grows. Richard Hubberthorne describes (Letters, p. 61) the meetings of this period " as full and large, where there is any to *declare the truth** among them," and "they that are great in the earth, the Power of Truth strives through them, and is drawing them in daily." Alexander Parker (Letters, p. 70) speaks "of a mighty thirst, and a desire and openness." This rapid growth continued till, in 1678, Friends numbered 10,000 in London alone,† such was the "result" that had attended the labours of those early preachers in the great city, so was realised that which Anthony Pearson wrote (Letters, p. 13), "there is like to be a great harvest here."

Throughout this early, vigorous, and increasing period the Society recognised two classes of meetings as before shown; the one for the "rude multitude," where the service was of such a nature as to be called "threshing," Bible in hand, as we see from the picture W. Crouch has left of Edward Burrough: the other, more retired gatherings in numerous private houses, where silence was a marked feature. In that day these arrangements were blessed as a means of in-gathering and building up; yielding in these respects large results, may they not serve as ensamples to encourage those in our large cities, surrounded, as in London, with masses of poor and ignorant people (not attending ordinary Friends' meetings) to adopt, as the early Friends did, special means suited to special circumstances, instead of thinking that a Friends'

---

* This is italicised, as showing the importance attached to preaching in these gatherings.

† From 1801 to 1811 the deaths amongst Friends of London and Middlesex averaged 50 per annum out of 2,270 members. At the same rate the 300 recorded deaths in 1678 would show a population of 13,620, say 10,000, to allow for supposed higher death-rate in early times.—*See Letters, p. 156.*

meeting, to be one, must be of the same kind, whether the awakened and the refined or the ignorant and rude are assembled.

Cromwell's decease occurred in the autumn of 1658; and though his son Richard promised fair as to relieving Friends from their sufferings, it proved that he was powerless unless the Parliament supported him, and it continued hostile to the Society.

London Friends were now again prominent in endeavouring to obtain relief for their members in the country, and a notable instance of their exertions occurred just before the feeble government of Richard Cromwell came to a close.

It would seem that, in some way not explained, 144 Friends still remained in bonds, on whose behalf Parliament was entreated with so great an amount of personal solicitation, that 164 Friends went to Westminster and offered themselves to lie in prison as substitutes for their suffering brethren; but, although they attended in the lobbies of the House to prove by their presence the sincerity of their appeal, the petition was refused; and three of their number being called to the Bar, were informed that the decision of the House was that they should go home and follow their callings, and submit themselves to the laws of the nation and the magistracy they live under.

Great changes in the governing powers were now at hand, for the King had been restored in 1660, with every demonstration of national joy, and the leading men in former Parliaments had to flee the country or suffer loss of liberty or life. At first reprisals and persecution seem alike to have been forgotten in festive revelry; but such scenes grieved our Friends, and awakened fears for the result. Richard Hubberthorne, who was in the crowd when Charles entered London, writes (Letters, p. 82), he thought the King "wore a pretty sober countenance," but fears those who brought him in "would lead him to do things which he himself is not inclined unto"; their pride and vanity was so great: and he adds, "the wickedness is inexpressible."

In Maitland's "History of London" this entry of Charles II. is described as conspicuous for its imposing character, even in a city where processions and shows had been so numerous. Perhaps their scarcity during the long period of Puritanical austerity now closing, quickened the zest for such displays, and added to the troops of gaily caparisoned

D

gentlemen and citizens who rode to greet the King. Foremost amongst these, are to be observed in the historian's narration the names of two men who each rose to civic honour and royal favour, and so used their power as to lead to their memory being associated with the cruel persecution of "Friends"; these were Alderman Richard Brown and Sir John Robinson, who, when the King entered, rode in procession at the head of their respective troops of gentlemen, decorated with "cloth of silver," brandishing their swords. The first of these civic dignitaries, now so loyal, had previously been a Republican and Puritan, but his principles were held subservient to his advancement, and a Knighthood became the reward for his change. His subsequent career of civic power was distinguished by zeal in suppressing the Fifth-Monarchy men, and harsh cruel treatment of Baptists and Friends. Sir John Robinson received his reward in a Baronetcy and the Governorship of the Tower, an authority which he used with almost equal severity to Sir Richard Brown in suppressing the Nonconformists.

Meanwhile, even Friends could rejoice in the accession of Charles II., for by Royal Proclamation all those in prison for conscience' sake were set free. The King, both by his manner and conversation, showed at first every desire to be lenient and liberal, but the temper of the times was unfavourable, and the High Church tendencies of the ruling ministers did not promote Toleration. Unfortunately, also, circumstances soon occurred after the King's accession which gave a pretext for refusing liberty of conscience to sectaries. This was an outbreak of some London fanatics, who proclaimed the hour was fully come for King Jesus to reign; and that his kingdom should cast down all other power and authority through them his agents. There had been, they asserted, four great monarchies in the earth, and now was to come the last and greatest of all, even the fifth and final one; hence arose their name of Fifth-Monarchy men.*

---

* *Burnet*, vol. i. p. 224 : "King not many days at Whitehall, when one Venner, a violent Fifth-Monarchy man, who thought it was not enough to believe that Christ was to reign on earth, and to put the Saints in the possession of the kingdom (an opinion that they were all unspeakably fond of), but added to this that the Saints were to take the kingdom themselves."

Maitland's History of London, 29th May, 1660 : "Just after, a horrid

Their doctrine excited but little attention, their numbers not being large, and the gallant Sir Richard Brown so soon killed or dispersed them by his trained bands, that in a few days the whole rebellion was at an end; but it served as a pretext for severity against Baptists and Friends, of which the ruling powers took full advantage. All their meetings in London were now greatly disturbed by Sir Richard's train-bands. The royal favour was lost, and a proclamation issued from the King in Council, especially directed against Friends, because "they meet in such great numbers, and at unwonted times," though no actual disturbance was ever proved to have been committed by them.

Now followed a day of strong measures; there were trials and judgments of regicides; a disinterring and burning of the dead; there was a purging of the Church by the Act of Uniformity in 1662 (when 2,000 ministers left), and these matters being regulated, Parliament proceeded to frame laws to put down all conventicles and unlicensed preaching; for which purpose, an act, carried mainly by the influence of Lord Clarendon, made the holding meetings a penal offence, and imposed heavy fines on all their attenders, viz.: £5 per head for the first offence, or three months in gaol; £10 for the second, or six months' imprisonment; and banishment beyond the seas for the third.

Its effects were soon seen, by peaceable citizens being taken from their families, and crowded into gaols with felons, because they dared not disobey the voice of God in their conscience to satisfy a High-Church Parliament.

Great exertions had been made by Friends in London to arrest the progress of the bill, in which Edward Burrough and others were especially engaged. He had even been permitted, with Richard Hubberthorne, Edward Pyot, and

---

and unparalleled insurrection happened in this city by a small number of wild, barbarous, most desperate, and bloody enthusiasts, called Fifth-Monarchy men, that ever appeared in this or perhaps any other nation;" they came out from a meeting-place in Swan Alley, Coleman Street, on Sunday, 6th January, in the evening, and were about sixty in number, headed by Thomas Venner, a cooper, who was their preacher. They said they would rather die than take the wicked oaths of supremacy and allegiance. Sir R. Brown suppressed them after a desperate fight in Wood Street between them and his train-bands. "Had their numbers," says Maitland, "been equal to their spirits, they would have subverted the city, kingdom, and world." About twenty of the troops were killed.

George Whitehead, to appear at the bar of the House, there to plead the cause of the Society, but though their simple eloquence evidently made an impression in their favour, it was but temporary, and eventually the bill was carried through both Houses, and received the Royal Assent.

It may be as well here to note the position and number of meetings in London, that were affected by the passing of this act.

The *public* meeting-places in use at this time comprised only two—the Bull and Mouth for the City, and the other at Westminster, near the Abbey. The more private meetings held in houses were numerous, and form quite a list as we extract their names from such works as those of William Crouch and Gilbert Latey. Thus :—

In the City, there were two in Aldersgate ; one being at the house of Sarah Sawyer, and the other near it at Sarah Yates', in Aldersgate Street ; another neighbour, one Sarah Matthews, in Whitecross Street, also opened her dwelling for the same purpose ; still more within the City, at the sign of the Helmet, in Basinghall Street, Samuel Vasse, or Vaux, allowed a meeting at his house. In the neighbourhood of Doctors' Commons, Gerrard Roberts, living in Thomas Apostles, freely opened his doors, and besides having meetings there regularly, so hospitably entertained all travelling Friends, as to long make his house a sort of headquarters for their conferences previous to obtaining premises in Gracechurch Street; Humphery Bach, or Bates, a goldsmith, at the sign of the Snail, in Tower Street, was another who sheltered a meeting ; so, also, Robert Dring, near him, in Watling Street ; and Simon Dring, his brother, in Moorfields. Then there was John Oakly, of Westbury Street, Spitalfields, and John Elson, at the sign of the Peel, in Clerkenwell, both founders of future well-known meetings, through having opened their houses to the service. More westward, we find the origin of the Savoy Meeting, at Nicholas Bond's, who was then living at Worcester House, in the Strand, and William Woodcock, in the Savoy itself; proceeding further westward to Westminster, one Elizabeth Trott, of Pall Mall, a widow, near (as they call it) James's House, long sheltered a meeting there ; so, also, did Stephen Hart, in his house, in the New Palace Yard ; and lying out in the country beyond this, we find a William Bond, of Chiswick, and afterwards one living near the Limekilns at Hammersmith, recorded as allowing meetings to be held in their houses; and others, whose names are not given, offered the same facilities to their friends at Mitcham, Croydon, Walworth, and Lambeth Marsh. Returning to the east, there was Captain Brock, of Mile End, or Stepney, whose house became the precursor of Ratcliff Meeting; and a Gilbert, or Gobert, Sikes is mentioned, as also allowing a meeting at his house in Hackney. In the borough of Southwark there were several: one at the house of the Widow Webb, in Jacob Street, thus originating Horslydown Meeting. Then Henry Clark and Thomas Hackleton, both of Bankside, and William Shewen, of Bermondsey Street, also Daniel Fleming, of Blackman Street —four separate gatherings, the germs of what became eventually the large meeting of Southwark.

Previous to the Proclamation of 1661, the London Friends, (as previously remarked) had known but little of collective and corporate suffering, but they were now, as a body, to feel the full effects of an act severe in its provisions, and enforced by men in power relentless as Sir Richard Brown (become the Lord Mayor) and Sir John Robinson, made a baronet and invested with the responsible post of the governorship of the Tower of London; between these two, as in a press, persecution was to be wrung out to them even to the dregs.

All Nonconformists suffered, but especially the Baptists and Friends, for whom these civic authorities showed great hatred, as the accounts given under the heads of the various meetings will more fully show. From the storm now thickly gathering there was no flinching on the part of the early preachers, though well aware that its force would be specially directed against them; yet, true to their charge, they exhorted Friends to keep to their meetings, and lost no opportunities of being themselves present there; as a consequence they were almost all soon in imprisonment, prolonged, in many instances, until death was their only release.

This was especially the case with Edward Burrough—he was absent from London at the time of the act becoming law, but returned to it at once from Bristol, to encourage Friends by his example, saying as he left, "I go to lay down my life for the Gospel." He had told the Committee of the House he should feel it his duty to exhort Friends to the maintenance of meetings, whatever law they might pass; and, true to his word, he now cast himself into the midst of the sufferers. Arrested by Sir Richard Brown, at the Bull and Mouth Meeting, he was thrust by his order, in company with many other

Friends, into Newgate,* at that time an old, ill-arranged prison; forming a scene of which the graphic pen of Thomas Ellwood (see his Journal, p. 149, &c.) has left full account. Morally and physically the air was pestilential—the over-crowding was shocking, and a gaol-fever setting in increased the sufferings of the imprisoned. Richard Hubberthorne presently succumbed to its effects; Edward Burrough also, after a four months' imprisonment, became ill, and it was evident his sickness would likewise be unto death. During his sufferings the heavenly fervour of his spirit made the prison seem radiant as the gates of heaven, for to him death had no terror, and when he departed it was as a conqueror rather than a prisoner, breathing forth nothing but love and forgiveness to all.† Nevertheless, though to him the change was gain, on his persecutors' memory must rest the responsibility of his death as much as if they had brought him to the gallows or the stake.

Though conspicuous in the severity of his sufferings as he had been in his ministry, he was but one among the many now cut off by this method of imprisonment, hardly less cruel than torture; and even these so killed in the city of London are but a representation in one city of the kind of cruelty which the government continued for some fourteen years to inflict all over the nation, under an easy and indifferent king.

Is it strange that those who knew of this cruelty, having seen it for themselves, believed that the cry of anguish so wrung throughout the land from many an orphan's heart and desolated home, was heard on high, and answered by judgment even as in Egypt of old? On this subject opinion may now

---

* *Maitland*, vol. ii. p. 951 : "But however ornamental this prison may be without, it is a dismal place within. The prisoners are sometimes packed so close together, and the air so corrupted by their stench and nastiness, that it occasions a disease called the gaol-distemper, of which they die by dozens, and cartloads of them are carried out and thrown into a pit in the churchyard of Christ Church without ceremony, and so infectious is this distemper that several judges, jurymen and lawyers, &c. have taken it of the prisoners when they have been brought to the Old Bailey to be tried, and died soon after, of which we have had an instance within these seven years. And to this wretched place innocent people are sometimes sent, and loaded with irons before their trial, not to secure them, but to extort money from them by a merciless gaoler; for if they have money to bribe him they may have the irons as light as they please." N.B.—This was after the prison had been rebuilt, it having been damaged in the Fire, and the imprisonment of Friends occurred before.

† Josiah Coales' testimony—"Near his departure he was heard to desire of the Lord, if it were possible, to forgive Brown," &c.

differ, but the testimony of history is clear, that during the time these scenes of persecution for conscience' sake occurred, London was visited by three afflictions, each so severe as to be by common consent called great—such as the great Plague, the great Fire, and the great Indignity when the Dutch burnt our ships at the Nore; whether these be taken as judgments or regarded only as incidents, they form a group of disasters happily unparalleled in our annals; and they occurred at a time when blameless citizens and honest tradesmen were treated worse than felons solely because their religious convictions would not permit them to conform to a law-established church.

To scenes like these the King and his court might give no *such* heed as to see in them "Signs of the times," but doubtless the men of England took the lesson to heart. The dynasty which refused to listen was rejected, and as a nation we so learnt to respect the rights of individual conscience as to make the recurrence of persecution in England for religion's sake almost impossible.

Surely the memory of the men who so greatly helped to teach us this lesson is to be prized; these humble prisoners, not only in London but all over the land, were, by patient suffering in those crowded and pestilential dungeons, waging a warfare seldom noted on the page of general history; yet, for all that, one having really no inconsiderable share in that noble contest for freedom against prejudice and human interference in sacred duties, which in its success has earned for us, as Englishmen, those rights of conscience now held so dear, and which conduce so much to our national greatness and our country's fame.

"Offences (as our Lord declared) must come," and those who bring them have their woe. Yet, doubtless, it behoves us, in regarding the past and its errors, to view it in that same spirit of forgiveness and charity the early Friends showed toward their persecutors when they suffered under them, and believe that those who inflicted these cruelties thought that thereby "they did God service."

For the little Church itself thus suffering, it was unto it as birth-pangs of that organisation by which it has since been distinguished. The fellowship of suffering* caused it to become

---

* See *Epistles*, 1653, Preface, where it speaks of "the danger that many lie in because of the oppressors," and arrangements are made for collections and periodical meetings so as to support one another under sufferings.

really "a Society," and the arrangements then made gave to it that cohesion and unity in action and purpose which has been alike its preservation under attacks from without and disorders within—giving it a permanence amid shocks under which others, such as the Seekers, Ranters, Muggletonians, Fifth-Monarchy Men, &c., disappeared. To trace this discipline somewhat more closely will be the object of the succeeding chapter.

NOTE.—It has been said that Friends arose from amongst many sects. Besides the more important ones already mentioned, two of these need some further mention, to show the evils Friends avoided. One of these passed by the name of Seekers, or the Family of Love, whose practice was to "wait together in silence." As W. Penn says in his Preface to G. Fox's Journal, " and as anything rose in any one that they thought favoured of a divine spring, so they sometimes spoke." But, becoming "exalted above measure, and for want of an humble dependence upon Him that opened their understanding, they run out in their own imaginations, and, mixing them with those divine openings, brought forth a monstrous birth to the scandal of those that feared God." The Ranters were a still more numerous body, and more mischievous in their tendencies: one in authority once thanked G. Fox, observing that "but for him the Ranters would have overrun England." They considered, says W. Penn, "that Christ's fulfilling the Law for us discharged us from its duties and obligations; that it was no sin now to do that which before it had been a sin to commit, if done with the mind and persuasion that it was good." Which views led "into gross and enormous practices." Thomas Story says of these (see Journal, p. 192), "They frequently come into our meetings, and rant, sing and dance, and act like anticks and madmen, throwing dust in the face of our ministers when preaching."

As a further illustration of the character of those who joined the Society, we may quote again from William Penn. He says, "though not great and learned in the esteem of this world (for then they had not wanted followers upon their own credit and authority), yet they were generally of the most sober of the several persuasions they were in (*i.e.* before uniting with Friends), and of the most repute for religion; and many of them of good capacity, substance, and account among men."

The following selection of names from the early marriage records is a slight indication of the mental bias of the parents:—Revolution Sixsmith, Hallelujah Fisher, Marvellous Scanfield, Obedience Waring, Returned Elgar, Damaris Davis, Silence Williams, Chasten Hoine, Temperance Poor, Obedience Cotter, Charity Harford, Discipline Matthews.

CHAPTER V.

SKETCH OF THE ORIGIN OF THE DISCIPLINE UP TO THE
ESTABLISHMENT OF THE SIX-WEEKS MEETING,

INCLUDING SOME NOTES ON THE YEARLY MEETING.

THE remarks on this subject are kept thus separate, as presenting a clearer view of the rise of the discipline than if intermingled with the incidents of the narrative.

From the earliest times in the history of the Society general meetings for conference, similar to those among other sects, especially the Baptists, were common also with Friends. They were confined to no particular place, nor at first held at any set time, but were convened as circumstances seemed to require them, being attended by deputies from various localities. In these we see the germs from which the Yearly Meeting eventually arose. Also out of other assemblies of a smaller character within particular districts, held usually once a quarter, we can trace the origin of Quarterly Meetings, and these (so far as the Society in general is concerned) would appear to have been the only meetings regularly established prior to 1666-7, when, in addition to such, the Monthly Meetings were settled all over the nation.

In London the circumstances of the case led to somewhat more special arrangements at an earlier date.

Here large numbers had been collected from a mixed multitude, having little or no previous knowledge of one another; and excessive labour fell upon the various ministers in attending numerous meetings among them; also in conducting disputes and debates with opposers, and answering in print the attacks of adversaries whose works were constantly issuing from the press. Hence arose in Edward Burrough's time, before the establishment of any Monthly Meetings, arrangements as to meetings for a care over the Churches, which may be best given in his own terms as abbreviated from an explanatory paper issued by him in 1662 shortly before his decease, and much treasured as "parting words" by his friends. (The Paper will be found *in extenso* in Letters, pp. 294—310) :—

"It having pleased the Lord God of Heaven and Earth . . . to move . . . divers of us . . to come to this 'great city' of London, to publish and declare the message of eternal life which we had received power from the Father to do . . . we entered this city . . . and though we met with . . . many trials and much opposition from men of all conditions, yet we were not discouraged . . . but went on in boldness and confidence in God . . . and . . . it pleased the Lord to bless us and prosper His work in our hands . . . and though we appeared at first in much weakness . . . and had no man to stand by us, or to help to bear our burdens, at our first coming to this place, as being strangers both in body and spirit to the whole city, yet . . . as we began so we went on in the name and power of Christ Jesus. . . . And in the space of about two years' time truth was much spread, and many were convinced . . . and we have in a measure seen the blessed effect of the travail of our souls, and are satisfied. And, as I have said, in some space of time after our coming to this city, the work of the Lord was much increased . . . and many occasions happened and divers matters came to pass daily . . . such as so properly did not belong to us of the ministry . . . as to the Friends of the city . . . to wit. Concerning providing convenient meeting-places for the publishing of truth, . . . care for the poor . . . the sick . . . weak and impotent . . . also placing servants in honest employment who had been turned out of their places for receiving the truth, which services . . . were not so proper for us . . . being wholly devoted to the work of the ministry. . . . in preaching . . . in answering books . . . and in disputes and contentions with such as opposed the truth. . . . Therefore . . . seeing the necessity . . . we did ordain and appoint that the men Friends of the city or the ancientest of them in the truth (not excluding any) should meet together at the Bull and Mouth, or elsewhere once in the fortnight, or once a month, as they in the wisdom of God should find it necessary, . . . that in all things in the respects before mentioned good and wholesome order . . . might be carried on. Thus was your meeting of men . . . appointed—not to be divided, . . .

ye contrary to us and we to you . . . but we to go on in the ministry. . . . to the gathering of more to the Lord and . . . ye to go on . . . in dear and tender unity . . . to the good government and well ordering of the affairs of Friends in outward things, and all this effected through the power and wisdom of the Lord God manifest in the hearts of his people, and in our concurrence together in the same . . . without the least grain of contempt one of another, or lordliness over one another." Edward Burrough next proceeds to discourse under different heads as to the objects and duties of this meeting. "First, it is to consist of just and righteous men . . . not limited to a number of persons, but freedom for all Friends in truth (none excepted) as they are moved to come for the service of truth. Second, that the meeting be kept once a week or fourteen days . . . to be conducted not as a worldly assembly . . . seeking to outspeak and overreach one another in discourse . . . not deciding affairs by the greater vote . . . but hearing and determining every matter coming before you in the love, coolness, gentleness, and dear unity. . . . Third, in case of difficulties arising, such to be left until more Friends that are anciently grown in the truth have the understanding of the matter. Fourthly, disputes between Friends, or a Friend and a stranger, concerning outward things, as bargains, debts, or the like, the meeting itself, or its committee, to inquire into and endeavour to settle it. Fifthly, record to be made by the meeting of all births, marriages, and burials. Sixthly, care for the poor that believe and profess the truth; the meeting of women Friends particularly to help in this service, which meeting," Edward Burrough says, "was appointed by us . . . some years since the appointment of the men's meeting . . . as it was not so proper for the men as for the women to visit the sick and to search out the necessities of the poor, weak, widows, and aged. Seventhly, care to be taken for collecting and preserving accounts of sufferings." Counsel and encouragement is extended under all these heads. "Being moved," as E. B. says, "so to write in the name, power, and authority of the Lord Jesus Christ." And he dates his paper as issued in the "ninth year of the publishing of truth in this city."

Such were the arrangements for conducting the discipline in London, during the time of Edward Burrough and the early preachers; the next change in London was the establishment of Monthly Meetings—these had been held in the north as early as 1653 (at Swarthmoor). Afterwards, when Friends' views had spread, such were held in Cheshire, Lancashire, Westmorland, Cumberland, Northumberland, Bishoprick [Durham], and Yorkshire, and edge of Wales; and at a meeting of Elders at Swarthmoor, composed of representatives from most places, it was settled to have Monthly Meetings everywhere; nevertheless, these did not become general in the nation, nor were adopted in London, until 1666-7-8.

It was under such simple arrangements as this Two-Weeks Meeting and Women's Meeting, described by E. Burrough, that the Society in London maintained its ground, and grew up a numerous body, numbering many thousand members; and during the first eleven years of its existence, no further organisation seemed requisite. But as persecution struck down the early preachers, one by one, restraining them by imprisonment from their swiftly circulating visits, or silencing them for ever by death, this large body gathered from all sorts of sects, becoming deprived of the services of those gifted men (whose prophetic fervour had called it into being), showed symptoms of internal disorder, which might well arouse the anxious thought of all concerned in its welfare.

It is evident from his Journal that George Fox felt this deeply, when he again visited London in the winter of 1666. He was himself but just released from an imprisonment of nearly three years' duration, under the rigour of which his naturally powerful frame had almost succumbed, and within and around the London circle he found signs of trouble and desolation. The city he had left so crowded was now a ruin, two-thirds of its citizens homeless, their dwellings having been burnt to ashes. He himself was weak in body, and his limbs swollen from cruel hardships. His early companions in the ministry (the valiant "sixty" that had gone forth two and two all over the land) were nearly all in prison, or had been removed by death, and the companies and congregations they had been the means of gathering had been sifted by persecution, and (still worse) were suffering from internal dissensions. It was clear some decided course must be taken, that the most pressing necessity existed to secure some power of self-regulation in the body itself, without which the London Society would to all appearances have become dispersed.

Amongst the troubles from within under which it was then

suffering, none occasioned more anxiety than the schism of John Perrot, who, without attracting such public notice as poor James Naylor had done, was really the cause of more dissension in the community.

"Little in person," (as Thomas Ellwood says,) "yet great in opinion of himself," John Perrot had in earlier life started for Rome, in the full persuasion it was his mission to convert the Pope to Friends' views, and although his imprisonment there might have shaken his belief in the soundness of his calling, it did not prevent him from continuing to be one of those who troubled his friends; he had now, under show of great sanctity, adopted the peculiar idea that it was wrong to raise the hat in prayer, whether when listening to others or when personally so engaged, and a great many were drawn away by his specious views (of which Thomas Ellwood himself was for a time one).*

The subject occasioned great dissension, and was threatening a schism at the time of George Fox's visit. On no occasion perhaps was his power over his fellow believers more strongly manifested: "Pure as a bell and stiff as a tree" (as his persecuting gaolers had said), he moved among his friends with an apostolic grace—still under physical suffering, active when nature would have asked for repose, scarce able to ride or walk for pain, his whole soul was poured out for his friends' and the cause's sake. He held meetings among them that lasted day after day for several days in succession, where feelings of tenderness and deep solemnity prevailed. Here the same voice that had struck the first key-notes which the early preachers had taken as their texts, now raised the clear sound of warning, and in a spirit of harmony and love which his presence seemed to beget, the eyes of objectors were opened to see their errors, and dissension was stayed. John Perrot, the author of the mischief, emigrated to America, where, subsequently leaving the Society, he ended his career in some political influence, but became in that official capacity a persecutor of Friends, though they held the same views which he had formerly (but in vain) sought to impress on the mind of the Pope.

This immediate cause of danger being removed, and brotherly unity restored, George Fox's next care was to provide some

---

* It was also noted by Sewel the historian, as one of Perrot's "extravagant steps, that he had allowed his beard to grow."

arrangements whereby a principle of self-regulation might become developed in the community, and disorders such as had arisen be checked or removed. The original Meeting for Discipline, held once a fortnight, had obviously become inadequate to exercise due care over so large an area as the whole London district presented, and under George Fox's advice, its sphere became now confined to the space within the walls, whilst the remaining extensive and populous districts were subdivided into five other Monthly Meetings, to which were committed more important duties of oversight than the earlier meetings had exercised. "Then was I moved of the Lord," are the words in which George Fox in his Journal records these arrangements, to recommend the setting up of " Five monthly meetings of men and women in the City of London . . . to take care of God's glory, and to admonish and exhort such as walked disorderly or carelessly, and not according to truth." Later on, some few months further, special directions are mentioned on the subject of marriage. " I was moved to exhort them to bring all their marriages to the men's and women's meetings, that so care might be taken to prevent those disorders that had been committed by some." The rectifying of these disorders became a prominent feature in the business of the Monthly Meetings when first established, as may be seen by reference to the account given of Southwark Meeting, which happens to be *only* one of the group in which the first volume of the records has been preserved. It contains ample evidence of the need there must have been for such meetings, and leaves no doubt but that in London it was, as G. F. says in his Journal of the country, " great reformation was made amongst people by these meetings, insomuch as the very justices took notice of the usefulness and service thereof." Thus the Society, previously knowing little of corporate aid and counsels, dependent upon the personal influence of gifted ministers and others, became associated together in groups, each member taking his share as a burden-bearer, all " watching over one another for good."

Thus remarks George Fox in his Journal :—" Since these meetings have been settled, many mouths have been opened in thanksgiving, and have blest the Lord God, that ever he did send me forth in this service. Yea, with tears, many have praised the Lord. For now all coming to have a care for God's honour and glory. All to see that all who profess the truth, do walk in the truth, and order their conversations aright. All having this care upon them, and being exercised in his holy spirit, may know and partake of the government of Christ." . . . "These come to inherit and possess—

'The joyful order of the joyful Gospel,
The comfortable order of the comfortable Gospel,
The glorious order of the glorious Gospel,
The everlasting order of the everlasting Gospel,'

and these shall see the government of Christ. . . . the First and the Last—the Beginning and the Ending—the Foundation of God, Christ Jesus, the Amen."

What George Fox's views were as to the manner in which Meetings for Discipline should be conducted, may be best illustrated by adding at length a paper which he drew up on this subject, which is to be found entered in MS. on the books of several of the London Meetings.

Friends' fellowship must be in the Spirit, and all Friends must know one another in the Spirit and Power of God.

First, in all the meetings of the country, two or three being gathered from them to go to the general meetings, for to give notice one to another, if there be any that walks not in the truth, and have been convinced and gone from truth, and so dishonoureth God, that some may be ordered from the meeting to go and exhort such, and bring to the next General Meeting what they say.

2ndly.—If any that profess the truth follows pleasures, drunkenness, gamings, or is not faithful in their callings and dealings, nor honest nor just, but runs into debt, and so brings a scandal upon the truth, Friends may give notice to the General Meeting (if there be any such) and some may be ordered to go and exhort them, and bring in their answer next General Meeting.

3rdly.—And if any goes disorderly together in marriage, contrary to practice of the holy men of God, and assemblies of the righteous in all ages who declared it in the assemblies of the righteous, when they took one another (all things being clear), and they both being free from any other, and when they do go together, and take one another, let there not be less than a dozen friends and relations present (according to your usual order) having first acquainted the Men's Meeting, and they have clearness and unity with them, and that it may be recorded in a book according to the word and commandment of the Lord; and if any walk contrary to the truth herein, let some be ordered to speak to them and give notice thereof to the next General Meeting.

4thly.—And all that be widows (which have children) and do intend to marry, let query be made what she hath done for her children. If there be no will made, then let such part of her late husband's estate be set out for her children as is equal and according to truth, and what they can do afterwards let them do also; and where there is a will made, let those legacies and portions be improved and secured before marriage for the children of the deceased, with what more they can do for them, and then, when these things are done, let them be recorded in a book at the next General Meeting.

5thly.—And, also, all widows in all your General Meetings, let them be taken notice of and informed and encouraged in their outward business, that there be not any hindrance to them in their inward growth, and so carefully looked after, that they may be nourished and cherished, and so preserved in the truth that love may be increased; and if they have many children to put out apprentices, or servants that may be a burden to them, to bring them up, let friends take care to ease them by putting them forth as may be meet. Let all those things be looked into by every meeting, and notice thereof given to the next General Meeting, and then some ordered to see that all things are done according to truth and righteousness.

6thly.—And all such as marry by the Priests of Baal, who are the rough hands of Esau, and fists of wickedness and bloody hands, and who have had their hands in the blood of our brethren, and are the cause of all the banishment of our brethren, and have spoiled so many of their goods, casting into prison, and keeps many hundreds at this day. Such as goes to them for wives or husbands, must come to judgment and condemnation of that spirit that lead them to Baal, and of Baal's priests also, or else Friends that keeps their habitations must write against them and Baal both; for from Genesis to the Revelations you never read of any priest that married people; but it is God's ordinance, and whom God joins together let no man put asunder; and they took one another in the assemblies of the righteous when all things were clear. Therefore, let all these things be inquired into and brought to the General Meeting, and from thence some ordered to go to them and to return what they say at your next meeting. And all these, before they or any of them be left as heathens or written against, let them be three or four times gone to, that they may have Gospel order, so that if it be possible they may come to that which did convince them to condemn their unrighteous doings that so you may not leave a hoof in Egypt.

7thly.—And all such as wears their hats when Friends prays, and are gotten into the old rotten principle of the Ranters, who set up the wearing thereof in opposition to the power of God, and therein upholds it which is condemned by it, and the power of God is gone over it, and them who are ranted from the truth, and have stopped many who were coming into it (that the very world can say you are in confusion and divided, and gone from your first principle, who said you were of one heart, and one mind, and one soul); and therefore that spirit must be cut off by the sword of the spirit of the Lord, that they may come to that which did at first convince them; and notice must be given to the General Meeting of all these things, and from thence some must be ordered to go to exhort them that be in such things to come to the first principle that did at first convince them, that they may come over such things, and Friends must stand up in the noble seed of God to judge the world and all the fallen angels.

8thly.—And in all your meetings let notice be given to the General Meetings of all the poor, and when you have heard that there is many more poor belongs to one meeting than to another, and that meeting thereby burdened and oppressed, let the rest of the meetings assist and help them, so that you may ease one another, and help to bear one another's burdens, and so fulfil the law of Christ, and so see that nothing be lacking according to the apostle's words. Mark, nothing lacking, then all is well. . . . So there is not to be a beggar now amongst the Christians, according to the law of Jesus, as there was not to be any amongst the Jews, according to the law of God.

9thly.—And also all men that hunts after women from woman to woman, and also women whose affections runs sometimes after one man and soon after to another, and so hold one another in affection, and so draws out the affections one of another, and after a while leaves one another and goes to others, and does the same thing, this doing makes more like Sodom than saints, and is not of God's moving nor joining where they are not to be parted. For marriage is God's ordinance and God's command one to another, and in that they feel the power of God.

10thly.—And that notice be taken of all evil speakers, backbiters, slanderers, and foolish talkers and idle jesters, for all these things corrupts good manners and is not according to the saints and holy ones whose words are seasoned with salt, ministering grace to the hearers.

11thly.—And all such who are tale carriers and railers whose work is to sow dissension, are to be reproved and admonished; for such do not bring people into the Unity of the Spirit, but by such doings comes to lose their own conditions.

12thly.—And all such as goes up and down to cheat by borrowing and getting money of friends in by-places (and have cheated several).

13thly.—And if there happen any differences between friend and friend of any matters, and if it cannot be ended before the General Meeting, let half a dozen Friends from the General Meeting be ordered to put a steady end thereto, that justice may be speedily done, that no difference may rest or remain amongst any (and let your General Meeting be once in every quarter of a year, and to be appointed at such places as may be most convenient for the most of Friends to meet in). So that the house may be cleansed of all that is contrary to purity, virtue, light, life, and Spirit and power of God. So that Friends may not be one another's sorrow and trouble, but one another's joy and crown in the Lord.

14thly.—And all Friends see that your children be trained up in the fear of the Lord, in soberness and holiness, and righteousness, temperance and meekness, and gentleness, lowliness and modesty in their apparel and carriage, and so to exhort your children and families in the truth that the Lord may be glorified in all your families, and teach your children when they are young, then will they remember it when they are old, according to Solomon. So that your children may be a blessing to you and not a curse.

15thly.—And that Friends do buy convenient burying-places, as Abraham did, who bought a place to bury his dead, and would not bury amongst the Egyptians and Canaanites; and Jacob was brought out of Egypt, and Joseph, and they were buried in their grandfather's and great-grandfather's burying-places: and so Friends to buy decent burying-places for your meetings (and to keep out of the spirit of the Sodomites, Egyptians, and Canaanites, which corrupts the earth), and let them be decently and well fenced—that you may condemn the world in all things.

16thly.—And also that Friends do buy necessary books for the registering of births, marriages, and burials, as the holy men of God did of old, as you may read through the Scriptures, that every one may be ready to give a testimony and certificate thereof if need require, or any be called thereunto.

17thly.—And also that the sufferings of Friends (of all kinds of sufferings) in all the counties be gathered up and put together, and sent to the General Meeting, and so sent to London, to Ellis Hookes, that nothing of the memorial of the blood and cruel sufferings of your brethren be lost, which shall stand as a testimony against the murdering spirit of this world, and be to the praise of the everlasting power of the Lord in the ages to come, who supported and upheld them in such hardships and cruelties; who is God over all, blessed for ever. Amen.

18thly.—And let enquiry be made concerning all such as do pay tithes, which makes void the testimony and sufferings of our brethren who have suffered, many of them to death, by which many widows and fatherless have been made, and which is contrary to the doctrine of the apostles and the doctrine of the martyrs, and contrary to the doctrine of the righteous in this present age; all such are to be enquired into, and to be exhorted.

19thly.—And let enquiry be made concerning all prisoners that are poor, that they may be relieved, and so encouraged in their sufferings, and also that care be taken for their wives and families that they do not suffer for want of supply of outward things, and let enquiry be made how many prisoners there are in all the prisons in the county. Let diligent enquiry be made into all these things at every Monthly Meeting, and at every Quarterly Meeting, and to take care accordingly.

Dear friends be faithful in the service of God, and mind the Lord's business, and be diligent, and bring the power of the Lord over all those that have gainsaid it, and all you that be faithful go to visit them all that have been convinced, from house to house, that if it be possible you may not leave a hoof in Egypt; and so every one go seek the lost sheep and bring him home on your backs to the fold, and there will be more joy of that one sheep than the ninety-nine in the fold.

And my dear friends live in the wisdom of God, that which is gentle and pure, from above, and easy to be entreated, and bear one another's infirmities and weaknesses, and so fulfil the law of Christ ; and if any weakness should appear in any in your meetings, not for any to lay it open and tell it abroad ; that is not wisdom that doth so, for love covers a multitude of sins, and love preserves and edifies the body, and they that dwell in love dwells in God, for He is love, and love is not provoked. And, therefore, keep the law of love, which keeps down that which is provoked, for that which is provoked hath words which is for condemnation, therefore let the law of love be amongst you, it will keep down that which is provoked and its words, and so the body edifies itself in love.

Copies of this to be sent all abroad amongst Friends in their men's meetings. G. F.*

In these minutes, or "Canons" as some have termed them, is to be found the germ of much of the subsequent disciplinary action of the Society ; they contain also, in a condensed form, the counsel which George Fox from time to time throughout his life felt it right to issue. This is to be found *in extenso* in a great variety of pastoral letters and addresses in the second of the three volumes of his works (the first of these is the Journal, the third contains his Doctrinal Treatises, and this second may be termed a collection of his Pastoral Letters and Epistles). No one can read these last, and compare them with the works of the other early Friends, without seeing the pre-eminent position he took (even among that array of devoted preachers and evangelisers) on all questions affecting the good order and discipline of the Church, which, says George Whitehead, " greatly was his Christian care." To him, as long as he lived (and his service lasted some forty-five years), all gave, as it were, an instinctive deference, admitting that he sought not his own, and, like Moses of old, was one of the meekest of men. "God" (says

---

* There is no date to this document, but it is believed to have been framed about 1668. It is found entered in the MS. books of most of the London Meetings, also at Bristol and elsewhere. G. Fox's advices used to be periodically read in meetings, notice of such being the case occurring as late as 1776.

William Penn) "had visibly cloathed him with a Divine preference and authority." Now George Fox's desire was to use this influence (he undoubtedly possessed) to bring his friends, not, as he says, to "myself, but to his glory that sent me .... and when I turned you to Him that is able to save you I left you to Him."—*Epist.* p. 341. Hence, as his life's work drew toward a close, the same principles that had led him to encourage the local self-government by Monthly Meetings, and their association into Quarterly Meetings, tended towards the development in power of that Annual General Assembly which might exercise among them a chief voice and control, which so long as he himself lived seemed instinctively accorded to him. Not until after the decease of George Fox and his immediate cotemporaries do we find the Yearly Meeting (although existing parallel with them) drawing forward towards that power in the Church it has now become. The history of this meeting, to become understood, requires much searching among its records and minutes; and it is to be wished this might yet more be done, as it would form an instructive picture of the progress of the discipline amongst the body. The epitome given in the Meetings of Discipline Book, as also that in the Preface to the published Epistles, is far from complete, and what is here said can be taken only as a sketch.

The Yearly Meeting was from its commencement of a twofold nature: first and chiefly, a gathering of public Friends (*i.e.* ministers), to confer together on matters of faith and doctrine, and watch over one another in their service (for, in the beginning, the brethren in the ministry watched over their fellow-labourers in the Gospel, no such order as elders being at first known—the term when used meaning, as explained in speaking of the Baptists, ministers). Then, in 1672, it was agreed to give the Quarterly Meeting a direct representation, viz. "one or two of each county y^t are concerned in the publick service of the Truth .... to be chosen p^r ye Qrly. Meetings .... for y^t purpose." But the next year, 1673, it was thought best to discontinue this representative element until "Friends in God's wisdom shall see further occasion; but that the General Meeting of Friends who labour in the work of the ministry do continue as formerly appointed." Thus for four years more the ministers alone formed the Annual Assembly in London; but in 1677 the invitation for deputies from the Quarterly Meetings was renewed, and the year after it was said in inviting them that they were to attend, not only as to sufferings (which would seem to have been their business when they came up in 1673), " but for the more general service of Truth and Body of Friends in all those things wherein we may be capable to serve one another in Love." Next year a similar invitation was issued, and ever since the representative element has been formally recognised, and thereby the Yearly Meeting has come to its position of legislative importance in the Church, though it acquired it but gradually. Its action may be somewhat traced in reference to one branch of its labours—the well-known Queries. These first appear four years after the meeting had thus become representative, and were as follow:—

1682.
1. What Friends in the ministry in their respective counties departed this life since the last Yearly Meeting?
2. What Friends imprisoned for their testimony have died since last Yearly Meeting?
3. How the Truth hath prospered among themselves since the last Yearly Meeting, and how Friends are in peace and unity?

These were the first Queries; and no change or increase in their number was made until six years after George Fox's death, when, in 1696, they were altered to the eight following questions:—

1. What sufferings?
2. What present prisoners?
3. How many discharged, and when?
4. How many died prisoners, and the time when?
5. How many Public Friends died, and when?
6. How many meeting-houses builded, and what meetings added in each county, since last year?
7. What signal judgments have come upon persecutors?
8. How Truth prospers, and Friends are in unity, in their respective counties?

Four years later (1700) an addition was made to the eighth Query, viz. How have the former advices of this meeting relating to their godly care for the good education of their children in the way of truth and plainness of habit and speech

"The Quakers Synod", from Francis Bugg, *The Pilgrim's Progress from Quakerism to Christianity*, 1698 [LSF]

White Hart Court, or Gracechurch Street: print taken from a steel engraving in Picart's folio *Cérémonies et coutumes religieuses* (1723–43) in *Quaker Pictures – second series* (1897)

been practised? and it was "advised Friends bring brief and direct answers to the Questions drawn up at the Quarterly Meetings, and brought in writing to the Yearly Meeting."

In 1701 it was agreed to suspend the question No. 7— "seeing through the good providence of God and favour of the government we have our liberties;" and instead of this, two years later (1703) No. 7 was made to read thus:— "How are the several advices of this meeting being put in practice?"

Up to this time it would seem (notwithstanding the advice six years before) that all these questions were answered verbally by one of the representatives; for in 1706 a minute is made, that "for more ease and dispatch of business," Nos. 7 and 8 should in future be answered in writing, "to be sent up by faithful and understanding Friends, yet not to limit any from giving a lively verbal account." Eight years after a caution is given—"Those sent up be men fearing God, of good conversation, of weighty spirits, prudent and sincere, and well acquainted with the affairs of truth at home."

In 1720 another Query was added to the list, viz. No. 9— "How are the poor Friends among you taken care of?" and a year later (1721) the following addition was made to No. 7—" and particularly that against receiving or paying tithes." Also in 1723 a fresh Query, No. 10, was agreed to be added, "Do your Quarterly and Monthly Meetings take care to see that none under our profession defraud the king of any of his Customs Duties or Excise, or in anywise encourage receiving of goods? and do they severely reprehend and testify against all such offenders, and their unwarrantable, clandestine, and unlawful actions?"

Another alteration took place two years after in 1725, in the form of the 6th Query, making it to read thus :—" How do Friends prosper in the truth? and doth any convincement appear since last year?" leaving the rest of the Query as before. Complaint is at the same time made of the answers having been too general, and a distinct answer to each Query is asked for in future. No further change occurred for ten years, when (1735) a fuller answer was desired as to the 8th Query, respecting the poor, introducing the subject of education in these words :—" How are the poor amongst you provided for? and what care is taken of the education of their offspring?" Two years after (1737) and the subject of Records is more specially referred to, by asking in the 9th

Query, "And do you keep a particular record of all the sufferings and prosecutions that happen in your county in your Monthly and Quarterly Meeting books?" It was in this year that rules concerning removals and settlements were so settled as first to define membership, and lead to lists of members being kept. Seven years now passed, when (1744) the 8th Query received the following form:—"Do ye bear a faithful Christian testimony against the receiving or paying tithes, priests' demands, or those called church-rates, bearing of arms, or paying trophy-money? and do ye admonish such as are unfaithful therein?" These continued for thirteen years, when the increasing conformity to the general habits of society led, in 1757, to the following more pointed form of the 7th Query:—"This meeting observing with concern, in reading the answers to the Queries from the several counties, a manifest defection in parents training up their children agreeable to the tenor of the 7th Query, it is now agreed that for the future the said Query shall stand as follows, viz.:—' Do Friends, by example and precept, endeavour so to train up their children, servants, and those under their care, in all godly conversation, in the frequent reading of the Holy Scriptures, also in plainness of speech, behaviour, and apparel? and are Friends faithful in admonishing such as are remiss therein?'"

In 1758 some minor changes were agreed to; and in the next year inquiry was added as to registering marriages, &c. In 1761 *Quarterly* Meetings were advised to get their *Subordinate* Meetings to make their answers to them full and explicit, and in writing. It would appear as if the first formal answering of Queries by the Monthly to the Quarterly Meetings was arranged for by the Yearly Meeting in 1755; and their advice had to be repeated on the subject three years later, in 1758, when it was especially directed to the Quarterly Meeting of London — as if their Monthly Meetings had hitherto failed in a compliance, for Monthly Meetings were, previously to this, very various in the nature of their answers to Quarterly Meetings, many of them retaining a strong feeling of independence towards the Quarterly Meetings, which were at first, in many cases in the country, as will be seen in London, merely meetings of *record* of marriages, births, burials, and sufferings, rather than of any administrative nature. It was the action and service of the Yearly Meeting through many years to bring about that regular gradation and representative dependence now so thoroughly observed. It was, in fact, through the Yearly Meeting that the Society, when showing signs of becoming dispersed, was gathered together into social order and unity. For becoming deeply concerned at the state of affairs manifested by the answers to the Queries, especially "the sorrowful neglect of the most important duty of worship," the Yearly Meeting (1760) encouraged all who felt a concern to offer their names as a committee, which, thus formed, spent *years* in visiting and encouraging the Churches. From this, great purging of the camp resulted, as the numerous disownments show, and great order and regularity became infused into the discipline of the body, eventually bringing about that the Queries answered by one meeting to another, and by the Quarterly to the Annual assembly, were but one complete and regular series, as they continued for a century, until again recently varied. In these recent alterations, it may be observed, that the lessening of the number to be answered and increasing those regarded as advices, is a return to, rather than a departure from, the more early forms. For it has been shown that, whilst there were MANY advices, there were but FEW questions, and those only relating to matters of fact, at first *required* to be answered. George Fox, though a lover of order, feared forms and formalities; and though he issued advices as to dress, manners, and habits, yet left it then to the individual conscience. He was very cautious as to disownments, as he was also to recognition of membership. The last was never defined in his lifetime; not, in fact, till 1737, when rules as to removals and settlements were arranged. As to disownments, the following may be taken as a specimen of his feeling toward delinquents :—

"And no condemnation ought to go further than the *Transgression* is known, and if he or she returns and gives forth a Paper of Condemnation against him or herself (which is more desirable than that we should do it) this is a testimony of his or her repentance and resurrection before God, his people and the whole world as David (Psalms 57) when Nathan came to admonish him."—*G. F. Epist.* vol. ii. p. 284. No doubt, the simple arrangements of the earlier half of the Society's existence, adapted to a state of the Church when much zeal was yet shown by travelling ministers, did not prove equal to the condition of affairs as the eighteenth century advanced and this zeal declined. In 1760 came a time of revival, when the whole body were aroused to take a much more *general* interest in the Society's welfare. Monthly Meetings ceased to be select gatherings of but a few invited ones—becoming open to attendance of the members generally, so with all the higher meetings and the Yearly Meeting. Accompanied with this a strict discipline became established, by which the Society was kept together, in a measure, of life under social influences that threatened disruption. It is interesting to observe a body thus enabled to act so differently at different times and freely use varied machinery to meet altered circumstances: such gives an interest even to its discipline. That the chief burden in the service of *first* settling the discipline lay on George Fox, is shown (among other ways) by the personal opposition he encountered from some of his disciples, such as John Wilkinson and Thomas Story, whose works, published about 1680, remain to show how adverse they were to his proceedings. This is also alluded to by W. Penn in his preface to G. F.'s Journal: "This man of God had his share of suffering . . . as one that sought dominion over conscience because he prest by his presence or Epistles a ready and zealous compliance with such good and wholesome things as tended to an *orderly conversation* . . . They begrudged of this *meek man* the love and esteem he had, and deserved, in the hearts of the people . . . They would have had every man *Independent*, that as he had the principle in himself he should only stand and fall to that . . . and so struck at the *spiritual unity* which a people guided by the same *principle* are naturally led into . . . some weakly mistook good order in the government of church affairs for discipline in worship . . . and ready to reflect the same things that Dissenters . . . had objected to the National Churches that have coercively pressed conformity to their creeds and worships, whereas these things related . . . to the civil part of the Church . . . But in all these occasions though there was no person the discontented struck so sharply at as this good man . . . he returned not reflection for reflection but forgave them their . . . bitter speeches . . . And truly I must say," adds W. Penn, "he held his place in the Church of God with great meekness and a most engaging *humility* and *moderation* . . . his authority was inward not outward, and he got it and kept it by the love of God and power of an endless life. I write my knowledge and not report . . . having been with him for weeks and months together on divers occasions, and those of the nearest and most exercising nature, and that by night and by day, by sea and by land, in this and in foreign countrys, and I can say I never saw him out of his place or not a match for every service or occasion, in all things he acquitted himself like a man, yea, a strong man, a new and heavenly-minded man." And the Yearly Meeting itself acknowledged his influence in one of its Epistles, 1673, " Yet the Lord hath laid it more upon some in whom he hath opened counsel for that end—and particularly in our dear brother and God's faithful labourer, George Fox—for the help of many."

N.B.—It is obvious to any (at all acquainted with the Discipline established in the Society) that the foregoing is but an imperfect sketch of its history, and that there are many subjects connected with it besides the Queries which it would prove interesting to develop—such as the rules concerning Marriage, Care of Poor, Education, &c.

The important action taken by the Yearly Meeting in 1760, and the results that followed, are well shown in William Thistlethwaite's Lectures on the Society; and William Tanner's Lectures on the Bristol and Somersetshire Friends supplies much general and collateral information.

CHAPTER VI.

GENERAL SKETCH OF THE PENAL LAWS WHICH AFFECTED FRIENDS' MEETINGS.*

It may be as well to note here, though in but general terms, what those laws were through disobeying which Friends experienced for many years so much suffering, to the loss of liberty, property, their country, and even life.

In so doing there will be no occasion to make reference to any general statutes affecting the individual person, such as the taking of oaths, payment of tithes, &c.; but to allude only to those laws which, through prohibition of *public assembling*, seem more pertinent to the subject in hand.

No act was passed in the time of Cromwell to restrain Friends specially from meeting; but his government, ever fearful of plots and insurrections, were averse to assemblies of the people; and as a consequence it was not difficult for ministers and teachers of other sects, working upon this feeling, to bring down the iron hand of the magistrate upon a sect, innocent of any revolutionary purpose, but persistent in assembling together, and awakening jealousy by its numbers and rapid increase. Hence, though without any special law passed against them, Friends suffered much under the semi-military government of Cromwell through holding their meetings, being (as subsequently proved) unjustly confounded with revolutionary zealots, or with those seeking to subvert all order, or else undistinguished from disaffected papists conspiring for a renewal of papal supremacy.

The first Act of Parliament specially directed against Friends' meetings was passed in 1662; a time when the Church party, re-established in power, two years previously, by the restoration of the King, were finding the difficulty of obtaining that settlement in religion which they desired, viz.—universal conformity to a State-Church.

Previously to the passing of this act the outbreak of the

---

* N.B.—Any more particular and accurate knowledge of these laws can be found in Joseph Davis' Digest, or in the pages of Besse's Sufferings.

enthusiasts, known as the Fifth-Monarchy Men, had drawn from the King in Council a Proclamation prohibiting as illegal all assemblies for worship other than those according to the ritual of the Established Church, and bringing down upon their frequenters the pains and penalties of acts passed a century before, in the days of Elizabeth. These ancient laws were four in number; three of them were to compel people to attend church under penalties differing in character—the earliest of them inflicted a fine of twelve pence per head on each absentee from worship on any Sunday or holiday; the second, passed some twenty years after, increased the amount of the fine very largely, making it as much as twenty pounds a month; the third (some five years later) added power to imprison offenders, and even to transport them beyond seas in case of confirmed obstinacy. The fourth went a stage further by making all these applicable, not only to those who absented themselves from church, but who "frequented conventicles," thereby endeavouring to stop the practice of many who (to evade the previously mentioned laws) only put in an appearance at church and then went off to assemble in the conventicle for their worship.

Charles II., by his proclamation in 1662, brought down, as before remarked, the powers of these old laws of Elizabeth on the Sectaries — the sharpness of which Friends (still holding to their meetings) had to endure, as well as those other penalties for non-payment of tithes, and for not taking oaths, even of allegiance, in any Court of Justice.

It was not however thought consistent, with due regard to British liberties, to leave the King alone to deal with this matter, and Parliament, ever jealous of a government through the exercise of Royal Prerogative, proceeded to take the matter in hand itself, and framed the Act of 1662 before alluded to, in which Friends are specially mentioned in these words—
" Whereas, of late times certain persons under the name of Quakers and other names of separation . . . under a pretence of religious worship, do often assemble themselves in great numbers in several parts of this realm to the endangering of the publick peace and safety, and to the terror of the people, by maintaining a secret and strict correspondence amongst themselves, and in the mean time separating and dividing themselves from the rest of his Majesty's good and loyal subjects, and from the publick congregations and usual places of divine worship."

In all this preamble we see what were the fears entertained by the Parliament of 1662 toward the "certain persons under the name of Quakers," and whether these fears were true or not let the History of the Society bear witness. Whether the Legislature *had* formed a correct judgment as to the motive in the "secret and strict correspondence," or the nature and object of the great assemblies "to the terror of the people," let their own subsequent acts say, whereby in twenty-five years after this the Friends (though in no wise changed, as their public acts and records testify, and still holding their great assemblies in public), were not only permitted the common protection then accorded to other Nonconformists, but received especial exemption from those things that had formerly been pressed on them, to the loss of liberty, property, their country, and even life itself.

By this act each person attending a meeting where more than five not of the household were present, became liable, for the *first* offence, to a fine not exceeding five pounds, or in default of payment to *three* months' imprisonment; for the *second*, the fine was limited to ten pounds, or *six* months' imprisonment with *hard labour;* and if after these convictions the offence was the *third* time committed, then *transportation* "beyond the seas" was the severe and extreme penalty.

Two years afterwards the provisions of this act were made more stringent, by one passed in 1664, and by it Elizabeth's regulations were confirmed, and more summary powers of imprisonment committed to the judges, enabling them, without any appeal to a jury, to imprison for three months for the first offence; and, in case of the second, if the party accused declined to plead to the indictment framed against him, the judges had power, without the appeal to jury, to transport him "beyond seas" for seven years.

In reading notices of those "Friends' trials," which occurred during the operation of these acts, many may have thought the parties often treated the questions put to them by the judges in that evasive manner which has given the name of "Quaker answer" to such mode of reply; but if any will be at the pains to read for themselves the text of the acts as given in Besse, it will be seen in what straits a person so arraigned was placed, because an admission on his part such as the judges sought to extort would have placed him out of court as to any trial by jury—(which Friends were anxious to obtain)—leaving to the judge power at once to pronounce sentence. Of the fact of their being Friends and of their assembling together there was no secret, but whilst they suffered, they did not court prosecution, and felt it no part of their duty to ensnare themselves in legal penalties which any direct admission, such as the judges' questions sought to obtain, would involve them in. These acts really deprived Britons of the right of trial by jury;* to obtain that right —the heritage of all Englishmen—was what Friends were striving for, and their evasive answers to judges' questions must be regarded from this point of view, if their motive is to be rightly estimated.

This Act of 1664 gave magistrates the power, with such " companies of horse or foot," . . . " and by the best means they can, to dissolve and dissipate, or prevent all such unlawful meetings. It also bears throughout it evidence of being specially directed against " seditious " and " disloyal " persons, whose part in " insurrections," it mentions, " late experience " had shown. Hence the frequent objections made by Friends on their trials, that such provisions, directed so obviously against " insurrectionists," should be turned upon their " peaceable " meetings, and horse and foot employed to break them up with violence. This act was to remain in force for three years, within which time it was no doubt hoped that the stringency of its powers would remove the necessity for its continuance. " There is a new statute," said Judge Turner to Francis Howgill, at this time, " that will make you fewer." That these words cannot be regarded as prophetic, is shown by the necessity being found for a third Conventicle Act six years later.

This last one, of 1670, somewhat changed the line of attack, by reducing the fines for mere attendance at a meeting, but greatly increasing them on any one who might be found preaching or praying there. Such an individual was liable to £20 penalty for the first offence, and £40 for every subsequent one ; the legislators thinking, no doubt, that if the

---

* See *T. Ellwood*, p. 250, on the Act of 1670, the same in principle as this of 1664 :—" It breaks down and over-runs the bounds and banks anciently set for the defence and security of Englishmen's lives, liberties, and properties, viz. trial by juries ; instead thereof, directing and authorising Justices of the Peace (and that too, privately, out of session) to convict, fine, and by their warrant distrain upon offenders against it, directly contrary to the Great Charter." [Ellwood ref corrected to "p.273" in annotated copy]

shepherd be smitten, the flock will disperse.* Distress of goods and imprisonment followed also, as a consequence of nonpayment. These provisions were in themselves severe, but the chief edge of the cruelty lay in the inducements which by the provision of this act were offered for persons to become informers, inasmuch as it allotted to these one-third share in the produce of all the fines, thereby a class of persons was developed who made this work their business, and lived upon "the spoil and ruin of conscientious people."

To these grievous hardships the King's attention became directed; and he undertook, by a Royal Declaration† (issued after the act had been in operation some two years only) to suspend all Penal Laws in matters ecclesiastical, excepting only Roman Catholics from the benefit. But the Parliament, finding these to avail themselves of such clemency, grew alarmed both at this and the exercise of the King's prerogative, and compelled Charles to withdraw his "Declaration," thus enabling informers to return to their old employment. In 1680, the Parliament, ever concerned for the Protestant cause, and further roused at the discovery of another Popish Plot, became conscious that, in prosecuting Nonconformists, they had so subdivided the anti-Papal interest as greatly to weaken the strength of the Protestant cause in the country. Desiring now to remedy this, and to hold out the hand of friendship to all peaceable Nonconformists, they passed a resolution to cease from this prosecution as "grievous to the subject, weakening to the Protestant interest, an encouragement to Popery, and dangerous to the peace of the kingdom;" they also brought in a bill to this effect, and

---

* "Dear Friends," wrote G. F. to Bristol, "Now is the time for you to stand. . . . You that have been Publick men, and formerly did travel abroad, mind to keep up your Testimony. . . . Go into your meeting places as at other times . . . that none faint in the time of trial . . . that their heads may not sink in the Storms," &c.—*Epistles*, vol. ii. p. 317.

† King Charles, in his Declaration, 15th March, 1671-2, says: "Our care and endeavours for the preservation of the Rites and interest of the Church have been sufficiently manifested to the world by the whole course of our Government since our happy Restoration, and by the many and frequent ways of Coercion that we have used for reducing all erring and dissenting Persons, and for composing the unhappy differences in matters of religion which we found among our subjects upon our return. But it being evident by the sad experience of *Twelve* Years that there is very little Fruit of all these forcible methods," &c. &c. N.B.—It was during the respite from suffering obtained by this Declaration that George Fox visited America.

likewise appointed a committee to inquire into the sufferings of the Quakers—all which being unpleasant to the Papal party, the King was induced to dissolve the Parliament, and thus persecution again raged, and continued so until the end of his reign, giving the informers, like beasts of prey, opportunity to make sad havoc among the conscientious people—1,500 Friends alone, without mentioning the Nonconformists, being in prison at the time of Charles II.'s death, besides the losses of many thousands of others, through fines and distress on goods, which, though all recorded in the original books of sufferings, still at Devonshire House, are too numerous to quote, and difficult to summarise.

James II., during his short reign of three years, relieved these sufferings by putting a check on informers and releasing prisoners, proceeding so far as to suspend, by Declaration, (as his brother had done six years before) the operation of all Penal Laws against Nonconformists, a benefit they received but suspiciously at his hands, knowing his object to be not so much their toleration, as to promote the cause of his co-religionists—the Catholics. Happily, under William III., Parliament was able to deal with the whole question, and passed an act by which all those former laws, treating Nonconformity as a penal offence, were repealed in favour of all persons who would take a simple oath of allegiance to the King as chief magistrate. Places for divine worship, though conducted in other modes than that of the Establishment, if properly *registered*, and held with *open* doors, were both to be permitted and receive legal protection. For Friends some special arrangements were made to meet their conscientious objection to all swearing; and thus after so long a struggle they were successful in maintaining the right to "assemble themselves together."

Seldom, perhaps, since the days of early Christianity was a cause maintained with more perseverance than Friends exhibited at this time. Denounced as fanatical and blasphemous when the fierce Puritan was in power; confined in the filthiest of gaols, treated as a common felon, outlawed and transported when the Bishops of Charles II. had recovered their places; regarded with suspicion by Parliaments for their "secret correspondence and great assemblies;" dreaded as possible plotters and insurrectionists by each party as it in turn ascended to power; branded by all as heretical opponents to Ministry and Magistracy, and subjected to the sharp penalties of law; the Friends, bearing all—enduring, but not relinquishing—kept up their meetings, though fine, "cruel mockings" and imprisonment were, with little or no intermission, their portion for more than forty years. Through all, it was met by patience, and a confidence that the Lord they served would in due time make a way of escape. In hope they persevered and suffered, yet used all lawful and peaceable means to convince those in power of their innocence. As to themselves, in love they drew nearer and closer to each other in the hour of mutual trial; encouraged by martyr spirits such as Burrough, coming cheerfully to meet their death in gaol; cheered by such as Dewsberry, who, though pining as to the body, said, "In the prison I sang praises, and esteemed the bolts and locks as jewels."* Stimulated by the self-sacrificing zeal of such men as Fox, Whitehead, and others, who counted it a joy to spend and be spent in the cause, the band held together during the strongest efforts for their dispersion; hoped on, though long and dark the trial, and relief came at last—the victory was won. The meetings they were, during forty years, persecuted for holding, were, by the same high authority of the Legislature which had formerly made them penal, now as formally permitted, and, though in no respects changed as to their nature from the day when they had been denounced as treasonable, they were now recognised as among the gatherings of Christian people; for each of the other sects, as well as the Established Church, had at last come to acknowledge that the Quaker had proved his cause,—that men could meet together for worship without Liturgies or Rituals, or formally

---

* Basil Montagu, whose name is so honourably associated with the subject of prisons, &c. in his account of a visit he paid to Warwick Gaol in 1815, says: "This offensive vault, which may now be seen in the prison, is 18 ft. 10 in. underground. In the middle is a cesspool; on the side is a stream for the prisoners to slake their thirst. There is a large heavy chain now in the dungeon that passed through a link in the chains of each of the felons, which was then carried up the steps and secured to the outer door of the vault. The only light and air is through an iron grate on the top and nearly even with the surface of the ground."

Life of William Dewsberry, p. 120, and p. 176: "We that are here [*i.e.* Warwick] are kept close from coming one to another. There were some of our Friends here a little time since put into a close cellar, where they had not room to lie one by another; and one of them being near dead for want of room and air was brought forth very weak, and he yet remains sick and weakly."

appointed priests; and yet have no ulterior motive dangerous to the peace of the realm, being refreshed by the Divine presence experienced among them. Such long persecution, met as it was by such Christian zeal and immovable resolution in maintaining their right of publicly assembling for the worship of God, is (as " Besse, Preface," p. 511, remarks) " an indication that in those assemblies they were made partakers of that solid comfort and celestial sweetness which attend the true and evangelical worship which they valued above all the delights, pleasures, and enjoyments of this world, and which . . enabled them cheerfully to undergo not only the spoiling of their goods, but imprisonments, banishments, and even death itself. . . . May their constancy (adds this author) stir up those who now freely enjoy what they so dearly purchased. . . "

In no one case was it ever proved that Friends held secret or treasonable meetings; not one of their gatherings was ever tumultuous, or true cause of terror; and though the indictments under which they suffered were based on such charges, their accusers seldom dared to bring them to an *independent* jury. But time brought the whole matter before the bar of public opinion; and that, clearly expressed, acquitted the Friend, and admitted his scruples and practices as peaceable and conscientious.

What these meetings were, what was the mind and desire of their chief promoters, at a time when those in authority were denouncing them as heretical, insurrectionary, and treasonable, let the following extract show. It is taken from a paper issued in 1660 (the time of the King's first Proclamation against meetings) by Alexander Parker, who was one of the earliest, also one of the most gifted and judicious, of those by whose Gospel labours these meetings were established. It shows the great and solemn importance with which these assemblies were regarded by the first Friends. (The paper will be found *in extenso* at page 361 of the Letters.)

"And now dear souls . . mind every one your particular duties . . in your meetings and solemn assemblies . . come orderly in the fear of God . . be not careless nor wander . . either in body or mind . . but sit down in some place . . and wait upon God singly, as if none were present but the Lord. . . And so all . . coming in, in the fear of the Lord, sit down in pure stillness . . this is a sweet and precious meeting where all meet with the Lord. Those who are brought to a pure, still waiting upon God in the spirit, are come nearer to the Lord than words are . . here is the true feeding in the spirit . . and this is the end of all words and writings to bring people to the eternal living Word. . . If any be moved to speak, see that they speak in the power; and when the power is still be ye still. . . In such a meeting where the presence and power of God is felt there will be an unwillingness to part asunder . . and when your meeting is ended do not look upon the service of God to be ended, but . . dear friends, in all companies, at all times and seasons, so walk, that ye may be examples of good unto all . . and that God over all may be glorified." Then follows some judicious advice as to being " still and quiet," amid the " overturnings " in the political world, and not siding " with any parties." But enough is quoted to show the spirit and power under which Friends set up their meetings, and the source of that strength which enabled them to maintain them whilst other Nonconformist assemblies were for *a time* almost dissolved.*

---

* As an illustration of how among other communities there was no cohesion in the congregation without a minister, we find in G. F.'s Journal, " That, at the time of the first Proclamation against Conventicles, the Presbyterians had arranged for a great gathering at Lemster, where they said they would stand to their principles; but before meeting there they had heard of this proclamation, and though the people came, ' the priest was gone, and then they were at a loss.' "

To this may be added what may be regarded as an independent and impartial testimony to the tenacity of Friends from a recent author, viz. Skeats, *History of Free Churches*, p. 76 : " The sufferings of ministers and people during this period were unspeakable. Their congregations were scattered; they were fined, pilloried, imprisoned, and banished. Many Presbyterians took refuge in the Church ; others identified themselves more closely with the Independents ; and the denomination, as such, began to decline. The Independents and Baptists gave up their meetings, or met by stealth ; while watchers stationed on roofs, or as outposts in the streets, were ready to give warning of the approach of informers. The members of one denomination alone continued by meeting to defy, and not to evade, the law: these were the Quakers. The brutality with which the members of this sect were treated exceeded anything which had been known in the recent history of persecution in England."

CHAPTER VII.

LONDON AND MIDDLESEX QUARTERLY MEETING.

In most parts of the country, the origin of Quarterly Meetings may be traced to those periodical gatherings of Friends from different but adjoining counties, known as GENERAL MEETINGS, and held at intervals with more or less regularity in different places.*

By means of such assemblies, Friends resident in different counties became associated together for the transaction of affairs in which they had a common interest.

In London it is not so easy to trace the development of these occasional General Meetings into those held regularly every quarter, on account of its having been necessary at an early period to establish certain meetings, which only by degrees became assimilated to those arrangements which Quarterly and Monthly Meetings indicate.

The earliest meeting in London for the care of the Church, seems to have been composed of men Friends in the ministry only, who met at first in the house of Gerrard Roberts, as often as occasion needed, forming a body which has doubtless gradually developed into the present " Morning Meeting."

The Society had grown, as we have seen, rapidly into a large community, spreading from the city itself as a centre to all those surrounding parts, then distinct in themselves, but now composing London as a whole.

Amid such a numerous body, its members no doubt but little acquainted with one another, and scattered in so many directions, the need for some bond of union was soon manifested; for subjects of general want and care rapidly arose, whose necessities required more time than Friends in the ministry could devote to them. This occasioned the setting apart of others well concerned for the truth, but not so engaged, who might take charge over these matters

---

* Not to be confounded with the General Meetings of a later date, which were meetings for worship.—*See* T. Story's Life, &c.

of external arrangement and discipline, whereby all things might be done "decently and in order," among the newly gathered people.

Thus, within some two years of the rise of Friends in London, a meeting was set apart for these general objects, and met once every fortnight, being known from such circumstance as the Two-Weeks Meeting, the history of which will be given in Chap. VIII. Subsequently to this, the whole London district being found too large for only one such meeting, it became divided, at George Fox's suggestion in 1668, into six parts, five of these being known as Monthly Meetings; whilst the Two-Weeks Meeting retained its name and the care over that portion of the district comprised within the line of the walls, and known as the City proper. A few more years and a meeting of appeal and general oversight over these six subdivisions was established, known as the Six-Weeks Meeting, which long held a position among them, similar to that now taken by the Quarterly Meeting; and in consequence it is difficult to trace the exact origin of this latter meeting.

The earliest allusions to its existence are found in George Fox's Journal (*circ.* 1666) and in a paper by him on the Six-Weeks Meeting (see Chap. VIII.), also in a letter from Ellis Hookes, our first recording clerk (see Letters, p. 188). Writing from London, under date Eighth Month (October) 1672, E. H. says, "Friends here did at the Quarterly Meeting take into consideration my pains and care in the service of the truth, and are willing to allow me a man to assist, which is some encouragement to me," &c. (This was the year when the General Meeting for the Society at large, held in London since 1661,* was agreed to be held there regularly every Whitsun week, making it thereby the Yearly Meeting that has since continued; it would no doubt bring more labour on Ellis Hookes, as recording clerk.)

Unfortunately, there are no minute-books remaining of the Quarterly Meeting's proceedings earlier than the year 1690.†

---

* See *Letters*, p. 313.

† Some of its transactions are nevertheless entered in the minute-books of the various Monthly Meetings. The following is one of the earliest of these:—

"At a meeting of Friends at Devonshire House, the 25th of the Third Month, 1668, concluded and agreed as followeth (viz.)—

At which time we find the following to have been the Monthly Meetings represented, viz.: London (*i.e.* Bull and Mouth, or City Meeting); Devonshire House (or Wheeler Street Meeting); Ratcliff, Southwark, Peel, Westminster; and besides these of the London district were the following Suburban Meetings, viz.: Hendon, Hammersmith, Uxbridge and Endfield (Barking was transferred to it from Essex Quarterly Meeting in the following year).

In early times the business of the Quarterly Meeting* comprised much of a routine character, being for many years one of record and registration, rather than of discipline. To it were brought reports of births, marriages, and burials; copies of marriage certificates, also a statement of the number of prisoners for conscience' sake; and further the clauses of all wills relating to legacies, trusts and bequests which were duly entered on its records.

The first business of a legislative character would seem to have been the setting up or discontinuance of meetings for worship in various places, also alterations in the times of holding them.

" That all Births, Marriages, and Burials, and also all Friends' Sufferings, be brought in and recorded in every Monthly Meeting, and copies thereof (once every quarter) sent to the General Meeting, there to be recorded also, that, if one book should be lost, the other may remain as a testimony thereof.

" And that all Births of Friends' children that were born before their parents were convinced, and could not for conscience' sake register their names in the World's Books, should be registered in a book distinct, and to have a distinct title.

" Persons are appointed in the several meetings to take care of the several things before mentioned, and to give notes for the burying of the dead (and none else)."

[Here follow the names of Friends appointed to attend to the above affairs in the various Monthly Meetings.]

* George Fox thus defines the qualifications for members of the Quarterly Meetings: " Now concerning them that do go to the *Quarterly Meetings*, they must be *substantial Friends* that can give a *Testimony* of your *Sufferings*, and how things are amongst you in every particular *Meeting*. So that none that are raw or weak, that are not able to give a *Testimony* of the *affairs* of the *Church* and *Truth*, may go on behalf of the particular *Meetings* to the Quarterly *Meetings*, but may be nursed up in your Monthly *Meetings*, and there fitted for the *Lord's service*. So that two may go one time from every particular Meeting, and two at another time, or as it is ordered in your Monthly Meetings . . . for the Quarterly Meeting should be made up of *weighty, seasoned*, and *substantial* Friends."—*G. F. Epistles*, vol. ii. p. 290.

Another department of business under its control was that of assisting to find situations for those in want of employment, by keeping a registry of such on its books. Thus we read, in 1694, that "the widow French's children at Endfield are wanting places as apprentices." And again, "John Stringfellow reports that Richard Owen wants imploye and may be heard of in Hanging Sword Court in Fleet Street."

At this time, although there were several country meetings nominally members of the Quarterly Meeting, yet, in fact, no such union really existed either then or for long after, but a distinction existed between them, so that when spoken of in technical language those of the London district were called of London Quarterly Meeting, and those of the suburban ones of Middlesex. In answering Queries to the YEARLY Meeting, separate statements were drawn up for each; and in sending representatives to that body, whilst the London Monthly Meetings each chose their own, the Quarterly Meeting itself appointed individuals to act for the Monthly Meetings of the country districts. This last feature was continued for twenty years, when an alteration was made in 1710, allowing the country Monthly Meetings to nominate their own representatives, subject, however, to the Quarterly Meeting's approval.

Nevertheless, the distinction between London and Middlesex as two distinct Quarterly Meetings was long maintained, even though meeting together as one body at the same time and place, it being thought best on account of certain vested interests in funded properties, thus technically to keep them separate. But the introduction of suburban residence among the London Friends so intermingled those of town and country as gradually to break down this distinction, though not until a long period after this. Ultimately all distinction was removed, except that of funds, which last ceased only so late as 1862, on the establishment of a Quarterly Meeting's Stock common to all the meetings.

It may be noted here, in connection with the appointment of representatives, that those to the Yearly Meeting were, until 1793, appointed by the separate Monthly Meetings, since which time only the present plan of electing them in the Quarterly Meeting itself has been adopted.

Thus the Quarterly Meeting of London and that of Middlesex, commencing amid other meetings by which all important matters of discipline were transacted, was concerned at first with subjects of a purely secular and routine nature; yet by degrees it gradually rose in character, chiefly through its value becoming recognised as a court of appeal from the decisions of Monthly Meetings; being preferred as such to the Six-Weeks Meeting, on account of its more open and representative character. In consequence, matters of importance came under the care of the Quarterly Meeting, until (as we shall have to show in the next chapter) the Six-Weeks Meeting, from being so long the "prime meeting of the city," became simply the steward of the Quarterly Meeting's property. There seems, however, before this to have long been an anomalous connection between these two bodies. Both had control over one common purse, and business was occasionally referred by the Quarterly Meeting to the Six-Weeks Meeting, or reported by this body to have been attended to. It was not until 1745 that the Quarterly Meeting relieved the Six-Weeks Meeting of any management in the Church business of the London and country meetings, committing to it only (as its cash committee) the financial and other comparatively secular affairs.

As the business of the Quarterly Meeting increased in interest, and especially when appeals to it were frequent, it seems to have been the arena of much earnest discussion. Hence arose, in 1713, the necessity for the following quaint regulations:—

"This meeting considering that the observing a due method in matters of debate greatly tends to the dispatch of business and prevents heat and disorder, doth therefore recommend the following particulars to be observed and put in practice by all the members of this meeting:

"1. That when a debate arises upon any matter, no person speaks above thrice on it, unless he has leave from this meeting.

"2. That every one that speaks be careful not to make digressions from the subject matter in debate.

"3. That several speaking together be carefully avoided, and no person interrupt another, or begin to speak before he has fully done.

"4. And in order to prevent more than one from speaking at a time 'tis desired, That he which speaks would stand up, thereby to be seen, and the better heard by the members of the meeting, and the others, as much as may be, keep their seats.

"5. That when any one speaks, he speak to the meeting, and not be talking to those that sit by.*

"6. That all personal reflections or indecent expressions be carefully avoided; and if any one shall give them, that the meeting condemn it as disorderly.

"7. That this minute be read at the opening of the next Quarterly Meeting, to put Friends in mind of this necessary and tender recommendation."

Up to the year 1759 the Quarterly Meeting seems to have been a meeting for discipline only, without a previous meeting for worship; but in that year we find men Friends inviting the women to join them in a time of religious worship before proceeding to transact the affairs of the Church. In their reply to this requisition, the Women's Meeting state that "ever since the Women's Meetings in London were established, a time for retirement before they entered upon business has been constantly in use, wherein living testimonies to the truth have been frequently delivered to the comfort and edification of our meetings, and we trust may be continued among us if we keep our women Friends together in our usual manner." "If this has not been the practice of our brethren, it becomes us not to inquire into the cause thereof, and we only submit the account of our practice as a reason why we think the alteration cannot avail, at least to our advantage." They also urge that the proposed change will "prevent giving seasonable advice to many of our own sex," and will "perhaps straiten our brethren."

Notwithstanding this opposition to the proposal, it was subsequently carried into effect, and continued to the present time. There was a minute made in 1810 connected with this subject. It directs women Friends at the Meeting for Worship to sit on their own side upstairs and down, in front of the table and in the gallery over the entrance, before going elsewhere in the meeting-house; and, when the Meeting for Worship is over, to go to their own house without stopping to talk in the meeting-house or yard; "which latter the

---

* The need for such directions were not peculiar to Friends, see Stoughton's *Eccl. History*, vol. ii. p. 176, Presbyterian Divines, bye-laws, Sion College, 1645—58 : "That private whispering shall be forborne," and "that no man shall use irreverent or uncomely language or behaviour."

Quarterly Meeting intends to take further means of clearing from any obstruction on the part of men Friends."

The Quarterly Meeting was originally an afternoon gathering, being long held at 2 p.m. on a Second-day. In 1784, after meeting in the afternoon for more than a century, Friends concluded that " the fore part of the day is the most proper to set apart for meetings of worship and discipline"; and accordingly have since held the Quarterly Meeting, as at present, in the morning.

Referring to the distinction already mentioned as existing between the London and Country Meetings, we find that during the course of the eighteenth century considerable dissatisfaction was expressed by the country meetings in respect to it, so that in 1773 the subject was referred to a large committee, but without result; and the matter rested for eleven years more, until in 1784 country Friends again pressed the question upon the Quarterly Meeting's attention, and so far successfully that a union was agreed upon as concerned answering the Queries, but nothing further. This could only be a temporary arrangement; and in 1788 Tottenham Monthly Meeting was especially energetic in pleading for a complete union; when, after various deliberations by the Quarterly Meeting itself and a large committee appointed on the subject, extending over nearly two years, a proposed plan of union was entered on the books.

The real cause of the difficulty felt in this union of London Meetings with those of Middlesex was one respecting property. During the century that had elapsed since Friends arose in London, some institutions had been established to which, through donations and legacies, important property belonged, the chief of these being the school and workhouse. Now, as these funded properties had been bequeathed by their donors for the benefit of the London district, it was felt to be a difficulty how far others not resident within those limits could be admitted to share in these advantages; and besides these, there were the funds which had been raised and invested with a view to extinguish the quotas.

It was now proposed to raise a common Quarterly Meeting's stock; and, in order to be admitted to this so as to participate in the full benefits of the school and workhouse, Tottenham Monthly Meeting should pay to the common stock £1,300, Longford £700, and Barking £345. This suggested arrangement was kept before the Quarterly Meeting for another year, and then taken off the books without a decision. It was left for Friends of a later period [1862] to effect these arrangements, of which mention will be made in the next chapter on the Six-Weeks Meeting.

The amount of business devolving upon the Quarterly Meeting in modern times has led to one or two propositions of interest. In 1824, it was sought to extend the proceedings over two days, by commencing on Third-day morning with a Meeting for Worship, holding the Quarterly Meeting of Ministers and Elders in the afternoon, and giving up Fourth-day entirely to the meetings for business. A similar plan was advocated in 1833, after Kingston (transferred from Surrey in 1800) and Longford had both complained that the Quarterly Meeting was " inconveniently and unprofitably large." But no changes resulted from these suggestions.

Having now mentioned some of the leading points in the history of London and Middlesex Quarterly Meeting as a corporate assembly, we proceed to note a few matters of interest which from time to time have occupied its attention.

Care of the Churches.

The Quarterly Meeting at an early date felt a responsibility as to the state of the meetings within its borders. In 1697, it appointed a committee to visit the Monthly Meetings, and recommend them to read George Fox's advices at least once a quarter,* which celebrated advices are to be found transcribed at length in the records of most, if not all, the London Meetings; and as late as 1775 and 1776, the fact of their having been " read to good satisfaction" is entered on the Quarterly Meeting's books.

The Quarterly Meeting was frequently concerned in the issue of special advices on particular subjects to its subordinate meetings. Thus, in 1699, it advised Friends against " selling what they could not wear." In 1707, it directed Friends "not to send for their children home from school on holy days, or masters to release them, or Friends to shut up." In 1717, it was so concerned on account of a great declension in plainness of apparel and language, as to issue a document on the

---

* It must not be supposed that this statement refers exclusively, if at all, to the rules or canons previously quoted, but to the doctrinal and moral exhortations issued by G. Fox at various times, most of which are to be found in the second volume of his works.

subject, from which some extracts will show that our ancestors (a hundred and fifty years ago) had the same tendencies to contend against as their successors in more modern times.

In this "Paper on Pride, Plainness of Dress, &c.," dated 1717, the Quarterly Meeting first inveighs against the men for wearing extravagant wigs, and for wearing their "hats and clothes after a beauish manner;" they grant that "the wearing of modest, decent, or necessary wigs" is allowable, on account of age, loss of hair, &c., but condemn the prevailing modes. They then exhort the women about their decking themselves with "gaudy and costly apparel," and about their wearing "gold chains, lockets, necklaces, and gold watches, exposed to open view." "The immodest fashion of wearing hooped petticoats" next comes in for reprobation, and also the practice of "men and women making a show of mourning," and the "declension in plainness of speech," &c. "Likewise," they add, "there is a declension crept in amongst us, by unbecoming gestures in cringing and bowing of the body by way of salutation, which ought not to be taught or countenanced in our schools or families."

The document then proceeds to ask, "How shall any persons reputed Quakers, wearing extravagant wigs, open breasts, their hats and clothes after a beauish fashion, gold chains with lockets, and gold watches openly exposed, like the lofty dames, or hooped petticoats, like the wanton women, be distinguished from the loose proud people of the world?"

The paper concludes by advising Friends "not to run into every new, vain, fantastical fashion," and to "train up their children rightly," and "not in fineness and vanities," but to "impress the same Divine principle on them as reached and convinced themselves."

Unfortunately there is too much evidence to show that those in authority needed to be concerned, not only about hooped petticoats, and lockets, and wigs, and watches, for positive irreligion, veiled by outward conformity, was becoming increasingly prevalent in the Society. And as the century grew older, secret irreligion became manifest in open immorality, and hence in after years arose the supposed necessity for maintaining a strict legal and disciplinary spirit, which in turn has produced results not always beneficial.*

---

* For confirmation of these remarks see Table of Disownments at a subsequent page.

In 1720, at the instigation of George Whitehead, the Quarterly Meeting exhorted Friends "to keep clear of vile and wicked practices in stockjobbing and bubbles." In 1728, we find them concerned about the Meetings for Worship, and mourning over the great neglect of the time, &c. They also caution Friends "to avoid drowsiness and light, airy, affected gestures" on these occasions. In the same year they complain of meetings being disturbed by the "rattling and noise of coaches when there are burials." They advise against too much company or extravagant entertainments, and that "no more coaches from the meeting-house to the burial-ground be made use of than are necessary for the aged and infirm;" and strongly recommend "the ancient and honourable practice of bearing our dead Friends to the grave on our own shoulders." We find in this same year, 1728, a concern is expressed about "divers going to playhouses." It would only become tedious to mention further occasions upon which the Quarterly Meeting showed a care over the subordinate meetings, but it may be said that in the revival of the discipline in the latter part of last century, it gave very considerable aid and co-operation to the work of reformation.

Church Arrangements.

There are one or two matters of Church arrangement that may be here alluded to, which came under the notice of the Quarterly Meeting at various times. In 1700, Barking applied to know the proper status of Friends having businesses in London, but residences in the country. The Quarterly Meeting decided "that Friends having country houses may assist the country Monthly Meetings, provided they don't neglect the service of the city meetings to which they belong." (The modern plan has been, as many of our readers will know, to allow Friends thus situated to choose which of the two meetings they would prefer to be in membership with.)

In 1710, at the suggestion of Devonshire House, the Quarterly Meeting ordered doorkeepers for the Yearly Meeting to be appointed, and directed each Monthly Meeting to send up for this office "one weighty, solid Friend," who was not to be considered a member of the Yearly Meeting. Two years afterwards we find these doorkeepers advised to be careful about "evil-minded persons who, with design of scorn or envy, intrude themselves." In order to show that at that

The Paper,
from the Quarterly meeting in London,
by Adjournm.t the 5th 6m 1717.
To the monthly meetings in London and
Middlesex, &c.

Pride of } As Pride of Heart, Haughtiness, Highminded=
Habits &c } ness, Arrogancy, Disdain and Despising them
not to be } that are Good, under what pretence or Habit
Indulged } Soever, ought in no wise to be Indulged or
allowed amongst us, the same being Judged
and Condemned by the Light of Truth, even
by the meek Spirit and humble Example of
our Lord Jesus Christ, and all true Christians.
So, where Pride of life, the Fruits, the marks,
the vain and foolish Habits and Garbs thereof
are manifest and apparent to the Scandal &
Reproach of our holy Profession & Society; It
becomes very necessary and Requisite That
some Serious Notice should be taken thereof
and —

Opening of the paper on plainness, issued by the Quarterly Meeting in 1717 to the monthly meetings in London and Middlesex, in the QM minute book [LSF]

MINISTERS.

DEV. HOUSE.		GRACE.		SOUTH.		RATC.		WEST.		TOTT.		LONG.		PEEL.		KING.				TOTAL MINS.	DATE.
M.	F.	M.	F.	M.	F.	M.	F.	M.	F.	M.	F.	M.	F.	M.	F.	M.	F.	M.	F.		
3	4		4	1	1	3	1	1	1	2		1	1	1	1		1	12	13	25	1792
...	...	...	...	1		...	...	...	...	...	...	...	1	...	...	...	...	1	1	2	1793
...	...	1		1	1	...	...	...	...	...	...	...	...	...	...	...	...	...	2	2	1794
...	1	1		...	...	...	...	1	1	...	1	...	...	...	1	...	...	1	5	6	1795
...	...	...	...	..	...	...	...	...	1	...	1	...	1	...	...	...	...	...	3	3	1796
...	...	1		1		...	...	...	1	...	1	...	1	...	1	...	...	...	6	6	1797
...	...	...	...	...	...	...	...	...	...	...	...	1		1		...	...	...	2	2	1798
...	...	...	...	...	...	...	...	...	...	...	...	1		...	...	...	...	...	1	1	1799
...	...	...	...	...	1	...	...	...	...	...	...	...	...	...	...	...	...	...	1	1	1800
1		...	...	...	...	...	...	...	...	...	...	...	...	1	1	...	...	2	1	3	1801
...	...	...	1	...	...	...	...	...	...	...	...	...	...	...	...	...	...	...	1	1	1802
...	...	...	...	...	...	...	...	...	...	...	...	...	1	...	...	...	1	...	2	2	1803
...	1	...	...	...	...	...	...	...	...	...	...	...	...	...	...	...	...	...	1	1	1804
...	...	...	...	...	...	...	1	...	1	...	...	...	...	...	...	...	...	1	1	2	1805
...	...	...	...	...	...	...	...	...	...	...	...	...	...	...	...	...	...	...	...	...	1806
...	...	...	...	...	...	...	...	...	...	...	...	...	...	...	...	...	...	...	...	...	1807
...	...	...	1	...	...	...	...	...	1	...	...	...	...	...	1	...	...	...	3	3	1808
...	...	...	2	...	...	...	...	...	...	...	...	...	...	...	...	...	...	...	2	2	1809
...	...	...	...	...	...	...	...	...	...	...	1	...	...	...	1	...	...	...	2	2	1810
...	...	...	2	1	4	...	...	...	...	...	1	...	...	1		...	...	2	7	9	1811
...	...	...	1	...	...	...	...	...	...	...	...	...	...	...	...	...	...	...	1	1	1812
...	...	...	...	...	...	...	...	1	1	...	1	...	...	...	...	...	...	1	2	3	1813
1		...	1	...	...	...	...	...	...	...	...	...	...	...	...	...	...	1	1	2	1814
...	...	...	...	...	...	...	...	...	...	...	1	1	...	...	...	...	...	1	1	2	1815
...	...	...	...	...	...	...	...	...	...	...	...	...	1		...	...	...	1	...	1	1816
...	...	...	...	...	1	...	...	...	...	1	1	...	...	...	...	...	...	1	2	3	1817
1		...	...	...	1	...	...	...	...	...	...	...	...	...	...	...	...	1	1	2	1818
...	...	...	...	...	...	...	...	...	...	...	...	...	...	1		...	...	...	1	1	1819
...	...	2		...	1	...	...	...	...	...	...	...	...	...	...	...	1	2	2	4	1820
...	...	...	...	...	...	...	...	...	...	...	...	...	1	...	...	...	...	...	1	1	1821
...	...	...	1	...	...	...	...	...	...	...	1	...	...	...	...	...	1	...	3	3	1822
...	...	...	...	...	...	...	...	...	...	...	...	...	...	...	...	...	...	...	...	...	1823
...	...	...	...	...	...	...	...	...	...	...	...	...	...	...	...	...	...	...	...	...	1824
...	...	...	1	...	2	...	...	...	...	...	...	...	...	...	...	...	...	...	3	3	1825
...	1	...	...	...	...	...	...	...	...	...	...	...	...	...	...	...	...	...	1	1	1826
...	...	...	...	...	...	...	...	...	...	...	...	...	...	...	...	...	...	...	...	...	1827
...	...	...	...	...	1	...	...	...	...	...	...	...	...	1		...	1	1	1	2	1828
...	...	...	...	...	1	...	...	...	...	...	...	...	...	...	...	...	...	...	1	1	1829
...	1	...	...	...	...	...	...	...	...	...	...	...	...	...	1	...	...	1	1	2	1830
...	...	...	...	1		1		...	...	...	...	...	...	...	...	...	...	1	1	2	1831
1	1	2		...	...	...	...	...	...	...	...	...	...	...	...	...	...	1	3	4	1832
...	...	...	...	1		...	...	...	...	...	...	...	...	...	...	...	...	1	...	1	1833
...	...	...	...	...	...	...	1	...	...	...	...	...	...	...	...	...	...	...	1	1	1834
...	...	...	...	...	...	...	...	...	1	...	...	...	...	...	...	1	1	1	2	3	1835
...	...	...	...	...	1	...	...	...	...	...	...	...	...	...	...	...	2	...	3	3	1836
7	9	2	19	5	15	3	4	3	7	5	9	1	6	4	10	3	7	33	86	119	...

This TABLE shows the number of Ministers and Elders of each sex belonging to the Quarterly Meeting of Ministers and Elders at the time of its institution in 1792, with the additions annually made to each class up to 1836.

DATE.	TOTAL ELDERS			DEV. HOUSE.		GRACE.		SOUTH.		RATC.		WEST.		TOTT.		LONG.		PEEL.		KING.	
		M.	F.	M.	F.	M.	F.	M.	F.	M.	F.	M.	F.	M.	F.	M.	F.	M.	F.	M.	F.
1792	41	24	17	2	3	4		3	2	3	2	1	2	4	5	3	1	4	2	...	...
1793	8	4	4	...	...	...	...	1	2	1		1	1	...	1	...	...	1		...	...
1794	2	...	2	...	...	...	1	...	...	...	...	...	1	...	...	...	...	...	...	...	...
1795	1	1	...	...	...	...	...	...	...	1		...	...	...	...	...	...	...	...	...	...
1796	1	1	...	...	...	...	...	...	...	...	...	...	...	...	...	...	...	1		...	...
1797	1	1	...	...	...	...	...	...	...	...	...	...	...	1		...	...	...	...	...	...
1798	...	...	...	...	...	...	...	...	...	...	...	...	...	...	...	...	...	...	...	...	...
1799	...	...	...	...	...	...	...	...	...	...	...	...	...	...	...	...	...	...	...	...	...
1800	1	...	1	...	...	...	...	...	1	...	...	...	...	...	...	...	...	...	...	...	...
1801	1	...	1	...	...	...	1	...	...	...	...	...	...	...	...	...	...	...	...	...	...
1802	1	1	...	...	...	...	...	...	...	1		...	...	...	...	...	...	...	...	...	...
1803	1	...	1	...	...	...	...	...	...	...	...	...	...	...	...	...	...	...	...	...	1
1804	...	...	...	...	...	...	...	...	...	...	...	...	...	...	...	...	...	...	...	...	...
1805	3	2	1	...	...	...	...	...	...	...	...	...	...	...	...	2	1	...	...	...	...
1806	...	...	...	...	...	...	...	...	...	...	...	...	...	...	...	...	...	...	...	...	...
1807	...	...	...	...	...	...	...	...	...	...	...	...	...	...	...	...	...	...	...	...	...
1808	...	...	...	...	...	...	...	...	...	...	...	...	...	...	...	...	...	...	...	...	...
1809	3	1	2	1	2	...	...	...	...	...	...	...	...	...	...	...	...	...	...	...	...
1810	1	...	1	...	...	...	...	...	...	...	...	...	...	...	1	...	...	...	...	...	...
1811	...	...	...	...	...	...	...	...	...	...	...	...	...	...	...	...	...	...	...	...	...
1812	3	1	2	...	...	...	...	1	1	...	...	...	...	...	1	...	...	...	...	...	...
1813	4	2	2	...	...	1	2	...	...	...	...	...	...	1		...	...	...	...	...	...
1814	...	...	...	...	...	...	...	...	...	...	...	...	...	...	...	...	...	...	...	...	...
1815	4	2	2	...	...	1	1	...	...	1	1	...	...	...	...	...	...	...	...	...	...
1816	...	...	...	...	...	...	...	...	...	...	...	...	...	...	...	...	...	...	...	...	...
1817	4	4	...	...	...	...	...	...	...	...	...	...	...	2		...	...	2		...	...
1818	1	...	1	...	...	...	1	...	...	...	...	...	...	...	...	...	...	...	...	...	...
1819	...	...	...	...	...	...	...	...	...	...	...	...	...	...	...	...	...	...	...	...	...
1820	4	2	2	...	...	...	...	2	2	...	...	...	...	...	...	...	...	...	...	...	...
1821	6	2	4	1	1	...	...	...	...	...	...	1	3	...	...	...	...	...	...	...	...
1822	...	...	...	...	...	...	...	...	...	...	...	...	...	...	...	...	...	...	...	...	...
1823	...	...	...	...	...	...	...	...	...	...	...	...	...	...	...	...	...	...	...	...	...
1824	3	2	1	...	...	...	...	...	...	2	1	...	...	...	...	...	...	...	...	...	...
1825	3	2	1	2	1	...	...	...	...	...	...	...	...	...	...	...	...	...	...	...	...
1826	...	...	...	...	...	...	...	...	...	...	...	...	...	...	...	...	...	...	...	...	...
1827	...	...	...	...	...	...	...	...	...	...	...	...	...	...	...	...	...	...	...	...	...
1828	1	...	1	...	...	...	...	...	...	...	...	...	...	1		...	...	...	...	...	...
1829	...	...	...	...	...	...	...	...	...	...	...	...	...	...	...	...	...	...	...	...	...
1830	2	...	2	...	...	...	2	...	...	...	...	...	...	...	...	...	...	...	...	...	...
1831	3	3	...	...	...	...	...	3		...	...	...	...	...	...	...	...	...	...	...	...
1832	7	2	5	...	...	...	2	...	...	...	...	...	...	...	...	1	1	1	2	...	...
1833	...	...	...	...	...	...	...	...	...	...	...	...	...	...	...	...	...	...	...	...	...
1834	...	...	...	...	...	...	...	...	...	...	...	...	...	...	...	...	...	...	...	...	...
1835	2	2	...	...	...	...	...	...	...	1		1		...	...	...	...	...	...	...	...
1836	...	...	...	...	...	...	...	...	...	...	...	...	...	...	...	...	...	...	...	...	...
...	112	59	53	6	7	6	10	10	8	10	4	4	8	8	8	6	3	9	4	0	1

Table after p.78: adapted from original folded sheet between pages 78 and 79

The London Quaker

Probably late seventeenth-century engraving [LSF]

facing p.79

early date all hours were held alike suitable for public worship, we may mention that in 1722 the Quarterly Meeting advised that "week-day meetings should be held at such hours as were likely to result in the largest attendance."

About the year 1789, after the camp had been cleared of the mixed multitude that troubled it, and the Discipline firmly established, we find the Quarterly Meeting much occupied in interpreting the Yearly Meeting Minutes and deciding legal questions. Such, for instance, as the distinction between overseers and elders; the status in the Church of the offspring of mixed marriages, and the explanation of the rules of settlement. In connection with this latter subject, they decided that being appointed a representative from a Preparative, or Monthly Meeting, was a Church service, and, as such, gave a settlement in accordance with the then existing rules. In 1792, the Quarterly Meeting of Ministers and Elders was established; some statistics in connection therewith are shown in the annexed table.

Appeals.

Amongst the appellants who from time to time came before the Quarterly Meeting with complaints against their Monthly Meetings, there were several during the course of the eighteenth century respecting whom many interesting facts might be given. One of the most notorious of these was William Gibson.

This Friend was the son of that eminent preacher and controversialist of the same name, who, first in Lancashire, and afterwards in London, did good service for the Society in its days of storm and conflict (and was buried from Gracechurch Street Meeting, as mentioned in the account of that Monthly Meeting). The first appearance of the younger William Gibson upon the Quarterly Meeting books is in 1706, when he appealed against a judgment of the Bull and Mouth Monthly Meeting concerning him. The Quarterly Meeting ordered the judgment against him to be withdrawn, but also directed William Gibson to call in and destroy the book he had printed, entitled "Bigotry and partiality Ruinous and Destructive to True Religion." This he did to the best of his ability and signed a paper condemning it, and Friends were advised "to carrie it gently towards him."

The affair does not seem to have injured his position

amongst Friends; for in 1714 we find the Quarterly Meeting giving him a certificate for religious service in the North of England, couched in terms of full unity, and signed by George Whitehead, Richard Claridge, Joseph Wyeth, Theodore Ecclestone, and about seventy other Friends.

A few years afterwards, however, W. Gibson began to show signs of mental aberration. Thomas Story describes him as "a sort of lunatic." He was a popular preacher, especially with the young, whom he sometimes treated to a joke from the minister's gallery. For these peculiarities, as well as for certain stigmas upon his moral character, he was severely satirised by Elias Bockett, of whom more presently. W. Gibson's failings soon became so manifest and scandalous to the Church, that in 1723 the Monthly Meeting refused to let him "put his name in their book," *i.e.* for attendance at various meetings for worship. In 1726, the Bull and Mouth disowned him as a minister, and in 1727 as a member. On all these three latter occasions he appealed to the Quarterly Meeting, but without procuring anything else but a confirmation of the previous judgments.

Long after his disownment W. Gibson continued to trouble Friends' meetings, and pour forth sermons; which must have been decidedly comic in their character, if the fragments given by Bockett and others are to be relied upon as authentic. So troublesome did this disturber and his son become, that much expense was incurred in keeping him out of meetings by the employment of constables, and also in prosecuting him for his riotous behaviour.

Elias Bockett, before alluded to, was a distiller in George Yard, Lombard Street; and appears to have been of a satirical turn of mind, and to have had his attention directed to some glaring inconsistencies which were but too evident in some of his fellow professors. Between 1717 and 1727 he issued over twenty works, mostly bearing on this subject; and in several cases especially directed against the William Gibson just mentioned. His zeal appears to have far outrun his discretion, and led him beyond the bounds of truth and propriety; and he was disowned by Devonshire House Meeting for his scandalous imputations on members of the Society. He appealed to the Quarterly Meeting, and afterwards to the Yearly Meeting, but could not procure a reversal of his sentence.

We can but allude to Aquila Rose, the friend of Elias

Bockett, and probable coadjutor in his writings; to James Hoskins, of Westminster, another satirist, who endeavoured to heap calumny upon the venerated name of Thomas Story; to Benjamin Lay, disowned by Devonshire House for his repeated public opposition to approved ministers; and to John Wall who kept a school on Devonshire House premises, and who came at least five times to the Quarterly Meeting, chiefly on questions relative to his own ministry. All these occupied much of the time of the Quarterly Meeting with their complaints.

One case, that of John Hewlett, requires more than a passing notice, inasmuch as it resulted in the establishment of an important principle, viz. that no disciplinary power was vested in any meeting of Ministers and Elders.

This John Hewlett went to America from England in 1704, having been previously married in this country, and having also separated from his wife. In America he was convinced of Friends' principles and joined the Society, saying, however, nothing of his marriage. He became a minister, and as such had a certificate granted him by his meeting on Rhode Island, in which it was stated, amongst other matters, that he was clear of all marriage engagements. With this certificate he travelled in the ministry, but in Pennsylvania, in the following year, met with some who had known him in England, and the circumstance of his marriage was at once made known. Accordingly Philadelphia Friends wrote a statement of this fact on the back of his certificate, expressing their opinion that he ought to have told Friends of the circumstance.

John Hewlett next proceeded to England, and whilst there, according to his own subsequent confession, copied out his certificate afresh, with the signatures, omitting all reference to clearness from marriage, and also the Philadelphia endorsement.

After his return to America this was discovered, and he was judged by his own meeting in Rhode Island, and made full confession to their satisfaction, and refrained from appearing in public supplication or the ministry.

In 1721 he removed to England, and received a certificate from Newport, Rhode Island, in which the above facts were set forth. Thirteen years afterwards the Morning Meeting, finding John Hewlett sitting amongst them as a minister, and having their attention called to the facts, revived the whole affair, and proceeded to take measures equivalent to banishing him from amongst them. Hence resulted an appeal by J. H. to the Quarterly Meeting, and afterwards to the Yearly Meeting, in which it was decided that the Morning Meeting could rebuke, exhort, &c. its members, but should stay all proceedings on receiving notice from a Monthly Meeting of its taking a case under its serious care. "And we are of opinion," they add, "that the Morning Meeting or any other meeting of ministers have no power to disown any minister, or other person in any capacity whatever."

During the present century, two celebrated appeal cases attracted so much attention at the time, that they may be deemed of sufficient importance to be alluded to here.

It was in the year 1800 that a talented female minister from America, named Hannah Barnard, was travelling with certificate amongst Friends of Ireland. At the close of her service in that land the Dublin Yearly Meeting gave her a clear certificate of unity, and she then crossed over into England, and commenced labouring as a Gospel minister in this country. But reports became speedily circulated, from which it appeared that although nothing objectionable had been officially proved against her by the Irish Yearly Meeting, yet many individuals in that country were very uneasy about the unscriptural tendency of some of H. B.'s utterances whilst among them.

The Yearly Meeting of Ministers and Elders in London was the first body to notice these reports, and it referred the case to the Morning Meeting. This latter meeting investigated the charges, and became satisfied of H. B.'s unsoundness on several points. She held that the Almighty had never in the history of the world sanctioned the taking away of human life, or war in any shape;* also, that she could not assert the truth of the miracles recorded in the Scriptures, because they were not revealed to her own mind. These, and other views of a similar character, were held by the Morning Meeting of Ministers and Elders to be so objectionable that it desired Hannah Barnard to refrain from appearing as a minister, and go to her own home as speedily as possible.

Hannah Barnard refused compliance with this recommendation, on the ground that the Morning Meeting possessed no disciplinary power.† Accordingly, that body brought the case before the Monthly Meeting of Devonshire House, which,

---

* Even in the Patriarchal or Mosaic dispensations.
† Referring to the case of John Hewlett above cited.

after due inquiry, confirmed the recommendation alluded to. H. B. now appealed to the Quarterly Meeting of London and Middlesex; but here also she was met by a confirmation of the previous decision.

The last resort, an appeal to the Yearly Meeting, was now essayed. The appellant conducted her own case with great ability during the protracted proceedings of several days' duration; but the respondents, headed by Joseph Gurney Bevan, tracked her subtle intellect through all its devious windings, and, finally, the Yearly Meeting set the seal of its deliberate approval on the previous judgment given by the subordinate meeting.*

Conspicuous amongst a few Friends who encouraged and aided Hannah Barnard at this period was Thomas Foster, of Bromley, to whose pen is generally attributed a long narrative of the proceedings, which afterwards appeared. This Friend soon gave further evidence of following in Hannah Barnard's track. He published in pamphlets and magazine-articles, comments on the Yearly Meeting Epistles, and other official documents, issued by the Society, and also subscribed to the Unitarian Book Society. In 1812, the Monthly Meeting of Ratcliff and Barking, of which he was a member, disowned him for his evident profession and dissemination of Unitarian views. He appealed to the Quarterly and afterwards to the Yearly Meeting, but these bodies remained firm to their Evangelical principles, and confirmed the decision arrived at by Ratcliff Friends.

There now remain one or two miscellaneous matters connected with the business of the Quarterly Meeting to be noticed.

FINES.—In 1692, it seems the Government had discovered that the money recovered from the Friends by the Conventicle and other similar acts, had never been paid into the Exchequer. Certain individuals who had been appointed to discover the whereabouts of this money and procure it for the Government, keeping one-third for their trouble, came to Friends and offered them ten per cent. for their aid in finding out to whom the money had been paid. Friends, however, in their Quarterly Meeting, declined to have anything to do with it unless

---

* Hannah Barnard returned home, and was soon afterwards disowned by her own Monthly Meeting in America. She lived eighteen years longer, but was never reunited to Friends.

they received the whole, and the matter seems to have dropped.

INFORMERS.—The Quarterly Meeting used to keep a list of these. In the Seventh Month, 1694, we find Benjamin Bealing, Recording Clerk to the Society, was ordered to give a list of late informers to Thomas Lacey and John Edge, that inquiry may be made what judgments befell them; and the recording of judgments that had happened to persecutors and informers was continued until 1717, when, with grateful allusions to "the mild government under which we now live," &c. the periodical inquiry upon this subject was ordered by the Quarterly Meeting to be dropped.

MALDON MEETING-HOUSE.—As an illustration of assistance to an object beyond the limits of the meeting, it may be noted that, in 1710, London and Middlesex Quarterly Meeting voted £25 towards the building of the meeting-house at Maldon; Coggeshall Quarterly Meeting having asked for assistance, stating that they had gone over their subscription lists again and again without being able to raise the desired amount.

PRIVACY OF MEETINGS FOR DISCIPLINE.—In 1804, one of the provisions of the Toleration Act, which "gives liberty to Dissenters to hold their meetings without molestation, provided the doors are not locked, barred, or bolted during the time of such meeting," was attempted to be imposed on Meetings for Discipline by a person who had been disowned. Being prevented by the doorkeepers from forcing his way into the Quarterly Meeting, he brought an action against John Batger and others for assault and false imprisonment, &c. which was tried on the 23rd of Second Month, 1805, and the plaintiff nonsuited. The Chief Baron said, "I take this meeting to be entirely for the purpose of Church government (and if so, it is a place of business at that time), though it may be interspersed with acts of worship."

BIBLES.—It may be interesting to state, in conclusion, that in 1812 the Quarterly Meeting directed the Monthly Meetings to make inquiries as to what servants, or single persons, residing within their boundaries, were unprovided with copies of the Scriptures. In accordance therewith, due inquiries appear at once to have been instituted, and the deficiencies, where existing, supplied.

CHAPTER VIII.

THE TWO-WEEKS MEETING—SIX-WEEKS MEETING—AND MEETING OF TWELVE.

The Two-Weeks Meeting.

This meeting which was also called the Fortnightly Meeting was earlier in the time of its origin than any other of the London Meetings for Discipline, excepting only those periodic conferences among the Friends in the ministry, held from the beginning in the house of Gerrard Roberts, and developing into the so-called Morning Meeting.

It was established and continued many years before the London district was sub-divided into several Monthly Meetings, and exercised a care over the whole area, which it only gradually relinquished as these Monthly Meetings increased in their efficiency. It forms a connecting link between the time when the Society was in the first stages of its ingathering, and those succeeding periods wherein efforts for consolidation and regulation were the conspicuous features.

Unfortunately no minute-books of this Two-Weeks Meeting exist earlier than 1671, the previous documents having, as is supposed, been either destroyed by fire or lost; but there remain independent testimonies which show both its early origin and the nature and importance of its duties.

William Crouch, one of the early London Friends, mentions in his Memoirs that this meeting was commenced soon after the taking of the Bull and Mouth [1655], and was held in an upper room on those premises, and that it was composed of men Friends, who met "there to consult about and consider of the affairs of truth, and to communicate to each other what the Lord opened in them for the promotion thereof; and also to make such provision to supply all necessary occasions, which the service of the Church might require."

Edward Burrough, in the paper issued by him in 1662, from which quotations have been previously given (see p. 42), bears testimony to the early origin of this "Fortnightly" Meeting, carrying the period of its commencement back to within two years of the rise of the Society in London. He shows also the importance of its position and duties, by the earnestness of his exhortations to its faithful maintenance.

It was evidently considered in his time to be the one meeting for matters of discipline and arrangement in the London district, embracing the whole area, subsequently divided into six Monthly Meetings; and as Friends were already numerous, its duties must have become greatly multiplied and somewhat onerous. Such an important position may well have drawn forth from one so zealous for the welfare of the Church as Edward Burrough, the earnest yet loving counsel which he administers in this document—exhortations which, to the grief of his friends, proved to be almost his closing words, as the paper is dated 1662; and in the Twelfth Month of that same year, his decease took place in Newgate Gaol.

From this same document may be traced the causes which led to its establishment, as also the manner of its first appointment. Edward Burrough, after stating how, in about two years' time, truth had become much spread in London, and many were convinced, shows "that the service it required advanced greater and greater daily," so that such as himself, "being wholly devoted to the work of the ministry," could not suitably attend to the many external matters which were, nevertheless, required to be "managed with all heavenly wisdom and prudence, for the prosperous carrying on the good work." Such being the need (he adds) "we therefore, in the name, power, and wisdom of the Lord Jesus Christ, as we were endued with the same," did "ordain and appoint, that the men Friends of the city, or the ancientest of them in the truth (not excluding any), should meet together at the Bull and Mouth, or elsewhere, once in the fortnight, or once a month, as they in the wisdom of God should find it necessary." This shows that the meeting was commenced through the counsel of the early ministers, and for their relief in the care of the Churches; and the free nature of our institutions is seen in the caution that none are to be held as excluded from attending.

Edward Burrough further defines, under several heads, the

character of the duties thus committed to the care of this Fortnightly Meeting:—

1st. That the meeting do consist of "just and righteous men."

2nd. That they meet "once a week, or fourteen days, as Truth's necessities do require."

3rd. That cases found to be difficult be suspended until "more Friends that are anciently grown in the truth, can have understanding of the matter," and the ministers be called in to assist.

4th. Disputes as to bargains or debts between Friend and Friend, or a Friend and a stranger, be inquired into, and "all possible fair means used for their settlement."

5th. Records be kept of all births, marriages, and burials.

6th. That especial care be taken concerning provision for the poor, including servants out of place.

7th. Accounts of Friends' sufferings to be collected and preserved.

The earliest of the variations that occurred in these arrangements was the appointment of a meeting of women Friends, to attend more especially to the sixth item, which refers to the care of the poor. Edward Burrough himself thus mentions it in the same paper, viz. that "some years after the appointment of the men's meeting," the "affairs of truth being grown more large daily," and seeing "that it was not so proper for the men as for the women to visit the sick," &c. that, "therefore, the women Friends should keep a like meeting, to be assisting in what was convenient to the men, especially in that particular of visiting the sick and weak, and looking after the poor, widows, and fatherless"; and this, E. B. adds, "was the occasion of the first setting up of that meeting of women which hath been happy and prosperous in the work to which it was appointed."

It will have been observed that Edward Burrough alludes to the "daily" growth of service required by the spread of truth, and such is confirmed by allusions to be found in George Fox's Journal and others. It must have rendered the concentration in one meeting of the service involved by so many Friends a burden difficult efficiently to support, and this difficulty must have increased when, either by death or imprisonment, many of the fathers in the Church had been removed.

In 1666 some further arrangements had evidently become needful, and we find George Fox in his Journal thus alluding to them; he had but just been released from his severe imprisonment in Scarboro' Castle, and, with an enfeebled constitution, but chastened and earnest zeal, was moving as an elder brother, worthy of honour among the Churches. He records the spirit of disunion that had become apparent in London, chiefly through John Perrot's influence, and adds (Journal, vol. i. p. 310): "Then was I moved of the Lord to recommend the setting up of five Monthly Meetings of men and women Friends in the city of London (besides the Women's Meetings and the Quarterly Meetings) to take care of God's glory, and to admonish and exhort such as walked disorderly or carelessly, and not according to truth." (See the account of Southwark for the evidence of need of this, especially as to marriages.)

Thus a new arrangement was established at the suggestion of George Fox in the London district, and one similar to that which he was at this time engaged in recommending to the adoption of Friends throughout the kingdom. For, whereas, he says (Journal, p. 310), "Friends had had only Quarterly Meetings, now truth was spread, and Friends were grown more numerous, I was moved to recommend the setting up of Monthly Meetings throughout the nation."

The establishment of these five Monthly Meetings in London would appear, from their nature, so likely to absorb the service previously borne by the Two-Weeks Meeting as to render the continuance of that meeting unnecessary; but the words of George Fox, when he alludes to London being divided into five Monthly Meetings, must be taken with some qualification, for though the area of service formerly discharged by the Two-Weeks Meeting was very greatly lessened by this change, there was still left an important district which remained for some years longer under its peculiar care. Of these five Monthly Meetings, known respectively as Wheeler Street or Devonshire House, Southwark, Peel, Ratcliff, and Westminster, neither comprised much, if any portion of the space enclosed by the walls of the ancient city, which large, populous, and influential section remained under the care of the Two-Weeks Meeting for at least five years more, when it became merged as a sixth section into the group of London Monthly Meetings, being known first as the Bull and Mouth, or London, or City Meeting, and subsequently as that of White Hart

THE
TESTIMONY
OF THE
LORD
CONCERNING
LONDON.

WITNESSED

In truth and faithfulnesse, to the consciences of all People in it, that they may returne to the Lord, and repent.

ALSO,

The great Abominations discovered of this People, who draws near God with their mouths, and professes self-separation, when as their hearts be far from the Lord.

WITH

A WARNING to all sorts of People in it, what the Lord requires of them.

By a *Lover of all your soules*, E. B.

LONDON:

Printed for *Giles Calvert*, at the Black-spread-Eagle, near the West end of *Pauls*, 1657.

Title page of *The Testimony of the Lord Concerning London* by Edward Burrough, 1657 [LSF]

TABLE showing the NUMBER of MARRIAGES at the MEETING-HOUSES in the QUARTERLY MEETING of LONDON and MIDDLESEX, in Quinquennial Periods, from 1658 to 1864.

DATES.	DEVON-SHIRE HOUSE.	WHEELER STREET.	BULL AND MOUTH.	GRACE-CHURCH STREET.	HORSLY-DOWN.	PARK.	RATCLIFF.
1658 and 1659	...	...	...	...	...	...	...
to 1664	...	...	11	...	5	...	...
,, 1669	14	19	8	...	19	...	3
,, 1674	67	9	26	1	26	...	12
,, 1679	87	11	63	...	55	...	27
,, 1684	111	...	74	...	31	5	17
,, 1689	103	4	54	...	19	5	15
,, 1694	66	...	35	...	30	5	21
,, 1699	89	...	27 + 8* B.H.	5	17	10	13
,, 1704	66	...	37 + 4	4	19	15	16
,, 1709	82	...	35	...	29	6	13
,, 1714	49	...	37	...	30	13	17
,, 1719	58	...	25	2	23	15	9
,, 1724	62	...	20	...	16	11	9
,, 1729	42	...	17	...	18	13	9
,, 1734	30	...	8	2	8	12	11
,, 1739	28	...	9	3	8	8	7
,, 1744	29	...	1	16	14	2	5
,, 1749	27	...	...	12	14	3	8
,, 1754	21	...	...	13	11	2	8
,, 1759	24	...	...	5	9	...	12
,, 1764	21	...	...	11	9	1	9
,, 1769	29	...	...	13	3	9	5
,, 1774	28	...	...	20	5	3	6
,, 1779	22	...	...	12	6	3	8
,, 1784	24	...	...	11	8	2	15
,, 1789	8	...	...	13	9	2	2
,, 1794	10	...	...	11	10	1	6
,, 1799	13	...	...	4	6	1	3
,, 1804	12	...	...	10	...	9	4
,, 1809	14	...	...	9	...	12	3
,, 1814	14	...	...	6	...	9	7
,, 1819	9	...	...	6	...	5	7
,, 1824	13	...	...	5	...	4	3
,, 1829	14	...	...	8	...	6	3
,, 1834	8	...	...	5	...	3	3
,, 1839	6	...	...	...	...	3	1
,, 1844	4	...	...	2	...	...	1
,, 1849	4	...	...	1	...	5	...
,, 1854	6	...	...	...	...	2	...
,, 1859	5	...	...	...	...	1	1
,, 1864	6	...	...	...	...	...	...
TOTALS	1325	43	499	210	457	206	31

* These twelve marriages were celebrated at Brewers' Hall during the occupation of that edifice as a Meeting-house instead of the Bull and Mouth. (See Chap. IX.)

DEPTFORD.	WAPPING.	WEST-MINSTER.	SAVOY.	PEEL.	PRIVATE HOUSES.	PLACE NOT GIVEN.	COUNTRY MEETINGS.	TOTALS.
...	...	...	...	...	1	1	...	2
...	...	1	...	7	2	21	...	47
...	...	6	...	25	6	27	2	129
...	...	17	...	25	1	...	10	194
...	...	4	20	2	...	3	23	295
...	...	18	5	...	...	...	26	287
...	...	15	...	17	...	...	31	263
1	...	6	6	34	...	...	19	223
2	...	11	10	37	...	...	25	254
1	3	5	15	23	...	...	33	241
1	6	1	22	28	...	...	18	241
...	2	...	19	11	...	...	19	197
2	...	...	8	18	...	...	26	186
...	2	3	4	20	...	...	15	162
1	...	...	15	16	...	...	19	150
...	2	1	11	6	...	...	11	102
...	...	...	8	4	...	...	15	90
...	...	...	6	10	...	...	18	101
...	...	...	3	9	...	...	9	85
...	...	...	5	7	...	...	11	78
...	...	...	2	8	...	...	27	87
...	...	1	4	6	...	...	25	87
...	...	...	5	6	...	...	22	92
1	...	...	5	2	...	...	11	81
...	...	...	7	5	...	...	14	77
...	...	3	...	8	...	...	20	91
...	...	5	...	4	...	...	18	61
1	...	1	...	7	School 1	...	23	71
...	...	4	...	5	...	...	22	58
...	...	13	...	4	...	...	29	81
...	...	4	...	3	...	...	25	70
...	...	7	...	9	School 1	...	24	77
...	...	2	...	3	...	...	31	63
3	...	6	...	4	...	...	29	67
1	...	5	...	7	...	...	43	87
1	...	1	...	6	...	...	48	75
1	...	4	...	1	...	...	32	48
1	...	2	...	6	...	...	23	39
...	...	1	...	4	...	...	38	53
...	...	4	...	2	...	...	28	42
1	...	1	...	2	...	...	32	43
...	...	8	...	3	...	...	22	39
18	15	160	180	404	12	52	916	4816

Table after p.88: adapted from original folded sheet between pages 90 and 91

Whereas Tho. Taylor & Rebecca Clifton having for
some time made a profession of the Truth among us did
p. 24 did after a clandestine manner go to one Matt Stoute at Isling-
Agt ton ye 3 or 4th and by their own appointment, & belonging
Tho. Taylor to ye Meeting, did then & there pretend to take each other in
& marriage, not only contrary to ye good order, nor thing wholesome
Reb. Clifton of God is established among us, but not to be patricious
& of an ill consequence —— they did Tho. Taylor and
Rebecca Clifton having according to gospel order been admonished with much tenderness to bring to a sence of their outgoings
& of ye ill consequence & reproach, if they have & may bring upon
ye name of ye Lord & his people; & all our tenderness & labour
being in vain, they continuing in ye hardness of their hearts, & in
opposition to all ye good counsel & advice ye have given to them

Peel Monthly Meeting condemnations book: entry in 1705 for the attempted disorderly marriage in Stoke Newington described on p.212. Permission for this marriage had already been refused by Two Weeks Meeting. [LSF]

Court, or Gracechurch Street. Subsequently a more complete fusion took place in 1671 (a year before the establishment of Yearly Meetings). Henceforward the Two-Weeks Meeting, though no longer having any special district under its care, was maintained for nearly 120 years, *i.e.* almost up to the present century, as a meeting having especial charge over all the marriages among Friends within the compass of any of the London Monthly Meetings.

It is an evidence of the great care bestowed by Friends to see that these important and life-long engagements were rightly undertaken, that whilst all other matters have been committed (as we have seen) to the charge of Monthly Meetings only, the care over marriages was supplemented by the retention of an ancient meeting for discipline, with no other object than to exercise a general superintendence over all these marriage engagements, wherever occurring within the London district. Those about to marry had to appear twice before the Two-Weeks Meeting, in addition to obtaining the consent of their respective Monthly Meetings, before proceeding to solemnise the marriage. The books of the Two-Weeks Meeting, from 1671 to 1789, are still extant. The meeting was held once a fortnight, alternately at Devonshire House and the Bull and Mouth, and in early times mostly eight or ten or more marriages were under inquiry at one time. The annexed tables will show the comparative frequency of marriages at different periods, and the difference in social stations of the persons about to marry at two different epochs.

In 1789, the Two-Weeks Meeting proposed its own discontinuance, alleging that its business could be transacted equally well by the Monthly Meetings, and that it was not desirable to multiply unnecessary engagements for Friends. The Quarterly Meeting consented to the proposed change. The last marriage passed by the Two-Weeks Meeting was that of Osgood Hanbury and Susannah Willett Barclay, in the Eighth Month, 1789. The records of this meeting were deemed important, and as a precautionary measure against fire, &c., it was agreed by the Quarterly Meeting to deposit the *rough* minute-books at Westminster, where they still remain; the fair copies being at Devonshire House.

COMPARISON OF 250 MARRIAGES ABOUT 1680, WITH 250 MARRIAGES ABOUT 1780, WITH REFERENCE TO DESCRIPTION GIVEN OF THE BRIDEGROOMS.

	About 1680.	About 1780.
Banker	—	7
Merchant	14	20
Salesman, Warehouseman, Wharfinger	1	7
Brewer, Distiller, Wine Merchant	7	6
Vintner, Victualler, Tobacconist, Tobacco-Cutter	2	5
Schoolmaster	5	2
Yeoman	—	1
Surgeon, Doctor	—	6
Stock Broker, Money Scrivener, Land Surveyor	—	4
Goldsmith, Silversmith, Builder, Founder, Coal Merchant, Meal-factor, Maltster, Flour-factor, Skinner, Leather-seller, Saddler, Leather Cutter, Corn Dealer, Miller, Mealman	8	41
Manufacturer, Dyer, Tanner, Currier, Soapmaker, Sugar Baker, Calico Printer, Tallow-chandler, Staymaker	2	22
Chemist, Druggist, Perfumer, Printer, Stationer	1	9
Block-maker, Tinplate-worker, Cabinet-maker, Upholsterer, Watch-maker, Enameller	4	13
Hatter, Draper, Clothier, Shopkeeper, Slopseller	—	17
Seedsman, Farmer, Florist	—	5
Brazier, Cutler, Ironmonger, Pewterer, Tinman	10	11
Butcher, Baker, Chandler, Confectioner, Grocer, Cheesemonger	21	13
Hosier, Glover, Haberdasher, Linen-draper, Silkman, Mercer	12	12
Woodmonger, Basket-maker, Cordwainer	8	6
Cowkeeper, Husbandman	5	3
Spectacle-maker, Instrument-maker, Patten-maker, Castor-maker, Clock-maker	16	3
Woolstapler, Callenderer, Woolcomber, Woolcardmakers, Threadman, Felt-maker, Cloth-worker	12	5
Smith, Sawyer, Blacksmith, Joiner, Lathrender, Turner, Carpenter, Cooper, Sailmaker, Ship Carpenter, Shipsmith, Mastmaker, Wheelwright	29	9
Bricklayer, Brickmaker, Mason, Plasterer	9	1
Mariner	10	—
Weaver, Silk-throwster, Woolsorter	19	4
Shoemaker, Tailor	39	5
Cook, Brewers' Man, Porter, Labourer, Waterman	8	—
Undescribed	8	13
	250	250

N.B.—A comparison of the numbers in this Table will show how many more were engaged in the humbler class of industrial pursuits in the former period than in the latter.

Reverting now to the year 1671. When the city district became formed into one of the regular Monthly Meetings, and as a consequence the Two-Weeks Meeting, which formerly had had it under its care, confined its attention to the regulation of marriages only, a want was felt for a new meeting of a more *select* nature than the " open " gatherings of the Monthly and other meetings, where, as in a sort of senate, matters could be considered which, though affecting the interests and welfare of all, could not be so suitably introduced into an open meeting: hence arose the Six-Weeks Meeting now to be described.

THE SIX-WEEKS MEETING.

Of the three meetings mentioned in the title of the present chapter, the Six-Weeks Meeting is the only one now in existence. But such are the changes it has undergone, both in its constitution and functions, that few of its ancient features now survive but the name—given to it from the circumstance of its meeting once in six weeks.

The Six-Weeks Meeting of the present day acts as the Cash Committee of the Quarterly Meeting. Its transactions, though important, are chiefly secular in their character. It is composed of about 30 men Friends, chosen by the associated Monthly Meetings as their representatives; and has charge over all their meeting-houses, burial-grounds, and matters of finance or property in which these have a common interest. But the Six-Weeks Meeting, as originally instituted in 1671 (nearly two centuries ago), was a very different body. It was then a selected assembly of "grave and antient" Friends (both men and women) chosen out of all the meetings in the metropolis and its district; to whose management and control all matters affecting the common interest of these meetings were committed, forming also a court of final appeal among them in all cases of difficulty that might arise. George Fox termed it, in after years, "the prime meeting of the city."

Great therefore have been the changes it has undergone between its former and present position, to understand which some detail is necessary in its description.

The records of this meeting commence in 1671, a time which may be noted as one year before the Yearly Meeting was settled in London on a representative basis, also as being the year George Fox left England on his visit to America.

The first minute in this book is under date Eighth Month 28th, 1671, when the chief business of the meeting was agreeing that the Bull and Mouth, or "City" meeting, previously holding a Two-Weeks Meeting for Discipline, as established from the first, should conform to the later arrangement, and, becoming a Monthly Meeting, be associated in that capacity with the five others established five years before, in 1666—making henceforward six Monthly Meetings in the London district. That the settlement of this matter was through the action of the Six-Weeks Meeting, shows its influence and importance at the time of its commencement.

In the first page of this earliest volume there is entered a statement in the same hand-writing as that of the minutes—which shows the meeting at its establishment to have been composed of 49 men and 35 women Friends, who (as the heading above these names states) were "to meet once in six weeks to consider of such affairs relating to Truth and the service thereof as might not be judged fit to be publicly discoursed of at the Fortnight's Meeting, who have power to add to their number such other Friends as they shall see meet." Then follow the names of these its first members, amongst whom are found—George Whitehead, Alexander Parker, Gilbert Latey, Francis Camfield, Thomas Yoakeley, William Crouch, Thomas Rudyard, William Mead; and of women Friends—Rebecca Travers, Ann Whitehead, Mary Elson, Mary Foster, Mary Woolley, Ann Stodart, and many others well known in their service for the spread of Friends' principles, and as "mothers in Israel."

These 84 men and women Friends, chosen (possibly by George Fox* himself before he left for America) out of all

---

* Towards the close of his life G. Fox thus addressed the Six-Weeks Meeting; in it he speaks as one having authority :—

"The *Six-Weeks Meeting* is for to see, that all their *Meetings* are preserved by the wisdom of *God* in the *unity* of the *Spirit*, the *Bond of Peace*, and in the Fellowship of the *Holy Ghost;* being ordered by the pure, gentle, peaceable, heavenly Wisdom, easie to be intreated, Holy and vertuous *Examples* to all other *Meetings* both in City and Country. And that all may be careful to speak short and pertinent to matters in a *Christian Spirit* and dispatch Business quickly, and keep out of long Debates and Heats ; and with the *Spirit* of *God* keep that down which is doting about

the London Meetings, formed a sort of senate, or court of appeal, from the more public Two-Weeks or Monthly Meetings, and to find amongst the number of those charged with these important duties so many as 35 women Friends, shows, by the large proportion they bear to the rest of the assembly (more than one-third), how important was the position early assigned to women Friends in the arrangements of the Society; their duties in this case, as members of a "prime meeting," requiring more of an administrative and legislative nature than the care over the poor that had still earlier been committed to them.

It is also interesting to observe that the term "antient," previously quoted as applied to the members of this meeting, applies rather to their length of standing "in the Truth" than to the period of their life, for where able (as in many cases) to test what the ages of these members of the "prime meeting" were at this time, we find them to average about 45. So that, as to years, these "grave and antient" Friends were in the vigour of middle life.

Although the assembly which had thus met might have been the germ of the Six-Weeks Meeting, it would appear from the opening minute of the next recorded meeting, held some seven months later, that neither the name nor time of assembling had been then determined, for under date 1672, 14th Third Month, is the following minute:—" It is assented to and agreed by Friends now present, that this meeting be in the future held and kept duly every six weeks by the name of the Six-Weeks Meeting, the ffirst of which to comence this day 6 weeks being the 25th of the 4th Month next at the 8th hour in the morning at this place [viz. Bull and

---

Questions and *Strife* of *Words* that tends to *Parties* and contention . . not to speak more than one at a time ; nor any in a fierce way ; for that is not to be allowed in any *Society* neither Natural nor Spiritual ; but as the Apostle saith, *Be swift* to hear *and slow to speak; and let it be in the Grace which seasons all words.* And if there be any *Differences* that cannot be quickly ended in the meeting, let the *Six-Weeks Meeting* order some *Friends* to hear the Matter out of the *Meeting*, without respect of Persons, and bring in the Report to the same *Meeting* the same day (if possible [the Six-Weeks Meeting used at this time to meet at 8 a.m.] and the *Meeting* may give judgment ; that no Business be delayed from time to time. And so with my Love to you all in the *Seed* of Life, *Christ Jesus*, in whom ye have all *Peace* and *Wisdom* from Him who is the *Treasure* of *Knowledge* and *Wisdom*. Amen.—G. F."—*Epistles*, vol. ii. p. 555.

Mouth]." A clerk (William Welch) was also at this time appointed to keep the Books and Papers.

From this time forward the meeting has been regularly held unto the present time. Thus constituted as a body of reference among the six Monthly Meetings, it also took the chief care over any outward matter that might affect their general interests, of which the property in meeting-houses and burial-grounds, and care of casual poor, became prominent subjects. These involved so much of a financial nature as to render needful the appointment of a less numerous body than the eighty-four Friends of the Six-Weeks Meeting to discharge them efficiently; and accordingly a sub-committee, known as the Meeting of Twelve, was early set apart to have charge over all rents, receipts, and disbursements. Of this Meeting of Twelve a separate notice is hereafter given. It commenced two years after the settlement of the Six-Weeks Meeting, and was continued up to the commencement of the present century. Appointed, originally, by the Six-Weeks Meeting as its cash committee and trustees, it soon became, to a partial extent, a representative body; for in 1674 six of its number voluntarily retired, in order that the six Monthly Meetings might each appoint one of their own members to it, who were in future to retire annually, that a fresh appointment might be made.

Thus, itself a large and non-elective body with a small committee, partially composed of delegates, the Six-Weeks Meeting continued for some years from its foundation to be the meeting of reference and appeal among all the six Monthly Meetings of London; and in 1679, after seven years of existence, it was still so far from being a representative body as to itself add many Friends to its number to replace losses by death or removal. But at the next general settlement, some four years later, in 1683, the principle of representation became partially recognised, for we then find the Monthly Meetings desired to *nominate* suitable Friends to attend the service of the Six-Weeks Meeting.

There is extant a paper by George Fox referring to the constitution of this meeting, which we give *in extenso*. It is without date, and is entered on its records in 1691; but as George Fox was then no longer living, and the circumstances of the meeting in 1683 make it applicable to that time, which was one, as the Journal shows, when George Fox was himself in London and giving much personal care to the

Friends who were undergoing great trials from persecutions, we think it may safely be considered as written in this year.

The paper, if it can be referred so far back, shows that the change in the constitution adopted in 1683 was a suggestion of George Fox, who ever seems to have favoured the open and representative form of government, rather than any self-elected and select arrangements. The document is as follows :—

"*George Fox his papers abbreviated relating to the Six-Weeks Meeting.*

"The ancient Friends that formerly served the Six Weeks Meeting being some dead, some dwell out of town, some gone beyond the sea, some grown feeble that they cannot come. So let the six Monthly Meetings of the Citty choose some faithfull Friends, men and Women, that have known the affairs of the Church and have stood sufferings, and such as are impartiall, and that will not respect persons nor relations in Judgement, approved men and women that will not by respect be drawn away by affections into sects and parties, but have a generall care of the peace of the Church of Christ, and the prosperity of Truth, and a Care of God's Glory, and none but sencible men and women of good lives and conversations should be members of this Meeting as it was in the beginning, for it is the chief meeting of the Citty which all the Monthly Meetings appeal to."

It would seem as if the Quarterly Meeting also made it a court of appeal, for G. F. proceeds—

"And if there be anything in the Quarterly Meeting y^t concerns the 6 Weeks Meeting, wch canot there be well determined, let it be recommended to the 6 Weeks Meeting."

Now follow directions as to how the monetary affairs are to be conducted :—

"And the 6 weeks Meeting recommends things to the twelve, which twelve give an account to the Six Weeks Meeting of all the mony they receive, how it is laid out, and what they have in stock, once a year (when six of the twelve are chosen anew) and their account (after examination) appearing right to be signed.

"And the twelve, which are to be chosen out of the Six Monthly Meetings, are to be wise faithfull men, fearing God, vertueous, and of good example, and well grounded on their Rock and foundation Christ Jesus.

"And these of the twelve to attend the Six Weeks Meeting."

An extension of the area of the meeting is next suggested—

"And it were well if the 4 Monthly Meetings of Middlesex, as Enfield, Henden, Hammersmith, and Staines, did each meeting choose one faithfull friend to attend the Six Weekes Meeting."

By the following paragraph it is seen that, although the Six-Weeks Meeting was a limited body, yet all Friends in the ministry were to be at liberty to attend it.

"And the friends in the Ministry to have their liberty of coming when in ye Citty, and not otherways imployed in their testimony and service."

The Six-Weeks Meeting was to have control over all property transactions, as follows:—

"And if any meeting-place be bought, built, or repaired, or any burying-place bought, it should be with consent of the Six Weekes Meeting; and if their Monthly Meeting, to whome it belongs, canot defray the charge themselves, then they lay it before the Six W. M., and what sum the Six W. M. do agree to contribute, they order to be rec^d of the Twelve."

The Six-Weeks Meeting was at this time, as it still is, the custodian of all the title-deeds of the several Monthly Meetings of the London district.

"And as the Quarterly Meeting calls for wills, Deeds, and publick legacies concerning the Church, so to recomend them to the Six Weekes Meeting, and thence to ye Meeting of Twelve to be safely kept and registred—and to see the Trustees be faithfull to their Trusts, and that ye Trusts be faithfully performed, and that according to the donors, or Testators mind or will."

It was also the duty of the Meeting to order and regulate collections for the general service of the Monthly Meetings, i.e. independent of that for the needs of each particular meeting.

"And if any paper be given forth for a Collection for the

service of the Church of Christ in this Citty or County, it should be given forth from this Meeting to all ye aforesaid Monthly Meetings, and by this Meeting's order it should be disposed of to the 12, or otherwise, as they shall see meet."

The Committee of Twelve were to have control over the recording clerk as follows, viz. :—

" And the 6 W. M. should order ye twelve to oversee the Clark or Clarks at the Chamber [*this they did rather strictly, as may be seen further on*], (who pay them their half sallary) that they register all Births, Marriages, Sufferings, and Deaths, and that the Meeting of Sufferings assist therein."

The duty of sending round testimonies of denial to all the Monthly Meetings was committed to this meeting, that all the rest might know what any one had so issued.

" And any written Testimony y^t is given forth against any looseness and scandalous persons, or practises, it is to be read in the 6: weekes Meeting, and from thence communicated to the quarterly and monthly meetings, as they shall see cause —and no such paper to be brou^t to the 6 W : M : but first to be agreed upon at ye Monthly Meet: or some other Meet : and also that friends take care that what papers any of them bring in are proper for this Meeting's consideration.

" And every businesse of great concern and difficulty to be considered of in 2 meetings, if this Meeting shal see a real cause."

All funds of any kind common to the meetings of the London district were under the control of the Six-Weeks Meeting.

" And it is an old order among friends at every Quarterly Meeting, y^t Inquiry be made what poor friends' children in all the Monthly Meetings, both in the Citty and Middlesex, are to be set forth as Apprentices, and what friends' Children they have sett forth, and if the want assistance, they lay it before the Six weeks Meeting, and then the 6 W : M : gives a note or order to the Twelve to assist the Monthly or Quarterly Meeting with what the 6 weeks Meeting judgeth needfull.

" And if any of the Six weeks Meeting dy, or decline the service, the Monthly Meeting should choose and appoint another faithfull man or woman, to be approved of by the Six Weeks Meeting."

H

In the following clause is to be seen the importance G. F. attached to the character of the meeting, and his solicitude for its right maintenance:—

"And so the 6 weeks Meeting *being the prime Meeting of the Citty*, is to see that all the Meetings are preserved by the wisdom of God in the unity of the Spiritt, the bond of peace, and in the fellowship of the Holy Ghost, being ordered by the pure, gentle, heavenly, peaceable wisdom, Easie to be entreated, holy and vertuous examples to all other meetings, both in Citty and Country, and that all may be carefull to speak short and pertinent to matters in a christian spirit, and dispatch businesse quickly, and keep out long Debates and Heats, and with ye spirit of God keep down that which is Doateing about questions and strife of words, that tends to affections and parties, and contention for in the Church of Christ, there is no such custome to be allowed—and not to speak 3 or 4 together, nor in a forced way, for that is not to be allowed in any society, either naturall or spirituall, but as the Apostle saith, to be swift to hear, and slow to speak, and let it be in the Grace wch seasons all words.

"So wth my love to you all in the seed of Life, Christ Jesus, in whome you have all peace and wisdome from him who is the Treasure of Wisdome. Amen.

"And if there be any difference which canot quickly be ended, let the Six Weeks Meeting order half a Dozen to to hear the matter out of the Meeting, without respect of Persons, and bring in the report to the Meeting the same day, (if it can conveniently be). That the Meeting may give Judgement. That no businesse wch can be ended presently, be delayed from time to time.

"And at the end of every 2nd or 3rd Meeting, let the names of ye friends y^t belong to the Meeting be read over, and any that do not come to the Meeting ye second or third time, then to know the reason, and if they decline the service, then let others be put in their Roome."—G. F.

"And that the Quarterly Meeting be desired to appoint some friend to keep a generall Register what poor friends have been, and shall be bro^t up, and put to Apprentice at the Charge of Friends."

Such, then, was the estimation in which G. F. held the Six-Weeks Meeting, and such the qualifications expected in those composing it; and doubtless, whilst its members possessed these, a ready assent and submission would be accorded to their decisions. A list of the names of the members of the meeting is given at this time. It includes for Peel, 7 men and 6 women; Westminster, 8 men and 8 women; Southwark, 10 men and 7 women; Ratcliff, 6 men and 4 women; London, 14 men and 6 women; Devonshire House and Wheeler Street, 17 men and 12 women.

Continuing its future history as a meeting, so as to show the change in its objects and constitution, the particular subjects under its care will, after this is done, receive subsequent notice under separate heads.

In 1696, the Six-Weeks Meeting was definitely established on a representative basis, and a fixed number of delegates from each of the six Monthly Meetings was determined upon—these were 8 men and 8 women Friends from each of the four Monthly Meetings of Peel, Westminster, Southwark, and Ratcliff; and 10 men and 10 women from each of the other two, the Bull and Mouth and Devonshire House, *alias* London district. Public Friends to have the same liberty to attend as before.

Theoretically, the Six-Weeks Meeting remained unchanged for about half a century after the date just mentioned. But, in point of fact, as years passed on, various modifications in its duties took place from the operation of causes which may be briefly noted.

In the first place, the Monthly Meetings gradually became more independent of it, and settled for themselves many cases which in former years would have been considered sufficiently "difficult" to send up to a superior meeting.

Secondly, the Meeting for Sufferings was increasing in weight and authority, and as it met more frequently than the Six-Weeks Meeting, its advice was often sought in emergencies. Thus sundry affairs came to be included in the province of the Meeting for Sufferings to which the Six-Weeks Meeting had formerly attended.

But perhaps the most important of the causes referred to as affecting the functions of the Six-Weeks Meeting, was the development of the authority of the Quarterly Meeting described in the preceding chapter. When that body, from being simply a formal bond of union between the metropolitan meetings, with little to do but record statistics, began to advise as to establishment and discontinuance of meetings, to settle appeals from the decisions of Monthly Meetings, and in various other ways to assume a position as the Representative Body of the London Monthly Meetings, it was only natural that the Six-Weeks Meeting should gradually decline in power and importance. Thus was it, by the operation of various causes, that the once "prime meeting" became, in about fifty years, no longer that senate or court of appeal it had been at first, but found itself confined to duties more and more of a financial nature, in administering funds collected for services of common benefit to the associated Monthly Meetings. It is now in connection with this financial service that those further changes in its constitution arose, to understand which reference to some pecuniary details will be necessary.

The duties remaining to the Six-Weeks Meeting at the end of fifty years, as above, were—"To inspect the condition of the several meeting-houses and tenements belonging to Friends in this City, and order the building, rebuilding, and repairs thereof; to take care of burial-grounds, repairing their walls, &c.; to make purchases for the general service of Friends in this City; receive the rents of tenements and parts of meeting-houses let out; pay taxes for the same; the clerk's wages, and the expense of public Friends' horses; to provide for the *casual* poor;—[N.B. Each Monthly Meeting provided for the poor among its own members]—also such other contingencies as affected the Society in general, including the distribution of testimonies of denial to the several Monthly Meetings."

The discharge of these duties involved much expense, and the funds at the command of the meeting were at first derived chiefly from the liberal free-will offerings and bequests of London Friends; also from moneys deposited with it by widows and others for investment, &c., on condition of their receiving interest as annuities during their lives, and with or without a power of disposal of the principal at their death. These collectively amounted to large sums, and, aided by occasional collections, long sufficed for the meeting's requirements without any stated contribution in the way of quotas being necessary. All moneys were handed over to the "Committee of Twelve," which was appointed to receive and disburse them according to the orders of the Six-Weeks Meeting; to have also the care of deeds and wills, registration of births and burials, and generally act as an executive body to carry out the decisions of the Six-Weeks Meeting, of which its members, *ex officio*, formed a part.

In 1677 notice occurs of the widows' and orphans' money, amounting to about £1,200.

All this time, when money was needed for any special object, the Six-Weeks Meeting used to send a request to the other meetings to raise it. As for example :—1673. Collections ordered for Friends, sufferers by fire at Shadwell and Wapping. 1674. Collection ordered for Southwark Meeting-house. 1681. Collection ordered for Friends suffering from fire at Bradwick and Collumpton, in Devon. 1684. Fire in Hunts, £100 to be collected. 1676. £25 to be gathered for Longford. £30 to be collected towards Hammersmith. 1678. Monthly Meetings to collect for Friends suffering by dreadful fire at Northampton. 1679. £50 to be raised for Friends, sufferers by fire at Limehouse. 1683. Ditto £133 for fire at Wapping.

When the meeting itself needed money it asked the Monthly Meetings to collect and furnish it. Thus, in 1678, the Meeting of Twelve complained of being in arrear, and the Monthly Meetings were requested to raise £860 among them, no proportion in the collection being assigned. A new meeting-house at Devonshire House was built at this time. Four years after (1682) the Meeting of Twelve report being in debt £250, and a collection of £300 is then ordered. In 1688, an audit shows a debt to Treasurer of £40 6s. 8d., but the meeting holds £1,484 14s. 8d., on which interest has to be paid, and only £700 of it invested. 1690. Collection of £400 ordered; a note is again found that the disbursements of Meeting of Twelve are much more than income, and agreed—" Poor Friends be lodged in ' Pairs' to save expense": the charge for the casual or general poor was becoming heavy. The purchase of Peel was now in hand; £300 was borrowed from " Captives' money." In 1693 money is said to be urgently wanted, and in 1694 comes further borrowing £500 of Meeting for Sufferings—the cause of this is stated, in 1695, to be partly by reason of charges for the poor; and the collection for the same falling short, and purchasing and expending money for meeting-houses, from all which a deficiency of £1,000 has accrued, a collection is ordered for such; and in future each Monthly Meeting was to pay its own repairs and taxes.

1696. The meeting was reconstituted and put on a representative basis, and it now appears able to free itself from debt by the amount of the collections. But two years after, in 1698, £500 is noted as borrowed again from the Meeting for Sufferings. It is obvious that every effort was made at this time to increase the individual responsibility of Monthly Meetings, rather than merge their liabilities in a common stock. Thus four years previous the repairs and taxes of each meeting-house had been thrown on the Monthly Meeting to which it belonged, and now, in 1699, it is concluded that the families of poor Friends travelling in the ministry are to be maintained, if needful, during their absence by the particular Monthly Meeting of which the Friend may be a member. Notwithstanding these arrangements, it is found that, in 1700, a debt of £1,400 has been incurred by the Six-Weeks Meeting, which is thus explained:—

	£	s.	d.
By taking in moneys instead of making collections when wanted and spending it	905	0	0
By interest and annuities for money not improved	250	0	0
By three meetings drawing out more than they bring in	194	13	2
By repairs and charges of out meetings	59	6	1
	£1,408	19	3

The meeting in face of these difficulties now orders of the Monthly Meetings what is called a tenfold usual *quarterly* collection,* and apportions it thus:—

Devonshire House	£300
City	240
Westminster	120
Peel	120
Southwark	120
Ratcliff	150
	£1,050

---

* It is evident that at a very early date the Monthly Meetings collected *quarterly* for the Six-Weeks Meeting, besides responding to the orders for General Collections. These quarterly collections had gradually become regular assessments.

By raising this amount the Six-Weeks Meeting hoped to secure the right investment of legacies the interest of which alone it ought to use. Among these thus wanting investment is the now well-known one of " Pollard's Trust." In 1703, the meeting is again in financial difficulties, its debt being £1,200, which increased in 1704 to £1,339; but efforts by collections were made; some houses also in Red Lion Street were sold, and the solvency restored. In 1707, there was a surplus, and at this time the estimated annual income of the meeting was found to be £778, and its expenditure £776. Three years afterwards (1710) income had again fallen short of expenses by £500, " occasioned by purchasing burying-ground, assisting in building and altering meeting-houses, and supplying the poor this dear time." This last seems now to have been the chief cause of expense, and frequent are the complaints from the Monthly Meetings that the poor are a " heavy burden." In 1714 Devonshire House is found unable, through " loss of many ancient and wealthy Friends," and " great increase of its poor," to contribute to the meeting. Other Monthly Meetings make similar complaints at this time, and the funds of the Six-Weeks Meeting are so low that when Friends of Staines ask for a contribution from it towards a meeting, they are told such help cannot be given. Frequent notices of "adjournments" occur at this time. " Stating numbers insufficient to proceed to business," once, it says, " 11 Friends met and waited till near 12 o'clock [*i.e.* 4 hours] but numbers being insufficient, adjourned." The time of meeting was in this year changed to 9 a.m. A new settlement is made, 1718, on this basis:—

1. A new general collection quarterly at each Monthly Meeting.

2. The same to be paid into their own Monthly Meetings as before.

3. The present quarterly payments to the Meeting of Twelve to cease. Each Monthly Meeting to keep account of what they collect, and all their disbursements. Deficiency to be made good, or surplus received by the Meeting of Twelve.

In this is seen a further attempt to throw increased responsibility upon Monthly Meetings; and it was hoped, whilst expenditure might be thus reduced, that the debts of the Six-Weeks Meeting could be paid off by accumulated surpluses from the Monthly Meetings. Bad attendance at the Six-Weeks Meeting continues to be noted. Thus, in 1719,

Monthly Meetings are requested "to order" their members to attend next meeting to consider how to prevent same for the future; and to endeavour an improvement, the hour of meeting is changed from 9 in the morning, that had been settled in 1714, to 3 in the afternoon. The leaving Monthly Meetings to expend as they thought fit, and adjust surplus or deficiency, instead of realising any income, as by the last settlement, produced, after some years' trial of it, an accumulation of heavy debt, needing the renewed efforts by collections for its discharge, to aid which the meeting called for lists of subscribers in the various Monthly Meetings and the sums they paid. The time is spoken of as a difficult juncture, chiefly as to amount of poor. In 1724, the following minute shows the anxiety of the meeting to obviate a recurrence of this in future.

1724, Tenth Month 1st, a paper brought in to prevent an over liberal expense of the Poors Stock: "Whereas it is manifest that very great inconveniences have accrued to this meeting by their, or the Quarterly Meeting, disposing of money or engaging in expenses when this meeting have not wherewith to answer the same. And whereas by such methods this meeting hath been brought into debt above £2,000, which it hath required the utmost industry to raise and discharge, and which, notwithstanding the same, is not fully discharged. To prevent the like inconvenience for the future, it is resolved and agreed that this meeting will not consent to any new expenses of more than £50 on any one particular article or occasion, nor more than £100 upon all pretences whatsoever till they have effects in their power to make good the same, and that a copy of this resolution be sent to the next Quarterly Meeting." The power of the Monthly Meeting to come upon the Six-Weeks Meeting to make good any deficiency, as given in 1718, was now revoked; each was to maintain its own poor, and to pay quarterly a sum to the Six-Weeks Meeting for general expenses, which was thus allotted:—Bull £30, Devonshire House £30, Southwark £15, Peel £13, and Westminster £12. Thus, by their quarterly payments, raising an income of £400 per annum from the whole. Even this does not work to satisfaction, for in four years' time it is found that, in 1728, Southwark formally complains "of the Six-Weeks Meeting running yearly into debt, and not to the reputation of a Christian Society," but no action seems taken, and the next disagreement is ten years later, in 1738, when it is Peel gives notice it intends "for the future to be independent of the Six-Weeks Meeting, their manner of proceeding towards us is not equal, and the methods they are pleased to take seems to us so disagreeable, except only our proportional contributions towards the charge of casual poor, horse-bills, servants' wages, candles, and such other small contingencies as properly belong to that meeting." The chief cause of complaint seems to have been the non-allowance by the Six-Weeks of some items of expenditure by Peel, which, by an appeal to the Quarterly Meeting, were ultimately adjusted.

1738. Ratcliff is the one dissatisfied. "They never have been on the same bottom with other meetings, and desire that all Quarterly Meeting expenses of records, horse-bills, casual poor, and rents of Wapping, be kept as a separate account, of which they will pay their part, but no more." £752 is found to be the debt of the Six-Weeks Meeting in 1739, which becomes increased by new works at the White Hart Court Meeting, and repairs at Devonshire House. A large collection (£1,500) is therefore ordered, the result of which not being wholly satisfactory, the Monthly Meetings are advised "to amend their subscription lists; some names not down at all; others have not given enough." A few years later, and in 1741 the whole question of the compact is under discussion. Four out of the six Monthly Meetings think it would be best to be independent of one another, and only contribute to some general expenses. But Peel thinks "the only just and equal method is for all the collections to come into one common stock, and then be paid out to the poor;" and Devonshire House, though willing to try, says "it has many poor who come to that quarter for low rents."

In 1745 matters came to a crisis. Peel and Ratcliff had openly declared their secession from the federal compact; Westminster was insubordinate, and other meetings, though nominally associated, had ceased to contribute fully and fairly to the common stock. The Six-Weeks Meeting had no power to enforce its claims, and no superior meeting to fall back upon for support. Deeply in debt, frequently unable to get its members together in sufficient numbers to form a quorum, and with its decisions constantly set at nought in one quarter or another, the once "prime meeting of the city," found itself compelled to approach the Quarterly Meeting, which had, in growing up beside it, absorbed its strength and vitality. The

Six-Weeks Meeting asked the Quarterly Meeting to take under its own management those affairs which it now found itself unable to transact efficiently.

In response to this application, the Quarterly Meeting appointed a committee (including John [Dr.] Fothergill, Thomas Corbyn, Jacob Hagen, and several others) to investigate the whole case. These presented a report, in which, after detailing the circumstances which had led to the changes we have referred to in the functions of the Six-Weeks Meeting, they state as follows :—

"Part of their business (*i.e.* of the Six-Weeks Meeting) having thus gradually devolved upon other meetings, for upwards of twenty years past, as well as at present, the Six-Weeks Meeting seems chiefly to have been engaged in the following affairs:

"They inspected the condition of the several meeting-houses and tenements belonging to Friends in this city, and ordered the building and rebuilding and repairs thereof; took care of the burial-grounds, repairing their walls, &c.; made purchases for the general service of Friends in this city; received the rents of tenements, and parts of meeting-houses let out; paid taxes for the same, paid clerk's wages, and the expense of public Friends' horses; provided for the casual poor, and such other contingencies as affected the Society in general: set on foot collections to answer these purposes, and distributed testimonies of denial to the several Monthly Meetings; which affairs they appear to have conducted in a regular and reputable manner, till the difficulties and inconveniences occurred which induced them to request this Quarterly Meeting to take the immediate management of affairs into their own hands.

"Your Committee, upon inquiry into the occasion of the difficulties which have thus embarrassed the Six-Weeks Meeting, apprehend that they don't so much arise from the nature of the affairs themselves as from the want of a regular dependence upon some superior meeting, whose judgment might be appealed to, and admitted as decisive in cases not easily determinable amongst themselves.

"Wherefore your Committee appointed to consider in what manner the business of the Six-Weeks Meeting may be most conveniently taken into the management of this Quarterly Meeting, propose for this purpose the following method:—

"That the same number of Friends who at present constitute the Six-Weeks Meeting, viz.: Devonshire House, ten; Peel, eight; Southwark, eight; Gracechurch Street, ten; Ratcliff, eight; Westminster, eight, besides the Meeting of Twelve, chosen by the respective Monthly Meetings out of their own members, and approved by the Quarterly Meeting, be formed into a Committee.

"That the Committee meet every six weeks, under the same appellation as before, to manage the usual business of the Six-Weeks Meeting, and to act thereon as the deputies of the Quarterly Meeting, before whom they are to lay the state of their affairs and accounts as often as this meeting shall require."

The suggestions contained in the above report were carried into effect, and the Six-Weeks Meeting became henceforth simply a Committee of the Quarterly Meeting for the settlement of all matters connected with the finances and trusts property of the associated meetings,—retaining the Meeting of Twelve as its executive branch. A new appointment was made, in which the names of Mildred, Moline, Partridge, Besse, Corbyn, West, Elliott, Weston, &c., are noticeable, and vigorous efforts were at once made to get out of debt, and commence a career of financial soundness.

It was soon found that the difficulties of the case were not to be so summarily disposed of. The quotas were apportioned as follows—Devonshire House £50, Gracechurch Street £60, Peel £20, Westminster £20, Horselydown £30, Ratcliff £20. But much trouble was experienced in obtaining these sums from one or two of the meetings, especially when in 1750 it was found necessary to call for a five years' quota, to pay off debts, and also to impose an annual addition of 50 per cent. to guard against future embarrassments.

By 1754 the Six-Weeks Meeting had, however, managed, by strenuous and persevering efforts, to discharge its debts.

Repairs to the workhouse and meeting-houses, the rebuilding of Park Meeting-house, &c. proved heavy; far beyond the settled income of £300 per annum, and large collections were made to meet deficiencies. It is evident a generous spirit prevailed about this time, for an attempt was made to raise by private subscription a fund to such an amount that, if invested, its annual interest might prove sufficient for the current expenses of the meeting.

As this fund (usually called the fund for extinguishing the quotas) reached in course of years to the substantial amount of £15,000, and forms at the present time a large portion of the Invested Funds of the Six-Weeks Meeting, it may be as well to trace its origin and progress a little further; for this purpose the minute under which it was raised may be given *in extenso* :—

"Six-Weeks Meeting, 2mo. 1772.—Amended Proposition.—The state of this meeting being now under consideration respecting the deficiencies of some Monthly Meeting in the payment of their annual quotas to this meeting's stock, whereby we are embarrassed in our circumstances, and also that there seems a danger, lest the chain or connection between the six Monthly Meetings of this city, by which the said stock hath been many years raised and supported, may at length be broken, and the important and necessary purposes for which this meeting is constituted be left unprovided for, such as building and repairing our several meeting-houses and the walls of our burial-grounds, taking and renewing leases, with the rents and taxes with other incident expenses of a public nature; and there appearing a disposition in the minds of some Friends arising from the foregoing considerations to contribute by legacies or donations towards raising a fund, the produce of which might be £300 a year, being the sum of all the quotas of the six Monthly Meetings (which, if paid, are often inadequate to the expenses attending); and that then the said quotas might cease and be abolished; provided the Quarterly Meeting of London do, by a proper minute, guarantee and secure the application of such legacies and donations to the above-mentioned purpose, the interest of which to be applied as above in lieu of the quotas now paid by the Monthly Meetings."

The Quarterly Meeting of the Third Month of that year considered the foregoing proposition, and decided in its favour. And at the same time it guaranteed the permanent investment of the fund, and the application of the interest only towards diminishing the quotas, which it agreed should become reduced 10 per cent. for every thousand pounds added to the so-called quota fund.

By this it is apparent that the Quarterly Meeting has pledged itself as trustee to a permanent investment of the fund for a special object; that of reducing the annual contribution of the various Monthly Meetings to the general expenses of the Six-Weeks Meeting.

The donations for this purpose commenced, as shown, in 1772, and it was only after a prolonged interval of seventy-two years they reached the amount of £15,000. Some differences in the rate of contribution between the several years may be noted: thus, by the expiration of the first thirteen years from its commencement, the fund had reached £8,000, of which £3,000 was a legacy from Thomas Talwin (a munificent benefactor to the London meetings, especially that of Devonshire House, of which he had been a member); in six years more another £1,000 had become added, when the rate of contribution became somewhat accelerated, for in two years' time another £1,000 was reported, and so again in the next two years; then it was three years before another £1,000 had been received; after that it took twelve years before a further increase of £1,000 had accrued; the total amounting then in 1819 to £13,000. After thirteen more years it had reached £14,000; and finally, in 1844, after fourteen years' interval, the donations, &c., had become increased, so that the sum of £15,000 was attained. Although the amount originally contemplated had, by this continued perseverance over a period of time so extended, been thus secured, it was not attended with all the benefit its projectors, in the days of Dr. Fothergill and Thomas Talwin, had looked for. The quotas were from time to time reduced, until, in 1844, the original quotas were declared to be extinguished. But in reality the object was not attained, because during the formation of this Quota Fund additional contributions were from time to time called for instead of increasing the quotas; and these *contributions* were continued under that name as regular periodical payments from the Monthly Meeting; so that for some years the Monthly Meetings were paying a decreasing *quota*, but an increasing *contribution*, thus practically retaining a similar annual assessment, though under a different name.*

---

* The contributions to the fund for extinguishing the quotas were as follow:—1774, Devereux Bowley £200; 1775, Sarah How £100; 1781, John Miers £200; 1784, Jacob Agar £100; 1785, John Sherwin £100, Joseph Lum £100, Thomas Talwin £3,000; 1786, Richard Sterry £200, Peter Cockfield £200; 1788, Sarah Shewell £50; 1789, Daniel Mildred £200; 1791, Jacob Woodward £20, Thomas Corbyn £500; 1793, Thomas Smith £50, John Paris £1,000; 1795, Abraham Gray £100; 1798,

The above arrangement, whereby the amount paid every year by each Monthly Meeting became divided as between quota and contribution, was evidently adopted to enable the Quarterly Meeting to fulfil its pledge to the various donors, with regard to the fifteen thousand pound fund; this distinction is first to be noted in 1812, when the additional contributions were assessed as follows :—

		£	s.	d.		£
Devonshire House	Quota	27	0	0	Contribution	50
Gracechurch Street	do.	18	0	0	do.	45
Peel	do.	9	0	0	do.	25
Ratcliff	do.	9	0	0	do.	15
Southwark	do.	15	15	0	do.	70
Westminster	do.	11	5	0	do.	35
		£90	0	0		£240

And the Country Meetings, which had no participation in the benefit of the Quota Fund, were assessed to contribute—

Barking	...	...	...	...	£4
Kingston	...	...	...	...	5
Longford	...	...	...	...	6
Tottenham	...	...	...	...	10
					£25

Previous to thus fixing regular contributions in 1812, recourse was had, from time to time, to large collections; thus, in 1780, £2,400 was raised; Dr. Fothergill giving £200, and eight other Friends £100 each; fourteen £50; the remainder being subscribed in smaller amounts. 1798, a subscription to the amount of a twelvefold quota was ordered for purchase of land, &c., at Bunhill Fields. 1802, £3,216 was also raised, being needed for further purchases; building Ratcliff Meeting-house, repairing Peel, &c. 1808, a twentyfold quota was

---

Thomas Broadbank £400; 1799, William Bowrey £100; 1805, Mary Halsey £200; 1809, Hannah Plumstead £200; 1814, Joseph Smith £100; 1817, Mary Sterry £500; 1823, Anthony Neatby £50; 1826, Anthony Sterry £100; 1829, John Row £1,000. These legacies (£8,770), with the accumulations of interest, amounted to £15,000 in 1844, then invested in Three per Cent. 1726 Stock. This was sold out in 1853, and Three per Cent. Consols bought to the amount of £16,262 8s. 3d.

ordered; and in 1811 a collection of £1,500 was ordered, but only £1,100 was realised, which might have been a proximate cause for the arrangement of a settled contribution from each meeting, adopted in 1812, as already described.

Some adjustment took place in the character of the meeting which should be noted; in 1810, the number of members was reduced to twenty-seven, viz. six each from Devonshire House, Gracechurch Street, and Southwark; three each from Ratcliff, Peel, and Westminster, but the system of retiring by rotation was introduced instead of the previous mode of appointment for life, or during consent of individual. Thirteen years after, 1823, the six meetings were put on an equality as to representation, being allowed to send five members each. Passing on now to 1856, we find the contributions (as the quotas were now called) were as follow: Devonshire House £105, Peel £25, Ratcliff £60, Southwark £40, Westminster £40. The three country meetings of Kingston, Longford, and Tottenham, were not as yet associated with the London Monthly Meetings as regards finances and property, but paid a small sum towards the Quarterly Meeting expenses.

A still more important change took place in the constitution of the Six-Weeks Meeting, at a comparatively recent date, viz. 1862. Hitherto, as we have seen, the associated Monthly Meetings were independent of one another as regarded the maintenance of their own poor, and management of their trust-funds, but made contributions to a common stock under the management of the Six-Weeks Meeting—out of which all expense of repairs and maintenance of the meeting-houses and burial-grounds were met, as well as some other charges considered likewise as general to the meetings; yet the three country meetings of Kingston, Longford, and Tottenham, though forming part of the Quarterly Meeting, were not included in this arrangement, but only made a small annual contribution to this common stock, in respect of the use their members might make of the other meeting-houses and burial-grounds; but they sent no representatives, nor were considered part of the Six-Weeks Meeting.

In 1862 radical changes were effected. The distinction between the country and town portions of the Quarterly Meeting was removed, and the Six-Weeks Meeting was constituted a Cash Committee for the *whole* Quarterly Meeting. Each Monthly Meeting was still to have control over its funded and other property; to pay all its current expenses for the poor, also for repairs, rents, taxes, &c. Yet at the end of every year these to be so adjusted that none pay more than at a certain rate per meeting, to be determined by the Six-Weeks Meeting, on a scale according to the ascertained contributing power of each meeting. Thus each would pay over to the Six-Weeks Meeting any funds remaining between the expenses incurred by it, and the amount of contribution for which it was assessed; and on the other hand, receive from the Six-Weeks Meeting any excess of expenditure that had been incurred over the amount of income from investments, and its particular quota, or contribution. Thus practically a common stock was formed, and arrangements that had become antiquated were simplified, and all difficulties about maintenance in moving the poor from one meeting to another were removed. But whilst the meetings thus pay their own expenses during the year, they are restricted from incurring any of a special nature, such as repairs, without the sanction of the Six-Weeks Meeting being first obtained.

At this date the excess of the average general expenditure and the care of the poor over the proceeds of invested funds in the whole Quarterly Meeting was estimated to be about £800 per annum, and for the repayment of this sum the Monthly Meetings were thus assessed:—Devonshire House £200, Ratcliff and Barking £100, Westminster £125, Kingston £150, Longford £75, Tottenham £150. The contributions have since been raised 50 per cent., and some other modifications in the assessment introduced. The country meetings were at this time empowered to send from three to five representatives to the Six-Weeks Meeting.

The Meeting of Twelve.

To understand the origin of this meeting, it will become needful to retrace our steps to quite an early date. In a meeting having under its charge such important affairs, as for a long period formed the business of the Six-Weeks Meeting, attention to matters of detail connected with finance and trust property was so obvious a burden, that from the earliest times a committee, known as the Meeting of Twelve, was set apart for the special care of these monetary affairs.

This committee became representative in its character earlier than the Six-Weeks Meeting itself, viz. in 1673, when six of its members voluntarily resigned, that each of the Monthly Meetings might send a delegate. The plan of six retiring annually was now adopted—the vacancies being filled up by appointment from the Monthly Meetings, subject, however, to the veto of the Six-Weeks Meeting.

George Fox's paper on the Six-Weeks Meeting (see *ante*, p. 95) furnishes some information as to the duties devolving upon the Meeting of Twelve. Some additional details are found in the following statement, entered on the books of the Six-Weeks Meeting under an early date, Twelfth Month, 1674-5 :—

"It was agreed that the charge of Friends' horses' meat that travel in the ministry of truth, the rents of meeting-places, burying-grounds, and the fines and charges of renewing, together with the charge of writing, leases and other things incident thereto ; as also rents and coals for the poor, relieving prisoners in any prison in or about this city, requiting gaolers when they have showed kindness, and Ellis Hookes, his salary as formerly proportioned, be all accounted public charges, and to be defrayed from time to time by the Meeting of Twelve.

"And as for answers to books wrote against truth, and others given to magistrates and parliaments, first being approved of and allowed by the Second-day's meeting of Friends of the ministry [now the Morning Meeting], it is agreed that such of them as are given away in and about the city to congregations and the like, be defrayed by the Meeting of Twelve, and that those that are given to magistrates, parliament, &c. being of a national concern, be defrayed by those five Friends as appointed for that purpose for the Yearly Meeting."

Such were the duties of the Meeting of Twelve, in addition to those previously mentioned, and their work appears to have been for many years efficiently performed. The men elected to serve upon it were evidently business characters. In 1679, even the age and standing of an Ellis Hookes did not preserve him, in the twenty-second year of his clerkship, from the following minutes :—

"7th 5th mo., 1679. Agreed that Philip Ford pay not any moneys for quartering or other unto Ellis Hookes, until he has first entered all former agreements made by the Six-Weeks Meeting relating to this meeting, in the book of this meeting appointed for that purpose, as he ought to do.

"Agreed, that E. Hookes, as he is a public servant to

Friends, do give an account what work and service he does, once every quarter, to this meeting in writing, that it may appear whether his work deserves his yearly salary, and before he has his last year's bill paid, to show cause why he charges Friends with 101 sheets of writing at 12d. per sheet."

The salary thus to be inquired about in connection with work for the six Monthly Meetings in and about London, was £20 per annum. Two years after this Ellis Hookes' decease occurred. His original appointment, in 1675, as recording clerk to the Six-Weeks Meeting was evidently the source of some thoughtfulness, possibly on account of his age and other Society engagements, for in the minutes of the Six-Weeks Meeting, 18th Eleventh Month, 1675, " Upon consideration of the proposal made by Ellis Hookes, and upon his solemn promise made that he will personally and duly, if the Lord will, give his attendance as a scribe to this meeting, it is agreed that the order made last meeting in his case be reversed, and he be desired duly to attend this meeting accordingly. Thomas Zach, being present, voluntarily resigned."

The Meeting of Twelve shared, of course, in the difficulties of the Six-Weeks Meeting, and want of funds often made it powerless to perform its duties. It was retained after the reconstitution of its superior meeting in 1745, and existed till 1810, when a committee was then appointed in its place, known as the Committee of Accounts of the Six-Weeks Meeting. This committee was dissolved in 1821.

Having now given a brief sketch of the origin and history of the Six-Weeks Meeting, Two-Weeks Meeting and Meeting of Twelve, some further particulars will be added in reference to the character of the business transacted by the first-named, especially in its earlier years.

Care of the Churches.

" A general care of the peace of the Church of Christ and the prosperity of truth," was stated as being one of the objects set before the Six-Weeks Meeting at its commencement. Accordingly, it kept a watchful eye upon the London meetings and their members, and from time to time issued its advices and counsels, warnings and reproofs. It was frequent in its exhortations to the Churches to be diligent in the maintenance of their principles and testimonies, and especially to take proper care of widows, the fatherless and the newly convinced.

1688. Appointment made of Friends "to draw up a few lines to be read at next Quarterly Meeting against going into privileged places for debt."

The following are specimens of the advices which, in its Christian zeal for the good of the Monthly Meetings, the Six-Weeks Meeting found it desirable to issue:—

From the Six-Weeks Meeting, 22nd Second Month, 1690.

The Six-Weeks Meeting advise "that faithful endeavours should be used, and a godly care taken in ye respective Monthly Meetings in order to prevent ye prejudicial preachers of ye separation . . . from imposing their lifeless preaching and talk upon public assemblies . . . and considering that wee have been constrained in ye great meetings and mixt assemblies many times without public interruption to bear their forced empty preaching, and feigned talk (though mixt with good words and fair speeches) . . . for ye sake of many ignorant, and undiscerning, weak and unstable souls, and y^t ye world might not have occasion to reproach us as a people in strife and divisions, . . . although both in private and in public, their spirit and work of division and separation has been . . . clearly testified against . . . to remove and blow away the chaff, mist, and smoke raised by that dividing, self-separating spirit . . . which has set up . . . separate meetings in the city and country, which are made refuges and nurseries for both prejudiced, envious, loose spirits, apostates, and backsliders, who in some places have shut Friends out of their own meeting-houses and properties therein . . . It is, therefore, by the said S. W. M. recommended . . . to ye several monthly meetings of our dear Friends and brethren in and about this City of London, &c. to use their Christian endeavours . . . to prevent and stop such pernicious preachers by some ancient and substantial Friends and elders (of every meeting where they come), privately giving them plain and faithful warning or admonition not to impose their ministry or preaching upon our assemblies . . . If they were in this wise taken aside and plainly and faithfully dealt withal . . . it would bring a weight over them, and a load upon their spirits, and weaken their perverse designs; and more clear Friends, rather than to let them go off quietly and whole, without showing any dislike unto them, when sometimes they have preached one part of ye day (in our public meetings, to draw more disciples after them into their meeting the other part of the day," &c.

In 1690, persecution being now over, it is clear that many professed to join themselves to Friends whose character and conduct were not consistent with their profession, and the following document is issued respecting these:—

"*From the Six Weeks Meeting in London, 10th of 12th mo., 1690-1.*

"Dear Friends,—We tenderly salute you in the holy and blessed truth that the Lord in mercy hath made us partakers of, in which we find it is our Christian duty to watch over one another for good, and to see that all who are convinced thereof may in their conversations answer it. But to our great grief we hear and understand that there are some that come amongst us and make profession of the Truth, that do not answer it in their conversation, but are loose in their minds and take a liberty, neglect their watch, keep not to the daily cross, but run into the spirit and friendship of the evil world in keeping ill hours, ill company, sitting idly, and excessively drinking &c., tippling, and haunting ale-houses and taverns, gaming and neglecting of their own affairs, ruining their families, which is contrary to our holy profession, and brings a reproach upon us and it, and greatly obstructs the prosperity of Truth, by their loose and disorderly conversations and evil practices which they have been and are found in.

"Wherefore we do beseech you for the Lord's sake and for the sake of our holy and Christian profession that you faithfully deal with, admonish, reprove and rebuke all such in your several Monthly Meetings, without respect to persons, that are found in anything which is scandalous or inconsistent with the holy Truth and our Christian profession; and if they slight and disregard such admonition, reproof, and counsel that in the love of God, good to their souls and concern for the Truth shall be given them, and do not condemn their evil practices but continue therein, that you do for the clearing of Truth give forth a testimony against them, and their ungodly practices, that we may manifest ourselves to be such that cannot have any fellowship with the unfruitful works nor workers of darkness, but do reprove and deny both them and their works, until they shall come to unfeigned repentance and amendment of life. So, dear friends and brethren, let us be diligent, fervent and zealous herein, and with one heart and mind let every one set hand and shoulder to this work, for such must be thundered out of these wicked and scandalous practices, or else the power of God will thunder them out of his camp and society of his people; that it may be kept clean, His Truth may spread, His name be honoured and exalted over all, who is God blessed for ever. Amen.

"To the Friends and Brethren
of the several Mo: Meetings in London."

In 1691 a testimony was issued by the Six-Weeks Meeting against "those that have imitated the world, whether it be in men in their extravagant periwigs, or modes in their apparel; or whether it be women in their high towering dresses, gold chains, or gaudy attire; or whether it be parents like old Ely, not sufficiently restraining their children therefrom . . . or whether it be in voluptuous feasting without fear, or costly furnitures, and too rich adorning of houses, &c."

The next extract bears date Ninth Month 8th, 1698:—

"*Advice against great Dinners at Marriages, &c. &c., prepared by the 2 weeks Meeting, directed by the Six Weeks My. to be sent to the several Monthly Meetings.*

"At our Two Weeks Meeting the following particulars were mentioned as hurtful to our profession, and therefore recommended to the care of the Six Weeks Meeting in order to have them avoided.

"1st.—At Marriages great Dinners, together with other vain practices and conversations, both then and in the evening, and having any Dinners at public-houses.

"2nd.—At or after Births of children; costly Treats and giving of gloves.

"3rd.—At Burials, the frequent use of Hearses and Coaches in great numbers, too pompous for our self-denying testimony unless upon a case of necessity.

"4th.—Upon the decease of a near relation some women have been observed of late to go into Black, too much imitating the world's custom in that they call mourning.

"5th.—Sleeping in Meetings a great fault, a dishonour to our holy profession, a grief and exercise to all the faithful amongst us; which such that are concerned are desired to watch against, and be very sparing both in eating and drinking before they go to meetings, for the contrary ('tis believed) is one great occasion thereof."

The care of the Churches was a matter which, as we have

seen in the last chapter, gradually devolved upon the Quarterly Meeting, and from this latter body subsequently emanated the advices and admonitions referring to the " Peace of the Church of Christ and the prosperity of Truth." But under the following heads:—Delinquency ; Meetings for Worship and Discipline ; Friends in the Ministry ; Marriages ; Care of the Poor ; Education, and Miscellaneous, further examples will be given of the influence of the Six-Weeks Meetings, but we first subjoin a few notes as to its general care over the Churches ; thus, *e.g.*—

1673. Monthly Meetings, to "consider of the most effectual way and means for gathering Friends to accompany corpses to the ground."

1678. The act for burying in woollen being presented to the consideration of the meeting, " Doe agree that the compliance therewith as to wollen is a civil matter and fit to be done, and to promising the making oath thereof they meddle not therewith, but leave it to Friends freedome in the Truth, and this to be sent each Monthly Meeting."

Another minute as to burials is as follows :—

" Dear Friends,—Our love salutes you, and these are tenderly to recommend unto you the need there many times is as to more men Friends being at burials than sometimes there are to help to perform the last office of love unto our deceased Friends, and in order that service may be made more easy, we entreat you to stir up young men in the respective monthly meetings that may be serviceable herein to attend the same, as also to procure, as much as may be, light coffins of wainscot or deal, that Friends may not be oppressed with the weight of them, and when corps are large, and coffins heavy, that they get pads at the coffins, and take particular care to get them that are able to bear the same, and that such that are carried from their dwellings to meeting-houses be buried from the nearest to the burial-ground, that so we may in no wise oppress one another, but with ease and readiness of mind discharge that office of love one for another, not knowing how soon any of us may stand in need thereof, and therefore we do request and hope that none for the future may be backward herein, and in brotherly love remain," &c.

1674. Monthly Meetings requested " to visit widows, fatherless and newly convinced."

1674. Agreed to erase the name of a Friend from the meeting books, and in same year two Friends' names are mentioned whom the Monthly Meetings are to see that "they be kept out" of certain specified meetings.

Even to minute particulars of conduct, the watchful care of the Six-Weeks Meeting was extended, *e.g.* in 1674 it minuted, "Agreed that in future no maidservants desert their service to live at their own hand without consent of their Monthly Meeting, and the like as to young men."

1677. The following was directed towards any failing in business:—"It is the counsell and judgment of the Meeting that it is the duty of every person that breaks and are not able to pay their debts that they forthwith disown and surrender up their Estate, both real and personal, unto their creditors. Together with their persons, or that they condemn their actions to their creditors." And again, as to meetings at houses of any not conducting themselves properly, "It is the mind and counsel of this Meeting that if a meeting of Friends be at the house of any particular Friend, and it appear that the Friend of that house comitt anything that is dishonarable to the truth, then forthwith the Meeting be removed from that House."

1682. "Friends transporting themselves beyond seas" to have certificates to the meetings they go to, as to conversation and debts; and if single, as to marriage engagements. Six years later is a notice as to settlements for maintenance, viz.—

1688. "Friends not to be taken care of by a Monthly Meeting into which they remove without bringing a certificate from the Monthly Meeting they leave."

1690. Tenth Month. "No books or papers to be sold in Friends' meetings that Friends have not approved of, and particularly Joan Whitrow's books,* to be stopt from being sold amongst Friends' books."

In the same year a paper was also issued, advising the several Monthly Meetings to be cautious how they granted permission for any to be buried in the Society's burial-ground, who, though attending our public meeting, had been married by a priest, without having condemned their actions.

"At a Six Weeks Meeting att ye Bull ye 5th 2mo. 1692.

"It is agreed yt each monthly meeting bee advised yt if any Friends of any Monthly Meeting be sent for by any Friend to advise with in relation to making any Will or Trust or Bequest, any Legacy for ye service of poor Friends,

---

* See Joseph Smith's Catalogue.

that they doe rather encline to advise y^m to bestow their gifts soe as itt may be handed to y^m y^t keep ye general poors stock in reguard y^t great sums are by y^m disburssed for poors Rents, Coales and other incident charges y^t attend y^t meeting."

In 1694 George Keith seems to have personally submitted his case to the Six-Weeks Meeting. "There being a straight upon some Friends about receiving his testimony," a committee was appointed; but eventually the matter proved of that importance as to be undertaken by the Yearly Meeting.

1695. Occurred a long-continued case of appeal between Philip Ford and Samuel Waldenfield, which shows that the Six-Weeks Meeting was referred to as a "Prime Meeting" in the London district; one also in 1697 between William Mead and another; in 1699 between Philip Ford again and Nathaniel Markes.

In 1699 : "The Six Friends appointed to attend the Yearly Meeting to have in charge—

1. How the charge of the Meeting for Sufferings shall be defrayed.

2. That a due correspondence be settled as well beyond seas as in this nation.

3. The regulating the press and sending of books into foreign parts.

4. To present what they do in writing to the Yearly Meeting."

1698. The meeting arranged the number of representatives from the London meetings to the Yearly Meeting, "each to send 2 solid Friends to attend, also one to keep the door."

1700. The bounds of Monthly Meetings being now fixed, "Friends to be members of the Monthly Meetings in which they live, unless by consent of the two meetings concerned."

1702. A paper was issued against "Friends going to law with each other."

1702. Mention made of ministers having certificates. "This meeting desires that the Yearly Meeting Minutes be inspected in relation to those that travel abroad, from or to this city, about having certificates. In the interim care to be had in this city or county that they take notice to mind to speak with any disorderly preachers that may happen among them (or go abroad) in order to reclaim them."

1703. There was a standing appointment of Friends of the different Monthly Meetings of such as "are free to accompany public Friends out of Town."

1695. A minute is made discountenancing "separatist preachers coming amongst us."

1699. Advice is issued against "overcrowding of Ships."

1700. Thomas Lewis, a young man bred to the law, and slighted by his relatives, to be employed to draw the leases, &c.

It would seem as if the Six-Weeks Meeting was regarded as a court of appeal in *pecuniary* matters later than on other subjects.

Thus, when a difference had arisen between Bull and Mouth and the Women's Meeting about the possession of "276 ounces of weighty money," sent from Jamaica, the case was thus settled by the Six-Weeks Meeting, 30th of Sixth Month, 1720. "Now this meeting being the last resort for differences between the six monthly meetings of this city, relating to Legacies for the Poor, are of opinion that the Bull and Mouth Monthly Meeting in so doing, do act out of unity with this meeting, and in opposition to the ancient practise the Monthly Meeting of this city."

In 1735 some action was taken respecting residence of Friends in one meeting who were members of another. "All such Friends to desire a recommendation to Monthly Meeting they reside in; and in default for 6 months after they are removed, the Monthly Meeting in which they reside authorised to demand a recommendation from the Monthly Meeting he, she, or they did belong to." In this year commence, however, signs that the Six-Weeks Meeting is no longer a court of final appeal, as it has itself to come before the Quarterly Meeting in a case where Westminster Monthly Meeting has declined to abide by its decision in respect of some widows' children. Westminster had eventually to acknowledge itself in the wrong. But three years afterwards another appeal had to be sustained as against Peel, which yet further shows the declining influence of the Six-Weeks Meeting.

Nevertheless, so late as 1741, the meeting was applied to as an arbitrator, to settle a case of four years' standing (respecting the poor) between Devonshire House and Peel.

1748. Had to testify against a disorderly marriage where two Friends came in to one of the meeting-houses on a First-day, and, at the close of the meeting, without having passed through any preliminaries, stood up and declared that they took one another in marriage, some friend reading a certificate for them.

1749. Issues advice to Monthly Meetings that they arrange for "sober women Friends" to attend them.

Delinquency.

Inasmuch as it was one of the duties of the Six-Weeks Meeting, which it exercised so late as the year 1825, to record any testimony of denial or disownment, whenever issued by any of the London Monthly Meetings, and till 1796 to circulate copies of the same amongst all the other metropolitan meetings, we have thereby a means of forming an approximate idea of the state of the Society in London at various epochs, as shown by the disownments.

From the first general Rules or Canons of the Society (p. 95, *ante*), issued about 1668, and signed G. F., copies of which are to be found in the Records of the Six-Weeks Meetings, and also in the books of most of the London Monthly Meetings, it is evident that even in the times of its primitive fervour, the Society numbered amongst its members many who, whilst "professing truth," were far from evidencing the possession of "truth" in their daily lives and conversations. Even at the early date referred to, "such as walk not in the truth, or have been convinced and gone from truth"; those "that profess the truth and follows pleasures, drunkenness, gaming, or is not faithful in their callings and dealings"; also "evil speakers, backbiters, foolish speakers, idle jesters, talebearers, and railers," are mentioned as to be laboured with, and, if not repentant, testified against.

There is sufficient evidence to show that these advices were not merely precautionary, but were called forth by the circumstances of the hour. But whilst such evils were not unknown amongst those who had joined Friends at the beginning on the ground of convincement, they became still more conspicuous when the children of the first convinced began to be numbered in the ranks of the Society.

George Fox had much trouble with that second generation. He had to complain to Friends of their showing less care over their children "than when you were in the form of a profession." The leaving of the young and inexperienced to their *own convictions* had been wrongly interpreted by many, and had brought about results not anticipated. G. F. strongly rebukes the "lightness and frothiness" of the youth, which he says is so great, "that when they are set to apprentices, or places, many times they run into worse things than the world."

Strenuous exertions were no doubt made by the faithful leaders and teachers of the Church to stem the advancing tide of declension. But whilst membership was undefined, the task was found impossible. For more than half a century matters grew gradually worse, till the Churches began to make out definite lists of their members,* and active measures were subsequently taken to purify the camp. The settlement of membership in itself dissevered many who had hitherto been looked upon as Quakers; and out of those who were registered as Church members, many more were afterwards disowned by the six London Meetings for their disorderly conduct, as is more plainly shown in the annexed table, which illustrates the action of the discipline at this middle period of the Society's existence.

TABLE OF DISOWNMENTS AND RESIGNATIONS IN THE SIX LONDON MONTHLY MEETINGS, ARRANGED IN PERIODS OF FIVE YEARS, FROM 1735 TO 1824.

	Immorality.	Disorderly Conduct, Drinking, Gaming, &c. &c.	Bankruptcy and Fraud.	Marriage by a Priest, &c.	Oaths, Tithes, War, Inconsistency, Absence from Meetings, &c. &c.	Resignations of Membership.	Total.
1735 to 1739	...	2	...	...	...	...	2
1744	2	1	2	8	2	...	16
1749	1	7	1	8	...	...	17
1754	4	9	8	10	2	...	32
1759	5	13	6	13	6	...	43
1764	13	37	8	44	8	...	113
1769	17	29	19	63	4	...	132
1774	9	31	9	55	10	2	116
1779	13	15	14	37	11	7	97
1784	15	35	20	65	21	10	166
1789	19	29	17	91	24	21	201
1794	12	9	12	47	37	8	125
1799†			152			3	155
1804			132			2	134
1809			154			2	156
1814			132			8	140
1819			130			14	144
1824			123			30	153
							1,943

* In accordance with the Rules of Settlement, Yearly Meeting 1737.
† After 1794 disownments are simply recorded by the Six-Weeks Meeting without assigning cause.

After 1796 the Six-Weeks Meeting was relieved from the duty it had discharged of circulating copies of disownment, &c. among the Monthly Meetings; and in consequence, it was in future only informed of the fact of one being issued without stating the cause, so that no distinction is made in the above table after that date. In 1825 it ceased to take cognisance of disownments in any way.

Up to about 1780, or after, most of the cases of marriage by a priest were also in connection with disorderly conduct, frequently of a gross character. Many of the earliest bankruptcy cases are also ascribed to excess in drinking, and similar causes.

A large proportion of the disownments were for crimes and offences not often heard of at this day amongst us, and all of them, be it remembered, were gross or unpenitent cases. Many others, equally guilty, were, by the exercise of patient labour, led to repentance and renewal of life. And here, again, we are reminded of George Fox's Rules (already quoted from), in which he directs, "and all those before any of them be left as heathens, or written against, let them be three or four times gone to, that they may have Gospel order, so that if it be possible, they may come to that which did at the first convince them, to condemn their unrighteousness."

Meetings for Worship and Discipline.

It was only natural that the "prime meeting of the city" should exercise some degree of care over all other meetings established in London, and this was even extended towards arrangements for the Yearly Meeting itself. Thus, in 1681, we read, "It is agreed that Ellis Hookes do signify to the next Quarterly Meeting the desire of this meeting that *only those twelve persons* that are appointed by the Monthly Meetings do attend the Yearly Meeting, and that others forbear, that there be no example given for people that has no business to obstruct the affairs of those meetings."

As regards the right maintenance of the meetings for worship in the Metropolis, the Six-Weeks Meeting was frequently exercised, though their burden in this respect was shared by the "Morning Meeting" of men ministers.

From the advices of George Fox we find that he desired that meetings should begin "between the tenth and eleventh hour when the priest and his company are over their dishes and pleasures, and to break up your meetings as you feel the power about the third or fourth hour,"—"this was the practice of Friends at the beginning, therefore continue in it, and do not lose it." In the same document (we quote as before from the Six-Weeks Meeting records) he exhorts against "sottishness and dullness, and sleeping in meetings, for it were a shame for the priest and his company to come in and see you sit nodding."

From time to time, whilst the matter continued in their province, the Six-Weeks Meeting issued its advices with reference to the proper maintenance of the various meetings for worship in London. We subjoin two examples :—

In 1678 they complain of the young men crowding in upon women Friends under the gallery, and request them not to sit on that side, and order a form to be made to prevent them.

Further arrangements in this respect seemed necessary, for, under date 10th of Seventh Month, 1678, " E. Hookes to draw up a paper of Friends' advice and exhortation to Friends in general, that the women do sit on one side of the meeting-place, apart from the men."

In 1684 it is recommended that after meetings, " Friends stand not about the door, or in the street, talking, but immediately pass away."

The meetings known as " Retired Meetings" are mentioned. Thus, in 1688, an appointment was made " to enquire for a convenient place between Bishopsgate and Tower Hill for Friends to meet in more retiredly, and report it to the Second-day's Morning Meeting, who are to do in it as they see meet." Notice is also made at this time of the week-day meetings being at two in the afternoon.

In 1692 it was held needful " to stir up Friends to diligence in attending week-day meetings."

1698. Retired meetings mentioned at Southwark and Devonshire House at three in the afternoon, and " upstairs " at Gracechurch Street and Ratcliff, at eight o'clock in the morning.

1703. It is evident the women's meetings were not attended so well as formerly. " It is agreed by this meeting that a few lines be drawn up and sent to the women's meeting and to the several Monthly Meetings in and about the city, that the antient women may be desired to visit the young faithful women, and stir them up to frequent the Monthly

Meetings and the women's meetings, and encouraged in their service, and employed therein,—and the Friends employed in the said meetings and the business not to be kept among a few antient women Friends." Ten years further, and matters do not seem to have improved, for, in

1713, a minute from the women's meeting, "intreating" the Six-Weeks Meeting's "advice and assistance, so that their meeting may be better attended." A paper was in consequence prepared and sent round to the several Monthly Meetings.

1740. Monthly Meetings were requested to appoint suitable friends to sit in the galleries with the ministers.

Friends in the Ministry, and Care of their Horses.

Although Friends in the ministry or "Public Friends," as they were called in the early days of our Society, had their own assembly known as the Second-day's Morning Meeting, which commenced in the house of Gerrard Roberts, in which they took charge of such Church affairs as were connected with their own office and calling, and arranged for the distribution of ministers amongst the London meetings,—yet for travelling and other expenses when engaged in active service in London they were dependent upon the Six-Weeks Meeting.

The wants of country ministers labouring in or passing through London were carefully attended to during their stay in town; sums of money for their benefit being handed to certain Friends by the Meeting of Twelve, "*without requiring an account.*" But it is evident that these visitors were chiefly dependent on the hospitality of individuals. At a later period, viz. in 1736, we find the Six-Weeks Meeting lamenting that "many of our ancient friends who used to entertain ministering friends when they came to visit us in this city are very much worn off by death, and some (*i.e.* ministers) have been to seek for a place of entertainment."

But though many merchants and tradesmen could entertain the ministers, few, if any, could accommodate the horses, which formed the usual means of transit in those times. A committee of six Friends was accordingly set apart to take charge of these, and the stabling and provender thus required formed a considerable annual item in the accounts of the Meeting of Twelve.

It is curious to observe, in connection with these horses,

notices of Friends as innkeepers in the days of primitive Quakerism. Thus, in 1674, "The stables of the Castle and Falcon are reported as suitable for Friends' horses, the hostess being a Friend." In 1680, "John Netherwood has taken the Cock Inn, and desires encouragement from Friends travelling." In 1682 an appointment is made "to give notice to Friends in the country that the Friend at the Falcon is deceased, and that the Friend at the Platter can accommodate them." In 1701, "Richard Cooke has given up inn-keeping, and a stable and man are to be sought."

After the establishment of the Friends' Workhouse in Clerkenwell, the stables of that Institution were made use of for the horses of ministers visiting London.

1702. As a reason of debit is noted : "Friends' horse-bills very great and chargeable, and that we reckon several that are capable of paying for their own horses are charged therein ; some whereof not concerned in the ministry."

In 1703 stables at the workhouse were fitted up for the Friends' horses.

In 1706 a Friend gives a horse, saddle, and bridle, and £10 towards keep of the horse, for use of public Friends.

1708. Renewed complaint about horse-bills. 10d. per night at grass, or 14d., with hay and corn, is considered 2d. too much. At this time the bills for horse-keep were about £90 a year. Directions now given to shift the brown horse from the workhouse to the Ship Inn, Southwark, at request of Friends there.

Not only did the Six-Weeks Meeting take care of the horses of those "Public Friends" who had them, but occasionally supplied those who had not.

In 1713 the meeting spent £6 in buying a mare, the said mare being for the general use of "Public Friends" visiting the outlying meetings, &c. In the following year another mare was presented for the same object. On one occasion, in 1709, a sum was voted to purchase a horse for a "Public Friend," who, by some mischance, had lost his own, but "it was not to exceed £5."

Some years elapse without notices of horses occurring on the minutes, and it would seem as if attention on this head had declined, for, in 1722, complaint is made of public Friends visiting distant meetings beyond a walk, but seldom owing to want of horses. Authority given to provide them when needful.

Marriages.

The marriages of early Friends in London were, as we have stated, solemnised under the joint care of the Two-Weeks and Monthly Meetings. But the Six-Weeks Meeting often gave its advice and counsel as to the right ordering of these important events.

In the rules of 1668, George Fox enjoins that, at the marriage ceremony, "not less than a dozen friends and relations be present." It was long before the practice of marrying at the established week-day meetings only came into vogue. Marriages were very frequent about the close of the seventeenth century, and the Six-Weeks Meeting found it desirable to instruct the Two-Weeks Meeting "not to permit more than two marriages to take place at one time and place." In 1691 the latter body was advised "to give due notice of time and place, and not confine the marriages to one day in the week."

The above are matters of arrangement, but the Six-Weeks Meeting was also careful as to the order observed on these occasions. In 1672 a paper was issued against such young men and young women as intending a marriage do go and dwell or lodge in one house together before the matter of marriage is approved by Friends. In 1683 they were troubled about disorderly crowdings and inconveniences, "through bringing wine into rooms near the meeting-house at marriages," and "Friends are advised wholly to discontinue that practice." In 1700 the Monthly Meetings are directed to appoint "ancient Friends to attend the marriages to prevent disorders." These appointed Friends were not merely to witness the ceremony, but to be present with the wedding party until the guests separated.

The following, in 1672, reads quaintly :—

"Upon consideration of the matter proposed by Rebecca Travers touching a couple who formerly propounded a marriage among Friends, and between them such discontent being arisen betwixt them as to the allianating their affections, &c.," a committee was appointed, and at next meeting report made that the woman's affections were engaged to another even whilst betrothed to this man—that she had been admonished and reproved, and told that, as they had bound themselves, Friends could not release her. The man said he intended "not to look for another till she was married or laid down the body," and Friends record satisfaction " in great measure as to his part."

In cases of difficulty George Fox would seem to have been consulted, thus:—1673. "Agreed that the matter now proposed by Rebecca Travers and Ann Whitehead touching marriages be taken into consideration next meeting, and that in the interim dear G. F. be conferred with."

1674. Rules issued for marriages when parties members of different meetings.

1688. "Attenders at Marriages and inviters to Burials and gravemakers not to be over-craving and receiving too much money of persons relating thereto; not to receive more than 2s. each for inviting to burials,* and their attendance about the same, and one shilling for making a grave; and for attending at a marriage and cleaning the room one shilling."

1731. A Testimony is issued against a Friend for his unwarrantable marriage with his deceased wife's sister.

Care of the Poor, &c.

The care of the poor in the Society in London appertained to each particular Monthly Meeting. But a joint action was early taken as regards the payment of their rent (chiefly widows') and the supply of coals, also as to those called "Casual Poor." The free rent-roll for all the London meetings was under the care of "the Women's Meeting," and the autograph receipts of Ann Whitehead, Mary Elson, Grace Bathurst, and others, are still extant for the £30 or £40 expended quarterly for this purpose only.

In the rules of 1668 George Fox had directed that there should be "no beggar in the church," that "nothing be lacking, according to the Apostle's words," and meetings were to help each other if any meeting was overburdened with its poor. It became the duty of the Six-Weeks Meeting to see that the Monthly Meetings did not fall short of their duty in these respects. In 1677 we find them ordering a poor-box to be put up at Devonshire House, and another at the Bull and Mouth. In 1679 they decided that no relief for

---

* The employment of bidders to funerals was an old English custom, and is still in vogue in Holland, instead of the modern plan of sending letters or memorial cards.

K

poor Friends should be received from the parish. Shortly afterwards they decided that " poor persons professing Truth, but not owned by any Monthly Meeting, should be relieved."

This free charity in some cases paved the way for imposition. About 1668 George Fox had declared against " all such as goes up and down to cheat by borrowing and getting money of Friends in by-places, and have cheated several; all such are to be stopped and judged, as there is a woman tall in her person and freckled in her face, and also one John Harding, who are for judgment and to be condemned." The Six-Weeks Meeting, in its watchful care for the interests of the Churches, had occasionally to caution them in a similar manner to the above.

1701. Settled that a residence of two years if married, and three years if single, was to confer a settlement in a Monthly Meeting. In connection with a care over the poor was that desire to find some employment for them, which ultimately led to the establishment of a workhouse; and of this a separate account is hereafter given. But as early as 1676 minute is made that it is proposed to employ the poor in spinning, and the Meeting of Twelve were directed to provide £100 out of Annuities money in their hands to buy flax to employ poor Friends in spinning; one person in each Monthly Meeting to receive the flax and dispense it to spinners and pay them, and deliver it to the weavers. Two years after, it was found necessary to have some superintendent, and one Margery Brown is appointed to sort the flax, oversee the spinners, and direct them in their work.

The mentally afflicted were another object of care. As early as 1673 we read of a " John Goodson offering to the meeting to take a large house for distempered and discomposed persons." This Friend was a surgeon, and seems to have settled in the quiet locality of Bartholomew Close.

But not only towards the poor and afflicted in their own borders were the sympathies of London Friends drawn out. By the continuous sufferings of early times their hearts had been brought into fellow feeling with their brethren all over the world. Thus we find the Six-Weeks Meeting frequently voting money, or ordering collections for Friends and others in various counties, sufferers from oppression, fire, flood, loss of cattle, &c., and also according liberal grants from time to time to Friends in Holland, Friends in Holstein, captive Friends in Algiers, &c. In 1668, in the accounts, we find physic for the German, £2 10s. 6d. ; and again, for the German's clothes, £2 17s. 0d. In 1677, £120 was raised for Friends suffering at Dantzig, Emden, and Holstein ; also certain moneys for release of " captives at Sally." Captives' money amounted to quite a fund, from which notices are frequent of sums having been borrowed. In 1679 a committee was appointed for release of captives in Algiers, to meet with the Meeting for Sufferings from day to day, and attend to the business. We may remark, in passing, that at one time Friends in captivity in Algiers were so numerous as to hold a meeting there, and epistles were received from them. 1679, £60 to John Lodge, in Amsterdam, for a " present supply to the sufferers—more to follow." 1706, Woman Friend in distress assisted back to Pennsylvania.

Furthermore, Friends had compassion on the stranger within their gates. A Dane (recommended by W. Penn), a Spaniard, a Silesian widow, and others, are examples of this class of recipients, who, as " casual poor," were relieved by the Six-Weeks Meeting. And, as a further illustration of the wide sympathies of Friends, we may cite the following minute made in 1693 :—

"Friends having under their consideration the poor condition of the Pietists now in England, about forty, the Friends undernamed are desired to draw up a few lines to be read in the public meetings at the conclusion thereof next First-day, for a collection towards their relief, viz. George Whitehead and John Vaughton, and the friends that are free to visit them and sit with them are Wm. Mead, Theodore Eccleston, John Vaughton, Gilbert Latey, or any others."

Education.

One of the subjects that early claimed the care of the meeting was education. Thus, two years after its establishment, occurs, under date Second Month, 1674, proposal to erect a school for teaching poor Friends' children gratis, which being unanimously agreed to, a committee was appointed to carry it out. The master was to be one well skilled in Latin, writing, and arithmetic. At a subsequent time, report is made of Richard Richardson (afterwards recording clerk) being chosen ; he is to have " the lower room in Devonshire House, where the meeting is, gratis." Poor Friends' children to be paid for by the Monthly Meetings:

others he is "to agree for as he can, with their parents;" an offer came from the Women's Meeting to bear part of the cost of this education. The master, R. Richardson, was to have £20 a year, each of the six Monthly Meetings to pay £2 a year, and send any poor children gratis. Women's Meeting to pay £8, and send any poor children gratis.

Beginning thus with the poorer class, it would seem that George Fox suggested some arrangements suitable for a somewhat higher, since 11th Third Month, 1675, this minute is found,—"That the proposition made by G. F. touching Wm. Thomlinson setting up a school to teach the languages, together with the nature of herbs, roots, plants, and trees, be taken into consideration the next meeting, as also his fitness, abilities, and qualification for the said employment." Two Friends, Thomas Rudyard and Christopher Taylor, are also appointed "to prepare a book for teaching children at the schools courthand and lawyer's Latin, the better to enable them to read a writ and other law proceedings."

This, no doubt, involved some amount of care, as in 1677 Friends' schoolmasters were requested to meet a Committee of the Meeting, to agree upon a method of teaching Latin, that might prevent differences and reflections for the future. Many Friends had been burdened by the use of some of the heathen authors.

1677. Allusion is found to the school at Shacklewell in the appointment of a committee to go there and treat with the schoolmistress about her school, and to see her, and the result seems to have been a loan of £50, on bond of her furniture, and "women Friends are to try and procure scholars for the school." Each Monthly Meeting having in all cases to pay the cost of education of poor of their own members, no occasion arises after first establishment to bring the subject on the books of the Six-Weeks Meeting.

Miscellaneous.

Examples of the miscellaneous business that came under the notice of a meeting, whose province was so extensive as that of the Six-Weeks Meeting, might, of course, be cited to an almost indefinite extent. One or two will suffice as illustrations.

The Six-Weeks Meeting at one time rented rooms in the Fleet Prison, and afterwards a house in the "liberties," for the accommodation of Friends sent up as prisoners from the country.

In the days of persecution, the Six-Weeks Meeting " requited gaolers," as G. F. advised ; and in securer times we find them invoking the aid of the law on their own account. Twenty pounds was once voted to the city marshal for protecting Friends' Meetings from one or two noisy disturbers of the period ; and on another occasion, fifty-five pounds was paid to the same functionary " for protecting Friends' houses on rejoicing nights."

The following, under date 1680, is a curious instance of quaint shrewdness : —

" It being proposed to this meeting by G. Watts that there is a complaint that Friends do employ some of the world's people in printing and binding of Friends' books, it is upon consideration of this meeting desired and advised that henceforth such as print Friends' books do for the future employ only Friends in printing and binding, provided it be by the said Friends done as well and as reasonably as the world's people will do it."

Our forefathers were evidently alive to the dangers of monopoly, and whilst desirous of helping each other, were not willing to pay too dearly, or be content with an inferior article.

Care over documents was early shown ; thus, in 1672, a minute is sent round to the Monthly Meetings, that " each should procure a chest for its writings, and appoint two caretakers." Minute articles of expenditure were also looked after, *e.g.* in 1684 enquiries are to be made " who ordered the watch and larum," at the chamber, *i.e.* the Recording Clerk's Office, then 3, King Court, Lombard Street.

We have now adverted to most of the points of interest in the business of the Six-Weeks Meeting. But of that which formed a prominent feature of its transactions from the commencement, and its almost exclusive business in modern times, viz. the building and repairing of meeting-houses, and care of burial-grounds, we have said but little, inasmuch as its operations of this character will more properly come under notice in connection with the various meetings referred to in the subsequent chapters of this volume.

CHAPTER IX.

GRACECHURCH STREET MONTHLY MEETING.

Including the Bull and Mouth (or City, or London Meeting, as it was at different times called), also that at White Hart Court, Gracechurch Street, and that at Stoke Newington.

THE records left us of this Monthly Meeting are unfortunately but few, and those which remain do not date back further than the year 1821, in consequence of the destruction in that year of all earlier documents in the fire which burnt down the meeting-house premises in White Hart Court. Such a circumstance is the more to be regretted as the former importance and early origin of this meeting would have made its records highly illustrative of the rise and progress of the Society in London as containing information which cannot be thoroughly supplied from other documents.

It follows that what is to be noted of these meetings must be gathered from other sources, and for this purpose use will be made of early letters as given in Barclay's series, and the records of sufferings, still preserved at Devonshire House and epitomised by Besse.

BULL AND MOUTH, OR CITY, OR LONDON MEETING.

When Francis Howgill, Edward Burrough, and others of the early preachers in the Society of Friends, found that in London a "great and effectual door" was opened for their ministry, it became with them an earnest desire to secure some place of public assembly capable of holding a large congregation, where they might proclaim their message more widely than the meetings held in Friends' houses and other places would admit of. For this purpose the premises known as the Bull and Mouth, in Aldersgate Street, were taken within some six months (as we learn by the Letters) of F. H. and E. B.'s coming to London.

The meeting-place thus taken formed part of an ancient Inn

or Hostelry, known by the sign of the Bull and Mouth, in Aldersgate Street; the room is described as holding 1,000 persons, though that probably meant "standing," inasmuch as forms for sitting were not anywhere much used at first; over it were other rooms which Friends either sub-let or used for various purposes.

The situation of the place is well known, though all traces of the building have disappeared amid the many changes and rebuildings that have occurred. To find it, a visitor must place himself at the north-east corner of the General Post Office, in St. Martin's le Grand, when he will see nearly opposite to him the Queen's Hotel quite a modern building, but still having on its front a carving of a Bull standing in an open mouth,* that shows such was formerly the sign of the Inn. Crossing over, and passing down the narrow thoroughfare on its northern side, still known as Bull and Mouth Street, the visitor can enter through some carriage gates at the back of the hotel, where he will find himself in a large yard, in the occupation of railway carriers and surrounded with sheds for storage of their goods. As he looks around on the busy and crowded scene, he may be sure he is upon the site of the former meeting-place, though unable now to define its exact form or position.

The spot is one that must always have been somewhat retired from the public thoroughfare, yet conveniently situated for access and within a short distance of the old cathedral where so many scenes of stirring interest went forward; thus whilst sheltered it was not a secluded place.

It was taken, as has been mentioned, in 1654, and a meeting was regularly held there (or else in the street adjoining, when magistrates had boarded up its doors), until the building itself was destroyed in the Great Fire of 1666. On its being rebuilt, a tenancy by Friends was resumed until the year 1740, when it was decided to relinquish it, since which time the premises have been used as a carrier's yard, long retaining, even amid the change of occupation, the shell of the building erected by Friends; but now even this has thoroughly gone amid adaptations for increased requirements of the modern carrying system.

Here, amid crowded congregations of eager and vociferous

---

* Underneath this sign as a motto is, "Milon, the Crotonian, slew an Ox with his Fist, and eat it up at a single meal."

disputants, the early preachers were to be found, gaining adherents from the heterogeneous mass of human beings around them. Here would often burst in the "rude multitude and wild savage apprentices," raising scenes of uproar, that put all the physical, mental, and spiritual powers of the preacher to the fullest stretch; even a George Fox (strong at all points) finding himself at times spent among them.* But here also, amid these difficulties, the divine power by which they were animated, rose into dominion, and, upborne through it to the wonder and astonishment of their friends, the early preachers succeeded in bringing down disorder, subduing opposition, and converting meetings, that commenced in wrangling and confusion, into times of earnest listening and deep conviction.

In the commencement of the work thus carried on by Friends in the Bull and Mouth Meeting-place, none were permitted to have more successful share than Edward Burrough, whose lot it often was there to confront the noisy and rude London crowds. "Bold," as Ellwood says, "in his Master's cause," this north country youth, not yet come to man's estate, would fearlessly arise among them, and drawing forth a Bible, begin in a loud and powerful voice to pour forth such full and eloquent discourse, as arrested the attention of disputants, and withal changing, as he found order and attention secured, to such heart-melting and tender appeals as made him a "son of consolation," as well as "a son of thunder." He himself called this meeting-place a threshing-floor, and a rich harvest of convinced people soon arose to bear witness to the successful "ploughing and threshing" carried on there by himself and the other early preachers.

Thus contending at first with conflicting elements, order was gradually secured, and large and "heavenly" meetings were maintained throughout the thirteen years of the Commonwealth, and also during the first six months after Charles II. had returned to the throne, during all which time Friends of the Bull and Mouth Meeting had experienced, as a body, no interference from legal authorities, but shared only as individuals in the prosecutions for non-payment of tithes and other causes, and on the whole their difficulties during the

---

* Barclay's "*Letters*," p. 27, "G. F. was at the great meeting-place two First-days before we came; and his voice and outward man was almost spent amongst them."

Commonwealth were chiefly from opponents of other sects. Like other Nonconformists they hoped for continued permission, and even fuller liberty from the newly-restored King, whose message when in exile had been so full of promise for liberty of conscience to all.

The time of this liberty had, however, not yet arrived, and the congregation of the Bull and Mouth were to experience their full share of suffering under the vigorous attempts which were made in the name and by the power of the law to put down all other modes of worship than those of the Anglican Church. For such harsh measures an excuse was found in the fear of Papists on the one hand, and wild enthusiastic Republicans on the other, each plotting under the guise of religion against the Government, and it wanted but a spark to set the whole ruling powers ablaze in a crusade against all nonconformity to the Church as now by law re-established. This exciting cause arose from the mad conduct of some Fifth-Monarchy men, who, on the 6th January, 1660, some eight months after Charles's accession, issued from their chapel in Coleman Street, armed, and crying out, "Down with King Charles, for King Jesus is come to reign!" One Venner, their preacher, a cooper by trade, was the leader of the band, which numbered only fifty or sixty, but they fought with such desperation as to rout the train-bands the Lord Mayor (Sir Richard Brown) had led against them. Retiring for the night to Hampstead, they were attacked next day by a troop of horse; but rallied again the day after, and re-entering London, engaged in an obstinate conflict in the streets, but were at last defeated. Venner—wounded and taken prisoner—was, with eleven companions, executed. A Royal Proclamation against the meetings of all Dissenters was issued in 1660, and before three months had elapsed, its evil effects were shown in the imprisonment of nearly 400 Friends, mostly taken at different times from the Bull and Mouth Meeting, all of them quiet and peaceable tradesmen, or householders, yet deprived of their liberty, and shut up with felons in the then filthy gaol of Newgate, and all for no other crime than because it had pleased the King and Council to proclaim as illegal their assembling together for worship. In this common gaol they were crowded in defiance alike of health and decency—more than a hundred in a room—producing a closeness which soon developed mortal sickness among them.

The chief agent in this persecution against the Bull and Mouth Meeting, was Alderman Brown, who lived close by in Ivy Lane, and being now entered on the office of Lord Mayor, was showing a zeal for King and Church which contrasted strongly with his former Presbyterian views, and caused much suffering to his fellow Nonconformists. Being charged (as chief magistrate of the city) with the execution of the King's Proclamation, he broke up all conventicles, but seemed to lay his hand with relentless force on this particular one, that met so near his doors. To any plea for mercy his language was coarse even in that age. An instance may be given. The wife of one Nicholas Ridley had been sent by his orders to Bridewell prison, and had there fallen ill. Nicholas appeared before the Lord Mayor, and stating his wife's case, pleaded for her release. "Let her die and rot," said this heartless magistrate, "thee mayst get another wife the sooner." Even the sight of a Quaker seemed to awaken his rage. "Art thou a Quaker?" said he one day to Philip Harwood. "They call me one," replied Philip, and forthwith he was seized and sent to Newgate, and lay there for three months. For merely not taking off their hats to him in the street, he would send Friends to Newgate. In one such instance the offenders were two, who, having come up some seventy miles out of the country, were quietly transacting their business in the open market, when, for not lifting their caps (as the Mayor rode by), he had them imprisoned in Newgate, when they owed their release, after a fortnight, merely to his term of office having expired. Such allusions to the personal character of Alderman Brown seem needful to understand how, when armed with powers greater than a Royal Proclamation, a man of his temper would relentlessly inflict the penalties any Act of Parliament might impose.

The first so-called Conventicle Act which succeeded to this Royal Proclamation passed the Legislature in 1662, and being especially directed against the "Quakers" on account of the "Mischiefs and Dangers" apprehended from them, they soon felt the force of its penalties; these were those of fine or imprisonment arranged on a graduating scale, according to the number of times a person was convicted, and the enforcement of them was left to the jurisdiction of the Justices of the Peace, of whom, in London, Alderman Brown, in virtue of his official position there, would be one. He was now foremost in a systematic effort to rid the city of these assemblies, and for months in succession the record as to the Bull and Mouth becomes monotonous in its statement of unsparing cruelty toward the worshippers there, and especially of Alderman Brown's personal brutality to them—even his own train-bands sickened of the work, in thus disturbing Sabbath after Sabbath a congregation who, as they said, had such "good honest countenances;" one soldier confessed that he knew in doing it " he was serving the devil." But the Alderman's zeal knew neither scruple nor bounds, and when he found personal violence, or fine, or imprisonment alike unavailing to keep Friends from meeting, he had the door itself covered over with thick strong-nailed planks. But even then they met in the street, and whilst doing so he had a personal adventure with them which neither reflected credit on his character as a gentleman nor a rider. He was one First-day morning returning on horseback, accompanied by the sheriffs, from attending service at the cathedral, when he encountered the Friends (whom his thick planks kept out of their meeting-place) quietly assembled in the street. Enraged at the sight he charged in among them, and knocking some over spurred his horse to trample them when on the ground; but the animal, more merciful than its master, refusing, reared up so straight as to let the Alderman slip off into the gutter, when the sheriffs, as if ashamed of his conduct, led him away. Under this first legal persecution for attending Friends' meetings many hundred Friends of London suffered imprisonment in Newgate, and among these, as before mentioned, was Edward Burrough. He had been among the most active of those who laboured with the House of Commons during the time the bill was under discussion, and was one of the four Friends* permitted to plead against it at the bar of the house. Though absent from London at the time the act came into operation, he declined thus to escape, and knowing how strongly the storm would break out there under the management of Alderman Brown, he quickly returned; was arrested by that magistrate at the Bull and Mouth, and formed thenceforward one of the crowded band in the filthy Newgate, soon falling ill from its pestilential atmosphere, and dying there as a martyr rather than violate his religious convictions.

After two years' trial of the working of this first Conventicle Act it was thought fit to have a second one passed, whereby

---

* Edward Burrough, Richard Hubberthorne, Edward Pyot, and George Whitehead; the two first died under its provisions.

fuller powers were given and heavier penalties provided, even to transportation for a third conviction; notwithstanding which, no better result was obtained in suppressing Friends' meetings all over the country, and the Bull and Mouth one was also regularly held, for the Friends felt themselves bound to obey a power higher than any human law, and preferred to suffer rather than forego the duty and privilege of "assembling together." It would be interesting to learn, if we could, how far Friends in these trials were but as fellow sufferers with other bodies of Nonconformists; but it seems as if these were not so concerned to gather together in any number when the Parliament had made such assembling illegal; for Skeats, in his "History of the Free Churches," speaking of this time, says, p. 76, "Many Presbyterians took refuge in the 'Church.' . . The Independents and Baptists gave up their meetings or met by stealth." If again we search Neale's "History of the Puritans," we fail to discover instances of congregational suffering such as Friends now underwent. The records of other Nonconformist sufferings refer rather to those of the minister than his congregation—2,000 of these, as is well known, vacated their livings rather than conform, and in almost every gaol was some Baptist or Independent minister confined, like Bunyan, during long-continued periods; but here, in their case, the persecution stayed without extending to the general congregation, for these, on the smiting of the shepherd, mostly became dispersed as a flock; some London Nonconformist congregations "nestled," as a writer in the *British Quarterly* observes, "under the protection of the City Companies, secure from all parochial molestation within the boundary walls, which girdled in their halls and quaint gardens." But the more we examine into such histories as are extant, the more "peculiar" becomes that persistent assembling which Friends suffered so much to maintain. Neale, before quoted, speaks (vol iv. p. 378) of Nonconformists going "openly and boldly to their meetings," as a sign of less stress of persecution in 1667 (on the fall of Earl Clarendon); is it not fair then to doubt whether *they* went openly and publicly during it, which we find the Friends persevered in doing?*

---

* "The behaviour of the Quakers was very extraordinary, and had something in it that looked like the spirit of martyrdom."—*Neal's History of the Puritans*, vol. ii. pp. 673—676.

Throughout the first four years of this storm the Bull and Mouth Meeting was regularly held, so was it also through that succeeding trial, greater even than persecution, which the ravages of pestilence caused—that Great Plague of 1665, when citizens were dying at the rate of forty to fifty an hour, and the weekly bill of mortality swelled to six or seven thousand a week. All through Friends kept their meetings; but to this scourge under which (as George Whitehead says) good and bad alike perished, succeeded a disaster before which the meeting was obliged to leave, for its premises were utterly destroyed in the Great Fire of 1666, when the cathedral itself also perished.

Looking back on this first attempt by law to suppress Friends' meetings, as begun under the Royal Proclamation, and continued under the two first Conventical Acts, and revering, as we cannot but do, the zeal and constancy with which so much oppression and cruelty was endured, we are bound to admit that the congregation had in it elements of a ruder nature than are to be found in this more civilised day. Thus it will be found, if Besse's Sufferings are consulted, that several cases are mentioned by him, whereby expression was given to feelings in a manner which, in the present time, and to our ideas of propriety, seems extravagant and fanatical. Thus, for instance, we read of two women entering St. Paul's Cathedral during time of worship, their back hair down, and so saturated with blood placed upon it, as to wet the pavement of the church as they walked along. In this state they approached even to the altar, on which they poured blood, and uttered some words in doing so. All which, if taken by itself, seems like religious feeling worked up to that pitch which becomes ranting or fanatical, and may have been so in these particular women, but the body must not be judged for the acts of individuals; and even these women are entitled to have the circumstances under which they acted fully considered, when any judgment is passed on their conduct. Now, in their eyes, there is no doubt the place, though a cathedral, had no sacredness, and only two years before it had been considered as but a common place by the citizens; moreover, the provocation had been great through the brutal conduct of persecutors, by whom blood had been freely drawn from innocent people, even women and children; and some had been beaten so as to cause death. Take, for example, a case that had occurred just before at the Bull and Mouth, which was near this cathedral, where the Mayor worshipped. He had himself entered the meeting-place, after Friends had been sitting there two hours, and were just preparing to go; but he caused the door to be locked, and with his men began so to beat, strike and wound, that six or eight were soon drawn out and laid on the ground half dead. The neighbours now came and cried out shame, and well they might, for one of the Mayor's officers was laying about him with a cudgel "a yard long," as much "as he could well hold for bigness and weight;" one man was knocked down five times, and another was so beaten that he died ten days after. When such things were done in the name of the King and the Law, and men like Richard Brown placed in command, an official who forgot himself alike of dignity and humanity, "pinched the damsels" and "knocked down women with his fist," surely it is little cause for wonder some such scenes as the two women Friends enacted should occasionally have occurred, even in churches, seeing what disgraceful and even bloody actions were done in the Church's name and for the maintenance of its system. Happily the bishops no longer order human beings to be cudgelled and imprisoned as felons for not coming to church, and we hear no more of such scenes as this defilement of their buildings, nor of men such as Solomon Eccles * going in street and church without his garments, as a sign of impending judgment.

It was not until some five years had elapsed after the Great Fire that Friends resumed their occupation of the Bull and Mouth; and meanwhile another meeting-place in the city had been secured by them, viz. "part of a great house without Bishopsgate, called Devonshire House;" they had also entered into treaty for a piece of land in White Hart Court, on which to build a meeting-house themselves, showing how little persecution had served to slacken their zeal for "meeting together."

In 1671 they were again re-established on the former spot,

---

* *Besse*, vol. i. p. 393.—The said Solomon Eccles, at the time of Bartholomew Fair, passed through with his body naked, and a pan of fire and brimstone burning on his head, calling to the people to repent and remember Sodom... For this he was committed to Bridewell. [Bartholomew Fair was a scene in those days of great wickedness, and whatever may be thought of the propriety of the action, pestilence and fire did fall on the city.]

the premises having been rebuilt, and apparently affording considerable accommodation; for above the meeting-house, capable, as before, of holding 1,000 persons, were rooms in which the elder Friends met to administer the affairs of the Church,* and over these two more storeys, sub-let for the purposes of education to one John Field, a schoolmaster, who kept a school for Friends' children there. John Field's rooms are described in the agreement as being up "two pair of stairs," where were "two chambers, and over them a schoolroom;" and upon the same floor "two other little rooms, one having a chimney in it." Some interruption appears to have occurred in 1685 to Friends' tenancy, for we find in records of the Meeting for Twelve, under date 29th Fourth Month, 1683:—"Friends of this meeting minding that the Quarterly Meeting in course should be at Bull and Mouth, which place at present by authority is made a prisoner, and there being no other meeting to appoint a convenient place at present, it is desired by this meeting that the next Quarterly Meeting be held at Devonshire House."

The lease of twenty years, under which Friends held these premises, having expired in 1691, a fresh term of five years was arranged for at £66 per annum, and when it was expired, some difficulties arising as to a renewal, Friends left the premises, remaining absent from them as long as three years, during which time they obtained the use of the Hall of the Brewers' Company at £35 a year, being allowed for this the "hall, little parlour, music-room, and long gallery," twice a week, on First and Sixth days, and on others, if not wanted by the Brewers' Company. Here also the Six-Weeks Meeting and Two-Weeks Meeting were held.

In 1700 this absence was brought to a termination by agreeing with the proprietors of the Bull and Mouth for a new lease of nineteen years, at a rental reduced to £40 per annum, because an outlay of £200 was needed to put the buildings in repair. The premises were evidently showing signs of weakness, so common to those erected after the fire, and due to the haste with which they were constructed; in this instance, doubts arose as to its security, and in 1703 we find notice of a column being put up for the support of some portion. Nevertheless its radical defects, as a building, did

---

* This is supposed to have been the morning meeting of men ministers, first held at Gerrard Roberts'.

not deter Friends from again renewing the lease, in 1719, for twenty-one years, and at the same annual rent of £40, agreeing also to pay a fine of £210 for this extension of their term. But the structure was now becoming expensive to maintain; notices of defective drains, insecure vaults, and "ruinous gable end," occur, and as the term drew towards its close, probabilities of further expense were so evident, that Friends declined to renew the lease, unless the "Widow Hampson," who owned the property, would remit the fine, in consideration of the outlay required by the state of the premises, and herself undertake the cost of repair. To this the widow would not assent, and as no other terms could be arranged between them, Friends decided to leave the place when the lease expired, which they did, holding their last meeting for worship there on the 15th of Fourth Month, 1740; thus closing in free-will and quietness a meeting which had been maintained for some eighty-six years. Thenceforward the Friends met at the premises in White Hart Court, Gracechurch Street, where also the Six-Weeks Meeting and Women's Box Meeting were transferred; but though the premises were given up, the name of Bull and Mouth was retained as that of the Monthly Meeting for two years after this change, until, in 1742, it was agreed that it should take the title of Gracechurch Street Monthly Meeting.

In a notice remaining of this removal we read of Friends taking away their "seventy-six forms" from the old Bull and Mouth, but they left there traces which long continued to mark their former occupancy; for even after the place had become a carrier's warehouse, and in the memory of those now living, there could be seen the ministers' gallery, suggestive of days of earlier zeal and strangely incongruous with the chests and packages that lay around. It has now quite disappeared, but surely a people more relic-loving than Friends would have taken some means to preserve a memorial of such interest in their early history.

Gracechurch Street, or White Hart Court.

Turning now to the meeting-house whither the Monthly Meeting of the Bull and Mouth was transferred, we find that at the time of this junction in 1740 the premises at White Hart Court had been a long time built.

When the old Bull and Mouth had been destroyed in the

Great Fire, and Friends were uncertain as to obtaining it again, a choice of some fresh locality became needful, and although the want had been to some extent met by taking a part of a large house without Bishopsgate, known as Devonshire House, it was concluded also to build another meeting-house more in the heart of the city, where Friends were then resident in considerable numbers and commencing those trading pursuits in which they were ultimately to become so influential.

A plot of land, formerly occupied by the White Hart Inn, that had been cleared by the fire, was found to be obtainable, and its situation near the junction of Lombard and Gracechurch Streets, with access by passages from both, gave it all the advantage of centrality, whilst its removal behind the houses that lined those streets secured also that quiet so essential to the comfort of a place of worship. The land comprised a space larger than needed for a meeting-place alone, but Gerrard Roberts* and some other Friends took portions of it, and built their own houses there. So that when all was erected, the meeting-house with its committee-rooms and these private houses adjoining—as also some others in the court known as Million Bank Yard, close by (where some other Friends lived, and into which the meeting-house had a door), all these combined, made the place quite a settlement of Friends with the place of worship in their midst. The ground-rent was £46 for the meeting-house and £34 for the houses in the court. Among the Friends thus living around Gracechurch Street Meeting was Isaac Sowle, the bookseller, and his successor Tace Raylton, whose names are so familiar as imprints on the works of early Friends; John Osgood and James Brayne were those who, with Gerrard Roberts, built the houses in White Hart Court (the latter also had the vaults under the meeting-house).

There is some obscurity about the original tenure of the meeting-house premises, and it would seem, so far as the minutes in the Six-Weeks Meeting are a guide, to have been at first only a parole lease by which Gerrard Roberts held them. Other matters were also involved in some degree of uncertainty, for when Gerrard Roberts (who seems to have joined with Friends in taking the place, or to have done so

---

* Up to this time Gerrard Roberts (so hospitable to the early preachers) had lived at the sign of the Fleur-de-Luce, in Little St. Thomas Apostle, where he carried on his trade of a wine-cooper.

L

on their behalf) sent in once an account of taxes and other expenses defrayed by him, the Six-Weeks Meeting could not understand the matter, but agreed that it should be "left to the witness of God in the conscience of Gerrard Roberts." Twenty years after this, in 1688, the interest of this Friend in the property was purchased by the meeting for £60.

After an occupancy of seventy years this first building lease had become expired, and arrangements were made with the Fishmongers' Company, as freeholders, for a renewal of twenty-one years, with the same rent as before of £46 for the meeting-house; but an outlay of £1,000 was needed on the meeting-house, another proof, no doubt, of the unsubstantial style of building after the Fire. The Friends also, at the same time, renewed the lease of the houses, but the rent of these was advanced from £34 to £104. It is interesting to note among the names of those tenanting them at this period (1748), that of [Dr.] John Fothergill,* whose house was rented at £45 per annum. One thousand pounds was now spent (chiefly in repairs) on the meeting-house building.

Twenty-one years afterwards (1760), when this second lease was also expired, a third renewal for the same term and at the same rent (£46) was obtained from the company, who, however, required a further outlay of some £400 to be made on the property (the lease for the houses was not now renewed by Friends).

Seven years before the term of this third lease was concluded, Friends had become desirous for an enlargement and reconstruction of the premises and had bought a house in Nag's Head Court adjoining. Coming now to their landlords, they received from the company permission to surrender the remainder of their lease, and to take a new one on a building term of ninety-two years, without any increase in the rent of £46; for this they agreed so to enlarge, alter, and renew the old building erected after the Fire, as to make it equivalent to a rebuilding, in which work some £2,000 was spent; and they hoped it might not only serve the purposes of the Friends meeting there, but also be suitable for the accommodation of the Yearly Meeting. But this meeting not finding these enlargements gave to it the space required, and learning some few years afterwards that it could purchase the Dolphin Inn, in Bishops-

---

* For some further particulars of this Friend, see account of Westminster Meeting.

gate, concluded to acquire that property; where it built the large meeting-houses and gradually formed the extensive premises it now occupies there.

Reverting to the premises in White Hart Court, thus rebuilt by Friends in 1774, and leased to them for a term of ninety-two years, it so occurred that they did not last out the period of this fourth lease; for after standing some forty-seven years, they were totally destroyed by a fire that broke out in some adjoining premises on the morning of First-day, 9th September, 1821. Not only the building and all its appurtenances were razed to the ground, but some lives were lost, and also the books, records, parchments, and papers of the Monthly Meeting; these last were the more to be regretted as they comprised those of the old Bull and Mouth Meeting, and many other early documents; amongst them a MS. Journal of "remarkable passages" connected with Bull and Mouth and Gracechurch Street Meetings, a MS. Journal of Claude Gay (a native of Jersey, and one who travelled on the continent as a minister before Sarah Grubb and Lewis Dillwyn's visit), also a black-letter Bible (Luther's) which had been presented by George Fox to the Women's Box Meeting, and many other documents curious in themselves, and valuable as illustrating the Society's history.

So far as any loss on the building was concerned, this was lessened by the insurance; and Friends were able to effect an arrangement with the Fishmongers' Company on favourable terms; whereby, on condition of giving up to the company some adjoining property which they possessed, and re-building a larger meeting-house, an extension of fifty years was to be added to the former building lease, and the rent for this additional fifty years to be £50 per annum. The company also showed their courtesy to Friends by permitting them to make use of their hall during the re-building, and there are those yet living who will remember gathering First-day after First-day in that place, surrounded with the pictures and heraldic devices so common in the halls of the City Companies, and not unfrequently is yet to be heard the anecdote, how on one of these occasions a venerable and respected Friend* of the meeting rose with the words of the city motto as his text, "Domine Dirige Nos."

The meeting-house when rebuilt was large and had a some-

---

* John Lister.

what imposing appearance; round three of its sides were galleries sustained on pillars, and as the only light it received was from above through one lanthorn in the ceiling, this feature became its most prominent characteristic. It was one that occasioned anxiety and great exercise of skill before a thorough balance was obtained for its support by the timbers of the roof instead of any columns from below.

This new building, being the third constructed by Friends since their tenancy had commenced, was completed in 1822, and cost about £4,000; but, like its predecessors, was not destined to last to the end of the building lease under which it was granted, as will now be explained.

The practice of suburban residence began to prevail soon after its re-erection, and in about ten years' time Stoke Newington Meeting-house was built, chiefly by members of Gracechurch Street Monthly Meeting. Through the operation of this and other causes its meetings became so thinly attended that, at the junction of the two Monthly Meetings of Gracechurch Street and Devonshire House, all meetings for worship on First-day were discontinued there. But its week-day evening meeting (highly prized by the young Friends) was still maintained, and a Friends' library and reading-rooms grew up in it to a sphere of usefulness.*

From this last institution arose the prompting motive, if it was not the actual cause, of the meeting-house passing out of the hands of Friends before their lease was expired. For as the Institute became year by year more useful, its closer connection with the Society's large premises in Houndsditch was desired, and an opportunity for this occurring in the offer of some property adjoining the meeting-houses in Bishopsgate, the change was decided to be made.

A large sum of money had to be paid for the lease of these premises, and a still larger sum in altering them. For these reasons, and because money was also required for a new meeting-house intended to be built in the suburb of Holloway, it seemed best to part with the Gracechurch Street Meeting-house and realise its value in money, as its chief use would be gone on the removal of the Institute to Bishopsgate.

---

* This was established in 1852, chiefly through the exertions of John Pryor, who acted as treasurer until its re-establishment, in a greatly enlarged form, under the name of the Friends' Institute, in the premises at Devonshire House.

It might have been expected that premises covering so much ground as this meeting-house, and situated in the very heart of a district where property had, during the last few years, increased so enormously in value, would have realised a very large amount to the Society for the value of their term, of which some fifty years remained unexpired.

But the value was lessened by a clause in the lease, which prevented any assignment without consent of the company; and although such assent is not usually withheld, the Fishmongers' Company felt themselves warranted in doing so in this case, chiefly because Friends had never had their rents raised by them during 190 years, on the ground of their being a religious body and using it for the purpose of public worship.

It became evident, through this refusal of assent, that, if parted with, the company must be the purchasers, and as they were the freeholders also of a large surrounding property, the leases of which were expiring, they were willing to come to terms. The company eventually agreed to give Friends £6,000 for their interest, and on the 2nd of Sixth Month, 1862, the premises were given up.

The last meeting for worship held there was one during the Yearly Meeting, 1862, when J. T. Eddy, of America, and B. Seebohm, with other ministers, were largely and powerfully engaged, closing thereby the use of that spot for Gospel service which had continued nearly 200 years.

The subsequent history of the place may be briefly told. When Friends left it, the firm of Barclay, Bevan, Tritton & Co. took it of the Fishmongers' Company for some two years, whilst their new bank was in course of building, and the former place of worship became thus a busy scene of banking use. After this the Fishmongers' Company had the ground cleared, together with much of the adjoining property, and let the whole on a building lease to the Agra and Masterman's Bank, who, subsequently, and before they had set up any building, parted with their interest at an enormous premium to the Freehold Estates Company. By them a great outlay has been made in the erection of an unusually handsome pile of building, of which the site of the old meeting-house forms a small part. It is still possible, as in the case of the Bull and Mouth, to go in and stand on the spot so long regarded with a feeling of reverence by us, but not the slightest trace of the original form remains, and the scene is one busy with exchangers and traffickers, and awakening no reminiscences of its former use.

[It may be noted, that the outlay made by Friends on this locality during their occupation of nearly two centuries, had become considerable, for, on adding together the sums spent in the three rebuildings, as also the great repairs in maintenance, rents, taxes, &c., the sum is found to amount to some twenty thousand pounds.]

Among the six Monthly Meetings of London, that of Gracechurch Street may be said to have held for a long time somewhat of a chief place, for it comprised within its limits all the more important portions of the city, within which those most largely engaged in mercantile pursuits lived and traded, and its members were therefore a more influential and prosperous class than those of other meetings.

Many leading firms, both in banking and commerce, originated in members of this Monthly Meeting, such as the Barclays, the Hoares, the Hanburys, Lloyds, Jansons, Alexanders, Dimsdales, Fowlers, Mastermans, Gurneys, Osgoods, among the bankers. Harman, Sanderson, Tindalls, Harris, Birkbecks, Woods, Bevans, Christy, Sturges, Sterrys, &c. &c., among merchants and traders. Dr. Fothergill and Dr. Lettsom, eminent in their profession, lived within its compass, also Joseph Gurney Bevan, founder of the well-known firm of Allen and Hanburys; Luke Howard, originator of the chemical works his descendants conduct at Stratford; William Allen, eminent in science, in philanthropy and religion; and Elizabeth Fry, were all, with many more prominent individuals, once members of Gracechurch Street Meeting.

The number of those who can recollect the state of this meeting before its members began to disperse, is now reduced to but few; yet it may easily be conceived with what pleasure they recall the time when, within the narrow compass of a few acres of streets, lanes, and courts, such social intercourse could be enjoyed as this circle of Friends would provide. Then without much of formal visiting, a large amount of general hospitality prevailed, both between the Friends of the meeting themselves and their relatives and acquaintance from the country. A London house in those days resembled an Inn for the number of its guests, with their frequent arrival and departure. Friends all were far more on a measure of general equality and intercourse than ultimately prevailed, when certain firms strode forward into greater prominence. One of the first great breaks in this circle occurred at the time of the threatened French invasion, when many of the wealthier Friends through supporting the formation of volunteer defence corps became disunited from the body; the Lloyds, Hanburys, Osgoods, Mastermans, &c., left at this time.

As London trade increased in its prosperity, and with it the green fields that once lay within a stone's-throw of the city gates* became covered with buildings, so that meadows, such as Moorfields, were changed into Finsbury Square and Circus, Friends solicitous for the health of their families took houses in the suburbs, where yet green fields were to be found. For a time only the wealthier members could avail themselves of this advantage, but the numbers even of these became apparent, when, on a First-day, their carriages were to be seen waiting in long rows (both in Gracechurch Street and Lombard Street) to take them back to their country homes. Eventually the public stages enabled the practice of of suburban residence to extend to those who did not keep their own conveyances; but these, though thus able to go to and from the week-day meeting, found an attendance at a city meeting all but impracticable on a First-day. Hence arose new meeting-houses, such as those of Plaistow and Stoke Newington, and with their settlement came the decline of that at Gracechurch Street, and the Stoke Newington Meeting was formed so especially from a migration of Gracechurch Street Friends, that, by arrangements with other Monthly Meetings, a district was formed for it, and officially connected with the old city meeting by a narrow strip, giving to the area of Gracechurch Street Monthly Meeting thus altered, when seen on the map, an appearance of two lobes, one towards the north, and comparatively in the country, and the other southward, and comprised within the city-walls, the two united by a narrow and elongated portion cut out of other Monthly Meetings.

* Elizabeth Beck (*née* Lister), born in London in 1767, who died at Stoke Newington, 1857, at the age of 89 years, used to amuse her young visitors, in narrating how she and her sister were able, when children, to go before breakfast in the fields, outside the city-walls, and return fresh with handsful of primroses and cowslips. Such things seem impossible as we look at the smoky squares now covering this spot, where hardly a tree can grow; but much later than this, a Friend had a garden in the City Road, where he claimed to grow better grapes and finer pears than any of his country acquaintance. [This Friend noted as "Joseph Taylor, father of John" in annotated copy]

As thus united in 1827, Gracechurch Street and Stoke Newington continued, until the almost complete relinquishment by Friends of any residence within the city district rendered the maintenance of the London Meeting impracticable, and the union already mentioned with Devonshire House took place on the 1st of Fifth Month, 1850.

Historical Associations.

It now remains to revert to some of the earlier historical associations connected with the premises in White Hart Court, for which, in the absence of the records and MSS. of remarkable passages, alike destroyed in the fire of 1821, we depend on Besse and letters of early Friends.

Gerrard Roberts, one of the principal London Friends, had, as before shown, a chief share in the erection of the meeting-house in 1668, after the Great Fire; and other Friends, such as John Gouldney, James Brayne, and J. Gold, built houses there with him. It is on record, also, that George Fox was present, and preached at its opening, and the mention of its name becomes frequent in the account of sufferings Friends had to undergo in consequence of their meetings there.

For some two years but little, if any, official notice appears to have been taken of this new meeting, although severe penal acts were still in force, whereby no conclusion can be drawn that Friends were more tolerated, but rather that, through pestilence and desolating fire, there was less disposition to seek out and worry those who attended meetings; and that this seems to have been the case, may be warranted by the violence of the proceedings undertaken against it, so soon as affairs in the city were more settled, and its rebuilding completed.

In 1670, a fresh Act of Parliament against "seditious conventicles" came in force, under which the civic authorities made a vigorous and persistent attempt to break up the Friends' meetings within the limits of their jurisdiction, devoting for that purpose much of their attention to this one in White Hart Court; every Sabbath, for some months in succession, it was duly visited by city officials, the sheriffs or constable, accompanied by soldiers, whose presence was used to keep Friends out of the buildings, and their drums to overcome the voice of any preachers as they arose amongst their brethren gathered in the street. Week after week has had its story of this persecuting interference duly kept, and may be seen in the original writing of Ellis Hookes, in the books at Devonshire House, and in print in the pages of Besse. Its narative presents little change in the incidents, though we note less mention of personal violence, such as Sir Richard Brown ten years before used himself to inflict at the Bull and Mouth; less also of that grievous imprisonment in pestilential gaols, but great spoliation of property by fine and distress on goods. It was marked also by two incidents, one of which may be noted, and the other alluded to; the latter is the trial of W. Penn and W. Mead, whose offence had been preaching in Gracious Street, during the time when Friends were kept out of their meeting-house in the court adjoining. The character and incidents of this trial are too well known by those interested in the history of the Englishmen's struggle for liberty of conscience, to require further note here, save to observe that an English jury were on this occasion kept for two days without meat, drink, or fire, were fined and imprisoned, all because the verdict of their conscience did not accord with the wishes of a prejudiced and persecuting court. The other circumstance may not be so familiar. It was the resolution of the civic authorities—when, after some weeks of trial, Friends could not be deterred by soldiery and beating of drums from assembling as near to the meeting-place as they could get—so far to change their mode of opposition, as themselves to use the building for a style of worship they could approve. Hence, a clergyman was appointed to conduct a service there according to the manner of the Established Church, and for weeks in succession the singular feature was presented of this canonical worship being conducted in a Friends' meeting-house. It brought no credit to the parties engaged, for few of any respectability would attend after the first feelings of curiosity had passed away, and the minister, left in the society of a rude rabble, hardly restrained from uproar by the guard of soldiers, was unable to conduct the service with propriety. His first sermon was on Love and Charity, but when he had done, George Whitehead took up the theme, and continued the discourse, showing, amid the quiet attention of those present, how contrary to this "all persecution for religion was," and though this boldness cost him a charge before the Lord Mayor, and a sentence of £40 fine, the people were impressed, and failed to see the logic of the magistrate, when he said, in giving sentence, that so soon as "the minister had done, it was a conventicle."

Next week the minister found Friends so early on the ground as to have fully assembled in the court by the time he came; seeing this he "slunk away," till the serjeant, assembling a "double guard," brought him up to the door. But then again "his heart failed him," and he turned off amid, it is said, the "derisions of the people." A week afterwards, and Friends were the forestalled parties—for military guards had assembled there as early as four in the morning, and under this protection the minister went through the service in the building, whilst Friends, debarred from entering their own meeting-house or the court, assembled in the street; the week following, even the streets were kept clear by train-bands picketted in them all night; and so the priest again had his service in the meeting-house, but only "a rabble was there"; "few persons of credit," says the account, "appeared to countenance their proceedings," and eventually it ceased; for, as William Crouch, an eyewitness remarks, "it held not long, for the priest's work did not prosper, and he grew soon weary of it." During it, however, whilst Friends were thus kept out of their building, occurred the arrest of W. Penn and W. Mead for preaching in the street, as before alluded to.

Funerals connected with White Hart Court.

Like Bull and Mouth, Peel, and Devonshire House, there was no space for burial attached to the meeting-house in White Hart Court, but notices remain of several of the very many funeral companies that used to assemble there to worship before carrying the remains to Bunhill Fields for interment. One is that of William Gibson in 1684, when more than a thousand Friends are said to have followed the remains from Lombard Street to the grave; and some one, knowing how great a sufferer the Friend had been in his lifetime, remarked how "oft the poor body had been beaten and imprisoned for Truth's sake." George Fox's funeral also took place from here, and as no other one will be mentioned, its importance may warrant a more extended notice —obtained chiefly by grouping facts to be found dispersed through the Letters and his memoirs.

Devoted to the last to the cause of his youth, George Fox,

like a true soldier, died in harness, and the closing scenes of his eventful life occurred in White Hart Court, where the room in which he died used to be shown with affectionate interest by its recent occupier though not himself a Friend. It will be observed by any reader of the Journal, that a large portion of his declining years had been spent by him in London, where he felt the calls of duty so urgent as to forego that comfortable home his affectionate wife would fain have had him enjoy with her in the North. Willing rather to spend and to be spent in his Master's service, his once powerful frame, "stiff as a tree," as a persecutor said, was now yielding to the effects of age, prematurely hastened by toil, hard travel, cruel imprisonment, and, if possible, harder than all these, "the care of the Churches." To the last he dictated Epistles, visited friends, attended meetings, counselled the Churches, answered opponents, memorialised authorities—and though for short intervals, his kind sons-in-law could draw him away to their country houses at Kingston or Gooses, he was ever, as recruited strength permitted, returning to the post of labour, until, whilst so engaged, and in the service itself, the hand of death was laid upon him. It was on First-day morning, First Month 11th, 1690-1, that George Fox, in coming out of Gracechurch Street Meeting, felt, on encountering the cold winter air, a chill which he said "went to his heart." He had become much heated during the meeting, where he preached a powerful sermon to the crowded assembly, and had concluded in one of those approaches to the Throne of Grace, the fervour of which his biographers have especially noted ; above all, says William Penn, " he excelled in prayer."

Feeling thus unwell, he passed into Henry Gouldney's rooms that adjoined the meeting-house, and lay down on a bed, his friends at first thinking little of it, as his habit had been thus to rest between meetings ; but it was evident a rest other than that of sleep was approaching, as greater weakness drew on, showing a close was at hand. He thus lay for two and a half days without signs of being in any great pain, but in extreme weakness, yet able to see his friends and impart his dying counsel to them. Gradually the bodily powers gave way, until on Third-day evening the spirit winged its flight, and he was a corpse. All was most peaceful ; death had no terror for him ; he said his work was done, " I am clear, fully clear." He declined all medicine ; without it he had known what it was to arise from a sick bed many times before, but he felt that now his hour was come, and desired peacefully to submit, thus making a "heavenly and harmonious conclusion" to an astonishingly active and eventful life, in the 67th year of his age. As he thus gradually passed away such a beautiful expression settled on the countenance, that a friend who was present has left it on record he was the "most pleasant corpse he had ever seen." It was also noted as an incident in this solemn scene, that "he himself closed his own eyes, and that his chin never fell, nor needed any binding up, but that he lay as if he had fallen asleep."

On the following morning (Fourth-day), at the conclusion of the usual week-day meeting, several of the leading ministers and Friends—such as William Penn, Stephen Crisp, George Whitehead, and others—retired into a room on the meeting-house premises to make arrangements for the funeral, at which an overwhelming attendance was to be expected. It was long before their grief allowed other expression than "deep sighs, groans, and tears." A few testimonies followed. One Friend said, "A valiant is fallen this day, and a place is vacant, if some faithful ones do not supply that glorious station he was in"; to which another replied, "He had faith that the spirit which had so largely dwelt in that body would expand itself into a thousand." Another recounted some of his services; and a fourth exclaimed, "He was as a fixed star in the firmament of God's glory, and there he should shine for ever." These utterances of affectionate admiration did not, however, prevent careful and practical arrangements following for the funeral, whereby one (himself so great a lover of order) was carried to his rest with great quietness and propriety, though nearly 4,000 Friends assembled. "The London Friends (say the Letters) were very discreet to order all passages and concerns relating thereto with great wisdom every way."

During the interval of three days that elapsed between the decease and the interment, though there was no lying in state of the remains, Friends were freely admitted to Henry Gouldney's house, and felt comforted in witnessing for themselves the peaceful and heavenly expression that had settled on the countenance.

On Sixth-day, being that appointed for the funeral, Friends assembled about noon in such numbers as to fill the meeting-house, its court, and the passages leading to it, they overflowed also into both Lombard Street and Gracechurch Street.

Library of the Religious Society of Friends

Gracechurch Street: meeting for worship, Isaac Sharples ministering (his hat is on a peg on the wall behind him); anonymous oil painting circa 1770 [LSF]

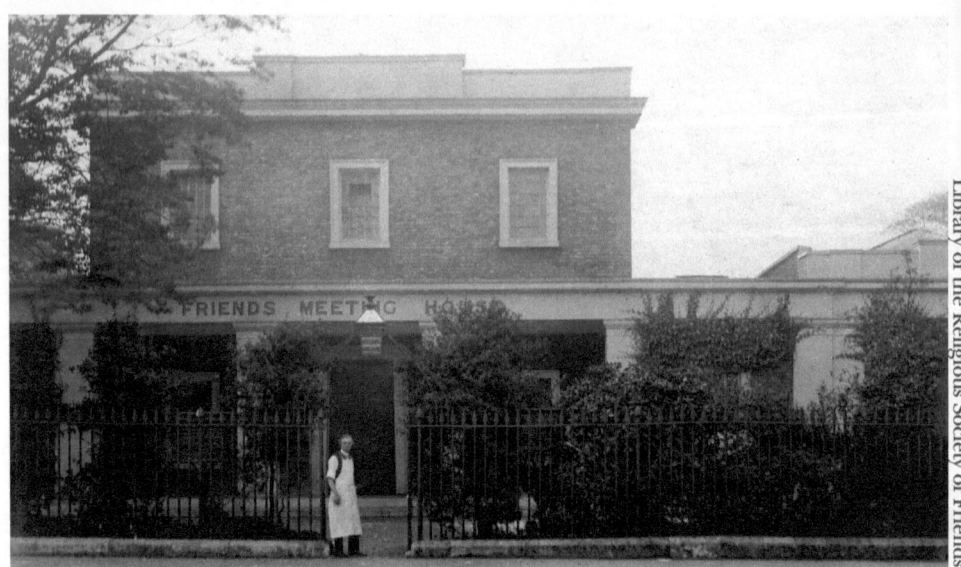

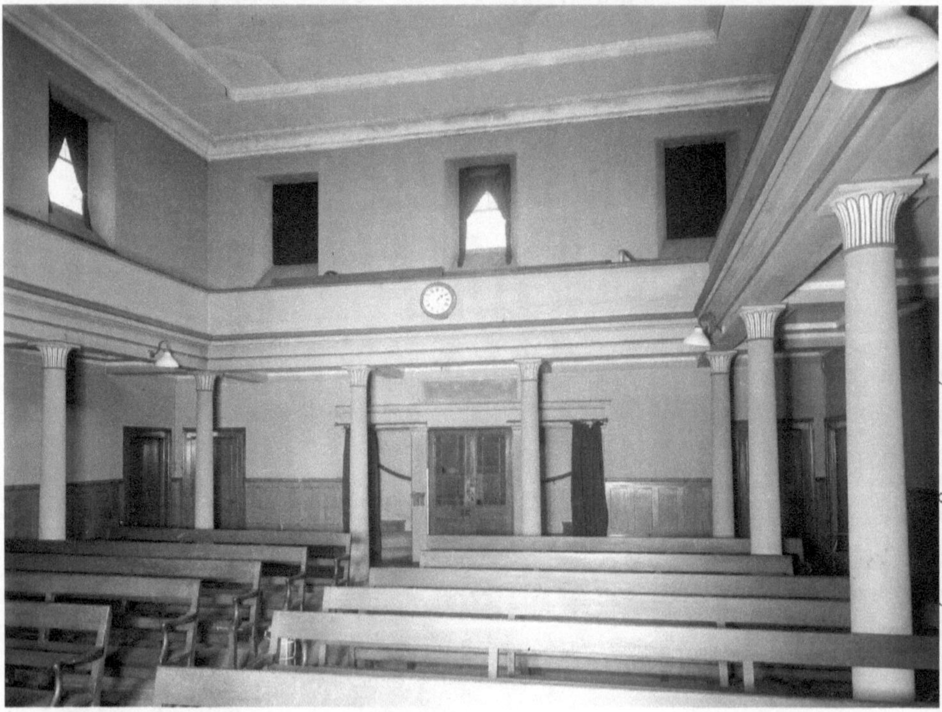

Stoke Newington meeting house:

Front view in 1907, the year William Beck died; this was his own meeting. [LSF]
Interior view from the 1940s. Other than light fittings little would have changed from William Beck's day. [LSF, Lidbetter collection]

facing p.157

Twelve Friends spoke in testimony, and when a two hours' meeting was over, some "ancient" Friends approaching the coffin carried it to the meeting-house door, and delivered it to the bearers, then the great company proceeded to accompany the remains to the burial-ground at Bunhill Fields. Like all funerals at that time, and for long after, no carriages were used, or any hearse; "Friends carried the coffin on their shoulders without any bier, cloth, or cover, but the natural wood, yet the coffin was very smooth and comely." Thirty-six Friends were specially appointed for the purpose, being six from each of the six Monthly Meetings, and the general company following were ranged in order, three abreast, and kept on one side of the street, so as to interrupt the traffic as little as practicable by its progress. It was supposed about 4,000 Friends thus walked from the meeting-house to the burial-ground, which became quite filled by the company. They must have taken some time arriving there, as the procession could not have been less than 900 yards long; its head would have traversed half the distance before the end had left the meeting-house. The interment itself took place about four o'clock. Thus ended this nearest approach to a public funeral which perhaps any Friends' meeting has had conducted within it.

The Second Stoke Newington Meeting.

We shall hereafter describe the first Stoke Newington Meeting (1698 to 1741) in our chapter on Peel Monthly Meeting. For nearly ninety years afterwards there appears to have been no settled meeting of Friends in Stoke Newington. At the expiration of that period the city meetings had become affected by that growing tendency to reside at a distance from the place of business, which now forms so conspicuous a feature of modern mercantile life.

In 1827 Gracechurch Street Monthly Meeting held a conference with Friends of Peel Meeting, to consider the propriety of taking some joint action with a view to the establishment of a meeting for worship at Stoke Newington, on account of so many members of the former meeting having removed to this locality. (Peckham Meeting was settled about this time.)

From this conference no satisfactory result was obtained, and Gracechurch Street Monthly Meeting then applied to the Quarterly Meeting for permission to commence a meeting of their own at Stoke Newington. The desired leave was obtained, and a committee then appointed by the Monthly Meeting to carry it out. The names of this committee it may be interesting to mention: viz. Edward Harris, William Allen, James Foster, John Beck, Richard Low Beck, Frederick Janson, John Lister, John Sanderson, Banks Farrand To these names were added, William Clay, Thomas Hunton, Thomas Pace, and Jonathan Barrett, to represent the Six-Weeks Meeting.

A suitable site having been found in Park Street, Church Street, it was taken by the Six-Weeks Meeting on a lease of 500 years, at £24 per annum, with right of purchase for £480. After paying one quarter's rent, this right was exercised, and the freehold became the property of the Society.

The edifice erected on this site was built at a cost of about £2,000, which was raised by a special subscription. Since its erection, various sums of money have been spent in necessary repairs and minor alterations. In its design, though severe in taste, much skill is shown in proportion. Its architect was a young man of great talent, William Alderson, from Dent Dale, Yorkshire, a pupil of Harrison, of Chester, and one who subsequently became famous by having his design for the Hanwell Lunatic Asylum chosen in a competition. (The late Samuel Tuke had assisted him in this design.)

In 1835 the north wall of the burial-ground was blown down, and the cost of rebuilding (£76) borne jointly by Friends and the trustees of Michael Yoakley's Almshouses.

In 1849 an addition was made to the burial-ground by the purchase of a piece of land, lying to the south of it, for £400.

Stoke Newington Meeting-house was opened for divine worship on the 15th of Third Month, 1829; and the usual First-day and Week-day Meetings were established. With reference to the latter, it is interesting to notice that the committee, seeing that the congregation was likely to be mainly composed of persons engaged in business in the city, proposed that the Week-day Meeting should be held at 6 o'clock, on Fifth-day evening. This proposition was overruled by the Monthly Meeting, who fixed the time for Third-day morning, at 10, and subsequently altered it to Fifth-day, as at present.

At the dissolution of Gracechurch Street Meeting, in 1850, Stoke Newington Friends became united with Devonshire House, and now form the largest congregation in that Monthly Meeting.

In the burial-ground attached to the meeting-house lie

many well-known Friends, who spent the evening of their day in this locality. Amongst these we may mention especially William Allen, John Lister, John Yeardley, &c.

APPENDIX.

WILLIAM DEWSBERY'S LAST SERMON.

IN connection with White Hart Court, it may be mentioned that William Dewsbery, who was at the same time one of the earliest and most gifted of the ministers in the Society, preached his last sermon in this meeting-house. He had come up from his residence in the North to attend the Yearly Meeting of 1688, being urged thereto by a pressing desire to be once more present at its deliberations; though his advanced age and great bodily weakness rendered it somewhat imprudent for his health's sake. Thus exercised in spirit, he attended the meeting on First-day previous, when a discourse of some length was delivered by him, which has been preserved to us by some one who was there having taken it down in short-hand, and by Sewel, the historian, incorporating it in his history. Apart from its intrinsic value, the discourse possesses a melancholy importance through its being in reality William Dewsbery's closing testimony; for increased illness came on, and though its severity abated so far as to allow of his reaching home, no opportunity was left for any subsequent public service, and his long and useful career soon terminated. Few of his contemporaries among the Friends were more gifted than William Dewsbery; his ardent piety was tempered by discretion, and undaunted in danger, or undismayed by suffering, he loved the truth, and rejoiced to suffer for it. A man of some culture, and fair outward means, he left house and home to serve the cause; in fact, piety had marked his conduct from early youth, and spiritual exercises had so engaged his attention that, when George Fox first met with him in a town near York, his native place, William Dewsbery assented to the views preached, not so much as new, but as being in accordance with what he had independently and in his own experience found to be Truth. Thenceforward he became one of the most valuable of George Fox's coadjutors, and no doubt this, his last discourse, though abrupt through frequent abbreviations and omissions, will show somewhat of the depth and soundness of William Dewsbery's views on Christian doctrine :—

"Except you be regenerated and born again ye cannot inherit the kingdom of God. . . . This know for certain that no man or woman can be quickened and raised up into the life of the second Adam till the life of the first Adam be taken away from them. . . . Now all of you that come to be regenerated you must come to the light of Christ. There is no other way to it. He will search your hearts, and try your reins, and set your sins in order before you. . . . You must see yourselves a lost people, a sinful people. . . . You must bring your deeds to the light of Christ and abide in the sentence of condemnation ; if you save your lives you lose them; if you will lose your lives for Christ's sake there is no danger of your eternal life. . . . I stand here as a witness of the Lord of life this day ; there is no way for people to come to salvation but they must know Christ revealed in their hearts. . . . He will baptise thee with the Holy Ghost and with fire. If thou knows not this thou art not a true Christian, thou wilt never look death in the face with joy, nor go down to the grave in triumph. . . . You must come to Christ to purify you in the fiery furnace. . . . Do not make the way to heaven easier on your minds and imaginations than indeed it is; and think it not sufficient to live in an outward observance of the ways of God. If your own wills be alive and your corruptions remain unmortified the judgment of God will be your portion. . . . Come and examine thy conscience. Dost thou strive to enter in at the strait gate and the narrow way? . . . The justice of God will not suffer thee to make a Saviour of thy duties and qualifications, and to take God's jewels and to deck thyself with them ; thou canst not be saved without the righteousness of God in Christ Jesus. . . . It is God's infinite goodness to men that he will hide pride from them and humble them under his mighty hand. . . . God will make short work in the earth. He will set thy sins before thee and make thee watchful unto prayer, and lead thee to holiness of life and conversation, and make thee abhor thyself and despise all the pomps and pleasures and vanities of this world. . . . All this thou oughtest to do, . . . and all this will not justify thee, . . . for these services thou owest unto God. If thou diligently wait thou shalt see more light ; then the sword that proceeds out of the mouth of Christ, who is called the Word of God, will cut thee off from all thy hopes of salvation—from anything thou hast done, . . . so that thou wilt be a hopeless soul—nothing in thine own sense and apprehension, . . . and wilt cry out, I am a dead, lost, and undone creature, . . . then become as a little child humbled and slain as to thy own will, . . . thou wilt not question [whether] I shall live a holy life, but will give all that life thou hadst for that life which is hid with Christ in God. O ! there is none come so far that ever miss of eternal life. All shuffling people that would have salvation by Christ and will not let him exercise his heavenly power—his princely glorious power— to baptise them into his death, it is they that come short of salvation, . . . I stand here as a witness for the God of heaven ; I never heard the voice of Christ (as his follower) till I was slain and baptised, and lay as a little child under his heavenly chastisements ; as soon as ever my soul was brought to this in my humiliation, O ! then, the dreadful judgment was taken away, . . . and the Lord spake comfortably to me, ' I have loved thee with an everlasting love,' and I was made a Christian through a day of vengeance and burning as an oven, and the haughtiness and pride of man in me was brought low. . . . Those that will [thus] die with Christ and be willing to die for him, he is revealed as a Saviour to *them*. . . . O ! let not your eyes slumber nor your eyelids take any rest till you be sure the Lord is your God. What remains now ? Christ is in me, and we are all one in him. Christ laid down his life for thee and me. Now he reigns in me, and he hath prepared my body to die for the truth as his prepared body was laid down for my sin. . . . O Friends, let us empty ourselves that Christ may fill us. Let us be nothing in our own eyes that we may be all in him and receive of his fulness. . . . And so I commend you to God. I have been long held in durance in great weakness; and I was restless till I could come up to this great city of London to preach the everlasting Gospel among you. . . . Let not these words passing through a mean vessel be as a bare empty discourse of truth to you which you only hear and take no further care of your salvation; . . . press forward to the heavenly work that is laid in the power of Christ Jesus, even through judgment into death, and then he will give you eternal life."

DESTRUCTION OF GRACECHURCH STREET MEETING-HOUSE.*

An account is here given of the destruction of the meeting-house in 1821, taken from a cotemporaneous letter, under date Ninth Month 14, 1821 :—

"The destruction of our good old meeting-house and nearly all its records, library, &c., is a dull and melancholy affair to many of us. Grandfather, who has been a member of it 60 years, shed tears over the ruins, and even now his spirits are considerably affected by the loss. Early on First-day morning, or at midnight on Seventh-day, the fire broke out, and before the watchmen discovered it, the back part of the premises close adjoining the meeting-house were all in flames. Our poor doorkeeper, his wife and family, had only just time to escape, saving barely clothes enough to cover them. Soon after escaping, their house and the meeting-house were, as I have understood, one dreadful flame, and the whole court seemed doomed to destruction; Ryan's, the cheese-monger, Samuel Fossick's, and a stationer's shop fronting Gracechurch Street, are completely destroyed, and not a wall of our meeting-house is standing, but it is one confused heap of ruins. I am sorry to confirm the report, too, of several lives being lost. One poor fellow was dug out yesterday rather unexpectedly, as the two that had been missing were dug out the day before. *They* were firemen, but some suppose this poor fellow got in to plunder the warehouse. I was present when they cleared the rubbish away and took off the body on a shutter. It was a dreadful spectacle. One of the firemen they found standing nearly erect, with a book under his arm, and the other flat on his face, and the poor fellow discovered yesterday nearly in the same position. They all appeared to have been making their way for a window that opened into the court, when the wall fell and destroyed them. Two firemen besides, only just escaped; one so much injured that he has died since in the hospital; but the other, who had his thigh broken, is in a very fair way of recovery. It is not ascertained, nor will it ever be, I suppose, at whose house the fire broke out, but it must have been at one of the three fronting Gracechurch Street. There is no reason whatever to think it happened from design, but from accident."

CLOSING MINUTE OF GRACECHURCH STREET MONTHLY MEETING.

"5th mo. 1, 1850.

"Being now assembled for the last time as Gracechurch Street Monthly Meeting of Friends, we desire thankfully to acknowledge the unity and harmony that has so generally prevailed amongst us, and we trust that Divine goodness and mercy will continue to follow us in our future association with our Friends as members of Devonshire House Monthly Meeting. "Signed, JOSEPH T. FOSTER, Clerk."

---

* "Letter by R[ichard] L[ow] Beck; grandfather is John Lister" [annotated copy]

CHAPTER X.

DEVONSHIRE HOUSE MONTHLY MEETING, INCLUDING WHEELER STREET AND DEVONSHIRE HOUSE.

WHEELER STREET.

The meetings of Friends, as we have seen in a preceding chapter, were originally held in private houses. It is to one of these little gatherings that we have to look for the origin of Devonshire House Monthly Meeting.

It was about the year 1656 that a few of the convinced, resident in the then half-rural district of Spitalfields, began to assemble in a "little upper room" in the house of one John Oakley.* This Friend's dwelling-place was situated near the corner of Westbury and Wheeler Streets.

It was a day of much convincement, and the congregation rapidly increased in numbers. The "little upper room" became insufficient for them, and two rooms were made into one. But a further increase soon compelled the worshippers to meet outside in the adjoining garden. Here they raised at first a canvas tent to protect them from the weather, and ultimately erected a meeting-house. For a time this was the only building of the kind in the extensive district afterwards known as Devonshire House Monthly Meeting.

Although all visible traces of that ancient meeting-place, have disappeared, yet is a memento of its existence left us in the name—Quaker Street—which the former Westbury Street afterwards acquired, and still retains.

Within this building, generally known as the Wheeler Street Meeting-house, grew up a meeting of considerable size and importance, which, after flourishing for a number of years, gradually fell away till its discontinuance in 1741.

In the times of persecution, Wheeler Street Meeting-house

---

* John Oakley, or Okeley, Citizen, and Merchant Taylor, afterwards married the widow Elizabeth Hatch, of Edmonton, and settled down for the evening of his life at Winchmore Hill. We shall hear of him again in connection with that meeting.

was the frequent scene of violence and injustice. For a long period the meeting was seldom held without a number of arrests being made. On one occasion the entrance-gate and the doors were broken down, and as many as fifty of the attenders taken to prison. The persecutor, whose name is chiefly connected with the outrages committed here, was Sir John Robinson, already mentioned as prominent in "the Great Cavalcade," being then an alderman. He had subsequently served as Lord Mayor, had been made a baronet, and through Court influence was appointed Governor of the Tower of London.

In this position he signalised himself by his zealous endeavours to suppress the sectaries. Against the Quakers he was especially bitter, and hurried off the worshippers at Wheeler Street in scores to the New Prison.* At this place was a worthy co-worker, Joseph Green the gaoler, who spared no pains to render miserable the lives of his captives. He thrust them into his most unwholesome cells, denied them even straw to lie on, cruelly beat and starved them, and even set on the felons to rob them of the provisions with which they were supplied by their friends outside.

William Penn, on 5th of Second Month, 1670, was taken from Wheeler Street, and, with his usual boldness, confronted the haughty governor. (This was five months after his famous trial for preaching in Gracious Street.) After nobly pleading the rights of conscience, he exclaimed, "I scorn that religion which is not worth suffering for, and able to sustain them that are afflicted for it; mine is."

About the year 1670 it seemed as if the troubles of the Wheeler Street congregation were to culminate in the utter destruction of their place of worship. Already had the Ratcliff Meeting-house been destroyed by soldiers from the Tower, and now Sir John Robinson expressed his determination to proceed to the same extremity with the Quakers of Spitalfields.

In view of this impending danger Friends turned to Gilbert Latey, the owner of the building, and of whom we shall have more to say in connection with Westminster. But Gilbert was far away, travelling in the west of England, and

---

* The "New Prison" of two centuries ago has passed out of existence. On its site stands the House of Detention, recently made famous by its attempted destruction by the Fenians.

accordingly a deputation waited upon the Governor, asking for some delay that the owner of the property might be communicated with. Robinson was induced to grant a respite of three weeks, threatening, however, not to leave one stone upon another if the owner did not then appear and show cause why the building should not be destroyed.

In those days of slow communication it required much promptness of action to acquaint Gilbert Latey with the threatened danger, and provide for his timely appearance. Nevertheless, matters were so managed that he returned to town some days before the allotted time had expired.

During that long journey back from Cornwall, Gilbert had had ample time to arrange his plans. He instructed his attorney to make out a formal lease of the premises in question, which was duly executed, letting them to a certain poor Friend whom he constituted his tenant. He then located this said poor Friend at the meeting-house, thus giving to the premises the privileges of a home, and at the appointed time waited upon Sir John Robinson.

"So you are the owner of this place?" bluntly exclaimed the governor.

"I am," replied Gilbert, with his usual stately demeanour, "and of several others too."

"How dare you own any meeting-house contrary to the King's laws?"

"I owned that meeting-house before the King had any such law."

"I find you are a pretty fellow!" said the governor; "and pray who lives in the meeting-house?"

"My tenant."

"Your tenant! What is your tenant?"

"One that I have thought good to grant a lease to."

"Then," replied the governor, "you have a tenant that hath taken a lease from you?"

"Yes!" calmly replied G. L.

At this the baffled governor, turning to the deputation that had first waited on him, said, "I think you have now fitted me. You have brought a fellow to the purpose; had your Friends been all as wise as this fellow, you might have had your other meeting-houses as well as this."

And thus was the Wheeler Street Meeting-house preserved from destruction, though the assemblies held there continued subject to frequent interruption till the cessation of persecution.* Friends, generally, profited by Gilbert Latey's example, for "after this," as he naïvely remarks in his Journal, " Friends taking the same care have ever since preserved their meeting-houses."

There is an Indenture of Lease extant, which is probably only a continuance of the precautionary tenancy above referred to. In this ancient document, dated 1686, Gilbert Latey let to Dennis Dodman, weaver, a messuage in Westbury Street, consisting of "one large room from top to bottom, surrounded by galleries, and two other rooms, and a large hovel or shed thereunto adjoining, together with all forms or benches, chairs or stools, &c." This indenture bears the clerkly signature of Gilbert Latey, and a sprawling " D.D." as the mark of Dennis Dodman.

It would appear that the building in question was not one that would have given Sir John Robinson any very great trouble to demolish. It must have been slightly built, for during its comparatively short existence, frequent complaints were entered on the minute-books of the Monthly Meeting respecting its defective condition. It was severely damaged in November, 1703, when that terrible storm passed over England which swept away the Eddystone lighthouse and destroyed life and property to an extent unprecedented in English history.† The damage done in London was estimated at £2,000,000, and Friends' meeting-houses bore their share in the common disaster. On this occasion we find a minute speaking of the injury done at Wheeler Street (and Devonshire House), and appointing "William Kent and John Hope to cause the same to be repaired so soon as well may be with Tyles if they can, and if they can't be gotten, then

---

* There is an old record-book of Wheeler Street Meeting preserved at Devonshire House, in which for a time an account of each meeting for worship was entered. Thus in the year 1685 we find that the meetings were very frequently held in the street. During the year fifty-six men, including George Fox, George Whitehead, William Penn, Francis Stampers, and twelve women (including one "Elin, not owned") were engaged in ministry or prayer at the meetings. Many of the names appear several times, but are only counted once in the numbers just given. The same names do not often appear twice running.

† It is to this memorable storm that Addison alludes in "The Campaign":—

" So when an angel by Divine command
 With rising tempests shakes a guilty land,
 Such as of late o'er pale Britannia passed."

with deals for the present." Henceforth threatening signs become increasingly frequent. In 1707 it is reported as likely to fall, and prompt action had to be taken to ward off the danger. Soon afterwards the damp low floor, the rain coming through the roof, and other discomforts are complained of. From time to time repairs of various kinds are reported and effected, until, in 1727, a new lease is obtained, and it is decided to rebuild.

But Wheeler Street Meeting itself now begins to show signs of decay, and the idea of rebuilding the meeting-house is abandoned. In 1740 we find the Week-day Meeting given up, "its smallness not being to the reputation of the Society." On the 2nd of the Seventh Month, 1742, the Monthly Meeting (with the sanction of the Quarterly) agreed to discontinue Wheeler Street Meeting entirely "after next Firstday." In 1745 the building partially fell, and in the Third Month, 1749, report is made that "Wheeler Street Meetinghouse has tumbled down." The materials were sold and the lease disposed of to the great brewers, Truman & Co. But the new occupiers were at once served with a notice of ejectment by Granville Wheeler, and Friends were reminded of an ancient covenant to build two tenements on the spot. These were accordingly erected at a cost of £190, and let for a few years till sold to Benjamin Mills, a weaver, for £187 in 1755, and so even the very site of this ancient meetinghouse passed into other hands.

It may not be out of place here to allude to the fact, that exactly a century afterwards, viz. in Third Month, 1849, Friends again became tenants in Quaker Street. A house was taken in which a First-day School was established. This lasted until 1864, when notice to quit the premises having been given by the Great Eastern Railway Company, which had become its purchasers, Friends obtained some land not far off, and erected the new building known (in memory of Peter Bedford, who lived in that neighbourhood so long) as the Bedford Institute. Into these new premises the First-day School was transferred on the first First-day of 1865, since which various other branches of Christian labour have grown up and are prospering there,—thus retaining the interest and influence of Friends in this locality.

The Bedford Institute building of 1865 in Wheeler Street, designed by William Beck, who was effectively the Institute's founder. T. Frederick Ball was employed here. The building was replaced in 1894. [LSF]

Devonshire House courtyard:
etching with aquatint by Sylvia Smee (1886–1969) [LSF]

Devonshire House.

The Meeting of Devonshire House, though some years younger than that at Wheeler Street, soon became the more important of the two, ultimately giving its name to the Monthly Meeting.

Its origin is different from that of other of the London meetings as it does not seem to have developed out of any gathering of Friends in a private house, but to have arisen somewhat suddenly through the force of circumstances.

The Great Fire of 1666 had deprived Friends for a time of their headquarters at the Bull and Mouth, and it was felt necessary to procure some premises in which temporarily to transact the affairs of the Society, and hold a meeting for worship for the ejected congregation.

It happened that at this time the great mansion of the Cavendish family known as Devonshire House (which had long been so prominent an object to the south of Moorfields), had been divided into several messuages or tenements, and a portion of it was unoccupied. Accordingly, from John Colville and William Edwards (who held the property from Christian, Countess Dowager of Devonshire, and William, Earl of Devonshire), Friends took an under-lease, for £70 a year, of certain rooms thus enumerated in the indenture :—

"The lobby, the great parlour, and dining room lying next the said lobby, with all the cellars lying under the said lobby, and half of the arched vault or cellar lying before the garden under the said great dining room and parlour, and three chambers lying over the said lobby and dining room, and over the three said chambers one large garret and the evidence room, and over the said evidence room large leads."

From a schedule attached to the indenture we learn that the building presented all the internal aspects of an old princely residence. The "turned carved pillars" in the lobby, the "fair carved portals" and "carved chimney-piece" in the dining-room, the "chambers curiously wainscotted with carved work," were all so many relics of its former grandeur.

Once located in these convenient premises, Friends seem to have been desirous of retaining possession, even after regaining the Bull and Mouth. Till 1678 meetings were held in the old mansion, when need was pressingly felt for increased accommodation. For a time the idea of procuring Crosby Hall for the purposes of the Society was entertained, but this project was, after due inquiry, abandoned.

It would appear that the proprietors of the Devonshire House property were now letting portions of the estate on building leases, and Friends took the opportunity to procure a lease of the ground on which Devonshire House Meeting-house was afterwards built. How close to the site of the rooms previously occupied by them was this piece of land now taken, cannot be ascertained. It was evidently not identical in position, for it is described as a toft or tofts containing walls, sheds, erections, and buildings, "being part of Devonshire House and Grounds." It was rented from one Dr. Bearbone, and two builders were at once engaged to erect a meeting-house at a cost of £630. William Mead and Gilbert Latey were the Friends concerned on behalf of the Six-Weeks Meeting in taking the necessary care on this occasion.

Upon the Devonshire estate arose Devonshire Square and the adjacent streets and courts. Eastward from Devonshire Square (in the centre of which originally stood a pedestal surmounted by a gilt Mercury) was a passage leading towards Gravel Lane. In this passage was a flight of steps, at the top of which was a noted Anabaptist meeting-house. To this fact we now particularly allude, inasmuch as Maitland the historian, and Ogilby the topographer, erroneously place the Quakers' Meeting-house in that position. The latter building was, however, situated in Sandwich or Sandy's (since Cavendish) Court, then, as now, a passage leading into Houndsditch. Rearwards it abutted on the stables of the Dolphin Inn, a large old-fashioned rambling place, (similar to the Talbot in Southwark), opening into Bishopsgate Street, near the present meeting-house entrance.

It was an unobtrusive, though for the period a sufficiently commodious, building that Friends erected on the site above described. Retired from the main thoroughfare, it could only be approached from Cavendish Court, the original entrance from which was near the south-eastern corner of the present meeting-house, opening into a wide lobby. To the right of this lobby was the large room, 40 feet by 40 feet, and 19 feet in height, lighted by three windows upon the court on the eastern side. On the western side was a narrow gallery, and there was a fire-place in the north-east corner. Over this room was another, used by the Two-Weeks and other disciplinary meetings. To the left of the lobby mentioned above, were two rooms, which with the lobby itself could on special occasions be added to the larger room by the removal of shutters; and over these were rooms for the tenant whom Friends had found it needful to locate on their premises, and two or three attics inhabited by poor widows. These rooms cannot all have been constructed in accordance with modern ideas of comfort, for there is an order extant for the removal of one Mary Taylor to Wheeler Street, she " being desirous of having a room with a chimney to it."

Cavendish Court, in the olden time, was one of the dark places of London, and Friends found it needful to hang out some sort of light in the winter evenings. In 1697 we read in the minute-book that John Cooper has offered to present the meeting with a lanthorn, which was gratefully accepted, and "it is desired that he and Isaac Jennings" (the meeting-house tenant) "do agree together where it is proper to be placed," &c.

Very numerous have been the alterations, improvements, and repairs in Devonshire House Meeting-house since the early times of which we have been speaking. To recount the details of these would be tedious and uninteresting; we may, however, briefly allude to two or three of the most conspicuous facts in the history of the building.

Here, as elsewhere, the ministers' gallery was at first only occupied by men Friends. In 1706 we read of the erection of "a standing for ministering women Friends in time of ministry."

In 1741 extensive alterations were effected. The meeting-house was enlarged by throwing open an adjoining room. The ministers' gallery was removed from the western side to its present position, and "a sufficient number of seats with backs" were ordered to be placed all round. These and other improvements cost the meeting £570, of which sum we see by the accounts that £2 7s. 4d. was spent in a raising supper, and £7 in breakfast-money and drink for the workmen.

In 1745 the interior of the meeting-house wore a novel aspect. It was made use of by the militia as a guard-room at the time when the metropolis was thrown into a state of alarm by the advance into England of the Young Pretender and his forces. This was done with the consent of Friends, to whom application had been made by the authorities. The

Monthly Meeting gave the desired permission, "desiring that they may take care not to damage the house or anything therein." But the soldiers were very far from carrying out Friends' wishes, and considerable expenditure was necessitated in order to repair the damage done to the place by its military occupants.

In 1762 a gallery and staircases were erected at a cost of £300. These were taken down in 1797, and sold for £10 10s.

In 1766, when the lease, which had been once or twice renewed, had still forty years to run, the property came into chancery. At this time Thomas Talwin, an ancestor of the late Joseph Talwin Foster, and a man of the highest character and liberality, bought the freehold for £700 and generously presented it to the Monthly Meeting for £300.

Towards the close of the last century the Meeting for Sufferings was desirous of building more suitable accommodation for the Yearly Meeting, hitherto held at Gracechurch Street. Whilst engaged in searching for a proper site, the Dolphin Inn, in Bishopsgate Street, with its yard and stables, was offered for sale. This extensive property was purchased, and upon the ground thus obtained were built in 1789 the two large meeting-houses in which the annual gatherings of the Society, and the Quarterly Meetings of London and Middlesex are now held. In consequence of this the premises of Devonshire House Monthly Meeting were adapted to face the courtyard of the new buildings, and Cavendish Court entrance closed. Considerable alterations and improvements have also been made during the present century. The purchase at various dates of certain houses in Cavendish Court, Houndsditch, and Devonshire Street, with the taking on lease of some property in Bishopsgate Street, has completed the extensive and important premises which, instead of being, as at first, simply part of a mansion, now comprise three meeting-houses, thirteen dwelling-houses, a Literary Institute, and about twenty rooms used for committees and other Society purposes.

Boundaries of the Monthly Meetings.

The Monthly Meeting, whose headquarters were first at Wheeler Street and afterwards at Devonshire House, comprised an extensive district within its limits. At first the boundaries were not defined with much accuracy, and Friends

Library of the Religious Society of Friends

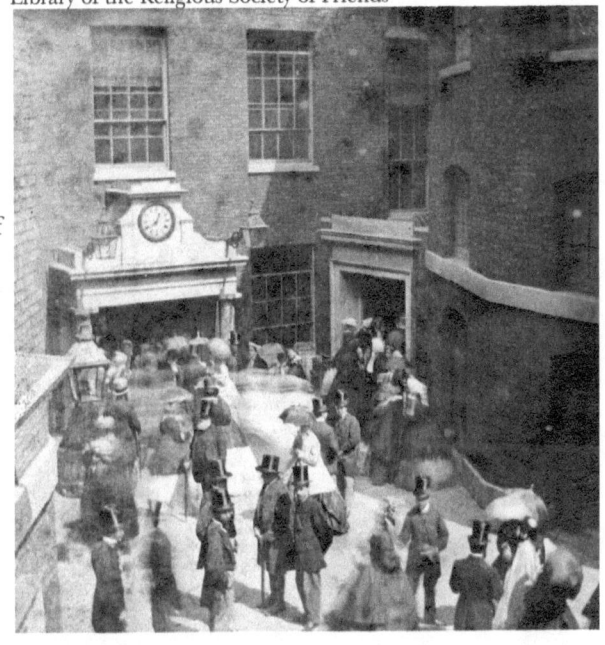

Devonshire House:

Right: The courtyard at Yearly Meeting 1865, from a series of stereoscopic photographs [LSF]. See also J.J. Willson cartoon p. xii, and Women's Yearly Meeting, p. 354.

Below: The Institute reading room, from a series of photographs by Walter Benington of Devonshire House in 1925, before the Society's offices and the Institute moved to Euston [LSF].

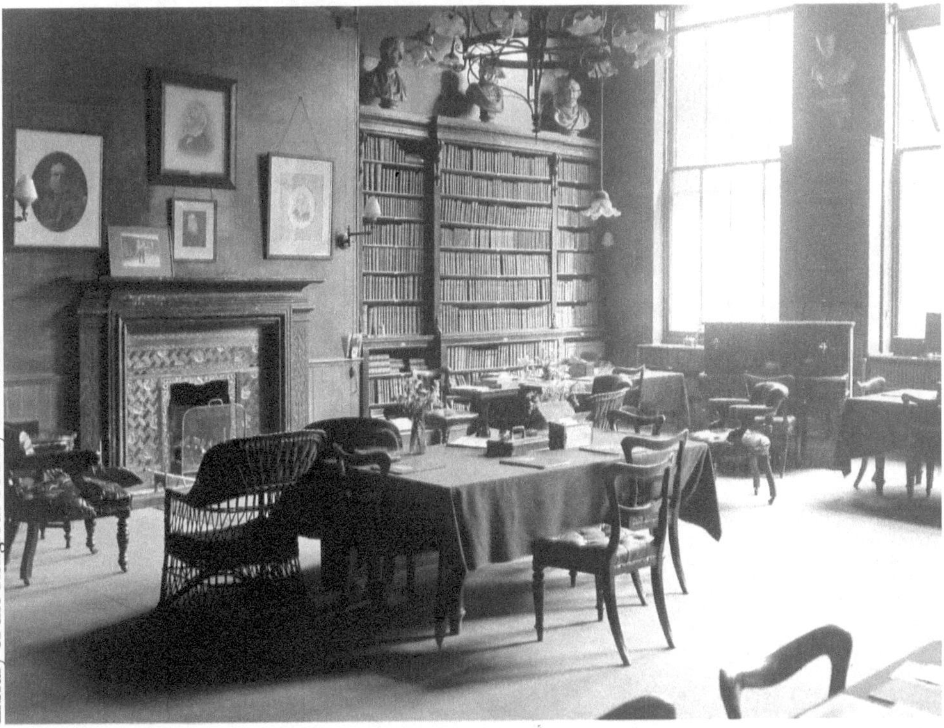

Library of the Religious Society of Friends

Bishopsgate entrance to Devonshire House. Left: ink drawing by Henry S. Newman, 1845. Right: photo c.1900 [LSF].

facing p.171

were left free to attend the service of such meetings as were most convenient or congenial to them. But as the Society gradually settled down into order and system, a definite district was mapped out within which each Monthly Meeting exercised its discipline and authority. In 1673 a boundary line was fixed upon between Wheeler Street Monthly Meeting and the Bull and Mouth Monthly Meeting; but in 1699 we find the first detailed account of the boundaries of the Monthly Meeting in its entirety. We extract the following from the minute-book, preserving the original spelling:—

"From London Bridge all ye East Side of Fish Street Hill and Gratia Street and Bishopsgate Street to Bishopsgate and without ye gate on both sides ye way to Shoreditch Steeple House & all petty france, old bedlam, and from the postern gate by petty france all y^e East Side of morefields, Long ally, Hoge Land, Holloway Land & Hogdesdon & all y^t part about annisseed Cleare, to y^e new Hospitall all Shorditch, Dolston, Shackellwell, hummerton, Bednell Green & oldford, & from y$_e$ doge roe Stone Bridge on the North Side of whitechapell road to London. And on y^e South Side from y^e Dunghill opposett to friends burriall Ground at whitechapell townsend on both sides of y^e Road to whitechapell steeple House and all white Chapell so down taking in Church Lane and well Close on The west Side & salt peeter bank East Smithfield, Nightingall Lane, & Rosemary Lane, so up the West part from the Hermitage bridge to London Bridge by the theams side & both Tower Hills & ye Minoriese, & within the Walls to Bishopsgate and on London bridge ye East Side of the Buildings belongs to Devonsheir House monthly meeting as far as the drawbridge & on the West side to the city monthly meeting within ye walls to ye said drawbridge, on both sides London bridge beyound the drawBridge belongs to Southwark monthly meeting."

Much difficulty was found in inducing all Friends to fall in with these arrangements. Small committees had frequently to be appointed to admonish such persons as being resident within Devonshire House boundaries would persist in attending Peel, Ratcliff, or the Bull and Mouth. Ultimately these difficulties were overcome, and the limits of the Monthly Meeting remained very much as described till its comparatively recent junction with other London meetings. Of the union of these to Devonshire House we shall have hereafter to speak in making our round of the metropolis.

Numerical Condition.

At the close of the seventeenth century, a very considerable body of Friends dwelt within the compass of Devonshire House Monthly Meeting. We have seen how at the commencement the little band of worshippers could manage to collect in John Oakley's upper room; but at the time of the building of the new meeting-house in Cavendish Court, only twenty years afterwards, out of the ten or twelve thousand Friends considered to have been then resident in London, probably about two thousand belonged to this Monthly Meeting.* In 1695 the numbers were so large that it was proposed to divide the district into two Monthly Meetings. This idea was, however, abandoned, and probably because the most influential and wealthiest members were for the most part dwellers in the same locality. As an evidence of the populousness of the meeting, we may cite the fact that eight or ten Friends were usually appointed to make collections, who divided the Monthly Meeting into four or five districts, and reported the sums separately raised in each. Although the meeting decreased in size during the eighteenth century, it continued for many years much larger than at the present day. In 1734 there were 333 subscribers for Barclay's Apology in the meeting, and in 1755 we find that there were required "200 Yearly Meeting Epistles," so that each *family* may have one."

During the early part of the present century Devonshire House Meeting was very large, and was held on First-days in the Women's Meeting-house from 1806 to 1834. In the former year £500 was spent in making it convenient and comfortable for this purpose. In the latter year about £500 was spent in altering the old meeting-house in such a way that 200 more members could be seated therein.

There appears to have been no regular list of members in this meeting before 1751, when the "Committee on Disorderly Walkers" (hereafter alluded to under the head of Religious and Moral Condition) were requested to produce one. This list of members was handed in, in 1753, by Thomas Talwin, a leading member of and great benefactor to this, as also to other London meetings.

---

* It now numbers, though united with all the former Gracechurch Street and part of Peel, only 600.

Persecutions.

The worshippers at Devonshire House had to bear their share of the persecution inflicted upon Nonconformists during the age of intolerance, although apparently not to the same extent as their brethren at Wheeler Street. Scarcely had they taken possession of their rooms in Devonshire House, in 1666, when the authorities seized it in the King's name, padlocked the door, and affixed the mark of the broad arrow as a sign of its being Government property.* No guard, however, was set to maintain the seizure, and accordingly Friends quietly removed the padlock and continued their meeting. But these meetings, especially after the meeting-house was built in 1678, were frequently interrupted by violence, and Friends turned out of doors. George Whitehead, John Burnyeat, William Simpson, and other preachers, were often arrested, and occasionally a score or two of their hearers were dragged off with them to Newgate. To be allowed to hold their meeting in the adjacent court, or street, even in hard frost, or pelting rain, was often the best treatment they could hope for. Occasionally we hear of a relenting watchman allowing them to bring out their forms, which was no small boon when we call to mind the protracted meetings of the period. But too frequently this open-air worship was disturbed by the drum-beat of soldiery as they rushed up with swords and staves, and cruelly maltreated the unoffending Quakers. One instance of oppression may be particularised as it culminated in the martyrdom of the sufferer.

It was on the 1st of Second Month, 1683, that the meeting was violently broken up by Lieutenant Minchard and a band of soldiers. These laid about them unmercifully, and the lieutenant himself struck John Sparsfield so violently on the head, that the poor man went home ill, and died in about ten days. The authorities thought it only decent to go through the forms of an inquiry. An inquest was held, but during the proceedings the guilty lieutenant sat beside the coroner. The witnesses were snubbed, and the jury browbeaten, and a verdict of "death from natural causes" was finally recorded. Thus had our forefathers to contend, not only against cruel laws harshly administered, but even against the perversion of the very forms of justice themselves.

---

* By Conventicle Act buildings where these were held became forfeit to the Crown, but if any tenant there, then a fine on the tenant.

But not only whilst actually at meeting were Friends in danger of suffering for conscience' sake. There sprang into existence through the provisions of the Conventicle Act a vile tribe of informers, who got their living by going to meetings, and then laying informations against the preachers and prominent attenders. Many a worthy tradesman was thus accused in his absence, heavily fined, and only made aware of the circumstance by the entry into his premises of the minions of intolerance, armed with a warrant of distraint, which they speedily proceeded to put into execution. Numerous were the sufferers through this iniquitous system amongst the members of the Monthly Meeting now under notice, and conspicuous amongst these was the man whose name stands foremost on the list of Devonshire House worthies— George Whitehead.

George Whitehead and other Worthies.

"That ancient and honourable elder, George Whitehead" (for fifty years a member of Devonshire House Meeting), was originally from the north of England. He was one of the sixty preachers raised up in the northern counties through the ministry of George Fox, who from thence went forth spreading the principles of Christianity, as held by Friends, through the length and breadth of the land. As we have seen in a preceding chapter, Burrough and Howgill came to London,—G. Whitehead's field of service was at first mainly in the eastern counties. In that district he spent his youth and early manhood, disputing with clergymen or ministers, convincing multitudes, raising up and establishing churches.

It is said his occupation in early life was that of a schoolmaster, but of this circumstance no definite confirmation appears. In his own memoirs it is mentioned that, about thirty, he settled down to a married life, taking as his partner the widow Grenwel, who under her maiden name of Anne Downer had been known as one of the earliest members of the London Society. They now kept a grocer's shop in Houndsditch, the back windows of his house overlooking the yard of the Dolphin Inn, now the court-yard of the meeting-house. His dwelling was thrice broken into in the name of the law, and property taken away to the amount of £14, £26, and £33 respectively, in consequence of some informer's having given evidence of his preaching at meeting. To such losses were citizen Quakers of that day subjected, whilst maintaining their numerous poor, and subscribing liberally for the "service of truth," and other important matters. After seventeen years of married life, his wife, who was older than himself, deceased. He remained two years a widower, and then took Anne Goddard, a tradeswoman of Whitechapel, as his second wife, who proved to him, as he says, "an ingenious and careful spouse."

The worthy minister whose pecuniary sufferings we have just alluded to was equally familiar with other forms of oppression. We shall have to mention his name again in connection with the persecutions at other meeting-houses. So frequent were his imprisonments, that he took the precaution of taking his nightcap in his pocket to meeting, to prepare for the too probable contingency of having to spend the next night in Newgate or Bridewell.

G. W. was one of the four who had been allowed to plead the cause of Friends at the bar of the House of Commons, when the Bill of 1662, for the suppression of conventicles, was under debate, and records in his autobiography (called Christian Progress) what there occurred, with the substance of that said by himself and his companions, adding, "as we passed out, some of the members near the door gently pulled me by my coat-sleeve. I turned and asked them what they would have with me? They said *nothing but to look upon you*, I being but a young man, about twenty-four years of age." His three companions were also young, and it no doubt raised some interest to see such youths pleading so simply and earnestly the cause of their friends. He himself became one of those many prisoners confined in Newgate by Sir Richard Brown, and mentions in the above-named work how severe were the sufferings they underwent in that close and pestilential gaol, where two of those that had stood beside him at the bar of the House soon succumbed. During one of his examinations at the Old Bailey, Sir Richard Brown gave a specimen, whilst sitting on the bench, of his insulting vulgarity, for one of the prisoners attempting to warn the court against persecution, Sir Richard, to drown his speech, imitated in a loud voice some of the common street-cries, "Any kitchen stuff—bring out your kitchen stuff." For a magistrate thus to act in his judicial capacity was strangely indecorous.

George Whitehead was a man of ready speech, and seldom at a loss for an answer; thus, when the same Sir Richard Brown, in one of his mad assaults on the Bull and Mouth, undertook to imitate the tone and manner of the preachers, calling out, "The devil is among you!" "This is *my* testimony," he was quickly told, "Then it's since thou came here."—

G. W.'s conduct during the Great Pestilence proved how ready he was at all times to incur any danger to help his friends. When it commenced he was absent on religious service in Surrey, but at once yielded to an impression of duty to go to London, though kind friends, anxious for his safety, endeavoured to dissuade him. There, throughout the height of the disorder, he attended meetings, visited Friends in prison and their own houses, and in all that time he adds, "the Lord preserved me by his power, through Faith, from that infectious Distemper." The Nonconformist preachers generally showed great courage at this time, when many of the beneficed clergy had deserted their posts. And says Maitland ("History of London"), "if ever preaching had a better effect than ordinary, it was at this time, for the people as eagerly catched at every word as a drowning man at a twig."

G. Whitehead was one of the principal of those engaged in pleading with Charles II. on behalf of Friends in prison, when success so crowned their efforts as to obtain that royal pardon issued under the great seal, which is still preserved in the archives of Devonshire House, where those of other denominations sometimes come to see how John Bunyan's name had been allowed by Friends to be included in the same order of release. G. Whitehead was also one of those who undertook to travel round the country with this great document (eleven large skins of parchment), showing it to the sheriffs of the several counties, and so obtaining release of the prisoners.*

As calmer times followed, G. Whitehead became, as it were, the patriarch of Devonshire House, and, indeed, succeeded in great measure to that prominent position amongst Friends which George Fox had occupied till his death in 1690. G. W. was the chief adviser of Friends in all matters touching the development and maintenance of their liberties, and frequently appeared before his sovereign on their behalf.

This Friend, whilst avoiding any expression beyond the bounds of Christian simplicity and truthfulness, had naturally so courteous a manner and such a felicitous style of address, as to give him great place with those in authority, and on several occasions both Charles II., and his successor, James,

---

* This labour was fortunately lessened by seeing the sheriffs of some of the more distant counties when in town.

showed him marked favour, when on not a few occasions he pleaded before them the cause of his friends.

In the presence of four sovereigns in succession—Charles II. James II. William III. and George I.—he stood forth as the undaunted champion of religious freedom whenever the course of legislation seemed to threaten the rights and privileges of his brethren. He was also distinguished as a polemical writer, bringing forth book after book in defence of the Society of Friends against Francis Bugg and other apostates or adversaries of the period. In 1723 his long and laborious career came to a close. He gently passed away in his 87th year, having been a minister of the Gospel for threescore years and ten. His mortal remains were interred at Bunhill Fields. A forcible testimony concerning him was placed upon the books of Devonshire House, signed by forty Friends. G. W. had been much concerned in his lifetime for the poor and afflicted, and at his death he left sums of money for them to all the London Monthly Meetings, as well as to the Friends' Workhouse and the Box Meeting.

It would be needless to enumerate the long succession of ministers and other worthies who, since George Whitehead's days, have borne their faithful testimony and accomplished their day's work in connection with Devonshire House Monthly Meeting, especially as of many of them little is now known. We may, however, mention as prominent, William Crouch, Theodor Eccleston, Thomas Story, Richard and Benjamin Partridge, Henry Fowler, Sarah Beck, Thomas Letchworth, Daniel Mildred, and Thomas Bevan, amongst the ministers; William Mead, described as a linendraper, at the sign of the Ship, in Fenchurch Street; John Eccleston, Thomas Talwin; and coming to our own times, John Thomas Barry, John Kitching, and Peter Bedford, as worthy labourers in other lines of service; Michael Yoakley, William Westwood, William Weston, James Vaston, and John Row, are among the benefactors to the meeting, whose names (with some others) still survive in the important trusts by them founded.*

Of William Crouch and Thomas Story interesting biographies have been published. There is another name on the

---

* For complete information as to the trust property of Devonshire House Monthly Meeting, see the work on that subject, published by authority of the Monthly Meeting in 1861.

list we have given which seems to merit more than a passing notice—that of Theodor Eccleston. No life of him has been published, but he was in his day one of the leading minds of the Society. Theodor Eccleston was born in London in 1650 of religious parents, of the description then known as Seekers, who were convinced in 1659 of the principles of Friends. Theodor began to speak in the ministry before he was twenty, and ultimately became an earnest and leading member of the Society in its church business, as well as a fervent and active preacher of the Gospel. He worked hard for the release of the captives in Algiers, and also for the relief of Friends in the matter of tithes, &c. His ministerial labours were chiefly in the neighbourhood of London, but he occasionally travelled to a distance; for instance, visiting Holland and Germany in 1698. He wrote five or six treatises, and was of great assistance to William Sewel in furnishing materials for the "History of Friends." He died at Mortlake in 1726, and was buried at Wandsworth. (His son John was a director of the East India Company.)

We have now to speak of the Monthly Meeting of Devonshire House in connection with its internal economy and discipline.

Meetings for Worship.

First, as regards the Meetings for Worship. There are, of course, no changes to record as regards the *manner* of holding these. Silent waiting upon God, as the basis of all true worship, was the practice of our forefathers; and when they thus waited they were content with simple accommodation. Upon rude forms without backs sat a portion of the congregation, whilst the remainder filled up the available standing room. Devonshire House was popular in those days, and in 1688 the Six-Weeks Meeting had to advise Friends "not to throng to that meeting and neglect others."

The meetings at Devonshire House were held for the first twenty years amid much opposition from the authorities, and after this had ceased (at the accession of William III. in 1688) they were still troubled by annoyances from the populace. Two Friends were placed at the door of the meeting-house in 1695, and soon afterwards this guard was increased to four, they being appointed (as the minute says) "to keep rude people away" and "keep down rude boys." The same plan was adopted at Wheeler Street. In 1702 we find a curious complaint made, that Friends "allow their children to play outside during meeting-time," and two Friends were appointed to prevent it. During the same year (1702) several private meetings were held at Friends' houses, some of them in the night; but these were soon suppressed by Friends as disorderly. Henceforward, with the exception of rather frequent annoyances from the preaching of persons whose conduct and ministry were not approved of, the Meetings for Worship appear to have been kept up with regularity and propriety from the cessation of persecution to the present time. In connection with this subject, it may be interesting to notice that, in the answers to the Queries in 1756, report is made that "the Advices are occasionally read in the Meetings for Worship."

In the times of holding these meetings some considerable change is apparent. The First-day hours for worship were in the year 1800 altered to 10.30 a.m. and 2.30 p.m., having previously been 9 a.m. and 2 p.m. The Morning Meeting was afterwards altered to 10 a.m. and more recently to 11 a.m., when the Afternoon Meeting was also changed to its present hour, 6 p.m., all the year. About the middle of the eighteenth century an additional Evening Meeting was held in the summer months at 6 p.m., which appears to have been intended, not for members of Devonshire House only, but as a general gathering of any London Friends who might find an evening meeting desirable.

The week-day meetings were at first afternoon gatherings, being held at 2 p.m. on Fifth-day at Devonshire House and on Sixth-day at Wheeler Street. For several years they were held as late as 4 p.m. in the summer. The present day and hour of Devonshire House Week-day Meeting was first adopted in 1759.

Meetings for Discipline.

As regards the Meetings for Discipline, these were first established at Wheeler Street, and afterwards removed to Devonshire House. The records of the first twenty-three years are unfortunately missing, no minutes being extant prior to 1689. At that time the business of the Monthly Meeting was very great; so much so, that adjournments from week to week were necessary. In 1689 twelve Friends were appointed, by the recommendation of the Quarterly Meeting, to act in the intervals of Monthly Meetings, any five to have the power of a Monthly Meeting. Amongst the first twelve were William Mead, William Crouch, Charles Bathurst, Theodor Eccleston, and William Sherlow. It is believed that the "Interval Friends," as they were called, were the precursors of the "Overseers." In 1691 two Friends were engaged to "attend the service" of the meeting, one of whom was remunerated with £6 per annum and all marriage fees (the marriages in Devonshire House at this time were at the rate of thirteen per annum); the other with £4 per annum and all burial fees.

The Women's Monthly Meeting was not established until 1753,* and was not at first held simultaneously with the Men's Meeting. But four years prior to this, in 1749, certain women Friends were invited to attend the Men's Meeting, a practice which was then spoken of as the revival of an ancient custom, and it lessens our surprise at this late origin of the Women's Meeting that women Friends were

---

* Minute of Devonshire Monthly Meeting. "1753, 7th mo. 4th.—This meeting taking into their serious consideration several minutes of the Yearly Meeting, on which the setting up or keeping up of Women's Meetings for discipline is strongly enforced, and their service as well as the authority of their first institution clearly asserted; and having reason to hope for the good effects proposed therefrom, by our religious exemplary women Friends taking upon them that part of the discipline of the Church which more immediately and most naturally belongs to them, to wit, the watching over, visiting, and admonishing such of their own sex who walk disorderly, or act any part inconsistent with our holy profession; and that by such a meeting they might be excited to strengthen one another's hands in their several and respective duties, in particular that important care of recommending and inculcating a religious education among the youth, as well as to administer the necessary relief and advice to poor women, of whose wants and circumstances they should be the best judges. This meeting, therefore, concludes that a Women's Monthly Meeting for discipline shall be established, to be held for the first time on the 2nd Fourth-day in the 9th month next, at the 4th hour, afternoon, being the time when the men's adjourned Monthly Meeting is held, and so to continue to be held every succeeding month on the same days and times. And we earnestly recommend to our women Friends a diligent attendance of the same and the service thereof, as in the wisdom of truth it may be further opened to them, and that they would invite and encourage the youth of their own sex to attend them likewise, who by that means may be diverted from less profitable conversation, and have an opportunity of seeing the concern which subsists in the Society for their preservation from the vanities of a corrupt age, and their establishment in that which alone can make them truly honorable and happy."

largely engaged in the service of other meetings, in the service of which they took charge of much which now comes under the care of the Women's Monthly Meetings.

For more than a hundred years (from 1666 to 1783) the Monthly Meetings were held in the afternoon, mostly at 4 p.m. In 1781 two ministering Friends from Ireland, Martha Ridgway and Jane Watson, expressed their concern that they should be held in the fore part of the day; a proposition to which Devonshire House Friends declined at that time to accede. But, in 1783, two other Friends from Ireland, Christiana Hustler and Hannah Wigham, pressed a similar proposition upon the Monthly Meeting, and in the Tenth Month of that year the alteration was adopted.

The majority of our readers will scarcely need information as to the general character of Monthly Meeting business. In early times, as at the present day, it consisted mainly of matters connected with removals and settlements, records of births and deaths, inquiry as to marriages, care of the poor, trust property, delinquency, &c. &c. A few facts of interest may be mentioned in connection with some of these points.

Marriages.

The due care of all matters relating to marriages occupied much time and attention. Friends' marriages had for years no distinct legal sanction, and especial care was taken that there should be nothing of an unworthy or clandestine character about them. Several instances are on record of the desired permission to marry being refused on account of the recommendatory certificates not being sufficiently explicit as to the previous conduct of the individuals applying. We find one case of a woman being advised to wait because her husband, supposed to be lost at sea, had only been absent five years. As at its most populous period there were almost always three or four, or even more, marriages pending, it will readily be seen that the making of due inquiries, &c., in connection with these, formed a conspicuous feature of the Monthly Meeting business.

Nor was it only with regard to preliminaries that care was exercised. We find on the minute-book a paper from the Quarterly Meeting, dated 27th of Fourth Month, 1715, in which complaint is made that some Friends in marrying have spoken inaudibly, and advises "that all Friends concerned having caution therein aforehand, may avoid having to speak twice, and that each Monthly Meeting, when they observe any defective therein, do cause such *to speak twice* at the times of their proposing their marriage, that they may be prepared to an audible, grave method of speaking, before they come to the time of their marriage meeting."

Care of the Poor.

The poor were evidently numerous from the first amongst Friends of London, and especially so at Devonshire House. The care of these was a work involving much labour. Membership was not defined, and as early as 1698 the Monthly Meeting complains of having had to relieve " scandalous persons," and of the difficulty of knowing whether applicants for relief were Friends or not. The relief of individuals in various ways occupies a conspicuous space in the minute-books. For instance, fresh names are added to the list of those whose rents are to be paid for them; 2s. per week voted to a Friend and five children; a shoemaker is out of work, and " Friends are advised to let him have their shoes;" a widow's little store of *old* money is exchanged for new coins of full value; " Sarah Downes appearing here and requesting stuff to buy her a gown, John Simms is to lay out 10s. for her;" " Ellinor Cart, a small maid," is going into a situation " bare of cloathes," and to receive no wages for the first year, and 30s. is devoted to clothing her during that time. Ellinor, by the way, sadly troubled the meeting with her unapproved ministry in after years, till it was decided that " she shall be kept out if not quiet." As a final instance of the class of facts we have just alluded to, we may mention an undertaker's bill passed in 1700, " To coffins for six poore Friends *thirty shillings.*"

In connection with the subject of the poor, it may be mentioned here that the trust known as Michael Yoakley's Almshouses was at first offered to Devonshire House Monthly Meeting. The following is a minute dated Tenth Month 13th, 1699:—

" John Stoakes and John Kent brought to the meeting the charitable offer of Michael Yoakley to accommodate nine indigent persons, Friends, whom this meeting shall approve of, for several convenient rooms for them to enjoy gratis, provided they be qualified as a paper sent to this meeting directs; but there being some clauses in the paper which seem difficult to be performed, the meeting desires J. S. and J. K. to endeavour to get him to ease that part, and to acquaint him of the meeting's kind resentment of his charity bestowed on poor Friends."

The appointment to speak with Michael Yoakley was continued for a few months, and then, in the Third Month, 1700, report was made that M. Y. says, "he has settled the business of the poor to his content, with the advice of Walter Miers." Thus the affair became, what of course it has ever since remained, a separate trusteeship, unconnected with any particular meeting of Friends.*

Finance.

The collection of funds for the poor, and for various other objects, is a marked feature in the history of Devonshire House Monthly Meeting. What with contributions to the Six-Weeks Meeting for general purposes, the sums paid for "service of truth," the Monthly Meeting's own expenses, and collections for "the powre Pallatines," for relief of sufferers by fire and flood (there were no insurance offices then), and further pecuniary response to "Royal Briefs," Friends seem always from the first to have been subscribing for some charitable object or other. They were for a long period able to do so, for the meeting (as a whole) was by no means a poor one. There were plenty of weavers and handicraftsmen in it whose vicissitudes caused expense, but there were also numerous thriving tradesmen and merchants. As early as 1707 we read of "such Friends as have houses in the country." The subscriptions of the period also attest the populousness of the meeting and its outward prosperity. Thus, in 1700, a "general collection for the service of truth" being required, the result of it was thus reported:—

Within the Walls	£165 13 6
Tower Hill and Minories	73 9 6
Bishopsgate, Shoreditch, and Houndsditch	47 19 6
Spitalfields and Artillery Ground ...	51 2 6
	£338 5 0

---

* For some further allusion to Yoakley's Almshouses, see the account of Southwark Meeting.

This is more than any other of the six Monthly Meetings collected, but as it was a special subscription to free the Six-Weeks Meeting from debt, must not be taken as an average.

For the purpose of relieving the poor with greater economy and efficiency, the Six-Weeks Meeting at this time established the Friends' Workhouse at Clerkenwell, for which the following subscription was raised by Devonshire House, reported as follows:—

Spitalfields, &c.	£96	0	0
Minories	87	0	0
Bishopsgate, &c.	103	0	0
Within the Walls	305	0	0
	£591	0	0

The poor continued to increase during the first half of the eighteenth century, whilst many of the more affluent members died or removed away. In 1714 the Monthly Meeting speaks of "many ancient and wealthy Friends dead." In 1722 it tells "of the late calamity which hath befallen abundance of Friends in and about the city." This, it will be remembered, was the period of panic resulting from the bursting of the South Sea Bubble and other disastrous schemes. Commercial distress was prolonged for some time. In 1730 as many as thirteen names of insolvent members were brought to one Monthly Meeting at Devonshire House.

And now the maintenance of the poor, joined to the numerous other calls upon the liberality of Friends, became almost too heavy to be borne. Again and again did the Monthly Meeting appeal to the Six-Weeks Meeting to be relieved as to its quota to the general stock. But the Six-Weeks Meeting was itself getting largely into debt, and could not afford to reduce its income. As a consequence of this state of things Devonshire House was £328 in debt in 1739, and this debt, notwithstanding frequent attempts to reduce it, swelled to £530 in 1754. Very strenuous efforts had to be made to pay off this encumbrance; the Barnards, and Hanburys, and Vanderwalds, who were now prominent members of the meeting, setting a good example by their liberality. But still we hear of poor increasing, and subscriptions dying out, until the ejectment of disorderly characters a few years afterwards, and a more exact definition of membership, with other changes in the circumstances of the meeting, reduced the expenditure within more manageable compass.*

Out of the care of the poor arose those vexed questions of residence and settlement which, during last century were frequently leading to long correspondences and frequent appeals to superior meetings. The Monthly Meeting in 1709, having had judgment given against it in one of these cases, records its dissatisfaction, but " for peace and quietness sake we doe agree to sitt down sufferers." Similar expressions are made use of on other occasions.

Removals.

It may be interesting to give a specimen of an early certificate of removal issued in the year 1697, and addressed to Westminster Monthly Meeting :—

" Dear ffrds,—Whereas Phillip Harman (who now dwelleth in yor quarter) has desired of us a certificate to yor meeting, but he whilest here living privately and working

---

* Several of the trusts from the income of which Devonshire House now derives an income of £700 a year, date from the middle to the close of the eighteenth century (the period when the pressure of the poor was so much felt); they include valuable bequests, such as Margaret Bell's and Thomas Talwin's (see *Devonshire House Trust Property Book*). Most of the donors express a desire that the principal of their legacies should be invested, and only the annual income be used. A former generation had neglected this practice, using too often the principal to meet present emergencies. One donor, Robert Plumpsted, leaves £100, with the proviso that the interest is to be entered in the collection book as his annual subscription for ever. In 1735, William Weston, late of Hertford, but formerly of Devonshire House Monthly Meeting, left all his estates for its benefit, to be applied to the education, the apprenticing and setting up in trade, " so many boys, sons of poor Friends belonging to this meeting, as the yearly rents of all the estates and the interests of all the monies would admit." Then follows a limit as to what sums are to be paid in each case. Unfortunately, through an informality in the will, its validity was contested by the heir at law, in whose favour, after some years of litigation, it was settled that he was entitled to all the freeholds, leaving only the copyholds and the personal property, to found the trusts. These last, prudently managed, have become very serviceable to the meeting. James Vaston, one of the trustees, increased the fund by a gift of £1,000 in 1770, and in 1829, through a bequest by John Row, of £3,000 4 per cent. Bank Annuities, a charity of a similar character to William Weston's was added for girls, agreeably to the clauses of his will.

in his Chamber for the most part, was scarce known to any of us; but upon enquiry where he lodged they report that he was diligent in his buisiness, and was observed by them to spend no time out of his buisiness but in going to meetings when he had an oppertunity, wee cannot say much of him, (save that when before us he appeared in a tender broken frame of spirit) but must refferr him to you for a furth^r satisfaction of himself whose conversation whilest with you may certifie for him.

"from y^e mo. meetinge held ℔ adjournment at devon$^{s.}$ house."

The Quarterly Monthly Meeting.

There was an institution connected with the Monthly Meetings during the first half of the eighteenth century, which requires some notice. We refer to what were called the Quarterly Monthly Meetings. At one Monthly Meeting in each quarter all business, except that connected with marriages and other urgent affairs, was postponed, and a special character given to the proceedings. What took place at these times is thus described in the Monthly Meeting's answers to the Queries in the First Month, 1707:—"We doe Continue a Generall Monthly Meeting once in three months, to which are invited our young friends and friends' children and servants, among whom are sometimes abstracts of some seasonable exhortations Read, where also they have oppertunity of much Good and suteable advice given for their Edification and encouragement in the blessed truth."

This meeting was established early in the eighteenth century. It was twice revived, viz. in 1723 and 1740. At this latter date a part of the time was set apart for worship. In 1757, it became entirely a meeting for worship, specially for youths, and would seem to have been the precursor of the Youths' Meeting afterwards held under the auspices of the Quarterly Meeting.

Religious and Moral Condition.

As regards the moral and spiritual condition of its members, Devonshire House Monthly Meeting seems to have passed through the same phases of primitive zeal, declension and revival, which have been the experience of the Society of Friends as a whole. Composed at first almost exclusively of convinced and convicted souls, whose ardour had been intensified by persecution, the Church at Devonshire House manifested all the signs of vitality. But by degrees the lukewarm, the unconcerned, and even the immoral and irreligious began to make their presence known and felt. These were faithfully laboured with, and often restored. A "Paper of Condemnation" was usually required from the penitent individual. This document, in which the faults complained of were duly set forth and acknowledged, was then publicly read, and the repentant transgressor was thus retained.

If an individual was contumacious, and refused to appear before the Monthly Meeting, or persisted in evil courses, then, after due inquiry, a testimony was issued, condemning the misconduct of the said individual. But even this does not appear to have been always tantamount to a modern testimony of disownment. For specimens of the *early* documents above alluded to, see the Appendix to this chapter.

The following extracts from answers to the Queries sent up to the Quarterly Meeting in First Month, 1707, will give some idea of the state of the meeting at that date :—

"The sence of this meeting is that Truth doth really Prosper, for although many Friends have of late been removed by Death, yett meetings are large, & there appeares an encrease of Love to truth in many sober people, & an openness upon their spiritts, by their frequenting meetings, and serious attention therein.

"And 'tis hoped a holy zeal and faithfulness doe continue and encrease among friends & true spirituall exercise in meetings, and many are concerned to attend ye services of monthly meetings. And friends Generally in this monthly meeting are in Love unitie and peace one with another.

"And care is taken for the Good Education of Children and publike advice often given for their preservation in the way of Truth. And divers Schools taught by friends are within this Quarter—and hearty Labour and Endeavours are used for the puting in practise of yearely meeting's advice and that the Testimony of Truth be kept up which is not without some good effect."*

---

* Perhaps no department of discipline had become more familiar to the attenders of Monthly Meetings in our day than the periodic answers returned every quarter by them to the Quarterly Meeting, and yet the practice in all its completeness had not existed until after the first century of the Society's existence had passed. Previously to 1755,

Soon after the last of the ancient founders of Quakerism had passed away in the person of George Whitehead (who died in 1722), signs of great declension began to manifest themselves. In 1729 "too great liberty" and "coldness of zeal" are complained of. In 1741 "declension and remissness" increase and continue. In 1748 "diverse evils to the dishonour of truth, and our holy profession" are reported. By this time the Church had found itself encumbered with a mixed multitude of nominal professors whose conduct was a constant reproach.

The discipline had become almost a dead letter; "many such offenders for several years have passed uncensured, and without notice," reports the Monthly Meeting. But there were still faithful ones who mourned over these things, and in 1751 it was resolved "to purify the camp," and revive the discipline.

A committee was appointed to bring in " a list of disorderly walkers," and afterwards continued to deal with the delinquents; for *twenty-one years* the Monthly Meeting was resolutely engaged in reclaiming or disowning its unworthy members. The committee was reinforced from time to time, and occasionally subdivided, to deal with various classes of offences. A similar movement to that described was at this time being effected throughout the Society. To aid in this work, a large Yearly Meeting's Committee were engaged in travelling through the land, and encouraging the subordinate meetings to zeal and faithfulness in carrying out the great work of the revival of the discipline. William Dillworth, Samuel Fothergill, and other members of the Yearly Meeting Committee, visited London in 1761, and encouraged the work

---

Queries had been regularly answered by Monthly to Quarterly Meetings, but only once a year, when it was called preparing a paper to enable the Quarterly Meeting to answer the Yearly Meeting's Questions. This paper was not drawn up in the meeting itself, but was submitted to the Monthly Meeting for approval by a small committee it had previously appointed to prepare such answers. Thus the practice of answering Queries in the meeting itself was not known before about 1755. The earliest notice of Queries at all, as answered by the Monthly Meeting of Devonshire House, occurs 1706-7, when the Society had been more than fifty years in existence—a time when (having passed out of its first stage, during which the sifting test of persecution had kept a check on its members) it was now feeling the necessity of increased care in discipline. There is reason to think that, previously to 1707, verbal information as to the state of meetings had been given.

which was going forward, and also left a paper of advice. The Devonshire House Committee on Disorderly Walkers laboured on till 1772, when they reported that " all had been dealt with except two who can't be found."

The period of defined membership and settled discipline had now commenced. The meeting was still a large one, and remained so for many years, until the great increase in the practice of surburban residence transferred many of its members to other meetings. Meanwhile, its history has been of so regular and ordinary a character as to present nothing requiring special notice.

Its former needs attracted, as before shown, assistance from its wealthier members, whose legacies carefully invested, and the incomes judiciously applied, have put the meeting into possession of a larger income from funded property than any of the other London meetings, a circumstance which, no doubt, has had its influence in retaining residents of a certain class within its compass. Yet the general members became much reduced in number, and in 1850 a fusion with Gracechurch Street Monthly Meeting took place, whereby a large accession of numbers was gained through its comprehending the district of Stoke Newington, where so many Friends reside. Still more recently, in 1860, on the dissolution of Peel as a Monthly Meeting, Devonshire House received an accession, from Peel Meeting-house being added, together with a large portion of the district of that Monthly Meeting, comprising all not taken over by Westminster.

Devonshire House has had on the lists of its members names of those who were the means of much good in their day, some of which have been previously mentioned. It may also be noted that within its compass William Allen was born, his parents being residents in Spitalfields. John Row, who was a silk manufacturer there, was a man of great force of character and benevolence; and his successor in the business—Peter Bedford—is now known, even to the general public, as the "Spitalfields philanthropist." (See Memoir by W. Tallack.)

APPENDIX.

We insert here (extracted from the Devonshire House Records) specimens of the Testimonies of Denial and Papers of Condemnation issued in early times.

TESTIMONIES OF DENIAL.

I.

WHEREAS one Elizabeth Nicholls, a person seeming to be of us, the people called Quakers, having been complained of as one of a scandalous conversation, who, under pretence of having visions and hearing voices that speak locally to her, has presumed through dreams and imaginations to charge divers notorious forgeries, falsehoods, and reproaches upon several honest people,—we thought ourselves concerned for truth's sake to take an inspection into these matters alleged against her; and having fully heard the accuser and the accused, face to face, at sundry meetings where they did appear on that occasion, it was clearly evidenced unto us to our general satisfaction, that the said Elizabeth Nicholls hath acted extremely injurious towards the said Friends, and that she is possessed with a dark, dreaming, and unclean spirit, which has influenced her (without any just cause) very foully to defame divers innocent people; but by a faithful testimony of ancient Friends from the country where she pretends some of these matters she charges were transacted, is clearly detected of her notorious falsehoods.

And we who were present at the hearing of them, do conclude, having a true sense of it, that she hath been led both to believe and tell lies by that spirit of delusion and imagination, which also works in her, to report by fire and sword the destruction of this nation, which false prediction of hers we do reject, knowing that the Lord makes use of no such unsanctified vessels for his use: all the Lord's vessels are holy, and holiness is written upon them. Besides, we daily experience the Lord gracious and merciful, having showed great compassion and favour to the inhabitants of this land, by disappointing the wicked devices of those that imagine mischief against it, and blessing it with plenty and preservation equal with, if not above, all lands, still crowning the years with his goodness, and sparing the nation and people for the sake of the righteous therein.

Now, therefore, we do certify, any who may anyways have heard of the evil conversation and practice of the said Elizabeth Nicholls, that we have no fellowship with her, nor the unfruitful works of darkness she is found in; but do testify against her deeds, for they are evil; nor can she be in unity with us, or accepted into the communion of God's people, until she has unfeignedly repented of the great wickedness she is so manifestly found guilty of, and condemn the lying spirit that has seduced her, which, that she may come to a sight and sense of and turn to the Lord and be cleansed from her gross iniquities, is what we desire, and that she may seek for pardon and forgiveness from the Lord, for there is mercy with him, that He may be feared.

Given forth at our adjourned Monthly Meeting at Devonshire House, the 9th of the Eleventh Month, 1694.

II.

WHEREAS sometimes (to our grief) we are brought under a necessity to bear our testimony after this manner against disorderly and wicked persons, who, having had some conversation amongst us, and pretended by an outside show and profession to be of us, and thereby have been reckoned and accounted by their neighbours and others to be of our Society and fellowship; but after a space, such pretenders have discovered and made themselves manifest by their irregular and unwarrantable practices to be none of us, they being beguiled and governed by the lusts and corruptions of their own evil hearts.

And now the aforesaid necessity is renewed by the treachery and falsehood of James Sargent, a tailor by trade, whose place of abode hath been for some years past in Moorfields, in Three Needle Alley. He is a tall, thin man, his face thin and pale, his nose something long, he doth or did wear his own hair straight and lank, and is thick of hearing. He pretended himself to be robbed at the latter end of last summer, of a pretty considerable sum of money, upon Gadshill, in Kent; but upon inquiry and examination he could not stand by it, nor make it appear; and since that in a disorderly manner he hath unduly forsaken his lodging, being in arrears for rent, and conveyed away sundry garments, broad cloth, and other things, which were delivered him to make up, and being found out at his new lodging in Katherine Cage Court, in Golden Lane, he withdrew from thence also, and conveyed from thence much of the aforesaid goods.

Wherefore that others may not be deluded or deceived by him, under the cloak of being a Quaker, this is given forth, that, his person being described, he may be known, detected, and prevented from doing further prejudice or injury to any one whatsoever.

Given forth from the Monthly Meeting at Devonshire House, 2nd of the Third Month, 1698.

A PAPER OF CONDEMNATION.

THE 7th of Twelfth Month, 1691.—This may satisfy all Friends and others whom it may concern, that whereas I, Joseph Inman, and Sarah my wife, did some years past, contrary to the good order amongst Friends, take each other in the market-place in the town of Colchester, before several witnesses, so that we then and there became man and wife in the sight of God, and are really married in our own consciences and affections, and shall stand unto the same until that Almighty God shall by death part us; yet, however, I have been much concerned for this indecent and rash proceeding on our parts, it being not according to the good order amongst Friends, nor yet becoming truth, we being at that time overcome and captivated by the evil spirit, and so went according to our own fancies, and contrary to the truth, which since hath told us better things, so that I am fully satisfied that in that point I have grieved the good spirit of God and light in my own conscience, and also many good Friends which do wish for the good of all God's people, for which I have been deeply concerned by myself, and have often sighed and moaned alone, and have felt the terror of the Lord on me that I should be so led away; and my wife hath been often concerned for the same, and doth join herself with me in this testimony. In witness whereof we have both set our hands this 7th day of the Twelfth Month, 1691.

JOSEPH INMAN.   SARAH INMAN.

CHAPTER XI.

PEEL MONTHLY MEETING,

Including the Meetings at Peel Court and Sarah Sawyer's, and the First Stoke Newington Meeting.

THE PEEL MEETING-HOUSE.

IN the heart of the densely-populated district of Clerkenwell stands the Peel Meeting-house. Its vicinity is distinguished by many objects of historic interest—amongst others, the venerable gate of the monastery of the Monks of St. John of Jerusalem, the pleasant gardens of the Charterhouse, the ancient Norman church of St. Bartholomow the Great, the now transformed, but for ever martyr-hallowed, Smithfield, and not unworthy to be named with these, in the estimation of any earnest Friend who truly knows and reveres the endurance and devotion of his forefathers, is the simple edifice in St. John's Street, where our meetings have been kept up for more than two hundred years.

A large tract of land in this locality once formed part of the possessions of the Knights of St. John of Jerusalem, having been received by them from the Crown at the dissolution of the monastery. The estate of the Knights afterwards became parcelled out amongst various proprietors, and in 1670 we find the site of our meeting-house and the buildings then existent upon it described in a title-deed as "all that messuage and tenement, with the appurtenances, called the Baker's Peel, situate in or near St. John Street, &c., and now in the tenure of John Elson."

John Elson, over whose head the estate was conveyed by the above-named title-deed by the Buggins family to Elizabeth Plesaunce, had long occupied the premises described. He was one of those "of whom," William Crouch says, "having opened their hearts to receive the word of life, they opened their doors for meetings in their homes." He was a carpenter by trade, and about thirty years of age; and in this his workshop permitted the little flock of "convinced" in the neighbourhood to assemble for worship. As early as 1656

Friends began to meet in that carpenter's yard, and ever since upon that spot have they maintained, often in the face of bitter persecution, the meeting whose subsequent history we purpose narrating in the present chapter.

The meeting grew and flourished, and Friends were soon desirous of expending money in some needed improvements. They accordingly took a lease of the premises themselves, retaining John Elson as their under-tenant, at a rent of £10 per annum. At a later date, in 1692, Friends purchased the freehold for £450 from the Elizabeth Plesaunce previously mentioned.

Having now become the proprietors of the estate, Friends laid out £260 in rendering the premises more suited to the requirements of the Church; still, however, permitting the carpentering business to be carried on in the room, shop, and stall belonging to the house.

John Elson, of whom we shall have again to speak, died in 1701, at the age of seventy-seven, and the "adjacent yard and tenement" were then let to John Stodder, another carpenter and Friend, for £6 10s. per annum. Mary, the widow of John Elson, occupied a part of the building till her death, and one or two poor widows were also accommodated there.

Of this first meeting-house at Peel we have no description extant, but may conclude it retained much of the original shed character, notwithstanding the £260 Friends had spent upon it.

By a minute of Peel Monthly Meeting, dated the 30th of Eighth Month, 1706, we learn that "Mary Elson reports that some women Friends are much straitened for a conveniency in standing when they have something to declare, &c." A committee was appointed to consider of a proper conveniency for that service by altering the gallery or otherwise. At the following Monthly Meeting report is made that the said conveniency has been contrived "for women Friends to stand on when they have something on their minds to declare to Friends."

We may here observe that the arrangements for ministers in early times was not the same as in our day, as may be gathered from the following minute of the Two-Weeks Meeting received at Peel not long after the last-mentioned date:—

"There being an inconveniency from the public women's seats being placed under the men's gallery, their backs being towards the men, so that a man and a woman sometimes stand up together to speak, which to some is a cause of offence, in order to prevent this, it is recommended to the several monthly meetings to take care better to accommodate the women's seats for the future."

But however simple may have been the arrangements of this primitive meeting-house, within its walls a flourishing and increasing Church was established, and on account of "the great resort of sober people thither," £100 was spent in considerably enlarging it in 1708. So much was the carpentering department encroached upon by this alteration, that John Stodder the tenant's rent had to be abated. The minute in the Six-Weeks Meeting books of this date states that Peel "is an old patched building;" public Friends' gallery was to be removed to the south-east side; the late Mary Elson's kitchen to be thrown into the meeting-house, and room over it to be made into a gallery. This meeting-house now possessed a gallery, which was occupied by the inmates of the neighbouring Friends' School and Workhouse (established at Clerkenwell). In 1713 we find the authorities of that institution applying for a key to the gallery, in order that strangers might not enter it before their arrival. But the Monthly Meeting thought it best to advise them to come "softly and *early.*"

In 1721 it was found necessary to pull down the edifice which by adaptation and enlargement had hitherto been made to suffice, and erect a more substantial building in its place. The Six-Weeks Meeting was appealed to, and the arguments advanced by the Peel Friends were pronounced to be "savoury," and £300 voted towards the expenses of the project. A small additional piece of ground was purchased for £21 9s., to make the ground-plan square; then the old building was removed and a new one erected in its place by John Jennings, a member of the meeting, at a cost of £624. The sale of the materials of the previous building only realised £27 10s.

The next repairs of an extensive character were effected, thirty-seven years after, in 1758. Timbers and girders had decayed, and the lead was found very defective. The walls had to be taken down and rebuilt. "A porch, with two setts of strong doores, and *an elegant frontispiece* were added." The cost of these and other repairs undertaken at the same time was £343.

With various improvements and reparations of a minor character, matters went on till, 1789, the external and internal appearance of Peel Meeting-house was totally changed. Previous to this date the ceiling of the interior had been 2 ft. 6 in. lower than at present, and a considerable amount of room had been occupied by great square pilasters supporting the gallery. The front of the meeting-house faced the west, in close proximity to St. John's Lane, where the traffic caused so much interruption from noise, that it was decided to make this west wall blank, and have a new front facing the north. The north wall was rebuilt entirely, and the three others partially so. The roof and ceiling were renewed and raised, and the old pilasters replaced with more suitable columns.

At this time the opportunity occurred of purchasing some property to the north of the meeting-house, stretching from St. John's Street to St. John's Lane, at a cost of £750; an acquisition which led to the formation of a principal entrance from St. John's Street, and the subsequent erection (under a building lease to a tenant) of two houses, Nos. 53 and 54, St. John's Street, and on another portion a doorkeeper's house and other accommodations were built in 1819, by subscriptions among members of Peel Meeting, at a cost of £457. The total amount expended in 1789 for the purchase of land and the alterations was £2,051, of which the Six-Weeks Meeting paid £350, the Friends of Peel subscribed £1,155, and the remainder was raised on annuities.

Thus, then, from the little meeting-place in John Elson's yard, sprang the commodious premises now known as the Peel Meeting-house. But whence the name? it may be asked. From the title-deed already quoted, it would seem that in days when houses were distinguished, not as now by numbers, but by signs, John Elson's house was known by the sign of "The Baker's Peel;" but whether this was adopted from the fact of John Elson manufacturing baker's peels, or from his predecessor having been a baker, or from some other cause, must remain, we believe, only a matter for conjecture.

Sarah Sawyer's Meeting-house.

We have yet another building to speak of in connection with Peel Monthly Meeting. There was anciently in this district a meeting-house known as " Sarah Sawyer's," familiar by that name to the readers of our ancient literature. It stood at the further end of a winding cul-de-sac known as Rose and Rainbow Court, situated at or very near the spot now occupied by Blue Lion Court in Aldersgate Street. From the earliest days of London Friends a meeting had been held here even before the large rooms at the Bull and Mouth Inn had been taken. At first it was simply a meeting in the premises occupied by Sarah Yates, and afterwards by Sarah Sawyer. It gradually acquired a more public and officially recognised position. In 1673 Peel Monthly Meeting hinted to the Meeting of Twelve, the desirability of paying Sarah Sawyer £8 a year, " seeing that the two lower rooms belonging to her is employed for a place to meet in."

In 1675 Sarah Sawyer married Josiah Ellis at the Bull and Mouth Meeting, and Friends soon after took her house. About this time, we read in the Peel minutes that the house is "likely to be taken by a Baptist woman, and Jno. Elson is requested to make the best terms he can." A lease was obtained in 1689, and a sum of money expended in enlarging and improving the premises. In the same year it was registered as a meeting-house according to Act of Parliament, and is described in the registry as " a great building."

These premises at Aldersgate Street seem to have been made use of for various Society purposes, and amongst others for the Women's Meeting, since known as the Box Meeting. For some time there was a considerable meeting for worship held here, but towards 1724 the question of discontinuance was under discussion. The Quarterly Meeting advised its continuance for some time longer; but Peel Friends continued to report " no increase," and at Midsummer, 1726, the premises were given up.

One memorial of our occupancy was brought away. Benjamin Yates, probably a relative of the Sarah Yates mentioned by William Crouch as being at first the resident at the meeting-place, had died in 1711, and had left to Aldersgate Meeting-house various useful appurtenances, and amongst other things a leaden cistern. When Friends vacated the premises this cistern was taken down, brought to the Peel, and there set up to be made use of; a piece of it may still be seen in the yard, bearing the date 1654, and the initials $_{\text{S.}}{}^{\text{Y.}}_{\text{B.}}$ the only relic left us of the ancient "meeting at Sarah Sawyer's."

Boundaries.

The first definitely settled statement of the boundaries of Peel Monthly Meeting to be met with is as follows. It is copied from the fly-leaf of the third volume of the Monthly Meeting's minutes:—

"Bounds of Peel, 1708.

"Beginning at Moorgate eastward, and taking the west side of Moorfields, Bunhill Fields, Windmill Hill, and so to Newington Green and Newington Town northward, including Islington; thence westward to Pinner of Wakefield, and from thence southward to Red Lyon Street, that leads into Holborn, taking only the east side of the said street and thence down Holborn on the east side only unto Chancery Lane, and including that lane on both sides of the way, and all the alleys and courts on the west side of the way that are not thoroughfares and no others; and at the south end of the lane to turn westward in Fleet Street to Shear Lane and Temple Bar on the south side, and so southward unto the Thames, including the Temple and along by the Thames side unto Blackfriars, and so up by the Ditchside, excluding Blackfriars, and up Ludgate Hill to Ludgate, and from thence all without the city walls to Moorgate."

Alterations have been made in the above limits at various dates to suit the arrangements consequent upon the establishment or discontinuance of neighbouring meetings, but it would only be tedious to recount the details of these successive changes.

Peel Worthies.

Turning now to the dwellers in "Peel Quarter" who were accustomed to meet for the worship of God in the buildings already described, we find a goodly list of faithful standard-bearers who lived and laboured in connection with this Monthly Meeting.

The first place on the list is due to John Elson, already incidentally alluded to in connection with the meeting-house; and let it be remembered that he unflinchingly opened his premises to Friends for a meeting, when to do so was to become liable to severe penalties. He gave proof of his integrity in 1656, when he suffered fine and imprisonment for refusal to take an oath, and frequently was he harassed in after years by the officers of the law for permitting a conventicle to be held in his house.

One evening, in the autumn of 1683, a functionary of the period, known as the Headborough, in company with one Gabriel Shad, an informer, and "two red coat soldiers," came to the house armed with a warrant of distraint for £30. Of this £20 was for the meeting-house, and £10 for an unknown preacher. They broke open the doors and took possession of the place. John Elson being from home, his wife, Mary Elson, with a female servant and two poor widows, seem to have been the only occupants. The neighbours saw that something was wrong, and strove to enter, but the reckless soldiers threatened to run them through if they interfered, and closed the door against all intruders. All night these ministers of unrighteous law stayed in the house, making merry over what they could find, "wine, brandy, ale, syrup, bread and cheese, &c." It must have been a time of terror for those poor women with these revellers in the house and the master absent. Doubtless they waited together upon that source of strength to which Mary Elson in her public ministrations had so often directed others. In the morning four loads of household stuff, including a chest of valuable writings, some wearing apparel of the servants, and the personal property of the poor widows, were taken away.

John Elson on his return saw cause to lodge an appeal, and deposited the required £30 with a Justice of the Peace. But the Justice decamped with the money, as well as with some which he held belonging to other appellants.

Again and again did John Elson, on other occasions, see his goods or trade materials carried away for similar reasons. The neighbours sympathised with his losses, and admired his courageous integrity. On one occasion, after the bailiffs had been in possession a week, and had loaded their carts with timber and boards, a neighbour came in, and weeping at the outrage, paid the fine and liberated the goods.

But all these things moved not John Elson. Steadfastly

he adhered to his principles and practice, and after seeing the age of persecution come to an end, he lived on at the spot where he had suffered so much till the year 1701, and died at the age of 77, having been for forty-five years the resident guardian of Peel Meeting.

His faithful helpmeet, Mary Elson, survived him five years. She was an approved minister of the Gospel, and, associated with Grace Bathurst and Ann Whitehead, was one of the leading spirits amongst the noble band of faithful women who were so conspicuous in that early day for their care of the "prisoners for truth's sake," and their bereaved families, and for their constant labours on behalf of the poor or the afflicted. Active to the last, Mary Elson died on the 29th of Eleventh Month, 1706, at the ripe age of 83, the cause of her death being entered as "of old age."

A few days afterwards Friends bore upon their shoulders from a meeting at Peel to their last resting-place in Bunhill Fields, the mortal remains of their departed "mother in Israel," attended by a large concourse of those who had long regarded her with reverent affection.

It consorts not with our principles unduly to exalt the honoured dead; their names we canonise not, and o'er their graves we raise no costly monument; but whilst maintaining the spiritual faith *she* loved upon the spot where *she* lived and died, let us cherish the memory of the loving zeal and active piety of " dear Mary Elson."

"Dear Mary Elson," as the Peel minutes affectionately term her, left £10 to the poor, and to the meeting-house a number of articles, which are thus quaintly enumerated :—

"An account of what goods &c. y^t was Dear Mary Elson's y^t are now this 19 of mo 12 1706 Left as Standards for the use of friends at ye Peel Meeting :

" In ye clossit in ye Room next ye Grate roome,—a box with friends writeings, as also a little title box with a key, as also another box with friends' printed books in it.

" In ye little roome and in ye Grate Roome,—2 grate Caine Elboe Chairs with 2 other Caine Chares with 4 Cushings to them. 6 Leather Chaires & a Cubard with Drawers, 2 little window Curtins & a Rod to ye Windo, a Looking glass & a brush, 2 Joynt Stooles & 2 tables, a p^r of andirons, fier shovel, & tonges & a little trevit to warm Drink on it, 4 Napkins & a Pewter Tankard, a Coper pot, a settle in ye Grate Roome, 2 Turky Work Carpets, a pare of bellows & a fender, 2 Grate Brass Candle Sticks & a hanging candle-stick of brass, a paire of snufers & a standick, a tin hanging Candle Stick, 4 Large Q^t Bottles and a Steene, and a tinder-box and 2 locks & keys."

Passing on, we find the following names amongst the ministers of the Gospel at Peel; many of the early ones were also zealous sufferers in support of the truths they preached:—George Fookes, Ann Anderson, Ann Frame, Humphrey Wooldrig, Francis Camfield, Mariabella Farnboro, John Skelton (who travelled 1,665 miles in 1716–17, though aged 63), Sarah Clarke, Richard Claridge, Isaac Butcher, Benjamin Cowper, Thomas Butcher, Andrew Pitt, Elizabeth Honour, John Hunt, Thomas Whitehead, Nicholas Davis, John Townsend, John Eliot, Sarah Corbyn, Mary Lamb, Deborah Townsend, Robert Letchworth, Ruth Marriott, Abigail Pim, Mary Stacey, Elizabeth Townsend, John Withers, Ann Withers, Dorcas Coventry, John Pim, Ann Hubbert, and Richard Barrett. Amongst the elders we may name as the two earliest, Gilbert Mollesson and Richard Hutcheson (appointed in 1727), and later on, John Jennings, Thomas Corbyn, George Stacey, sen., and Jacob Post.

The most important, perhaps, of the names in the foregoing list is that of Richard Claridge. He was originally a priest in the Church of England, afterwards a Baptist minister, and in 1696 joined Friends. He first declared the truth in the meeting at Sarah Sawyer's, in Aldersgate Street. From 1700 to 1706 he lived at Barking, and distinguished himself by his opposition to priestcraft, as well as by his ministry. In 1706 he removed to Edmonton, and in the following year to Tottenham. Here he opened a school, and became remarkable as a gallant defender of the rights and liberties of Nonconformist schoolmasters. The Vicar of Tottenham and others essayed every artifice to crush his school and bring him under the operation of the penal laws, but their efforts were in vain. For an account of the proceedings against him at Doctors' Commons, and at the Queen's Bench, we must refer our readers to the interesting biography written by his friend Joseph Besse. In 1714, being 64 years of age, he gave up his profession and came to reside in George's Court, near Hicks's Hall. During the remaining nine years of his life he faithfully fulfilled his ministerial calling, dying in 1723, full of years and honour. He was the author of several controversial and religious works.

Joseph Besse,* the biographer of Richard Claridge, was for some time a member of Peel. He had been formerly a schoolmaster at Colchester, wrote many works (for particulars of which see Smith's Catalogue), but is best known for his two large folio volumes of the Sufferings of Friends. Whilst at Peel he seems to have been a sort of assistant-clerk and record-keeper to the meeting, and to have received a remuneration of £4 per annum.

Size of Peel Meeting.

As regards the size of the congregation, some of whose conspicuous ornaments we have above enumerated, we can of course, with respect to the earliest periods, only speak inferentially. It was not a small meeting that was held in John Elson's yard, when, on the 28th of October, 1662, 128 prisoners were haled away. There are also evidences to show that towards the close of the seventeenth and during the early part of the eighteenth century, a large and important meeting flourished at Peel, in proof of which assertion we may instance the necessity for again and again enlarging the meeting-house. In 1712 a committee, appointed to visit families, consisted of forty Friends, which was divided into four sub-committees of ten, and a district allotted for each to labour in. The meeting had evidently declined in strength, and apparently in numbers, about the middle of the eighteenth century, but evinced an upward tendency towards its close. In 1770, after more strictly defining membership and ejecting a number of "disorderly walkers," the list of members showed 228 names, classified thus— 61 men, 80 women, 27 sons of Friends, 32 daughters, 17 apprentices, 2 journeymen, and 9 maid-servants. In 1786 the number had increased to 270, and a larger increase followed in after years. There are those now living who can remember when it was difficult for a late comer to get a seat in Peel Meeting-house. But subsequently (through suburban residences) the meeting decreased very considerably, so that at its division between the Monthly Meetings of Westminster and Devonshire House, less than sixty members were added to the latter meeting by the change, and about twenty to the former.

---

* Son of Joseph Besse of Colchester; married Hannah De Horne in 1716, died at Ratcliff in 1757, aged 74. It is a question whether himself and wife were not of Huguenot extraction.

Meetings for Worship.

Let us now turn our attention towards the meeting for divine worship at the Peel—that institution for the due maintenance of which these men and women were banded together in so close a bond of union—and for whose accommodation so much money was (as we have seen) from time to time freely expended. The meetings for worship held at the Peel, like other London meetings of Friends, were for more than thirty years only maintained in the midst of many difficulties and dangers.

Hints occur of the first difficulties being from the intrusion of rude strangers. As early as 1668 we find an appointment of four Friends " to keep rude boys and unruly persons from disturbing the meetings."

"With unruly persons," accounting themselves members of the flock, Peel Friends were often troubled. In 1668 one of these characters, named Ann Blow, took a couple of pitchers to meeting and publicly broke them, as a testimony against Friends.

John Elson's case, already narrated, is only a sample illustration. Many of his co-members suffered grievously by the seizure of their goods for preaching at, or even for being present at, the gathering in St. John's Lane. But not only was the assembling together fruitful in such after-results of suffering—for going to meeting involved a liability to brutal violence, and immediate incarceration in pestilential gaols. Ruffian soldiers would rush in and lay about them cruelly with their muskets, and drag away both preachers and the more prominent of the listeners to a common imprisonment. The doors of their own meeting-house were often closed against them by authority, but still Peel Friends would meet in the adjacent street. They had thus often to meet in the open air in that terrible winter of 1683 when the Thames was frozen over, so that booths were built on it, and were dragged off from these open-air gatherings to even greater hardships, if not certain death, in the overcrowded wards of Newgate, " the smoke and stench of the place being ready to stifle them."—*See* Besse, vol. i. p. 460.

The vile tribe of professional informers made the Peel one of their harvest-fields, and resorted to any expedient to procure convictions. A miscreant of this class stationed himself at the door one day as Friends left the meeting, and marked with red ochre the coats of the worshippers as they passed out. On this evidence alone, twenty-three were convicted and punished.

In the pages of Besse there are recorded no less than 719 cases of arrest at the Peel Meeting-house.* This is in addition to the number subsequently informed against and distrained upon. Yet through all the meeting was faithfully maintained, and, in 1688, persecution by authority had gradually ceased.

There seems to have been a standing committee of four Friends in 1703 "to speak with disorderly preachers." A notable example of these unapproved ministers is to be found in the case of one James Jackson, who early in last century preached for several years in opposition to the wishes of Friends. He had been formerly a parish priest, and afterwards an Independent preacher, and had then joined Friends. He printed some works in defence of our principles, but, subsequently wrote a book reflecting on his co-members at Peel. They appointed two Friends "to keep James Jackson out of the gallery," but he continued so unruly that he was ultimately disowned. Avowals of want of unity with other preachers occur from time to time in the minute-book.

Times of holding Meetings.

The time for holding the meeting for worship was evidently considered a matter to be arranged in accordance with convenience. The meeting held on First-day afternoon was long the chief gathering of the week. Indeed it is doubtful whether this was not for many years the only meeting held at the Peel on First-days. At any rate it was at its close that Epistles and Briefs, and at one time Testimonies of Disownment, were read and collections made. After a time we find the Morning Meeting evidently the

---

* The Friends arrested at the Peel were often tried at Hicks's Hall, a building now no longer existing, but in the days of Charles II. a comparatively new structure—standing on pillars in the centre of the wide part of St. John's Street—comprising large rooms on the upper storey used by the magistrates for the purposes of the sessions, and furnishing, in this respect, an accommodation now much better provided for in the Court-house on Clerkenwell Green; the lower and open part of the building was for the purposes of a market.

most important, and heaviness and dulness at the afternoon meeting are complained of.

In 1761, at the suggestion of the Quarterly Meeting, the hour of gathering was altered from 2 p.m. to 3 p.m. Peel, however, reported no consequent improvement, "but we believe if Friends pretty generally would eat and drink sparingly, and not provide hot dinners, they might be fitter for the awful duty of worship, and also prevent the difficulty of their servants coming in good time." A much later hour was afterwards fixed upon.

The week-day meeting at Peel was an afternoon gathering till 1753, at which time the hour of 10 a.m. was adopted. This meeting was of course always smaller than that held on the first day of the week, but it is evident that our forefathers expected this to be the case. In 1715 the Monthly Meeting reports that its week-day meetings are "*well attended*," and evidently in consequence of advice having been extended in a recent family visit "that at least *one member of each family* should attend week-day meeting."

Between thirty and forty years ago the concern of Peel Friends was awakened on behalf of those engaged in business, who are unable to attend a week-day meeting in the daytime. In 1834 they asked the Quarterly Meeting to establish a week-day evening meeting at one of the London meeting-houses, and in 1843 they renewed their request. The proposition, as we know, has since been carried into effect.

The Monthly Meeting.

Turning our attention to the Peel Meeting as one of discipline, we find that the minutes of this Monthly Meeting are amongst the oldest official Society documents now extant in London, commencing as they do with the year 1668 (or two years after the settlement of the Monthly Meeting). They treat, as may be supposed, of the usual subjects which came and still come before such assemblies, marriages, apprentices, the poor, &c. &c. But with regard to these topics we may, perhaps, glean a few fresh facts of interest.

The presence of G. Fox and other ancient worthies is occasionally noted on the minutes of Peel Monthly Meeting. And here, as elsewhere, we catch glimpses of the paramount authority of the founder of our Society in the councils of the early Church. To give details might be tedious; but one case, in 1672, may be noted of a certain delinquent who is ordered to carry a paper of condemnation to George Fox before the following morning, as if it were sufficient to satisfy the meeting if but that he had it.

Peel Monthly Meetings for more than a century were held in the afternooon. In 1683 " Friends are desired to gather soon, that business may be despatched before candle-light." It was proposed in 1761 to meet in the forenoon, but the proposal was not acted on till 1783, when it was decided to hold the Monthly Meeting at the close of the Week-day Morning Meeting, a practice which has been since adhered to.

Our early Monthly Meetings were select gatherings, and with this fact one is particularly struck by an examination of the Peel records. Frequent were the appointments to invite certain Friends to attend, and occasionally an appointment is made to search the minutes, and see who are members of the Monthly Meeting. Not, be it observed, members of the Society, for this was a matter without definite settlement for a long period. One Friend writes to the Monthly Meeting to protest indignantly at not being admitted, urging that he used to be invited when formerly living in the compass of Devonshire House.

It was, however, found desirable to make some effort to interest Friends generally, and especially the young, in Society matters, and accordingly a Quarterly Monthly Meeting (similar to that described in our account of Devonshire House) was established in 1745, to which " all are to come." It had been proposed forty years before, but the proposition had not then been carried into effect on account of there being " one at the Bull so near and large," and apparently very popular amongst Friends of adjacent meetings. In 1761 it was decided to answer the Queries at the close of the First-day Morning Meeting previous to the Monthly Meeting, in order that they might become generally known.

The Women's Monthly Meeting was not finally established till 1760 (seven years after that of Devonshire House). In 1729 and 1742 we find certain women Friends urged to attend the Monthly Meeting " as was anciently the practise." In 1753 we read, " It is proposed that men and women Friends should meet together at the second hour, and wait some time on the Lord; afterwards that the women should withdraw into a chamber by themselves, to transact business that shall properly come before them." The consideration of this question was deferred a few months, and then the plan was tried. But in less than two years the arrangement was given up, having occasioned "differences and dissatisfaction." Women Friends again met with the men as heretofore, till in 1760 the Women's Monthly Meeting was revived, and this time successfully.

Care of the Poor.

The care of the poor seems to have been a heavy burden to Peel Monthly Meeting. In 1678 they complain that their district is one to which many poor resort whom they cannot refuse to help. The proper relief of these became a serious difficulty, and on various occasions the Quarterly Meeting had to assist Peel in making up its deficiencies from this cause.

It was evident that in the early days many were relieved, respecting whom little was known beyond the facts of their attendance at meetings and their evident distress. On one occasion it is decided that "Mary Holford is not so near us as to merit constant allowance, but something is to be handed to her as formerly." Such entries as the following are curious :— "To the poor palsy man, 10s.; to poor old Elizabeth, 2s. 6d.; to Ann Richardson for the lame maid, 2s. 6d.; ancient Esther, 2s. 6d.; poor Jones in Shoe Lane, 3s. 6d.," &c. &c. Some of the poor were accommodated in tenements at Bunhill Fields burial-ground, and two or three at the meeting-house. In 1709 report is made that about £90 had been lent to various poor Friends, and that there was little likelihood of getting it back. Confirmed cases of poverty were often recommended to the Women's Two-Weeks or Box Meeting.

Amongst the items of expenditure for other objects, it is noticeable for a long period that wine for Ministering Friends cost 7s. for a gallon quarterly; occasionally we find two gallons charged for in the quarter. This was refreshment supplied them after meeting at Peel, as elsewhere. An item of 6s. for a tankard and salver is doubtless connected with the foregoing. The salaries in 1726 were, £6 a year to the resident caretaker and cleaner, Elizabeth Carter; £2 a year to the non-resident doorkeeper and bidder to burials, J. Stokes; and £4 a year to Joseph Besse (the clerk), as before noted.

Delinquency.

With respect to delinquency, we see in Peel the same laxity of morals, &c. gradually creeping in during the progress of the seventeenth century amongst the "mixed multitude" who were associated with Friends, as in other Monthly Meetings. And the same sharp measures were resorted to in 1750 &c. to "purge the camp," as were generally common at the time of the revival of the discipline; such need not, therefore, be further alluded to.

The Library, &c.

The growth of the Peel Library deserves a passing notice. It seems that there was a chest of books in the time of the Elsons, and after Mary Elson's death some of these were missing, and a Friend was appointed to "ask her—that was, Mary Elson's maid—about them." In 1708 Benjamin Yates presented a large folio Bible, and the Monthly Meeting desired Gilbert Mollesson "to take care that a place be affixed for it to lie on, as also that *a chain be annexed* to the said book in this Monthly Meeting room." The Bible and chain are still preserved at the Peel Meeting-house. Gilbert Mollesson himself gave several books in the following year, and in 1723 the widow of Richard Claridge presented a number that had belonged to her late husband.

The mention of Benjamin Yates's Bible may introduce the fact that, in 1812, Peel Monthly Meeting appointed a committee to investigate the state of the meeting as regards the possession of Bibles by the members. Five cases of deficiency were reported, and the need supplied. There seems at this date to have been a fresh interest felt in this subject, for we find the use of the meeting-house granted in the following year for a Bible Association.

Funerals.

In connection with funerals there are one or two minor circumstances that may be mentioned. In 1716 Peel Friends complain of corpses from Westminster being brought to meeting at Peel, to be buried at Bunhill Fields, and of very few Westminster Friends coming to help to carry. They advise Westminster Friends to take their corpses direct to the graveyard in future, "in order that we may not sustain the hardship we have been at in that affair."

In 1724, on account of meetings being frequently disturbed by the bringing in of corpses during meeting time, Friends are directed to bring them to the meeting-house on the previous evening.

History of the Monthly Meeting.

Having now mentioned a few points of interest in the business proceedings of the Monthly Meeting, some account may be given of the principal points in its history as a corporate body, including the circumstances which led to its junction with Devonshire House.

From an early date Peel Monthly Meeting had to complain of troubles from "contentious spirits," and it would almost seem that the influence of these manifested itself in the action of the body, for its disputes with other London meetings on questions of maintenance and settlement were very frequent. Conferences, arbitrations, appeals, were the result; but Peel Friends often called in question the decisions thus obtained. They declined to relieve certain persons whom the Quarterly Meeting (for instance) adjudged to be their members, and impugned the authority of the Yearly Meeting itself by refusing to accept the "Settlement of 1737."

But it was with the Six-Weeks Meeting that the greatest difficulties arose. Peel had found the burden of its own poor so great, that it could with difficulty raise its quota for the Six-Weeks Meeting. After in vain endeavouring to procure abatement, Peel gave notice in 1736 of its intention to be independent, except only for "its proportional charge for casual poor, horse-bills, servants' wages, candles," &c. The difficulty, however (a matter of cash settlement), was on this occasion settled by arbitration.

But fresh causes of difficulty continued to arise. Peel (in 1740) complained that its extensive suburbs were a receptacle for "poor and irregular Friends of London, and, indeed, of England." They besought the Quarterly Meeting to take charge of all the poor of the London meetings. Meanwhile the Six-Weeks Meeting had become very heavily in debt, and was pleading for enlarged contributions. In 1742 Peel again seceded in disgust, declining to raise any quota in future. The Six-Weeks Meeting sent back the minute, but Peel Friends pertinaciously adhered to their purpose. They paid their share of the outstanding debts, but resolutely held aloof from any further connection.

Matters had now reached such a crisis, as we have seen in our account of the "Six-Weeks," that the Quarterly Meeting was compelled to reconstitute it on a different basis. The result of it being that Peel again joined the compact at the end of 1745.

Peel *Monthly* Meeting was a very small gathering, though a resolute one at this period of its history. We find it frequently not held on account of there not being a sufficient number present to conduct business. On one occasion "the wetness of the weather" is alleged as a reason.

On the 14th of Tenth Month, 1748, Peel sent up an address to the Quarterly Meeting, alleging that it was greatly reduced by deaths, &c., and that Friends had used their utmost endeavours to keep up a Monthly Meeting. "But we fear we shall not be able to continue it in such a manner as we apprehend a meeting ought to be maintained." The address asks "in the most earnest manner" for assistance without delay. Thomas Corbyn, John Hunt, and others, went up with this appeal. Three months afterwards Peel again addressed the Quarterly Meeting, asking to be dissolved and joined to some other meeting, " such a course being more agreeable to us, and more reputable to the Society."

The affairs of Peel did certainly look ominous. The poor were numerous and increasing, its active members few and decreasing; it was from £800 to £1,000 in debt (more than £400 having been advanced by John Jennings), and might well be excused for desiring its own dissolution.

It was some time before affairs were settled; for, to complicate matters yet further, the Six-Weeks Meeting was again itself in debt, and requiring money in contributions. Peel left its poor for a time quite unrelieved, recommending them to the care of the Quarterly Meeting. Great distress ensued, and the Quarterly Meeting was compelled to promise that for four months, whilst affairs were in process of settlement, it would reimburse Peel for all expenditure on behalf of the poor in excess of its own collections. Peel accepted this, and in 1750 a further compromise was effected. The Quarterly Meeting paid Peel £240 and its actual debts, and Peel paid £100 towards the settlement of the debts of the Six-Weeks

Meeting; also engaging to pay its annual quota, and do its best to maintain its poor for the future.

In 1754 we find Peel Friends again approaching the Quarterly Meeting in despondent accents. They give it as their "solid judgment" that it would be best to be dissolved as a Monthly Meeting and united with some other. In their answers to the Queries on the same occasion, they confess "that things are low with regard to solid, substantial, religious experience," "worldly concerns being preferred."

The Quarterly Meeting agreed to give Peel Monthly Meeting financial aid when necessary, and appointed ten Friends as a committee to attend the Monthly Meeting, and assist in the business.

For some time after this date, the names of all present at Peel Monthly Meeting are minuted—the number varies from twelve to about seventeen members of the Monthly Meeting, and a few of the Quarterly Meeting committee.

Matters seem now to have taken a turn for the better, though chequered with occasional complaints, and the consequent extension of Quarterly Meeting aid, until, at the time of the extensive alterations of the meeting-house in 1789, there was evidently a flourishing and wealthy meeting. Church business was again conducted with zeal and efficiency for upwards of half a century more.

But about the year 1856 great weakness had again become manifest. There were no recorded ministers, and but one elder, and the congregation had dwindled down to a very small number.

The Quarterly Meeting appointed a committee on the subject, but the meeting, which had twice in former times begged to be dissolved, was now four years before it could be brought to acquiesce in its dissolution. After various propositions had been made and discussed, it was agreed to divide its area into two portions. The recently established meeting at Holloway and its adjacent district was transferred to Westminster, and the Peel Meeting proper was joined to Devonshire House.

An equitable division of the funded and other property was effected. The Holloway premises were allotted to Westminster, whilst the Peel premises—the house in Field Lane (recently purchased by the Holborn Viaduct Commissioners), and Mariabella Briggin's legacy of £200, the interest of which is annually divided among the poor by the overseers of the Peel Meeting—were retained for Devonshire House.

Peel:
Left, Courtyard, drawing by A.S. Hartrick, from the *Pall Mall Magazine*, 1905 [LSF]
Right: photo from St John Street, undated [LSF]

facing p.210

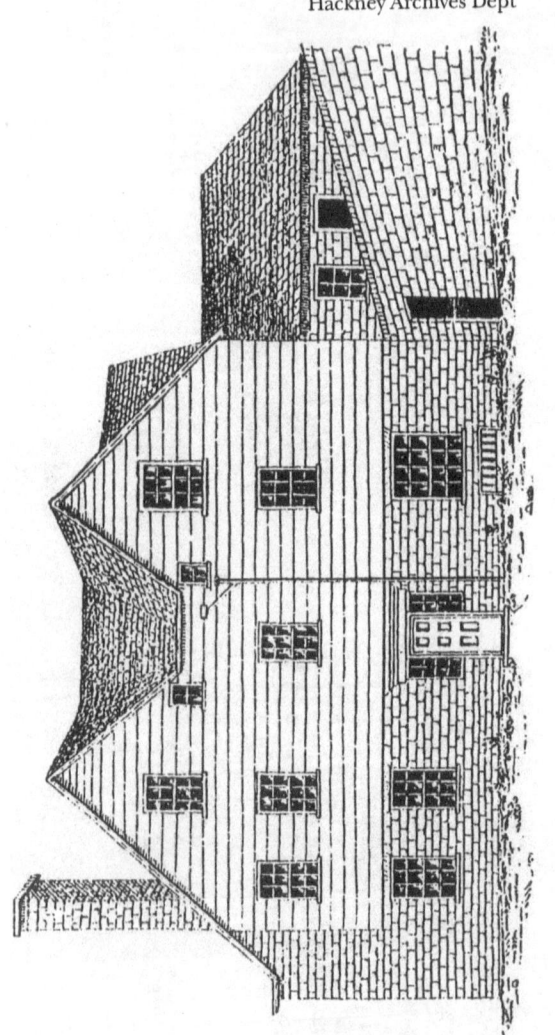

Hackney Archives Dept

Stoke Newington: the building used by the first meeting, from 1698 to 1741: a drawing of 1825, when it became the first premises of Mary Lister's Invalid Asylum; it seems unlikely to have changed significantly in the interim. From I. Prideaux Moline, *A Short History of the Home Hospital for Women (Invalid Asylum)*, 1916 [Hackney Archives Dept]

On the 1st of the Eighth Month, 1860, Friends of Peel met for the last time in the capacity of an Independent *Monthly* Meeting; and the following minute closed their records, kept without intermission from 1668 to 1860, a period of 192 years:—

"This being our last sitting as a Monthly Meeting, in accordance with the minute on record received from the Quarterly Meeting, and having completed what appeared to remain for our attention—our women Friends being present, and being about to separate, we desire to commend each other to the care and keeping of Him whom we reverently acknowledge as Head over all things to his Church.

"Signed on behalf of the meeting,
"JOSEPH ARMFIELD,
"Clerk this time."

THE FIRST STOKE NEWINGTON MEETING.

In the pleasant suburb of Stoke Newington is situated at the present day a large and flourishing meeting of Friends. This meeting, as we shall presently see, is of comparatively recent origin.

But towards the close of the seventeenth century, when Stoke Newington was a retired hamlet, separated from the Metropolis by an extensive district of meadows and corn fields, a meeting was established here, on the premises of a gardener, which after being maintained for nearly half a century, was given up for want of attenders.

In 1698 it had been first proposed to the Quarterly Meeting to set up a meeting at this place to be held *once a month;* but the subject was referred to the Six-Weeks Meeting, who hired two rooms and arranged for a meeting to be held *fortnightly* on those First-days on which no meeting was held at Tottenham. It was placed under the care of Peel Monthly Meeting, in whose territory it was situated, the rent of the rooms, however, being paid by the Meeting of Twelve.

The deed of registration of this meeting is in the possession of Robert Alsopp, who has kindly permitted a copy of it to be taken. The original is engrossed on a small strip of parchment, $3\frac{1}{2}$ inches wide and 13 inches long. The text is as follows, viz.:—

"Middss. These are to Certifie That att the Generall

Sessions of the peace held for the county of Midss at Hicks Hall in St John's Street in the said county on Monday the ffith day of this instant December it was certified to the Justices of the peace of the same County That an Assembly of persons dissenting from the Church of England for religious Worship called Quakers would be held in the house of Robert Walburton gardener situate in the parish of Stoake Newington in the s^d County which was recorded att the said Sessions according to the statute in such case made and provided. Dated this ffifteenth day of December Anno. Domini 1698. Anno q^r· Regni Regis Gulielmi," &c.

Five years after its establishment much scandal was created by two Friends going down to this rural meeting, and, without having taken any of the preliminary steps required by the rules of the Society, standing up before the congregation and taking each other in marriage. Friends had had much trouble in procuring a legal sanction for their marriages, and were fully alive to the danger of any proceedings of a clandestine or informal character. To clear Friends of the reproach, Devonshire House Monthly Meeting, to which the parties belonged, formally disowned them for "their disorderly works of darkness," and, in accordance with the custom of the time, circulated copies of the testimony amongst the London meetings.

In the year 1716 we find on the minutes of Peel a complaint that "Friends of Tottenham have settled a meeting *every First-day* without the consent of the Quarterly Meeting, whereby ours at Newington has much declined." It is also stated that "there is hardly a public Friend seen there for several meetings together," and that the attendance has dwindled down to some eight or ten worshippers.

The Quarterly Meeting decided that it was not in good order to set up a meeting for worship without its consent, and desired Enfield Monthly Meeting to hold its meeting at Tottenham fortnightly as heretofore.

A feeling appears now to have set in, that Stoke Newington and Tottenham Meetings were mutually prejudicial to the interests of each other. In 1723 we find Enfield Monthly Meeting putting the question to Peel whether Newington Meeting is of any service, and advising its discontinuance.

But Peel Friends did not seem to like the idea of giving up their suburban offshoot, which they evidently regarded somewhat in the light of a mission Church *in partibus in-*

fidelium. They accordingly took measures for sustaining its efficiency. To secure a better attendance and give time for London Friends to get out to it, they fixed the hour of its assembling at 1 p.m. in summer, and 2 p.m. in winter. They also specially besought the members of the Morning Meeting " to visit for the sake of strangers who come in there."

Peel Friends themselves also resolved to do what they could to keep up the meeting by frequent attendance. For many years they minuted each month the inquiry, " What Friends have attended Newington Meeting since our last Monthly Meeting?" and received reports as to its condition.

An evident improvement followed the adoption of these measures, and the attendance for a time considerably increased. But these artificial efforts for its maintenance were not permanently successful, and in 1728 we find the Six-Weeks recording it as their opinion that " Newington Meeting is of little or no service, and therefore had better be laid down." But this judgment seems only to have stirred up Peel Friends to renewed efforts for its continuance.

In Twelfth Month, 1733, report was made that the house wherein Friends rented rooms for their meeting at Newington had been taken for the parish workhouse. It transpired, however, that the tenancy of Friends would not be interrupted, and the meeting was still kept up for some years.

But it became increasingly evident that the meeting was dying a natural death for want of resident Friends to maintain it in efficiency, and in 1741 it was at last discontinued.

CHAPTER XII.

SOUTHWARK MONTHLY MEETING,

Including the Meetings in Horslydown, the Park, Peckham, and Deptford; also Long Lane, and the Park Burial-grounds.

SOUTHWARK.

PERHAPS no portion of the Metropolis has been more conspicuous in the annals of Nonconformity than the borough of Southwark, whose intimate association in modern days with the ministry of a Rowland Hill, a Newman Hall, or a Charles H. Spurgeon, seems but the continuance of its ancient fame as a stronghold of religious dissent.

Two centuries ago, when the citizens of London were for the most part vieing with each other in frenzied devotion to the restored monarchy, and the restored national religion, the multitudinous sects of Puritanism continued to flourish in Southwark and Bermondsey, and indeed in all the metropolitan parishes of North Surrey. Presentments from grand juries and petitions from " well-affected" inhabitants are still extant, showing that at the period referred to the " sound Churchmen" of this district had really worked themselves up into an almost hysterical condition of terror and alarm at the rapid growth of Nonconformity amongst them. But in vain were the Penal Laws evoked and carried into execution, for in spite of severity the Dissenters manfully asserted their rights, and occupied a prominent position in the borough.

In 1682 we find the grand jury praying for a more rigorous suppression of conventicles, complaining that " we of this borough more particularly labour under this grievance." They assert that notoriously disaffected persons have become "the majority of governors of a hospital of royal foundation amongst us," the disposers of all offices and employments relating thereto, and the managers of its revenues. They earnestly beseech to be protected from their Nonconformist neighbours, "that so the numerous party of honest trading men of this vast body be no longer discouraged in their industry, or cramped in their loyalty by the artifices of those who meditate our ruin."

Such, then, was the position occupied by Puritanism in South London, and such the feeling which animated those by whom it was feared and hated. It is evident that amongst these troublers of the official and parochial mind of Southwark, Friends were numerous and important. In the locality under notice they effected an early footing, and for many years maintained a prosperous career.

It was in the summer of 1654 that Francis Howgill and Edward Burrough were preaching and teaching (as we have previously stated) in London and the neighbourhood. One day they addressed an assembly at an Anabaptist Meeting-place in Southwark. Much disputation followed; some pleading on one side and some on the other, but the result was that a number of the Anabaptists seceded and became Friends, and this appears to have been the origin of our religious Society on the south bank of the Thames.

As in other places, our first glimpses of the newly-convinced reveal to us the little companies meeting in private houses to wait upon God. They told others of the treasure they had found, and from time to time "public Friends" came among them; and from day to day the Churches were edified and multiplied. In 1654 we find one little company meeting at the house of Daniel Fleming, in Blackman Street, and another "in the little parlor at William Shewen's house in a yard at the sign of the two brewers in Bermondsey Street." Then shortly afterwards a widow named Mary Webb allowed Friends to meet in the garden of her house in Fair Street. This assembly was the parent of the future Horslydown Meeting. About three years later, viz. in 1658, we find a meeting established at the house of Thomas Hackleton, near the Falcon, in the Upperground, which developed into the future Park Meeting. About this period also, as Friends increased, Henry Clarke of Bankside, Robert Benburke, Adam Walker of Newington Butts, David Barrow of Marygold Stairs, and a Friend at Lambeth Marsh, all sheltered meetings of Friends in their houses. There was also a large meeting at Walworth, of which we read that it "was much disturbed by rude people."

HORSLYDOWN.

The meetings enumerated above have all ceased to exist. Two of them, however, when located in buildings specially built for their reception, maintained a long and prosperous career, under the name of Horslydown and Park (subsequently Southwark) Meetings. The former was for a long period the most important assembly of Friends in South London.

The meeting at Horslydown commenced about the year 1655, in Widow Webb's garden. The assembly is described as being then "pretty large." The widow was a woman of property, and shortly afterwards she built some houses " on Artillery Wall," and with the assistance of Friends erected a meeting-house at the back of them. But in 1663 Mary Webb found occasion to sell her houses, and the meeting-house, being included in the same lease, was sold with them. It was, however, resold to Amor Stoddart for the use of Friends, at a peppercorn rent for the remainder of the term by the purchaser Thomas Jones.

The history of the Widow Webb's meeting-house is a thrilling narrative of cruel persecution on the part of the authorities, and of meek endurance on the part of Friends. During the year 1662 eighty persons were at different times taken from this edifice to prison, of whom several died in gaol. In the following year we read of the silence of the meeting being broken by the sudden inrush of excited soldiers, firing their muskets as they entered. They would follow up this demonstration by bruising and cutting the unoffending worshippers, and even amused themselves by firing their muskets, charged with powder, whilst the muzzles were pressed against the dresses of the women, so that their clothes were burnt and their bodies scorched. In succeeding years the meeting at Horslydown was still kept up in the face of similar violence, and the dragging off of twenty, thirty, or even sixty, of the attenders to prison. Some of these never regained their freedom in this life. Amongst those who thus perished was the noted preacher and controversialist, Samuel Fisher, who died in the White Lion Prison in 1665.

But it was in 1670, after the passing of the second Conventicle Act, that Horslydown Friends seemed to have passed through their severest trials. Through May and June of that year fines, imprisonments, and cruel beatings, were unscrupulously tried as means for preventing the meeting from being held. Friends were kept out of the meeting-house, but they still, as at other places, assembled in the adjacent street. Then the cavalry strove to ride over them, but the horses, more merciful, refused to go forward. But not to be foiled in their cruel endeavours, the soldiers turned their horses round, and backed them on to the crowd of worshippers to do what mischief they could.

In July, 1670, a Royal Mandate was issued, commanding that the meeting-house itself should be pulled down. The King, with Prince Rupert and the bearers of the historic names of Ormond, Ossory, Ashley, Oxford, &c. &c. were present at the passing of this order in council. It was committed to the charge of the great architect, Sir Christopher Wren, as Surveyor of Works, to see to its execution.

It was on Saturday, the 20th of August, that the soldiers and a number of carpenters arrived and pulled down the meeting-house, carrying away the boards, windows, benches, and forms. On the following day Friends met and held their meeting on the heaps of rubbish till the soldiers appeared on the scene and dragged them away.

It is hardly needful to recount in detail the harrowing scenes that occurred at this spot during the next four months. Friends were beaten and cut with clubs and pikes and halberts till their blood lay conspicuous in the street. Women and even girls were not spared; they suffered blows and wounds like their fathers and mothers, were dragged along the streets fastened to the saddle-bows of the cavalry, and otherwise maltreated, and still through all the meeting was kept up.

"If you knew what orders we had, you would say that we dealt mercifully with you," said a soldier on one occasion, although it seemed as if almost everything short of actual murder had already been attempted. After a time the violence of the persecutors seemed partly to wear itself out, though for many a long year the Church at Horslydown was liable to occasional interruption in its religious meetings and its members to frequent sufferings from fine, distraint, and imprisonment.

It is wonderful to notice how little can be gathered with reference to these events from the records of Horslydown Monthly Meeting. It is from the pages of Besse, or Whitehead, that our information respecting them has to be gleaned.

We do indeed find on the 7th of September, 1670, an order for a carpenter to make a boarded fence across the end of the meeting-house, to keep the boys from climbing over. This was done at a cost of 9s. 6d. The destruction of the building by the soldiers had been probably only partial, and chiefly confined to the end nearest the street, and to the interior. Another entry about this time is for six deal boards (probably for seats) and planing, 7s. 6d., also for clearing away bricks, rubbish, and timber, £1 2s. 6d. These simple entries are about all the hints furnished us by the records of the Monthly Meeting concerning the circumstances that have been described, the minutes referring only to care of their apprentices, their poor, their marriages, their delinquents, &c. &c.

Friends rebuilt their demolished meeting-house in 1671, and seem to have studied comfort as well as convenience in its fittings, for we find William Crouch charging them £2 7s. 6d. for "carpets and curtains." There was a gallery to this second meeting-house, which seems frequently to have occasioned trouble. At one time it has to be lowered, being "such a strain to ministering Friends"; at another time it is to be plastered to keep dust and dirt from falling through; and then again, a door or gate has to be placed on the staircase to keep the boys from running up and down. Rude boys, by the way, seem to have been a standing nuisance both at Horslydown and Park, and there was a monthly appointment of two Friends for each of these places to keep this class of attenders in order.

The lease from Thomas Jones seems to have expired in 1697, when a fresh one was obtained from the ground landlords on payment of a fine of £140, for forty-one years, at a yearly rent of £8. This property, now taken, included two messuages, or tenements, in front of the meeting-house. The expiry of this term brings us to 1738, when the lease of the same or an adjacent site was obtained from the Rector and Churchwardens of St. Olave's for ninety-nine years, at £5 rent, with covenant to spend £400.

Friends far exceeded their contract by spending £1,134 in erecting a new meeting-house, the Six-Weeks Meeting contributing £500 towards it. This building was opened for divine worship on the 18th of First Month, 1739. In 1800, when the lease had still thirty-seven years to run, it was thought best to concentrate the whole meeting at one meeting-house, viz. at Redcross Street, and the Horslydown

Meeting-house was sold for £500. The building is still in existence, and has been used since Friends left it for a temperance hall, and other purposes.

The Old Park Meeting-house.

Once more turning our attention to the earliest periods of Quaker history, we find that, in 1674, the meeting held at Thomas Hackleton's had outgrown its accommodation. Friends accordingly took on lease a piece of ground forming a part of the extensive park once attached to the palace of the Bishops of Winchester. This ground was rented from one James Ewer, a builder, who seems to have given his name to the street soon afterwards built there, for in the angle of Ewer Street is the site of the Old Park Meeting-house. It was a substantial brick building, standing clear of other houses on three sides. Two sides fronted the road, and, in fact, it seems to have been just the sort of building, as regards position and convenience, for a military guard-house, and for this purpose it was seized by the Crown and used about a dozen years after its erection.

It was in the Third Month, 1685, as George Whitehead informs us, that the soldiers came and turned the Park Meeting-house into a guard-house, "and did great spoil and damage about and in the same, by pulling down pales, digging and cutting down trees, carrying away and burning them; and also the wainscotting and benches about the room, and they carried away many of the out-doors and many of the casements." After doing this damage (estimated by the Monthly Meeting at £40) and occupying the place so long as suited their convenience, the military passed on to the camp, leaving the dismantled house open to anybody.

John Potter, the reputed owner, took possession, but in October of the following year the occupants were again ejected. George Whitehead states, "a quartermaster belonging to Colonial Haile's regiment came to the chambers of the said John Potter's tenants and demanded entrance; which being denied, the quartermaster, with the help of soldiers, broke in, handed away their goods, and turned out three aged women to another house: and when they had taken possession of our said meeting-house and rooms below, they pulled down the galleries and made a brick wall across the lower room, with many other alterations, as if they intended to have the sole and perpetual possession to themselves, having made a sort of place for prayers or a mass house in one end, inclosed from the rest by the said partition wall."

It appears that Friends were not disturbed in the possession of the adjoining tenement, but the occupant thereof was sadly annoyed by the soldiers amusing themselves by making holes through the wall into his house. He complained to the Monthly Meeting, who appointed Robert Paile to have the damage repaired, and to speak to the "Coronall" to prevent the soldiers from indulging in future annoyances of the kind.

In the Tenth Month, 1686, George Whitehead and Gilbert Latey went to the King and expostulated with him about the seizure of the Park and Savoy meeting-houses for guard-houses. Colonel Hailes was present, but for the details of the interview we must refer our readers to G. W.'s deeply interesting biography. Suffice it now to say that the King declared, "I am resolved to invade no man's property or conscience," adding, that he would inquire further into the matter, the result being that in a few weeks the meeting-house was restored to Friends. But the King still coveted his convenient guard-house in Southwark, especially with the supposed improvements effected by the military during their occupancy. In the Fifth Month, 1687, an application was made to the Six-Weeks Meeting apparently through William Penn, for the purchase of the Park Meeting-house by the King.

"At which meeting" (we quote from the Six-Weeks Meeting minutes) "it was unanimously agreed that Friends cannot take any money of the King for the meeting-house in the Park, having a tender conscience to God in the matter. That 'tis the mind of this meeting that the King have the said place during his pleasure. That Friends are desired to withdraw from appearing in that place, and to get some conveniency at the burying-ground in the Park side by the building of a shade." Several Friends were then appointed to "signify the mind of the meeting to William Penn to present it to the King," and to expend £30 in the proposed temporary erection.

For about a year and a half the King's troops used the Park Meeting-house, and not till the time of the great Revolution did Friends regain possession. At a Monthly Meeting held at Horslydown, on the 7th of Ninth Month (November), whilst the Prince of Orange was marching towards London, the following minute was made:—

"Agreed that Thomas Hudson, Wm. Chandler and Walter

Above: Cambrian Chapel, formerly Horslydown meeting house.
Below, Southwark New Park meeting house, exterior.
Engravings with watercolour by G. Yates, 1825 [City of London,
London Metropolitan Archives, from Manning and Bray collection]

facing p.220

Southwark New Park meeting house interior: above, "Monthly Meeting House" (women's, first floor); below, main room. Engravings with watercolour by G. Yates, 1825 [City of London, London Metropolitan Archives, from Manning and Bray collection]

facing p.221

Miers should go to Coronall Hales about seeing to gett yᵉ meeting-house in yᵉ Park againe yᵉ King having as we here ordered* that we should have it."

On the 5th of the following month we read:—

"Agreed that the Friends formerly appointed about to gett the meeting-house in yᵉ Park bee still continued, &c." "to see to gett yᵉ Gards out, they having already possession of the part that was made up for their chapel."

We find that the soldiers now withdrew, and Friends returned to their ancient meeting-place; transforming their temporary structure at the burying-ground into a home for two poor women.

In the year 1689 the well-known Richard Scoryer, who afterwards kept a celebrated training-school at Wandsworth, occupied the upper storey of the Park Meeting-house as a school, with permission "to make a window in the roof, provided he cuts no rafters."

Occasional repairs, the building of two galleries, renewals and transfers of lease, &c. &c., seem to be the only historical facts that have come down to us in connection with the old Park Meeting-house for the next sixty or seventy years. In 1759 there was some talk of rebuilding, on an estimate of £300; but nothing was done, and in 1762 the house was declared to be dangerous to meet in, and was ordered to be shut up. The meeting was now held for a time at a schoolroom in the Green Walk, belonging to a Friend.

New Park Meeting-House.

Before proceeding to speak of what was long known as New Park Meeting-house, and afterwards as Southwark Meeting-house, we should premise that about the distance of a quarter of a mile from the premises whose history has been narrated Friends possessed a burial-ground. It was here that the temporary meeting-house had been erected in 1687. This burial-ground had been long used by Friends; as early as 1666 we find them already in possession of a lease, and paying twenty-two shillings a year rent. It was originally a rural spot, separated by wooden pales from the surrounding gardens, and was situated to the south of the present Worcester Street, being known as the Park † or Worcester

---

* Originally written "granted" and altered to "ordered."
† Grounds of the palace of the Bishops of Winchester.

Street burial-ground. In connection with this burial-ground we may observe that there is amongst the Southwark papers an original bill presented by John Elson, the worthy carpenter of Peel, in which, amongst other matters, there is a charge for " mending the fence which rude lads broke down and carried away, and burnt, leaving the burial-ground open."

This ancient burial-ground became very thickly populated with the dead, and in 1733 it was raised to accommodate more.

In 1762 Friends found that they could procure a lease of the land lying between this Worcester Street burial-ground and Redcross Street, which they took accordingly; and here, at a cost of about £640, the new meeting-house was erected. The old building in Ewer Street was now sold for £140.

The New Park Meeting-house was opened on the 15th of Tenth Month, 1763. In 1799, on the giving up of Horslydown Meeting-house, more than a thousand pounds was spent in its enlargement to render it capable of containing all the Friends of the borough.

A strong meeting continued to flourish here for many years, attended by families engaged in wool, hop, corn, and other trades, for which the borough was a favourite locality. Eventually, by adopting the practice of suburban residence at Peckham and elsewhere, the original meeting became greatly reduced in its attenders. In 1860, in consequence of the formation of New Southwark Street, the premises were compulsorily sold to the Metropolitan Board of Works for £2,619, and the last meeting for worship was held here on the 28th of the Tenth Month in the year mentioned.

The adjacent burial-ground (which had been closed for interments since 1794) was included in the above sale. This was carefully dug over under the superintendence of a Friend who attended daily whilst the work was in progress, and about a thousand skeletons and nineteen entire lead coffins were dug up. All wood coffins had disappeared. The bones were packed in 111 shells of ordinary size, and carried by hearse to the Long Lane burial-ground. Here two large deep pits were dug and the remains re-interred. (For further particulars as to this re-interment see Appendix.)

Long Lane, Bermondsey.

The burying-ground at Long Lane just referred to was purchased for £120 in 1697. It has been extensively used, and once or twice raised in consequence. It seems formerly to have contained large trees growing in it, the roots of which are complained of in 1751 as obstacles in digging. This burial-ground was closed in 1854, and it is now let to a tenant who rents it of Friends for a small consideration, on condition of keeping it in order.

Deptford.

We now turn to the meeting-house at Deptford, which has long been under the care of Southwark Monthly Meeting. Our readers will find in our account of the Westminster meetings an allusion to a Court official named Nicholas Bond, who sheltered a meeting of Friends in his lodgings at Worcester House. On being removed to Greenwich he allowed a meeting there for a time, which was subsequently transferred to Deptford. Gilbert Latey was a frequent attender at Greenwich Meeting, and tells us in his Journal of the dangers to which he and his friends were exposed by going there.

This first meeting, however, subsequently fell away, but about 1691 it was proposed to be re-established. In the following year "two brick tenements and gardens in Butt Lane, part of a field formerly called Hart upon Hope, or Coney Wall, measuring 100 feet by 32, was purchased for £140, and £60 laid out in repairs. In 1694 the Six-Weeks Meeting established a Monthly Meeting at Deptford, under its own care financially, but to be assisted by Horslydown in disciplinary matters. This latter Monthly Meeting had a standing committee of twelve Friends, whose duty it was to attend the Monthly Meetings at Deptford, an arrangement which lasted until 1729, when (on account of the increasing weakness of the smaller meeting) the two were completely joined; but a meeting for worship has been maintained at Deptford, as at present. There is a small graveyard on the premises, which was closed, by order of the Government, a few years ago.

Deptford Meeting-house possesses a curious relic in an old form, upon which tradition confidently asserts Peter the Great used to sit. It is well known that this wonderful man, whom

Macaulay has daguerreotyped in eloquent picture-language,* attended the Friends' meeting during his stay at Deptford. It was one of those strange contrasts which entered so strikingly into the character of this extraordinary monarch that he, at times so convulsively restless, should choose for his place of worship the silence of a Quakers' meeting. (See Appendix for some further account of Peter the Great and Friends.)

WOOLWICH.

About 1674 there was a small meeting of Friends at Woolwich, which was then joined to Horslydown Monthly Meeting. They rented a room or rooms, but little can now be gathered with reference to the subsequent history and decline of this little gathering.

PECKHAM.

The most recently established of the meetings in the district is at Peckham, which, from being originally an offshoot, has now become the headquarters of Southwark Monthly Meeting. In 1821, several Friends having become resident in this locality, it was proposed that a meeting should be established here. A carpenter's shop in Baker's Row was accordingly hired for £28 a year, and £120 spent in fitting it up for the required purpose. Seats were borrowed at first from Deptford, and the meeting opened on the 23rd of Twelfth Month, 1821.

Four or five years afterwards, Peckham Meeting-house was built, being completed in 1826, at a cost of £1,650, of which £1,494 was collected specially, and the rest defrayed by the Six-Weeks Meeting. In 1844 nearly £700 was spent

---

* Macaulay, in his *History*, vol. v. p. 75, draws this picture of Peter,—"His stately form, his intellectual forehead, his piercing black eyes, his Tartar nose and mouth, his gracious smile, his frown black with all the stormy rage and hate of a barbarous tyrant—and above all a strange nervous convulsion which sometimes transformed his countenance during a few moments into an object on which it was impossible to look without terror—the immense quantities of meat which he devoured—the pints of brandy which he swallowed, and which it was said he had carefully distilled with his own hands—the fool who jabbered at his feet, the monkey which grinned at the back of his chair, were, during some weeks, popular topics of conversation." Macaulay also alludes, as one of the contrasts in his character, to Peter's love of retirement.

Deptford:

Above: undated reproduction from a watercolour [LSF]
Below: photo 1907, soon before demolition [LSF]

Peckham: undated lithograph by Howard Dudley [LSF]

in enlarging. There is a small burial-ground at the back of the meeting-house, which is now closed. Recent interments from this district have usually taken place at the general cemeteries at Nunhead and Norwood, or Peckham.

Populations, &c., of the Monthly Meetings, &c.

Turning now from questions more immediately connected with houses and lands to the consideration of the Church and its members, we see, in the first place, that the Monthly Meeting of Southwark was from early times large and influential. During the latter portion of the seventeenth century there was evidently a great mixture in the composition of the Society of Friends in Southwark. There were many rich and many poor —many faithful and zealous, and many lukewarm and disorderly. In addition to the earnest ones, who managed disciplinary matters and cared for the Church, there were numerous persons whose connection with the body was of so loose a character, that it was often an open question whether such and such individuals were Friends or not. And then again it was evident that many reputed Friends were only vaguely known to the heads of the meeting, thus for instance — "the combmaker in the Boro'," "Will the Chandler," "a woman of the name of Tanner," "one Shaw's wife," are descriptions of individuals in the early Southwark minutes. Of the oft-recurring delinquencies amongst this numerous class we shall have to speak presently.

Through the eighteenth century the Society continued large, and upheld its two meetings at Park and Horslydown. In 1723 we find twelve ministers recorded as living within its bounds at one time, viz. :—John Gopsill, Zachary Routh, Joseph Willet, Simeon Warner, Lawford Godfrey, Isaac Peckrill, John Padley, George Chalkley, Philip Harman, Thomas Bentley, Gilbert Hagen, Richard Bickham, and Nicholas Davis. We may remark, in passing, that about five years afterwards, two of these were requested not to sit in the gallery, and to refrain from preaching, both having failed in business—one through "joining with an alchymist in attempting to transmute metals."

Friends of Southwark were not only numerous during last century, but thriving in business, and to some extent becoming opulent. The plated coffin-handles that were found in digging over the Park burial-ground told of wealth, and the

Q

following analysis of the subscriptions for the building of Horslydown Meeting-house in 1738, shows it to have had a fair number of prosperous members. Out of the total subscription of £717 9s., £642 4s. was raised in the meeting by 104 subscribers as follows:—sixteen Friends gave amounts varying from 10s. to £2; thirty-four gave from £2 to £5; thirty-one gave between £5 and £10; six gave £10 10s. each; thirteen gave £15 15s., while three gave £20, and one (John Warner) headed the list with £35.

In 1786 Southwark was strong enough to appoint sixteen overseers at one Monthly Meeting. Towards the close of the eighteenth century there was probably a falling off in numbers, as in 1800 Park and Horslydown Meetings were both concentrated in one; Southwark Meeting still, however, remained strong and influential for many years; but as the present century advanced, the causes which we have seen operating in other metropolitan meetings effected similar results here. Its own suburban offshoot at Peckham outstripped it in size and power, and when in 1860 the premises were compulsorily sold, it was not thought needful to continue to maintain Friends' meetings in Southwark. The name of Southwark Monthly Meeting was still retained, and Peckham became its headquarters, the metropolitan portion of its territory being divided between Devonshire House and Westminster.

Meetings for Worship.

In connection with Meetings for Worship we have had in other chapters to speak of the class of meetings known as "Private," or "Silent," or "Retired" meetings, in which the edification of the flock, rather than the gathering in of those who were outside the pale, seems to have been the special object in view. In 1679 we find these for Southwark to have been held at the houses of E. Tidman, John Rouse, William Shewen, and others. Frequent allusions to such meetings occur in the minutes, and they were continued all through the times when Friends were an increasing body. Indeed during most of the eighteenth century a meeting of this character was held at the Park and another at Horslydown on week-days. The meeting at Park existed as late as 1794, though called at that time Park Evening Meeting. In 1720 we find the Monthly Meeting encouraging Friends to attend the Park Evening Meeting on Fifth-day, and also as much as possible the public meeting on Third-day. In

1755 the Park Evening Meeting on Fifth-days at 6 p.m. is reported as being well attended. In 1761 we find an appeal to the Morning Meeting, requesting that body to notice* this Evening Meeting as they do other meetings. In 1794 the Monthly Meeting inquired into the origin of this meeting, and traced it from the so-called private meeting of ancient times.

As in most other Monthly Meetings a Quarterly Monthly Meeting was for some time held in Southwark for the edification, more especially, of the youth and servants by the reading of epistles, exhortations, &c.

It may be noted, in passing away from the Southwark Meetings for Worship, how even the small matters of detail received attention; thus in 1707 occurs the following minute: "It being taken notice of that several women Friends at the Park Meeting do usually hang their riding-hoods on the rail of the gallery whereby the Friends that sit under the rail of the gallery are incommoded, It's left to Robert Fairman and Mary Fairman to take order for remedying the same."

At first, in Southwark, as elsewhere, no accommodation was provided for any women Friends to stand on when addressing the meeting, the gallery being occupied exclusively by the men ministers; but at the commencement of the eighteenth century a change was made in this respect, and Southwark uniting with this, there is found in 1709 an order entered on their minutes for women ministers to have a standing-place erected for them.

Meetings for Discipline.

The Meetings for Discipline were select gatherings originally, here as elsewhere. One of the standing orders of the Monthly Meeting was that "Friends who talk loosely out of Monthly Meeting about its business" are to be disqualified from sitting therein. Occasionally a more extended invitation to Monthly Meeting was given,—"A general meeting of all good Friends" in this Monthly Meeting is sometimes ordered to be held in the following month "for a special collection." Ordinary collections seem to have been made by appointing two Friends to stand at the door after a First-day meeting for worship.

---

* This means for ministers to attend it. (See Chapter on Morning Meeting.)

Troublesome Characters.

Respecting the state of this meeting in early times, it is evident it shared (perhaps more largely than others in the Metropolis) in the need for exercise of discipline. When George Fox revisited London after his long imprisonment in Scarborough Castle, he mentions in his Journal the need he found for the watchful care of Friends over one another, " especially those as walked disorderly or carelessly, and not according to the truth."* This was in 1667, and the minutes of Southwark Monthly Meeting show alike the care then exercised by it, and the need existing for such; a few instances of these may suffice.

It may be mentioned, as before alluded to, that Southwark is the only one of the six London Monthly Meetings which has preserved its earliest minute-book, a circumstance which prevents any comparison of its state at this time with that of any other meetings.

In Fifth Month, 1667, we read, "John Whithouse a madman who cryed ag^t Maiges [marriages] amongst ffrends who afterwards tooke a woman, the like spirit with him and its reported beats her, and its to be queried wheare he was Mared" [married]. This Whithouse, it seems by a subsequent minute, afterwards came to the meeting and "testified against Friends with his hat on."

Again, in 1667, " Richard and Ann Corkbree has denied Meetings; he is given to study astrologie and is run into imaginations and speaks against Friends."

In the same year, "Cobell and his wife to be spoken to about jeering Friends."

In 1668 Sara Pratt has " spoken flightily of Friends and Truth,"—"has taken part in a superstitious burying,"—has " too much familiarity with Doctor Howker, and says it is her liberty."

---

* Josiah Coale, writing to George Fox under date 11th of Ninth Month (November) 1663, says, in speaking of Friends at Southwark, " At Southwark, Friends were taken at two meetings together, and sent to prison, to the number of about 4 score, where the most of them still remain upon the account of not paying twelvepence a-piece for not coming to Steeple House. And truly, George, they are a very poor divided company, and several very bad spirits amongst them, and very unruly, and not subject one to another."—*Devonshire House MSS.*

In the same year "Susan Atkins has desired Robert Hogell to put away his wife and take her, Ranter-like, and has endeavoured this matter several times, saying it was a revelation from the Lord," and persists in her conduct and "wont condemn it."

Thus we see from the foregoing extracts signs of that spirit tending to make the liberty of the truth degenerate into licence and rant, which George Fox, the lover of order, so resolutely encountered and defeated.

Marriages.

After a general establishment of meetings for discipline in London, George Fox felt their care was especially needed in the case of marriages, to prevent disorders that had been committed (see Journal, p. 315), through lawless conduct or misplaced ideas of spiritual guidance leading to neglect of the customary restraints and usages.

It seems from the old Horslydown minutes that irregular marriages were by no means infrequent. The following are examples:—

Tenth Month 18th, 1667. — "John Farant and Ann his wife was here at this meeting, and was spoke to about the manner of their marriage, and they have declared that they do accept of one another as man and wife, and have declared they intend to and will live lovingly together until their lives end."

In the following year we find a notice of, " Will the Chandler, and the woman that has accompanied as man and wife without due publication," who promised satisfaction to the meeting. This probably means some public appearance and declaration.

In 1672 two Friends appear to propose marriage, and are described as "pretty tender and submissive." Friends order the young woman to take a lodging till the marriage. "She confesses she came to live with him through ignorance."

In Sixth Month, 1675, "two came and acknowledged their sin in living as man and wife, and promised to be faithful to each other."

The subject of marriage claimed in many ways increasing care and attention on the part of Horslydown Friends. Looking upon themselves as a distinct people, and, in fact, "*the* people of God in scorn called Quakers," they were very severe on those who took "a man of the world," or "a woman of the world" in marriage. Thus we read, in 1667, of three Friends being appointed "to go to Thomas Gesope and Thomas Sturgess to lay their wickedness upon them for their taking of wives of the world." They would hardly recognise the going before a priest as a true marriage, and in judging another Friend they speak of him as "taking the woman he calls his wife." In many cases they obliged those who had been thus married to go and testify against it to the priest who had married them, as well as to Friends and to their neighbours.

Not only did the Monthly Meeting judge those who had married contrary to rule, but took care to give advice beforehand when necessary. In 1670, we read of a Friend having to be visited, "to warn him from the woman that sells oranges, as to marriage, for she is a bad woman, and Friends cannot own him if he join himself to such a one." This Friend persisted in marriage with the orange-woman and was subsequently "denied" for the same.

The following minute (written in 1672) is a further instance of the care exercised with regard to matrimonial connections:—

"Thomas Blake, Prudence Mags, he lives in Whitt Shaple and she in Southwarke Parke, has propounded their intention of marige and ffriends does find A simplicity in the Man and a tenderness though but lately convinced. Themselves Advised and counseled them to wait to feel that true [*word illegible*] that first convinced them and as they find that to lead them to proceed in it."

Delinquency.

We find that Horslydown Monthly Meeting in its early days was troubled, not only by those who pleaded or practised an unscriptural liberty, but also by a numerous class who made profession of the Truth, but were very far from evidencing its possession by their daily lives and conversation.

From 1666 to about 1670 numerous are the cases recorded on the books of drunkenness, fraud, gambling in alehouses, beating wives or servants, &c. Thus we read of an appointment to visit "old Patin, the smith, about his getting drunk and beating his daughter—he used to beat his wife formerly." Again, "Ralph Yonge, at Horslydown stairs, plays at ninepins and passes bad money." Ninepins was evidently a favourite game; one Friend seems to have beguiled the period of his imprisonment with it. One Will Stuart, a little Scotchman, is judged and denied as "an habitual cheat." In 1670 one woman wants to be assisted in a passage to Jamaica, but the Monthly Meeting informs her that "she is so bad" that they won't help her. In many cases the misconduct was long continued; in 1668 William Horton brings in a paper "condemning his actions for fourteen years past," so that his misdemeanors must have commenced with the very origin of the Society in Southwark.

And here we may pause to remark that the disciplinary notice extended to these delinquents seldom terminated in the disownment of the individuals. If, by persevering in visits and exhortations, the offender could be got to write and circulate a paper of condemnation he was again received into unity, though of course under watchful oversight. But those who persisted in their ill-doing or refused to repent were "denied" in plain terms. Thus, in 1668, they record that "William Styles, once a pretty Friend, has become wholly apostatised and at present lost as to truth." Those who were denied, or, as it was afterwards termed, disowned, were considered "out of unity," or "of the world," and if they died in this state, their bodies were denied sepulture in Friends' burial-ground. We find in one case of this kind a turbulent relative threatening "to break the door down" if he couldn't have a burial-note.

It is a strong evidence of life and power in the Monthly Meeting that its treatment of delinquents did so frequently result in the repentance and reclamation of the offenders. And in a few years, doubtless in part owing to this care exercised by the faithful members, we find the cases referred to above becoming much less frequent. But of course the Conventicle Act and other cruel laws had also a large share in winnowing the chaff from the wheat. As a further illustration of what the Monthly Meeting when first established had itself to do in this way, we may mention that the subject of fraud was one of the delinquencies that needed care in early times, and in 1667 we find some Friends brought under notice for using false measures. The Monthly Meeting was very anxious that its members should stand clear before the world as honest traders. In 1670 they order Friends that are coopers to have their casks exactly measured, and if they are not exact they are to write on the casks a statement of such deficiency. Shortly afterwards the Monthly Meeting ordered an exact gallon-gauge to be obtained and kept for purposes of comparison.*

PRISONERS.

The care of such of their members as were in prison was a matter likely to claim attention from a Church whose members were at one period liable to be dragged off in the very act of worship, and afterwards had to hear its treasurer (for instance) report, as he did in 1683, that being under a " Ritt of excommunication," and expecting daily incarceration, he had sent in his accounts, for a new treasurer to be appointed. Amongst various evidences as to the care of their friends, we find this entry in 1684:—

"Paid Thomas Hudson for canvis to putt Round the Greate Bed where friends lodge, y^t are prisoners in ye Compter in tooley's Strete, and is to remaine there for the service of friends y^t are prisoners hereafter."

Horslydown Monthly Meeting, moreover, did not neglect the counsel of George Fox " to requite gaolers when they have showed kindness to Friends." For this cause two Westphalia hams and other matters, to the amount of £1 18s. 10d., were presented to the marshal of the King's Bench, and on another occasion £2 to Stephen Draper for the same reason.

POOR.

The poor claimed and obtained a large amount of care from Friends in this as in other quarters, and we find frequent entries as to their rents and allowances and funeral obsequies, &c. As regards these latter, five shillings for a coffin and one shilling for a grave seems to have been the regulation cost at the commencement of last century. In 1710 there is a com-

---

* Thus varied were the subjects needing the exercise of discipline, so as to restrain, correct, and reform disorderly walkers, in the early years of the Monthly Meeting, when the "mixed multitude," attracted by the fervour of the early preachers, came to be moulded to a life of regular and orderly walk. The extracts are interesting, as Southwark is the only one of the six London Monthly Meetings whose records at the commencement are preserved; they evidence the state of the Society in the period succeeding that activity of missionary effort which marked the time of the early preachers, the loss of whose formerly frequent presence through death or imprisonment soon showed itself in the increase of disorderly walkers. The contact of the early meetings for discipline with these is thus shown us on these Southwark books. By them we can appreciate the cause of that joy so evident in the pages of George Fox when he found Monthly Meetings well established.

plaint of there being too few Friends present at a certain poor Friend's interment to carry the body to the grave, and the Monthly Meeting agreed to pay the "Bidders" for summoning Friends in future.

It may be mentioned that Friends receiving relief were expected to make over their property to the Monthly Meeting.

A custom appears to have prevailed in Southwark, about the year 1687, which we have not observed elsewhere, of occasionally holding a sort of review or inspection at the meeting-house of all the poor members receiving relief. Occasionally others than members were helped, but in such cases the recipient is distinctly recorded as a "necessitous person, and not a Friend."

The following document, copied into the minute-book of Horslydown, connected with the establishment of Yoakley's Almshouses, bears on the subject now under notice:—

"I being left executrix to my dear husband, Michel Yoakley's will, by which he left the disposing of those rooms or tenements in Hope Court, in Wentworth Street, to such poor as I shall see meet amongst Friends, my mind is that always two Friends out of Southwark Meeting shall be admitted into said rooms in my lifetime, if such as are qualified for such charity can be found there, and at my death it's left to the Executors and Trustees as they shall see meet, as witness my hand the 21st 12th month, $17\frac{12}{13}$.

"It was also her desire after this was writt that two after her death might be allways in said roomes belonging to Southwarke.

"Witness, Robert Fairman.   "MARY YOAKLEY."

MISCELLANEOUS.

Adverting now to one or two facts of a miscellaneous character, we find in early times the usual wine-bills presented quarterly. "Paid Gabriel Erwood for wine for Friends that come to his house after meeting" is the entry on one occasion; on another, "for wine for Friends that declared at this meeting." The amount is generally about one pound or thirty shillings a quarter.

The following may serve as an instance of a custom which we believe was once not infrequent, i.e. the holding of committees at public-houses. There being a difference between two Friends in Fourth Month, 1686, the six Friends on the appointment were directed "to meet at the King's Head in Pudding

Lane on Sixth-day before the next Monthly Meeting at 3 o'clock in the afternoon." At the next Monthly Meeting we find them again directed "to meet to-morrow *after Change* at the same place."

It may be interesting to quote, at least as illustrating the coins of the period the following statement of a collection made at Horslydown in Twelfth Month, 1695-6:—

	£	s.	d.
" 18 ginneys, each worth 30s.	27	0	0
3 pistolls (22s. each) and one broad piece and quarter of gold (32s. each)	5	6	0
Silver	23	10	9
	£55	16	9 "

It may not be generally known that Southwark Monthly Meeting was for a long period the proprietor of two fire-engines, one being kept at Park and one at Horslydown. The latter was purchased in 1706 for £30, and the other soon after. Appointments of Friends to inspect the engines, reports as to their being damaged at certain fires; orders to purchase buckets or mend the pipes, &c., occur occasionally for many years. What method was adopted for the use of these is not stated. We know that there was a standing committee for each engine, but whether or not this committee was composed of young and active Friends who were expected themselves to run with and work the engine in cases of emergency is a matter that must remain in obscurity.

In the year 1721 we find a somewhat curious circumstance taking place. One Sixth-day, Tenth Month, 1721, a solemn meeting was held at Park in the morning, and at Horslydown in the afternoon, " with reference to the great calamity the Lord has been pleased to inflict on our neighbours in France." These meetings were large and full, and held to general satisfaction, and the Monthly Meeting records that " the Lord's presence was felt as it was last year on the same solemn occasion." From the minutes of Devonshire House we learn that similar meetings were held there on both the occasions above referred to.

But we find subsequently that some Friends at Horslydown strongly objected to the above procedure, and it was ultimately agreed that the circumstance should not be a precedent for the future.

The general course of the Monthly Meeting's history offers

so little of a character different from that of the others, as to require but few further extracts. There are ample evidences on its records of the low state to which, after a period of judicious maintenance of the discipline, it had lapsed towards the middle of the eighteenth century;* and yet even then it had sufficient life remaining within it to furnish a fair contribution towards that large General Committee which, appointed in 1761, at the advice of the Yearly Meeting, spent five years in "clearing the camp." With the rest, Southwark at this time experienced a revival of the discipline. Many disorderly walkers were reclaimed, the rest disowned; and in order to better care in future, as many as sixteen overseers were then appointed in this Monthly Meeting alone.

Amongst the ministers and other worthies who have been members of Southwark Meeting, we may mention the following, in addition to some whose names appear in the preceding pages. William Shewen, who removed to Enfield in 1686, and whose wife's name is connected with the demise of land there to Friends; Thomas Padley; Walter Miers, one of the early convinced, who was living in 1706, at which date he wrote a MS. account of the rise of Friends in Southwark, which is still preserved at Devonshire House; Gerrard Roberts, a well-known name to all readers of our ancient records, of whose house in St. Thomas Apostles we have spoken in a previous chapter, seems at one time to have been a member of this meeting; Robert Curtis, Daniel Stevenson, Ellis Hookes, the first Recording Clerk of the Society of Friends; Francis Davis, John Estaugh, Benjamin Walker, William Pitt, Mary Pace, Benjamin Chandler, Nicholas Davis, Mary Freeman, Samuel Sturge, and Thomas Norton whose remains have been consigned to the tomb during the compilation of the present chapter.

---

* In the report made by the Quarterly Meeting to the Yearly Meeting in 1755, it states of Southwark, "they have no separate Monthly Meeting of Women, nor ever had. But their women Friends sit with their men in their Monthly Meetings, and are jointly concerned in carrying on the business thereof." We mention this fact not as a proof of the declension alluded to in the text, but as illustrative of the character of the Meetings for Discipline at the period referred to.

APPENDIX.

Report by the Surveyor to the Six-Weeks Meeting.

It may be as well to inform you respecting the removal of bodies from the ancient burial-ground in Lower Redcross Street, Southwark, that George Leake, the undertaker, has now completed the work in manner as specified in his agreement.

During its progress E. D. Hayward, one of the members of the Society, has been engaged to attend on the spot daily, and to take charge of the remains as they were found, so as to secure proper care over the same. (N.B. No interments had taken place since 1799.)

The ground has been dug over its whole surface down to the level of the virgin soil; and in those cases where a deeper interment had taken place, to the needful distance into it. With the exception of lead coffins in various stages of preservation, the remains were found to have become reduced to skeletons; and although there was a considerable amount of loose coffin wood, no wooden coffins were raised entire. It may also be remarked that no bodies were found nearer the surface than seven feet, showing the care Friends had taken not to overcrowd the ground. The bones, as thrown up by George Leake's workmen, were carefully collected by the Friend in charge, who packed them into shells of the ordinary size, each of which it was found would hold about nine complete sets of bones. In this manner 111 shells were used. For the lead coffins (of which nineteen were raised) a separate shell was in each case provided—making the total number of shells that were used 130. These were all removed (by hearse) at various times to the burial-ground at Long Lane, Bermondsey, and re-interred in that place, according to the permission obtained from the Council of State. For this purpose, two large and deep pits, about eight feet square and fifteen feet deep, were made in a part of the ground that had been but little used, and into these the shells were stowed as closely as practicable, placing them head and foot in regular tiers to economise the space; and when these graves were thus filled up to within about three feet of the surface, the ground was thrown in and levelled over them.

Reverting to the burial-ground from whence the bodies were taken, it may be mentioned that the latest remains were found, as before-mentioned, to commence at a depth of about seven feet below the surface, and then in three tiers lying transversely. Also, from the loose manner in which many of the bodies were found buried, it is concluded they had been previously taken up from the space occupied by the meeting-house and re-interred, which may have been done when the meeting-house was enlarged in 1800.

As Friends may feel interested in some of the minor details connected with the works; the following particulars may be given. In reference to the coffins none when only made of wood were found remaining whole, they having been forced asunder by the pressure of the earth, and, in by far the greater majority of cases, the wood was entirely perished. Yet, strange as it may appear, in the lowest row of the three layers of interments several bottoms of coffins of common deal were found undecayed, though the oak and elm ones had perished, showing how this wood, which in most cases decays so readily, becomes occasionally the subject of a marked exception. [It is presumed that the circumstance was due to the entire exclusion of the atmospheric air.] Of the coffin furniture, such as the handles, fewer were found than might have been anticipated; but some of these being plated, showed that expense had not been spared in the interment, and the very good state of their preservation indicated the original excellence of their quality.

The remains of all bodies not buried in lead, were found, with scarce an exception, to be merely bones, without any offensive matter attached or near them. A few skulls retained some of the hair; and in one instance a vertebra was raised with its spinal marrow entire. It was also very observable that in most cases the teeth were very perfect, though worn, showing there was less of imperfection in these parts then than at the present day. Generally speaking the bones were of the average size, but in one instance a set of thigh bones were found of unusual length, measuring as much as twenty inches, so that if the owner of them had been a person of correct proportion he would have been at least six feet eight inches high.

Out of the whole number of 956 remains thus exhumed, there were nineteen for whom their friends had sought the more costly mode of encasing them in lead to ensure better preservation; but practically there was little difference, except where the lead coffins had been made of unusual substance, and thereby enabled to resist the corrosive influences of the earth. Where only lead of ordinary thickness was used, it had become worn into holes, and thus allowing the wet to penetrate the lead to the inner coffin; this inner coffin of wood became destroyed, and the lead, being unequal to the support of the earth above, was in consequence so crumpled and broken that the bodies within were found to be nothing but mere bones.

As, however, some of these lead coffins were of a thickness of metal that had secured them against corrosion, and were very perfect in form—the outer coffin alone having decayed—it became a curious question to know how far they had preserved the remains enclosed within them. For this purpose some were opened in the presence of several Friends, and also our friend Dr. Hodgkin. One of these which bore a date of 1765, and the name of Elizabeth Crosby, proved to have its inner wooden shell *quite perfect*, and on raising its lid, and removing the long wool with which it was closely packed, the body was found wrapped in a winding-sheet of fine linen; the smell was pungent, but could not be called very offensive; of the body, so far as was seen, it may be said to have had all the shrivelled appearance of a mummy. A shroud expensively worked on its front, and ornamented with rosettes, remained quite uninjured. The feet were bare, and the flesh on them and the lower part of the limbs, which alone were exposed to view, had shrunk down to the hardness of a board, every muscle and tendon being as strongly marked (as if it had been dissected)—the feet were much arched and twisted, for which we could see no reason to account.

The next lead coffin opened had no inscription, but, from the very good state of its preservation, it was judged to have been more recent than the former; here the remains were found more perfect. It was evident that it was a female, the colour of whose hair showed that her life must have been cut short in the midst, and whose fine and portly figure bore evidence of a once stately presence ; her features were remaining in a state recognisable by any one who might have known her in life ; but though thus preserved (by the excellence of this casing) from the slightest intrusion of moisture, and therefore free from any approach of the *active* elements of destruction, though all, even to the finely-crimped cap-border was perfect, yet the general effect of this large and full-featured corpse was affecting, and anything but an encouragement for us to take much care in delaying our deceased relatives from returning to that inevitable dust which all, whether rich or poor, must sooner or later share.

The third coffin opened also further illustrates the folly of expensive interments. The corpse had been enclosed in lead, nearly quarter of an inch thick, and fitted to the general form of the body, going round the head, and in at the neck, coming out again to the shoulders, forming a complete mummy case of lead. But all this care had been in vain—even this great thickness of lead had become so corroded that the body was reduced to a skeleton, which fell out through the holes as it was being raised. The head portion of the case remained entire, and on opening this it was found to be packed close with feathers of excellent quality, yet nothing but a skull was left, except only a profusion of fine auburn hair, that fell down in long tresses, and in its midst remained a pad (still perfect), one which ladies used to wear on the top of their heads to keep up the hair when it was worn as a tower on the crown.* In this hair, also, was a tortoiseshell-comb of first quality, and though plain, yet quite perfect. Thus the remains were evidently of a young female, whose vanity in life was perpetuated in the grave, but the extreme care of whose relatives had been productive of no result in preserving the body.

It is, perhaps, needless to add that these examinations were made in the presence of several Friends, and under the management of an undertaker; also a medical man (one of our members) was in attendance. Their result gave no encouragement to open any of the remaining entire lead coffins, and at the conclusion the inner coffin-lids were replaced, the lead well soldered down over them, and they were re-interred shortly afterwards. Thus these Friends, over whom their relations thought a last farewell had been taken, were again seen by fellow-creatures nearly a century after their interment, and those who thus looked upon them felt that the sight was an affecting one, proving that all art or device is in vain to save from the destructions of the grave. Better in simple faith to give to the worm its food, and let earth claim its dust, than thus to attempt to preserve the body when life is gone. Except only for any present purpose—such as to avoid spread of infection, or in some cases where a journey is needed, &c.—it is well, doubtless, to avoid burying in lead (expensive in its first instance and profitless in its result).

---

* This report was obviously written at a date before the revival of this foolish practice.

Peter the Great and Friends.

In Thomas Story's Journal, page 123, will be found a somewhat detailed account of an interview he and Gilbert Mollyson (Robert Barclay's wife's brother) had with Peter the Great when in London, and it would appear that the next First-day after this, Peter (anxious, no doubt, to know more of Friends) came to their meeting at White Hart Court, entering it whilst one Robert Haddock was engaged in the ministry: he had risen with the subject of Naaman as his text, and though unconscious of the high rank of one among his auditors, delivered in the course of his sermon a sentence very pointedly addressed to the highest of earthly kings, saying, "Thou art not too great to make use of the means offered by the Almighty for thy healing and restoration, if ever thou expect to enter his kingdom, into which no unclean thing can come." The Czar's interpreter was observed by Thomas Story (who alone had recognised the distinguished rank of the visitor) to whisper to his master, doubtless in translation, but through people coming in to gaze at him, the Czar suddenly rose and left the meeting. Not that Peter was offended with Friends' plain-dealing, for he showed, nineteen years after this, that he retained an appreciation for them.

In the same Journal, page 494, will be found an account of how this Emperor, when, in 1712, his troops had occupied a Friends' meeting-house at Frederickstadt in Germany, ordered them out of it, and sent word that if the few Friends there would come to meeting he would attend it, which he not only did, but, as his Muscovite generals were ignorant of the German language, Peter acted as interpreter, "with much gravity and seriousness commending what he heard, saying, that whoever could live according to that doctrine would be happy." He promised afterwards to have Robert Barclay's Journal translated, and printed in his own language.

CHAPTER XIII.

WESTMINSTER MONTHLY MEETING,

Including Meetings at the Little Almonry, Peter's Court, Savoy, and Long Acre.

IN the earliest period of the history of the Society of Friends there appear to have been three places in or near the city of Westminster, at which meetings were regularly held, viz. at Worcester House, in the Strand; at Stephen Hart's, in New Palace Yard; and at William Woodcock's, in the Savoy. There was also a large room near the Abbey capable of holding a thousand persons, which was made use of for a time as a place in which to "plough and thresh" among the people of the world, as at the Bull and Mouth.

The first named in the above list of meetings was held in the lodgings of one "Nicholas Bond, who had a place at Court." His official duties afterwards transferred him to Greenwich Palace, where, as we have seen, he continued to accommodate a meeting of Friends.

The meeting at Stephen Hart's may be considered as the precursor of the present Westminster Meeting. It was established about the year 1655. We catch a glimpse of this assembly in troublous times in the diary of Pepys, who says, under date February 7th, 1660,—"In the palace yard I saw Monk's soldiers abuse Billing and all the Quakers that were at a meeting-place there: and, indeed, the soldiers did use them very roughly and were to blame."

Amongst the early convinced in this locality was a well-to-do woman named Elizabeth Trott. She occupied a good house in Pall Mall, which she opened to Friends, and thither the meeting was transferred.

A constant attender at this meeting was Gilbert Latey, of whom we shall have more to say hereafter. He was acquainted with a neighbouring Justice of the Peace, over whom he exercised an influence so considerable, that for some time the meeting was held without interruption. But at length, in

1662, this Justice informed Gilbert that he had been blamed for suffering a conventicle to be held so near the Duke of York's residence (St. James's Palace), and that now in obedience to higher authority he must come and " break up the meeting."

But Gilbert Latey and his friends continued to assemble as usual. In consequence of so doing he and others were haled away to prison. The worshippers were often forcibly prevented from entering the house, and compelled to assemble in the street. But the Justice found it impossible to obey his orders and really break up the meeting, which continued to be held at this place till Elizabeth Trott's decease in 1666.

Elizabeth Trott's house was situated on the south side of Pall Mall; on the opposite side of the road was a row of elms, beyond which were the open fields. From this rural spot, Gilbert Latey and his friends thought it would be best to remove the meeting to a more central situation, as Friends belonging to the meeting mostly resided in the city of Westminster, then very populous.

Little Almonry.

A lease of a house or houses, with a plot of garden ground, situated in the Little Almonry, was now purchased for £150, and here for more than a century a Friends' meeting was maintained.

The lapse of time has completely changed the appearance of the district in which this ancient meeting-house was situated. Even the Little Almonry itself has disappeared. It was a street, occupying with the Great Almonry, from which it diverged, the site of a long-perished ecclesiastical building once connected with the Abbey. This street was not a thoroughfare, and at the further end of it, in one of those retired spots which Friends seem to have sought after for the erection of their meeting-houses, lay the irregular plot of ground of which Latey and his friends had now possessed themselves.

The whole affair was rustic and simple enough. A piece of land whose sides measured respectively 60, 84, 94, and 129 feet, partly abutting on the parish workhouse and partly separated from adjacent gardens by wooden palings, that were often wanting repair. Palings might well decay, for on the south side ran "a great ditch or milldam," whilst on the west there was " a great ditch or common sewer stretching towards Longditch."

These ditches were subsequently either filled up or covered and built over. But the place seems always to have retained a dampness which made itself seriously felt in after years.

Here, then, stood the meeting-house, at first evidently only an adaptation of the original tenements. But even at its best, the structure was small and unpretending, for forty years after the acquirement of the property, when much money had been spent in alterations and repairs, the insurance value of the whole, including the accommodation for two tenants, was only £300.

The property formed a portion of the Cathedral Close, and it may seem surprising that the Dean and Chapter should tolerate a nest of schismatics in the very shadow of the Minster Towers. Friends were for awhile only undertenants of original leaseholders, and do not seem to have rented the land direct from the cathedral authorities till 1688; but in that remarkable year of tolerance and revolution, they seem to have found little or no difficulty in renewing, on their own account, the lease which then expired.

We have mentioned the fact of Friends having two tenants at Westminster. For many years one of these was a schoolmaster, John Jeffreys, who paid forty shillings per annum for the use of "the gallery room" as a school. The Monthly Meeting apparently thought it best to be on the safe side as regards the tendencies of erratic schoolboys, and especially covenanted with John Jeffreys that he should keep the windows in repair.

As the second lease terminating in 1717 began to draw to a close, it seemed probable that Friends would have to vacate the premises. Frequent were the appointments by the Monthly Meeting to plead with the Dean* and Chapter for a renewal of the lease. It appears that the Archbishop of Canterbury wanted Friends' piece of garden-ground for some purpose, and the Monthly Meeting offered to present him with this if he would induce the Chapter to grant a fresh lease of the meeting-house.

But it seemed as if all these efforts were to be in vain. In

---

* The Dean of Westminster (and also Bishop of Rochester) was at this time the notorious Dr. Atterbury, afterwards banished for treasonable practices. He had a great dislike to Friends, whom he had publicly maligned in the House of Lords as on a level with Jews, Pagans, and Mahometans.

the Second Month, 1717, we find Friends leaving the building and carting away all their moveable property.

Scarcely had they departed when a change seems to have come over the spirit of the ecclesiastical authorities. They sent a polite message, expressing their regret that Friends had removed, inviting them back, and promising that meetings might be held in the interim (till a fresh lease was granted) without disturbance or opposition.

Friends accordingly returned, and on payment of £300 received a fresh lease of the premises, which was subsequently once or twice renewed, either on expiry or on occasion of extensive repairs, &c. The last occasion was in 1751, when a lease of forty years was granted, which, as we shall see, was not suffered to run out its full term.

Extensive repairs, sometimes involving the closing of the meeting-house for two or three months at a time, had been several times effected during the long occupancy of Friends. About the year 1772 it became evident that a new meeting-house must be built. It was accordingly resolved upon to look for a site on which to raise an edifice capable of accommodating all the Friends of the quarter, and thus obviate the necessity of keeping up two or three meeting-houses, as had hitherto been the case.

Peter's Court, or Hemming's Row.

In 1776 a suitable piece of ground was found, being a part of the estate of the Earl of Salisbury, situated near the angle of Hemming's Row and St. Martin's Lane, with approaches from each of those thoroughfares. On this site, of which a ninety-nine years' lease was obtained, were erected a meeting-house and premises, and the remainder of the land was sub-let on a building lease, which having expired in 1845, the four dwelling houses erected on it are now rented of Friends by the tenants.

The new meeting-house in Hemming's Row was opened on the 28th of Second Month, 1779. Friends had been debarred for some time from using their meeting-house at the Little Almonry on account of "the dampness and unwholesome smells." The remainder of the lease of this latter meeting-place was sold to the Dean and Chapter for £137.

The cost of the new edifice was £2,684, of which Westminster Friends raised at the time £1,265 from amongst themselves, including the above amount received from the Dean and Chapter for the old premises. Other Friends in London subscribed about £710. Of the remainder (£707 18s. 6d.) £500 was borrowed of the bankers on a note of hand in the names of J. Fothergill and B. Marshman, and £207 18s. 6d. was lent on interest by the Marshman family, which amounts, being spread over a number of years, became gradually liquidated by surplus of annual contributions over expenses. In this work of building the meeting-house, Dr. Fothergill took a great and generous share; he not only gave £314 16s. 4d. to the actual building, but most largely assisted in the preliminary expenses involved by clearing the site; for it would appear as if numerous interests had to be purchased, and houses pulled down, involving an outlay of not less than £1,332 8s. 4d., of which Dr. Fothergill advanced as much as £1,000. (It is said one of the buildings which had thus to be removed was that formerly occupied by the celebrated sculptor Roubilliac as his studio.) Dr. Fothergill was also at this time actively promoting the foundation of Ackworth School, one among the last of his many benevolent endeavours. His life, now far advanced, closed in about two years, i.e. 1780, at the age of 69. It would seem that at his decease some lien was held upon the property by his sister Ann, who survived him, which claim was generously relinquished by her in favour of the meeting.

The meeting-place under notice is doubtless well known to most of our readers as being one of the most commodious and well-fitted of the London meeting-houses. It is not, however, a freehold, and the building lease has only a few more years before its term expires. For some time past a Sabbath-school has been carried on in the basement storey of the premises, which has been adapted for the purpose.

SAVOY.

Turning our attention now to the third meeting-place named in the introductory paragraph of this chapter, we find that the meeting first established in the house of William Woodcock existed almost without interruption for 120 years. It became known as the Savoy Meeting, and the Monthly Meeting of Westminster was held alternately at the Savoy and Little Almonry during the greater portion of the eighteenth century.

As the name would indicate, the meeting was held in the precincts of the old Savoy palace, on ground which, though now for the most part appropriated to the purposes of trade, is still interesting to the antiquarian for its historic associations. Here Peter, Earl of Savoy, built his palace in 1245, which was afterwards transferred to the friars of Montjoy. Then Eleanor, queen of Henry III., bought it for her son, the Duke of Lancaster. It was the prison of John of France in 1357, at which time it was one of the finest palaces in England. The Kentish rebels burned it down in 1381, and the ground devolved to the Crown. Upon the site of the ancient palace Henry VII. and Henry VIII. built a hospital for destitute persons, with a corporation of chaplains, &c. which passed through various vicissitudes, as monarchs of varying opinions successively mounted the throne, but managed to maintain a separate existence and hold its revenues till dissolved for corruption and misappropriation in the reign of Queen Anne. This latter fact bears immediately on our subject, as we shall see that it made an important change in the tenure by which Friends held their meeting-house property.

About the middle of the seventeenth century the principal gate of the Savoy Hospital opened into the Strand nearly opposite to the present Burleigh Street. Over this gateway was a tower known as the Great Tower, and in 1660 we find the Master of the Savoy and his chaplains leasing the said Tower and the five adjacent houses to William Woodcock for forty years at £7 5s. per annum. In one of these houses W. W. had previously resided, and had there sheltered a meeting of Friends, and in this house the meeting would appear to have been held till 1669.

In that year an extensive fire destroyed considerable property in this neighbourhood, and amongst the rest the houses, &c. leased to W. Woodcock, and then in the possession of his widow, Jane Woodcock.

There was at that time sitting in Clifford's Inn a commission (of which the celebrated Judge Hale was the principal member), empowered to settle all disputes, &c. arising from the destruction of property by fire. Their special business was probably in connection with the Great Fire of 1666, but all other conflagrations taking place during the next few years seem also to have come under their cognisance. Before these judges Jane Woodcock laid her case, and obtained a decree empowering her to hold the property at the old rent for sixty years from Midsummer, 1671, on condition of at once rebuilding.

Jane Woodcock now arranged with Friends to build a meeting-house on her property. In conjunction with one Martha Fisher they accordingly erected a building, spending £160 upon a large room to meet in, whilst the said Martha Fisher spent £330 upon the vaults underneath, and a set of apartments, &c. above. It was arranged that Friends should hold the building of Jane Woodcock at a peppercorn rent, and that Martha Fisher should hold her portion of the building from Friends on the same terms. Both Jane Woodcock and Martha Fisher devised to Friends absolutely their interest in the property at their respective deaths, till the expiry of the term decreed by the judges.

Upon the Strand front of her property Jane Woodcock built four or five houses. It is probable that, as at White Hart Court, a little Quaker colony was formed here. In one of these houses dwelt the worthy proprietor herself; another was let to Gilbert Latey, and, sheltered from the main thoroughfare by these dwelling-houses, stood the meeting-house.

Under the east side of Gilbert Latey's dwelling was a passage four feet wide, leading to a stone staircase which terminated in a yard paved with stone. Here stood the meeting-house abutting southwards on Chapel Yard. The building consisted of one large room on the ground floor, under which were two brick vaults and a kitchen. The space above the meeting-room was partly covered by a lead flat, and partly by the three chambers, one garret, &c. occupied by Martha Fisher. Till the erection of the premises in Hemming's Row this meeting-house was the best in Westminster quarter. Its insurance value in 1704 was £400.

The term for which Jane Woodcock and her assignees held the meeting-house and the adjacent premises from the Hospital expired in 1731. But in the meanwhile, as we have said, viz. in 1702, the whole estate had reverted to the Crown. Accordingly the meeting-house, &c. was henceforth held under the King's sign-manual, during the royal pleasure. George III. renewed in 1762 the permission granted by his predecessor, but in 1781 the property was required for other purposes, and Friends received notice to quit. The poor widows, &c. then residing at the meeting-house were accordingly removed elsewhere; and the meeting, after having been held in the Savoy for more than a century, was transferred to the new and commodious premises previously described in Hemming's Row.

Long Acre.

There was anciently a Friends' meeting-house and burial-ground situated in the space now surrounded by Long Acre, Hanover Street, Castle Street, and King Street. This property when purchased by Friends was known as the "Hole in the Wall," and was approached by a court from Long Acre. We find the Six-Weeks Meeting complaining in 1675 of Friends of Westminster for having procured this plot of land for a burial-ground without their consent. The tenements standing at one end of the property were let to a Friend named Daniel Waite in 1677. In the following year Westminster Monthly Meeting agreed to the holding of "a silent meeting" in Daniel Waite's house. Whether this "silent meeting" was originally of a distinctive character or not it evidently became a regular meeting for worship. In 1679 the Monthly Meeting bought back Daniel Waite's interest under this lease, and such alterations were made in the tenements as were necessary for the construction of a meeting-house.

Very little is known respecting this now vanished edifice. It was the lowest in value of the Westminster meeting-houses, its insurance in 1704 being only rated at £200. Its arrangements were evidently primitive in character. In 1690 William Chamberlayne is appointed "to prevent the smoke from offending the meeting, and to make a stool for a Friend to stand on," doubtless whilst addressing the assembly.

This meeting-house, like the one in the Little Almonry, was used in the week for a school, being let for this purpose to Thomas Hart, to teach writing, "he covenanting to repair broken forms and broken windows."

At the expiry of the lease in 1716, the property passed for a time out of the hands of Friends. It was purchased however by a couple of builders. From these persons was procured in 1717 a lease of their burial-ground, but not the Long Acre entrance and meeting-house. They obtained however, in lieu thereof, five tenements on another side of the ground, and a new entrance from what had been known as Knockall's Alley, but was just then being widened into the present Hanover Street.

The tenements were pulled down with the intention of building a substantial meeting-house on the spot, this being about the time of the flight from the Little Almonry previously narrated. But the design was never carried into effect. A part of the ground was let to Thomas Hart, who built himself a school-house there. The rest of the ground seems to have lain open for a long time, as in 1720 complaint is made of its being a gathering-place for rude boys, much to the disturbance of Thomas Hart's scholastic arrangements. A wall was then built, still with the intention of its forming ultimately part of a meeting-house; but, however, time passed on, and nothing was done, and in 1757 the lease again expired. It was never renewed, and at this day a dense mass of buildings covers the site of the ancient burying-ground.

Meeting Arrangements.

A few years before the revival of the discipline in 1760, the Yearly Meeting was concerned to ascertain, through the Quarterly Meetings, the state of their subordinate meetings, chiefly as to Women's and Week-day Meetings. Westminster thus answers through the Quarterly Meeting, under date First Month 1st, 1755: " This meeting takeing into consideration the minute from the adjourned Quarterly Meeting, dated ye 4th 11th mo. 1754, relating to perticular meetings where no week-day meetings are established, we answer there are three meeting-houses within the compass of this Mo. Meeting, viz. one at Hammersmith, held once a month in the winter and twice in the summer. But no week-day meeting, being very few friends that reside there—likewise one at Westmin^r held every first-day afternoon, but no week-day meeting, the week-day meeting for this Quarter being always held at Savoy on fifth-day morning, but not so well attended as could be desir^d. Wth respect to Womens Meetings for Disoplying we are not in the practice of.—John Hole is desir^d to carry a coppy of this minute to the adjourn^d Quarterly Meet^g."

This shows incidentally that it was not the practice to have meetings at Westminster and Savoy twice on the First-day, but only once at each; and, subsequently to this minute, annoyances from rude persons so increased in the afternoons at Westminster as to cause the meeting to be held there in the morning and at Savoy in the afternoon—no doubt the latter place being in the more public thoroughfare of the Strand was better lighted and protected after dark than the retired spot in the Little Almonry of Westminster.

Boundaries.

The boundaries of the Monthly Meeting whose places of worship we have now described were in 1700 as follow:—
"Beginning Eastward at Shear Lane in Fleet Street, taking both sides of the way, and all alleys or courts to the Westward to Chancery Lane that are thoroughfares, and then including Lincoln's Inn to go up unto Turnstile Alley, and then down Holborn only on the South side unto Chancery Lane End and from Turnstile aforesaid up Holborn on the South side to Red Lion Street, and down Red Lion Street, taking in only the West side thereof, and go northward to Marylebone, and from thence Westward to the first lane beyond Knightsbridge, that goes out of the road that leads to Kensington, and from thence down to the Thames Southward, and so by the Thames side to the Temple, and so up to Temple Bar."

Alterations in the foregoing have been made from time to time, more especially upon the junction of Westminster Monthly Meeting with that of Hammersmith in 1750, with part of Peel in 1860, and with Longford Monthly Meeting in 1865.

Numbers.

The number of Friends dwelling within the boundaries of the Monthly Meeting has always been large. In the early days there was some infusion of the aristocratic element amongst the convinced. About 1658 we read of several from Fleetwood's family, many lords and ladies from the Court, the Earls of Newport and Pembroke, &c. &c., being either at Worcester House or at William Woodcock's house. But after the King came in Quakerism did not make much headway amongst the upper classes. Tradesmen and handicraftsmen were the chief upholders of Westminster Meeting for many years. Not till modern times was the monied interest much represented in that quarter, the more affluent Friends being found amongst the merchants and bankers of the city.

MINISTERS.

Amongst the ministers of the Gospel in Westminster Monthly Meeting may be mentioned Gilbert Latey, John Vaughton, John Bell, James Hoskins, Daniel Bell, George Thompson and Mary Keane; Claude Gay also resided for a short period of his life at Hammersmith. Dr. Fothergill, having moved from White Hart Court, spent the few last years of his life within the limits of Westminster Meeting.

The first name on the above list, that of Gilbert Latey, is one so intimately associated with the establishment of the Society of Friends in Westminster, that we might well have been excused for dwelling on it at some length. We have already had to mention him in connection with meeting-houses, and shall probably have to do so again, but for the full details of his laborious career we must refer our readers to the narrative of his life, compiled by his nephew, Richard Hawkins, which, though brief, is not the least interesting among our early Quaker biographies. Suffice it to say now, that he was by birth a Cornishman, and had come up to London, where he became a prosperous tradesman in the Strand. He was convinced in 1654 by the preaching of Edward Burrough, at the house of Sarah Matthews in Whitecross Street, and became useful in the councils of the early Church by his clear common sense and good judgment. He was a master tailor, and had by tact, business attention, uprightness of conduct, and pleasing manner, so come into esteem with the gentlemen of fortune about the Court, as to have a large and profitable business among them; but becoming a Friend, or one of the "children of the Light," as they were then termed, and no longer easy to make such gay clothing as the fops required, he by declining such orders lost all his fair prospects of making a fortune, and for a time seemed to imperil the business itself. But his integrity was blessed, and a good steady custom remained. He placed his talents at the service of his friends, giving them the benefit of such access as he had to people at the Court, where he would often plead in their favour. Gilbert was personally much esteemed by the authorities, although they might either deride or object to his peculiar views; and even Charles II. would have a kind word for the conscientious tailor. The King, when out hunting one day, saw Gilbert Latey coming along the road on his way to a meeting, and the merry monarch calling out made the Friend come up alongside and exchanged words of cheer, parting quite affectionately—he to his hounds and Gilbert to the meeting. But for the complete narrative of his experience, his toils, his disputations in steeple-houses, his Gospel labours in the provinces, his sufferings in the Gatehouse dungeon, his interviews with kings, princes and nobles on behalf of suffering Friends at home or abroad, his visitations of the imprisoned and the poor in that terrible year of the Plague—for these and other incidents of this worthy man's career we must refer to his published memoir before mentioned. He died in 1705, aged 79 years. George Whitehead, a co-worker, says of him, "He was constant in his love and true to his brethren . . a sensible man, and of a good judgment." In another testimony, that of Richard Hawkins, his nephew (founder of the Library), it is added of Gilbert—" His parts were quick, and his apprehension lively; his memory good, and his judgment sound and strong; his example shining in self-denial." " No woman hath parted with a better husband, nor children with a more tender father, or sincerer man," is the loving testimony of his bereaved wife, Mary Latey.

Sufferings.

As regards the sufferings of Friends of Westminster for conscience' sake, we may have already mentioned how the patient and defenceless worshippers were harassed by soldiery and others at Nicholas Hart's, also at Elizabeth Trott's. Experience of this kind was often the lot of Friends at the Savoy and at the Little Almonry, at both which places meetings were occasionally held out of doors in the cold and wet. On one occasion, 10th Seventh Month, 1670, when Friends (through having been denied the use of their meeting-house) were assembled in the street, the coachman of one of the justices drove his master's coach and horses up and down to clear the street of Friends, and endangered many; another coachman, following his example, some severe injury was actually inflicted on a woman Friend (delicate and unable to move quickly) through crushing her leg between the wheel and a post. Notwithstanding this cruelty, it would seem that persecution did not rage with such persistency or severity in this quarter as in the City and Tower Hamlets, where Brown and Robinson had command.

In 1686 the Savoy Meeting-house was seized and used as guard-room. Friends were, therefore, kept out of it for a considerable time, but through the earnest efforts of Gilbert Latey, and his friend George Whitehead, the King was induced to order the soldiers to give up possession to the rightful owners.

Discipline, &c.

The meetings for worship and discipline at Westminster do not appear to have presented any very distinctive features of interest as compared with those held elsewhere, and already described. The Monthly Meeting was established in the Second Month, 1667, and was at first held in the afternoon. The minutes extant do not commence before 1674, those of the previous seven years being missing, as in most of the other London Monthly Meetings.

It was long a practice in Westminster to term every third Monthly Meeting a Quarterly Meeting, making it an occasion when, besides the ordinary business, financial matters received attention. The subscriptions were then made up, and the expenditure for the quarter ascertained, and all duly recorded on the minutes. The Monthly Meetings were not for more than a century open (like those of the present day) to all members, but were select gatherings of the more influential Friends, the men and women sitting together. In 1723 there would seem to have been about sixty thus considered eligible to attend the Monthly Meeting, but the number present seldom at that time exceeded twelve, and once or twice is noted a failing to reach that number, and so having to adjourn. In answering the Queries, it was usual to commit them previously to a small sub-committee to prepare and bring in answers for the meeting's adoption.

Up to 1739 the Monthly Meeting was not preceded by one for worship as is now the case; but in that year the Quarterly Meeting " recommended " setting apart a time to wait on the Lord before the general business commenced.

A few general minutes may be here introduced more or less abridged, viz. :—

" 5 mo. 2, 1707. Friends having it on their minds that it may be of benefit to the youth amongst us to appoint a meeting after each Quarterly Meeting, and to invite them to come and sit amongst us in order to receive such good counsel and advice as may arise from the minds and spirits of Friends on these occasions : thereby to have an opportunity of hearing the good order and discipline read amongst us as may tend to their edification and growth in the blessed Truth."

As showing a difference in practice as regards the suitable time for meetings for the young, it may be observed that the above proposition was deferred, after being considered for several meetings, till October had arrived, "till the days begin to lengthen sufficient for them to return home in due time."

"2 mo. 7, 1708. Friends taking it into their serious consideration the benefit that may arise to the edification of the youth amongst us, both as to our children and servants, by appointing a meeting to be held after each Quarterly Meeting during this summer time, in which to read the good and wholesome advice of our ancient friends and brethren, John Vaughton and William Beech are desired to search the books and papers, and to mark out such as may be suitable to the occasion."

The first meeting of this character is recorded as follows:—

"At an adjourned Quarterly Meeting held at the Savoy, 14th of 2nd mo., 1708—To give our youth an opportunity to come and behold the good order of truth used amongst us—

"The Friends being met, the exhortation was read, which directs us to keep to the ancient principles of Truth in bearing a testimony against the world's ways, manners, and fashions ; as also an Epistle of Caution against going out into the world for wives or husbands, and marrying by the priests, and other good counsel and advice therein contained, which we hope will have the desired effect as well upon the youth as the aged."

This arrangement was suspended in 1709, and young people advised to go to the Bull and Mouth, where a similar meeting was held.

"3 mo. 5, 1708. A paper being brought in from Mary Willis, widow, and read, wherein she condemns herself for going to and joining with those they call the French Prophets, and suffering the agitation spirit to come upon her, and to exercise herself thereby in our meetings, ' she is advised to forbear imposing her preaching upon our public meetings for worship till Friends are better satisfied.'"

"1 mo. 5, 1712. Agreed that the Friends in their several quarters do take an opportunity to bring the names of such as they believe may be fit to frequent our Monthly and Quarterly Meetings for the service of truth against next meeting."

"1723. Divers worthy women Friends deceased that we used to have the company of at our Monthly Meetings—others to be invited.

"7th 6 mo. 1723. About 60 members of this meeting, men and women; very few met; all who are absent earnestly entreated to come.

"5th mo. 3, 1728. This meeting taking into consideration that marriages being [solemnised] at this place on the fifth day of the week, do very much lessen the meeting for worship of Almighty God held in the afternoon of the same day; and notwithstanding a minute some years past, desiring all Friends as much as in them lay to avoid marrying at this place on the said day, and though frequently repeated, hath had little or no effect, this meeting doth, therefore, now agree that for the future none be admitted to solemnise their marriage here on that day of the week."

1740. 9th mo. The Fifth-day meeting altered from the afternoon to 9 a.m., to secure a better attendance, it having become much neglected.

1749. Monthly Meeting renewed its invitation to certain women Friends to attend the Monthly Meeting; a minute advising this course having been issued by the Quarterly Meeting.

"2 mo. 3, 1751. To proceed therein [*i.e.* marriages] with such decency and good order as becomes our Christian profession. That they should be careful neither to endeavour after too much privacy, nor too popular invitations to the solemnity. But that suitable notice be given of the intended marriage. That they keep punctually to the hour appointed. That as much as possible they would avoid all superfluity in apparel, and unnecessary dinners and publick entertainments, these things being altogether inconsistent with the simplicity and moderation we profess, injurious to the circumstances of some, and even in such as can afford it, but an ill example to those of less ability." (Marriages were usually solemnised at meetings specially appointed, and not at the ordinary meetings for worship.)

"7 mo. 4, 1751. A minute from the Two-Weeks Meeting held at Gracechurch Street, the 5th 6th mo., 1751. Relating to some young men under our profession rowing on the river Thames, and giving a publick ball, on which inquirey has been made amongst us and do not find any within the compass of our meeting concerned therein."

Here follow the minutes relating to the disownment of Hannah Lightfoot, who was a member of Westminster Meeting; these may be of some interest, as the case has excited of late public attention, but they do not cast much light on the disputed points in the controversy.

"1 mo. 1, 1755. This meeting being informed that it is currently reported that Hannah Lightfoot is married by the priest, and since absconded from her husband, on which this meeting appoints Mich. Morton, Jms. Marshman, and Mary Keene to visit her thereon, and make report."

"9 mo. 3, 1755. The Friends appointed to visit Hannah Lightfoot report they have made inquiry concerning her; were informed by her mother that she was married by a priest, but was not fully satisfied she was absented from her husband. 12 mo. continued—To bring in minute of denial."

"1 mo. 7, 1756. The Friends appointed to visit Hannah Lightfoot report that they have made Inquiry after her, and cant hear where she can be spoke wth or where she is, on wch this meeting appoints said friends wth Wm. Donne and Nathl. Wright to prepare a Testimony of Denial against Hannah Lightfoot for marrying by a priest against the known Rules of the Society, to be brought to our next meeting."

"3 mo. 3, 1756. A Testimony of Denial against Hannah Lightfoot was brought in, pursuant to the Direction of Last Meeting, wch was read and approv^d and is as follow, viz.—

"'Whereas Hannah Lightfoot, a Person Educated under our Profession, and who for several years past resided within the Compass of this Meeting, did then enter into a state of Marriage by the Priest with one not of our Society, which is directly repugnant to the good Rules & orders well known to be Established amongst us, on wch this Meeting appointed Friends to visit her, who several times Endeavered to find where she was in order to speak with her. But to no Purpose, nor could they obtain any Intelligence where she is, We therefore being desirous (as much as in us lies) to clear the truth which we profess, and ourselves from any aspersions wch through the misconduct of the said Hannah Lightfoot, may be cast upon Friends, do hereby testifie against such her Prosedings as aforesaid, and disown her for the same as one with whom we can have no fellowship, untill from a penitent mind and true contrition of heart, she shall be induced to signifie her unfeigned sorrow for her offence, and that this may be her case is what we truly desire."

It is observable, with respect to this matter, that the above testimony on being sent up as usual to the Six-Weeks Meeting was considered by that body at four different meetings before it would issue the customary order for its dispersion amongst the Monthly Meetings.

About 1700 we find that there was commenced a standing committee of some twelve men and women, known as "The Interval Friends," who seemed to fill the duties afterwards committed to overseers, and had committed to them the care over all business calling for immediate notice between the Monthly Meetings.

For upwards of a century, viz. to 1770, there was no separate Women's Meeting for Discipline in this Monthly Meeting, (the men and women sitting together), and there seems to have been in Westminster, as in some other quarters, considerable disinclination for the establishment of any separate Women's Monthly Meetings. When the subject was proposed to it by the Quarterly Meeting, in 1767, the meeting made a minute to the effect that, "it is not expedient to alter our usual method of their meeting with the men; our women friends so few that we think it impracticable for the present." The subject came forward again about three years after, and then the Women's Monthly Meeting, after considerrable and repeatedly adjourned discussion, was established. It may be noted that in the interval between the rejection of this proposition and just seven months before its adoption, Dr. Fothergill and his sister Ann had moved from White Hart Court into the meeting, also Judith Hill; possibly the altered view of the case might be due to their influence; both Ann Fothergill and Judith Hill became soon after appointed elders in the meeting.

Previously to this time traces are not wanting to show that at Westminster during the first half of the eighteenth century the same lack of zeal prevailed there as elsewhere. This was seen chiefly in the small attendance at meetings for discipline, the lukewarmness so often noted in answers to Queries, the marriages out and consequent disownment—and (when a more zealous feeling arose) in the many delinquents who had to be cut off for various and often grievous offences. The following minute from the Morning Meeting of Ministers and Elders, under date 16th Eighth Month, 1759, does not show a very satisfactory state as to ministry at Westminster:—

"This meeting takeing into consideration the Loss it suffers for want of due attendance of discreet and judicious Friends from the several Monthly Meetings, and observing that for a considerable time past none from your meeting have attended, wee therefore find ingaged to request you will, as in the wisdom of Truth you may be directed, appoint two discreet and judicious Friends the best qualified for the Weighty-service."

This minute of the Morning Meeting had been preceded by a record on the books of the Monthly Meeting, "No Elders; some care to put rules of Discipline in practise."

Nineteen years previously to this the Six-Weeks Meeting had had to call Westminster Friends' attention to the want of Friends "to sit in the Gallery where ministering friends usually sit."

Poor.

"The poor ye have always with you," was a fact well understood by Westminster Monthly Meeting, in early days, as well as by the other metropolitan meetings. In 1676 we find the meeting divided into five districts, namely, Westminster, Piccadilly, Covent Garden, Giles, and Strand. For each of these districts two or three women Friends were appointed, apparently in a sort of diaconal capacity, to oversee and report the wants of the poor and relieve them as directed by the Monthly Meeting. Our previously mentioned friends Jane Woodcock and Martha Fisher are both found on this appointment.

The relief of the poor and other increasing expenses pressed heavily on the resources of the Monthly Meeting during the eighteenth century. The experience of frequent collections, and occasional debt and forced economy was known at Westminster as in the City Meeting though to a less extent. In 1716 the meeting took under its consideration in what respects any diminution of expense could be effected. Amongst various suggested reductions of expenditure the following small item occurs:—

"Wee find in oure Quarterly Bills of expense, there was about the sum of £7 sett down for wine, and wee being in the mind that a Cupp of Warme Ale may be generally speaking as acceptable as ye wine, therefore [it] may be spared." This wine was the refreshment handed at the close of meeting to ministers who had visited it.

Library.

The large endowed Library of Westminster Monthly Meeting claims some notice here. It appears that there was a library of Friends' books kept at the Savoy as early as 1691, but in 1714 a number of books were added, as per minute, by Richard Hawkins. This friend is described as a yeoman of Covent Garden, and was a nephew of Gilbert Latey before mentioned:—

"1 mo. 3, 1714.—Our friend Richard Hawkins acquaints this meeting that he hath had it for some time weightily upon his mind under the consideration of the service it may be to truth, to propose that a library may be set up, for the preserving our ancient and honourable Friends' writings and testimonies which thereby may be ready to have recourse unto as occasion requires, and also for the use of the Friends belonging to this meeting, especially such as are not in a capacity to purchase large or many books, yet by having the opportunity of reading them may receive benefit and comfort from them, and further acquaints us that he hath divers such books of his own in quarto, folio, and octavo, which he is willing to give for the beginning of so good a work. Our friend John Whiting signified at the same time his desire to help forward the same work. This proposal was accepted, and it was recommended to other Friends to consider what help they can give. The books to be kept upstairs (at the Savoy)."

This Friend largely increased the collection at his death, when by will dated 1734 he gave "his books, to be placed in a regular and handsome manner for the giving liberty to any Friends, or the sober children of any Friends, who might desire it, to read any of such books."

Richard Hawkins also endowed the said library by the will just referred to, directing that from a portion of the rents of certain property* "Westminster Monthly Meeting do yearly cause to be laid out so much as they shall think proper in the purchase of Friends' books to be handsomely placed with the others, in order to the leaving a perfect collection of all Friends' books to posterity."

---

* A moiety of a house, No. 49, Strand, lately rebuilt under a building lease.

John Whiting (compiler of the catalogue of Friends' books only recently superseded by Joseph Smith's more comprehensive work) was a member of this meeting, and gave his valuable assistance in the formation of the library. It is very rich in pamphlets, of which there are no less than sixty-six volumes, chiefly relating to the early times of the Society of Friends.

In 1780 Dr. Fothergill also supplied a bookcase and many tracts, part of the library of the late John Nichols, thus mentioned in Dr. Lettsom's memoir: "Dr. Fothergill purchased likewise a pretty large collection of tracts, which Mr. Nickolls had picked up in his pursuit of Heads, written by those of his own persuasion from their first appearance, which the benevolent possessor has left to the meeting to which he belonged in Peter's Court, Westminster."

This may be the place to introduce some further notice of Dr. Fothergill, who, after passing by far the greater part of his very successful professional career in a house in White Hart Court, moved, when advanced in years, to within the compass of Westminster Monthly Meeting.

All through life he had, amidst his most varied, numerous, and arduous engagements, taken a share in the management of the Society,* becoming much interested in the settlement of the discipline engaged in by the Yearly Meeting, 1760, &c. &c., saying, during an illness that had threatened his life, "that if he had left anything undone which he wished to have done, it was perfecting the plan of Ackworth School, and likewise, the complete arrangement of the rules of our religious Society." Dr. Fothergill's active mind embraced also a wide range of philanthropy; he was a friend and supporter of John Howard in his work, became intimate with Dr. Franklin, and was one of three in a most important conference with that philosopher to endeavour on terms, so as to avert the disruption of the American

---

* His domestic correspondence or consultations within the kingdom were alone sufficiently extensive for ordinary occupation; but great as these avocations might be, and great they certainly were, they bore but a small proportion to the time and attention constantly devoted to the Society at large, of which he was a member, and which, though united in principle amongst each other, admitted of contingencies that demanded attention, influence, and abilities; which few men combined in a more ample degree than Dr. Fothergill did, or exerted them more ardently upon all interesting occasions.—*Memoirs*, p. 30.

colonies from the mother country. All social questions also engaged his attention, such as public baths, schools, and securing interments in cemeteries rather than in city churchyards. He was consulted by the wise and great of his day, and though at his decease it was decided to have the funeral at Winchmore Hill for the sake of privacy, it is on record that as many as seventy coaches and chaises went all that twelve miles filled with those anxious to do respect to his memory. Of one so eminent the following description of his personal appearance may be interesting :—

"The person of Dr. Fothergill was of a delicate, rather of an extenuated make ; his features were all character ; his eye had a peculiar brilliancy of expression, yet it was not easy to mark the leading trait so as to disengage it from the united whole. He was remarkably active and alert, and with a few exceptions enjoyed a general good state of health. He had a peculiarity of address and manner, resulting from person, education, and principle ; but it was so perfectly accompanied by the most engaging attentions, that he was the genuine polite man above all forms of breeding. I knew him well, and never knew a man who left such pleasing impressions on the minds of his patients.

"His dress was remarkably neat, plain, and decent, peculiarly becoming himself ; a perfect transcript of the order, and I may add the neatness of his mind. . . . . At his meals he was remarkably temperate ; in the opinion of some rather too abstemious, eating sparingly but with a good relish, and rarely exceeding two glasses of wine at dinner or supper ; yet by this uniform and steady temperance he preserved his mind vigorous and active, and his constitution equal to all his engagments."—*Memoirs, Dr. Fothergill*, p. 87.

He bought Ham House, Upton, of Admiral Elliot in 1762, as a country seat, where he formed an arboretum unrivalled at that time in England, for botany was one of his most ardently followed pursuits. But the ruling principle of his life is shown in the following, selected from among his memoranda :—

"I wished at my first setting out," he observes, "I wished most fervently, and I endeavour after it still, to do the business that occurred, with all the diligence I could, as a *present duty*, and endeavoured to repress every rising idea of its consequences ; knowing most assuredly that there was a hand which could easily overthrow every pursuit of this kind, and baffle every attempt either to acquire fame or wealth.

Westminster, entrance: pencil sketch by Henry S. Newman, probably 1846 [LSF]

facing p.260

Left: Hammersmith, interior: photo by Oliver Dell; first half of 20th century [LSF, Lidbetter collection]

Below: Hammersmith, exterior: photo from *Home of the Ealing Free Library*, 1902 [LSF]

And with a great degree of gratitude I look back to the gracious secret preserver that kept my mind more attentive to the discharge of my present anxious care for those I visited, than either to the profits or the credit resulting from it ; and I am sure to be kept under such a circumscribed, unaspiring temper of mind, doing everything with diligence, humility, and as, in the sight of the God of healing,—frees the mind from much unavailing distress and consequential disappointment. Such were the maxims of this wise and good man."—*Memoirs*, xiii.

Before turning from Westminster to speak of meetings that have become affiliated with it, an historical fact may be mentioned in connection with the meeting-house in Hemming's Row.

When the Emperor Alexander of Russia was in London, just before the banishment of Napoleon to Elba, he once came to this meeting-house and sat down there as an humble worshipper. It is said that this mighty potentate afterwards acknowledged to William Allen and Stephen Grellet that he had felt in that hour, as he listened to the soul-stirring ministry of Richard Phillips and John Wilkinson, or waited in silence with the other worshippers, a communion with the Majesty of All, greater than any he had ever known in connection with the grandest church ceremonial. Certain it is that he rose from his seat in a very tender and affectionate spirit, and shook hands with all around so warmly and heartily as to evince how deeply he had been impressed.—*Vide* Letter at end of chapter.

Hammersmith.

We have now to speak of Hammersmith Meeting, which since 1750 has been subsidiary to Westminster, having had a previous independent existence of about ninety years.

It was about the year 1658 that one Sarah Blackbury,* a minister, came to Hammersmith, and under her ministry one Hester Matson was convinced of the truth. This woman entertained Sarah Blackbury, and asked her husband's permission to have a meeting appointed at their house. To this he consented, but it was only held once. It seems the

---

* Sarah Blackbury was incidentally, through a conversation she had with George Fox, the means of establishing the women's meeting for the poor known afterwards as the Box Meeting.—*G. F. Epistles*, p. 6.

husband had a situation at a brewhouse in Westminster, returning home but once a week. His fellow servants at the brewhouse on hearing him relate his wife's doings, so calumniated Friends that on again visiting his home he withdrew his previous permission. The meeting was then removed to the house of William Bond at Chiswick, and then to a place called the Hope near the Limekilns, half-way between Chiswick and Hammersmith. Soon after it was brought back to Hammersmith. Gilbert Latey, as his biographer remarks, " was a frequent attender and, in measure, supporter thereof, being a nursing father thereto."

The first regular meeting-house was built in Hammersmith in 1677, the Six-Weeks Meeting voting £30 towards it. The meeting was originally a pretty large one, and the attenders did not escape their share of suffering.

In connection with persecution at this place, there is a curious circumstance recorded in Latey's biography, which may be epitomised here as a Hammersmith association.

Gilbert Latey was once waiting on Lady Sawkell in connection with his business, when Sir William Sawkell, who commanded under the Earl of Oxford, came into the room. He had a kind respect for G. L., and presently asked him, " What meeting do you go to ? "

" Sometimes to one, and sometimes to another," said the worthy tailor.

" The reason," said Sir William, " why I asked you is, because I have orders to go and break up a meeting of your people at Hammersmith, which I have deferred executing, and now I have a fresh command laid on me, and I cannot avoid it, but must go there on Sunday next ; and therefore I speak in kindness to you, if you use at any time to go there, that you refrain coming that day, for I receive my command now from so high a hand, that I dare not omit executing thereof."

Gilbert Latey immediately found it laid upon him to be present on the occasion, and before parting, informed the knight that he should be there.

Gilbert went to the meeting on the following First-day, and was preaching when the troopers rushed in. They listened awhile, but presently one shouted, " This man will never have done, let us pull him down."

" Who commands you ? " said Gilbert, as the soldiers laid hands on him.

"Sir William Sawkell," said the troopers.

"Tell him I am here, and that my name is Gilbert Latey."

Sir William, who is described as a lusty, jolly man, came in trembling and exclaimed, "Latey, did I not tell you that I was commanded to be here to-day?"

"Thou didst so," said Gilbert; "but did I not tell thee I was commanded by a greater than thou art that I must be here also?"

"Go; get thee gone about thy business," cried the knight, "and I will take care concerning the rest here met."

"If thou hast any respect for me, discharge the rest and let me be thy prisoner," said Gilbert.

After some time the knight was persuaded to take this course. Gilbert was taken and fined. Some of the others present were also distrained upon, but through G. Latey's kind offices their goods were restored to them again.

This was no solitary instance; it ever was this Friend's delight to bear with his substance the sufferings designed for his brethren. At one time there have been warrants out against him for several hundred pounds. Whilst speaking of G. L. in connection with Hammersmith, we may also record that he preached his last sermon there.

During the eighteenth century the Monthly Meeting at Hammersmith gradually declined in strength and numbers. The average attendance at the meeting for discipline had only been three persons at a time for three years previous to its junction with Westminster. Many of its minutes (now preserved at Westminster) are quaint and suggestive. For instance, "Mary Scott brought three & sixpence which she had made of the mulberries, & we being indebted to her one shilling made her a present of the remaining two shillings & sixpence."

A respectable meeting for worship seems to have been kept up at Hammersmith for some time after its junction with Westminster. It was sufficiently large in 1765 to warrant the building of a new meeting-house, at a cost of £315. But towards the close of the eighteenth century, the meeting for worship was with difficulty kept up. The plan of holding it fortnightly, and even monthly, and of encouraging some Friends from Westminster to go there, was tried; but in 1798 it was decided to lay down the meeting.

It was reopened in 1805 as a regular meeting for worship, twice on First-day and once on Fourth-day, some Friends having gone to reside in the vicinity; but it was again discontinued. It still remains the property of Friends, but is at present allowed to be used as a chapel by some Nonconformists. The burial-ground adjoining was closed for interments some three years since.

HOLLOWAY.

In 1860, as we have said, that part of Peel Monthly Meeting known as Holloway Particular Meeting became united to Westminster. The meeting at Holloway was first held in the Eleventh Month, 1858, in a building in St. George's Place, which had formerly been a Wesleyan chapel, and of which Friends had taken a short lease for the purpose. The meeting then consisted of about thirty First-day morning attenders.

After the junction with Westminster, it was soon found out that the meeting had increased so much as to make the erection of more suitable premises desirable. Accordingly, a piece of ground in Mercer's Road, Upper Holloway, was taken on a building lease of sixty years from the Mercers' Company, at a rent of £24, on which the present substantial building was erected. The Six-Weeks Meeting, being in possession of funds from the sale of Southwark and Gracechurch Street premises, gave £2,500 towards the cost, and nearly £1,200 more was subscribed chiefly by Friends of Holloway and Westminster. The ministers' gallery is the one which formerly stood at Gracechurch Street previous to the sale by Friends of that property, and the oak forms came from the same building. These forms had been the result of great care bestowed on their shape and size by the committee who had the charge of rebuilding White Hart Court in 1821 (the original model came from Westminster), but the Gracechurch Street were an improvement, and have been copied since in many meeting-houses.

The premises at Holloway were opened for public worship with a large meeting on the 27th of Eleventh Month, 1864.

Respecting the other meeting-houses which have come under the care of this Monthly Meeting, through its junction with Longford in 1865, we shall have to speak in another chapter.

Holloway meeting house: foundation stone laying, 1864 (William Beck was present) [LSF]; interior, undated photo before 1938 [LSF, Lidbetter collection]

facing p.264

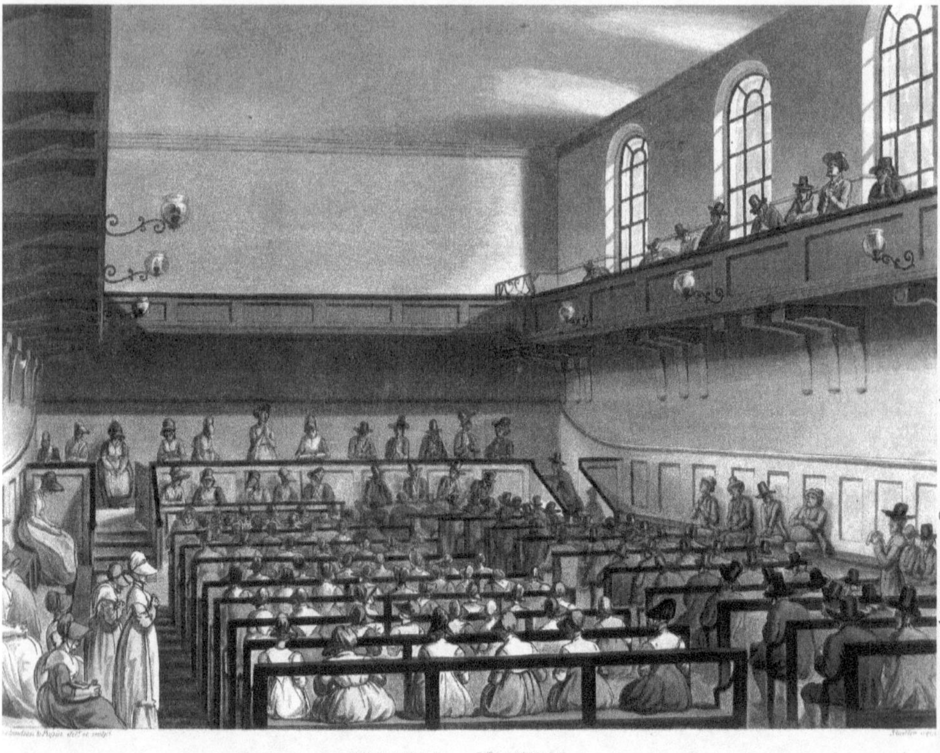

Westminster: "The Quakers Meeting", etching with watercolour, by Thomas Rowlandson and A.C. Pugin, 1808, six years before Emperor Alexander's visit. It is identifiable as Westminster from the drawing below, "from an old water-colour" in Hubert Lidbetter (1979), plate XXIV, different only in the stove and light fittings. This building was demolished in 1882 when the lease expired: the present Westminster meeting house is the other side of St Martin's Lane. [LSF]

Library of the Religious Society of Friends

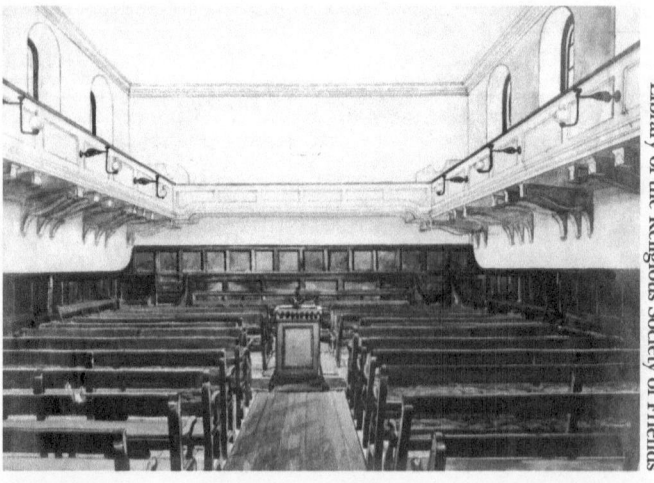

facing p.265

APPENDIX.

WESTMINSTER.

THE following,* on the subject of the Emperor of Russia's visit to Westminster Meeting on First-day, 19th Sixth Month, 1814, is an extract from a private letter written the same day by one (then a young man of two and twenty) to an intimate friend in the country :—" We have fine doings in town with the Emperor Alexander and the other grandees. Almost every day affords some novel and highly interesting spectacle. Yesterday there was a very grand procession to Guildhall, where the Emperor and all the rest went to dine. . . . The streets, windows, and tops of the houses were quite full long before they came. . . . But how shall I relate it? and how wilt thou credit it? when I tell thee I this day had the honour of shaking hands with the Emperor. I went to Westminster Meeting quite by accident, and found very few Friends there, owing, I suppose, to the wet weather, but about a quarter past eleven a noise at the bottom of the meeting announced the entrance of some strangers. When, strange to tell, who should it be but W. Allen introducing the Emperor Alexander, the Duchess of Oldenburgh, some foreign prince in his uniform, and several other foreigners. The sight was, as thou mayst naturally suppose, very gratifying, and my situation in meeting was so good an one that I sat almost opposite to him all the time, and therefore had an excellent opportunity of examining his features and behaviour. John Wilkinson was very fortunately at meeting, and spoke to some length very excellently. Richard Phillips also spoke and gave us a short and beautiful exhortation. The Emperor and rest showed the greatest attention and they really seemed to take great interest in the meeting. After it concluded the Emperor shook hands with Richard Phillips and several other men Friends. He then went to the women's side, and shook hands with Josiah Messer's and John Wilkinson's wives, and a great many other females, young and old, as he went down the meeting; the duchess was also condescending enough to do the same. The Emperor's gallantry seemed to lead him so much to the female side that I almost despaired of having an opportunity, but standing directly opposite to some forms where there were no females, I ventured as he was very slowly passing to place myself—hat on—a little before him and bow; he did the same, and in a very condescending way took my hand, and gave it a much warmer shake than any of the Dons at Westminster Meeting have ever done, and at the same time smiled in so gracious and pleasing a manner as quite penetrated my heart. The Emperor is a fine man; his face full, features small, with a most delightful expression—very animated and cheerful; his countenance very open, and his face altogether carries with it an evidence that he is of a kind and benevolent disposition, but I should hardly think he possesses *very great* strength of mind. In his habits he is regular and temperate, and as his reward, he carries with him a healthy and fresh appearance. Everybody seems delighted with him, and it is a very common acknowledgment with persons that they are Emperor mad. Farewell," &c. &c.

*By William Beck's father, Richard Low Beck [annotated copy]

CHAPTER XIV.

RATCLIFF MONTHLY MEETING, INCLUDING MEETINGS AT BROOK STREET AND WAPPING.

The Meeting at Captain Brock's House.

Amongst the early meetings of Friends established in London and its suburbs, was one held for some years in the house of Captain James Brock, of Mile End Green, in the parish of Stepney, at that time quite a rural hamlet. The exact date of Captain Brock's opening his house to Friends is now only a matter of conjecture. It may have been before the arrival in London of Edward Burrough and Francis Howgill, for it was possibly to visit Captain Brock that ex-Captain Amos Stoddart, with Isabel Buttery and another, were "walking in the fields *towards Stepney*," when Ruth Brown (afterwards wife of William Crouch) was convinced, through thus accidentally meeting and falling into conversation with them.

However this may be, it is certain that under Captain Brock's protection a Church was soon gathered. The aggressive character of early Quakerism drew attention to this assembly. In 1655 Ann Downer (afterwards wife of George Whitehead) went to the neighbouring "steeple-house" at Stepney, and publicly declared against the minister there.* For this she was sentenced to ten weeks' imprisonment in the House of Correction, and was beaten with a rope's end for refusing to work.

This "Conventicle" at Mile End Green was situated in the Tower Hamlets, and was consequently under the jurisdiction of Sir John Robinson, the Governor of the Tower. After the Restoration of the Stuarts, like many other time-servers of the period, he exerted all his power to crush the sectaries, and we read in "Besse's History" of many imprisonments resulting from attending the meeting at Mile End Green. In

---

* This being the time of the Commonwealth, the minister officiating would not be an incumbent such as were settled at the Restoration.

June, 1662, he particularly mentions two youths who were taken hence to Bridewell, aged respectively 13 and 16 years. They displayed a remarkable constancy whilst standing for two hours with their hands in the stocks, and could not be forced to work, nor to eat, except at their own charge. They wrote from their prison an epistle to Friends' children, exhorting them to stand faithful.

The size of the meeting at Mile End Green may be judged to have been considerable from the following statement of the number of persons seized there and cast into prison during thirteen consecutive Sabbath-days, commencing July 17th, 1664. The numbers are respectively 33 (including Alexander Parker), 22, 15, 50, 21, 11, 34, 16, 20, 21, 10, 27, 16. Sometimes these innocent sufferers were dragged off to the Tower, and sometimes to Bridewell, and fines or protracted imprisonment were generally their subsequent experience.

These East End Quakers did not quail in the presence of judges and magistrates. In December, 1664, the authorities took one John Otter, a shoemaker, from this Mile End "Conventicle." The justices before whom he was arraigned asked him where he dwelt.

"I have a dwelling," said he, "where neither thief, murderer, nor persecutor can come."

"Where is that?" queried the bench.

"In God!" was the reply of the undaunted cobbler. This was a logic which the justices could not appreciate, and by way of reply they sent him to Bridewell as a vagabond.

At the sessions John Otter was again brought to the bar, and asked where he dwelt. He gave the same answer as before, and, after a consultation with the other justices, the judge passed sentence of transportation upon him. He was consequently sent out to Virginia, in company with three malefactors, to be sold into slavery for seven years.

RATCLIFF MEETING-HOUSE.

The meeting at Mile End Green was removed to its present position at Ratcliff about the year 1666 or 1667. We may here remark, in passing, that some of the earliest marriages amongst us were, as shown by the registers, solemnised at James Brock's house. But the meeting had now outgrown its accommodation, and in 1666 Thomas Yoakley, on behalf of Friends, bought some land situated at the corner of Schoolhouse Lane and Brook Street, in Ratcliff. This land was originally copyhold, but was enfranchised in 1734 for £21.

On a part of the portion of land referred to, Friends erected a meeting-house; the remainder was made use of as a burial-ground. Hither, however, the implacable Sir John Robinson tracked them out, and especially in the year 1670 he seems to have spared no pains to break up the meeting. He kept them out of their premises, and in June, 1670, fined William Simpson £20 for preaching in the street. In August he sent his soldiers and carried away or destroyed sixty-one forms and two tables. But Friends still met all the same though having nothing to sit upon, and Sir John again came down and dispersed them. His followers were so indignant at the worshippers keeping their heads covered in his presence that they snatched away Friends' hats and threw them over the wall into the adjacent street, where the rude people outside were only too glad, as we are informed,* to have the opportunity of exchanging bad hats for good ones. All this, and other suffering, Friends bore with such meekness that one of the trained-band's men who stood near, named Benjamin Bangs, felt so drawn to them by their conduct here and elsewhere that he joined the Society, and became an eminent minister of the Gospel.

But neither the loss of their forms nor their hats could prevent Friends from meeting in Brook Street, Ratcliff, so Sir John determined to have the place itself destroyed. He sent on the 2nd of September his soldiers, who for a day and a night toiled at the work, and carried away twelve cart-loads of doors, windows, floors, glass, lead, &c. and also "made ruinous work" of the tiles, and other easily destructible portions of the building.

The persecuted ones, nothing daunted, met upon the ruins until they had again restored their premises; and the meeting was always kept up though maltreatment and arrest continued during the era of persecution to be the frequent lot of the zealous worshippers.

In 1681 we find that a gallery was added to the meeting-house, but it is not certain whether this was what we now call a "ministers' gallery," or extra accommodation for worshippers. In the same year some further alterations were ordered to be

---

* Life of Benjamin Bangs, in which will also be found an account of his attending a meeting at Westminster.

made, and we transcribe the minute of the Monthly Meeting, as it gives us some idea of the edifice. It was in the Third Month, 1681, that some Friends were appointed to " contrive to let ayre into the Uper and Lower meetings on each side of the chimney, if there be neede, and on window on the side of the back door in the lower meeting, and by taking downe the Uper parte of the Glace windows above and below where they shall see meet, and make new casements and put up a new piller in ye meeting."

We see from the foregoing minute that Friends had begun to call the building in which they met a *meeting*, just as their Episcopalian neighbours called the place in which the Church met a church.

Passing over various minor alterations, including the making in 1693 of " a little seat for children to sitt on in the gallery," we find that in 1712 the meeting-house was much out of repair, and about £330 was spent in improvements and reparations. The Six-Weeks Meeting had promised £30 towards the expense, but the anticipated cost had been doubled, and, considering that the work was " done so substantially," they increased their grant to £100, with the understanding that the arrangement was " not to form a precedent."

With necessary repairs from time to time the meeting-house, thus renovated, lasted till 1797, at which date it was rebuilt on an enlarged scale at a cost of nearly £2,200. This is the present building, and was opened for divine worship in the Eighth Month, 1798. During the process of demolition and rebuilding, Friends' Meeting was temporarily transferred to a commodious room near Ratcliff Cross, which was rented at £16 per annum.

WAPPING.

From 1700 to 1779 Ratcliff Monthly Meeting had under its care a meeting-house at Wapping. For at the close of the seventeenth century Ratcliff Friends found their own meeting-house so overcrowded that they resolved to erect a new one for the use of Friends residing in the south-western portion of their district. A piece of ground was accordingly taken on lease at £6 a year, and £100 paid down, situated behind the houses, with a court about 96 feet in length leading to it from the north side of Wapping Street, and south of a rope walk belonging to one Marmaduke Bushel. To keep this court clear, by the way, was often a troublesome task, for the neighbouring dealers in various maritime stores whose yards or workshops were contiguous, had a habit of piling their anchors, &c. about the passage, much to Friends' annoyance.

On this spot of ground it appears that a meeting-house was built at a cost of £620 (probably including purchase of lease), but of its subsequent history little is known. In 1754 we find the Quarterly Meeting consenting to an evening meeting being held there on Third-days, which was, however, given up in 1765. Friends had become less numerous in this waterside locality, and in 1779, at the expiration of the lease, the property passed out of the hands of Friends, and no attempt has since been made to establish a meeting in the district. There are entries in the registry of burials, which show that several Friends were buried in the ground attached to Wapping Meeting-house.

The Ratcliff Burial-ground.

The remainder of the estate purchased by Thomas Yoakley and others at Ratcliff, now built upon, was used till 1857 as a burial-ground. It was at first only an enclosed piece of a field, and was levelled in 1686. At that time the meeting found it necessary to order the gravemaker not to put more than three corpses in one grave. Such was at that time the population of the Monthly Meeting, that in 1689 complaint was made of more room being wanted on account of there being so many interments. Further accommodation seems to have been obtained by raising the ground. A list of the burials from 1789 to 1857 is preserved, in which there are about four hundred names, forming doubtless only a small proportion of the total number interred in this place. The ground has been buried in over and over again, and in the more recent interments the digging was frequently obstructed by the lead coffins, &c. of a past era.

Before passing from the subject of burial, we may quote a minute of the Monthly Meeting, dated Seventh Month 19, 1683, illustrative of the primitive manners of that early time. It reads as follows:—

"It is desiered that Friends be spoken to the next Monthly Meeting concerning the carrying the corpses to the ground, that thay be desiered to com timly at the hours appoynted, and *to set a helping hand to ye finishing ye same.*"

Ratcliff Monthly Meeting.

We are not certain as to the precise date of the establishment of Ratcliff Monthly Meeting. Its minutes now extant date from the Twelfth Month, 1680, and are headed, "A Booke of and ffor Busines in the Monthly and Quarterly Meetings of Ratclif."

From this book it is readily to be seen that the Friends of the district were largely tinctured with the nautical element. The description of individuals as mariners, sailors, shipwrights, &c., occurs frequently. There was also a considerable sprinkling of tradesmen and mechanics.

But the Church had also amongst its members large traders and merchants. In 1682 a great fire destroyed part of Wapping and Shadwell. Sixteen Friends were burnt out, whose losses are duly scheduled at various amounts from thirty shillings up to a thousand pounds. Collections in aid of the sufferers were set on foot amongst Friends generally. Fires, by the way, seem to have been frequent in this district. Readers of Thomas Scattergood's Journal will remember his description of the results of one that destroyed between four and five hundred houses, burning almost up to the walls of Ratcliff Meeting-house.*

---

* *Thomas Scattergood's Life*, p. 139 :—" Returned [from Gravesend] with Wm. Dillwyn and as we rode along we saw a very great smoke arise toward London, which we found to be a fire. It broke out in a boat-builder's shop adjoining the East India Company's large warehouse and saltpetre works, which were soon on fire and burnt violently. It continued burning many hours, and it was supposed that between four and five hundred houses were destroyed. It came very nearly up to Ratcliff Meeting-house, and extended over several acres of ground.

"7th mo. 24.—This was the day of Ratcliff Monthly Meeting, which I knew not, but found my mind turned that way rather than to Westminster week-day meeting. Joseph Smith went with me, and when we got there we found the yard pretty much filled up with casks, and no appearance of a meeting. It being early we took a walk amongst the ruins and rubbish caused by the fire yesterday, and in a little while returned and found two Friends standing in the graveyard, who hardly knew whether to go into the meeting-house or not, but I encouraged them to go in, and so we went and sat down. Our meeting amounted to four members of the meeting on the men's side and two women and a child on the other, with about as many from other meetings, and a minute was made by a Friend adjourning the meeting for one week. The clerk, we understood, is burnt out."

P. 162.—" 1795, 3 mo. 29, First-day. We found a very crowded meeting at Ratcliff, and it proved an open time. The afternoon meeting

Amongst the maritime and mercantile class above described an earnest and growing Quaker Church seems to have long flourished. It passed, as we have already seen, through sharp and severe trials in the days of persecution. Of this continued persecution we catch occasional glimpses in the minute-book. In 1682 reference is made to the meeting being broken up by justices and heavy fines levied.

Ten years afterwards, in the reign of William III., record is made of a case of suffering of a kind that had not been infrequent in the Stuart period, but had now become exceptional. A poor Friend named James Goodwin was forced by soldiers into the Tower, and detained there to be sent to Flanders. He was kept five days, and beaten and abused by the soldiers because he refused to take part in any military duties. He was then got off by Friends " as a great favour," at a cost to them of thirty shillings for his redemption, and two shillings and sixpence given to his family in his absence.

We have alluded in previous chapters to the " Retired Meetings" as a special feature of early Quakerism. One of these was established at Ratcliff in 1678, and was held on First-day mornings, "to begin at nine and break up at twelve." The public meeting for worship seems to have been in the afternoon.

The care of its members, scattered over a wide area, early claimed the attention of this Monthly Meeting. In 1681 we read, " It is concluded by the meeting that ffriends doe sett apart certain times ffor men and women ffriends to visett poore ffriends and other ffriends as it moveth in their harts soe to do. And this service to be minded and account given of it in Each Monthly Meeting. The quarter to be divided into four parts, from Blackwall to Samuel Groomes house one part, and from Samuel Groomes up Whithorse Street, and soe to New Grauel Lane the uper way and lower 2nd

---

was also large and favoured. I stood up near the close and told them that I had seen that day good things in store for the inhabitants of this neighbourhood if on their part they would embrace the visitations of the Holy Spirit ; and that as Divine Providence had suffered a devouring fire to lay waste their outward habitations, and they were now raising pleasant buildings on the ruins, so if they were willing to let the searching and overturning power of the Lord lay waste their old buildings spiritually to the foundations, and remove the rubbish out of the way, they in due time would be favoured to be built up a Church and people to His praise, and testimony-bearers would be raised up amongst them to promote the work." . . .

part, and from New Grauel Lane to the Hermitage and to Wellclose 3rd part, Milend, Stepney, and Bow 4th part." Then follow the names of sixteen Friends in sets of four, respectively appointed to the above districts.

It will be seen that we have culled but little from the Ratcliff minute-book. We might, of course, have presented many instances similar to those already detailed in previous chapters illustrative of Friends' care of the poor, apprentices, marriages, or other matters coming under the notice of the Church in its Monthly Meeting capacity. Like other meetings, Ratcliff had its times of prosperity and declension, its triumphs and its trials. As at other places, we find the meetings disturbed occasionally by would-be preachers. One of these, "a poor man," being forcibly ejected (in 1692) had ten shillings handed to him to repair his garments which had been torn in the struggle.

Ratcliff Monthly Meeting was conspicuous towards the middle of last century for its secession from the compact by which the London Monthly Meetings were financially connected with the Six-Weeks Meeting. This circumstance was one amongst other of the immediate causes of the reconstitution of the Six-Weeks Meeting in 1745.

In 1729 the Quarterly Meeting joined Ratcliff and Barking as one Monthly Meeting, but in 1732, on account of the strenuous opposition of the Ratcliff Friends the arrangement was rescinded. In 1821, however, the junction was successfully carried into effect. By this arrangement Plaistow Particular Meeting was brought into the Monthly Meeting, and has continued to be its main support. Ratcliff meeting for worship declined so much in numbers that as early as 1833 it was proposed to discontinue it. The meeting-house is now largely made use of for religious and philanthropic purposes connected with the Bedford Institute Association, which are kindly permitted by the Monthly Meeting. A very encouraging attendance of the poor marks its meeting for worship every First-day evening, at the close of which a Scripture-reading Meeting is also held, to the evident appreciation of a class who, but for this, would seldom, if ever, hear the Scriptures read.

CHAPTER XV.

BARKING MONTHLY MEETING,

Including Meetings at Barking, Plaistow, Wanstead and Harold's Wold.

BARKING.

PRIOR to the year 1691, the Monthly Meeting of Barking included the meetings of Waltham Abbey and Epping, as well as those hereafter mentioned, and formed with them a portion of the Quarterly Meeting of Essex. But the two meetings were in that year transferred to Enfield (afterwards called Tottenham Monthly Meeting), and Barking, with its subsidiary meetings at Wanstead, Plaistow, and Harold's Hill, became one of the Monthly Meetings of London and Middlesex Quarterly Meeting.

Over these rural districts, at an early date, the principles of Friends spread from the adjacent metropolis. Small congregations met at the houses of the yeomen or farmers, till the needs of the increasing Churches prompted the purchase of land, and the erection of suitable premises, or some wealthy adherent presented to the Society a place to meet in.

The earliest separate meeting-house in the locality now specially under notice was at Barking. Here in 1672 Friends purchased of Edward Burling half an acre of ground, formerly an orchard, for a burying-place. In the following year they gave £87 for *part* of the adjacent mansion known as Tate's Place, including the Great Hall, measuring 28 feet by 26, two parlours, a staircase, and some chambers. The place was out of repair, and in the Barking cash-book is an entry at this date for £18 11s. for timber, boards, and workmanship.

In the Ninth Month, 1703, there occurred a terrible tempest, which unroofed the building and blew down chimneys, and also the wall of the burial-ground, occasioning Friends considerable expense to set matters right again.

This old meeting-house, adapted out of Tate's Place, seems to have served the purposes of Friends till 1758. At this date a new building was erected at a cost of £233; about £78 being raised in Barking Monthly Meeting, whilst the two country meetings of Longford and Tottenham subscribed nearly £20, and the Six-Weeks Meeting voted the rest. A meeting for worship was kept up in this building till the Ninth Month, 1830, since which time it has been closed, except on special occasions.

In the adjacent burial-ground, now a large plot of land, were interred William Mead and his wife, and in modern times, Elizabeth Fry and Samuel Gurney.

WANSTEAD.

A building to be used as a meeting-house at Wanstead, with the ground it stood on was bought in 1673 for £30, of Abraham Shapton. The origin of the meeting at this place we have not been able to ascertain. In 1700 the building was out of repair, and there was some talk of selling it. But £25 was the highest bid that could be obtained, and rather than part with it at the price, it was agreed to lay out a few pounds in repairs. Fourteen years afterwards the building and ground it stood on was sold by the Monthly Meeting at a still greater loss, viz. for £21 10s. to a Friend named Joseph Wright.

It seems this step had been taken without the concurrence of the Quarterly Meeting, which expressed its strong dissatisfaction, but reluctantly consented to the arrangement, and ordered Joseph Wright to pay the money to the Six-Weeks Meeting. This, however, was not what Barking Friends had intended, and they directed Joseph Wright to pay no one but themselves, alleging that they wished to erect a new meeting-house at Stratford. The Quarterly Meeting now ordered Thomas King, of "The Beehive," near Wanstead, who was a trustee for the property, not to convey to any one else till the money was lodged with the Six-Weeks Meeting. Matters remained thus at a dead-lock for two years, when Barking Friends gave in, and agreed that the Six-Weeks Meeting should receive the money. An understanding was, however, come to, that it should be repaid to Barking Monthly Meeting as soon as the site for the proposed new meeting-house should be found. The design alluded to was never carried out.

Quite recently a meeting has been commenced in this neighbourhood, on a First-day afternoon, for the accommodation of the families of Friends resident at Woodford and Leytonstone; it is held in the Court-room of some alms-houses at the latter place.

Plaistow.

The meeting at Plaistow was transferred thither from Ham, as stated by William Crouch. Persecution at Ham Meeting is alluded to by Besse, as early as 1662, and in the ancient account-book of Barking Monthly Meeting, "our meeting at Eastham" is spoken of in 1670.

In 1677 there was living at Plaistow Ann Eccles (widow of Ralph Butcher), who had married Solomon Eccles, the Friend whose walk through Bartlemy Fair in 1663, in very primitive attire, forms such a striking passage in the history of those days of excitement. Ann Eccles possessed two copyhold messuages, and some land adjacent, which she held of the manor-courts of Westham, Burnett, and Plaise. This property she left by will to her husband during his life, and after his death to William Penn and others, "for the service of truth for ever."

In one of the messuages on this land, after due adaptation had been effected, the meeting was held till 1703. In that year we find the Monthly Meeting complaining of Plaistow Meeting-house as to the "great inconveniency to Friends' health on account of the straitness" of the building, it being "crowded on First-days with young Friends from London." It was accordingly resolved to take down an adjacent barn, build a new meeting-house, and make the old one into two rooms, thus preserving the chambers over it. These plans were carried into effect in 1704, at a cost of £80, the Six-Weeks Meeting paying half.

This edifice could not have been a very substantial one, for in 1714, only ten years after its erection, it is stated in the minutes of the Six-Weeks Meeting, "that ye Friends of Plaistow and Barking have neglected to Repair and Support the Meeting-house at Plaistow, so that part of one End is in Danger to fall to the Hazard of the lives of Friends, which will oblige this Meeting to complain to the Quarterly Meeting, in order to discourage Friends about ye City from Resorting thither, till they can do it with Safety, by its being Secured, wch this meetg desires the Friends of Plaistow & Barking will forthwith do."

Ratcliff: Above, undated watercolour by William Edward Fox [LSF]. Below, interior photo 1901, from Clement Y. Sturge, *Leaves from the Past*, 1905 [LSF]

facing p.276

Barking: 1758 building, undated photo (before the new building of 1908) [LSF]

Plaistow, exterior: undated photo (before 1923) [LSF, Lidbetter]. See also p.281.

The necessary repairs in the building were attended to on this and many subsequent occasions. In 1823 new and very commodious premises were erected, forming one of the best of the suburban meeting-houses belonging to the Society. More than £1,400 was subscribed amongst Friends and attenders of the meeting, and £300 was given by the Six-Weeks Meeting towards this erection.

Plaistow Women's Meeting.

At Plaistow we find the records of an ancient Women's Meeting commencing with the Fifth Month, 1675. This meeting was chiefly occupied with the care of the poor, and also with seeing after the cleaning, &c. of the meeting-houses. It was held at Plaistow, Barking, Harold's Wood, &c. and its prominent members were Sarah Mead, Alice Townsend, Mary Bridgstock, Mary Kemp, Elizabeth Fryer, Margaret Taillor, and several others. After some years we find Mary Claridge taking an active part.

At these meetings a collection was made and records of the various disbursements required. For instance, we find "for a poor gyrle 1s. 4d.," "for dorothe Eastcotte 10s. 0d." (this Friend seems to have been a standing recipient for many years), "for the nursing of a boy by the hand of Elizabeth Mortimer 1 . 0 . 0," "for cleaning Plaistow Meeting-house for one quarter 1s. 0d." With entries of this character, interspersed with charges for cutting grass in the burial-grounds, for the supply of mops, &c. the minutes run on till 1721, when the Women's Meeting seems to have dropped.

The following is rather a curious specimen of an account passed by the meeting just referred to:—

"A note of what have been laid out by Henry Loveday for the burying of Alice Mander:

	s.	d.
for a coffin	6	6
for bread	1	0
for beer	1	8
for cheese	0	10
for the woman that stript her	1	0
for the evidence and the woman that went to the justice	1	0
	12	0 "

Plaistow Meeting is in modern times associated with the names of many of the great and good. It is hardly necessary to do more than simply mention Elizabeth Fry, and the late Samuel Gurney, who long worshipped in this place, and whose mortal remains were interred in Barking burial-ground.

Harold's Hill, or Harold's Wood.

Not far from the town of Havering-atte-Bower, is Harold's Hill, where a meeting was early established. It was contiguous to the mansion called Gooses, the residence of William Mead, who married Sarah, daughter of Margaret Fell, of Swarthmoor. Of this meeting the Mead family were doubtless the chief support. Hither, in his declining years, George Fox often came for those periods of retirement which advancing age rendered necessary, and several entries in the Journal mention this staying "at my son-in-law's house at Gooses."

The meeting at Harold's Wood, like many, if not most, of the country meetings round London, was held every other First-day. In 1695 we find William Mead coming to the Quarterly Meeting to ask permission for a Retired Meeting to be held there on the intermediate First-days on account of those aged Friends of the locality who could not get to more distant meeting-houses. It was left for Barking Monthly Meeting to settle "as they in the wisdom of God shall see meet," and at the next Quarterly Meeting, the said Retired Meeting is reported as arranged to be held.

There is no evidence extant of there being any separate meeting-house at Harold's Wood, and it is probable that the assembly was held on the premises of some Friend (most likely David Harding), who had a convenient room for the purpose. It is chiefly its connection with the Mead family which gives interest to this bygone Church.

William Mead, whose name is associated with that of William Penn in the memorable trial when the jury brought in a verdict of guilty of "speaking in Gracechurch Street," besides being a minister of the Gospel, and a frequent and active labourer in the business and discipline of the Church, seems also to have been a sort of banker to his Monthly Meeting. In 1706, when a cottage, called the Yard Room, at Barking (near Fern Hall), left for poor Friends by Anne Bayley, was sold to one of the trustees named Thomas King for £50, the money was deposited in William Mead's hands at 5 per cent. Other sums were also handed at various times to W. Mead for investment, and at his death he left £100 to the Monthly Meeting, so that for some time his son and executor Sir Nathaniel Mead of the Inner Temple was paying interest on £330 to Barking Friends.*

Sarah Mead died soon afterwards, and left £100 to Barking Friends for the erection of a meeting-house at Romford, and the transfer of Harold's Hill Meeting to that place. This £100 Sir N. Mead refused to give up until the proposed work was taken in hand. Apparently, without seeing the necessity of it, a site was selected, but after some delay the project was abandoned on Sir N. Mead's agreeing to pay the money conditionally, on the maintenance of one John Dennis, probably some old retainer of the family at Gooses. Barking Friends did not receive the whole of the principal and interest due on these various accounts from Sir N. Mead till 1732.

It may here be mentioned that in 1717, in accordance with his father's wish, Sir Nathaniel distributed amongst the various meetings in the county of Essex a library of Friends' books collected by his father.

The Monthly Meeting.

The minute-book of Barking Monthly Meeting, previous to the changes detailed in the opening paragraph of this chapter, is not now in the possession of Friends, having been given up

---

* In Friends' burial-ground at Barking is a stone with this inscription :—

"Here lieth the body
of William Mead
esq. who departed
this life the 3rd day
of April anno dni
1713 in ye 86 year
of his age
and also Mrs. Sarah Mead
died the 9th of June 1714
in the 71st year of her age."

There is a tradition that this stone was removed from its place by some Friends of Barking Meeting, and used as a part of the pavement leading into the meeting-house. But the family insisted on its being replaced, which was done.

to the Government authorities at the time of the collection of non-parochial registers. The present minutes commence in 1691, but their continuity is not preserved, as there are several large gaps in the records. The earliest Monthly Meetings were often held at Friends' houses, for instance, at David Harding's at Harold's Wood, at Henry Loveday's at Beentary (probably Beacontree) Heath, &c. Friends were evidently widely scattered over South Essex, as we find allusion to them as of Romford, Dagenham, and other parts where none are now resident.

The Barking minutes present little of a distinctive character, though much might be adduced corroborative of remarks made in connection with other meetings.

In 1703 we find the Quarterly Meeting instituted, and "Friends are to bring their wives and children, and servants, next Monthly Meeting day." Richard Claridge (who was at this time a member of Barking) and John Farrand are appointed "to *prepare papers of advice* suitable to the occasion." It appears that our ancestors had not always that dread of a prepared document which influences some of us at the present day.

Barking Monthly Meeting seems to have grown smaller and weaker as the century advanced. The Quarterly Meeting often had to expostulate with them on account of continued absence. Amongst other apologies for this, Barking Friends alleged their remoteness and the fact of their being sometimes compelled to stay all night in town after an afternoon meeting. They also complained of being in some degree neglected, and begged that more public Friends might visit them, and that city Friends having country houses in their district might help them in their discipline, &c. To this latter proposition the Quarterly Meeting consented conditionally,—on such Friends not neglecting the service of the city meetings to which they belonged.

In 1727 the Quarterly Meeting appointed a committee to visit Barking Monthly Meeting, its condition having become so low as to threaten an entire abeyance of the discipline. There are no minutes for five years from this date. In 1729 the Quarterly Meeting joined the meeting to Ratcliff. But Friends of the latter place declined to be associated with it, as to monetary matters, though willing to assist in the discipline by sending Friends to attend at Barking. The Quarterly Meeting agreed to pay the debts of Barking, and guaranteed its future inexpensiveness to Ratcliff. But the opposition continued so strong that in 1732 Barking was reinstated as a separate Monthly Meeting to be held at Plaistow.

Affairs were now carried on with more or less efficiency till, in 1821, not only Barking but Ratcliff also had become weak, and a junction was now effected, which has since continued to the present time.

In commencing the previous chapter on Ratcliff, a footnote was made as to the minister disturbed by Ann Downer not being one of the Episcopal Establishment; the following in confirmation of this may be quoted from the works of Anne Docwra :—" In those days," speaking of the times when Friends went into churches, " the Common Prayer-Book was tied to the troopers' horses tails in some places, and the boys run after it; this made sport for those priests that clamoured against it in the pulpit and their followers; this was F. Bugg's Established Church and ministry that he clamours so much against the Quakers for their going into their Steeple-houses in many of his books. I never heard that the Quakers, so-called, disturbed the episcopal clergy in their worship by going in amongst them, they only disturbed F. Bugg's established ministers of the late professing times."—p. 22, Second part of " Apostate Conscience Exposed." Anne Docwra lived at Cambridge, and was a person of considerable talent and some position in society. Previous to becoming a Friend she had been both a Royalist and an Episcopalian. F. Bugg was her nephew, and his apostacy from Friends, and his scurrilous abuse of them, gave her much trouble.

Plaistow, interior: undated, before 1923 [LSF, Lidbetter]. See also p.77.

CHAPTER XVI.

LONGFORD MONTHLY MEETING,

Including Meetings at Longford, Colnbrook, Staines, Uxbridge, and Brentford.

UNDER the name of Longford Monthly Meeting, Friends resident in the western portion of the county of Middlesex long maintained a separate Monthly Meeting until their recent junction with Westminster in the year 1864. To the preaching of Edward Burrough the Churches of this district appear to owe their origin, for we learn from a report presented to the Quarterly Meeting in 1703, in answer to inquiries on the subject, that that indefatigable evangelist was the first to proclaim the principles of Friends in those parts. He held a meeting at a very early date in the house of William Winch at Uxbridge.* About the same time, as the said report goes on to state, " Thomas Gilliam and William Simpson declared the Truth in Uxbridge Street." As in other localities during this extraordinary era, the earnest efforts of a few devoted men soon resulted in the establishment of meetings. Further labourers followed in the footsteps of those mentioned, and amongst the convinced themselves faithful preachers were raised up. Friends rapidly increased in numbers, till in 1669 we

---

* The following letter addressed to George Fox in 1658, the original of which is preserved in the Swarthmoor MSS., affords some additional information with respect to the meeting for worship at Uxbridge :—

" Dear frend, this is to Certifie thee that their is a metting hear in uxbridge one the morrow : it being the fourth day of the week : and this metting was appointed by edward burrough for a month meeting : and now he being absent and not in these parts : the metting hath been neglected, becaus he is not hear abouts to suplye it or to declare amongst the people : their for it did lye upon me : to writt to thee : that thou mightest consider of it : and to send some frend in the ministry to the metting if the Lord will soe,—I remain thy loveing frend in truth,
"JOHN SANDS.
" from uxbridge this 22 day of 12th month.
" *Directed*,—For the hands of Georg fox this to be given speedely.
" *Endorsed*,—J. Sandes to gff—1658—Read."

find the Monthly Meeting of Longford fully established, with meetings for worship at Longford, Colnbrook, Staines, and Uxbridge.

Longford.

It is uncertain at what date the meeting for worship at Longford was set up. In 1670 we find the Monthly Meeting making a grant of twenty shillings to Edward Swift for the "use of his room next the street," and agreeing to give him eight shillings a year for the future. It was about this time that the Friends of the meeting began to find the necessity of having a separate burial-place. The Quarterly Meeting and also the neighbouring Monthly Meeting of Kingston were consulted, and inquiries made, which issued in the purchase for Friends, by John Northcott, of a piece of land situated beside the high road not far from the town of Longford. Seventeen pounds was collected in the meeting, and some additional subscriptions procured from London; which enabled Friends to purchase the land, and properly ditch and fence it, in the year 1673. The original acquirement of this property is, however, a little obscure, for the earliest title-deed extant is dated 1675, and is a *lease* from John Northcott of the burial-ground for 498 years at a peppercorn rent—the said burial-ground being therein described as a portion of a field belonging to the lessor.

In 1675 we read, "at our Monthly Meeting at Longford it was agreed on by Friends that the next First-day, being the 4th of the 5th month, that Richard Ashfield should desire Friends to stay together after the meeting for worship was ended, to consider by a mutual consent about building of a meeting-place on part of our burial-ground, &c." Friends considered the matter as requested, and set some of their number to look about for timber, &c., and others to collect subscriptions among Friends in the various parts of West Middlesex. Each of the London meetings contributed four or five pounds, and the building was soon erected.

Colnbrook.

Of the meeting at Colnbrook we know but little, and, as to its duration or period of discontinuance, nothing. In 1672 we find it ordered, " to be still continued in the shoop," and in 1676 two Friends were appointed to look out about Coln-brook for a room to meet in, and this is about the sum of our information on the subject.

STAINES.

The meeting at Staines seems to have been originally held once a month, but in 1676 was made fortnightly. We may here remark, in passing, that all the meetings noticed in this chapter were subjected from time to time to varying arrangements for the purpose of carrying out the ancient practice of Friends in country districts of closing their meeting-houses once or twice a month. This was done in order that the attenders might assist in maintaining the efficiency of meetings held elsewhere.

Friends of Staines seem to have met for some time at the house of Patience Ashfield. In 1685 it was agreed to pay her forty shillings a year for the accommodation. But as years passed on the want of a meeting-house began to be felt, and in 1710 John Tanner left £30 towards building one. Two years afterwards a piece of freehold ground with an old barn upon it, situated in the lane described as leading from the market house down to the Thames, was purchased of Thomas Berryman, of Chertsey, for £33.

Upon this piece of ground a meeting-house, measuring 38 feet by 22, was erected. For this purpose about £120 was raised amongst Friends of the Monthly Meeting, and about £70 amongst the London meetings.

The present meeting-house in Staines was built in 1844 upon some land purchased a year or two previously. A shop and tenement in High Street and six cottages in the rear were cleared away for the purpose. At this time the old meeting-house in the lane was sold to Margaret Pope for £200, and the money applied towards the erection of the present edifice.

This meeting-house is substantial in construction, and complete in its arrangements. Samuel Daukes (who built also those at Gloucester and Hitchin) was its architect.

Friends of Staines also possess an old burial-ground at the back of Church Street with a passage leading from that thoroughfare. This plot of land, measuring 80 feet by 56, was presented to the meeting by John Finch in 1765.

It was originally copyhold, but was enfranchised in the Manor Court in 1824 for £30.

UXBRIDGE.

The meeting at Uxbridge was held prior to 1691 in a room for which Friends paid £4 per annum, letting off a corn-loft over it for 13s. 4d. per annum. In 1676 they raised a subscription, and fitted up this room with forms and benches, &c.

In 1691 it was proposed to build on the burial-ground at the back of the George Inn, which Friends had then possessed for fifteen or sixteen years. This burial-ground, which was paled in in 1676, was probably a gift from the Heale family, and had formed part of their grounds. There appears, however, to have been no legal transfer of the land until the erection of a meeting-house upon it as just mentioned; the earliest extant title-deeds dating from 1692.

The building now erected cost about £160, nearly half being raised in the Monthly Meeting of Longford, and the remainder in other parts of the Quarterly Meeting. An appeal for contributions was made to the Yearly Meeting of 1691, and a minute was then made, commending the case to the assistance of Friends. It speaks of "the regard to truth, the service and spreading thereof," as having been the prompting motive—the Friends themselves being "but few in number and in debt £19, yet have themselves subscribed £80.

In 1723, through want of care, the landmarks of the Uxbridge property had disappeared, and a committee was appointed to stake it out. Partly from inspection of the deeds, and partly from the memories of Friends, the boundaries were settled; Daniel Heale testifying to the spot where, when a boy, he used to stand upon the landmark and spin round upon his heel. On this occasion Daniel Heale and Deborah Heale added six feet in length to the burial-ground as a gift, and then, in presence of many Friends with their children, the stakes were driven into the ground. The Heale family were frequent benefactors of Uxbridge Meeting; in 1722 Deborah Heale had accepted £40 as payment in full of £140 due to her late husband Joseph Heale.

In 1723 the elm trees at Uxbridge were cut down, and 162 cubic feet of timber sold for £5 8s.

In 1754 the meeting-house at Uxbridge had become dangerous, the foundations were giving way, and the walls cracking in several places. A new building was accordingly erected in the following year at a cost of £245. There were many rich Friends now in the Monthly Meeting. Rebecca Mildred and her son headed the subscription list with twenty guineas; the total amount received from individuals being £151 10s. To this was added £50, being a legacy from John Hudson, about £15 from Tottenham Monthly Meeting, and £50 from the Quarterly Meeting. A surplus was in hand after the completion of the works, out of which £10 was sent to Barking Friends towards the erection of a new meeting-house at that place.

BRENTFORD.

The earliest meeting held at Brentford, as we have seen in a previous chapter, afterwards became transferred to Hammersmith, and formed a distinct Monthly Meeting. But one was subsequently settled at Brentford, subsidiary to Longford.

In 1706 the settling of a meeting at this place was proposed, and Longford Friends consulted with those at Hendon and Hammersmith on the subject, with a view of making it a joint undertaking. Hendon Friends declined co-operation, alleging the fewness of their numbers, their distance from Brentford, the badness of the roads, &c. Hammersmith Friends, however, responded to the appeal, and a barn was procured and fitted up as a meeting-place. For this accommodation, situated in Old Brentford, £3 per annum was paid, and a meeting established which was held at first on the last Fourth-day in each month.

This Brentford assembly must have been rather intermittent in its character, and have been subjected to many changes. Our information respecting it is very fragmentary. We hear of its being *revived* in 1707, and at one or two other dates.

In 1721 Hammersmith Friends proposed to the Quarterly Meeting to lay down the one at Brentford because it damaged theirs, and they felt their proportion of its cost to be a burden. The Quarterly Meeting, however, advised its continuance but agreed to be responsible for its cost in future.

In 1731 we find Benjamin Holmes bringing a paper to the

Longford: undated photograph [LSF]

Staines, exterior: photo by H.W. Sale, before 1935 [LSF, Lidbetter]. See also p.294.

Above: Uxbridge, exterior and interior, H.W. Sale [LSF, Lidbetter]
Below: Brentford & Isleworth, exterior: undated sketch [LSF]

facing p.287

Quarterly Meeting from Jonathan Gurnel, asking permission to build a meeting-house at Brentford. For this purpose J. G.'s father-in-law had left £50, to which he himself would add £50, and Edward Halsey would give £10. The present place of meeting was alleged to be inconvenient and in bad repair, and dangerous to health. But on account of the smallness of Hammersmith Meeting, the Quarterly Meeting declined to assent to the erection of new premises at Brentford. Four years afterwards, however, permission was given to Jonathan Gurnel and others to build at that town.

In 1784 Longford Monthly Meeting proposed to build at Brentford End. To this the Quarterly Meeting gave its consent, and a piece of freehold ground was purchased for £35 in Conduit Lane, in Isleworth parish, adjoining the grounds of the Duke of Northumberland. Here a meeting-house was erected for £582 (including the cost of the walls of the burial-ground), and a meeting for worship established in Tenth Month, 1785. It was at first only held on the fourth First-day in each month, and on Third-days. It was made fortnightly in 1786, and in the following year was agreed to be held on three First-days in each month.

In 1824 Sarah Angell gave an adjoining piece of ground, some 350 feet long by 60 feet wide, extending from these meeting-house premises to the high road, and a portion of this has been devoted, since 1855, to the purpose of interments from the several Monthly Meetings of London.

The Monthly Meeting and the Discipline.

The earliest records of the Longford Monthly Meeting date from the close of the year 1669. The minute-book commences with the following prefatory note:—

"th. booke of the menes meeting containeing in it what is monthly done by the members of the said meeting of Longeford in the county of midellsektes for the sirves of trewth. And according to the praktes of the Anshant primetive saintes for too aktte for the trewth and too presirve peaces Love and unety in the body."

The Monthly Meeting thus inaugurated was held for a few years at the house of John Northcote, in Longford, until removed to the meeting-house, built in 1676. The meeting was afterwards held periodically at Longford, Uxbridge, and Staines; but in this arrangement changes were made from time to time to suit the varying requirements of successive periods.

The Monthly Meeting, though zealously maintaining the recently introduced forms of "Gospel order," had evidently in its early days but little business to transact. Their poor were duly attended to, and proper care taken as regards marriages, &c. Occasionally we find somebody visited and judged for taking a wife "out of the unety," and "contrairey to the good ordder of ffrendes." Now and then a case of paying tithes occurs, or an over-zealous member goes about preaching to the dissatisfaction of the Church and is advised to keep his station and rest at home. In 1672 one Thomas Talbot, "being cunstabell or ofeser," so far forgets himself as to press men for the King's service "too fight, it being contrairey to the principal of Trewth which Friends one." But these matters were insufficient to keep a Monthly Meeting in vigorous ecclesiastical action, and we find on sundry occasions a simple minute declaring that there was "noe bissness judged necessary to be registered." But there still might be, and doubtless was, much valuable conference on the spiritual condition of the scattered Churches of West Middlesex.

These Churches were not wanting in primitive zeal and fervour. In accordance with G. F.'s advice to bring back as on their shoulders those who strayed from the fold, they strove earnestly to provoke to repentance their erring brethren, and very generally their labour was not in vain. Even when testimonies had been publicly read against individuals, they were retained in the body if repentant. Frequently the individuals themselves were induced to produce papers condemning their own actions, as we have seen was elsewhere the case. Thus, in 1696 one Friend testifies, "I do declare and acknowledge that I did, contrary to the principle of truth, in going out to wrestle with some persons at the King's Arms, about seven weeks since." The Friend then enters into further condemnation of his conduct, and expresses his hopes that the Lord will forgive it for his Son's sake, and his desires that Friends will pass it by.

With the eighteenth century came the signs of decreasing zeal. In 1700 the Monthly Meeting had reported full meetings, and some convincement. In 1712 they still speak of full meetings, but "can't say that any are added." Cases of delinquency began to occur more frequently. In 1719 they complain that the enemy has sown misunderstandings amongst them, and in the following year, "can't say that truth doth prosper," and acknowledge that "the unity is not good." Again and again, indeed almost as a rule for many years, "no convincement" is recorded, and about 1739 considerable declension is sorrowfully acknowledged. In 1740 the Monthly Meeting state, "we don't pretend to prosperity."

During the period we have just rapidly glanced through in the preceding paragraph, we find the Monthly Meeting frequently omitted on account of Chertsey Fair, or Uxbridge Fair, or for some similar reason. Sometimes the badness of the weather prevented, and on one occasion the minute-books were not forthcoming. In 1740 it was agreed to hold the Monthly Meetings on First-days, which was for a time put in practice.

It is evident that there were those in the meeting who longed for an improvement in the state of the body. But no Friends could at one period be induced to take office in the Church. Thus, in 1743 a minute which had been long on the books, respecting the visiting of families, had to be dropped, because there were no Friends suitable or willing to undertake the service. In 1755 the Monthly Meeting reported that there were no overseers for similar reasons.

Some financial difficulties were also experienced. In 1740 the annual expenditure was about £20, the income only £10. The Six-Weeks Meeting made a small grant in aid.

To this low state a better time succeeded. The meeting shared with so many others in the revival kindled through the vigorous and pastoral care of the Yearly Meeting exerted about the middle of the eighteenth century, and, as a consequence, between 1760 and 1770 matters were improving. Some thriving families had settled at Staines and Uxbridge, and the better state soon becomes apparent in more subscribers to the meeting's funds. The Meeting now settled down into orderly routine and commenced a long period of quiet usefulness and respectability. A hundred years passed away without any marked vicissitudes requiring to be dwelt upon, till, in 1864, the Monthly Meeting was found to have so far decreased in number as to render its junction with some other one desirable. It elected to be joined to Westminster, and with the consent of this latter Monthly Meeting, the proposal was carried into effect.

General Monthly Meeting.

Towards the close of the year 1682, the three Monthly Meetings of Longford, Hendon, and Hammersmith, met in conference at Ealing, and agreed that their members should be free to attend all three Monthly Meetings for mutual help and encouragement. About three months afterwards we find that the idea had been further developed, and that a general Monthly Meeting was agreed upon to be held on the second Fourth-day, in each month by turns, at Hammersmith, Longford, and Hendon.

The Quarterly Meeting, and also George Fox, consented to the above arrangement. The minutes of this meeting are extant, commencing with First Month, 1683. The business seems to have been chiefly the passing of marriages through a preliminary stage before going to the Monthly Meetings, and the collecting of funds for defraying some ecclesiastical appeals then pending. The following letter from George Fox, addressed to this general meeting, and still preserved at Devonshire House, throws some further light on its origin and proceedings:—

"Fords Green, 8th 2 mo. 1684.

"Dear Friends,—Whereas there hath been some jumble concerning a meeting out of your 3 meetings lately erected, namely, Longford, Hammersmith, and Hendham, you know it was settled by several that came to me to have it 4 times a year; you did allege that you had a good service about some that were slack as to meeting, as about Uxbridge. So it was yielded unto that 4 times of the year you might have 4 quarterly meetings, whereby you might be helpful to any other meeting where any slackness was, or running out or corrupted with bad spirits. This at first was the ground of your meeting; you were not to meddle with the marriages nor stock that belonged to another. But every Monthly Meeting were to keep the authority and power among themselves that know both the poor and also the parties concerned in the state of marriage. But since you have taken the marriages into your flying meeting from the monthly meeting, which doth disturb some Friends' minds. Therefore let it come into the same channel again 4 times a year once a quarter, and let every monthly meeting keep their marriages among themselves, and not let your meeting be concerned with the marriages nor poor stock, nor with that which belongs to another meeting. So let every meeting be concerned with that belongs to them. If your flying meeting will have a stock, you may collect it for charitable uses as they do at London at the Quarterly Meeting there. And that money you had out of the Poor's-stock to pay for a dinner (if any be dissatisfied), let that be collected among yourselves and return it back again. If you will bespeak a dinner, let that be collected for among yourselves by your own quarterly meeting, and so let all things that have been past of differences be blotted out of your remembrance and live in love.—So with my love,

"G. F."

Whether or not this epistle resulted in discouraging the meeting from being held is not recorded, but the minutes of the General Meeting terminate abruptly about two months after the date of the letter.

Appointed Meetings.

It is interesting to observe that in the rural districts now under notice appointed meetings were frequently held in the outlying districts, not only at the request of travelling ministers, but as periodical gatherings. About the beginning of last century Friends' houses were often made use of for these assemblies by appointment of the Monthly Meeting. They appear indeed to have been regularly held about twice a month during the summer season. Moses Neave's house at Hanworth was one of the places where appointed meetings were held; and the house of Michael Biddle, of Langley Park, in Buckinghamshire, was frequently made use of for the same purpose. At this latter place these appointed meetings were held so frequently, that a number of forms, boards, &c., belonging to the Monthly Meeting were kept there.

Care of the Young, &c.

It is a noticeable fact that in the Longford minutes, under date of 1669, we find the earliest record known to us of the adoption of any plan for numbering those convinced of Friends' principles. In that year it was directed that a correct list of Friends should be brought to each Monthly Meeting, but no statistics have been preserved. Three years later, lists of children were called for, and this class from time to time called forth the interest of the Church on their behalf.

Some years after, viz. in 1694, the Monthly Meeting permitted Edward Griffin, of Horslydown, to come and open a school in Longford Meeting-house. But this undertaking did not answer, and Edward Griffin and family had to return to their *original trade of pin making.*

In 1698 a Quarterly Monthly Meeting was established for instructing the young, &c., at which meetings " the wholesome and good advices of George Fox " were ordered to be read.

In 1712 the Monthly Meeting purchased a supply of R. Barclay's Catechism, Stephen Crisp's Primer, and George Fox's Primer, for distribution amongst their young people ; and increased their stock of these books a few years afterwards for the same purpose.

SUFFERINGS.

Friends of West Middlesex were by no means exempt from the general persecution which befel the Society all over the country in its early day. We have not many details of these sufferings, and from what is described it would seem that the experience of Friends in this locality was not marked by any special features of interest ; but that here as elsewhere they suffered in property and in person through the agency of harsh laws, called into action by the aid of bigoted priests and unprincipled informers, and administered by prejudiced and intolerant judges.

These sufferings were evidently severe enough to attract the notice of Friends elsewhere. In 1671 £10 was received from London for the sufferers, and £8 or £9 was collected in the Monthly Meeting for the same purpose. In the following year £10 was received from London on this account, and afterwards £8 from Friends in Jamaica, and £5 from Friends in Ireland. These latter sums were portions of larger amounts sent over for suffering Friends generally, and apportioned to various meetings by Friends in London.

MARRIAGES.

The Longford minutes would give many instances of the care of Friends in relation to marriages. But the details, if furnished, would be only similar to those which have already appeared in previous chapters. On one of the earliest occasions recorded in these minute-books, the two Friends concerned, after appearing twice and being fully cleared, are given permission to marry by the Monthly Meeting's declaring that it "Lefte them to doe it in theire one freedom & According to the good order of Frendes and praktes of the holy men of ollde."

Care of the Poor.

There appear to have been many poor in the early times of the Monthly Meeting of Longford within its extensive limits. In the Twelfth Month, 1670, two Friends are appointed to *continue* overseers for the poor; so that at a very early date a special appointment for this service was required. The nature of the assistance rendered does not appear to have differed from that elsewhere adopted, but it is noticeable that in several instances, either entire or partial support for individuals was accepted from the parish. Instances occur in 1690, 1694, 1717, and at some intervening dates. These may possibly have been cases where the connection with Friends was of a somewhat doubtful character.

Ministers.

With the names of some of its Ministers we conclude our chapter on Longford Monthly Meeting. Richard Heale, died 1700; Elizabeth Richardson, visited the North 1702, Scotland 1711; Joseph Gilby; Richard Gove, who came from Pennsylvania, died 1710; Margaret Burton; Joseph Heale, visited Holland 1710, died in 1722; he was a physician by profession, and his death was evidently a great loss to the Church; Michael Biddle; Anne Swift, respecting whom it is curious to notice that the Monthly Meeting was in some doubt whether to report her death to the Yearly Meeting or not, because her public testimony for truth had been confined to her own meeting at home; Elizabeth Richardson; Mary Roake, who was born in 1676, began to preach in 1696, travelled much in various parts of England, and died in 1756; her voice is described as being clear and strong, though preaching at such an advanced age. "She spoke very distinct and correct notwithstanding she had but little school-learning" (*vide* Testimony).   Richard Richardson ;   John Finch ; Joseph Russell, who died 1750 ; Thomas Finch ; Elizabeth Morton, daughter of Thomas Morton of Barnsley, visited the Eastern Counties in 1782, shortly afterwards married Joseph Dell, of Kelvedon, and travelled in the ministry to an advanced age ;* Thomas Ashby ; Mary Steevens ; Sarah Rudd ; Ann Crowley ; Mary Browne ; Elizabeth Ashby ; Elizabeth Lynes.   Dr. Pope, an old resident at Staines, enjoyed a large professional practice all around, extending through the highest circles to the Royal Family, where he was medical attendant to the Princess Amelia, yet through all he preserved his character of a consistent Friend, and was remarkable for punctual attendance of meetings. His daughter, Margaret Pope (whose decease at an advanced age has so recently occurred), ever manifested a warm interest in the affairs of the Society, and filled the station of minister during her later years.

---

* This Friend was grandmother to the well-known family of the Dells, of whom W. R. Dell and R. Dell are at present ministers in Westminster Monthly Meeting. There is a story in the family that the first appearance of their grandmother in the ministry met with a severe rebuff from an elder in the gallery, who, rising, said, "Sit down, thou prating hussy !"   E. M. lived, some time before her marriage, with her brother, John Latimer Morton, who kept a boys' school at Wandsworth, formerly conducted by Richard Scoryer.

Staines, interior: before 1935 [LSF, Lidbetter]. See also p.287

CHAPTER XVII.

TOTTENHAM MONTHLY MEETING,

Including Meetings at Waltham Abbey, Epping, Flamstead End, Chipping Barnet, South Mimms, Winchmore Hill, Enfield and Tottenham.

WITHIN the limits of that extensive district known as Tottenham Monthly Meeting, stretching from Chipping Ongar on the east, to Chipping Barnet on the west, and from Lea Bridge northwards almost to Hoddesdon, there are now three meetings of Friends, viz. Tottenham, Winchmore Hill, and Epping. It may not be generally known that these three meetings are the remaining representatives of a considerable number of such assemblies with which this rural district was once dotted over.

To the founder of our religious Society North Middlesex and the adjacent parts of Essex and Hertfordshire seem to have presented strong attractions. During his short visit to London in 1644, in the days of his probationary exercises, we behold him wandering through Enfield Chase absorbed in his solitary musings, when he "looked upon the great professors of London and saw that all was dark and under the chains of darkness." Years passed away, and his followers became numbered by thousands, and many of his richest and most influential adherents had their country residences in the district now under notice, and hither would he often come, especially in his later years, to escape from incessant labour and recruit his exhausted frame in rural homes that were always ready to receive him.

But in this locality G. Fox found not only his peaceful retreats, but also one of his most successful fields of service. Many a large and precious meeting in the neighbourhood of Waltham, Edmonton, Barnet, Enfield, &c. &c. has he recorded in the pages of his Journal. Great was his service here in the summer of 1690, his last upon earth. He had spent the winter of 1689 at the residence of his son-in-law, William Mead, at Gooses, near Havering-atte-Bower. He was at the Yearly

Meeting in the spring of 1690, and spent a short time in town; after which he came down to the district under notice "moving to and fro among Friends thereabouts and attending or holding meetings wherever opportunity offered." He gratefully records that the Lord was with him, "opening many deep and weighty truths and heavenly mysteries to his people through me to their great refreshment and my joy."

Waltham Abbey.

Probably one of the oldest, if not the oldest, of these meetings was that held at Waltham Abbey. George Fox tells us, in his Journal, how a meeting which he held here in 1654 was interrupted by rude people who collected round the house and broke the windows. Whereupon he, undaunted, went forth, *Bible in hand*,* and desired them to step in and he "would show them Scripture both for our Principles and Practises." Satisfactory service followed, and when over, the people went away quiet and satisfied. "A meeting," he adds, "hath since been settled in that town."

Waltham Meeting became possessed of landed property in 1672, when Mary Bennett devised to Edward Mann, for the use of Friends as a burial-ground, a certain orchard situated in East Street, Waltham, Holy Cross, for a thousand years at a peppercorn rent, if demanded. This Edward Mann was a prominent Friend of the district, a citizen and haberdasher of London, having a country house at Ford Green, near Winchmore Hill, where he was occasionally visited by G. F.

The assembly at Waltham appears to have been long held in a barn, but a meeting-house was subsequently erected on the piece of ground above referred to.

Here, in the early days, flourished a considerable Church, and one which had to pass through the scathing fire of persecution. The sufferings of its members attracted notice. We find, in 1685, the neighbouring Monthly Meeting of Enfield, to which at present it had not been united, sending £4 for "poor persecuted Friends" of Waltham. The Meeting for Sufferings also sent relief,—in part from a fund at their dis-

---

* This is italicised as showing how at meetings for the declaration of truth, G. F., like Edward Burrough, used to produce the Bible; whenever such notices occur they do so in a way that indicates an ordinary practice.

posal, raised in Ireland, for the benefit of persecuted Friends in this country.

Prior to 1691, Waltham Abbey gave its name to a Monthly Meeting held in turns at Epping, Chingford, Walthamstow, Wanstead and Barking, and forming part of the Quarterly Meeting of Essex. But in that year, at the request of the Friends concerned, all these were added to London and Middlesex Quarterly Meeting; Waltham and Epping being added to Enfield Monthly Meeting, afterwards known as Tottenham Monthly Meeting, whilst Friends of Barking and the adjacent parts were formed into a separate Monthly Meeting, of which we have spoken in a previous chapter.

We find that at Waltham Abbey, as at many other places, a period of weakness and decline set in after the first generation of the convinced had passed to their rest. As early as 1702 the members pleaded inability to contribute to the general collection. During the latter half of the seventeenth century the meeting for worship on First-day was only held fortnightly—for some time alternately with Epping. About the year 1817 we find it only held at quarterly intervals, and soon afterwards discontinued.

In 1840 the meeting having long since died out, the premises and burial-ground were sold for £120. A bond was taken to use them for a school and not to disturb the graves for twenty years.

Epping.

Friends of Epping (where a meeting is still kept up) also acquired property in 1672. In that year Thomas Brand, of Theydon Garnon, devised an orchard to the Edward Mann already mentioned, on the same conditions and terms as the property given by Mary Bennett at Waltham. In 1705 a meeting-house was here erected, towards which the Six-Weeks Meeting gave £20.

During last century Epping Meeting was evidently small, but some increase is perceptible about the year 1773. At that time Friends asked to be allowed to meet every First-day instead of every other. Permission was given them to meet on three First-days out of four. On the remaining First-day it was doubtless intended that Epping Friends should assist in keeping up Waltham Meeting. At this date, also, a Week-day Meeting was established.

In 1850 an exchange of some part of the Epping property was effected with an adjoining owner, by the terms of which he was to build Friends a new meeting-house on an adjoining site. When this was done he received the old one and the ground it occupied in exchange; the old building he took down to form an entrance to his mansion, but the ancient burial-ground remains the property of the Society.

Flamstead End.

Flamstead End, or, as it is called by George Fox, Flamstead Heath, lies near the town of Cheshunt, in Hertfordshire. A meeting was held here in a building hired for the purpose from the Widow Cooke in and before 1672 for the sum of £8 10s., afterwards increased to £11 per annum. It was doubtless but a simple place. From an entry in the cashbook we find that the forms cost 13s., and one or two additional ones afterwards purchased are charged 1s. 6d. each.

The meeting at Flamstead End belonged to Enfield Monthly Meeting; but, as it was situated in Hertfordshire, some contribution towards its maintenance was expected and obtained from Hertford Quarterly Meeting. In 1686 we find Hertford giving £8 6s. towards repairs. They also engaged to pay 40s. per annum towards the rent, but about 1698 we find Enfield Friends complaining to the Quarterly Meeting of the nonfulfilment of this engagement. The authority of the Yearly Meeting had to be invoked to obtain the money, whereupon, in 1702, Hertford Quarterly Meeting paid £20 in full of all demands, and declined any further care in the matter.

The meeting existed under the charge of Enfield Friends for some time longer. In 1707 we find it was registered as a place of worship, but of its subsequent history we can furnish no further information.

Chipping Barnet.

In 1689 the house of John Huddlestone, in Chipping Barnet, was registered a place of worship for the Society of Friends, in accordance with the provisions of the Toleration Act. In 1743 this meeting was laid down, its continuance being considered "disreputable to the Society."

South Mimms.

North of Chipping Barnet lies a village known as South Mimms. G. Fox often mentions this place about the year 1677 *et seq.* Amongst the Friends of this town was one Samuel Hodges, a butcher, who was heavily fined for a meeting at his house in 1683.

In 1686 this Friend sold for £5, to William Wyld, senior, of Chipping Barnet, for the use of Friends, a piece of ground known as Chantrey Mead, and situated near Mimms Green, abutting on the lane leading from South Mimms to Ribble. On this piece of land, measuring about eleven yards square, a meeting-house was built in 1697, towards the cost of which the Six-Weeks Meeting gave £20.

The remainder of the property was used as a burial-ground. It was of course of very small dimensions, but in 1737 some land adjoining was added to it.

The Meeting for Worship at Mimms was another of those which declined during the progress of the eighteenth century.

In 1771 it was held only three times a year, in the Fourth, Seventh, and Tenth months, and then badly attended. In 1773 it was made half-yearly, and in 1787 discontinued.

In 1818 occurs the following minute on the books of Tottenham Monthly Meeting:—

"The Mg.-House at Mimms having been now for many years disused, and the Burial Ground not having been lately opened, it is decided to sell the same."

Two years afterwards report was made that the sale of the estate had been effected for £120.

Kit's End.

In 1701 a meeting was set up at John Hickman's, at Kit's End, near Mimms, which was joined to the meeting at Mimms about six years afterwards.

Winchmore Hill.

The meeting at Winchmore Hill is of ancient settlement. Previous to 1682 we find Friends of that place meeting in a barn, for which they paid a rent of 40s. per annum. One of the leading Friends here was John Okeley, who occasionally saw his cattle and stock driven off his farm for his attendance at meetings. In the year last mentioned he gave to Friends an acre of ground on which was a tenement and barn. The tenement and part of the ground was then let off, and the barn continued for a time to be the meeting-house. "To plaistering the barn 8s.; to Archer, for tyling the barn 4s. 6d." are items in the cash-book.

It will be remembered from the account given in that of Devonshire House this was not the first meeting John Okeley had been instrumental in settling, for, as is there shown, it was in his own house in Westbury Street, Spitalfields, that gathering commenced which grew subsequently to so much importance as the Wheeler Street Meeting.

In 1687 a meeting-house was built. The Six-Weeks Meeting gave £45 towards it, and subsequently an additional grant of £40. The meeting increased in size; in 1705 the Quarterly Meeting gave permission for it to be held fortnightly instead of monthly. But the building was still rustic, if not barn-like, in its character; for, as late as 1757, we find a charge for "straw and thatch 19s. 4d." In 1758 the ground was properly drained at a cost of £18, which was defrayed by David Barclay, sen. and jun., Joseph Freame,* and Jonathan Bell.

In 1787 report was made that the premises and the walls of the burial-ground were in a ruinous condition, and it was decided to rebuild. The new meeting-house, &c. was completed in the Seventh Month, 1790, at a cost of about £700, which was raised by a special subscription.

The neighbourhood of Winchmore Hill is very pleasant, being diversified in its surface and well timbered. From an early period various influential Friends had their country residences here.

There is a special fund for the care and maintenance of Winchmore Hill Meeting-house, to which it may be desirable to make some brief allusion. In 1796 David Barclay, Isaac Smith, Samuel Hoare, jun., and Joseph Osgood, gave £100 each to be invested as a fund, the interest of which was to be applied as follows:—One shilling a week to be given to the resident doorkeeper in addition to the Monthly Meeting

---

* One of the original partners in the now well-known Banking firm of Barclay, Bevans, &c. &c.

Winchmore Hill, exterior: photo 1940s? [LSF, Lidbetter]

facing p.300

Tottenham:
Above, meeting house from High Road, 1905: the gabled part is 1879, later than this book; the lower structure behind to the right is the earlier building [LSF]. Below, plan of burial ground, from Six Weeks Meeting records: a reference grid of letters and numbers along the walls enabled location of individual plots [LSF].

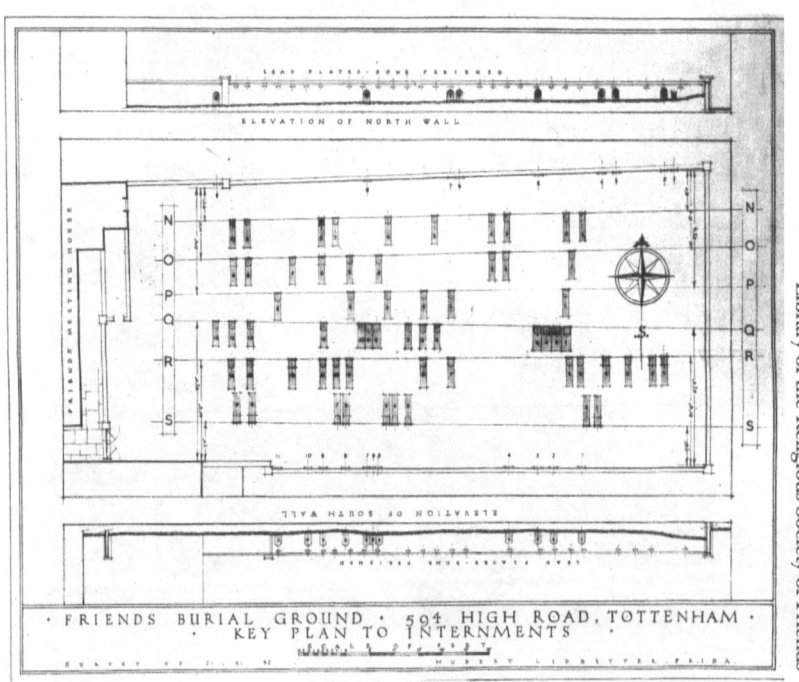

facing p.301

allowance, for taking care of the building, and keeping the ground in decent order, and the remainder for repairs as needed. This fund was further increased in 1830 by £100 from Robert Barclay, in 1838 by £100 from John Osgood Freame, and in 1858 by £100 from Lydia Catchpool.

Enfield.

Turning to Enfield we find that the meeting at this town, though of ancient origin, and at one time the headquarters of the Monthly Meeting, did not acquire property till 1696. At Enfield lived Elizabeth Dry, in whose house G. Fox was cared for during the winter of 1667, and also Amor Stoddart, whom G. F. visited in 1670, when A. S. was near his end, "very weak and almost speechless." The Monthly Meeting was held at different Friends' houses in this town, sometimes at Elizabeth Dry's, sometimes at Thomas Hart's, &c.

At Thomas Hart's, in 1682, a Monthly Meeting was held, at which a certificate of removal, signed by twelve men and five women Friends, was given to Christopher Taylor and his wife and family, they being about to remove to Philadelphia. Readers of G. F.'s life will remember this Christopher Taylor and his brother Thomas, who had been "preachers amongst another sort of people" until convinced by G. F.'s ministry.

In 1696 John Payne conveyed to Friends of Enfield, for five shillings, a piece of land and a barn. Ann Shewen also gave £100 towards building a meeting-house, on condition of receiving interest for the same during her lifetime. It seems probable that the barn just mentioned had been previously used for meetings for worship. A new building was now erected, and completed in 1697. Thirteen years afterwards this structure was reported to be unfit to meet in in the winter. The cost of a new meeting-house was estimated at £160, and the Quarterly Meeting gave £40 towards it.

During the eighteenth century Enfield Meeting declined in proportion as Tottenham increased in size and importance. The Monthly Meeting came to be held more frequently at the latter place than at the former, and the name of Tottenham Monthly Meeting was gradually adopted.

Enfield Meeting was, however, of sufficient importance to justify the laying out of nearly £70 on the meeting-house in 1788. But after being held for some time on every other First-day, it was given up in 1794. In the following year it was decided to sell the property, and in 1803 the sale was effected for £90, and the money applied to the general purposes of Tottenham Monthly Meeting.

We have now to speak of the present headquarters of the Monthly Meeting, viz. the premises at Tottenham.

TOTTENHAM.

George Fox speaks of attending a meeting at Tottenham High Cross, and it is said that this was one that had been settled at his request. It appears to have been held in a hired house near the Cross, and in 1698, the terms upon which the house was held having nearly expired, the Six-Weeks Meeting encouraged Friends of Enfield Monthly Meeting again "to hire it, or some other house thereaway."

In the Sixth Month, 1698, a new place was taken "about half a mile farther on, near the pound," at a rent of £3 10s. per annum, which was paid by the Six-Weeks Meeting, or rather its cash committee the Meeting of Twelve.

The meeting at Tottenham was held alternately with the meeting at Stoke Newington for many years. It was evidently a growing assembly, and in 1706 a proposal was made to build a meeting-house. Nothing was done, however, for some years, but in Sixth Month, 1712, notice to vacate the meeting-room having been received, some action became necessary.

At this time the meeting had increased, and was still increasing; there were also two Friends' boarding-schools carried on in the village. The question of building was again mooted and discussed. During the next two years the meeting seems to have been held first at Richard Claridge's, (a schoolmaster), and then at Alice Hayes's.

Meanwhile inquiry was made about a site, &c., and the estimated cost of the new building was stated to be £200. Tottenham Friends offered to raise £70 towards it (which the Quarterly Meeting and Six-Weeks Meeting held to be insufficient), and Waltham Abbey Meeting declared it was so poor it could not contribute. Finally the Six-Weeks Meeting agreed that if Tottenham Friends would purchase the ground and erect thereon a substantial meeting-house, they would give £100 towards the cost. Some delay was now occasioned by considerable difference of opinion amongst Friends of Devonshire House, Newington, Enfield, and

Winchmore Hill, as to the proper place for building a new meeting-house.

A site was obtained in 1714, by the purchase from James Larkes and Richard Baker, for £25, of a plot of ground by the roadside, having 50 feet of frontage and 140 feet of depth, adjoining the almshouses. On this ground a meeting-house was built, which we find some years afterwards was insured for £300.

The meeting for worship was still held on alternate First-days, but in 1717, for the sake of the aged people and children, the Quarterly Meeting gave leave for it to be held every First-day. As we have seen in our account of Stoke-Newington, an informal attempt to do so had been made in the previous year, which arrangement the Quarterly Meeting had then refused to confirm.

It is curious to notice that for many years there was an open ditch before this meeting-house, but in 1763 it was resolved to cover it over, provided the neighbours agreed to do the same in front of their houses,

Tottenham Meeting continued to increase, and in 1772 report was made that the meeting-house is too small for the numbers that congregate there in summer. It was decided to enlarge it, and a subscription was set on foot, but the committee who had it in hand could not agree as to the method to be adopted, and the idea was temporarily abandoned.

In 1776 the subject was again resumed; a plan produced and fresh estimates obtained. The proposed alterations were expected to cost £375, " but the sum subscribed not being sufficient, endeavours are to be used to obtain the amount, and carry out the work with all convenient despatch."

In the Third Month of the following year the alterations were commenced, Friends of Tottenham attending for a time the meetings at Winchmore Hill and Enfield. A room, however, was provided in Tottenham, in which the scholars and others who could not go to a distance might meet. The enlarged meeting-house was opened in Sixth Month, 1777, the sum of £484 having been spent. £418 had been collected and £8 received for old materials, leaving £58 for the meeting still to pay.

In 1779 we find a meeting set up at Tottenham at 5 o'clock First-day evenings, during the summer months, from Lady-day to Michaelmas.

The burial-ground attached to the meeting-house was

considerably enlarged in 1803, at which time a piece of ground, forming part of an orchard, was bought of Thomas Shillitoe for £30. This piece of land, measuring 63 feet by 100 feet, is now the eastern part of the burial-ground.

In 1821 extensive repairs, &c., to the amount of £542 were effected at Tottenham Meeting-house. £108 was spent in a similar way in 1824, and in 1833 the meeting-house was practically rebuilt at a cost of £1,677, of which £1,528 was raised by a special subscription. Some further improvements in the premises have been since effected at various dates.

General Survey.

We have now briefly sketched the history of the various meetings that have been or are still held in the extensive area under notice. Doubtless some of those in the early days in the houses of Friends have eluded our search, and of course we have not noted the special gatherings in orchards or barns, &c. &c., convened to listen to George Fox or other travelling ministers since his day.

There is one circumstance in connection with those meetings which have been described which claims prominent mention. We allude to the fact of many of them being held alternately with the meetings elsewhere. And this principle was not only carried out amongst the meetings having a disciplinary connection with each other, but, whenever small meetings were contiguous, mutual arrangements seem to have been made for the benefit of both. Thus Tottenham alternated at one time with Stoke Newington, and Mimms with Mill Hill in Hendon quarter.

There were doubtless benefits connected with this plan. The members of small meetings were encouraged and strengthened by the visits of their brethren from a distance. A social feeling was kept up by the fact of worshipping together. But not only to Friends as individuals, or to small meetings, would benefit accrue from the plan under notice. The cause of truth itself must have been benefited by this periodic upholding of a testimony in a number of places instead of only in two or three. Considered in this light, the effect upon the outer world must surely have been greater by the holding of meetings at intervals in seven or eight places, instead of regularly in two or three.

In illustration of these remarks we may state that in 1786,

after Barnet and Flamstead End had been given up, Firstday Meetings were held as follows:—On the first First-day in the month at Tottenham, Winchmore Hill, and Epping; on the second, at Tottenham, Winchmore Hill, and Waltham Abbey; on the third, at Tottenham, Enfield, and Epping; on the fourth, at Tottenham and Waltham Abbey, and on the fifth, at Tottenham, Winchmore Hill, and Epping. At this time it was customary also to hold a meeting at Mimms twice in the year.

Meetings for Discipline.

Turning now to the Meetings for Discipline, it is to be regretted that the materials at our disposal are but scanty. Amongst the records wanting are the minutes of Waltham Abbey Monthly Meeting from 1672 to 1691, and the minutes of Enfield Monthly Meeting from 1689 to 1756, and other valuable records, some of them more ancient than those just named. From what remains we may gather one or two facts of interest. The books missing are at Somerset House, having been given up to the authorities there on account of the books containing registers of births, marriages and burials.

It seems that at the commencement Enfield Monthly Meeting maintained a somewhat divided allegiance. In 1675 they made this entry: "That upon the question put, wether this Monthly Meeting should be related to the Quarterly Meeting at London, or to that at Hartford, it was remembered that at the first establishing this meeting, it's granted that if anything fell amongst us here which this meeting be willing or see it convenient not to determine of ourselves, but rather to have refured to a Qurterly Meeting; in such a caire and on such ocation if it falls out on that prt of this meeting that belongs to Middlesex, that then one or two friends at that part of this meeting belonging to Hartfordshire are to goe along with Midlesex's Friends to the Qrterly Mecting at London and lay the matter before Friends there. And so likewise if the Ocation hapen among any of the Hartfordshire Friends belonging to this meeting, that then on or two of Midlesex's Friends acompany them to the qrterly meeting at Hartford, and there to lay the matter before friends."

The business affairs of Enfield Monthly Meeting were much the same as at other places; marriages, care of the poor, and of apprentices, treatment of delinquents, &c. &c., occupied Friends' time and attention as at other places without exhibiting, so far as can be seen from the documents preserved, any novel phases.

1760 to 1770 we see troubles apparent here as elsewhere. Great difficulty is experienced in finding suitable Friends to fill the stations of elder and overseer, laxity and declension in many are complained of, collections run short of expenses, and the meeting finds itself £59 in debt in 1773, £63 in 1779, and £96 in 1781. One or two unapproved preachers are troublesome and have to be ejected. But the exercise of vigorous measures overcomes these and other difficulties, and the nineteenth century found the age of strict discipline established at Tottenham as in most other meetings.

We have alluded in our account of the Quarterly Meeting to the anomalous position occupied therein by the country Monthly Meetings. We find that this state of things was by no means satisfactory to Friends of Tottenham. In the First Month, 1761, they record the following minute:—

"Whereas it was signified at the Quarterly Meeting held last sixth month, that the Friends of the county of Middlesex are no part of the Quarterly Meeting of London. And a Committee being then nominated upon a certain occasion belonging to the said Quarterly Meeting, the Friends of Middlesex were accordingly excluded from having a right to be any part of the said Committee or any other of the like extent. But inasmuch as we do not apprehend or conceive how such a distinction can properly take place, in an assembly so reciprocally congregated in one and the same place, and at the same instant of time, where the occurrences of matters relating to Religious Discipline, are called for by one and the same clerk, and recorded in one and the same book. To be short, as there appears not to be any constituent part wanting to denominate an assembly so constituted, to be but one single Quarterly Meeting consisting of members mutually connected, and whose authority is or should be the power of God, so we cordially desire that those Friends who are of different sentiments would please amicably to favour us with their reasons why; that we may know in what relation we stand in respect of being members or not of the said meeting."

This protest was taken to the Quarterly Meeting by Josiah

Forster* and Jonathan Bell, but the arrangement, as we have seen, was not altered for some years after.

The original select character of our Meetings for Discipline is evidenced by the Tottenham minutes. In 1789 we find some relaxation in this respect, directions being given that when the Queries were answered, members generally and young Friends were to be invited.

The Women's Monthly Meeting at Tottenham was established in 1769, a previous attempt at its establishment two years before having been unsuccessful. There were still difficulties in connection with it, for there is a letter extant written in 1769 by women Friends of Epping, in which they state that the shortness of the days and the badness of the roads render it impracticable to come to Tottenham in the winter, but that they will attend Monthly Meeting when it is held at Waltham.

The following names may be mentioned as conspicuous members of Enfield (afterwards Tottenham Monthly Meeting), besides some who have been alluded to already:—Samuel Waldenfield, Alice Hayes, William Forster, and Thomas Shillitoe.

It used to be said by the late Paul Bevan that Richard Claridge kept school at Tottenham, in the premises now known as the George and Vulture Inn—recently pulled down; previous to its use as a school, the mansion had been the residence of the Reynardsons, whose almshouses are on the east side of the high road, near the Cross.

Priscilla Wakefield—a member of this Monthly Meeting—so well known for her writings, resided in the Ship Yard, and among her benevolent engagements was one originating the movement in favour of Savings Banks, of which that at Tottenham, founded by her, is said to be amongst the earliest.

---

* Grandfather to our present much revered friend of the same name.

CHAPTER XVIII.

HENDON MONTHLY MEETING,

Including Meetings at Mill Hill and Guttershedge.

HENDON.

HEMMED in, as it were, by the two large Monthly Meetings which divided the greater part of North Middlesex between them, there yet existed for many years the small Monthly Meeting of Hendon. It had two meeting-houses very near to each other, situated, one at Mill Hill, in the parish and manor of Hendon, and the other at Guttershedge, about a mile farther south.

Our first notice of this latter meeting is in the Journal of George Fox, who speaks, in 1677, of staying at the Widow Hayly's at Guttershedge, and holding a large meeting there. A similar entry occurs in 1680.

The meeting protected by the Widow Hayes acquired some copyhold property in 1699, when Stephen Hubbersty surrendered to Friends in the Court of the Manor a tenement and garden at Guttershedge. Of the meeting for worship held at this place we hear but little. In 1715 died William Jordan, husbandman, who bequeathed £10 for the repairs of the meeting-house and the palings of the burial-ground. In 1733 Hendon Friends had decreased in number, and had omitted to keep up the Guttershedge Meeting. The Quarterly and Six-Weeks Meetings accordingly directed Peel Friends to stir up Hendon Friends to diligence in keeping the meeting-house open at the appointed times. But about six years afterwards it became evident that the meeting had died a natural death and accordingly the meeting-house was sold, the burial-ground being reserved to the use of Friends by a bond.

MILL HILL.

The origin of the meeting at Mill Hill is involved in obscurity. A meeting-house was built for it in 1678, on a piece of land held on a lease at £5 per annum. As a further illustration of the reciprocal character of the country meetings, we may mention that, in 1693, we find George Whitehead suggesting in the Quarterly Meeting that this meeting should be held on the same day as Mimms, first held at Samuel Rodgers' house, instead of on the same day as Winchmore Hill. In the year just mentioned some alterations were made in the meeting-house to render it more commodious, which would imply a still increasing Church. But in the eighteenth century evidence of decline soon presents itself. The meeting grew smaller and smaller until, like its sister Church at Guttershedge, it disappeared.

The Monthly Meeting, although having these two meetings for worship under its care, can at no time have been a large or important one. There are no minutes extant; but a book once belonging to it is preserved at the Peel, containing some cash accounts and a few miscellaneous records. In 1690 the total of the Monthly Meeting collection varied in amount from 2s. 6d. to 8s., which implies but a small assembly of those likely to be competent to transact the business of the Church.

In 1709 we find them proposing to the Six-Weeks Meeting that their meetings for worship at Mill Hill and Hendon should be held fortnightly instead of monthly, from which it would seem that previously there was no meeting at all on two First-days in each month, within the compass of the Monthly Meeting.

As time wears on a low state of things is acknowledged in the answers to the Queries. No convincement is reported, and earnest appeals are made to the Quarterly Meeting for more frequent visits from public Friends. In 1715 William Jordan (mentioned above) left £10 for the entertainment of travelling Friends coming to Mill Hill Meeting. This fund was many years in hand, the annual expenditure from it averaging 10s. or 12s.

In 1719 the Monthly Meeting was so small that the Quarterly Meeting proposed to join it to Hammersmith or some other neighbouring meeting. But nothing was done for ten years longer, when in 1729 the Quarterly Meeting decided to join it to Peel.

The Friends of this objected, on the ground that its junction with some country meeting would be more suitable. But the Quarterly Meeting adhered to its decision, guaranteeing, however, to make up any pecuniary loss to which Peel might become liable through the union. But there seemed small likelihood of this; the scanty income of Hendon had more than sufficed for a still scantier expenditure, and it now handed over to its new ally an accumulated balance of £6 9s. 1d.

Peel Friends endeavoured in vain to uphold the meeting for which they had become responsible. As we stated in speaking of the two meeting-houses, the meetings were dying for want of Friends to keep them up, and no outside aid could avail in arresting the process of inward decay. In 1740 nothing remained to Friends but a burial-ground, where the graves of their forefathers bore silent witness to the fact that there had once been a Hendon Monthly Meeting.

CHAPTER XIX.

KINGSTON MONTHLY MEETING,

Including Meetings at Kingston, Croydon, Wandsworth, and Esher.

KINGSTON, CROYDON, AND WANDSWORTH.

THE establishment of Friends' meetings in the more metropolitan districts of Surrey has been described in preceding chapters. Similar meetings appear to have existed in the rural districts of the same county at an equally early date. One of these, viz. Kingston Monthly Meeting, comes within our province in the present volume, as it now forms a part of the Quarterly Meeting of London and Middlesex.

In the Monthly Meeting referred to, meetings for worship are now held in the meeting-houses at Kingston, Wandsworth, Croydon, and Esher.

The oldest of these would appear to be the meeting at Kingston. With reference to the gathering of the convinced at this town, we are informed, in Gilbert Latey's Journal, that amongst those who offered up themselves and their houses for the truth's sake in times of hardship and trial, " were the worthy servants of the Lord, John Fielder and Ann his wife, who were convinced at Kingston-upon-Thames; and as faithful followers of the Lamb not only received the Lord's ministers that then laboured for his work and service, but also gave up their house for a meeting-place. Accordingly a meeting was there settled; and Oliver Cromwell, then called Protector, residing much at Hampton Court, this meeting became of great service, and many were there convinced and turned to the Lord, and directed to wait in silence for the arising of the pure gift in themselves. Several that then belonged to Oliver were also convinced at this meeting, and continued faithful, of whom there are some (viz. in 1706) yet alive."

The earliest history of the Church at Kingston is, one might almost say of course, a story of persecution and violence. To recount the details of these trials would be only to repeat a similar narrative to what has been already described in connection with other meetings. Edward Burrough (to whose preaching John Fielder's convincement was doubtless instrumentally due) was imprisoned here, with several of his hearers, in 1656. For thirty years the attenders of meetings in this town maintained their allegiance to truth, despite of kicks and blows, cruel beatings with clubs and carbines, heavy fines, and long imprisonments. As late as 1685 we find the meetings broken up with brutal violence—one woman thrown into a ditch, and her arm broken, and many Friends so cruelly pinched, bruised, and maimed, that they were kept to their beds long after. In addition to their sufferings for persisting in the maintenance of their religious assemblies, Friends of Kingston and the adjacent districts suffered fearfully from the rapacity of the rural clergy, and the tithe-renters in the matter of tithes, &c. Fine and imprisonment was the lot of many who were cited, under old Acts of Parliament, for non-attendance at the services of the Established Church.* Some of them, who resided in the town, were prosecuted and punished for opening their shops on Christmas Day or other ecclesiastical festivals or fast-days. But here as elsewhere the blind rage of the persecutors signally failed in its object, and the Church was confirmed and strengthened by the very means intended to destroy it.

In 1663 Friends of Kingston purchased by subscription a burying-ground for £24 18s. This was situated in Norbiton Street. In it Gilbert Latey was interred in 1705. We had

---

* Here as elsewhere attempts were made to prove that Friends were popish recusants. The following document, copied from the fly-leaf of the Kingston minute-book (1667 to 1691), shows one of the precautions taken on this account:—

"This is to be put in the front of Friends' wills to clear us of that scandal that the Quakers lives and dies Papists.

"'My body, soul and spirit I have given up to the Lord, with which I have glorified God, which all are the Lord's, and have been long given up to him. And now I do commend my body, soul and spirit unto my Saviour and Creator's hand, for all is his, and I die in the Lord (in whom I have lived and moved and had my being) a true and real Protestant Christian and a member of the true Reformed Church in Christ Jesus as was in the Apostles' days before the Apostacy was, of which church Christ Jesus was and is the holy head and husband, Mediator, Redeemer, and Saviour, and no pope nor false christian, by whom I have been a great sufferer for bearing a true testimony to the Lord's holy name, in whom I rest.'

"Spread this among Friends."

it (says a remaining record) placed under the care of the women Friends in 1690 at their request; and the minute of consent quaintly concludes, " are very free they should have it, provided they keep it in good order." Friends of Kingston appear to have had a separate building in which to hold meetings till 1673, at which time a meeting-house was erected, with accommodation for residents in the cellarage. In these basement apartments one Sarah Lyons was placed, and also one Elinor White and her child, to live there " as they two can best contrive." The minute-books show that between these two women differences arose. Sarah Lyons was a midwife, and when she was absent on her professional engagements, Elinor would decline to " mopp the door and sweep." The Monthly Meeting decided to eject Elinor, but on her evincing penitence and promising amendment, she was permitted to remain.

In 1674 we find a minute ordering a " convenient place for Friends to stand on to minister to be made." But it seems the congregation were still sitting on forms without backs. In 1686 two new forms with backs were made, and placed in the meeting-house, doubtless at the upper end. At this innovation offence was taken ; and to get over the difficulty, the Monthly Meeting ordered all the forms on that side to have backs made to them.

The meeting-house we have now alluded to sufficed for the needs of the meeting for about a century. In 1771 fifteen and a half rods of ground, situated in Eden Street, Kingston, were purchased, and upon this plot of ground, in 1773, the present meeting-house was erected, at a cost of about £540.

In addition to their meeting-house and burial-ground property, Kingston Monthly Meeting, prior to its junction with Croydon and Wandsworth, and since that time Kingston Preparative Meeting, has long been the possessor of a considerable amount of landed property, the revenues from which are applied to the relief of the poor. As early as 1688, Richard Harris left by will £300 for certain purposes, the remainder of which was to be used in the purchase of land " for a yearly payment for ever to the poor people worshipping of God, known and distinguished by the name of Quakers." A small estate was thus procured, and other donors followed the example of Richard Harris, so that in 1677 Kingston Friends were possessed of the following property, viz. five acres near Norbiton Common; nine acres of woodland in Cleygate, Thames Ditton; four acres in Lilsworth, Esher; half an acre by Weston Common; and half an acre in Marshfield, Thames Ditton. There is a memorandum of this date extant, declaring the said property to be "first for poor of Kingston, then for others of the same judgment elsewhere."

In 1678 John Fielder (the Aquila of Kingston) left £20 to be used in the purchase of land. Ground was then purchased to the amount of £27 15s. 6d., the Monthly Meeting making up the deficiency. The estate at Littlefield (one and a half acres) was the result of this bequest.

In 1693 Ruth Lilley left £40, which was put out to interest till 1730, at which time land was bought to the amount of £70.

It is somewhat difficult to trace all the enlargements and alterations of the Kingston property; but in 1804 it is stated to consist of twenty-two acres in Kingston, Esher, and Thames Ditton, besides a meeting-house and ground at Kingston.

Kingston Meeting maintained its existence as a separate Monthly Meeting till 1778. The Quarterly Meeting attempted to join Wandsworth to it in 1674. But Kingston Friends resisted the arrangement; making, however, a quarterly appointment to attend Wandsworth Monthly Meeting and assist in its affairs. This appointment was kept up about three years.

In 1761 the Quarterly Meeting joined both Wandsworth and Croydon to Kingston as a Monthly Meeting. But as we shall see hereafter, the opposition on this occasion was from the two meetings attempted to be united, who succeeded in dissolving the compact after a few months.

The three meetings named above were, however, finally united seventeen years later in 1778, under the name of the United Monthly Meeting of Kingston, Wandsworth and Croydon; and twenty-four years after, in 1802, this Monthly Meeting was transferred to the Quarterly Meeting of London and Middlesex, and its name altered to Kingston Monthly Meeting.

The minutes of the ancient Kingston Monthly Meeting date from Fifth Month, 1667. There appear to have been held at this time what was called a "General Monthly Meeting," as well as "our men's Monthly Meeting." It was at the latter that the Church business seems to have been transacted.

It is very interesting to notice the aggressive character of the much persecuted Church of Kingston. It was not content with its own local gatherings, but frequently appointed by minute meetings for worship at Waybridge, Hounslow, Cobham, Esher, and other adjacent places. There was a meeting set up at Walton for a time, which was removed to Kingston about 1678. The meeting at Cobham, spoken of in 1673 as being attended by "many of the world's people," became settled, and a burial-ground was here purchased of Lady Vincent in 1677, and a meeting-house built by subscription. This meeting-house was sold in 1739 for £15, and the burial-ground, which long formed part of a garden, was disposed of not many years ago for £5.

Esher.

The meeting at Esher, mentioned in 1666 as being held in the house of John Edler, and afterwards in that of Thomas Boskett, also became a settled meeting, and continues so to this day.

The little village of Esher is pleasantly situated in a rural district some mile or so from a station on the South Western Line. Near adjoining to it are the Royal seat and grounds of Claremont, so associated with the residence and abruptly terminated happiness of Leopold and the Princess Charlotte, and more recently identified with the long exile of the much respected ex-Queen of the French. At Esher, in former times, some wealthy Friends had their residence, one of whom gave a portion of his lands for a burial-ground and site for a meeting-house. It is in one corner of the property, and adjoins a high road; on it is a meeting-house, which, though small, is convenient and complete, and with the burial-ground, nicely planted and surrounded by trees, exhibits more rural taste than can be found in most other suburban meeting-houses. Among the families formerly resident at Esher may be mentioned the Biddles, with which the Alexanders, of Ipswich, are connected by alliance. There are very few Friends now at Esher, and the meeting-house is only used once on First-days; but other communities are permitted its use, of which the Baptists in Conference courteously acknowledged the obligation. (See Appendix.) A Friend there has lately commenced mission work, and meets with encouragement; and whenever Friends are drawn to hold public meetings, a willingness is shown to attend them.

The following shows that 100 years ago Esher stood well as to attendance, in comparison with the other Surrey meetings:

Report of a Committee appointed to visit the various meetings in Surrey, 17th of Eighth Month, 1761:—

"Dorking. First-day meetings pretty well attended in the morning. The afternoon & week-day meetings not well attended.

"They hold a First-day meeting at Riegate & Capell. No week-day meeting held at Riegate, & but one in the month at Capell.

"Croydon. They have but one meeting on the First-day, & that is pretty well attended. The meeting on week-days small.

"Wandsworth. The First-day meeting pretty well attended, but that on the week-day not so well.

"Esher. The meeting on First & week days pretty well attended.

"Kingstone. Only one meeting is held on First-day. None on the week-day.

"Guildford and Godalming. It appeared that meetings for worship were well attended by some, tho' others, we fear, are greatly deficient in that respect. The settling of week-day meetings where none are held was earnestly recommended.

"Meetings for discipline too much neglected."

Kingston Monthly Meeting.

The following minute, dated Second Month 16th, 1669, shows the spirit which animated Kingston Friends in their efforts for the establishment of meetings in the surrounding country:—"Ordered, that where any tenderness is found in any place that some Friends do draw forth out of their established meetings and visit them, as in the wisdom of the Lord they shall be ordered."

In arranging for their meetings for worship, general convenience seems to have been the principle by which questions of time, &c. were regulated. The First-day meeting in 1674 was held at 11 p.m.; on Fifth-day at 1 p.m. In 1670 there

Right: Kingston, undated ink drawing formerly owned by Thomas Chalk of Kingston [LSF]

Below: Esher, interior, photo H.W. Sale?, 1942 [LSF, Lidbetter]

facing p. 316

Wandsworth, exterior photo H.W. Sale; interior probably also, 1940s? [LSF, Lidbetter]

was a meeting for worship held at 7 p.m. on Fourth-days. So that our modern evening meetings are not the entire novelty which some have supposed.

In the early periods of its history this Monthly Meeting was evidently strict in its discipline though it refrained from cutting off any erring members who evinced penitence for their faults. In 1678 we find as follows: "Ordered that Robert Hunter write a paper in denial and disowning of himself for drinking excessively, whereby a scandal hath risen upon Truth, and give that paper abroad to the world, and especially in such places where such disorderly actions have been done." At the next meeting this was reported to have been attended to.

Again in 1669 we find a Friend who had been induced to acknowledge his "outgoings," ordered "to stick up his paper at Guilford, Kingston and Brentford markets."

Though possessing landed property for the support of its poor, the Monthly Meeting had nevertheless to resort to collections in addition. Both at Kingston and Cobham, a "box with a hole in the top" was made use of, into which the worshipper might drop his contribution "according as the Lord had prospered him."

The wants of the poor were thus efficiently cared for. Some times sums of money were disbursed to them; sometimes flax provided for spinning. One rather frequent method of relief seems to have been for the Monthly Meeting to purchase a cow and resell it in a few months, allowing a poor Friend to make the best use he could of it in the meantime.

The business of this Monthly Meeting was not usually very complicated or protracted. In 1675 we read, under date of Ninth Month 25th, "At our Men's Monthly Meeting, Friends did meet according to former order, and did call over and examine things concerning the affairs of the church, and all things were found well and in very good order, and so the meeting dismissed itself for that time with very good satisfaction. Blessed be the Lord for it." The above forms the whole record of the meeting on that occasion.

Kingston Monthly Meeting originally formed part of Surrey Quarterly Meeting. The Quarterly Meeting was held at a number of places in turns, viz. Wandsworth, Croydon, Cobham, Guildford, Kingston, Reigate, Dorking, Capel, Esher, Godalming, Gatton, &c. The long journey to some of these places was usually performed on horseback, and the Monthly Meeting paid the horse-hire of its representatives or officials, if they had no horses of their own, *i.e.* they paid the expenses of those who would otherwise be prevented from acting as representatives.

Before passing from Kingston, we should note that hither in 1672 came Gilbert Latey, and took to wife Mary, the daughter of the John and Ann Fielder already alluded to. Amongst other worthies more or less connected with this meeting, may be named Francis Holden and Stephen Hubard.

At Kingston the house may still be seen in which George Fox is said to have taken up his abode when retiring to this place for the sake of a quiet retreat. It was here that he penned some of his epistles to rulers and others in authority.

In his Journal, in 1683, he says, "After some time, having several things upon me to write, I went to Kingston, that I might be free from interruptions. Whilst I was there I wrote a little book, entitled, 'The Saint's Heavenly and Spiritual Worship, Unity and Communion, &c.'"

In his Journal, First Month, 1683, he says, "I went to Kingston-upon-Thames, and it being then a time of persecution, as I went to the meeting I met the chief constable, who had been at the meeting-place, and had set watchmen there to keep us out; yet he was pretty civil, and the watchmen let Friends have a couple of forms out to sit upon in the highway; so we met together there, and a very precious meeting we had; for the refreshing presence of the Lord was with us, in which we parted in peace."

WANDSWORTH.

The origin of Wandsworth Meeting is involved in obscurity. The first meeting-house was built in 1673 (thus being coeval with that at Kingston), at a cost of £202. The property was copyhold, being renewable with fines from time to time. The building was partly occupied by Friends' tenant, and was a plain and simple edifice. In 1731 what were considered extensive repairs were effected, but the building was far from perfect. Before long the rain began to come in, and, besides, the chimneys seem to have been radically defective. In testimony to this we may cite Andrew Hasgood, who in 1740 was tenant, paying £5 rent for his accommodation, and also rendering some services to Friends. The following is a statement of account sent in to the Monthly Meeting by him:—

"The first winter of our coming into this troublesome

house wee Lighted the fire 30 times, and the next Winter wee Lighted the fire 36 times, and this last Winter 26 times, in the whole it is 92 times at 1½ per time, and my wife sollomly Declares to me that she has been above one hour and half a Laying and Lighting and Blowing of the fire to bring the fire to a good heat."

This meeting-house lasted, however, more than a century, till 1778, at which date the present one was built at a cost of £600.

The Church at Wandsworth had its share of persecution to undergo in the early days. Besse tells us how in 1680 a Justice came into the meeting and, after gazing awhile at the silent gathering, exclaimed, scoffingly, "The Spirit does not move them." He then proceeded to impose fines, for which heavy distraints were afterwards levied. For non-attendance at "church" and for tithes Friends of Wandsworth, like their brethren at Kingston, often suffered.

The minutes of Wandsworth Monthly Meeting commence with Sixth Month, 1695. It was in that year that a junction with Croydon was effected by mutual consent and with cordial unanimity. This union (one Monthly Meeting in three being held at Croydon) lasted till 1719, when serious disagreement manifested itself. It was complained that Croydon Friends subscribed little to the public stock, but withdrew much for their poor. The charges for public Friends was also a matter of difference. Then again Croydon Friends wanted more Monthly Meetings held at Croydon, to which Wandsworth Friends replied, that to alter the arrangement " would be to reflect on the ancient Friends who formed the compact," and thus expostulated, " You seem to think your branch is almost as bigg as the tree into which you are grafted and may be bigger."

Wandsworth soon passed from words to actions; they decided that as Croydon Friends neglect coming to Wandsworth, a Monthly Meeting shall be " fixed irrevocably " always to be held at Wandsworth. The Quarterly Meeting saw that a separation was desirable for peace' sake, and from Second Month, 1720, the Wandsworth and Croydon were separate Monthly Meetings.

A Women's Monthly Meeting had been established in 1702, but in 1727 the men's meeting, having got very small, it was minuted that it would be " very much to the benefit and advantage of this Monthly Meeting if women Friends would sit with us as one Monthly Meeting." Women Friends did not agree to this proposal; a lengthy paper of "Reasons" was sent to them, and much joint conference and discussion, &c. &c. ensued, but without result. Women Friends declined to comply, and "advised men Friends to stir up one another." For several months the agitation was kept up, but at last the men had to give in, recording on their minute-book that "it will be the Women's fault if this Meeting drops."

In 1758 we find the Monthly Meetings being regularly held on First-days, in order to procure a larger attendance.

In 1761 occurred the attempt on the part of the Quarterly Meeting of Surrey to unite Kingston, Wandsworth, and Croydon as one Monthly Meeting. But for the opposition of Wandsworth, the arrangement would have been effected. In Tenth Month, 1761, we read, "Wandsworth Friends left the meeting, not being able to proceed to business, Kingston Friends insisting upon acting in conjunction."

An appeal was made to the Yearly Meeting of 1762, which, whilst appreciating the good motives of Surrey Quarterly Meeting, found itself obliged to reverse the decision of that Quarterly Meeting, on the ground of irregularity in its mode of procedure. Sixteen years afterwards, as we have seen, the effort to unite these three meetings was successful.

Having now briefly noted the prominent facts in the history of the Monthly Meeting, we may proceed to touch upon one or two curious phases of social life, &c., of which we get a glimpse in the Wandsworth records.

"Minute of Wandsworth Monthly Meeting, Eighth Month, 1695 :—

"Agreed that the Meetings on Fourth-days begin at the first houre dureing this ensuing winter."

Again, Fourth Month, 1697 :—

"It's agreed that Friends do gather together precisely at the twelfth hour on First-days and week-days' meetings, both for the summer and winter season, and it's desired that Friends be very circumspect to meet exactly at the said above time."

Again, Fifth Month, 1697 :—

"Last meeting it was agreed that the Fourth-day meeting should begin exactly at the 12th hour all the year round, which hath been performed this month ; and some inconveniencys haveing attended, it's proposed to the meeting that it be altered to the first hour all ye year round ; which is concluded so to be by this meeting."

In 1711 we find a minute upon the occasion of a complaint having been made that Wandsworth Friends did not sufficiently encourage the printing of Friends' books, which describes their social condition. "As for the Friends belonging to Wandsworth Monthly Meeting, they are for the most part Handycrafts, who with labour and industry administers to the necessity of themselves and families; and when Trading in general is bad, as now it is, they are willing to live more meaner and sparing, not counting gain as godliness, but having food and raiment being therewith content. Desiring our Friend the Printer will be of the same mind with us herein until it shall please God (if he sees meet) to make way for us all to enjoy a more plenteous trade."

But though, as stated above, the townsmen of Wandsworth were mostly handicrafts, we find mention made of "divers Friends of London who have residences in this quarter," and who seem to have been very reluctant in many cases to "join the service" of Wandsworth Monthly Meeting, being mostly desirous of retaining their city membership.

It is evident that Wandsworth and other outlying meetings depended very considerably for support upon the city.* The appearance of ministering Friends from London at the regular meetings for worship was frequent; and upon the occurrence of extraordinary occasions, such as funerals, at Wandsworth or Croydon, notice used to be sent to the Recording Clerk, B. Bealing, to speak to some ministering Friend to be present.

At Wandsworth, as at other places, we find that wine was supplied for "labouring Friends."

"Agreed by this meeting that Richard Almond be desired and impowered to provide some wine for the refreshment of Labouring Friends after meetings; and that this meeting do reimburse him his charges again." 1698.

Some of the bills are still extant. Thus, for the year 1718, we find twelve pints of wine, at 2s. per pint, and sixpennyworth of "biscakes" charged for.

Not only was refreshment provided on ordinary occasions for ministers, but a good substantial meal for all Friends present was furnished whenever the Quarterly Meeting was held at Wandsworth during the earlier portion of last cen-

---

* As did most of the country meetings near London from the first. See account of Uxbridge, *ante*; also the following :—"At Kingston and Tibbalds are constant meetings set up, and SOME SENT TO THEM EVERY FIRST DAY."—James Naylor to George Fox, 1654.

tury. From documents still existing we are able to state, as an example, what took place on the 1st of Fifth Month, 1728.

On the occasion referred to twenty men and twenty-one women dined together at the Rose and Crown. The following statement shows the cost of the meal and other incidental expenses connected with it:—

"25 lbs of Loyn of Beef & Suet @ 3½d. ... 7s. 0d.
29¼ lbs of Veal @ 4½d. ... 11 0
6 lb 14 oz of Bacon @ 9d. ... 5 2
Beans, one peck 10
Pudings 9 3
Bread 2 6
Cheese 8
Dresing & Butter 10 0
Breakfast 2 5
Beer, 8 gallons 8 0
Wine & Tobacco 5 4
Servants 1 10
                                    ─────────
                                    3 4 0
Collected 2 3 3
                                    ─────────
Paid by Mo. Mg. 1 0 9
                                    ═════════

Sent in Gratis by John Kuweidt 6 cabbidges, 6 colloflowers, & cucumbers with sallatt."

Other statements similar to the above are to be found amongst the Wandsworth papers. At the bottom of one of these accounts four names are written, with the following remark attached:—"The 4 above-named Friends refused dineing with all ye other Friends at ye Rose and Crown, but stayed and eat by themselves at the Ram."

We have alluded to the fact of Kingston Monthly Meeting paying for the horse-hire of its representatives. The same practice obtained at Wandsworth. The following is the account paid for a Friend who went on official business to the Quarterly Meeting:—

"for ye horse ... ... 3s. 0d.
my own expenses 1 2½
time of going 2 0
                            ─────────
                            6 2½"
                            ═════════

Another instance in 1734:—

"hier of horse	...	...	3s.	0d.
diner	...	...	1	2
hors standing	...	...	1	0
			5	2"

There is a circumstance of historical interest to Friends, as being connected with the family of William Penn, which transpired at Wandsworth Meeting-house. This was the marriage of William Penn, the grandson of the Pennsylvanian legislator, to Christiana Forbes, in 1732. The readers of that interesting volume, "The Penns and Penningtons," will remember that this individual was not in all points the counterpart of his grandfather. In early life he had contracted a matrimonial engagement with an Irish lady named Ann Mansell. On passing the meeting at Wandsworth, William Penn and his intended bride had to listen to the reading of documents connected with his former love affair, including a full release from Ann Mansell and her family, in consideration of William Penn's having paid £1000 in compensation for his breach of promise. The marriage certificate, the release, and various other documents connected with this affair, are preserved in the Wandsworth archives.

It may be remembered that Richard Scoryer kept a training-school at Wandsworth, and was himself a leading friend of the meeting in early days, being valiant in suffering for the cause. Coming from time long past to the present, it may be mentioned that now a week-evening school for young women and adults is held in the Women's Monthly Meeting room, the use of which has kindly been granted by Friends there; the members interested in this school feel encouraged to persevere; there are some ladies not connected with Friends who also give it their assistance.

CROYDON.

Turning our attention now to Croydon we find in Latey's Biography an allusion to a Friends' Meeting in this town about the year 1657, but no particulars are given respecting it. Latey also mentions a meeting at Mitcham, of which we hear a little in Besse's Sufferings. It was at Mitcham in July, 1659, that a volley of stones was thrown at a bareheaded man engaged in prayer, and the congregation kicked, beaten, trampled upon, and sent away drenched with muddy water. A few days afterwards the meeting at this place was again broken up with violence. At this meeting that valiant servant of God, Rebecca Travers, and other preachers were present.

But the meeting at Mitcham, though settled for awhile, was of no permanent duration, and the gathering at Croydon became the headquarters for Friends of that district.

We do not find anything to record respecting Croydon Meeting during the first forty years of its existence. Not till 1696, at the time of its first junction with Wandsworth, does it emerge from obscurity.

Minute of Wandsworth and Croydon Monthly Meeting, Sixth Month, 1697:—

"It is agreed that the week-day's meeting be appointed to begin on the second hour on the fifth day of the week, at the meeting-house in Croydon."

Then, and for some years after, Friends of Croydon were meeting in a small building, where situated we are unable to state, which they rented for 40s. per annum of Thomas Beck, a well-to-do member of the meeting. In 1702 we find the use of this meeting-house granted gratuitously to Joseph Pierce, jun., to keep a school there. In 1707 the present burial-ground in Back Lane, now Park Lane, was purchased for £25 5s., and about £21 expended in building the west wall. On the ground thus acquired a meeting-house was built in 1721 at a total cost of £249. This building now forms the older portion of the present Croydon premises. The meeting-house now used was built for £900 in 1816, but has been altered and enlarged since that date.

In 1761 John Eliot left £100 as the nucleus of a fund for keeping Croydon Meeting-house and Burial-ground in repair. This was increased in 1764 by £50 from Frances Eliot, and £100 from Mary Eliot.

If, leaving the meeting-house, attention is turned to the meeting and its members, it is evident that at the commencement of last century Friends of Croydon were few in number. Some of them were farmers in the neighbourhood and suffered considerably for tithes. Thomas Beck, already named, had wheat, barley, &c. taken away on one occasion to the value of

£17, at another seizure £21, and at a third £23. Other Friends who were landowners or cultivators suffered similarly.

CROYDON MONTHLY MEETING.

The minutes of Croydon Monthly Meeting commence with the date of its separation from Wandsworth, from causes already described, in the year 1719. It was in the Eleventh Month of that year that Croydon Friends met, and after minuting their complaint that Wandsworth Friends had made Seventh-day the Monthly Meeting day, so that Croydon Friends could not attend "because it is our market-day," declared that for this and other reasons they would henceforth form an independent Monthly Meeting. To this arrangement the Quarterly Meeting consented. But differences on the subject of documents, trust-deeds, &c. continued for several years to rankle between Croydon and Wandsworth Friends till the Quarterly Meeting authoritatively desired "to hear no more of it."

After a few years had passed away it became evident that Friends of Croydon had, in forming a separate Monthly Meetting, undertaken a task more than they were equal to. Small in numbers, encumbered by several poor needing almost constant support, and with some of their most influential members so engaged with their own affairs in London that they could with difficulty be got to attend the service of the Society, it was no wonder that the Monthly Meeting became languishing, and after a time almost inert. We find on one occasion this minute: "only one Friend appearing, there was no business done;" on another it is recorded that the representatives "through carelessness neglected to attend" the Quarterly Meeting. These and various other signs show an increasing indifference and laxity, which culminated about the middle of the eighteenth century. But still there is not wanting evidence to show that there were a faithful few, of men and women Friends, who endeavoured to maintain the religious life of the meeting in the midst of much discouragement.

In 1755 matters had reached a very low state. Monthly Meetings had been held only four or five times a year for some years, and when held hardly anything but cash affairs seems to have been attended to. Indeed it would appear as if whoever relieved the wants of the poor, &c. only called a Monthly Meeting when money ran short. Occasionally representatives to the Quarterly Meeting were appointed, and their expenses mostly paid; but the Queries do not seem to have been answered from 1744 to 1756.

In 1755 the Quarterly Meeting felt it necessary to look after the state of Croydon Meeting. They sent down a committee who informed Croydon Friends "how much the Quarterly Meeting desires our Monthly Meeting may revive and be better attended, which we take in good part, and hope we shall be enabled to put in practice."

Considerable improvement now followed. The meetings were regularly held; two or three delinquents disowned; and a man and woman who had long worshipped with Friends, and who shortly afterwards took each other in marriage, were admitted members. Care was now ordered to be taken of the registration of births and burials which had been confessedly long neglected. A little tendency to be severe is manifested, and the " hardened, stupid, senseless condition " of one woman is commented on in a testimony against her.

In 1756 Croydon Friends agreed to hold their Monthly Meetings on First-day, in order to secure a larger attendance of the London men of business who might be members of the meeting.

The ancient dependence of suburban meetings in a considerable degree upon London Friends is evident at Croydon, as at other places. In 1758 "Nicholas Davis acquainted this meeting that being at the morning meeting at London, the week-day meeting of this place was not called over amongst the other country week-day meetings, and the reason given for it was, that it was never requested; this meeting therefore desires Nicholas Davis to get it entered and called over."* At the next Monthly Meeting Nicholas Davis reported that this matter had been attended to.

About 1760 the state of affairs was again very low at Croydon, and indeed through all the Monthly Meetings of Surrey. Only at Godalming were there any overseers. At Croydon, Kingston, and Wandsworth, the discipline was so neglected that the Yearly Meeting Committee, who travelled over England about this time, strongly advised the junction of these three meetings. Hence resulted that temporary and short-

---

* This means that it might lead to its being visited by public Friends, whose direction of service was arranged for at the Morning Meeting.

lived union which has been already described, which was annulled by the Yearly Meeting in 1762.

Croydon Monthly Meeting remained separate for sixteen years longer. It never seems to have relapsed into its former low condition, but nevertheless there was sufficient weakness still manifest to render desirable the junction with Kingston and Wandsworth, which was finally effected in 1778.

A proposal to establish a Women's Monthly Meeting in 1767 had not been found practicable. The attempt to hold two meetings on First-day in 1768 had also failed.

In 1774 the practice of collecting for the poor, &c., at a Monthly Meeting was discontinued, and the plan of an annual subscription adopted instead. It may be interesting to some to subjoin the list for the year 1774 :—

	£	s.	d.
" Jonathan Steel	7	7	0
Foster Reynolds	7	7	0
William Bell	7	7	0
Benjamin Bell	7	7	0
John Strellett	7	7	0
Francis Chamberlain	4	4	0
Joseph Reynolds	3	3	0
Richard Smith	2	2	0
	£46	4	0"

It should be mentioned that, even when at their lowest condition as a Monthly Meeting, Friends of Croydon did not neglect the virtue of hospitality, and whenever the Quarterly Meeting was held at Croydon, they gave the customary dinner either at the Greyhound or the White Lion.

Since 1778 Croydon Meeting has increased. In 1825 a large addition was made by the removal of the school from Islington Road to extensive premises adjoining the meeting-house (as mentioned in another chapter). At about the same time not a few families adopted Croydon as their suburban residence, and since the development of railways, it has become so favourite a locality, that the meeting is one of the largest round London. A Preparative Meeting has of course been held here, from whose minutes the following extract may be given, as bearing upon a question that has of late attracted some attention :—

" 7 mo. 28, 1782. The Advices to the Monthly and Quarterly Meetings were read at the close of our meeting for worship this day."

There is evidence to show that the same practice existed at other places about this time.

In conclusion, a few names of ministers and others may be mentioned who were connected with Croydon Meeting, in addition to some already alluded to:—John Lamb, Elinor Peters; Nicholas Davis, died 1762, aged 73 years, a minister forty-three years, attended meeting till within a week of his death; Rachael Trafford, a minister many years, and twenty-five years a schoolmistress in London, lived at Croydon in her declining years, but died and was buried at Wandsworth in 1772; Mary Sterry, Richard Barrett, Peter Bedford, &c.

APPENDIX.

The following minute from the Baptist Church at Esher was read at the Monthly Meeting of Kingston, held in the Eleventh Month, 1868:—

"At a meeting of the Esher Baptist Church, on Thursday, October 29th, 1868, it was unanimously resolved,—'That the heartiest thanks of this meeting be given to the members of the Society of Friends residing in Esher, for their prolonged Christian kindness and liberality in granting the Baptist congregation the gratuitous use of their meeting-house for divine worship, during a period of several years: and that the richest of God's blessings be implored to descend on our generous friends, that they may enjoy great spiritual prosperity, and a growing success may attend their works of faith and labours of love.'

"Signed on behalf of the Church—

"J. E. Perrin, *Pastor.*
"W. F. Hine,   } *Deacons.*"
"Rowd. Bartholomew, }

Copy of a letter from J. E. Perrin, to one of the Friends at Esher:—

"I have pleasure in asking you kindly to communicate to the members of your Society the expressions of gratitude sent herewith, for the multiplied favours you have conferred on my friends and myself. Will you permit me to express a hope, that while we retain our distinctive principles, we shall be willing, as opportunity is given, to co-operate in any practicable scheme for the religious welfare of this benighted neighbourhood.—*Oct. 31st, 1868.*"

Kingston Monthly Meeting has for several years granted the use of Esher Meeting-house, free of any charge, to the Baptists and Wesleyans in that locality. When the use of it was first agreed to at the Monthly Meeting, there were about sixteen public-houses or beer-shops in the immediate locality, but not a single place, even a cottage, in which these two small congregations could assemble for worship, owing in no small measure to a sectarian spirit which strove to keep these poor little flocks from forming congregations. The Baptists have at length succeeded in securing a new place of worship for themselves, hence the above minute of thanks, &c.

CHAPTER XX.

BUNHILL FIELDS AND WHITECHAPEL BURIAL-GROUNDS.

The isolated and indeed antagonistic position of our early Friends with regard to other bodies of professing Christians and the public at large, soon laid upon them the necessity of providing separate burial-places for their dead. Several of these have already been mentioned in connection with the meeting-houses to which they were attached, but two large burying-grounds yet remain to be noticed, viz. those whose names form the heading of this chapter.

The first of these is at Bunhill Fields, long known as the Chequer Alley Burial-ground, and now a broad level space surrounded by brick walls, around which the eye in every direction meets a dense mass of houses. But the small paled enclosure which formed the nucleus of the present extensive plot was originally almost in the country, lying as it did just at the extremity of the crowded and not over-reputable suburb of Cripplegate, almost in sight of the open fields that stretched toward " merry Islington."

In bringing their dead to this spot Friends were maintaining the traditions of the locality. Beneath the streets and houses of Finsbury and the adjacent parts lies an enormous population of the dead. In this neighbourhood were buried in huge pits the victims of the terrible plagues that so often visited the ancient city, and here too were interred the bodies of suicides, martyrs, malefactors, and similar persons denied Christian burial. Several skeletons were disinterred at the recent rebuilding of a Friend's premises in Old Street.* There were at one time many burial-places in the neighbourhood, some of which are now built over, but the large cemetery where John Bunyan's tomb stands amidst a thick forest of gravestones, is still a conspicuous object in the public burial-ground known as Bunhill Fields, on the west of the City Road. Amongst the almost forgotten burial-places alluded to, may be mentioned one that became the gardens of the houses in Broad Street Buildings, now covered by the present North London Railway Terminus, and in the erection of which

* "Sam[ue]l Hubbert's" [annotated copy]

great traces of burial were found. John Lilburne was carried from the Bull and Mouth Meeting to be buried here. It was one of the grounds used during the Great Plague, and so many leather shoes were dug up with the bones as to lead to the conclusion that the dead smitten in that pestilence died in their shoes and so were buried.

"Our burial-ground under Bunhill" (as it is sometimes termed in old records), or rather its western extremity, was the earliest freehold property possessed by the Society of Friends in London. If the visitor at the present day, entering by the Coleman Street gate, will turn to the right and walk forward till he stands about ninety feet from the western wall, he will face a nearly square plot of ground that may well by its associations awaken thoughts of earnest interest. There lie about 1,100 Friends who were carried off in that terrible year of the Great Plague. There were interred all that was mortal of Samuel Fisher, Richard Hubberthorne, Edward Burrough, and about ninety other of our martyrs who were carried to this spot on the shoulders of their brethren from the crowded prison in which they expired. Here also lie the sufferers who died on board the ship that was to have transported them to the western plantations.

Turning to other portions of the ground we may just allude to George Whitehead as conspicuous amongst a host of worthies who found in Bunhill Fields their last earthly resting place. But the funeral which makes this burial-ground pre-eminently worthy of notice in connection with the history of Friends, is of course that of George Fox.

We have already, in speaking of Gracechurch Street, described the memorable meeting held there on the 16th of the Eleventh Month, 1690, and the vast concourse of Friends who followed the body of their worthy elder through the streets. To this burial-ground the long procession wound its way. The "graveyard is a large plot of ground, yet it was quite full," says Robert Barrow. At this date the ground was only about half its present size, but nevertheless even then so large as to show that the crowd must have been a great one.

Amongst this crowded assembly of "tender hearts, watery eyes, and contrite spirits," several "living, open, powerful testimonies were published" by Joseph Batt, George Whitehead, John Vaughton, William Bingley, and William Penn. This latter Friend was in the post of danger by his presence here. An infamous fellow named Fuller, whom we have parliamentary authority for terming a "thief and a liar," had made charges on oath which had caused a warrant to be issued for the apprehension of William Penn. Only a mistake on the part of the officers as to the hour fixed for the funeral, prevented William Penn's arrest in this burial-ground at the interment of his friend.

For a curious account of the re-opening of George Fox's grave, see M. Webb's "Fells of Swarthmoor." There used to be a small stone on the spot, marked by the initials " G. F.," which it is said became so great an object of interest to Friends visiting London from the country, that a worthy member of some influence in the London meetings, caused it to be removed, applying to it the same term Hezekiah used in destroying Moses' serpent—"Nehushtan"—a piece of brass.* Tradition still preserves the locality of the grave, which is said to be found by standing on the spot where twenty-one paces from the east wall and fourteen paces from the north wall would meet.

On the east side of George Fox was buried two years afterwards his faithful friend and co-worker, Stephen Crisp. On the other side was buried George Watts, and at the south end of the grave was interred the worthy minister and writer Alexander Parker, who came up to London with George Fox in 1654, and who seems by his letters to have maintained an especially fraternal affection for George and Margaret Fox.

To allude in detail to the various individuals of note among Friends interred in this burial-ground would be to prolong this chapter to an almost indefinite extent. Few perhaps are aware, as they look at the flat unmounded surface, that the silent population of this graveyard is within a thousand of the whole number of the Society of Friends at present in England and Wales. The names of persons registered as buried here is very close upon 12,000. Allowing for unrecorded

---

* "There was once extant in Friends' Burial-ground at Bunhill Fields, a stone fixed in the wall, with the initials ' G. F.' and a date on it, to denote the spot where our honorable Elder George Fox was interred. But on occasion of enlarging the ground this stone was removed, together with the wall, and laid by. In the corner where it lay, however (no longer denoting anything real), it was found to attract too much of the attention of visitors, and my father [Robt. Howard, a tin plate worker in Old Street, formerly of Folkestone, where he had been instrumental in building the meeting-house] told me, he himself pronounced it "Nehushtan," and ordered it to be knocked to pieces."—*Luke Howard's Yorkshireman*, vol. iv. p. 115.

funerals at the commencement, and during the confusion at the time of the Plague, and also for hundreds of funerals not counted above, which are registered as being from the Bull and Mouth Meeting, from the Peel Meeting, &c., without the place of interment being specified, the comparison just made may be accepted as correct.

And taking this into account, how extraordinary is the spectacle. A green oasis in the great city, containing more than 12,000 corpses, many of them once the possessors of names held in high honour and veneration, and yet not a solitary gravestone,—not even a grassy mound to mark the resting-place of any individual! Surely the rich and the poor have here mingled together in a way few other burial-grounds can show.

Turning now to the history of the acquirement of the land, we find that on the 10th of October, 1661, Sir Reginald Foster, bart., and Dame Blandina, his wife, in consideration of the sum of £270, devised to Amor Stoddart, " for the use and service of the elect people of God in scorn called Quakers," that extreme western portion of the ground measuring about 90 feet square, which has been referred to in a preceding paragraph. A portion of this plot was re-sold to Sir Reginald for a time, but ultimately came again into the possession of Friends.

In about four years after this ground was pretty well filled, and in February, 1665, after the Plague had brought so many to the grave, Friends increased their territory in an easterly direction, by buying two messuages and gardens in Coleman Alley, now Coleman Street. For this addition £210 was paid.

To meet the growing needs of the Society, fresh purchases were made from time to time. Land to the value of £85 was added in 1687; £100 in 1689; £400 in 1696, and £190 in 1708. These four last-named purchases include the eastern part of the ground, but exclusive of the Coleman Street frontage. This was obtained in 1740, 1798, and 1799, by the purchase of seven houses and gardens. The western portion of the ground has been considerably widened by the presentation of a piece of ground in 1789 by John Eliot, and the purchase of land at various dates up to 1845. In 1839 one piece was bought and added by Westminster Monthly Meeting specially for their own use, being purchased with money left by Richard Hawkins for that purpose. The total amount expended in the purchase of the various plots of ground now included within its walls is about £3,600.

The ancient entrance to this burial-ground was by a court from Whitecross Street; subsequently it was approached from Chequer Alley, and in more recent times by the present chief entrance in Coleman Street. There appear to have been originally several tenements standing upon parts of the property at the time of purchase. These were either let to tenants or occupied by poor Friends, till demolished from time to time in order to make use of the ground on which they stood.

Under date of the Seventh Month, 1686, we find a curious minute on the books of the Six-Weeks Meeting, which gives us some idea of the place at that time. In avoiding superstitious reverence, some disregard for propriety seems to have crept in:

"A paper being read of yᵉ encroachments in yᵉ burying-ground in Chequer Alley, through severall Keys, drying-cloaths, settling-posts, &c. upon it, thereupon it is agreed, That yᵉ Keys be called in, That yᵉ washer-women and leather-dryers, mentioned in yᵉ paper be debarred at present, That yᵉ gravemaker have a note from Richard Richardson concerning Friends' minde, That yᵉ new door be opened only at a burial, & that also next to Chequer Alley. The graves lying open not to be suffered for yᵉ future, but filled up at every burial before night."

In 1716 we find Peel Friends expressing to the Six-Weeks Meeting their fear lest bodies should be stolen as had been done elsewhere. They were authorised by it to change the tenants for Friends, and it was ordered that in future all the gates but one should be locked up at dusk, and the excepted one not later than 10 p.m.

Occasionally sheep and cattle were allowed to pasture in this ground, but we find it forbidden by minute of the Six-Weeks Meeting in 1769. At the same time great complaint is made of the dirt and bones, &c., thrown into the graveyard by the neighbours—a nuisance which our present carekeeper complains of at this day.

Bunhill Fields burying-ground has been closed for interment since the year 1855. It remains in our day a broad walled-in space, surrounded by a teeming population mostly composed of the poorer classes.* It would afford an admirable

---

* There is a special fund for keeping Bunhill Fields in neat and decent order, not to be used for increase of salaries or repairs of walls and tenements, arising from a legacy of £50 left by John Smith.

site for the erection of a Mission Hall, with Schools, &c., and what fitter memorial could be raised over the graves of those zealous dead, who bore so good confession in their lives, and suffered much, even unto death, for the extension of the kingdom of Jesus?

Although closed by order of the Privy Council, the ground is far from full, and some portion has not been used at all for interment. Friends' anxiety to secure sufficient space had proved in excess of their needs, these being diminished through the practice of suburban residence, and obtaining burial-grounds attached to their meeting-houses there. One portion was let in 1840 on a building lease to a William Greig, and has had a British School erected thereon, which is now being worked by a general committee under the name of the Hope Schools For All; it is doing good service to the children of the dense population around. It serves also to show how much use might be made of a large open ground such as this if thrown open, under proper regulations, as a recreation ground for the occupants of the working homes all around.

WHITECHAPEL.

The burial-ground at Whitechapel resembles in many respects that at Bunhill, particularly in being a level walled-in space in the midst of a crowded district, though once almost in the open country. In 1687 we find the Six-Weeks Meeting purchasing the remainder of the lease of an acre of ground in Coverley's Fields, near Mile End Green for £140, said lease having then 105 years to run. In 1743 Lord Castlemaine, the proprietor, granted Friends a 500 years' lease, on payment of a 100 guineas, to date from the expiration of the lease then held. This latter did not expire till 1792, so that our present tenure is until A.D. 2292.

This burial-ground was under the particular care of Devonshire House, and a very large number of Friends who dwelt in the eastern parts of the Metropolis were buried there; but it would seem that ministers and persons of note were almost always buried in Bunhill Fields. The Whitechapel burial-ground was closed for interment in 1857.

There are frequent allusions to this burying-ground on the minutes of Devonshire House. Thus in 1690 we find twenty trees planted. In 1695 it is decided that, as some prejudice has

Bunhill Fields. Above: the Memorial Buildings, built in 1881 as the kind of mission hall suggested (see opposite page). The building behind on the left is the British School. The caretaker's cottage (left, behind the railings) is the only part of the building remaining after bombing in 1941 [LSF].

Below: Indenture for the original purchase of the land in 1661, and right, the same document folded [LSF].

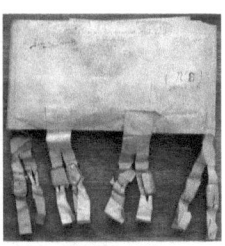

facing p.334

Whitechapel burial ground: undated photo after it had become a recreation ground [LSF]

Library of the Religious Society of Friends

arisen about it, no cattle, &c. are to be allowed to graze there in future. In the following year this prohibition is rescinded so far as regards sheep only. In 1698 a pond was filled up, and the ground raised and levelled, so that it must previously have been rather a rough piece of land. In 1700 a Friend agrees to pay £4 a year to keep his horse there. The house and gateway appear to have been erected in 1703, but of course there have been extensive repairs and changes since that date. The most recent of these is the rendering of the house commodious and comfortable for the residence of a few elderly or infirm poor Friends belonging to Devonshire House Monthly Meeting.

Three small houses fronting Baker's Row have also been at a comparatively early period erected on a portion of the land.

A curious circumstance occurred here in 1716. This was the stealing of a corpse from the ground by John Holmes (son of Michael Holmes, the gravedigger), and some of his companions. The Monthly Meeting dismissed Michael Holmes from his employment, and ordered him to quit his house by the gateway. They also authorised the payment of £10 for the prosecution of the offenders. This circumstance created a sort of panic amongst Friends about their burial-grounds, and at Bunhill Fields and elsewhere the precautionary measures were taken which have been previously alluded to.

One would suppose that the safety of corpses in Whitechapel burial-ground could not at this time have been guaranteed by any vigilance on the part of the gatekeeper, for it was only walled-in on two sides. In 1719 there is a complaint made of cattle walking in through the gaps in the fences. Subsequently walls have been erected all round it, and since it was closed by authority, in common with the other metropolitan burial-places, it has remained a comparatively useless possession. Here, too, as in Bunhill Fields, we see a poverty-stricken and vice-haunted neighbourhood, accompanied by a great deficiency of instrumental means for its enlightenment, and this eligible site for a Mission Hall and Schoolrooms in its very midst. Is not the opening out of circumstances to be sometimes taken as an indication of the mind of the Spirit? and is it for nothing that these teeming haunts of vice and irreligion have clustered round our once half-rural burial-grounds?

CHAPTER XXI.

MORNING MEETING—*i e.* OF MINISTERS AND ELDERS.

By the operation of the same principle of *mutual* oversight which led to the establishment of meetings for the care of the members in general, it is found that from the earliest time of the Society in London, meetings or conferences were held among those men Friends in the practice of publicly addressing the congregations—in which they gave counsel and encouragement one to another, and thus put in force the apostolic injunction to try the spirits, as also the declaration that the spirit of the prophets should be subject to the prophets.

But it is observable that at the first, and for about a century, such meetings (which were really the only oversight and control exercised over the ministry) were confined to *men* ministers; also that no persons (such as elders) not in the practice of addressing the congregations were present until 1727, about which time the Monthly Meetings *first* began to exercise any judgment as to who should be entitled to attend and be considered members of this select meeting. The conferences of men ministers, from which the so-called Morning Meeting took its rise, commenced at the hospitable house of Gerrard Roberts—a wine cooper by trade, carrying on his business near Doctors Commons; and were moved from thence to the Bull and Month, where one of the upper rooms was used for the purpose, and subsequently apartments at the White Hart Court premises.

After the taking of the Bull and Mouth, it would seem from W. Crouch (p. 94) as if these gatherings had been held in an upper room of these premises, and he calls it a meeting of elder men Friends, mentioning also that on the destruction of that meeting-house in the Great Fire, it was shifted to Devonshire House, then recently taken. Subsequently it was held again at the Bull and Mouth, and White Hart Court. Sometimes it is called the meeting of "travelling brethren." George Fox addressed it as the general assembly of the ministry in London, and eventually it became known as the Morning Meeting.

The records remaining of this meeting commence about the same period as that when greater regularity was becoming infused into the work of the various meetings—a time when those of the Six-Weeks Meeting commence, as also those of the Yearly Meeting—viz. the year 1672; any earlier records, if such ever existed, have not been preserved. This time was one in which, after twelve years of trial, a respite had been obtained through the King's Proclamation of General Indulgence to Nonconformists—during which George Fox and some others of the leading ministers made their journey to America.

The records of the Morning Meeting thus commencing, extend, in an almost unbroken series, from 15th of Seventh Month, 1673, down to the present time, and are contained in nine folio volumes; but for one year (viz. from 24th of First Month, 1678, to 3rd of First Month, 1679) there is an intermission; and one of the volumes is imperfect, through having been damaged in the fire at Gracechurch Street. The reason of the omission of the year above referred to is not easy to be accounted for; the time was one when persecution was somewhat allayed under James II. George Fox himself seems to have spent that year at Swarthmoor.

An inspection of these records shows plainly a watchful care in early times by the Men ministers over the services of Friends in the ministry—which was the primary object of the meeting; and also exhibits great vigilance over all works issued by Friends from the press, which was another and important department undertaken by this meeting and involved much scrutinising labour, especially in the earlier times.

There is entered upon the minutes, under date Second Month 24th, 1794, a report from a committee the meeting had appointed to inquire into its origin and duties, which is at once so concise, and yet explicit, in its information, that it is here given, as conveying the best information at hand on these points. Unfortunately there occur blanks which render the sense of some of the latter clauses somewhat doubtful; these arise from those portions having been destroyed or become illegible through the fire before mentioned.

"REPORT.

"1. That this Meeting appears from the Records to have begun in 1673, but not by appointment of any other, though it has been, since that time, frequently recognised by the Yearly Meeting. But we are inclined to think that the meeting of ancient Friends, mentioned by Wm. Crouch in 1660 (as having began after the taking of the Bull & Mouth Meeting House in 1656) gave rise to the Morning Meeting.

" 2. That in 1661 it was agreed there should be once a month a general Meeting of Ministering Friends in and about the City, in which the greatest part of its business was suspended, and afterwards a Quarterly Meeting of the like kind was added: which latter was discontinued in 1740 by minute, and the former has now fallen into disuse.

" 3. That it consisted first of Ministering Men Friends in and about the City; afterwards Elders were added from the six Monthly Meetings of London, pursuant to minute . . . [blanks] and Elders were introduced; except that Monthly Meeting's Women had sat in it . . . time. The first introduction of an Elder from either of the three Country Monthly Meetings appears to be in the year 1766.

" 4. That its first business seemed to be the general care of Books: most of which, except revising them, is now performed by the Meeting for Sufferings.

" 5. That as early as 1675 the orderly dispersion of Ministers to the several meetings for worship according to their concern or Freedom was a principal part of its care; and it was the practice for them to meet on a First-day morning to confer together; but that meeting has dropped into disuse, as well as the practice that gave rise to it.

" 6. That it has long been in the practice of giving Certificates to Ministers proposing to travel beyond Sea (except to Ireland) and of re . . . . those granted to Friends of Foreign Parts visiting this nation: and since 1821 of those . . . . London from any part of the Kingdom.

" 7. That it has also long been the practice . . . . decline of the First-day morning meeting reporting of such Ministers as had attended them, until the latter practice was dropt in 1793, as well as that of reporting their names.

" 8. That answering the Queries to the Yearly Meeting of Ministers and Elders and various other kinds of business have been from time to time either taken up by it, or committed to it, most of which are now turned into other Channels, except four of the before-mentioned, viz. :—

" ' The Revision of Books and Manuscripts.
" ' The Receiving accounts of Meetings for Worship.

"'The Granting Certificates to Ministers going beyond Sea.
"'The reading of such as are brought by Ministers visiting those parts.'"

After this report follows a minute, viz. :—

"Some doubts having arisen whether the Elders appointed by the three Country Monthly Meetings be proper members of this Meeting, it is the conclusion of this Meeting that they be considered as such, and they are desired to continue their brotherly . . . ." [as before mentioned, the blanks are caused by damage in the fire.]

In reference to a right conduct of the ministry, the records give full evidence of the care used by the brethren in this respect. One important branch of this was that, by previous arrangement, all meetings for worship in and around the city should be duly supplied with ministers, thereby guarding against some having too many present and others too few. Thus, as early as 1675, it was arranged for all Men ministers when in town to assemble at Ellis Hookes' chamber on the morning of every First-day as early as 8 o'clock, when, after a short devotional opportunity, they dispersed themselves among the meetings, according to an arrangement that had been agreed on; whilst those about to visit the more distant ones, mounted the horses that stood outside brought up in readiness for their use. The books in which these arrangements were made remain; they comprise ten folios, with the pages ruled so as to have the various meeting-houses under separate columns, with the Friends' names who had felt either free to offer, or had been appointed to attend, entered under the names of the respective meetings, which practice was kept up for a century, though in some of the later volumes the record is made subsequent, not previous to the meeting. On Second-day morning, the Men ministers again assembled at 10 o'clock, constituting practically the meeting now under description, when such advice as might be needed was duly given.

Ellis Hookes, as clerk to the Morning Meeting, had charge of the book in which those willing to attend meetings as ministers wrote down their names, and for a great length of time the tacit permission to do this was the only acknowledgment of any one being recognised as a minister; and the first sign of a Monthly Meeting being dissatisfied with the ministry of any particular person, is found in their objecting to such an one putting his name in the book.

Expressions of dissatisfaction with Ministers frequently occur in the Morning Meeting minutes. Sometimes caution is given, or care extended—thus to one engaged in a penny lottery, to another who confessed he had taken the sacrament; there are others recorded as dealt with—such as one on account of a "great failure," another, for bankruptcy, "to be silent till Friends are satisfied"; occasionally "further inquiry" is ordered to be made. Notices of prophesyings occur, and are reprehended. One Friend is "prohibited to minister"; another is "admonished to go home"; another is to be set to work; some are refractory—thus J. F. is mentioned as gone to America contrary to advice. Nor is the counsel confined to men ministers, since we note in 1682 one Mary K., "who gives trouble, rambling up and down in Suffolk," and the resolution come to was, "to speak to her husband about it." Again, "Modesty Newman to be required to produce her certificate." The following looks as if (when the eighteenth century opened) women Friends are thought to be given to too much speaking, for under date Eighth Month, 1700, it says: "Women Friends not to be forward to enter and speak in public places of worship"; and in another, whilst encouraging them to give in their names to Ellis Hookes as willing to be among those appointed to go to meetings, they were "to be careful not to interfere with the brethren." Later on came a minute which reads as if this caution was not followed, for it is entered that "Women Friends take up too much time in public meetings."

Respecting the ministry generally, caution was shown, as a minute occurs 1696 to the purport that the names of those who speak a few words not to be suddenly entered, nor to appear in the public gallery until proof have been given; notice also occurs, as to be subject for reprehension, of those "going about the streets pretending to preach as prophets."

The meeting itself underwent some changes in its constitution as time proceeded.

In 1681 it was agreed that once a month the meeting should be held between 8 and 9 on a Second-day *morning*, and all the usual business except "that of necessity" be postponed, in order that the occasion might be one of a devotional nature. (At this time the Morning Meeting met at least once a week for transaction of its business.)

During the Yearly Meeting much close work seemed entailed, the Morning Meeting being summoned as early as 6 a.m. to expedite business, which was of an arduous nature, as it undertook the answering of all epistles from foreign parts that had been addressed to the Yearly Meeting.

At other times it was also part of its functions to conduct the Society correspondence. George Fox having just before his decease, by a memorandum he wrote, requested all, both at home and abroad, that used to write to him, to write to the Morning Meeting.

In 1727 Friends not speaking in meetings, but chosen as elders, were to form part of the meeting, being called "discreet friends, not ministers, to advise young ministers;" two of these to be appointed by each Monthly Meeting, it needed some strong minutes in 1758, to secure an appointment of these. The first Yearly Meeting of Ministers and Elders was held at the suggestion of Samuel Fothergill, in 1758. At this time also the practice of annually answering Queries was introduced.

In 1773 women elders were agreed to.

In 1797, agreed to hold the meeting only once a month instead of every week as hitherto, "its business being much lessened." In 1860 this was still further reduced by the withdrawal of any care over MSS. intended for publication, and the meeting has met only once a quarter since that time. Its meetings now afford opportunities for religious fellowship and mutual encouragement among the ministers and elders, as also for considering the concerns of any who may be drawn towards foreign countries to travel in the work of the ministry, respecting which the meeting is expected, as from the earliest times, to exercise a judgment as to approval or otherwise. It is many years since the meeting issued any minute of counsel, though the earlier records contain instances of this having been its practice.

Thus, 1675, Friends finding arms, to be "admonished." Again, a care as to the elections, "to seek to be unanimous in voting for Members of Parliament who should engage to support liberty of conscience and the removal of popish and oppressive laws." Again, forms for marriage certificates brought in and considered. Care, also, that no marriage take place without notice that "the publique laborers as are free may be at them, there being a service for the Lord at them." These are instances of a general care which the meeting exercise, but it had no disciplinary power in any case that had been taken up by any Monthly Meeting. Thus, in 1800, when dissatisfaction was felt with Hannah Barnard, and the Morning Meeting had advised her to quietly return home by the first opportunity, such advice not being followed all future proceeding was deferred to Devonshire House Monthly Meeting, as a Meeting for Discipline, and by it was eventually issued a judgment in her case, subsequently confirmed on her appeal to superior meetings.

In respect to works proposed for publication, much business on this account devolved upon the meeting at its first establishment, to such an extent as to absorb the greater part of its attention. Frequent minutes occur to show the labour involved was great, and the censorship far from being a matter of form; indeed, for many years, the authors of MSS. before the meeting whose writings were discouraged or disapproved quite equal in number those whose works were passed. Under this system a marked change becomes observable both in the tone and style of works issued by members of the Society; all the quaint titles of a time previous to the establishment of the meeting disappear, and much more restraint in the language, and improvement in the general style becomes evident.

In 1675 the first formal order was made "that in future no books be printed but what are read and approved." George Fox's works are often noted as receiving revision to prepare them for the press, and after his decease, the Journal, when at length it issued from Thomas Ellwood's editorship, received long and continuous attention before being published. MSS. with such titles as "Hy. Pickworth dreams, &c.," "Ralph Fretwell's Epistle to the Behmenites," are minuted as "not to be published," "not suitable," "not safe," and the two printers of the Society were especially cautioned against any infringement of these restrictions.

Note.—Of the printers and publishers, one of the earliest employed was Andrew Sowle; then William Bradford, his son-in-law; afterwards Luke Hinde and others. A John Bringhurst had in early times printed for Friends and other Nonconformists, and suffered imprisonment and the pillory for printing George Fox's Primer in 1684, after which prosecution he is supposed to have gone to Holland. Giles Calvert, of George Yard, Lombard Street, printed for Friends, though not one himself, and was so employed even previous to the visit of Howgill and Burrough.

CHAPTER XXII.

WOMEN'S MEETINGS,

Including their Quarterly, Monthly, and Two-Weeks Meetings, as also the Box Meeting for the Care of the Poor.

THE cause of religion has owed so much in its progress to the faith and zeal of pious women, that it is impossible for a description of any age or period of the Church, or particular section of it, to be given, without finding this powerful influence to arise into some prominence.

It would, then, be strange if a narrative of any meetings belonging to a society, like the Friends, where the female character has been allowed so great a share in the Church arrangements, should fail in illustrating this marked feature, especially as the London meetings bear such ample traces of the influence of pious and gifted female labourers upon their history.

Indeed, it is with this that the narrative opens, for (as already shown, p. 19) it was a woman Friend—one Isabel Buttery—who was alike the first disseminator of Friends' views in London and the first to suffer in the cause; and though her humble endeavours were soon eclipsed by the vigorous ministry of the north country youths that succeeded, nevertheless their labours only opened up a fuller scope for that important line of service wherein their sisters in the faith became as "succourers of many" and "mothers in Israel."

In this respect it is interesting to observe how large a proportion of those who opened their houses as places of worship for Friends were women. Thus we found (see p. 36) three of of the name of Sarah—all living near Aldersgate—Sarah Matthews, Sarah Sawyer, and Sarah Yates, who thus permitted their dwellings to be used by the despised "children of the light"; then there was the Widow Jebb in Horslydown, Elizabeth Trott of Pall Mall, Jane Woodcock and

Martha Fisher of the Savoy, the Widow Dry at Enfield, and Widow Haly at Guttershedge, &c.

Some women Friends, such as Ann Downer (who became the wife of George Whitehead), were from the first engaged with the brethren in the work of the ministry; but during the early evangelising periods, the public meetings were frequented by too miscellaneous an assemblage to offer suitable scope for the exercise of this class of gifts, and it is observable in the minutes of the meeting of Men ministers which had care over such service, that the assistance of their sisters in public ministry was rather discouraged than promoted, a feeling which the arrangements of the meetings themselves confirm, for not until quieter days had thoroughly set in was there any provision made for women Friends as ministers in the gallery; yet, notwithstanding this discouragement, the ministry of women was a feature sufficiently marked to attract general attention, so that the earliest prints known of a Friends' meeting are taken as at a point of time when a woman Friend is addressing the assembly, not, however, from the ministers' gallery, but on a stool, tub, or bench.

Whilst thus permitted to share, to some extent, even from the first in the service of the ministry, it was in other and somewhat more social and practical duties that their energies and talents received the fullest development, and of these traces remain to the present day.

There are those mingling in the general society of the London Friends who may often hear a meeting familiarly spoken of as the Box Meeting, a name that sounds peculiar at first, but becomes associated with a pleasant sense of help, if the party may happen to be at all interested in some case of affliction or distress. To such it is not an unfrequent answer, on mentioning the circumstances, to say, "Oh! I will get so and so a gift from our Box Meeting." Gratified in thus obtaining some £2 or £3 for the object of his care, it is possible there may remain a curiosity to know more of this source of relief coming under so peculiar a name. If so, it will be found that it is regulated by rule both as to time and mode of dispensing and class of objects; that once a month, on a Second-day morning, the meeting is in session; that the objects to which its care is especially directed are those members of any one of the six London Monthly Meetings, who, not being in the receipt of Monthly Meeting allowances, may have become, through sickness or other trial, subject to temporary difficulty; besides which, assistance is afforded in such cases of "lying-in" where help seems desirable. But the sums given are confined to £2 or £3 each, and must not be had by the same party oftener than once in the twelve months. Should inquiry be pushed further, it will be found that women Friends alone are members of the meeting which conducts the affairs of this charity, and that they possess considerable funded property and freehold estate, from which the income is derived, that enables them to make such acceptable disbursements, and neither as to income or expenditure have they to give account to any other meeting as their superior. Any woman Friend, if a member of one of the London meetings, may attend; and it used to be the custom for each to drop a shilling into the box before taking her seat, but this practice is now very much fallen into disuse, owing to the invested funds furnishing sufficient income without this contribution. These funds arise from legacies and bequests that have accumulated during a long course of years.

Here most, if they had any curiosity at all as to this meeting, may have felt satisfied, and if so, can stay here; whilst some others, more inquisitive, will follow on to learn, if they can, somewhat as to the origin and history of this curiously-named and well-endowed assembly. If so, the actual name of the meeting will suggest ground of inquiry, for it runs, "The Women's Two-Weeks and Box Meeting for the care of the Poor." Why these two terms? Wherefore this two-weeks applied to a meeting holding session only once a month?

To answer this at all in full, we must become descriptive, and, at the risk of appearing tedious, go back to the beginning of the Society, and sketch some of its earliest arrangements, in doing which the reason of this combined title and functions may become more apparent.

Great strain fell (as we have shown, p. 42) on the early ministers as the numbers of convinced rapidly increased, involving care and duties, "such as so properly did not belong to them of the ministry." These, some men Friends, not ministers, but zealous for the truth, were willing to undertake, and thus places for meeting were secured, other external arrangements made, and the poor were inquired into and cared for; but as these men Friends in the work proceeded, they found the help of their sisters in the faith was desirable, for it was not so "proper for the men as for the women to visit the sick, and to search out the necessities of the poor weak widows and aged" (see p. 43); and thus a meeting of women Friends for the care of such matters came to be established.

Edward Burrough speaks of it as having followed soon after the settlement of the men's meeting; and Gilbert Latey has also given some account of the circumstances under which it arose. He seems when far advanced in life to have felt inclined to do this; and the epistle which contains it is printed in his memoirs.

By his letter he takes us back to the "early days, three or four years after the settlement of the men's meeting," when, on one occasion, some fifteen men Friends were met in their usual fortnightly gathering in an upper room at the Bull and Mouth, there providing for the things concerning the Church, when, says Latey, "our hearts were opened and we enlightened so as to see we wanted helpmeets for carrying on the service," and they saw clearly "that the women being added to us as helpmeets would answer" .... "for we could no longer do without their help and assistance." So it was agreed two of their number should go off to the house of Gerrard Roberts, where they knew some ministering Friends were assembled, and open up to them this new idea; there they found George Fox, with Edward Burrough, Francis Howgill, and Richard Hubberthorne, who, on hearing the proposal, "very well approved and fatherly consented." Forthwith names were taken down of all women Friends thought suitable, embracing "some from every quarter," and thus, as *supposed*, the women's Two-Weeks Meeting was formed, the special business being to look after and visit the *sick* poor, also the general poor of their own sex; to which was *subsequently* added a care over marriages, so far as for the parties intending to live together as man and wife to come and declare their intentions before them; but no record was made, that being left to the men's meeting.

Thus before the death of Edward Burrough, or the first persecution had commenced, there had been a line of service especially committed to the women Friends, for the discharge of which they were accustomed to assemble for conference at least once a fortnight, thus establishing the so-called "ancient Two-Weeks Meeting of women Friends."

The service being essentially one of relief, could not be

effectively discharged without some material means; these were supplied either by moneys from the men's meetings, or by collections made amongst the members by the women Friends, and gradually, with an instinct that seems to possess all societies, they acquired in after time some funded property from legacies and accumulations.

But to speak of invested property in connection with such a meeting, is to pass far on from the days when it arose; then the wants of the poor, the sick and aged, taxed all their energies even to *alleviate*, and when (as persecution set in) there were prisoners, and their *wants* added to the list, we may well believe the hands and hearts of the women Friends found overflowing occupation. Indeed, from some cause not easy to be explained, it would seem as if the earlier arrangements (as just narrated) had settled down into a regular course of Monthly Meeting relief, leaving a number of cases of special and suddenly occurring distress unprovided for, giving rise to another meeting even yet now in existence (as before shown), and the origin of which we seem to trace in an account given in George Fox's published Epistles, p. 6, &c. G. F. had been sent for during one of his visits to London (the exact year is not given) to see a woman and child in "Whitechappel," that were both thought to be dying; and though it was as unseasonable an hour as 3 o'clock in the morning when thus summoned, he immediately went, and records with thankfulness how both mother and infant recovered under his Gospel ministrations. Returning from this early service of love, he had no sooner re-entered Gerrard Roberts' house (where he was staying as a guest) than one of the leading women Friends of London, Sarah Blackberry,* came in about 8 o'clock to desire his attention, not to any one particular case, but "to complain of the poor, and how many poor Friends were in want"; and the Lord had showed me, proceeds G. F., "what I should do in his eternal power and wisdom, so I spake to her to bid about *sixty women* to meet me about the *first* hour in the afternoon, at the sign of the Helmet, at a Friend's house (Samuel Vasses, Basinghall Street), and they did so accordingly, such as were sensible women of the Lord's truth, and fearing God. And

---

* This Friend was instrumental in establishing Hammersmith Meeting. See also an Epistle, in 1680, by Ann Whitehead and Mary Elson, as to the origin of Women's Meetings in London.

what the Lord had opened unto me I declared unto them, concerning their having a meeting once a week every Second-day, that they might see and inquire into the necessity of all poor Friends who were sick and weak, and were in want, or widows and fatherless in the city and suburbs . . . . and this brought them into the practice of the pure religion, and to visit the sick, and for the relief of the fatherless and the widow, and to see that nothing was lacking among them . . . . which they have felt prosperous to this day . . . and very honourable it hath been in the eyes of all the faithful, yea, and commendable in the world also." Herein is described most likely the origin of the Women's Box Meeting; but it must be admitted there are difficulties in harmonising the accounts.

At first, some might think the narrative of G. F. to be but another version of the same circumstance described from Gilbert Latey's epistle, and that George Fox gives prominence to the part he himself took in the matter, not noticing the important share others had had therein. To this will at once occur the objection that there *are two distinct* meetings of women Friends, existing separately until comparatively a recent period, and now remaining in a combined form, both having a care over the poor for their object; each, too, bearing, in the possession of funded property and other circumstances, evidence of distinct origin. Then, again, how different is the manner of the appeal! In both George Fox is introduced; but Gilbert says the men, appointing two of themselves as a deputation, went to consult him and the other early ministers; whilst in George Fox's account the matter is introduced to him by a woman Friend herself; and it must be borne in mind that Gilbert Latey's account was not penned until years after the publication of George Fox's, to which, however, he makes no allusion, as would have been called for if both were speaking of the same meeting, so as to account for discrepancies. Gilbert, too, as a member of the Morning Meeting which revised all manuscripts, would have had full knowledge of what G. F. had written, and could hardly have allowed it to pass if what he himself says of the origin of women's meetings had been intended to apply to the same one described by George Fox.

It is, perhaps, a more difficult question (although of no practical importance) to determine which is the elder of the *two* women's meetings; there is in this respect, we think, ground for believing that the Box Meeting is somewhat the *later*, rather than the *earlier*, of the two.

It would seem as if when the early ministers found the care of the increasing Churches too heavy for them that the well-concerned Friends to whom they had committed all social and practical details, found the need on *their* part of assistance in a department of the work to which the services of the women would be acceptable. Hence, as *they* had a fortnight's meeting the women came to have one also themselves, in which poverty and sickness among the members was the especial care. Now the needs instead of diminishing increased as persecution set in, for it added *sufferings* and *prisoners* to the list. The earlier meeting, it may be supposed, had settled into its own ways of action and kind of relief (which meetings, as is known, so soon do). Meanwhile distress and want existed so greatly as to move Sarah Blackberry to see whether something more could not be done. George Fox realised the needs, and himself meets alone sixty women called together within five hours of Sarah Blackberry's visit, and then and there, at Samuel Vasses' house in Basinghall Street, a meeting exclusively of women, and unallied in any manner, like the former meeting with men Friends, was established, their object being to meet special cases of distress rather than those on the list for a regular allowance. As to funds, they were to get contributions where and how they could from Friends, at meetings or otherwise, to put all thus received into a common box, and distribute out of it according to the needs of the cases brought before them, when they met *once* a week. Such will, it is suggested, be the explanation that most readily meets the difficulties of the case in accounting for the origin of that Women's Meeting commonly known as the Box Meeting—entirely independent of any other—accounting to no superior body—making no statement of its income or expenditure, and jealously guarding its traditions of complete independence to the present day. The wants of the time when these meetings arose were, no doubt, very great, for parish relief had not become so thoroughly recognised as a successor to the old conventual system as it is at present, and the streets, as George Fox says in the Epistle before quoted, were full of "widows, strangers, and beggars," many of whom were no doubt glad, under plea of attendance of meetings, to find a share in the liberality of the "children of light." Thus we conclude that the Two-

Weeks Meeting first mentioned and the one alluded to by George Fox are distinct; that the Two-Weeks one undertook the care of the poor, relieved them by loans, or regular allowances, forming, in fact, poor for maintenance; whilst the other, and supposed later, meeting, known by the name of "the Box," was for handing relief to special cases and to persons under peculiar circumstances.

Hitherto the *origin* only of these meetings has been noticed, their individual history should now be alluded to. It appears that neither of them were considered meetings of record, so that the absence of any minutes is not a sure sign that there were any originally, and that they have been lost; those remaining show the same book to have been used for several meetings, *i.e.* Annual, Quarterly, Two-Weeks, and Box. An account-book exists commencing as early as 1669, when the chief entries are respecting loans of £3 to £5 made to individuals, for the repayment of which many Friends became responsible to the amount of 2s. 6d. or 5s. each. Considerable loss seems to have arisen from non-payment and decease of those become sureties, so that in 1685, under date Ninth Month 18th, it is agreed in future to let no loan stand over more than two years, without calling it in, or in default of payment coming upon the securities.

The Two-Weeks Meeting through its more definite alliance with the men's meetings, had the recognised right to gather collections from Friends at any of their meetings, and it seems to have been the custom (in days when lists in the clerk's office were unknown) for women Friends to be especially appointed to stand at the doors and passages as collectors, receiving contributions at the close of *all* our meetings, including even the Yearly Meeting, when the sums thus received were allotted among the different Monthly Meetings. It was also customary to divide 10 guineas three times in the year to the use of the women of the six London Monthly Meetings, for distribution among the poor. In 1788 it was 18 guineas annually. The circumstance of the women Friends uniting with the men Friends in a joint meeting for worship previous to the Quarterly Meeting (a practice commenced in 1762) led eventually to the abandonment of collecting on such occasions at the breaking up of the meeting, as interfering with the solemnity of the occasion. Thus, in 1769, it was thought "by placing the box in the large passage . . . for Friends to drop their collections as the meeting gathers," it might tend "to separating more quietly and satisfactorily than on the former method." But the men would hardly seem to have taken kindly to the alteration, for four years after men Friends are asked by minute "to drop contributions previous to coming out of meeting, so as to let the amount be ready for distribution."

At this time, 1780, a separation was made between the Quarterly and the Two-Weeks Stock, when, after certain payments, such as doorkeepers' salaries, servants' registry, were defrayed, the surplus of collections was to be equally divided; those in the autumn and spring quarters between the nine Monthly Meetings of London and Middlesex, and those of the summer and winter between the six London Monthly Meetings; the collections at the Yearly Meeting when it fell in the summer to be for the latter.

Some sixteen years later, in 1788, the Quarterly Meeting, which had discontinued the *men's* Two-Weeks Meeting, saw no reason why that of the women's should not also be relinquished, especially as the appearances of parties intending for marriage was transferred to their Monthly Meetings, but the women with a tenacity of purpose—not perhaps unusual—declined assent to the arrangement; nevertheless, they agreed two years later to a *fusion* of the two meetings for the poor; thus, 1790, Fourth Month 20th, at a Women's Two-Weeks and Box Meeting, agreed to meet only once a month, the first Second-day in every month, and to try for a more general and regular attendance. General collection to be made, and the poor in *both* lists to be relieved, to be called henceforward "Meeting of Women Friends of London for transacting the business of the Two-Weeks and Box Meetings."

At this point in the history, when the two meetings became fused into one, it seems natural to inquire what traces remain of the previous career of the Box Meeting, but as in 1764, when a similar inquiry was made, Friends were unable to discover this, there seems little prospect of learning much about it now, especially as it was at first no meeting of record.

One or two minutes seem, however, to refer to it; thus, in 1670, it is found to have been held once a week alternately at Devonshire House, Bull and Mouth, Aldersgate Street (Sarah Sawyer's), and the house of Rebecca Travers (a mother in Israel), whose name often occurs in connection with succour to the poor; it was at her house also G. Whitehead had lodgings before his marriage. When thus met they received collections and distributed to the necessities of the poor. If gifts to this meeting, by bequest or otherwise, were made, it was done as "for use and service of truth as managed by the women Friends." In 1675, notice of an extra collection at one time, when assembled at Devonshire House, " in order to pay debts which were contracted for such purposes, which we could not relieve from the box." From a minute under date 1680 it may be noted that a desire to keep a more particular account of moneys spent began in 1678, previous to which time Ann Whitehead says " only memoranda had been made." No doubt the minute-book in use at the time of the fire at White Hart Court in 1821, would, if preserved, have thrown some further light on the history of the Box Meeting, as during those twenty years, the records of which then perished, the various departments of Christian service had become more systematised; as it is, there is the meeting still in force, its management is still confined *exclusively* to women Friends, to them alone belongs the valuable funded and freehold property attached to the meeting, and it continues as from the first to be a means of succour and help to all cases of peculiar or temporary distress, similar in principle, though not in actual circumstance, to those which induced Sarah Blackberry, two centuries ago, to call George Fox's attention, when, by his advice, sixty women at a three hours' notice, gathered responsive to the summons at the sign of the Helmet (Samuel Vasses' house), thus supplementing the efforts of the previously established Two-Weeks Meetings, with which it has in course of time come to be blended.

It will be observed that, in describing these two meetings, the action of the women Friends as to the poor and distressed has alone been developed, leaving unnoticed any account as to how they came to have that share in the general discipline which is now allowed to them. Hence some few notes on this latter head may be desirable. At the first, in the days of the early preachers, it was observed that the *Men's* Two-Weeks Meeting and the *Women's* Two-Weeks Meeting were distinct, the latter having less of a disciplinary character, and more of the care of the poor; these respective meetings long existed, after varied systems of discipline had been adopted.

When at the instigation of George Fox, some twelve years after the first settlement of the London Society, Monthly Meetings were introduced, it was the practice for the women to sit with men Friends in these, which at that time were select meetings (not open like the Two-Weeks to any); they also formed, as before noticed, a large proportion of the members of the Six-Weeks Meeting at its origin—a time when it was a senate or meeting of appeal—a "prime meeting," as G. F. termed it, among the London Monthly Meetings. Thus the women Friends shared in the discipline with the men, but without having any *separate* meetings for it.

The whole subject, as to the state of Women's Meetings in 1755, is best described in a report from the London Quarterly to the Yearly Meeting, which is as follows:—

"In these meetings the men and women met together, so that all present making one Monthly Meeting, each might take their proper share of the discipline and necessary business of the Church . . . but there being of later years a pretty great declension in the attendance of the women Friends, it became our concern, in the year 1749, to recommend to the several Monthly Meetings to stir up the women Friends, to the continuance and support of such their antient and commendable practice, which had some good effect for a time, but is since dwindled, and in some Monthly Meetings not in practice."

We have also Two-Weeks Meetings composed of the members of all the six Monthly Meetings in London, the men and the women meeting separately. At the men's, certificates in order for marriage are signed, and at both the proposals by the parties concerned of their intention of marriage are received, and their clearness, &c., inquired into, as had before been done at the respective Monthly Meeting or meetings to which they belonged. There is likewise a collection made in each Two-Weeks Women's Meeting for the relief of such poor women as that Women's Meeting take under their care, and to whom is paid for the same service what the men collect in their Quarterly Meeting.

There is also a small Women's Meeting once in four weeks, heretofore held in Aldersgate Street, and then known by the name of Sarah Sawyer's Meeting, but since held at the chamber in Gracechurch Street, and now better known by the name of the Box Meeting, which likewise take care of their poor.

The particular situations of the several Monthly which make up the Quarterly Meeting are briefly as follow :—

"Southwark Monthly Meeting say, They have no separate

Monthly Meeting of women, nor ever had that they can find. But their women Friends sit with their men in their Monthly Meeting, and are jointly concerned in carrying on the business thereof.

"Ratcliff say, They have held a Women's Meeting time out of mind, and so continue to do, to visit and take care of the poor.

"Gracechurch Street say, That the antient Practice of that meeting was for grave and solid women to attend the service of their Monthly Meetings with their brethren, which continued many years, but latterly declined. That, however, from this meeting's advice on that head, in 1749, divers of their women Friends were prevailed on to come and attend that service, but by degrees dwindled, and is not now practised.

"Westminster say, That with respect to Women's Meetings for Discipline, they are not in the practise of it.

"Devonshire House say, They have a Women's Monthly Meeting which has been subsisting from the 9th month, 1753. The establishing whereof they ground upon the consideration of several minutes of the Yearly Meeting wherein the setting or keeping up of Women's Meetings are recommended, and the service they apprehend would attend it.

"Peel, have established a Women's Monthly Meeting, as appears by their minute of the 27th of 3rd mo., 1754.

> "Signed in, by order, on behalf of our Quarterly Meeting held by adjournment at Gracechurch Street, the 5th of 5th mo., 1755, by
> "BENJAMIN BOURNE, *Clerk.*"

Similar reports to this came up from other parts of the country, and the Yearly Meeting is found at this time earnest in its desire and advice for Women's Monthly Meetings to be established, which, so far as London was concerned, then took place, and a joint meeting for worship, of men and women Friends, came to be held previously, as is now the case. This was also arranged for on the Quarterly Meetings. Then, after some previous hesitation, the last link in the system became supplied when the Women's Yearly Meeting was settled, now about a century since. It had been wished for and was the subject of proposal by the Women's Quarterly Meetings some eight or nine years before the Men's Meeting finally consented to it.

Women's Yearly Meeting at Devonshire House:
from *The Illustrated London News*, June 1843 [LSF].
For other illustrations of Devonshire House,
see p.xii, and chapter X.

Jordans: etching by Schnebbelie of a drawing by H. de Cort, 1798, published by C.J. Smith, London, 1835 [LSF]

CHAPTER XXIII.

JORDANS MEETING.

It has been remarked, in the course of this work, how little attachment Friends as a body have shown to the outward relics of a former time, even taking care, as in some instances, to destroy anything which a too reverential regard for the past might invest with distinction. In like manner the Society observing no times or seasons as of any value in themselves; commemorating no occasions as special festivals; keeping no jubilees or centenary or bicentenary celebrations, have shown themselves content with the regular unvaried periodic round of monthly and quarterly gatherings, culminating to the general annual one in London at Whitsuntide.

There is, however, one occasion of periodical recurrence, when the surrounding circumstances impart to it somewhat of the character of a memorial festival.

Once a year it has been the practice now for some length of time past to hold a meeting at Jordans.

Here, as is so well known, are the graves of several of the Pennington family, that of Thomas Ellwood, also William Penn, both his wives, and some of his children. Hither, with that attraction which ever leads us toward the spot where the departed great are known to rest, pilgrimages have often been made, especially as in this rural ground the turf has been permitted to " heave in many a mouldering heap " over our great forefathers' dust, instead of merging the surface into one level uniformity according to the practice of our London grounds, where Burrough, Howgill, Whitehead and Fox were laid.

Other circumstances combine to render the occasion one of interest. It occurs in the early summer when the leaf is in its prime, and the toil and worry during the Whitsuntide assembly that has just passed prepare the eye to enjoy the green of the country, and appreciate the soft rural beauty of the Buckinghamshire lanes. There is all the exhilaration of a day's holiday,—the early start, the run down to Uxbridge on the Great Western, the ride some eight miles west from there in a hired conveyance, or, perchance, the slower yet pleasant tramp on foot.

The meeting premises of Jordans are beyond the limits of the London and Middlesex Quarterly Meeting boundary, and belonged, until the last few years, to Leighton and Upperside Monthly Meeting. They have for an extended period been closed as a meeting for worship, and not until a comparatively recent date has any use been made of them. But some fifteen years or so ago the Quarterly Meeting arranged to hold one of its Monthly Meetings there, and selected that of the Sixth Month as a time appropriate for a gathering in so rural a spot, and likely to attract the company of travelling ministers that had been up in London during the Yearly Meeting. Out of these arrangements has become developed that which is now looked forward to as an annual festival; and, although the Quarterly Meeting has itself been since changed, the altered meeting, so far from making any difference in the assembly at Jordans, has agreed for its yearly continuance.

Should the day be fine, the visitor cannot fail to enjoy the walk or drive through the Buckinghamshire lanes, by which the retired spot is alone to be reached; he will feel a thrill of classic interest as he passes the Grove at Chalfont St. Peters, once the residence of the Penningtons, and made so familiar to the readers of Thomas Ellwood's graphic story; he will pause and perchance enter the humble dwelling in Chalfont St. Giles, inseparably associated with the illustrious Milton as his rural retreat when the Great Plague made London dangerous; and as he nears the shady dingle where the Penns and the Penningtons met to worship and now lie at rest, he will find scenes of the present day strangely intermingled with his reveries of the past.

Various roads converge near that seemingly retired spot, and each one is alive with vehicles, all very different, yet evidently bent towards one object; there is the ancient one-horse chay, the large modern waggonette, horsemen turn in their saddles to exchange greetings, hired conveyances, carriages with post-horses, and nice private equipages, all intermingle to form a medley throng; some of which have come from twenty to thirty or more miles of dusty travel "to join the rendezvous."

Look into the long stable at the back of the meeting-house, there's not a vacant place in that close-set row of steaming horses; the dingle at the back is crowded with all sorts of traps, but more continually arrive, yet no need to fear for want of accommodation. There are farm-houses near (though not seen), and their barns are set open for the day; and, come who will, all horses seem, in some way or other, to be cared for.

What greetings under the trees, how pleasant the stroll in the neatly-kept graveyard, how smilingly the living stand around and above the dead!—there seems an absence both of levity and gloom—the flowers, the trees, and the sweet scented summer air are grateful, and the memories of the departed bring the line of the old poet to remembrance, how " the actions of the just smell sweet and blossom in the dust."

Instinctively, at about eleven, there is a drawing towards the open doors of the meeting-house, and, without strike of clock or bell, there is little want of punctuality in all becoming seated, though it often taxes the accommodation to the utmost to find room, not only for the Friends but the neighbours, who yet like to come to this gathering. The meeting-house (itself a fair-sized apartment) is soon filled; then the women's room upstairs is thrown in by putting down the shutters; then the parlour of the cottage, by taking down some framing, and soon (often to overflowing at the doors) all parts are full.

Excellent service now generally follows from our gifted ministers present, or some one or more from America or elsewhere, when the reverential attention of the strangers is very observable, and few who have attended on these occasions but can own to deep impressions received in listening to sermons at these " sepulchres of the fathers."

A meeting for business succeeds that for worship; at the close of which, a curious transformation takes place, and refreshment of all kinds for the body succeeds the instruction for the soul. Nothing can surpass the simple hospitality now shown; the impromptu tables in the meeting-house are well filled with cold viands, and, should the day be fine, are set in the open air; all friends are made welcome, the pedestrian is asked freely to share the substantial things the carriages have brought; and when the visitors have done, the numerous fly-men, coachmen, and servants sit down and also make their ample meal. The Friends of the Quarterly Meeting are particularly attentive and kind to others not of their meeting; it is only to be feared that as these gatherings grow year by year more popular, the numbers attending may overpass those limits which even the kindest attentions will be too far trespassed on to reach.

The long summer day leaves ample time after the repast is over to fill up the interval between its close and the start for the return, by a walk in the beautiful woodlands around, wherein the rare orchis or fern is sure to reward the intelligent seeker, and the general features both of scenery and society inspirit even the casual stroller. Some go off on longer walks, extending even as far as Hunger Hill, once the residence of Thomas Ellwood. By and by all again draw to the little estate and take a last look at the scene, over a quiet cup of tea. They stroll up and down the burial-ground, skirted on two sides by the road, and screened from it by lines of trees. At one end is the walled-in tomb of the Vandewalls, lying apart as wishing to have some more permanent memorial than a mound; then lower down, about central and opposite the red-brick meeting-house, occur row by row the honoured graves now lately distinguished by small stones, that give information as to name and date of the dead ones below, at the expense of some intrusion upon the past so modern an addition could not but involve. Yet they do not seem to check the enthusiasm and save the trouble of asking questions. None seem to cherish the spot more than the Americans; every blade of grass is searched over to find some distinctive memorial from William Penn's grave. A cowslip root, if found, is an especial treasure, and some will be content to put in their pocket-books leaves from the hawthorn hedge that blossoms hard by, welcoming even these as memorials of the place.

Gradually all disperse, and the Londoner, as he turns again towards the Great Babel, feels that, in going beyond his borders as an uninvited yet gladly-welcomed guest, he has had both body and soul refreshed by this visit to the annual assembly around the graves at Jordans.

In a small work published by Cash & Co.,[*] such full information is given of this meeting-house and all its circumstances, as renders the entering upon further particulars here unnecessary, especially as the meeting-house is not within the limits of the London meetings.

---

[*] This publication has not been traced in Friends House or the British Library. See Bibliography p.417 for other works.

APPENDIX TO CHAPTER XXIII. 359

APPENDIX.

1867.—Note made after a visit to Jordans.

When at Jordans, Fifth-day, Sixth Month 6th, there was a gentlemanly farmer-looking sort of person waiting to see Jos. Glaisyer, in order to show him certain extracts which he had made from the Registers of the parish of Chalfont St. Giles. In these Registers it appears are recorded the names of those interred in Jordans.

On looking down this list I observed the frequent recurrence of the names of the Mildreds and Mastermans, so that these families came I presume from this district. The Lanes, Butterfields, Pennys, also occur, and the Zacharys of Beaconsfield. (1786, first Masterman buried.) He informed me that the first name on their Register was the baptism, in 1584, of a daughter of the Russells, of which family Jordans was purchased, and some of them it is believed became Friends. Under date 1770, is recorded on the Register the burial of Joseph Rule, with the addition "a noted Quaker." Of this man there is a tradition of his having in life always dressed himself entirely in white, using also a white walking-stick, and that his funeral (though it took place in the month of June) was marked by a fall of snow, which most unusual circumstance was regarded by his friends as singularly appropriate to one who had been known when living as the white Quaker.—W. B.

The party before mentioned informed me that the land at Jordans was bought of the Russell family in 1671, by T. Ellwood and others.

In that same year, 1671, was the first burial. The meeting-house was commenced in 1688, and completed in the same year, as the first assembly there was held 7th August, 1688.

The meetings had formerly been held at The Grove, where John Pennington lived, which was thought suitable on account of its seclusion. The house of the Penningtons was old, dating as far back as 1580, and was one of the places where Queen Elizabeth is said to have been entertained.

Of the county of Bucks, it was observed that it is distinguished by its number of small freeholds held by yeomen, an evidence of which is seen in the cherry orchards attached to their homesteads. Such being a tree which only a proprietor cares to plant. (4,000 of these yeomen once rode up to support Hampden as their county member.) The original Friends in Bucks were of this yeomen class, and many of the families round Jordans were once connected with the Society. The memory of the body is still so respected, that every public meeting is well attended. Rebecca Collins had recently an overflowing one.

The first residence of William Penn is still standing, at present time occupied by a surgeon of the name of Endersen, and known as the Basing House, at Rickmansworth.

CHAPTER XXIV.

SCHOOLS &c. IN THE QUARTERLY MEETING.

In accordance with the frequently reiterated advices of George Fox, and the general care of the Society in all matters pertaining to the moral and religious well-being of its members —schools for the young early became a conspicuous feature in the arrangements of Friends.

In 1667 G. F. recommended the setting up of two boarding-schools near London, where youth might be instructed " in all things civil and useful in creation." One of these (for boys) was established at Waltham under the care of Christopher Taylor, formerly a clergyman in the Established Church, and the other (for girls) was at Shacklewell, under the care of the Widow Stott.

We have shown, in previous chapters, how from the first schools were carried on *in* nearly all the London *meeting-houses*. It will not be necessary to repeat these details, but merely recall attention to the great care taken to bring the means of education within the reach of all the members of the Society, in its most populous days. Amongst the schoolmasters were many who took a prominent part in Church affairs, *e.g.* George Keith, who kept a school at Theobalds; Richard Richardson, afterwards recording-clerk; Richard Claridge, of Tottenham and Barking; John Field, of the Bull and Mouth, and Richard Scoryer, who kept a celebrated boarding-shcool at Wandsworth, and also trained teachers, and in whose establishment Stephen Crisp was for a time an usher.*

In 1701 the Quarterly Meeting reported that there were schools in most parts of the city. Ten years after, in 1711, we find the schoolmasters asking the Yearly Meeting to be allowed to hold an educational meeting by themselves one day during

---

* In a document published in 1697, Richard Scoryer " offers freely to inform and direct schoolmasters in his method of teaching children, and take some pains in completing them in writing and arithmetic; they providing for themselves meat, drink, and lodging."

the time, which was acceded to, so that they must then have been a numerous and influential body.

Passing on to 1758 we find the Monthly Meeting reporting to the Quarterly their state as regards schools, from which we learn that in that year Westminster, Longford, and Barking had none. Devonshire House had two, viz. John Wall's day-school at the meeting-house for boys, not confined to Friends' children ; and Ann Barclay's boarding-school for girls.

Gracechurch Street reports one school taught by a Friend, not confined to Friends' children. Horslydown reports one boarding-school for Friends' sons, and four day-schools not confined to Friends' children.

Tottenham reports a school for boys, where they are taught reading, writing, English grammar, Latin, French, Greek, merchants' accounts, mensuration, trigonometry, geography, and other useful branches of mathematics, and frequent opportunities are taken to inculcate just sentiments of religion and virtue. This Monthly Meeting also reports a school for girls, where they are taught needle-work, reading, writing, and arithmetic, English grammar, Latin and French if required.

Ratcliff reports one boarding-school, and two day-schools, none of them confined to Friends' children.

Again, turning to the close of the seventeenth century we find at that time the establishment of the oldest endowed school of the Society of Friends, which was commenced at Clerkenwell, thence transferred to Islington Road, and is now conducted at Croydon.

Clerkenwell Workhouse.

We may open our narrative of the Clerkenwell School and Workhouse by stating that one of the London Friends, at the close of the seventeenth century, was John Bellers, who though not numbered amongst either the ministers or the controversialists, was nevertheless a remarkable man, and largely influenced the proceedings of the Society in his own day, the results of whose labours—though in a very modified and improved form—are still visible in our schools at Croydon.

John Bellers was evidently one of those who never see a wrong without wishing to smite it down—whose minds are ever engaged in shaping schemes for the regeneration of humanity; schemes, alas! too often incapable of being realised. He wrote many works in which he propounded his plans for leaguing all Europe in a peaceful confederation, for uniting all the Christian sects in a holy alliance against evil, upon the basis of those truths in which all unite, for reconciling political parties, for restraining bribery and corruption at elections, for abolishing needless oaths in civil affairs, for improving the science of medicine, for establishing hospitals for specific diseases, for facilitating *post mortem* examinations, for establishing prizes for curing diseases hitherto considered incurable, for encouraging science by public laboratories, for reclaiming the children of the streets whom he calls "the Black Guard," for clearing the town of "night walkers," and for the relief of the poor and the education of their offspring. He was a man in advance of his cotemporaries, and some of his ideas have the utopian tinge common to most fervent philanthropists. A few of his schemes have been carried out, and even far surpassed; others are still things to be desired. His ideas with regard to the poor and their offspring, after being apparently vainly pressed upon the attention of the legislature, were warmly espoused by the religious Society of which he was a member.

John Bellers threw his views on the care and education of the poor before his friends, in pamphlet form, in 1697.* This address was approvingly recommended to the Quarterly Meetings by the Meeting for Sufferings and Morning Meeting. Much interest was excited, and in 1701 the London Quarterly Meeting took action, and desired the Monthly Meetings to report what poor were in a condition to be placed in a co-operative home or workhouse such as was proposed.

Friends met and reported that there were in London 184 aged poor capable of some sort of work, and 47 children also fit for employment. The poor had already become burdensome, and doubtless J. B.'s plans were hailed with satisfaction as a probable means of relief. A subscription was at once ordered, in the full belief that "it may be of Service & benefitt to the Succeeding Generations, and a Testimony of our care & Simpathy of and wth our Poor Brethren and Sisters and their offspring according to the Admonition of the

---

* John Bellers died in 1725, aged 71, and was buried at Bunhill Fields. For complete list of his works see J. Smith's Catalogue.

Apostle, That every man as he purposeth in his heart soe let him give," &c.*

The sum of £1,888 was raised in less than a year, and a building formerly used for similar purposes was taken on lease in the Second Month, 1702. The site of our Clerkenwell Workhouse is now occupied by the north-western portion of the House of Detention. It was a building forming three sides of a square, enclosing a courtyard with the prison wall for its remaining boundary. The house contained 46 rooms, the largest measuring 20 feet by 85, being ultimately used as the boys' dormitory.

The institution was placed under the care of a committee of thirty Friends (five from each Monthly Meeting), whose minutes are still extant from their commencement in 1701. On meeting at the workhouse in 1702 they adopted rules to

---

* The following was the bill of fare adopted at the first settlement of the house in 1702:—

	Breakfast.	Dinner.	Supper.
"I.	Bread, 4 oz. Butter 1 oz. Beer, sufficient.	Bread, 5 oz. Mutton, 6 oz. and Pottage.	Bread, 4 oz. Cheese, 2 oz. or Butter, 1 oz.
II.	The Mutton Pottage well thickened with Oatmeal and Bread, 4 oz.	Half a pint of Pease Pudding, or Pease Soup. Bread, 3 oz. Butter, 1½ oz.	(as on I.)
III.	(as on I.)	Bread, 5 oz. Beef, 6 oz. and Pottage.	(as on I.)
IV.	(as on I.)	Bread, 5 oz. Furmety sufficient.	(as on I.)
V.	(as on I.)	(as on III.)	(as on I.)
VI.	(as on I.)	Pudding Pies, 9 oz.	(as on I.)
VII.	Bread, 4 oz. Water Gruel.	Tripe.	(as on I.)

Brot. in by Richard Hawkins."

Various changes were subsequently made in the above. As regards the furmety we find that before 1716 it was 12 qrts. of milk, 8 qrts. of wheat, and 1 lb. of sugar; it was then altered to 15 qrts. of milk, 12 qrts. of wheat, and 2¼ lbs. of sugar.

govern their proceedings in which they agreed to fine each member 12d. for non-attendance within half an hour of the time fixed for meeting. They were to meet monthly, each presiding as chairman in alphabetical order. They agreed that two persons should not speak at once, that frequent speaking on one subject be avoided, unless new matter be advanced; that the chairman should censure all personal reflections, and that the offending party should submit; that debate should be decided by the majority, and that if there should be an "equality of hands" when the chairman put the question, he should decide it as he pleased. A sub-committee of six Friends (one from each Monthly Meeting) were set apart to meet weekly, inspect everything, and redress grievances.

In the building above referred to, some thirty poor persons were at once placed. Some boys were introduced in 1704. The Quarterly Meeting directed that a meeting for worship should be held at the workhouse on Fifth-day mornings at 9 o'clock, and that "some chapters out of the old and new Testament should be read every morning and evening."

All its inmates were to be well employed, chiefly in spinning wool, winding silk, or spinning cotton. Some old people who were shoemakers, &c. worked at their trades. A quantity of old junk was bought to be picked into oakum, and it seems that picking oakum was occasionally given instead of other work to refractory individuals.

The children admitted were not to be under seven years of age; and, to keep order amongst them, one or two of the ancient people were to sleep in each bedroom.

As there was in connection with the workhouse some convenience for stabling and grazing Friends' horses, the committee requested the Six-Weeks Meeting to pay no horse-bills that might be incurred elsewhere. This was agreed to, and for many years the horses of Public Friends visiting London were here taken care of.

In 1706 a committee appointed to visit the workhouse reported that the ancient people and children were well looked after and meetings well kept up. The boys were kept to work, also taught reading and writing. Each have had Robert Barclay's Catechism given them for their instruction. They earn as much as can be expected, and one hopeful lad has been apprenticed. The committee proceed to state that there are thirty aged men and women in the house, who would cost £300 a year for as good a maintenance outside; "for besides all the common maintenance and other conveniences of the house, they are allowed attendance and nursing and other comfortable things when sick." The Monthly Meetings only pay £130 for these, and the Six-Weeks Meeting saves much in rent and coals. The average earnings of the old people is about a farthing and a half per day. False reports are flying about that they work beyond their strength. The committee suggest to alter the name to Hospital for Aged People, and Workhouse for Boys and Girls. They consider it would be more reputable for the old people to do no work but wait on each other. We may note, in passing, that in the year just mentioned, "deare Mary Elson," of the Peel, left the old people twelve pence each as a token of her love.

So far work had been the chief feature of the establishment, and a very little education had been superadded. In 1707 we find a visiting committee proposing to add a boarding-school at £10 or £12 per annum, "for the education of youth in all manner of useful learning," and also the reception of boarders at five shillings per week, "the said scholars and boarders to eat and drink separate from the poor. The Committee also suggest to call the place a "Colledge, which comprehends both hospitall, workhouse and school." These suggestions were only partially put in practice. The boarders or pensioners were admitted, and were a source of much trouble. The steward often had to complain of these pensioners—persons who paid a small sum for their board, and were admitted to the workhouse in order to eke out their private means.

A code of rules are entered on the committee's minute-book in 1709, from which we learn that the old Friends are to attend at all the times set apart for worshipping God, to cultivate love towards and wait upon each other, to sit in a reverent orderly manner at table, not to carry away or dispose of the food, &c., not to be contentious, not to go out without leave, to be in bed by 8 o'clock in winter and 9 in summer, to have no fire or candle in the bedrooms without leave. The boys are ordered after dressing to read as many chapters in the Bible as the steward shall think fit, to be called together as often as may be to worship God, to rise at 5 o'clock in summer and 6 o'clock in winter, and work one hour, and then, with clean hands and faces and combed hair, come to breakfast. They are to work the full time ordered by the steward, and not waste wool, and keep order in the workroom and at meals. Each boy's hat, knife, spoon and comb, is to be marked with his name, and laid by after use in an appointed place. "They shall not break the windows or walls about the house, nor go out of the gates without leave of the steward, nor speak untruths or naughty words, but avoid all idle discourse and use plainness of speech to all as well as to other." Any boy enticing another into a fault is to have double punishment, but a boy who has been led into a fault is to find favour if he confesses it before it is found out.

Passing on to 1710 we find in the building thirty-four old people, twenty-four boys and two girls. Report is also made that five old persons have been buried and five boys apprenticed during the year. Meetings are stated to be held on First-day and on Fifth-day, also that the Third-day meeting at Peel is attended, "soe that they have the benefitt of 4 meetings in the week, besides seasons set apart to wait upon and worship God in silence."

In 1712 it was proposed to establish a manufactory for the regular employment of the poor at the workhouse. This proposal was not agreed to, firstly, because the aged people are too infirm for regular employment; secondly, because the children are so quickly removed away to service. The place (it is agreed) must rather be accounted a hospital or nursery than a workhouse.

The committee at this time state, "We cannot but look upon the coming of this house into Friends' hands as providential, whether we regard the salubrity of its situation or the many conveniences for the comfortable entertainment of the aged and the good education of the children."

The Quarterly Meeting now ordered a fresh subscription in aid of the workhouse to be raised, and the stock to be kept entire, the interest only being used. It also guaranteed to pay the loss that might accrue from the Monthly Meetings not sending in a sufficient number of occupants at the reduced scale of three shillings for the aged, and one shilling for the boys and girls.

Much trouble was given by the rumours dispersed abroad as to the diet, &c., at this establishment.* In 1763 the "Bill

---

* The steward was perpetually having to combat some rumour or other. At one time he has to clear himself from the charge of having given them one herring each for their dinners, at another to prove that an invalid

of Faire" was read at the Quarterly Meeting and approved of, and Friends were directed to spread no more reflections on the subject As a further proof of comfort and plenty a paper was brought in, signed by the ancient Friends there, who warmly expressed their gratitude.

In 1714, a loss of £26 on the previous year had to be made up by the Quarterly Meeting. Bread is reported to have been dear, costing eightpence per head per week. "The number of girls is increasing, and they cost more than boys, and, besides, it seems necessary to have a woman to teach them sewing and prevent their mixing with the boys, which is found very inconvenient." The profit on yarn and mops during the past year has been £138. "There are now very good mopps made, and friends may have them cheaper than elsewhere." At this time there were twenty-two ancient Friends, twenty-eight boys, and sixteen girls.

In 1715 we find the Workhouse Committee wanting to clothe the children. A £100 legacy left for that purpose and £20 received from the Monthly Meetings is all spent. The boys require clothing, excepting coats, which last two years; and the girls' clothes will do for another year with some small additions. The committee press for some aid in giving the children clean and decent clothing, as it adds to their comfort and refreshment, and the reputation of the house. The Monthly Meetings were now ordered to contribute something for this special object, and legacies and donations were also received for it from time to time.

The Workhouse Committee also press for the appointment of a schoolmistress, that the girls may be as well instructed as the boys now are. They state that the girls cost more and earn less than boys, and that spinning does not suit their inclination or strength. The committee think that 2s. per week should be paid with each girl.

In the following year (1716) we find the Workhouse Stock

---

boy named William Brady had been properly cared for. With reference to this latter charge he states that he had roast beef, chocolate, &c., for his diet; conserve of roses in red-cow's milk for a medicine in the morning, and "the last thing when he went to bed at night he had a bit of bread toasted with a coffee-dish of claret burnt, with cinnamon and double refined sugar." These are but samples out of many recorded. By the way, the stewards, schoolmasters and other officials did not seem to stay long in the place. The changes were frequent.

has increased, on account of the extraordinary price and quick sale of yarn and the moderate price of bread, &c. The girls now have a mistress, and are learning sewing. Women Friends are exhorted to send in plenty of work, and allow reasonable prices for doing the same. The committee have still to regret that "notwithstanding the plentiful provision in diet (being more than the ancient Friends can dispense with), the large fires in winter, the opportunities of meetings and retirements, and no work required of them, only to be helpful to one another in the time of weakness, and to mend the children's linen . . complaints are still spread abroad tending to the discredit of the house and its conveniences." These complaints of false reports and rumours are very frequent in the statements sent in to the Quarterly Meeting by the committee.*

It was soon found that the sewing and knitting was much less profitable than the spinning had been—does not in fact pay the mistress's salary. Complaint is also made that the boys are not so profitable as they might be, because they are sent very small, and taken away by the Monthly Meetings and apprenticed far too soon, to save the cost of maintaining them at the workhouse.

In 1717 a new lease of the premises for 99 years was obtained from the Bench of Justices on payment of £100 fine.

In 1718 an order had to be issued to the ancient Friends that no tobacco was to be smoked in the lodging-rooms.

Passing on to 1725 we find false insinuations still complained of, also the notions of some that the children should do no work. The elderly people, it is stated, do not work;

---

* It seems the majority of the old people were weak and infirm, unable even to assist as above desired. Some of the Monthly Meetings had indeed alleged that they could keep the able-bodied poor more cheaply outside. In 1718 the committee speak of the ancient Friends being thus incapable, and request another servant. "One servant," they add, "has left from over-work; she used to mend the children's woollen clothes, make the beds, clean the rooms, take in and give out linen, &c., comb the heads, and dress their sore hands and feet in the winter season, having many of them sores, which business alone generally takes several hours every day, as may reasonably be supposed where there are so many small children." This was in the year 1718, in which year a profit of £89 was got out of the concern, towards which the labour of these children, who are complained of in the same year as being "sent in so small," materially assisted.

they consent to the rules when they come, but afterwards are "less agreeable when they can find nothing else to dislike." They also are found to exert idle influences over the children.*

The effects of the substitution of sewing, &c. for spinning came under special notice by the committee in 1728, and the

---

* As a specimen of the characters who were found in the workhouse and whose influence over the children was not likely to be always beneficial, we may state that, on the minutes of the Six-Weeks Meeting in 1728, it is stated that "Alexander Galloway, a poor Friend, twice expelled from the workhouse for misconduct, then disowned, and subsequently relieved to prevent his starvation, is reported to have been brought to the workhouse in a coach and left there." "The coachman opening the gate, put in his box, and set him upon it, he being unable to help himself, being lame of his limbs." The Workhouse Committee appealingly ask what *are* they to do with him, but no record is made as to the counsel given by the Six-Weeks Meeting in this dilemma.

But the most troublesome inmates were the Pensioners (see p. 365). They seemed to have dined at the steward's table, and to have been in various ways on a different footing from the rest. In 1711 the steward thus complains to the committee:—

"Some who have dined at our table have several times told us we were but their servants, and maintained there to wait on them, and they paid more than the rest, saying the house got by them but it got nothing by us; also said they had as proper a right to go into the pantry, and to be in the kitchen or parlor when they pleased, as we had; and as for the provision, they told us it was none of ours, and therefore they would have what they pleased and when they pleased." The MS. then states that these expressions got known amongst the children and poor maintained at the meeting's charge.

"When my wife has been cutting out Roast or Boiled Beef for the family at noon, those who dined at our table would come with a large copper spoon, like a ladle, and stand in her way, taking the gravy out of the great dish where the meat lay, thereby dropping upon and greasing her clothes, they not having patience to stay till we dined, when they might have gravy enough, and as she had been cutting pudding into shares if there was any place in the pudding that had more plums in than the rest they would cut that piece out for themselves . . . . . And when we have had roast meat, some of our table would run their fingers into the meat while it was roasting and frequently handling the meat at table very indecently, which is offensive to decent cleanly people, and yet when strangers dined with us they could behave themselves very discreetly.

"Also, under pretence of visiting and sitting with some who dined at our table, has come in an intruding sort of people (on First-days in the evening especially), who would place themselves in the kitchen, and there sit smoking tobacco and keep our servants from the fire, and being told they might be of more service in their own families than to be here keeping our servants from the fire, then such have returned unhandsome language, implying as if they had as good toleration as we, saying we could not hinder them." Much more follows of a similar purport.

following minute was made concerning it:—"The state of the Sewing School having been divers times inspected, and now more particularly examined. The committee found that keeping a person on purpose as a schoolmistress, hath all along been attended with a considerable yearly loss . . . and inasmuch as Ann Mercy Ellwood, a young woman apprentice in the house (in the last year of her time), is become capable, with the assistance of the stewardess, to instruct the girls in common sewing-work as far as is necessary for good servant maids, and as that is what we chiefly aim at for them, so we think that the educating them in seamstry of a nicer sort, tends rather to destroy the end proposed, by begetting apprehensions in them (and probably in their parents, &c.) that they are qualified for seamstresses, governesses, mantua-makers, quilters, &c., or some business by which they may live at their own hands (as they call it), and from whence we apprehend very ill consequences to arise." Therefore thought best to dismiss the schoolmistress, but the Women's Two-Weeks Meeting to be consulted. Soon after report is made of this arrangement being carried into effect.

In 1729 the committee were evidently making the concern pay.* They had spent £720 in repairs (without coming to the Quarterly Meeting) out of leases, profits, &c. They state that "we let off a small portion for more than we pay for the whole." The numbers at this time were 15 old people, 43 boys, and 14 girls. Up to this date 155 boys and 54 girls had been apprenticed. Complaint is again made of the "encouragement some Friends have given to divers of the ancient persons, who thereby have a liberty to insinuate things which are neither true nor for the interest of the house, in order to raise Friends' pity and charity towards them, which is often ill bestowed."

---

* Somehow or other, when the concern *paid* best, complaints thickened. In this year, 1729, the place is spoken of as a house full of dissatisfied persons, and the *running away* of the children is spoken of as frequent, and a cause of great inconvenience. This practice was not confined to the year now mentioned; two years before the following minute was passed by the committee:—

"1727. The committee having frequent complaints of the great inconveniency of the children's running away from this house, and thereby taking the opportunity of telling divers notorious lies to the prejudice of the same and scandalising the government thereof, resolves it shall be a standing rule, not to allow the steward to receive again any such child, till the Monthly Meeting to which the child belongs requests it."

In 1732 the gain for three years is stated to have been £197, which, with legacies, &c., has raised the stock of the house to £4,083. A committee, appointed specially to inspect the workhouse, reported that they examined the bill of fare, and saw the respective allowances cut and weighed. They deprecate the "groundless objections" current, and allude to a recent increase of the allowance of bread from 12 oz. to 14 or 15 oz.

The Committee of Inspection go on to state that the rule is for the children to get up at 6 in winter and 5 in summer, which order was made before we had any settled master in the house, only as one came in the evening after his own school was done to teach the children after their day's work from 6 a.m. to 6 p.m. They now proposed that the children should rise at 5 all the year round, finish work by dinner time, and have the rest of the day for school and play till they go to bed at 7.

The Quarterly Meeting declined to order children of seven or eight to be turned out of bed in the depth of winter at 5 o'clock to make mops.

There is reason to believe that, however careful the superior meetings might be to have the establishment well managed, disorders and abuses of authority did creep in. In 1735 some cases of hardship and severity were complained of by Horslydown, for which on investigation some foundation was found. The ignorance and imprudent management of some of the servants is alleged in extenuation.

In the year just mentioned it is stated, as worthy of note, that only thirteen children had died in twenty-five years.

The gain for four years ending 1735 is stated to be £213, but a time of loss now supervenes. Up to 1740 the loss is stated to be £135, but in 1741 the loss for one year is £227. This is accounted for by the extraordinary prices of food, the diminution of the yarn-trade, and the fact of the steward not having sufficient balances left in his hands to push the trade with vigour.

In 1746 a new subscription was agreed upon, and in this year the first printed report on the school was issued. It is entitled "An account of the Rise, Progress and present state of the School and Workhouse maintained by the people called Quakers, at Clerkenwell, London." In this pamphlet we are informed that the youth work in the mornings, and learn reading, writing, and accounts in the afternoon. That the girls learn needlework, also kitchen-work, housewifery, &c. The officers are enumerated as steward, stewardess, schoolmaster, schoolmistress, workmaster, and servants. A surgeon and physician attend gratis. The family are about 90 in number, 203 ancient people and 503 boys and girls having been received up to this time. The clothing is found very expensive; its cost was defrayed for some years by the late Anthony Crosfield.* An augmentation of stock is urged, also a considerable increase in the apprenticeship premiums, that better places may be found. Gratuities on expiration of time are also pleaded for.

Simeon Warner, Jacob Hagen, Daniel Vandewall, and John Fothergill took a conspicuous part in the effort now made to assist the institution. The subscription was headed by John Haward £100, John Warner £50, Simeon Warner £50, and Benjamin Horne £50.

In 1747 the committee complain of country children being introduced into the house through London meetings. They state that it is three years since there was a general clothing. The Quarterly Meeting, in reply, orders that the country children shall pay eighteenpence weekly, and that all the children be clothed forthwith, agreeing to find ways and means.

In the following year, notwithstanding the stock was now over £7,000, and the trade gain for the year was £29 in excess of that of the previous year, a debt for the year of £78 is reported. At the suggestion of a visiting committee (Jacob Post and others), the price for *all* children was raised to eighteenpence weekly. Still there was an annual deficit. In 1749 the accumulation of losses which it had been agreed to consider as a debt due from the Quarterly Meeting had reached £685. Unfortunately the Quarterly Meeting and its recently reconstituted cash committee, the Six-Weeks Meeting, were deeply in debt, and appealing to Friends for money, and therefore no further collection for the school and workhouse was at present feasible. More diligence and industry on the one hand, and stricter economy on the other, were meanwhile strongly recommended, and doubtless enforced. In 1750 the annual inspection committee report that the profits in trade have been reduced by the children not being

* It seems that the executors of the late Anthony Crosfield clothed the inmates at a cost of £219 16s. 1d. in 1738; and again at a cost of £211 10s. 9d. in 1752. On both these occasions leather-breeches at 3s. 9d., men's wigs at 10s. 6d., boy's wigs at 8s., figure conspicuously.

kept to work the stated hours, so that their earnings are one-third less in proportion to their numbers than formerly. Negligence in the officials is at this time complained of, especially as regards remissness in promoting sales. Through indolence 528 lbs. of yarn have been lost, as it is supposed, by omitting to make entries when sending out. Then again the inspectors state there is a remissness as regards frugality; the bill of fare is not kept to, and too many persons are entertained at the expense of the house. After commenting on irregularities of discipline, want of care as regards the morals of the children, and conformity to rules on the part of the old, also the neglect to keep the premises properly clean, or the children's clothes properly repaired, the visitors advise that the ancient people should be more fully employed either in shoemaking, tailoring, or carding wool, or in waiting on the sick, or mending linen.

The Workhouse Committee, in reply, stated that things were being improved. The Quarterly Meeting advised the Women's Two-Weeks Meeting to make appointments to visit the schools, &c.

In 1750 Friends' families are encouraged to buy mops at the workhouse, that trade being found profitable. The Quarterly Meeting now agreed to the employment of the ancient Friends. The charge for these was raised to 3s. per week, and that for children lowered to 1s. in order to encourage a larger proportion of the latter, they being found more profitable. Monthly Meetings are also directed to pay 40s. admission fee with each child, to defray in part the cost of its clothing whilst at school.

Passing on to 1754 we find that in consequence of taking an adjacent plot of ground, known as "The Mulberry Garden," some improvements in the premises had been effected. Some new windows were opened, and a drain, which washed the hog-yard of a neighbouring distiller, came through the Mulberry Garden, and ran *open* through the cellars the whole length of the house, was now turned in a different direction, having been previously found "a great and continued nuisance." In the same year the children are reported to have been new clothed, and their bedsteads, described in the Quarterly Meeting minutes as "old and full of vermin,"* were taken to

---

* Several years before one Christopher Fox had contracted with the institution to keep the house clear of the insects referred to, for 30s. per annum. It is to be supposed that his nostrums were not successful.

pieces and furnished with new sheets, blankets, and coverlids.

A fresh subscription was set on foot in the year just mentioned to pay off money borrowed, and add to a sum of £500 left by Samuel Brewster, and £100 left by Cornelius Taylor, as funds for increasing apprentice fees and rewards at expiration of terms of servitude.* This subscription was brought in in 1760, when it amounted to £1,085. Of this £400 was applied to payment of debts, and the remainder added to the Apprentice Fund.

To recount all the details of the financial experience of this institution would only be tedious. Reiterated losses raised the Quarterly Meeting debt to £1,127 by 1759, on which the workhouse received 3 per cent. Then we soon find the gains of some profitable years which were placed to the Quarterly Meeting's credit reducing the debt to £600 in 1771. But subsequent losses raised it again to £1,250 in 1785, when it was paid off by means of Thomas Talwin's legacy for that purpose to which reference has been made in our narrative of the Six-Weeks Meeting.

About this time the city authorities found they had occasion for the building at Clerkenwell, and bought the remainder of its lease from Friends. A new piece of ground of $1\frac{3}{4}$ acres was taken, situated between St. John's Road and the Goswell Road; it formed part of an estate belonging to the Brewers' Company, and the interest of their tenant being purchased for £252, a building lease was arranged for direct from the company for a term of 150 years, at a rental of £16 per annum for the first 85 years (being the extent of the tenant's term), and £50 for the remainder of the 150 years. On the land thus taken somewhat large premises were erected and the school transferred thither. William Allen and some other Friends strongly urged the removal of the school to some premises then vacant at Wandsworth, but the general feeling was in favour of retaining the institution as near as possible to its former site.†

---

* Devereux Bowley left £1,500 for the same purpose a few years afterwards.

† A few minutes of committee illustrating the history of the School and Workhouse at Clerkenwell may be inserted here—

1728. Richard Crafton reports that John Warner has left the three volumes of Foxe's Martyrology to every Dissenting Charity School about London; with the following intention, "And it is my mind and inten-

Plaistow Home for Ancient Friends.

It was only the children who were at first removed to the new premises in Islington Road. The experiment of maintaining the ancient Friends separately was tried for a time.

A large house and garden near Plaistow Meeting-house was purchased for £560, and another £200 spent under John Bevans' superintendence in altering the place to suit the requirements of Friends. Here, till 1792, the old Friends were located. We know very little of this institution, merely meeting with casual allusion to it. For instance, Wilson Birkbeck presents it with a pump, and a turret clock is repaired by subscription. The building was insured for £800.

After four or five years' occupancy it was thought cheaper again to reunite the families. An elaborate calculation, occupying several pages in the Six-Weeks Meeting books, shows that £172 17s. 7d. could be saved annually by having the old Friends again located with the children. Accordingly, the house at Plaistow was sold, and fresh accommodation was added to the Islington premises for the accommodation of twenty-four ancient men and women, to which they were transferred in 1792.

Islington Road School.

This building was erected on the plot of land anciently known as Hermitage Field, whose situation has already been

---

tion that some small time be spent every day before the school breaks up in causing one of the scholars to read a portion thereof."

1729. Holidays allowed, stated to be a week each at Christmas, Easter and Whitsuntide; only to go home three times between Christmas and Whitsuntide, and then only for one day, not a First-day.

1734. The old people to have half a pint of ale every evening to encourage them to be serviceable.

1736. No child to be corrected but in sight of the rest and at the same time the crime declared. Such corrections not to be frequent without consent of steward.

1761. For the future the ale to be regularly dispensed to old Friends, four days in the week, ½ pint at 12 o'clock and every evening the same. (This does not refer to the table beer at meals.)

1766. Committee directs that no servant of the institution be treated with a wedding dinner in future without consent of this committee.

1785. Some sail-cloth and tarred thread are to be bought, and the ancient men set to work at sack-making.

described, at a cost of £5,500, exclusive of the accommodation erected for ancient Friends in 1792. The architect was John Bevans. Malcolm, the topographer, speaking of the school, &c., in 1803, says, "The house, meeting, schools, apartments, and stairs are as white and clean as brushes and industry will make them. The ceilings are remarkably high and the windows large; consequently, the rooms are perfectly dry and well aired. The outside has the appearance of a villa, surrounded as it is by pleasure grounds, gardens, and trees."*

To this new building the children were removed in Twelfth Month, 1786. Almost all furniture, bedsteads, bedding, &c. of the old building was discarded, and an evident endeavour made to turn over a new leaf in many respects. Education and work changed places as regards priority of importance, though spinning flax continued for some time longer to be kept up in the afternoons.

Of course things had not yet arrived at modern excellence; for instance, the washing accommodation provided by the committee for boys and girls was two large troughs (one on each side of a partition) 18 inches across and 4 deep, into which water was laid on from an adjacent cistern.

It will be simplest briefly now to state a few facts in chronological order connected with the Islington Road Schools.

In 1795 was instituted the weekly penny for pocket money, which has continued as one of the school arrangements to this day.

We find in 1799 some able men appointed on an educational sub-committee, who introduced many reforms, some of which may be particularised. The names of the sub-committee were Robert Howard, Edward Janson, Wilson Birkbeck, Frederick Smith, and Joseph Gurney Bevan; subsequently Sparks Moline was added.

Through the influence of these Friends a rule was made that the school hours of boys above 13 being very valuable on account of their soon having to go out into the world, should not be interrupted, except to take their turns at the washing machine.

The same Friends drew up the following plan of study, &c. for the boys:—

To rise at 6; school at 6.30; breakfast at 8; school 9

---

* He gives an engraving of the school at page 412 of his *London*.

[see opposite page 378 for engraving and correct reference]

to 12; dinner 12.30; school 2 to 5; supper 6.30; to bed at 8.

They also arranged that the mornings should be spent over spelling and grammar; the forenoon over writing and reading; and the afternoon over arithmetic, spelling and reading; certain divisions alternating with each other as regards the acquirement and repetition of lessons. On Seventh-day morning, tables and mental calculation were to occupy the time till breakfast, and after breakfast on that day there was to be spelling for penny tickets till dinner time. On Fourth-day morning the boys were to attend Peel Meeting, on Sixth-day afternoon to be occupied *in mending their stockings*, and on Seventh-day afternoon to have a half-holiday.

An arrangement was also made at this time for giving three sixpenny prizes for writing and three shilling prizes for arithmetic on the occurrence of the quarterly committee.*

In the following year these Friends above named took measures to lighten the menial work of the place in which the children were still employed, though flax-spinning seems to have now been relinquished. They had the coals kept in a place on the ground floor, instead of being in the underground cellars, and instituted the afterwards well-known school pinafore, to save their clothes whilst engaged in these matters.

In 1806 the Education Committee divided the school into three writing divisions and three arithmetic divisions, and instituted three prizes for proficiency in each class, *i.e.* eighteen quarterly prizes in all.

In 1808, after the resignation of John Withers and wife, who had served the institution for twenty years, a considerable change was effected in the administration of the building when it was agreed:—

"1st, To place the whole establishment under the care of an able, steady Friend to be styled MASTER (instead of steward as formerly)—a person capable of managing the family and taking the general instruction of the children; one who is not much under middle age, who writes a good hand, is competent to keep the accounts, and has a good idea of the business of education. Such a person, it is conceived, by availing himself of improved methods of teaching, and of the

---

* The money procured from the fines for non-attendance of the Committee was applied to the payment of these prizes. There was often a considerable sum in hand from this source.

assistance of the elder boys, would have sufficient leisure for the superintendence of the family and other matters under his charge."

"2ndly, To commit the care of provisions and clothing, the necessary attention to the aged and infirm, and a tender oversight of the children, in short, those concerns that are properly within the province of females, to an able matronly woman Friend, as HOUSEKEEPER to the family; who should occasionally apply to the master for instruction and aid."

The above extracts are taken from a circular extensively issued at this time, signed "John Corbyn, clerk," and in response to which Thomas Salter was engaged as master.

In the year 1811 a change in the constitution of the school was effected by the adoption of the following (summarised) regulations by the Quarterly Meeting:—

"1. School to admit country children. Charge to be ten guineas per annum. Boys to be taught reading, writing, arithmetic, and English grammar; the girls the same, with needlework, knitting, and domestic work. The institution to be called *Friends' School under the care of the Quarterly Meeting of London and Middlesex.* Children to leave at 14.

"2 and 3. Each Monthly Meeting in London and Middlesex to raise a subscription for the school annually, and Quarterly Meetings adopting this arrangement may send children to the school.

"4. Ackworth plans for admission and agency to be adopted.

"5. London children to have priority of admission, as being on the foundation." (Since extended to London and Middlesex.)

The school was at this time under the management of a committee of eighteen London Friends. Agents were now to be at liberty to attend its sittings.

The ancient Friends were withdrawn from the institution by the 1st of the Seventh Month, 1811, and arrangements made for receiving 100 children.

Peter Bedford became a member of the School Committee in 1814. He was a warm friend to the institution till his death. Many now living will remember his earnest interest in the welfare of teachers and scholars during the closing years of his life, when residing near the school after its location at Croydon.

The use of "Kendall's Catechism of the Christian Religion" was introduced in 1815, and persevered in for a time.

We have now reached the time at which the annual reports

Engraving of the school at its Islington Road site
[City of London, Guildhall Library]

This is the picture Beck and Ball refer to on p.376. However, the illustration is not on p.412 of James Peller Malcolm's *Londinium Redivivum* but on p.412 of Thomas Kitson Cromwell's *History and Description of the Parish of Clerkenwell* with engravings by J. and H. S. Storer, published by Longman's in 1828.

facing p.378

Croydon School: photo 1874, from an album of Croydon and Saffron Walden Schools [LSF]

began to be published. These are readily accessible, and supply minute particulars as to the educational progress of the scholars year by year, and also the financial affairs of the institution. It is evident that to endeavour exhaustively to treat these would swell our volume beyond all reasonable compass. Our aim has, of course, been to present some of the striking points in the history of the school, and leave minute details to be investigated by those specially interested in them.

It was agreed in 1823 that one-third of the permanent income of the school should be annually paid to the Six-Weeks Meeting, to be applied to the maintenance of poor ancient Friends in London; they having originally had a claim on the funds. Two years after the above date, in 1825, the school was removed from Islington Road to its present position at Croydon.

Before proceeding to speak of Croydon School, a few facts as to the disposal of the Islington Road property may be given. This estate was held by Friends of the Brewers' Company, on a lease of 148 years from Sixth Month, 1786. It was, after removal of the School, underlet as building land, on leases of 70 years from Third Month, 1827. It has become laid out in streets and occupied with houses, the ground rents of which realise about £350 per annum. Of this amount two-thirds is applied to the general purposes of Croydon School, and the remaining one-third is paid to the Six-Weeks Meeting, by it to be distributed among the Monthly Meetings for the ancient poor Friends. After the expiration of the sub building leases referred to, the estate will revert to Friends, when of course a very considerable increase of income may be looked for during the remaining thirty-seven years of the term for which it is held from the Brewers' Company.

Croydon School.

In a work intended, like the present, to be for the most part a repository of facts drawn from the records of a more or less remote past, it will not be expected that any very lengthened notice should be given of an establishment so modern and so well known as Croydon School.

In 1820 the Monthly Meeting of Tottenham proposed to the Quarterly Meeting that the School should be moved into the country, Islington having become much built over. After due consideration this proposition was, in the following year, acceded to. A site was found at Croydon whereon stood an old mansion which, by the addition of two long wings, was rendered suitable for the required purpose. The purchase was about £5,500, cost of building about £8,000, of furniture, &c. £700. To defray these expenses a subscription was raised of nearly £12,000. Of this £10,160 was collected in the London and Middlesex Quarterly Meeting; £146 in the associated Quarterly Meetings, £515 amongst Friends of the country generally, and £250 amongst non-members. Besides these sums there was a grant of £460 from the Quarterly Meeting. £3,000 was also raised on annuities, and £356 obtained from sale of old materials on the Croydon estate. The premises have since been much improved at various dates, especially by the erection of an additional schoolroom and dormitory on the boys' side in 1848 (without increasing the number of scholars), also by the erection of a new schoolroom for the girls in 1853. At this date the boys' playground was considerably enlarged by taking in part of the shrubbery and gardens on the west; a paddock on the north side has also been since added.*

At the removal of the school to Croydon it was placed under the care of Henry and Edith Dymond. At the same time a lad came as an apprentice who afterwards rose to be head master, and subsequently superintendent, in which last position he became well known to several generations of scholars who learned to love and revere the name of John Sharp.

H. and E. Dymond were succeeded as superintendents by Edward F. Brady and his wife. After Edward Brady's decease, Elizabeth Brady continued for a time to direct the affairs of the school, John Sharp acting as second in command. He became superintendent in 1842, and died at his post in 1853. His much esteemed and valued successor, Charles Fryer, died one year afterwards, in 1854.

---

* Amongst the most conspicuous donors towards the buildings at Croydon may be mentioned Robert Barclay, £200; William Dillwyn, £250; Samuel Gurney, £300; Luke Howard, £300; William Janson, £300; John Overend, £300; William F. Reynolds, £300; Thomas Richardson, £250; Robert Warner, £300.

GENERAL APPENDIX.

At a Quarterly Meeting held by adjournment at Gracechurch Street, Eleventh Month 30th, 1761,—

Our friends Samuel Fothergill, Isaac Wilson, Isaac Fletcher, Wm. Dillworth, John Lindoe, Henry Wilkins, Sampson Lloyd, jun., and Robert Foster, being some of the Friends appointed by the Yearly Meeting to visit the Monthly and Quarterly Meetings in the nation, having visited the Monthly Meetings in this City and Middlesex, were present in this meeting, whose visit is kindly accepted.

Samuel Fothergill, from the aforesaid Friends, brought in the following observations and remarks upon the state of the Church amongst us, which account, as it contains, we believe, a just and impartial representation of the Society here, and many important and affectionate advices relative thereto, is accepted by this meeting in the same brotherly love wherein they are communicated, and at the same time that the several advices therein contained are earnestly recommended by this meeting to every individual member present, so we hope it will become the care of this Quarterly Meeting to put in practice such parts of these recommendations as more immediately relate to the discipline and good order of the Society. Copies are ordered to be prepared and sent to the several Monthly Meetings of London and Middlesex; the consideration of said advices and the manner in which they may be rendered most extensively beneficial is referred to the next Quarterly Meeting.

To the Quarterly Meeting for London and Middlesex, to be held at Gracechurch Street, 30th of Eleventh Month, 1761,—

Dear Friends,—In a sense of our Heavenly Father's love to his Church and people and his gracious willingness to extend a hand of help and salvation, we found our minds engaged to pay a visit to many Monthly and Quarterly Meetings in this nation agreeable to the appointment of the Yearly Meeting in 1760. The same motive hath drawn us to pay a visit to yours, wherein we have had occasion reverently to acknowledge the continued regard of the great Master of our assemblies, who, by the fresh visitation of his love and life, is drawing near for the help of all who embrace it, that our Zion may arise and shake herself from the dust of the earth and put on the beautiful garment of salvation and praise. And, dear Friends, though our enquiry into the state of the Church amongst you hath been in some respects pretty close, it hath been conducted in the spirit of love and meekness; far from any design to seek cause of complaint, we wished to have occasion to rejoice with you in beholding your steadfastness in love to Him who is ever worthy, and an increase of faithfulness before Him who hath often renewed the visitations of tender love to many of you.

The duty of individuals and the proper conduct of the members of our Society, in a religious and moral capacity, are briefly expressed in eight Queries sent from the Yearly Meeting in London in 1755, and recommended to be answered by the Monthly Meetings at each Quarterly Meeting.

From your reading and answering these Queries in the several Monthly Meetings we have been led to view the state of the Church, and make some remarks thereupon which we offer to the weighty consideration of this meeting, and, in order to render it more clear and intelligible, we insert the Queries, together with the state of the Church as it appeared to us in answer thereto :—

Query 1st. Are Meetings for Worship and Discipline duly attended, and do Friends avoid all unbecoming behaviour therein ?

Answer. There appeared a general shortness in the attendance of week-day meetings ; many families having entirely declined their duty in this respect. First-day Meetings in some places slenderly attended, especially in the afternoon. Meetings for Discipline very much neglected in some parts, scarcely a sufficient number attending to transact the affairs of the Society. No Women's Monthly Meetings in some of the quarters ; the youth, too, seldom brought into Meetings of Discipline, and of consequence unacquainted with it. Great hurt to the solid religious frame of meetings also arised from a neglect of the hour appointed, and a drowsy state which overtakes many ; and we wish levity of conduct and inconsiderate behaviour amongst some of our youth especially were not to be found amongst you—all which are very unbecoming a people professing spiritual worship unto that Holy One who is a Spirit.

Query 2nd. Are love and unity preserved amongst you, and do you discourage all talebearing and detraction ?

Answer. It appeared that love and unity are so far preserved amongst you that no open difference is depending amongst Friends except in one meeting, which we earnestly recommend to Friends' care ; and that they use their utmost endeavours to reconcile and thereby prevent further reproach to the Society as well as hurt to particulars. Yet the previous unity of the spirit which leads into oneness, in faith and practice, is too much wanting, and there appears great inconsistency in many with those testimonies our ancestors received to bear and to transmit to future generations ; were this spiritual unity more generally witnessed, it would bring up individuals in a conduct more consistent with the duties expressly pointed out in the Queries. Nothing appeared but the pernicious practice of talebearing is pretty generally discouraged, and so we wish all to bear in mind the positive command of God. (Lev. xix. 16), " Thou shalt not go up and down as a talebearer among thy people ;" also (Prov. xxvi. 26), " Where there is no talebearer the strife ceaseth."

Query 3rd. Is it your care by example and precept to train up your children in a Godly conversation and in frequent reading the Holy Scriptures, as also in plainness of speech, behaviour, and apparel ?

Answer. There seemed a care to rest on the minds of many amongst you to train up their children in a Godly conversation, in frequent reading the Holy Scriptures, and in plainness of speech, behaviour, and apparel, and in order to render this care more effectual many, we hope, are concerned to seek after that hand which hath ever been the preserver of all who depend sincerely upon it; that they themselves, being kept alive in righteousness, may be living examples to their children, and strengthen those principles they may find in their hearts to deliver to them. Themselves delighting in the statutes of God will be qualified agreeable to the ancient injunction to teach them diligently to their children, and to talk of them when they sit in their houses, and when they walk by the way, when they lie down, and when they rise up.

But many appear unqualified for this most certain and necessary duty, being insensible of the importance of early care to form the tender mind to virtue and religion, whereby the young and uninstructed fall an easy prey to the delusions of vanity, a dislike to the Cross of Christ ensues, and their minds being seduced into undue liberties and a variety of incitements thereto daily presenting, many have furnished cause of severe affliction to negligent parents, sorrow and suffering to themselves, and reproach and grief to the Society.

Query 4th. Do you bear a faithful and Christian testimony against the receiving or paying tithes, priests' demands, or those called Church-rates?

Answer. Though many amongst you appear clear in our testimony in these respects, yet there is a great remissness herein, and we fear that the necessary care to advise, instruct, and admonish the unfaithful, hath not been sufficiently extended.

Query 5th. Are Friends careful to avoid all vain sports, places of diversion, gaming, and all unnecessary frequenting of alehouses or taverns, excess in drinking, and intemperance of every kind?

Answer. Notwithstanding several meetings gave a pretty clear account of their members with regard to the contents of this very extensive Query, and we are sensible it is under the solid care of many amongst you to observe and put it in practice, yet it appears to our sorrow that there is a great deficiency amongst too many professing with us the self-denying doctrine of the holy Jesus, whose precepts, if received and faithfully obeyed, would lead out of all these things, and by convincing the mind of the importance and value of their precious time excite or redeem it.

We fear divers are not clear of resorting to places of diversion, whereby the mind hath been polluted and rendered insensible of their great duty and interest of keeping their hearts with all diligence, and watching unto prayer, not knowing at what time the Lord cometh. We, therefore, earnestly beseech parents, by their own example and precept, to teach their children the value of time, and amongst other branches of frugality to be above all frugal thereof, which once elapsed can never more be recalled.

We have little complaint of excess in drinking; but we fear divers resort to taverns as members of clubs there-held, which hath in many respects been very injurious to particulars; and we offer it to the consideration of parents in particular, whether the multiplicity of temptations in this city require not the strictest attention, and to keep them under their own eye, which, though painful labour in the parent and uneasy to the minds of imprudent youth, hath often furnished great peace to both. We earnestly wish Friends in general were more exemplary in the virtue of temperance. It would discover itself in bounding the pursuit after the fading things of this world in the plainness and uprightness of their conduct, and in true moderation in their apparel and houses, using this world as not abusing it, nor themselves with it.

Query 6th. Are Friends just in their dealings and punctual in fulfilling their engagements?

Answer. In general the account received was clear and satisfactory, and we entreat Friends carefully to remember the necessity of uprightness in their dealing, and punctuality in all their engagements, to which Temperance and moderation will greatly contribute, and that Friends be watchful over youth entering into trade and business, and tenderly advise them, where they judge it necessary, and that such youth pay a suitable regard to Friends' advice, and here we cannot well omit to remind you of a necessary part of justice as advised by the Yearly Meeting of 1759, viz. "That if any fall short of paying their just debts, and a composition is made with their creditors to accept of a part instead of the whole, notwithstanding the parties may look upon themselves legally discharged of any obligation to pay the remainder, yet the principle we profess enjoins full satisfaction to be made if ever the debtors are of ability."

Query 7th. Is early care taken to advise and deal with such as appear inclined to marry contrary to the rules of our Society, and do none remove from, or into your Monthly or Two-Weeks Meetings without certificates?

Answer. There appeared a care in some Friends to advise and deal with such as seemed inclinable to marry contrary to the rules of our Society, but some shortness in giving and receiving certificates or other usual recommendations, especially on behalf of servants, who being removed from the care of their parents or relatives, ought in an especial manner to become objects of the Society's notice.

Query 8th. Have you two or more faithful Friends deputed in each particular meeting, to have the oversight thereof, and is care taken when anything appears amiss, that the rules of our discipline be put in practice?

Answer. In many of your Monthly Meetings overseers are not appointed, which is worthy of the solid consideration of this Quarterly Meeting, as the want of such seems to be one cause of great relaxation in discipline, and the hurt of many particulars. The duty of an overseer being early and tenderly to advise such as may be in danger of falling into hurtful things, to endeavour to extinguish the first sparks of contention, to interpose timely with suitable advice, where any of our youth or others may be in danger of marrying contrary to the rules of the Society. To deal with and admonish such by whose misconduct, in any respect, the way of truth may be evil spoken of, and in case of refractory conduct, or notorious immorality, to lay such cases before the Monthly Meeting in order that the rules of our discipline may be properly put in practice where anything appears amiss. The timely and faithful discharge of this duty, we apprehend, would be the means of help to very many and greatly ease the burden of Monthly Meetings, in preventing the causes of complaint, and shortening the deliberation concerning what may be proper to be done in case of obstinacy. We believe it as prudent, by such an appointment of Friends, to endeavour to prevent misconduct, if possible, as to nominate to visit after the rules of our Society are transgressed, though we by no means design to discourage this labour, or the watchful care of Friends over one another for good, but previous labour wisely bestowed in proper time, hath been oftentimes blessed with success, to prevent what would otherwise be difficult to remedy.

We also found ourselves concerned to extend our enquiries into some other branches of our Christian profession, not expressed in the Queries aforementioned; and first, in regard to the Militia, in which we find our religious testimony much neglected, many we fear hiring substitutes. Secondly, respecting illuminations on those called rejoicing nights, too many we find concur with others in giving this public testimony of joy at the devastations of war, which is a dishonour to the Christian name. On the same occasion, and those of fasts, the keeping of shops shut is a tacit acknowledgment that the worship of God may be subject to the directions and appointments of men;—the foundation of many grievous and pernicious errors in religious worship, and against which our ancestors in the truth were led to bear (through much suffering) a noble and Christian testimony. A conformity to the world in some particulars in these respects, not only manifests a disunity in practice amongst us, but subjects the faithful to greater afflictions. Thus, dearly beloved Friends, we have laid before you what hath appeared to us to be the state of the Church amongst you, and earnestly entreat it may have proper weight upon all your minds, that being sensible of a sorrowful declension you may be excited to consider its cause. We are fully assured the continuance of Divine regard is strongly towards you, and that it is not of the Lord of all goodness and strength that a people He signally favoured and for whom He made bare his holy arm in the beginning and hitherto should fail of establishment before Him for ever. May we therefore regard the advice of the Lord's Prophet, and put it in practice (Sam. iii. 40), "Let us search and try our ways and turn again to the Lord." On such a search and trial, we must acknowledge righteousness belongs to Him, but unto us blushing and confusion of face.

A failure in obedience to that positive command which includes our duty and interest, "Thou shalt love the Lord thy God with all thy heart," hath now most certainly been the cause of loss and declension. The love of the world in its various alluring presentations hath prevailed over many, the life which hungers and thirsts after righteousness hath been greatly enfeebled, and in some we fear totally slain, and the whole bent of the mind directed to the world. To which sorrowful defection we have reason to fear divers have contributed, who, by their stations in the Church, ought to have set a better example. This is the unquestionable cause of your religious meetings being so much neglected by some on First-days, and by very many on other days of the week. The instituted means of renewing strength to live acceptably to God and profitably to the Church being neglected, weakness ensues, and such being deprived of that defence which is the alone means of safety and help become deficient in various branches of duty. As weakness and apostacy prevail in individuals, their relative duties are neglected, they cannot inculcate on their children or families those things themselves have ceased to consider as important and necessary.

Great is the advantage from a diligent assembling of ourselves together for the worship of our Heavenly Father; it unites and endears his children to Him, and one to another in Him; it becomes the truest source of fellowship and blessed communion; love and unity increase, and the living members become as epistles wrote in one another's hearts; they are not indifferent to each other's welfare in temporal or religious concerns, but kindly affectioned, having love without dissimulation.

The omission of this duty hath greatly tended to scatter out of the pure union and holy covenant, to render Friends strangers one to another, and introduce a shyness and distance which gradually loosens the bonds of affection and reciprocal regard, and scatters many from the enclosure of the Lord's fold.

By the prevalence of pure love, the care one for another would become extensive, and way be made for the performance of the Christian duty of visiting the families of Friends agreeable to the advice of the Yearly Meeting, a practice which hath been signally blessed with success in many places, and been a lively resemblance of the state of the primitive believers in breaking bread from house to house, and eating their meat with gladness and singleness of heart.

A visit to the families of Friends in this city might be attended with many excellent consequences. And in a particular manner to that part of the Society which, in all probability, is very numerous in this city, viz. the poor, many of whom we believe would rejoice at such an instance of the regard of the Society, and be induced to a careful endeavour to walk worthy of Friends' esteem, and be thereby preserved from mingling with the lowest class and dregs of the people, and if Friends would leave amongst them, where necessary, some suitable books, they might become a means of instruction to such as have few other opportunities to gain it.

Let not the poor amongst you, however circumstanced, be discouraged. He that judgeth with equity for the poor of the earth beholds their condition. As they seek Him, He will be found of them, and that Providence which clothes the fields and upholds the sparrows is over all his children, and will never fail the upright in heart.

As the love of God prevails it will engage many to join in the Lord's work and service, and prefer the interests of his house even before his own, and some would find the concern and weight of the Church rest upon them in such a manner as to create a willingness to be serviceable; the offices of elders and overseers would be supplied, and an holy engagement prevail to work in the Lord's vineyard in their day; the experience of these, as they have been preserved in faithfulness, hath been, that the reward of the faithful labourer is exceeding great.

And, dear Friends, as the discipline of the Church hath been an instrumental means of our preservation, we earnestly desire it may be maintained in a proper manner. It was first established in the wisdom of Truth, and can only be conducted therein to the edification of the Body and the glory of the Holy Head. There appears a necessity on our minds to recommend this to your weighty consideration, and we think it essential to the maintenance of the discipline that Friends wait to feel their minds in measure clothed with that power which is the authority of all our meetings, and sole help to profit for ourselves and others in them, and that it would tend to great advantage if the men and women Friends would meet together at their Monthly and Quarterly Meetings, and solidly wait for the arising of living power and virtue. We believe this a likely means to collect the youth together to enlarge your Monthly

Meetings, and add weight to their conclusions; and if the eight Queries were sometimes read, answered, and solidly spoke to in such meetings, it would more generally make known to the various members of the Society their duty, and impress their minds with proper thoughtfulness to walk, in some good degree, consistent. For we verily believe many amongst you, had they been early and suitably apprised of their respective duties with relation to our testimony in its several branches, would not have deviated so widely in their conduct and appearance as they do.

And as male and female are one in Christ, and ought to be mutually assistant in the promotion of his kingdom, we earnestly wish that Friends may keep in mind the recommendation of the Yearly Meeting to establish Women's Monthly Meetings for the care and oversight of their own sex, and which are in this city a very numerous body, and on whom very much depends with respect to the education of the youth, and other important concerns, and that the women Friends may be properly engaged carefully to mind the gentle leadings of Truth in this weighty affair.

We therefore earnestly beseech you, fathers, mothers, and all the principal amongst the people, to be roused in heart to diligence and labour in the Lord's cause, waiting for wisdom and counsel to act in your several stations so as to obtain a blessed portion in the sentence of "Well done, good and faithful servant, enter thou into the joy of thy Lord, and into thy Master's rest."

And, dear youth, our hearts are moved within us, for you may remember your Creator in the days of your youth, and may dedicate your first-fruits to Him from whom every mercy proceeds, and to whom are due the returns of obedience and love. Let the precious visitation of trembling, melting goodness prevail over the opposite nature in your hearts. Hereby you will be preserved innocent, the proper foundation of prosperity laid, an all-sufficient Guide and Helper will be with you through the future steps of life. Peace and serenity, the companions of virtue and religion, accompany you in all your ways, and having served God in your generation, you will be finally gathered to the Assembly of the Just.

We are comforted in tender sympathy with a living remnant amongst you who love the Lord, his Cause and Truth, and seek the exaltation of his name. May you dwell in the meekness of wisdom and therein wait to see your way open how to step along in your several services, abiding in the faith and patience of Saints, leaving the Lord's cause to the direction of his own Spirit, who can carry it on by means of babes and sucklings, yet standing with your loins girded, and your lights shining. Let your prayers ascend to the Son of his people for wisdom to go in and out before Him, being zealous for the Lord's cause, and the exaltation of his glorious name, yet carefully learn to know your own spirits properly subjected. Ever remember that meekness and love are never-failing recommendations to advise and labour, carrying with them their own evidence to convince, if they be not rendered effectual to reform.

We salute you in fervent affection, earnestly beseeching the Lord of all power to be with and bless you with an increase in righteousness that wisdom and knowledge may become the stability of your times and the predictions of the Lord's prophet may be fully accomplished: "I will turn my hand upon thee, and purely purge away thy dross, and take away all thy tin: and I will restore thy Judges as at the first, and thy Counsellors as at the beginning. Afterward thou shalt be called the City of Righteousness, the Faithful City."

We remain, your friends and brethren,
SAMUEL FOTHERGILL,
ISAAC WILSON,
WILLIAM DILLWORTH,
ISAAC FLETCHER,
HENRY WILKIN,
JOHN LINDOE,
SAMPSON LLOYD, Jun.
ROBERT FOSTER.

London, 30th of 11th Month, 1761.

THOMAS WILKINSON, of Yanworth in Cumberland, who died in 1836, aged 85 years, wrote a poem entitled, "Recollections of London," which is at Devonshire House in MS. We give a few brief extracts in which some of the honoured names in our Society at the beginning of the present century are pleasingly alluded to.

After describing the marvels of the city he says :—

" 'Mid these gay scenes when first I took my route
In my new robes, the little man of soot
Pressed by my side, the sable badge I bore,
Till Smith's kind cares the injured hues restore ;
But Smith's kind cares, ere home was left behind,
Had here for me a place of rest assigned,
While hospitable Beaumont and his bride
Received their Friend, and all his wants supplied.
Their words were kindness, come whene'er I might,
At early eve, or long protracted night.
At Messer's, too, I met a ready seat,
With greetings kind and conversation sweet ;
And when to Stacey's quiet home I went
The time was ever in improvement spent.

. . . . .

[Raw: "?John Row"; Dillwyn: "?George or William"; maids: "one of these mother of Dilwyn Sims" –annotated copy]

Not small the kindness when such Friends I saw
As cordial Capper, Lister, Pim, and Raw ;
As generous Dillwyn he whose ample mind
Expands with active zeal to human kind ;
With his sweet maids the evening wore away,
In pleasing converse, innocently gay :
With Knight and his the peaceful hour I past ;
Sweet, though by softening sorrow overcast.

. . . . .

Saw rapid Philipps, in his sweet career
Of ardent virtue—simple and sincere :
Saw gentle Allen with distinction move,
Among the Friends and characters I love :
Saw distant Gurney's plain uprightness shed
Like modest Truth a lustre round his head :

Saw friendly Howard—but we drew not near,
He sought the North,—I saw, and loved him there.   ["Luke Howard;
To crowded Sanderson's I now repair :   John Sanderson's"
The social board of Mildred Court I share,   –annotated
With Birkbeck, Philipps, Fell, and West I dine,   copy]
Or plunge in rural scenes with Sparks Moline.

And now with Fry, 'mid Plashet's tranquil bowers,
I view the setting sun and closing flowers :
With him and Conran through the fields I go,
While western clouds with ruddy splendour glow.

And now I sleep in Bromley's beauteous grove
Where liberal Foster in domestic love
Leads the soft hours of passing time along
Among his Friends—his family among.
I've walked to Kensington, and I have been
Where Newington o'erlooks the lovely scene ;
I've sat with Bevan in his classic shade ;
By ease and kindness more attractive made.

In Friendship's genial air I draw my breath
Whene'er I call on Sterry or on Horn ;
Our friendship was on Northern mountains born ;
Rocked in the cradle of the polar blast,
And will, I trust, in milder seasons last."

In a subsequent portion of the poem the author describes the ministry he heard whilst in London :—

" And I have seen the worthies of our day,
And with their names I'll sanctify my lay.
I saw a Kendal innocent and old,
Yet in the Faith maintain the goodman's hold.
Saw ancient Colley in the assembly rise ;
And light prevailed from Him that rules the skies.
Saw Birkbeck still with persevering mind,
Though he has left so many years behind.
Saw Wilkinson, who in his early days
Sounded the trumpet of immortal praise.
Saw Sterry's zeal her Christian life adorn ;
Saw female piety preside in Horn ;
Heard her sweet voice inspiring counsel bear ;
And fraught with love her drooping brethren cheer.
Saw serious Conran lowly and resigned,
In meekness keep the anchor of his mind.
Saw solid Price, concerned for Zion's weal.
Saw Cash that feels and makes the stranger feel.
Saw Alexander fervent for the Truth ;
And strength vouchsafed to dedicated Routh.
Saw gentle Gurney with a sweet address
Allure her Friends to heaven and happiness.
Saw Fowler's gift with love divine abound ;
Her precepts life, her voice a heavenly sound.

>The virtuous Tukes, that as a bulwark stand ;
>Saw long-loved Braithwaite join the chosen band ;
>Sweet charity and zeal in him unite.
>Saw Special West divide the word aright.
>Persuasive Philipps ;—thoughtful Howarth saw,
>Afraid to step beyond his Master's law.
>Saw Abbott to her old friends ever dear ;
>In life correct, in testimony clear :
>Of mind enlarged with moderation crowned,
>Saw Christian care in Bevan's counsel bound.
>Saw powerful Grubb, that sounds her Master's praise,
>In streets, in markets, prisons, and highways.
>Saw faithful Stacey unremitting keep
>A watch for Him who ordered 'keep my sheep.'
>I could proceed—for still a pious train
>Of those I love—beloved of Heaven, remain
>Who here have met to serve with reverent awe
>The God of all above and all below,
>While other worthies are dispersed afar,
>Who in his council urge the Christian war."

The Friend who composed these verses enjoyed the friendship and esteem of Wordsworth, who has handed down his name and character in one of his poems entitled, " To the *Spade* of a Friend, composed while we were labouring together in his pleasure grounds."

The following stanza culled from a poem called the *Country Quaker*, in a pamphlet book at Devonshire House, shows what was the prevailing idea of Friends' principles in the middle age of their history :—

>" Strong for a pow'r intuitive he pleads
>   Some emanation of th' eternal Light,
>An energetic rule ; beyond all creeds,
>   An home-felt fount and test of all that's right ;
>Not to one sect injuriously confin'd,
>   But like the orb of day enlightens all mankind."

The next stanza shows the hospitality of the time :—

>" His preaching brother, trav'ling to and fro,
>   Should he unbidden call to be his guest
>His bosom wakes to Friendship's cordial glow ;
>   And while he blesses finds himself more blest,
>Grasping his hand the pious kiss bestows
>   While his expanded soul in kind endearment flows."

The foregoing stanzas are somewhat eulogistic of the Society ; it pourtrays an inner life, retaining some vital powers. The following rhymes, are of an opposite character, viz.—

" Lines written after hearing an observation made in Public, by a Clergyman of the Established Church, to the effect that the Devil had, by offering gold to the Quakers, destroyed their vitality and religious influence.

>The Devil was out on his usual rout,
>   To walk to and fro on the Earth,
>With more business in hand than he well could command,
>   When the Sect of the Quakers came forth.

He took little heed, and let them proceed ;
  For he thought they'd soon die away ;
But, to his surprise, when they next met his eyes,
  They were increasing every day.

At this in a Pet he said I must set
  My old friends the Parsons to thin them,
And if persecution shall fail to reduce 'em,
  I'll try other methods to win them.

Their oppressors began and tried every plan
  The old boy could put in their heads,
They cast them in jail and wouldn't take bail,
All injustice was used, but naught would avail,
  And still the Society spreads.

He tried once more if ridicule's power
  Could move those sturdy men,
He gave them a rub in the Tale of a Tub,
  And his friend Bugg took up the Pen.

But they foiled him again,—all resistance was vain,
  And still they refused to bow down ;
Which, when Satan perceived, he was sadly grieved,
  And giving a hideous frown
He stamped with his hoof and he scratched his horned head,
And his tail swept angrily round.
' At length a people have risen,' he said,
' Who promise to bruise the serpent's head,
And all my Power confound.'

But I have one scheme more, which I tried before,
  And it answered exceedingly well,—
In the Church of old, I gave the Pope gold,
  And the true Church quickly fell.

He offered them Gold and you needn't be told
  That they bowed to the love of gain ;
If you wish to know, you have only to go
  To Capel Court or Mark Lane.

You see them there with a busy air,
  Bowing at Mammon's shrine ;
Whilst Satan, in fun that his end was won,
  With Cobbett is taking his Wine."

N.B.—This piece was written some forty years ago, when Cobbett and his doings, especially as to Tom Paine's bones, were topics of the day. *

* "By William Lucas of Hitchin, my father [Richard Low Beck] having repeated to him then a lad in London the remarks a Clergyman had thus made to him (W. Beck 4.xii.81)" – annotated copy

GENERAL OBSERVATIONS.

The work—such as it is—being now passed through the press, its compilers feel conscious how little they may have succeeded in presenting any clear view of the London Friends' Society, notwithstanding their labour in searching amid its voluminous records, both in MSS. and print.

They can only plead in extenuation that the task is not a light one—and would involve even more time than has been spent to render it at all complete; enough may, however, have been done to give at least a general idea. In doing so, it has been the aim to make the records as far as possible speak for themselves, and be the illustrators of the condition of the various periods in which they were made. Thus, both zeal and lukewarmness are found indicated on these pages, and revival, when it does occur, becomes also apparent. There has been a desire to select in fairness and report accurately. No roughnesses, where they exist, have been smoothed down, nor any shrinking from a full development of that state which led to a strict exercise of discipline. Thus, the London Friends' Society passes itself, so to speak, in review during its career of more than two centuries.

There will have been observed a certain amount of repetition, as to the same persons and, perhaps, the same incidents and circumstances; but, where so introduced, it has been the result of a desire to make the chapter illustrate itself without too frequently giving occasion to turn to other parts for information.

SUFFERINGS.

In this work—sketchy as it is—some may think too great notice has been given to the sufferings of the early Friends; but such will be those who have not searched for themselves into the history of that day; those who have done so will be aware it is impossible to avoid giving prominence in any description, however brief, to what was so obvious a feature in those times; and it is done not so much to reproach the persecutors as to exhibit the strength and power of those convictions which could support men amid sufferings of forty years' duration. It was through all this that the Friends, by enduring, became distinguished from the Ranters and others of that class, who succumbed and dispersed. By it each other of the recognised sects learnt to respect as conscientious and sincere—men—who would in patience suffer so much to keep up meetings which they themselves had had temporarily to suspend. And when to the fierce blast of the storm succeeded the wiser and milder rule of William of Orange, it was this hardihood under suffering which drew men from all classes to unite with Friends and so greatly swelled the ranks of the Society—the members of it now attracting attention, for, like their founder, they had stood "pure as a bell and stiff as a tree," under prolonged seasons of sharp and bitter trial. Clarkson in his portraiture of Quakerism says, " In the time of George Fox the number of those converted to his principles was immense."

Personal Influence.

No one can become at all acquainted with the history of the Society without observing the importance personal influence has had in forming it as a body, although its tenets are so spiritual in their character. All things, for instance, though so ripe, slumbered until some one man was raised up like Fox to give the word of command. Then, too, it was the personal zeal of the early gifted adherents that spread the good news throughout the length and breadth of the land, and their self-denying heroic conduct both drew and consolidated people around them. This personal devotion continued for some time, even after the first generation had passed away; but gradually this, in a great measure, declined, and the body became lukewarm until personal influence, under such men as Dr. Fothergill and many others, rekindled after a century somewhat of the zeal of former days, and renewed to the body, which seemed about to melt away, a life that has preserved it to our day, Ackworth School and attention to the discipline marking the turning point.

In the present and preceding generation it is observable how, whilst the views held are spiritual, they are also dependent upon the influence of gifted fellow-creatures. How often, for example, have eminent preachers from America been the means of rekindling zeal that seemed to flag. "Many ambassadors from America fraught with Gospel mission," is an expression used by a diarist; and, to mention but one example among so many, it was a William Savery from America that first led, by his influence and ministry, the young and engaging Miss Gurney to think of life in a way which developed into the career so eminent in all that is good as that of Elizabeth Fry. It is observable also how the influence, as to power, has rested with the travelling rather than the settled preachers. A bishop, in the persecuting days, said if we could but stop the travelling preacher we should soon stamp out the Society. In London in all times of zeal and revival the influence of the travelling preacher is seen. It was men from the North who began the work, and it is the frequently repeated visits of the missionary preacher that have sustained it; by these means variety and freshness is secured. Our London Meeting books show during an active period that it was seldom for the same minister to be at the same meeting for many months together, and a diary of a Friend in Essex, kept during the time of the Revival in 1770, &c., shows how great was the influence then of the *travelling* preacher.

Manners.

Let us not reflect harshly on the manners of the Friends as stiff, formal, and unnecessarily scrupulous; they formed what seemed to them a right line of conduct and kept to it; this was not for the time when they arose of the "straitest sect," for to the austere Puritans they seemed and were reviled as too free, and even persecuted for not being strict enough. They never were, as Burns would say, of the "unco pious"—and are found to have held a middle course as between the austere Roundhead on the one hand, or the gay Cavalier on the other; but having once formed their practices they kept to them, and *became* singular to a future generation through retaining the speech, behaviour, and dress common in a former one when they first arose.

Some would say they ought to have changed with the times, and so far imitated the practice of their forefathers, as to adopt all polite and civil forms; but when we remember the state of men and manners, from 1750 to 1800, the period of Friends attaching so much Society importance to strict discipline, in habit and language, is it not cause for thankfulness such a hedge was drawn? for it kept together a pure and correct body, dwelling in all parts of the land, separate from the surrounding world, which, under the influence of Infidel writers or Pagan modes of thought, became marked by irreligion, and developed into those gross public immoralities and general licence that marked the reign of the first Georges. Surely without such a hedge as the Friends formed, they could not have kept together or preserved their purity, and if *they* had been lost as a body, how much society would have suffered. For when at last the Friend issued as it were from his retirement, he was at the root of most of those social changes, from which society has received so much benefit; in him Prison Reform and Education found the staunchest advocate, Slavery her fiercest foe, Civil and Religious liberty the most consistent champion. The Bible Society and Temperance cause have owed in their early day much to the combined support of the Friends, so that those who have engaged in these efforts are ever ready to acknowledge that wherever they went, all over the land, at a time when persons of station, even in the religious world, stood aloof, the Society of Friends to a man were the firmest supporters; thus was this separated people permitted to be at the root and bottom of modern philanthropy, and realising the benefit thus conferred by them, how can he refuse to believe that the strict discipline which alone kept them had its great use, and was for its day the result of divine guidance?

In General,

it seems as if a body were unable twice in the course of its existence to take the same position, inheriting in a corporate capacity those infirmities which belong to the individual, and prevent a renewal of that "dew of the youth" when once passed away. So the Society of Friends, once young and vigorous, going forth battling with opposition, suffering, yet increasing, rejoicing as a young man to run a race, settled down gradually into a more steady existence, experiencing therein its times of lukewarmness, decay, and vigorous revival, yet never reacquiring that "fervour of youth" which once passed can never be recalled. It had around it, when consolidated by a century of experience, as much of a rude populace and wild spirits as ever called forth the powers of a Burrough or a Howgill, but the middle of the eighteenth century found no *public* voice or evangelising gospel message from the Friends to the perishing thousands of the cities. A John Wesley and a George Whitfield, standing on a similar spiritual platform to what Fox had occupied a century before, were then in the fulness and freshness of their youth to call in the multitude, and a Friend, such as Thomas Story (see his Journal), saw it was their mission, and could bid them God-speed in the work; the Friend's task was to reform himself, and so strengthen the things that remain, as not to let his candlestick be removed, and that he did do so at that time led, as we have said, to a result on general society, the good effects of which are only just becoming *publicly* acknowledged.

If it be allowable to trace any law on such a subject it would appear that the body gifted with a sound and abundant ministry is the one which increases. Have not some of us observed the contrast in this respect between the Latin and the Greek churches; the missionary, propaganding spirit of the former and its increase—the absence of it in the latter, and its dull, stationary character? Now the Friends had this missionary zeal once in a pre-eminent degree, and they were then a remarkably increasing body at home, and pushing outward to all the colonies.

No doubt there were causes which led them to have an abundant supply of ministers at one time, which has been wanting more or less ever since. During the time of their great increase, no provision existed for ministers other than those of the Establishment—the laws against any other being especially severe, so much so as to make it almost impossible for persons to become regular stipendiary ministers, unless conformed to the Church. Thus persons led to the ministry, very many of them found relief and exercise for their gifts in the assemblies of Friends, where, though fines awaited them, yet it was not quite so deterrent or prohibitory as if attached to a particular congregation; this also greatly favoured the travelling preacher.

Now when persecution was exchanged for toleration, it was not long before, under the altered conditions, it became manifest that those drawn to the ministerial office would be devoted to it entirely, and become ministers to particular congregations, thus withdrawing any fresh supply from such a body as Friends, who offer no *outward* inducement to persons to become ministers among them; thus the Society, deprived of these accessions, became more and more exclusively composed of tradesmen, correct in their habits, and prosperous in their concerns, and henceforth, elders rather than ministers, become inceasingly prominent in the body.

Nevertheless in the time of the revival a great number of ministers are found, and much *travelling* in the service, productive also of great influence for good in the body; and looking back to that day, it cannot but be observed, how men of naturally powerful minds grew up in quiet homes, trained to habits of endurance, and simple in their requirements, giving the bent of their powers to the work of the ministry, living themselves by the hands rather than the head, unconscious of that brain toil which professional life involves, or that strain which a vehement competition induces.

It seemed as if from these latter causes the stream of living ministry might have suffered a check in this day; it may have felt it, but the wants of Education do not lessen but increase the ranks of the Schoolmasters, of whom it is noticeable now, as at the first, how many become ministers, and the First-day School work in its rise and development has brought Friends into contact with the poor, and how many a heart has been warmed and tongue loosened in mission-work among them.

MYSTICISM.

Now that Friends are better esteemed than formerly, it is become the practice in this appreciation to adopt the views expressed by Vaughan in his hours with the mystics, also more recently by Cunningham, and regard them as one of that deeply spiritual though not very practical people. To those in this way of thinking, this work, founded on documentary evidence, may show that if mystical in *expression*, they were in all outward things very practical, and from the first were so governed by sound common sense, and in all the duties of social life and good citizenship, were so plain and practical in their conduct, that it is difficult to associate the idea of mysticism (as generally understood) with them. We see them regulating their marriages with care, taking record of all the events of life, obtaining meeting-houses, and burial-grounds, maintaining their poor, even keeping *fire* engines (see Southwark) to stop fires, reading briefs after meetings for losses by fire, helping all in some practical way or other, keeping a bed for prisoners (see Southwark), requiting gaolers, and on all occasions showing that their faith, if mystical in expression, was practical in its effects, and themselves were far too earnest citizens, and men of everyday life and duties, to be regarded as mystics.

In conclusion, it may be hoped this work may have given some information of the Society of Friends in London, under a few of its successive aspects.

It will have shown its early stage of missionary zeal, a work, it may be said, of the valiant North-men.

Then comes the hour of trial, amid which the work of consolidation commences, and a discipline becomes established.

It is reduced by dismemberment of the unworthy, and to some extent by emigration to America, though this latter movement lay at first more among the country than the London Friends.

The first century of their career found Friends at its close very numerous in London, but the light of their faith and example was not very bright. Stern upright men also (such as Dr. Fothergill) from the North, inaugurated a revival, conducted in a spirit of silence, awe, and weight of spirit, under which, baptised and exercised, issued a succeeding generation zealous in philanthropic effort.

Of this philanthropic period the records carry no trace, for the Society as a *body* was not indentified with the movements. Whether to any future compiler they may present traces of First-day School and mission-work now happily so in the ascendant, remains to be seen; there are signs even in London that such may be the case.

Bibliography

Part 1: Works cited

Part 2: Subject bibliography

    2A: London history (general)

    2B: Quaker history

    2C: Quaker London

    2D: Quaker social history, business and occupations

    2E: London Quaker meetings: arranged according to Beck and Ball's chapters

    2F: Subjects relating to later Beck and Ball chapters

Some items appear in both parts. Number of pages where given is a rough guide to extent, not a full collation.

Part 1: Works cited

These are references to published works in the original book, and the 2009 introduction. Some additional works by William Beck are included, although this is not a full list of his publications.

    Manuscript records etc are not included: the material consulted at Devonshire House is now in the Library of the Religious Society of Friends, Friends House (173 Euston Road, London NW1 2BJ), and references in the meeting records and other manuscript series are quite easy to locate from the context. The registers referred to on p.305 as held at Somerset House are those surrendered after the Civil Registration Act in 1837, which then became part of the Registrar General's records (the RG6 series) held now at the National Archives, Kew. Registers consulted by the authors would have been the Digest Registers copied up after the 1837 Act for the Society's own use.

An Account of the Rise, Progress, and Present State of Friends' School and Work-house, at Clerkenwell, London, (the school, 1754), 8pp.

Addison, Joseph, "The Campaign"; a contemporary edition was *The Poetical Works of Joseph Addison; Gay's Fables and Somerville's Chase*, (James Nisbet, 1859).

Allen, Richard C., *Quaker Communities in Early Modern Wales: From Resistance to Respectability*, (University of Wales Press, 2007), 314pp.

Ball, T.F., *Poems*, (A.W. Bennett, 1865), 168pp.

Ball, T.F., (ed.) *Anecdotes of Aborigines: or, Illustrations of the coloured races being "Men and Brethren"*, (S.W. Partridge, 1868; reprinted 1881).

Ball, T.F., *Queen Victoria: Scenes and Incidents of Her Life and Reign*, (S.W. Partridge, 1886), 244pp., ill.

Bangs, Benjamin, *Memoirs of the Life and convincement of ... Benjamin Bangs ... mostly taken from his own mouth by Joseph Hobson*, (Luke Hinde, 1757), 64pp.

Barclay, Abram Rawlinson and Barclay, John (ed.), *Letters, &c., of early Friends; illustrative of the history of the Society, from nearly its origin, to about the period of George Fox's decease...*, (Harvey & Darton, 1841), 418pp.

Barclay, Robert (1648–1690), *Apology for the Church and People of God called in derision Quakers*, (1676; repr assigns of J. Sowle, 1732). This would be the edition referred to on p.172.

Barclay, Robert, *A Catechism and Confession of Faith*, (1673; 4th ed. "corrected and very much amended" T. Sowle, 1701).

Barclay, Robert, "Journal" reference on p.239: apparently an error for *Apology*.

Barclay, Robert (1833–1876), *The Inner Life of the Religious Societies of the Commonwealth*, (Hodder & Stoughton, 1876), 700pp.

[Beck, William], *The Warder Trust*, (Devonshire House Monthly Meeting, n.d.). Catalogued at Friends House as by W.B., but otherwise anonymous.

Beck, William, *Six Lectures on George Fox and his Times*, (Samuel Harris, 1877; reprinted by BiblioBazaar, 2008?), 137pp.

Beck, William, *Ye Yoakley Charity, Drapers Hospital*, (the charity?, 1884), 21pp., ill.

Beck, William (ed.), *Biographical Catalogue: Being an account of the lives of Friends and others whose portraits are in the London Friends' Institute*, (the Institute, 1888), 878pp., ill..

Beck, William, *The Friends: Who they are, what they have done*, (E. Hicks, 1893), 277pp., ill.

Beck, William, *Family Fragments*, (privately published; printer, John Bellows of Gloucester, 1897), 150pp., ill.

Beck, William, *Birthright Membership: a historical sketch*, (s.n., 1899), 7pp.

Beck, William (ed.), *George Whitehead: his work and service as a minister for sixty-eight years in the Society of Friends; Compiled from his autobiography*, (Headley Bros, 1901), 133pp., ill.

Beck, William, *Devonshire House: historical account of the acquisition by the Society of Friends...*, (Headley Bros, 1903, rev. 1908); see also below, section 2E.

Beck, William, *Peter Bedford, the Spitalfields philanthropist*, (Friends' Tract Assoc., 1903), 40pp., ill. Catalogued by Friends House Library as by W.B., but Joseph Smith lists it as by William Tallack.

Beck, William, *A Description of Church Street, Stoke Newington*, (Edgar Publishing, 1927), 24pp., ill.

Bell, Erin, "Eighteenth-Century Quakerism and the Rehabilitation of James Nayler, Seventeenth-Century Radical", *Journal of Ecclesiastical History*, 59 (2008), pp.426–27.

Bellers, John, (ed. Clarke, G.), *John Bellers, 1654 to 1725, Quaker visionary: his life, times and writings*, (1987; repr. Sessions Book Trust, 1993), 293pp.

Besse, Joseph, *A Collection of the Sufferings of the People called Quakers*, (Luke Hinde, 1753), 2 vols. Besse's Sufferings has recently been reprinted in a series of facsimile volumes, including: Besse, Joseph with Gandy, Michael, *Sufferings of early Quakers: London and Middlesex, 1655 to 1690; with new introduction and newly compiled index of people and places by Michael Gandy*, (Sessions Book Trust, 2002).

Braithwaite, William C., *The Beginnings of Quakerism to 1660*, (1912; 2nd ed., prepared by Henry J. Cadbury, Cambridge U.P., 1955), 607pp.

Braithwaite, William C., *The Second Period of Quakerism*, (1919; 2nd ed., prepared by Henry J. Cadbury, Cambridge U.P., 1961), 735pp.

British Friend, The, Vol.1–49, New Series Vol.1–22 (1843–1913)

British Quarterly, i.e. *The British Quarterly Review*, vol.1–83 (1845–86).

Bugg, Francis, *The Pilgrim's Progress from Quakerism to Christianity*, (W. Kettleby, 1698), 175pp.

Burnet, Gilbert, Bishop of Salisbury, *History of His Own Time*, (1723–34); edition cited possibly *New edition, with historical and biographical notes*, (Henry G. Bohn, 1857), 3 vols.

Burrough, Edward, *The Memorable Works of a Son of Thunder and Consolation*, (s.n., 1672), 896pp.

Burrough, Edward, "see Letters" i.e. Barclay, A.R. (1841).

Butler, David M., *The Quaker Meeting Houses of Britain*, (Friends Historical Society, 1999), 2 vols, 946pp., ill.

Clarkson, Thomas, *Portraiture of Quakerism*, (1806; 3rd ed. amended and revised by Robert Smeal, 1847), 335pp.

Coffey, John, *Persecution and Toleration in Protestant England 1558-1689* (Harlow, 2000).

Crisp, Stephen: *Primer* cited on p.292 has not been identified, nor an appropriate entry in Longford MM minutes for 1712.

Cromwell, Thomas Kitson, *History and Description of the Parish of Clerkenwell*, ([Longman etc], 1828), 448pp., ill.

Crosby, Thomas, *The History of the English Baptists, from the Reformation to the beginning of the reign of King George I*, (1738–40), 4 vols.

Crouch, William, *Posthuma Christiana, or a collection of the papers of Willam Crouch*, (assigns of J. Sowle, 1712), 224pp.

Cunningham: the author cited on p.395 has not been identified.

Damrosch, Leo, *The Sorrows of the Quaker Jesus: James Nayler and the Puritan Crackdown on the Free Spirit*, (Harvard U.P., 1996), 322 pp., ill.

Daniels, Peter, "Quakers in Stoke Newington, to the mid-19th century", *Hackney History*, 8 (2002), pp.3-11, ill.

Daniels, Peter, "Quakers in Stoke Newington: the 19th and 20th centuries", *Hackney History*, 14 (2008), pp.24–37, ill.

Davies, Adrian, *The Quakers in English Society 1655-1725*, (Oxford University Press, 2000).

Davis, Joseph, *A Digest of the Legislative Enactments relating to the Society of Friends*, (Wansbrough & Saunders, 1820; 2nd ed. Edward Marsh, 1849), 144pp.

de Krey, Gary, *A Fractured Society: The Politics of London in the First Age of Party 1688-1715*, (Clarendon, 1985), 304pp, ill.

de Krey, Gary, *London and the Restoration, 1659-1683*, (Cambridge U.P., 2005), 472pp.

Devonshire House Monthly Meeting, *Trust Property Book*, (the monthly meeting, 1861), 126pp.

Dewsberry [sic], William, *The Life of William Dewsbury ... by the late Edward Smith*, (Darton & Harvey, 1836; facsimile repr. Sessions, 1997), 323pp.

Dixon, Simon, "Early Quaker meeting houses in London, 1654–1688", (University of York MA dissertation, 2001)

Dixon, Simon Neil, "Quaker communities in London, 1667–c.1714", (University of London PhD thesis, 2005).

Dixon, Simon, "Quakers and the London Parish 1670-1720", *London Journal*, 32 (2007), pp.229–49.

Dixon, Simon, "The Life and Times of Peter Briggins", *Quaker Studies*, 10 (2006), pp.185–202.

Dixon, Simon, "The priest, the Quakers and the second conventicle act: the battle for Gracechurch Street Meeting House, 1670" in Andrew Spicer and Sarah Hamilton (eds), *Defining the Holy: Sacred Space in Medieval and Early Modern Europe*, (Ashgate, 2006), pp.301–18.

Docwra, Anne, *An Apostate-Conscience Exposed*, (T. Sowle, 1699), 67pp.; and *The second part of An Apostate-conscience Exposed*, (T. Sowle, 1700), 48pp.

Ellwood, Thomas, *History of the Life of Thomas Ellwood*, (J. Sowle, 1714), 480pp.

Evenden, Doreen, *The Midwives of Seventeenth-Century London*, (Cambridge U.P., 2000).

Fothergill, John, Memoirs: various editions exist of John Coakley Lettsom's biography, of which the 4th ed. (1786) is called *Memoirs*, but the reference on p.261 does not match.

Fox, George, ms letter 8 2mo 1684 290: in A.R. Barclay mss (Friends House ref MS 324/193)

Fox, George, *Epistles*: refs match *A Collection of many select and Christian Epistles... The 2nd vol.*, (T. Sowle, 1698); "1653 preface" (p.39) is an error.

Fox, George, *Friends Fellowship must be in the Spirit: Directions to meetings* (1668); expanded version in *Epistles* p.276.

Fox, George, *Journal*: references match *A journal or historical account of the life...* (Thomas Northcott, 1694), except for preface by William Penn, from Luke Hinde's 1765 ed. The passage quoted on p.58 begins at "And as abruptly...", the earlier part in quote marks being a paraphrase.

Fox, George, Paper on Six Weeks Meeting: in SWM minutes, 1691.

Fox, George, *A Primer for the Schollers and Doctors of Europe*, (Thomas Simmonds, 1659), 55pp.

Fox, George, *The Saints (or they that are born of the Spirit) their Heavenly and Spiritual Worship*, (John Bringhurst, 1683), 20pp.

Fox, George, *To all that would Know the way to the Kingdom of Heaven*, (s.n., 1654).

Foxe, John, "Martyrology", published as *Acts and Monuments of these Latter and Perilous Days*, (1563), regularly reprinted for Protestant reading.

The Friend, vol.1–18 (1843–1860); New Series vol.1–71 (1861–1931); reverts to vol.90 (1932), continuing.

The Friends Quarterly Examiner, vol. 1–80 (1867–1946).

Gibson, William, *Bigotry and Partiality Ruinous and Destructive to Pure Religion...*, (s.n., 1705), 32pp.

Goldie, Mark, "The Hilton gang and the purge of London in the 1680s" in Nenner, H. (ed.), *Politics and the political imagination in later Stuart Britain* (U. of Rochester P., 1998), pp.43–73.

Hamm, Thomas D., "George Fox and the Politics of Late Nineteenth Century Quaker Historiography" in Pink Dandelion (ed.), *The Creation of Quaker Theory: Insider Perspectives*, (Ashgate, 2004), pp.11–18.

Harris, Tim, *London Crowds in the Reign of Charles II: Propaganda and Politics from the Restoration until the Exclusion Crisis*, (Cambridge U.P., 1987), 264pp.

Hawkins, Richard, see Latey, Gilbert

Hessayon, Ariel, '*Gold tried in the fire': the prophet TheaurauJohn Tany and the English Revolution*, (Ashgate, 2007).

Horle, Craig, *The Quakers and the English Legal System 1660-1688*, (U. of Pennsylvania P., 1988), 320pp.

Howgill, Francis, *Dawnings of the Gospel Day...*, (s.n., 1676), 736pp.

Howgill, Francis, *A Testimony concerning ... Edward Burroughs* [sic], (s.n., 1663)

"Lady Hutchinson"; presumably Hutchinson, Lucy (1620–1675), *Memoirs of the Life of Colonel Hutchinson... published from the original manuscript by J. Hutchinson* (1806; most current edition Henry G. Bohn, 1863), 523pp.

Kendall, John, *Catechism*: pubd as *Some principles and precepts of the Christian religion explained... for the use of children*, (James Phillips, 1783), 40pp.; reprinted under various titles, but "Catechism" not used until 1866.

Kennedy, Thomas C., *British Quakerism 1860–1920: The transformation of a religious community*, (Oxford University Press, 2001), 477pp., ill.

Landers, John, *Death and the Metropolis: Studies in the demographic history of London, 1670–1830*, (Cambridge U.P., 1993), 408pp.

Latey, Gilbert (ed. Hawkins, Richard), *A brief narrative of the life and death of ... Gilbert Latey, compiled... by R. Hawkins*, (J. Sowle, 1707) 156pp.; also a current ed. by Edward Marsh, 1851, 84pp.

Letters, &c., of early Friends, usually cited as "Letters", see Barclay, A.R.

Lettsom, John Coakley; see Fothergill, John.

Lidbetter, Hubert, *The Friends Meeting House: an historical survey of the places of worship of the Society of Friends* (1961; repr. William Sessions, 1995) 84pp.

Linebaugh, Peter, *The London Hanged: Crime and Civil Society in the Eighteenth Century*, (1991; 2nd ed. Verso, 2003), 492pp.

Macaulay, Thomas Babington, *The History of England*, (Longman, 1849)

Maitland, William, *The History of London from its foundation by the Romans to the present time...*, (1739; several continuations by John Entick up to 1756 and 1772 are in 2 and 3 vols.)

Malcolm, James Peller, *Londinium Redivivum, or an ancient history and modern description of London...*, (Nichols, 1802); for ref p.376 see Cromwell, Thomas Kitson.

"The Ministers' Morning Exercises": possibly Sangar, Gabriel, *The Word of Faith improved, by a providential concurrence of many eminent and pious Ministers ... in their Morning-Lectures...*, (s.n., 1656)

Moore, Rosemary, *The Light in their Consciences: the early Quakers in Britain 1646-1666* (Pennsylvania State U.P., 2001), 314pp.

Morgan, Nicholas, *Lancashire Quakers and the establishment, 1660-1730*, (Ryburn Academic, 1993), 319pp.

Nayler, James to Fox, George (1654) is Swarthmore MSS III.76.

Neale, Daniel, *The History of Puritans* (4 vols, 1732–38).

Nevitt, Marcus, *Women and the Pamphlet Culture of Revolutionary England, 1640–1660*, (Ashgate, 2006), 218pp.

Oxford Dictionary of National Biography, (2004), 60 vols. Available online through many libraries, www.oxforddnb.com

Pagitt, Ephraim, *Heresiography, or a description of the heretickes and sectaries sprang up in these latter times*, (1645; 3rd ed. William Lee, 1654) 150pp.

"Penns and Peningtons" see Webb, Maria.

Peters, Kate, *Print Culture and the Early Quakers*, (Cambridge U.P., 2005), 273pp.

"Posthuma Christiana", see Crouch, William.

Price, Jacob M., "The great Quaker business families of 18th century London: the rise and fall of a sectarian patriciate", in Dunn, R.S. and Dunn, M.M. (eds) *The world of William Penn*, (Pennsylvania U.P., 1986), pp.363–99. Also in Price, Jacob M. (ed.), *Overseas trade and traders: essays on some commercial, financial and political challenges facing British Atlantic Merchants, 1660-1775*, (Ashgate Variorum, 1996).

Quaker Pictures, second series, with notes by Wilfred Whitten, (1894; rev. ed., Headley Bros, 1897), 74pp. First series was 1892.

Reay, Barry, *The Quakers and the English Revolution*, (Temple Smith, 1985).

Robertson, F.W, *Expository Lectures on St Paul's Epistles to the Corinthians*, (Smith, Elder & Co, 2nd ed., 1860); this ed. on Google Books matches the ref.

Rowntree, John Stephenson, *Quakerism, Past and Present*, (Smith, Elder & Co, 1859)

Ryan, Michele Denise, "'In my hands for lending': Quaker women's meetings in London, 1659-1700", (University of California PhD thesis, 2003).

Scattergood, Thomas, *Memoirs of Thomas Scattergood ... compiled ... by William Evans and Thomas Evans*, (Charles Gilpin, 1845).

Scott, David, *Quakerism in York, 1650-1720*, University of York, Borthwick Paper, 80 (1991).

Sewel, William, *The History of the Rise, Increase, and Progress of the Christian People called Quakers*, (Assigns of J. Sowle, 1722), 723pp.

Skeats, Herbert, *A History of the Free Churches of England, from A.D. 1688–A.D. 1851*, (Arthur Miall, 1868), 638pp.

Smith, Joseph, *Catalogue of Friends' Books*, 2 vols., (Smith, 1867).

Story, Thomas, *A Journal of the Life of Thomas Story*, (Isaac Thompson, 1747), 768pp.

Stoughton, John, *Ecclesiastical History of England*, (4 vols., 1867–70).

Survey of London, vol.47 (ed. Temple, Philip): *Northern Clerkenwell and Pentonville*, (Yale U.P. for English Heritage, 2008).

Tallack, William, *George Fox, the Friends, and the early Baptists*, (S.W. Partridge & Co, 1868).

Tallack, William, *Peter Bedford, the Spitalfields Philanthropist*, (S.W. Partridge, 1865). 40pp., ill. See also under Beck, William.

Tanner, William, *Three lectures on the early history of the Society of Friends in Bristol and Somersetshire*, (Alfred W. Bennett, 1858), 148pp.

Taylor, Adam, *The History of the English General Baptists*, (T. Bore, 1818).

Thistlethwaite, William, "Lectures": possibly *Thoughts on Religious Education, presented to Friends Education Society*, (W. Simpson, 1856), 15pp.

Trust property book, see Devonshire House

Vaughan, Robert Alfred, *Hours with the Mystics: A contribution to the history of religious opinion*, 2 vols, (s.n. 1856).

Webb, Maria, *The Fells of Swarthmoor Hall and their friends ... a portraiture of religious and family life in the 17th century*, (s.n., 1865).

Webb, Maria, *The Penns & Peningtons of the seventeenth century, in their domestic and religious life*, (F.B. Kitto, 1867).

Whitehead, George, *The Christian progress of that ancient servant and minister of Jesus Christ, George Whitehead*, (Assigns of J. Sowle, 1725), 712pp.

Whitehead, Ann and Elson, Mary, *An Epistle for true love, unity and order in the Church of Christ, against the spirit of discord, disorder and confusion, &c.*, (Andrew Sowle, 1680), 15pp.

The Yorkshireman: a religious and literary journal, by a Friend [Luke Howard], vol.1–5 (1833–1837).

Part 2: Subject bibliography

2A: *London history (general)*

Beier, A.L., and Finlay, Roger (eds), *London 1500-1700: the making of the metropolis*, (Longman, 1985).

Brett-James, Norman G., and Collett, Charles H., *The growth of Stuart London* (London and Middlesex Archaeological Society [1935])

de Krey, Gary, *A Fractured Society: The Politics of London in the First Age of Party 1688-1715* (Clarendon, 1985), 304pp, ill.

de Krey, Gary, *London and the Restoration, 1659-1683*, (Cambridge U.P., 2005), 472pp.

Finlay, Roger, *Population and metropolis: the demography of London 1580-1650* (Cambridge U.P., 1981)

Griffiths, Paul, and Jenner, Mark S.R., (eds) *Londinopolis: Essays in the cultural and social history of early modern London*, (Manchester U.P., 2000)

Inwood, Stephen, *A History of London*, (Macmillan, 1998), 1111pp., ill.

London Topographical Society: their "A to Z of..." series is essential for historical locations: *The A to Z of Restoration London ... based on Ogilby & Morgan's map of 1676*, (Harry Margary, 1992), 93pp.; *The A to Z of Georgian London ... based on Rocque's plan of 1747*, (Harry Margary, 1981), 88pp.; *The A to Z of Regency London ... based on Horwood's map of 1813*, (Harry Margary, 1985), 116pp.; *The A to Z of Victorian London ... based on Bacon's Atlas of 1888*, (Harry Margary, 1987), 140pp.

Merritt, Julia F. (ed.), *Imagining Early Modern London: Perceptions and portrayals of the city from Stow to Strype, 1598-1720*, (Cambridge U.P., 2001). Includes: Smith, Nigel, "'Making fire': conflagration and religious controversy in seventeenth-century London", pp.273–93.

Picard, Liza, *Restoration London*, Weidenfeld & Nicolson (1997), 330pp., ill. Describes aspects of everyday life, from sources including George Fox as well as the expected Pepys and Evelyn.

Porter, Roy, *London: A social history*, (1994; repr. Penguin 2000), 541pp., ill.

Wilson, W., *History and Antiquity of Dissenting Churches in London* (1810)

2B: *Quaker history*

Not specific to London, but inevitably these works contain much concerned with it. These are mostly secondary: published editions of primary works include the Barclay *Letters* (1841, see Works Cited above).

Barbour, Hugh, *The Quakers in Puritan England*, (New Haven, Conn, 1964)

Barclay, Abram Rawlinson, and Barclay, John (ed.), *Letters, &c., of early Friends; illustrative of the history of the Society, from nearly its origin, to about the period of George Fox's decease...*, (Harvey & Darton, 1841)

Barclay, Robert (1833–1876), *The Inner Life of the Religious Societies of the Commonwealth*, Hodder & Stoughton, (1876).

Bauman, Richard, *Let Your Words be Few: symbolism of speaking and silence among seventeenth century Quakers*, (Cambridge, 1983)

Braithwaite, William C., *The Beginnings of Quakerism to 1660*, (2nd ed., Cambridge U.P., 1955)

Braithwaite, William C., *The Second Period of Quakerism*, (2nd ed., Cambridge U.P., 1961)

Butler, David M., "The Making of Meeting Houses" in: *Friends' Quarterly* 22:3 (July 1980) pp.316–24.

Damrosch, Leo, *The Sorrows of the Quaker Jesus: James Nayler and the Puritan Crackdown on the Free Spirit*, (Harvard U.P., 1996, 322 pp., ill.

Cantor, Geoffrey, *Quakers, Jews and Science: Religious responses to modernity and the sciences in Britain, 1650–1900*, (Oxford U.P., 2005) 420pp., ill.

Coffey, John, *Persecution and Toleration in Protestant England 1558-1689* (Harlow, 2000). Fell, Margaret, (ed. Glines, Elsa), *Undaunted Zeal: The Letters of Margaret Fell*, (Friends United Press, 2003), 510pp. Includes letters relevant to Quaker activity in London.

Fox, George, *Journal*, ed Nickalls, J.L., (Cambridge U.P., 1952; repr Philadelphia Yearly Meeting, 1997). See also Works Cited, p.401 for editions used by Beck and Ball.

Gwyn, Douglas, *Apocalypse of the Word: The life and message of George Fox*, (Friends United Press, 1986), 241pp.

Gwyn, Douglas, *Seekers Found: Atonement in early Quaker experience*, (Pendle Hill, 2000) 420pp.

Gwyn, Douglas, *The Covenant Crucified: Quakers and the rise of capitalism*, (1995, repr. Quaker Books 2006), 403pp.

Hill, Christopher, *The World Turned Upside Down: radical ideas during the English Revolution*, (1972; repr Penguin 1975), 431pp.

Horle, Craig, *The Quakers and the English Legal System 1660-1688*, (U. of Pennsylvania Press, 1988), 320pp.

Ingle, H. Larry, *First Among Friends: George Fox and the creation of Quakerism* (New York, Oxford U.P., 1994), 407pp.

Isichei, Elizabeth, *Victorian Quakers*, (Oxford U.P., 1970), 326pp.

Jones, Rufus, *The Later Periods of Quakerism*, (Macmillan, 1921), 2 vols.

Kennedy, Thomas C., *British Quakerism 1860–1920: The transformation of a religious community*, (Oxford U.P. 2001), 477pp., ill..

Kunze, Bonnelyn Young, *Margaret Fell and the Rise of Quakerism*, (Macmillan, 1994), 327pp.

Mack, Phyllis, *Visionary Women: Ecstatic prophecy in seventeenth-century England*, (U. of California P., 1992), 465pp.

Milligan, Edward H., "Unchronicled Barchester: and a few recent chronicles of our local meetings", *Friends' Quarterly* 22:3 (July 1980) pp.325–34. Considers the tradition of local meeting history.

Moore, Rosemary, *The Light in their Consciences: the early Quakers in Britain*, (Pennsylvania State U.P., 2000), 314pp.

Morgan, Nicholas, *Lancashire Quakers and the Establishment, 1660-1730,* (Ryburn Academic, 1993), 319pp.

Mullett, Michael (ed.), *New Light on George Fox 1624–1691,* (Sessions, 1991). Papers from the George Fox Tercentenary Commemorative Conference (1991: Lancaster)

Nuttall, Geoffrey F., *The Holy Spirit in Puritan Faith and Experience,* (2nd ed., 1947; repr. with new introduction by Peter Lake, U. of Chicago P., 1992).

Oxford Dictionary of National Biography, (2004), 60 vols. Available online through many libraries, www.oxforddnb.com

Penney, Norman (ed.). *Pen Pictures of London Yearly Meeting, 1789–1833, being extracts from the notes of Richard Cockin, James Jenkins and others.* (Friends Historical Society Journal Supplement 16–17, 1930), 227pp., ill.

Peters, Kate, *Print Culture and the Early Quakers,* (Cambridge U.P., 2005), 273pp.

Pink Dandelion, *An Introduction to Quakerism,* (Cambridge U.P., 2007), 277pp.

Pink Dandelion (ed.), *The Creation of Quaker Theory: Insider Perspectives,* (Ashgate 2004). Contributions on the development of Quaker self-consciousness; includes Thomas D. Hamm, "George Fox and the Politics of Late Nineteenth Century Quaker Historiography" pp.11-18.

Reay, Barry, *The Quakers and the English Revolution,* (Temple Smith, 1985), 184pp.

Trevett, Christine, *Women and Quakerism in the 17th Century* (Sessions, 1995).

Underwood, T.L., *Primitivism, Radicalism and the Lamb's War: the Baptist–Quaker conflict in seventeenth century England,* (Oxford U.P., 1997), 188pp.

Vann, Richard T. and Eversley, David, *Friends in Life and Death: the British and Irish Quakers in the demographic transition, 1650-1900,* (Cambridge U.P., 1992), 281pp., ill.

Vann, Richard T., *The Social Development of English Quakerism 1655-1755,* (Harvard U.P., 1969), 259pp., ill.

2C: *Quaker London*

The Library at Friends House contains the local meeting records for Greater London and many other primary sources. A manuscript history by George Edwards (Temp MSS 571) was intended as a successor to Beck and Ball in the 1960s, but has limitations; it contains excellent maps of historic sites prepared by David Butler, although some 1960s streets and landmarks are now out of date. Smaller secondary items not included here may also be of interest.

Besse, Joseph with Gandy, Michael, *Sufferings of early Quakers : London and Middlesex, 1655 to 1690; with new introduction and newly compiled index of people and places by Michael Gandy,* (Sessions Book Trust, 2002); pp.361–486 of the original, ill.

Bowers Isaacson, Lisa, *Quakers in the City: A walk around the City of London beginning at the gravesite of George Fox in Bunhill Fields*, 2nd ed., revised and enlarged (Bunhill Fields Preparative Meeting, 2001), 19pp., ill.

Brockbank, Elisabeth, *Edward Burrough: A wrestler for truth*, (Bannisdale Press, 1949), 176pp., ill.

Butler, David M., *The Quaker Meeting Houses of Britain*, (Friends Historical Society, 1999), 2 vols, 946pp., ill. Arranged by historic county, so the London area comes also in the sections on Essex, Herts, Kent and Surrey.

Cadbury, Henry Joel, "The first publishers of truth in London", *Journal of the Friends' Historical Society*, 36 (1939), pp.52–57.

Dixon, Simon, "Early Quaker meeting houses in London, 1654-1688" (University of York MA dissertation 2001), 72pp.

Dixon, Simon Neil, "Quaker communities in London, 1667-c1714" (University of London PhD thesis, 2005), 76pp.

Dixon, Simon, "Quakers and the London Parish 1670-1720", *London Journal*, 32 (2007), pp.229–49.

Dixon, Simon, "The Life and Times of Peter Briggins", *Quaker Studies*, 10 (2006), pp.185–202.

Dixon, Simon, "The priest, the Quakers and the second conventicle act: the battle for Gracechurch Street Meeting House, 1670" in Spicer, Andrew and Hamilton, Sarah (eds), *Defining the Holy: Sacred Space in Medieval and Early Modern Europe*, (Ashgate, 2006), pp.301-318.

Goldie, Mark, "The Hilton gang and the purge of London in the 1680s" in Nenner, H. (ed.) *Politics and the political imagination in later Stuart Britain*post-1869 (U. of Rochester P., 1998), pp.43–73.

Harris, Tim, *London Crowds in the Reign of Charles II: Propaganda and Politics from the Restoration until the Exclusion Crisis*, (Cambridge U.P., 1987), 264pp.

Holmes, Isabella (Mrs Basil), "Haunts of the London Quakers", *The Antiquary*, 35 (1899), pp.11–15, 210–13.

Landers, J. "Birth spacing and fertility decline among London Quakers", in Landers, J.M., and Reynolds, V. (eds), *Fertility and Resources*, (Cambridge U.P., 1990), pp.92–117.

Landers, John, *Death and the Metropolis: Studies in the demographic history of London, 1670-1830* (Cambridge U.P., 1993), 408pp. Includes chapter 4: "Mortality among London Quakers", pp. 131–61.

Landers, John, "Mortality in eighteenth-century London: a note". *Continuity and Change*, 11:2 (1996), pp.303-10.

Lidbetter, Hubert, *The Friends Meeting House: an historical survey of the places of* worship of the Society of Friends. (Quakers), from the days of their founder George Fox, in the 17th century, to the present day, (1961; repr. William Sessions, 1995) 84pp. plus unnumbered plates, ill. Arranged by architectural topic; examples include several London meeting houses.

North, Jon E., "Smashing Satan's Dominion: London Friends' meetings and the origins of the meeting for sufferings", *Friends Quarterly*, 19:6 (April 1976), pp.253-262.

Ryan, Michele Denise, "'In my hands for lending': Quaker women's meetings in London, 1659-1700", (University of California PhD thesis, 2003).

Southall, Kenneth H., *Our Quaker heritage : early meeting houses built prior to 1720 and in use to-day: photographs and word pictures from the past*, (Quaker Home Service 1974) , 81pp., ill.

Stell, Christopher, *An inventory of nonconformist chapels and meeting-houses in Eastern England*, (English Heritage, 2002).

White, Winifred M., *Six Weeks Meeting 1671-1971*, (Six Weeks Meeting, 1971), 119pp., ill. The only published overview of post-1869 Quaker London, written from the point of view of Six Weeks Meeting on its tercentenary.

2D: *Quaker social history, business and occupations*

This is only a brief selection of the works available, but should provide some further leads. Much on London Quaker life will be found in business histories such as banking (Barclays, Lloyds), and biographies of individuals in various fields, e.g. scientists (William Allen, Luke Howard), botanists (Peter Collinson) and physicians (John Fothergill, Thomas Hodgkin, John Coakley Lettsom).

Binyon, Edward. "Diary of a London Quaker apprentice, 1765–68", *Journal of the Friends' Historical Society*, 21 (1924), pp.45-52

Cantor, Geoffrey, "Quakers in the Royal Society 1660-1750", *Notes Rec. Royal Society, London* 51:2, (1997), pp.175-193.

Cole, Alan, "The social origins of the early Friends", *Journal of the Friends' Historical Society*, 48:3 (1957), pp.99-118.

Milligan, Edward H., *The Biographical Dictionary of British Quakers in Commerce and Industry, 1775-1920*, (Sessions Book Trust, 2007), 606pp., ill. This recent comprehensive work is an essential source for the later period.

Price, J.M., "The great Quaker business families of 18th century London : the rise and fall of a sectarian patriciate", in *The world of William Penn*, ed. Dunn, R.S. and Dunn, M.M. (Pennsylvania U.P., 1986), pp.363-99.

Raistrick, Arthur, *Quakers in Science and Industry*, (Bannisdale Press, 1950; repr. Sessions Book Trust, 1993), 361pp., ill. Useful on London scientists, and clock and instrument makers.

Walvin, James, *The Quakers: Money and Morals*, (John Murray,1997), 243 pp.

Windsor, David Burns, *The Quaker Enterprise: friends in business* (Muller, 1980) 176 p., ill.

Wrench, John Evelyn, *Transatlantic London: Three centuries of association between England and America*, (Hutchinson, [1949]), 262pp., ill.

2E: *London Quaker meetings*

Relating to Beck and Ball's chapter headings by historic monthly meeting, but also including histories of post-1869 meetings.

CHAPTER IX: GRACECHURCH ST (INCLUDING BULL & MOUTH)

Daniels, Peter, "Quakers in Stoke Newington: the 19th and 20th centuries", *Hackney History*, 14 (2008), pp.24–37, ill.

Edwards, George William, "The Bull and Mouth meeting house: its site and environs", *Friends' Quarterly*, 9 (1955), pp.78–84.

Harding, Vanessa, *Nomura House, no. 1, St Martin's-Le-Grand: a brief history*, (Nomura International, c.1990) 16pp., ill. About the Bull and Mouth site.

Metcalf, Priscilla, "Seven Centuries in White Hart Court", *Guildhall Studies in London History*, 4 (1979), pp.1–18. A very useful article putting the Quaker tenure of the site in a longer context. Including plans of the site from the Fishmonger's Company records.

Roberts, Evelyn (ed.), *Louisa: Memories of a Quaker childhood.* (Friends Home Service Committee, 1970), 53pp., ill. The early influences of Louisa Hooper Stewart (1818–1918) in Croydon and Stoke Newington.

CHAPTER X: DEVONSHIRE HOUSE

See also Anna Littleboy, under XXI Morning Meeting, below.

Beck, William, *Devonshire House: historical account of the acquisition by the Society of Friends...*, (Headley Bros,1903; rev. ed.1908), 20pp., ill. New version by Penney, Norman, *Devonshire House: an historical account [etc]* (Friends' Bookshop, 1920), with note on Beck: "Recent research having placed this book somewhat out of date, it has not been thought well to reprint it, but it was largely drawn on when the following article ... was in preparation".

Clark, Joanna *Eminently Quakerly: the building of Friends House* (Quaker Books, 2006), 36pp., ill. With an account of the last days of Devonshire House.

Devonshire House Monthly Meeting, Trust Property Book, (the monthly meeting, 1861), 126pp.

Hicks, Muriel A., "Friends' Reference Library 1901-1959", *Journal of the Friends Historical Society*, 49:3, (Autumn 1960) pp.123–34.

Knight, Frank & Rutley, *Particulars, plan and conditions of sale of the important block of property known as Devonshire House, Bishopsgate ... to be sold by auction, in one lot*, (Knight, Frank & Rutley, 2nd ed., 1923), 10pp., ill.

Sefton-Jones, Margaret, *Old Devonshire House by Bishopsgate* (Swarthmore Press, [1923]), 159pp., ill.

Wilson, Stephen Shipley, "From Devonshire House to Endsleigh Gardens" *Journal of the Friends' Historical Society*, 53:4 (1975) pp.293-313

CHAPTER XI: PEEL

See also XXIV Schools, below, for Clerkenwell Workhouse and School.

Daniels, Peter, "Quakers in Stoke Newington, to the mid-19th century", *Hackney History*, 8 (2002), pp.3–11, ill.

Pursaill, Olive O., *The sign of the Peel*, (S. Goss, [1913]), 49pp., ill.

CHAPTER XII: SOUTHWARK

Edwards, George William, "Quakers south of the bridge", *Friends Quarterly*, **21** (July 1967), pp.512–23.

Edwards, Irene L., "Early discipline in Southwark", *Journal of the Friends' Historical Society*, 31 (1934), pp.71–81.

Huzzard, Rosalie, *The History of Petts Wood Meeting, 1934–1994*, (Petts Wood Preparative Meeting, 1994), 25pp., ill.

Kinrade, Derek, "Quakers built a meeting house", *Peckham Society News* (Spring 2001), pp.26–29.

"Quakers' hall: Meeting house, Blackheath, London; architect Trevor Dannatt, 1973", *Architectural Review*, 153:914, (April 1973), pp.265–69, ill.

CHAPTER XIII: WESTMINSTER

See also Joanna Clark, *Eminently Quakerly* under X. Devonshire House; Friends House came within Westminster MM boundaries when built.

Cundy, H. William and Greenwood, John Ormerod, *Hammersmith Quakers' Tercentenary, 1677-1977*, (Hammersmith Preparative Meeting, 1978), 87pp., ill.

Edwards, G.W., "Friends' meetings in Westminster", *Friends' Quarterly*, 10:3 (1956), pp.125–28.

Lee, Doris, and Lee, Douglas, *Glimpses of Westminster Meeting 1655-1956*, (Westminster Preparative Meeting, 1983), 23pp.

Pryer, Christine A.H., "Quakers in Holloway", typescript at Friends House, L097.10 PRY

Chapter XIV: Ratcliff

Allen, John, (ed. Sturge, Clement Y.), *Leaves from the past: the diary of John Allen, sometime brewer of Wapping (1757-1808) written between February and July 1777*, (J. W. Arrowsmith, 1905), 96pp., ill.

Cozens, Ken, *Wapping 1600–1800: A social history of an early modern London maritime suburb*, (East London Historical Society, 2009). Includes Wapping Quaker meeting.

Hunt, Julia, *Enterprise of the Ratcliff Friends: three centuries of Quaker family networks*, (Stepney Historical Trust, 2000), 56pp.

Morris, Derek, "Quaker farmers in 18th century Stepney". *Quaker Connections*, 24 (2001), pp.26–28.

Poole, Roger, and Whistlecroft, Charles, *A History of William Gunn's Charity*, (the charity?, 2000), 150pp., ill. A Quaker charity operating in the Ratcliff & Barking Monthly Meeting area.

Chapter XV: Barking

Bambridge, David Edwin, "A history of Barking and Ratcliff [sic] Monthly Meeting of the Society of Friends: with particular reference to the Frys and Gurneys", (Battersea College of Education course dissertation, 1969), 101pp.

Davies, Adrian, *The Quakers in English Society 1655–1725* (Oxford U.P., 2000) About Quakers in Essex.

Fry, Elizabeth, (ed. Skidmore, Gil), *Elizabeth Fry: a Quaker life; selected letters and writings introduced and edited by Gil Skidmore*, (Altamira Press; International Sacred Literature Trust, 2005), 238pp. Elizabeth Fry lived within Barking Monthly Meeting; see also the biographies by June Rose (1980) and Jean Hatton (2005).

Martin, Mary Clare Hewlett, "Children and religion in Walthamstow and Leyton c.1740-c.1870", (University of London PhD thesis, 2000), 611pp., ill.

Philpot, Terry, "Barking Friends", in *The Barking Record*, 87 (June 1974), pp.5–10, ill. Also: Philpot, T., "The Quakers of Barking". *Essex Journal*, 9 (1974), pp.62–65.

Pollard, Myrtle, *Wanstead Friends Meeting: Stewardship of Epping Forest*, (the meeting, 1998), 16pp. Concerned with the title to the property in relation to Epping Forest land.

Chapter XVI: Longford

Crouch, K. R. and Shanks, S. A., *Excavations in Staines, 1975-76: the Friends' burial ground site*, (London & Middlesex Archaeological Society, and

Surrey Archaeological Society, 1984) 135pp., ill. Report of archaeological investigation of the former site of Staines Friends Burial Ground (finds mainly Roman, Saxon and medieval). The Meeting House was sold in 1936; the burials were removed to a communal grave at Jordans Burial Ground in 1960. Plan of the meeting house foundations and the burial ground, p.25.

Jones, Margaret Eiluned, "The Quakers in Brentford and Isleworth", in two issues of *St Francis of Assisi* magazine [parish magazine of St. Francis of Assisi, Great West Road, Isleworth], (Sept. 1974; Oct. 1974).

Trott, Celia, *The story of Uxbridge Quakers from 1658*, (Uxbridge Preparative Meeting, 1970), 19pp., ill.

Westminster and Longford Monthly Meeting, *An account of the trust property belonging to or under the care of Westminster and Longford Monthly Meeting ... : with a statement of the boundaries of Westminster and Longford Monthly Meeting*, (Headley Brothers [printers], 1904), 42pp.

Wilding, Joan, *Brentford and Isleworth Friends Meeting House 1785–1985*, (1985).

CHAPTER XVII: TOTTENHAM

Brown, Peter A.J.: a bound volume of his manuscript historical research on Tottenham Quakers has been recently deposited (2009) at Bruce Castle Museum, London Borough of Haringey.

Collicott, Sylvia, *Anti-slavers in Haringey*, (London Borough of Haringey, 1984), 25pp.

Collie, M.A., *Quakers of Tottenham 1775–1825*, (Edmonton Hundred Historical Society, 1978) 29pp., ill.

Compton, Theodore, *Recollections of Tottenham Friends and the Forster family*, (Edward Hicks, 1893), 74pp.

Edwards, I. L., "1688, Middlesex village to suburb of London, 1938: 250 years of Winchmore Hill Meeting", *Journal of the Friends' Historical Society*, 35 (1938), pp.23-40.

Olver, A. David, *A History of Quakerism at Winchmore Hill*, (Winchmore Hill Preparative Meeting, 2002), 66pp., ill.

Rowe, Violet A, "The Meeting House at Flamstead End, Hertfordshire", *Journal of the Friends' Historical Society*, 53:4 (1975), pp.326-334.

CHAPTER XVIII: HENDON

There is apparently no published material on the Hendon Monthly Meeting described in the book, but Peter Collinson lived in the area. Several meetings opened in the former MM area in the early twentieth century, included here as geographically appropriate.

Brett-James, Norman, *The history of Mill Hill School, 1807-1907,* (Andrew Melrose, 1911) 415pp., ill. Contains chapter entitled "Peter Collinson, the botanist of Mill Hill", p. 378-392.

Brett-James, Norman, *The life of Peter Collinson,* (Edgar G. Dunstan, 1925), 287pp., ill.

Harper, Rod, "Talk to Hampstead Friends on the centenary year of their meeting house", (the author, 2007), 5pp.

Muswell Hill: 75th anniversary 1926-2001, (Muswell Hill Preparative Meeting, 2001) 16pp.

Quakers in North London: a guide to Hampstead Monthly Meeting, (Hampstead Monthly Meeting, 2002), 36pp., ill.

Rubinstein, David, *Hampstead Quakers, 1907-14: the new meeting house and its members,* (the author, 1994), 18pp., ill.

Slack, Kathleen M (ed.), *A History of the Golders Green Meeting of the Religious Society of Friends 1913-1993,* (the meeting? 1993), 38pp.

CHAPTER XIX: KINGSTON

See also Evelyn Roberts, *Louisa,* under IX Gracechurch St, above.

Bashford, Louise, and Sibun, Lucy, "Excavations at the Quaker Burial Ground, Kingston-upon-Thames, London", *Post-Medieval Archaeology*, 41:1 (2007), pp.100-54. See also under Burial Grounds.

Edwards, W. J., *Wandsworth meeting house: a short sketch,* (the author, 1937), 27pp.

Finlow, Dilys, "A study of the Religious Society of Friends at Croydon, 1825–1875", (Coloma College of Education Dissertation, 1975).

Haynes, Richard T., *A brief history of Esher Meeting of the Society of Friends,* (Kingprint [printers], 1971), 36 pp, ill.

Marsh, Thomas W., and Marsh, Anne W., *Some records of the early Friends in Surrey and Sussex from the original minute-books and other sources,* (S. Harris. 1886). Meeting histories: Capel; Dorking; Guildford; Horsham; Reigate.

Mirwitch, Joseph, "The Society of Friends' Hall at Park Lane, Croydon", *The William Morris Society Newsletter* (Autumn 2006) pp.16–18; also *Twentieth Century Society Newsletter* (Winter 2006/7) pp.9–11.

Pulford, John Sydney Leslie, *The first Kingston Quakers,* (the author, 1973). 66pp., illus.

Pulford, J.S.L. *An index of Kingston Quakers in the 17th century,* (Walton on Thames Local Hist. Society, 1971), 46pp.

Steel, G. Gordon, *An outline history of Sutton Meeting 1932–2000,* (themeeting? revised ed. 2001), 38pp., ill.

2F: *Subjects relating to later Beck & Ball chapters*

Chapter XX: Burial grounds

See also Staines (under Longford); Kingston; and Quaker History and Quaker London sections above, for demographic works based on burial records by Richard Vann and John Landers.

Braithwaite, J.B. jnr, *Fifty Years Work at Bunhill Fields*, (1927).

Cox, Margaret (ed.), *Grave concerns* (Council for British Archaeology, 1998), 275pp. ill. Includes: Stock, Gwynne, "Quaker burial: doctrine and practice", pp.129–43; Bashford, Louise, and Pollards, Tony, "In the burying place: the excavation of a Quaker burial ground [London Rd., Kingston]", pp.154–66; Start, Helen, and Kirk, Lucy, "The bodies of Friends: the osteological analysis of a Quaker burial ground [London Rd., Kingston]", pp.167–78.

Holmes, Isabella (Mrs Basil), *The London Burial Grounds: notes on their history from the earliest times to the present day*; (T. Fisher Unwin, 1896), 339pp., ill. Quaker burial grounds on pp.139–43.

Chapter XXI: Morning meeting of Ministers and Elders

Including works on printers and publishers.

Bell, Maureen, "Elizabeth Calvert and the 'confederates'", *Publishing History*, 32 (1992), pp.5–49.

Bell, Maureen, "'Her usual practices' : the later career of Elizabeth Calvert, 1664-75", *Publishing History*, 35 (1994), pp.5–64.

Bownas, Samuel, (ed. Taber, William P.), *A description of the qualifications necessary to a gospel minister, containing advice to ministers and elders, how to conduct themselves in their conversation, and various services, according to their gifts in the church of Christ*, (Luke Hinde, 1767; republished with an introduction by William P. Taber, Pendle Hill Publications; Tract Association of Friends [Philadelphia], 1989), 112pp.

Hall, David J., "'The fiery tryal of their infallible examination': self-control in the regulation of Quaker publishing in England from the 1670s to the mid 19th century", in: Myers, Robin, and Harris, Michael (eds), *Censorship and the Control of Print in England and France 1600-1910*, (St Paul's Bibliographies, 1992), pp.59–86.

Littleboy, Anna L., *A history of the Friends' Reference Library with notes on early printers and printing in the Society of Friends*, (Friends' Historical Society, 1921 for 1920), 31pp.

Mortimer, Russell, "The first century of Quaker printers", *Journal of the Friends' Historical Society*, 41 (1949), 74–84.

Mortimer, Russell, "Biographical notices of printers and publishers of Friends' books up to 1750. A supplement to Plomer's Dictionary", *Journal of Documentation*, 3 (1947-8), pp.107-25.

Peters, Kate, *Print Culture and the Early Quakers* (Cambridge U.P., 2005), 273pp.

Terry, A.E., "Giles Calvert's publishing career", *Journal of the Friends' Historical Society*, 35 (1938), pp.45-49. .

Trevett, Christine, "'Not fit to be printed': the Welsh, the Women and Second day's morning meeting", *Journal of the Friends' Historical Society* 59:2 (2001), pp.115–44.

Chapter XXII: Women's meetings

The subject of Quaker women is much broader than the women's meetings discussed by Beck and Ball in this chapter, and has been a very fruitful area of research and publication in recent decades. Many works will contain references to the women's meetings as well as women's manuscripts, pamphlet literature and other sources; for some of these see under Quaker History and Quaker London, above.

Edwards, Irene L., "The women Friends of London: the Two-Weeks and Box Meetings", *Journal of the Friends' Historical Society*, 47 (1955), pp.3–21.

Ryan, Michele Denise, "'In my hands for lending": Quaker women's meetings in London, 1659–1700", (University of California, PhD thesis, 2003).

Tolles, F.B. (ed.), *Slavery and "The woman question": Lucretia Mott's diary of her visit to Great Britain to attend the World's Anti-Slavery Convention of 1840*, (Friends' Historical Society Journal Supplement 23, 1952).

Chapter XXIII: Jordans

Caudle, Jack, "The grave of William Penn: some problems of history", *Journal of the Friends Historical Society*, 50:1 (Spring 1962), pp.9–14.

Hayward, Arthur L., and Macmurray, John, *Jordans: the making of a community: a history of the early years*, (Home Service Committee, 1969), 186pp., ill.

Littleboy, Anna, *A History of Jordans*, (1909; 10th rev. ed. Home Service Committee, 1949) 28pp., ill.

Newman, George, *Quaker inheritance: an address to American Friends at Jordans, in Buckinghamshire, on August 18, 1920*, (Loxley Bros, [1920]), 23pp.

Smithson, Sue, and Pinder, Hilary, "The historical importance of Jordans Meeting House", *Journal of the Friends Historical Society* 60:2 (2004) pp.107–12.

Stefferud, Alfred Daniel, and Showler, Karl, *Jordans Quaker meeting*, (1974; repr. Quaker Home Service, 1985), 20pp. ill.

Warner, Ernest, *Jordans, a Quaker shrine, past and present: with a brief outline of the faith, doctrine and the practice of the Society of Friends*, (Friends Bookshop, 1921), 28pp. ill.

CHAPTER XXIV: SCHOOLS (WITH SOCIAL CONCERNS AND PHILANTHROPY)

The Library at Friends House has annual reports and school magazines for the Islington Road and Croydon periods of the Friends School, Saffron Walden. The Quaker educationalist Joseph Lancaster is also relevant to the subject of Quakers and education, although he is not discussed by Beck and Ball; Susannah Corder's and other schools in Stoke Newington are discussed by Peter Daniels in *Hackney History* (2003 and 2008).

Bartle, George F., "Joseph Lancaster's 'house lads': who they were and what happened to them", *History of Education Society Bulletin*, 58 (1996), pp.45–54.

Beck, William, *Peter Bedford, the Spitalfields philanthropist* (Friends' Tract Assoc., 1903), 40pp., ill.

Bellers, John, (ed. Clarke, G.), *John Bellers, 1654 to 1725, Quaker visionary: his life, times and writings*, (1987; repr. Sessions Book Trust, 1993), 293pp.

Besse, Joseph, *The life and posthumous works of Richard Claridge*, (3rd ed. Darton, 1836), 314pp.

Bolam, David Whielden, *Unbroken community: the story of the Friends School, Saffron Walden, 1702–1825*, (the school, 1952), 184pp. History of Saffron Walden School going back to Clerkenwell. See also Radley (2000) below.

Braithwaite, William Charles, "The Adult-School movement", in Mudie-Smith, Richard, *The Religious Life of London*, (Hodder and Stoughton, 1904), pp.331–33.

Brown, Sidney William, *Leighton Park: a history of the school*, (the school?, 1952), 198pp., ill. Founded by Quakers in 1828 as Grove House School (Tottenham); re-formed as Leighton Park School 1890.

Campbell Stewart, W.A., *Quakers and Education: as seen in their schools in England*, (Epworth Press, 1953), 310pp.

The Croydon School monthly magazine No. 1–12 (1846–1847).

Ellinor, Jennie, "Clerkenwell in the eighteenth century: a study in Quaker attitudes in education", *Journal of the Friends' Historical Society*, 52:4 (1971), pp.277–91.

Glover, Morris, "The work of the Bedford Institute Association and its relation to English social structure 1849-1948" (University of London thesis for diploma in Social Studies, 1948), 36pp.

Hawkes, H.G., *Some reflection on education in Tottenham over the past three centuries*, (Edmonton Hundred Historical Society, 1993), 26pp., ill.

Hoare, J. "One hundred years of Friends' service in East London", *Friends' Quarterly*, 3 (1949), pp.207–15.

Hutton, Richard, (ed. Hitchcock, Timothy V.), *Richard Hutton's Complaints Book: the notebook of the steward of the Quaker Workhouse at Clerkenwell, 1711-1737*, (London Record Society, 1987), 110pp.

Pyper, Hugh, *Mary Hughes: A friend to all in need*, (Quaker Home Service, 1985), 28pp., ill.

Radley, Farrand, "300 years of Friends School, Saffron Walden: a four-site saga", *Journal of the Friends' Historical Society*, 59:1 (2000), pp.3–18. See also Bolam (1952) above.

Reader, John, *Of schools and schoolmasters: some thoughts on the Quaker contribution to education*, (Quaker Home Service, 1979), 74pp.

Stone, Patricia, *Ragged, British, Quaker, Soldier: 19th century Croydon schools*, (A.C.M.D., 1992), 50pp.

Taylor, Joyce, *Joseph Lancaster, the poor child's friend: educating the poor in the early nineteenth century, with an introduction by Roy Porter*, (Campanile, 1996), 125pp.

INDEX

At Friends House there is an index bound in to several copies of the book, typed from an early twentieth-century manuscript index by the librarian Norman Penney. This has some mistranscription (e.g. "Fire, Great" and "Plague, Great" as "Fire Street" and "Plague Street"), some genuine headings of debatable use, and long strings of undifferentiated page numbers. It has been converted into a spreadsheet by Gwynne Stock, during his research on burial grounds, and the library staff kindly made this available to me.

I have made my own index entries from the text, but used the Friends House index as a check for missed items while entering my own, and sometimes it has suggested cross references or other inspirations. I would like to record my thanks for its help during the indexing.

The indexing of personal names is comprehensive. Places included some very incidental references (e.g. in describing monthly meeting boundaries), but not where a mention contains no actual information about a place. Passing mentions of meetings are not included: this often occurs where a meeting is mentioned as a comparison, but the full discussion of that meeting's case will be found elsewhere. I hope the subject terms chosen will be those that occur to the readers, but that is hard to predict. PD

Abbreviations: MM monthly meeting; QM quarterly meeting; SWM Six Weeks Meeting.
Illustration references are in bold (page numbers are the pages facing the picture).

Abbey (Little Almonry) 240, 242–43
Abbott [surname, female] 390
Aberdeen, Cromwell's troops in 12
aborigines, T.F. Ball on xxvii
absconding children, workhouse, 370n
accountants: T.F. Ball xxvii
accounts: *see also* finance
Ackworth School, 244, 259, 378, 393
Acts of Parliament 31, 60-68
   Affirmation Act (1696) xxiii
   Conventicle Acts q.v. (1662, 1664, 1670) 61–65, 83, 138, 139–40, 141, 152
   Marriage (Soc of Friends) Act (1860) xvi
   Toleration (1689) 65, 84, 178, 298; registering of meeting places 196
   Uniformity (1662) 35, 37
Addison, Joseph, on Great Storm, 165
adjournment of business (Devonshire House), 179, 180n
adult education: Bedford Inst., Ratcliff, 273
adverse literature (*see also* literature, not approved) 41, 42, 113, 177
advices (*see also* discipline; queries) 122, 179, 280, 292, 327–8
   G. Fox's 52n, 76
   in relation to queries 57
   Quarterly Meeting 118
   from Six Weeks Meeting 115–21
affirmation: *see* Acts; oaths
afternoon meetings: *see* times of meetings
Agar, Jacob, legacy to SWM 109n
Agra and Masterman's Bank 149
alchemy: business failure in 225
alcohol: *see* drink
Aldersgate 36, 343
   Bull & Mouth 134–44
   Sarah Sawyer's 136, 196, 351
Alderson, William, architect 158
ale, see beer
Alexander I of Russia 261, 265
Alexander, [surname] 389
Alexander, family 150, 315
Algiers, captives in 130, 131, 178
Allen and Hanbury's 150
Allen, William 150, 158, 159, 189, 265, 388
   and Alexander I of Russia 261,
   and Friends' School site 374,
Almond, Richard 321
Almonry, Little: *see* Westminster
almshouses (*see also* elderly people; poor; tenements)
   Leytonstone 276
   Tottenham 303, 307
   Yoakley's 158, 182–83, 233

420

Alsop, Robert, 211
alternating meetings: *see* times of meetings, fortnightly
Amelia, Princess: Dr Pope and 294
America
  G. Fox travels to 64n, 92, 337
  Hicksites xvi
  ministers from 81, 82, 149, 393
  Pennsylvania 81, 131, 193, 293, 301
  Rhode Island 81
  Virginia 267
  transatlantic community xxiii
  travel and emigrants to 45, 81, 340, 396
Amsterdam, sufferings in 131
Anabaptists (*see also* Baptists) 168, 215
"ancient Friends": *see* elderly people, elders; ministers; Morning Meeting
Ancient Friends, Plaistow Home for, 375
Anglicans *see* Church of England
Aniseed Clear (MM boundary) 171
Anderson, Ann 200
Angell, Sarah 287
anniversaries (*see also* times and seasons) xx
antiquarianism xiii
appeals, to QM 73, 79, 100, 107
appeals, to SWM 95, 106–7, 120, 121
Appleby Castle, F. Howgill's death 21
"appointed" meetings (*see also* meetings, private) 291
appointments
  difficulties 306, 325
  Peel MM, to attend 205
  rotation 111, 113
apprentice teachers 360, 370, 380
apprentices (*see also* occupations; young people) 122, 201, 370
  financial support 97, 98, 185n, 374
  (non-Quaker) disrupt mtgs 25, 26, 136
  placement of 48, 72, 366, 368
arboretum, Dr John Fothergill's 260
Archbishop of Canterbury and Little Almonry lease 242
architects
  William Alderson 158
  Beck, William xxiv
  John Bevans 375, 376
  Samuel Daukes 284
  Harrison of Chester 158
archives: *see* records
aristocratic membership 249
Armfield, Joseph 211

arms: *see* militia, peace testimony 56, 341
arrests, see sufferings
Artillery Ground 183, 184
Artillery Wall, Southwark 216
Ashby, Elizabeth 294
Ashby, Thomas 294
Ashfield, Patience 284
Ashfield, Richard 283
assembly, laws against (meetings) 60–68
astrology 228
asylum, John Goodson's 130
atonement xvii
Atkins, Susan 229
attendance
  Church of England 61
  local meetings 212, 252, 256, 263, 316
  ministers, Morning Meeting 338
  MMs 209, 210, 325
  penalties for non- 23, 364, 377n
  QM report (1761) 382
  SWM 96, 103
  weekday meetings 79
  women at MM 353
Atterbury, Dr. [Francis], Dean of Westminster 242n
Audland, John 20

Bach (or Bates), Humphery 36
Back Lane, Croydon 324
Baker, Richard 303
Baker's Peel, sign 192, 195
Baker's Row, Peckham 224
Baker's Row, Whitechapel 335
Ball, T. Frederick xxvii–xxix
  and Bedford Institute xvii, xxvii–xxviii
  as historian ix, xxx, xxxi
  portrait **xxiv**
Bangs, Benjamin 268
banishment (transportation) *see* sufferings
banking:
  Agra & Masterman's 149
  Barclays 149, 150, 300n
  Joseph Freame 300n
  William Mead 278
  Priscilla Wakefield (savings bank) 307
  other firms 150
bankruptcy xxvi, 119, 123, 124, 184, 340, 385
Bankside: Henry Clarke's 37, 215
baptism 14
Baptists 41, 196
  Anabaptists 168, 215   *contd*

421

Baptists *contd*
   Richard Claridge 200
   doctrinal controversies 14–17
   at Esher 315, 328
   persecution of 34, 35, 37, 68n, 140
   and Quaker origins xv, 11–13, 18n, 215
   Adam Taylor xiv
Barclay, family 150
Barclay, Abram Rawlinson (ed.) *Letters* **xv**, 25, 67, 70, 134, 136, 156
Barclay, Ann, boarding school for girls 361
Barclay, David sen and jun 300,
Barclay, Robert (1648–1690): *Apology* 28, 172; *Catechism* 292, 364; "journal translated into Russian" (error for *Apology*?) 239
Barclay, Robert (1833–1876) xiv, 301, 380n
Barclay, Susannah Willett, marriage 89
Barclays Bank (Barclay, Bevan, Tritton & Co) 149, 150, 300n
Barking 274–5, **277**, 286, 297
   Richard Claridge at 200, 360
Barking MM 274–81, 361
   and QM 71, 75, 78
   and SWM 110, 111, 112
   union with Ratcliff 273
Barnard, family 184
Barnard, Hannah xvii, 82–83, 342
Barnet 295, 298, 299
barns, for meetings 296, 300, 301
Barnsley, Thomas Morton of 294
Barrett, Jonathan 158
Barrett, Richard 200, 328
Barrow, David: Marygold Stairs 215
Barrow, Robert 330
Barry, John Thomas 177
Bartholomew Close, asylum 130
Bartholomew Fair, Solomon Eccles at 142
Bartholomew, Row[lan]d (Baptist) 328
Basing House, Rickmansworth 359
Basinghall St: Samuel Vasse's 36, 347, 349
Bates, William 7n
Batger, John 84
baths, public: Dr John Fothergill and 260
Bathurst, Charles 180
Bathurst, Grace 129, 199
Batt, Joseph 330
Bayley, Anne 278
Beaconsfield, Bucks 359
Beacontree Heath 280
Bealing, Benjamin (Recording Clerk) 84, 321

Bearbone, Dr, Dev Ho rented from 168
beards: John Perrot 45n
beating: *see* sufferings; violence
Beaumont [surname] 388
Beck family xxiv
Beck, Elizabeth (née Lister) xxvi, 151n
Beck, Ernest xxiv, xxv
Beck, John 158
Beck, Joseph xxiv
Beck, Richard xxiv
Beck, Richard Low xxiv, 158, 161n, 265, 391n
Beck, Sarah 177
Beck Thomas 324
Beck, William xxiv
   and Bedford Institute xxv, **166**
   clerk of Devonshire House MM xxix
   evangelical sympathies xvii
   historical work ix, xv xxx
   London Friends' Meetings, publication xxxi
   other works xxvi
   portraits xxiii, xxxvi
Becontree Heath (Beentary) 280
Bedford Institute xix, 166, 273
   T F Ball and xvii, xxvii, xxviii
   W Beck and xxv, **166**
Bedford, Peter 166, 177, 189, 328, 378
Beech, William 253
Beehive, The (Wanstead) 275
Beentary (Beacontree) Heath 280
beer/ale (*see also* brewers; drink; food and drink; temperance) 257–58, 277, 322, 375n
behaviour, disorderly: *see* disorderly conduct
Behmenites, Ralph Fretwell's epistle to 342
Bell, Benjamin 327
Bell, Daniel 250
Bell, John 250
Bell, Jonathan 300, 307
Bell, Margaret, bequest 185n
Bell, William 327
Bellers, John xxiii, 361–62,
Benburke, Robert: meeting in house 215
benches: *see* seating
Bennett, Mary 296, 297
Benson, Gervaise 18–19
Bentley, Thomas 225
bequests: *see* legacies
Bermondsey
   Long Lane burial ground 223, 236
   nonconformists in 214

Bermondsey Street 37, 215
Berryman, Thomas 284
Besse, Joseph sen of Colchester 201n
Besse, Joseph (1683?–1757) 201
  biography of Richard Claridge 200
  clerk of Peel 206
  on Six Weeks Meeting 107
  Sufferings 60, 62, 67, 134; Bull & Mouth 141, 142n; Gracechurch St 152, 153; Ham 276; Mile End 266; Mitcham 323–24; Peel 202–03; Southwark 217; Wandsworth 319
Bethnal Green: MM boundaries 171
Bevan, family 150
Bevan [surname] 390
Bevan, Joseph Gurney xvii, 83, 150, 376, 389
Bevan, Paul 307
Bevan, Thomas 177
Bevans, John, architect 375, 376
Bible
  authority of xvii, 11, 12, 13–14, 15–16, 82
  E. Burrough and 21, 25, 32, 136
  G. Fox and 147, 296,
  J. Nayler and xviii, 30
  New Testament (Acts) xxi
  Old Testament 8n, (2 Kings 18:4) 331
  provision of 84, 207
  reading 56, 273, 364, 365, 382
Bible Society 394
bibliography 397–418
  Smith, Joseph 259, 362n
  Whiting, John 258–59
Bickham, Richard 225
bidders to funerals 129n, 233
Biddle, family 315
Biddle, Michael 291, 293
bill of fare, workhouse 363n, 366–368, 369n, 371, 373
Billing, Edward 240
Bills of Mortality xxii
Bingley, William 330
Birkbeck family 150,
Birkbeck [surname] 389
Birkbeck, Wilson 375, 376
birthright Friends, "second generation" 122
births (*see also* midwives)
  Box Meeting 345
  costly treats at 117
  births, records xxii, 71n, 87, 101, 326
Bishoprick (Durham), early MM 44
bishops 9–10, 393

Bishopsgate (and Bishopsgate St) 125
  collections in 183, 184
  Devonshire House 142, **171**
  Dolphin Inn 146, 168, 170
  MM boundaries 171
Blackbury, Sarah (Blackberry) 261n, 262, 347n, 349
Blackfriars: MM boundaries 197
Blackman St, Southwark: Daniel Fleming's 37, 215
Blackwall: Ratcliff poor district boundary 272
Blake, Thomas 230
blasphemy, J Nayler trial 30
blood, poured at St Paul's 141
Blow, Anne 202
Blue Lion Court, Aldersgate St 196
boarding-house keepers [James Withers] xxvii
boarding schools: *see* schools
Bockett, Elias, satirises William Gibson 80
body snatching 333, 335
Bond, Nicholas 36, 223, 240
Bond, William of Chiswick: meeting 36, 262
bones: exhumation 236
  Tom Paine's 391
Book of Common Prayer 281n
books: *see also* libraries; literature; manuscripts; records
  printing and binding 133
  for records 51, 94
booksellers: Tace [Sowle] Raylton and Isaac Sowle 145
borrowing: *see* funds
Boskett, Thomas 315
botany 132, 260
boundaries of monthly meetings 120, 121
  changes 151, 226
  descriptions 170–71, 197, 249, 272–73
  ignored by residents 171
Bourne, Benjamin 354
Bow: Ratcliff poor district boundary 273
Bowden, James xxix
bowing (*see also* plainness) 77, 265
Bowley, Devereux 109n, 374n
Bowrey, William 110n
Box Meeting 144, 147, 196, 206, 261n, 344–48
  G. Whitehead legacy 177
  and Women's Two-Weeks Mtg 348–49, 351
boxes, for collections: *see* funds
boys, admitted to workhouse 364
boys' schools 360–61

Bradford, William 342n
Bradwick, Devon, fire at 101
Brady, Edward F. 380
Brady, Elizabeth 380
Brady, William 367n
Braithwaite [surname] 390
Braithwaite, William C xiv, xxi
Brand, Thomas 297
Bratt, brothers **xii**
Brayne, James 145, 152
bread, price of 367
Brentford & Isleworth 286–87, **287**
    Brentford market 317
Brewers' Company 374, 379
    Hall, used for meetings [*table after* 88], 143
brewers: Blackbury, husband of Sarah 262
    Truman & Co 166
Brewster, Samuel 374
Bridewell 20, 138, 142, 267
Bridgstock, Mary 277
briefs, charitable 183, 203
Briggins family? (given as Buggins) 192
Briggin[s], Mariabella, legacy to Peel 210
Briggins, Peter xxii
Bringhurst, John 342n
Bristol 20
    E. Burrough in 37
    G. Fox epistle to 64n
    J. Nayler in 30
    records 52n
    William Tanner lectures on 59
British Friend xxxi
British Schools: lease of Bunhill land 334
British Workman (temperance pub) xxv
Broad Street Buildings (site of station) 329
Broadbank, Thomas, legacy to SWM 110n
Brock, James (Captain) 37, 266, 267
Bromley [by Bow], Thomas Foster of 83, 389
Brook St, Ratcliff 268
Brown, Margery 130
Brown, Richard, Sir (Lord Mayor)
    at Bull & Mouth 37, 138–39, 142
    E. Burrough and 37, 38n
    comparisons with 153, 251
    and Fifth Monarchists 35, 137
    at Restoration 34
    G. Whitehead on 175
    and women 142
Brown, Ruth (later Crouch) 19, 266
Browne, Mary 294
Buckinghamshire 291, 359

Bugg, Francis 177, 281n, 391
    "The Quakers Synod" **54**
Buggins family [Briggins?] 192
builders: James Ewer 219
buildings: *see* houses; meeting houses, Six Weeks Meeting, tenements; workhouse
Bull & Mouth ("City" or "London" mtg) 24
    Box Meeting at 351
    E. Burrough arrested 37
    Sir Richard Brown at 37, 142, 175–76
    William Crouch at 25
    John Field's school at 360
    Great Fire 142–43, 167
    John Lilburne, funeral 330
    marriages at [*table after* 88], 196
    Morning Meeting at 336, 338
    poor box 129
    public meetings 36
    sign 135n
    Six Weeks Meeting at 93, 119
    Two Weeks Meeting at 42, 85, 86, 89, 346
    youth, meeting for 253
Bull & Mouth MM: **24**, 71, 134–44
    boundary 171
    burial registers 332
    city district becomes MM 91
    William Gibson and 79–80
    Gracechurch St MM, change to 144
    Quarterly Monthly Meeting 205
    and Six Weeks Meeting 99, 102, 104
    plan **24**
    records lost 147
    Two Weeks Meeting and 88, 92
    and Women's Meeting 121 330,
Bunhill Fields burial ground 329–34
    funerals: Mary Elson 199; G. Fox 156–57, 330; William Gibson sen 79, 154; Peel and Westminster 207
    Memorial Buildings **334**
    MM boundaries 197
    purchase of land 110, **334**
    tenements for poor at 206
    G. Whitehead buried at 177
Bunyan, John 13, 140, 176, 329
burial grounds (*see also* coffins; funerals; gravediggers; undertakers)
    body snatchers 333, 335
    cemeteries outside city 225, 260
    exhumations 222, 236, 329, 331
    G. Fox on 50–51   *contd*

burial grounds *contd*
  gravestones, G. Fox 331; Jordans 279n, 331, 358; William and Sarah Mead 279n
  locations: Barking 74–5, 278, 279n; Brentford 287; Broad Street Station (site of) 329; Bunhill Fields q.v. 110, 329–34; Chequer Alley *see* Bunhill 315; Croydon 324; Deptford 223; Epping 298; Esher 315; Hammersmith 264; Hendon 308; Isleworth *see* Brentford; Jordans 355–59; Kingston 312–13; Long Acre 247–48; Long Lane, Bermondsey 222–23, 236; Longford 283; Mill Hill 310; Peckham 225; Plaistow 277; Ratcliff 268, 270; South Mimms 299; burial grounds: Southwark (Old Park) 220, (New Park, Lower Redcross St or Worcester St) 221–22, 236–38; Staines 284; Stoke Newington 158; Tottenham **301**, 303–04; Uxbridge 285; Waltham Abbey 296, 297; Wapping 270; Whitechapel 329, 334; Winchmore Hill 260, 300
  Meeting of Twelve and 101, 113
  public health 4
  Six Weeks Meeting and 91, 96, 100, 103, 106, 118
  tombs, enclosed: Vandewall 358
burial registers 71n, 87, 101, 326, 331, 332, 359
Burleigh St, Strand 245
Burling, Edward 274
Burnet, Gilbert (Bishop) 12, 34n
Burnett, manor court 276
Burnyeat, John 173
Burrough, Edward 20–29, 32, 215, 282
  Bible, use of 296n
  at Bull & Mouth 134, 136
  buried at Bunhill 330
  discipline, paper on 41–44, 86–87
  and R. Hawkins 250
  imprisonment, Kingston 312
  in Newgate, and death 37–38
  and Parliament 35, 139
  predecessors in London 266, 342n
  Testimony of the Lord concerning London **88**
  and Women's Two Weeks Meeting 346
Burton, Margaret 293
Bushel, Marmaduke 269
business (meetings) (*see also* discipline; gospel order)
  attendance at SWM 103–04
  lack of 288

  men's and women's joint 235
  method 73–74; G. Fox on 92n-93n, 98; voting, Workhouse Ctee 364
  pressure of 179
  reduced, for worship 186, 340
  and worship, court decision 84
business (trade)
  failures 119, 225
  honesty in 231, 384
  and residence 157
businessmen
  attendance at week-day meetings 204
  Croydon 326
Butcher, Isaac 200
Butcher, Ralph 276
Butcher, Thomas 200
butchers: Hodges, Samuel of S. Mimms 299
Butler, David xiii
Butt Lane, Deptford 223
Butterfield, family 359
Buttery, Isabel 19, 20, 28, 266, 343

Calvert, Giles 342n
Calvinism 14
Cambrian Chapel, former Horslydown meeting house **220**
Cambridge, Anne Docwra of 281n
Cambridgeshire (Streatham) 14
Camfield, Francis 92, 200
Camm, J[ohn] 20, 22
candles, in workhouse 365
Canterbury, Archbishop of, and Little Almonry lease 242
Capel Court 391
Capel, Surrey 316, 317
Capper [surname] 388
captives, "Sally" and Algiers 131
"Captives' money" (SWM fund) 101
caretakers (*see also* doorkeepers)
  Peel, Elizabeth Carter 206
  Plaistow, cleaning 277
carpenters:
  John Elson 192–93, 222; John Stodder 193;
  shop acquired for Peckham mtg 224
  yard at Peel 193, 194
carpets and curtains, Horslydown 218
carriages/coaches 72, 151, 157
Cart, Ellinor, maid 182
Carter, Elizabeth, caretaker (Peel) 206
Cash [surname] 389

Castle and Falcon 127
Castle Street (Long Acre) 247
Castlemaine, Earl of 334
casual poor (*see also* poor) 94, 106, 129
  SWM responsibility 100, 105, 131
Catchpool, Lydia 301
Catechism
  Robert Barclay's 292, 364
  John Kendall's 378
Catholics
  fear of Papists 137
  Friends portrayed as 60, 312n
  toleration alongside Nonconformists 65
cattle
  at burial grounds 333, 335
  cows for poor 317
  distraint of 300
Cavendish Court 168–70, 172
cemeteries (*see also* burial grounds)
  outside city 225, 260
censorship by Morning Meeting 342
centenaries, disregard for xx, 355
certificates
  for marriage 181, 341, 353
  of removal 119, 384; Philip Harman 185–86, Christopher Taylor 301
  for travelling ministers 80, 120, 338, 339, 340; John Hewlett 81
Chalfont St Giles, and St Peter 356
Chalk, Thomas, Kingston drawing *facing* 316
Chalkley, George 225
Chamber (Recording Clerk's office) 97, 133
Chamberlain, Francis 327
Chamberlayne, William 247
Chancery Lane: MM boundary 197, 249
chancery, Devonshire House in 170
Chandler, Benjamin 235
Chandler, Will the 225, 229
Chandler, William 220–21
Chantrey Mead, South Mimms 299
Chapel Yard, Savoy 246
Charles II, King 33–35, 217
  and G. Latey 220, 250–51
  proclamations (1660) 137, (1662) 61, 138
  Proclamation of General Indulgence (1671/2) 64, 337
  and G. Whitehead (royal pardon) 176
cheating 231
cheesemongers: Ryan (Gracechurch St) 161
chemists: William Allen q.v. 150; Richard Low Beck, xxiv; Luke Howard (q.v.) 150

Chequer Alley, Bunhill 329, 333
Chertsey::Thomas Berryman of 284
Chertsey Fair displaces Longford MM 289
Cheshire, early monthly meeting 44
Cheshunt 298
Chief Baron (judge) 84
childbirth (*see also* births; midwives)
  Box Meeting 345
children (*see also* apprentices, education, schools, young people)
  epistle to 267
  education (*see also* schools) 76, 131–2, 187
  at meeting 179, 186, 269, 280, 292; Reading 2
  orphans/fatherless (*see also* widows) 48, 101, 115, 118, 121, 348
  upbringing 50, 54, 77, 253, 382–3, 384
  at workhouse (*see also* poor) 362, 364, 368, 369, 370n, 372
  working (*see also* apprentices) 97, 362, 368, 371, 373
chimneys: Dev. Ho. 169; Wandsworth 318–19
Chingford 297
Chipping Barnet 298
  boundary of Tottenham MM 295
  William Wyld of 299
Chipping Ongar: boundary of Tottenham MM 295
Chiswick 36, 262
Christ
  as head of church 12
  within 28–29
Christmas Day (*see also* times and seasons) 312
Christy, family 150
Church of England 9–10, 15–16, 17
  clergy 281n, 312, 390; Richard Claridge 200; James Jackson 203; Christopher Taylor 360
  ecclesiastical courts
  laws on attendance 61, 312
  and nonconformists, Southwark 214
  preaching at Gracechurch St 153–54
  rates (*see also* tithes) 383
  at Restoration 61, 137
  speaking in church 266, 281n
  Westminster Abbey 242–43
church government: *see* business (meetings); discipline
Church Lane, Whitechapel: MM boundary 171
churches, unity: John Bellers' proposals 362

City, not initially covered by MMs 88
City Companies xxiii, 140
    Brewers 374, 379; Hall [*table after* 88], 143
    Fishmongers 146, 147, 149
    Mercers 264
City Corporation buy workhouse site 374
City Marshal, payment to 133
City meeting *see* Bull & Mouth
City Road 151, 329
City Within the Walls: collections in 183
civil liberty 394
Claipoole, Ellin; member of SWM 31n
Clarendon, Earl 35, 140
Claridge, Mary 277
Claridge, Richard 80, 280, 302, 307
    schools 200, 360
    widow donates books to Peel 207
Clarke, George xxiii
Clark(e), Henry: Bankside 37, 215
Clarke, Sarah 200
Clarkson, Thomas 392
class xxv, xxvii, 249
classics, teaching (heathen authors) 132
Clay, William 158
Claygate, Surrey 314
cleaning (*see also* caretakers; doorkeepers)
    Devonshire House xxvii
    Plaistow 277
clergy: *see* Church of England
Clerkenwell (district) 36, 192
Clerkenwell workhouse: *see* workhouse
clerks (*see also* recording clerk)
    Devonshire House MM: W. Beck xxix
    Peel (Joseph Besse, assistant) 201, 206
    Six Weeks Meeting 94, 100; and remuneration 106
Clifford's Inn: commission on fires 245
clothing (*see also* dress; plainness)
    for poor 182
    school/workhouse 367, 372, 373; mending stockings 377
clubs: QM report (1761) 383
coach and horses, use in persecution 251
coaches/carriages 78, 117, 157
Coale, Josiah 38n, 228n
coals, for poor 129
Cobbett, William 391
Cobell and Wife 228
Cobham, Surrey 315, 317
Cock Inn 127
Cockfield, Peter, legacy to SWM 109n

coffins (*see also* burial grounds; funerals) 118, 157, 236–238
    cost of 182, 225, 232, 277
Coggeshall MM 84
cohabitation 128, 229
coins: *see* money
Colchester, Essex 191, 201
Coleman St (Alley) 35n, 330, 332, 333
    Fifth Monarchist chapel 137,
collections: *see* funds
College of Industry *see* workhouse
Colley [surname] 389
Collins, Rebecca 359
Collumpton, (Cullompton) Devon 101
Colnbrook 283
Colville, John, leaseholder of Devonshire House 167
combmaker (anonymous) 225
committees
    Ctee of Accounts, SWM 114
    Ctee on Discipline 188, 235
    Ctee on Disorderly Walkers (Devonshire House MM) 189
    Education Ctee (Islington Road) 376–77
    on London and country meetings 75
    Stoke Newington meeting, ctee to set up 158
    Ctee of Twelve, *see* Meeting of Twelve
    public houses, ctees held in 233
    workhouse committees 363–64, 371
Common Prayer, Book of 281n
Commons, House of, *see* Parliament
Commonwealth, conditions under (*see also* Cromwell, Oliver) 136–37
communion (Lord's supper) 14, 340
Companies: *see* City; East India
complaints, workhouse 370n
Compter, The (prison) 232
compulsory purchase: New Park, Southwark 222
condemnations book, Peel MM **89**
condemnation, papers of (*see also* discipline; disorderly conduct; disownment) 187, 191, 205, 231, 253, 288
    G. Fox and 57
    William Gibson jun 79
conduct, disorderly, *see* disorderly conduct
Conduit Lane, Isleworth 287
Coney Wall, Deptford 223
Congregationalists: John Stoughton xiv
Conran [surname, twice] 389

conscience
  G. Fox and 57
  liberty of 30–31, 341; Penn–Mead trial 153; swearing, objection recognised 65
conscription (pressing) 272, 288
conservative Quakerism xvi, xvii
constables 80, 152, 288, 318
  Thomas Talbot (Longford) 288
contention: *see* debates, disputes
contributions: *see* funds
controversies: Quaker v. Baptist 14–15, 17
Conventicle Acts (1662, 1664, 1670) 61–65, 83, 138, 139–40, 141, 152
  informers encouraged by 174
  and meeting house property 173n
  in Parliament (1662) 175
  severe persecution after 2nd Act 216
  winnowing effect of 231
conventicles
  Gracechurch St as 154
  Mile End Green 266
  Pall Mall meeting too close to palace 241
  Southwark 214
conversation (i.e. behaviour), disorderly; *see* disorderly conduct
convincements 55, 115, 118; lack of 288–89
Cooke, Richard, innkeeper 127
Cooke, Widow 298
Cooper, John 169
coopers
  and exact measure 231
  Gerrard Roberts 145n, 336
  Venner (Fifth Monarchist) 137
copyhold: Wandsworth 318
Corbin, Thomas 106, 107, 109, 200, 209
Corbyn, John 378
Corbyn, Sarah 200
Corkbree, Ann and Richard 228
corn trade 222
Cornwall
  R. Hawkins from 250
  G. Latey returns from 164
coroner 173
Correction, House of 266
correspondence 120
  conducted by Morning Meeting 341
Cort, H. de, drawing of Jordans **355**
country Friends, prisoners in Fleet 132–33
country meetings
  children at workhouse/school 372, 378
  ministers in London 126

  and Morning Meeting 326, 338, 339
  and QM 72, 75, 78, 306
  and residence: *see* residence
  and SWM 110, 111, 112
  variable frequency 284
"Country Quaker, The" (poem) 390
court (Royal) officials: Nicholas Bond 223
courts: *see also* legal system; juries; justices
  Chancery, Devonshire House in 170
  coroner's 173
  Doctors Commons: Richard Claridge 200
  ecclesiatical courts 290
  manor courts 276
  Middlesex Sessions 212
  records xxii
Covent Garden poor relief district, Westminster MM 257
Coventry, Dorcas 200
Coverley's Fields, Whitechapel 334
Cowper, Benjamin 200
cows (*see also* cattle), for poor 317
Crafton, Richard 374n
craftsmen (Wandsworth) 321
Cripplegate 329
Crisp, Stephen 156, 292, 331, 360
Cromwell, Oliver
  appeals to 31
  Commonwealth 3–7, 8, 136–37
  death of 33
  followers at Kingston meeting 311
  and liberty of conscience 30
  persecution under 60
  and soldiers 12
Cromwell, Richard 33
Cromwell, Thomas Kitson, engraving of Islington Rd Schools xix, 376n, **378**
Crosby, Elizabeth 237
Crosby Hall, acquisition considered 168
Crosfield, Anthony 372
Crouch, Ruth (born Brown) 19, 266
Crouch, William 19, 36, 177, 276
  on E. Burrough 25–26, 32
  on John Elson 192
  at Gracechurch St disturbance 154
  Interval Friend 180
  Morning Meeting 336, 338
  Six Weeks Meeting 92
  Southwark carpets etc 218
  Two Weeks Meeting 85
crowds (*see also* disturbance, preaching) xxii, 24–26

Crowley, Ann 294
Crown, reversion of Savoy estate 246
Croydon 316, 317, 323–25
Croydon MM, union with Kingston and Wandsworth 314, 319, 326, 327
Croydon School (Friends' School; *see also* Islington Road School; workhouse) 361, **379,** 379–80; T. F. Ball at xxvii; Peter Bedford resident near 378
Cullompton, (Collumpton) Devon 101
Cumberland
  early MM 44; Thomas Wilkinson of 388
Cunningham [surname], on Quakers as mystics 395
curtains, Horslydown 218
Curtis, Robert 235
customs duties, query on 55
Czar, see Alexander I; Peter the Great

Dagenham 280
Dalston (Dolston): MM boundaries 171
dancing: young men give public ball 254
Dane, relief for 131
Daniels, Peter xxiii, xxxi
Danzig, sufferings in 131
Daukes, Samuel, architect 284
Davis, Francis 235
Davis, Nicholas 200, 225, 235, 326, 328
de Cort, H. drawing of Jordans **355**
De Horne, Hannah 201n
de Krey, Gary xxii
deacons, Baptist 13
Dean and Chapter of Westminster 242, 243
deaths (*see also* burial registers; statistics)
  death rate xix, 32n
  query on reporting 54, 293
debate, Baptist meetings for 13
debate in meetings (*see also* business; disputes) 73, 92n, 98
debts (individuals': *see also* bankruptcy; for meetings' debts see funds), advice on 115, 119; disputes about 87; G. Fox 47; Yearly Meeting (1759) 384
deceased wife's sister (*see also* marriage) 129
deeds (*see also* records)
  care of: Meeting of Twelve 100
  of registration, Stoke Newington 211–12
defence corps: *see* militia
delinquency *see* disorderly conduct
Dell family 294
Dell, Elizabeth, prev. Morton 294

Dell, Joseph 294
Dell, Oliver: Hammersmith photo **261**
Dell, R 294n
Dell, W.R. 294n
demography: *see* statistics, population
denial, testimonies of: *see* disownment
Dennis, John 279
Dent Dale, William Alderson from 158
Deptford 223–24, **224**
  marriages at [*table after* 90]
  MM 223
Detention, House of 163n, 363
Devon 101
Devonshire House (*see also* Friends' Institute) 160–70
  Bishopsgate entrance **171**
  Box Meeting at 351, 352
  building 101, 105, 142, 146, 165
  courtyard **xii, 167, 170**
  doorkeeper: Thomas Ball xxvii
  Friends' Institute reading room **170**
  marriages at xxvii, [*table after* 88]
  meetings for worship 125, 178–79, 234
  poor box 129
  Quarterly Meeting at 143
  schools 81, 131–32, 361
  Strong room **xv**
  Thomas Talwin 109
  and Tottenham meeting house 302
  Two Weeks Meeting at 89
  Women's Yearly Meeting at **354**
Devonshire House MM 71, 78, 88, 109, 162–91, 361
  boundaries 148, 152, 158, 170–71, 201, 210, 226
  disownments etc 188–89; T.F. Ball xxv–xxix; Hannah Barnard 82, 342; Elias Bockett 80; disorderly marriage 212; gravedigger 335; Benjamin Lay 81
  and Gracechurch St MM 148, 152, 158
  marriages xxvi
  members lists xxv
  ministers and elders [*table after* 78]
  and Peel MM 121, 201, 210
  poor 121, 129
  and QM 70, 78
  records **xx. xxviii**
  Six Weeks Meeting 99, 105, 107, 110; quota 102, 103, 104, 107, 110, 111, 112
  and Southwark MM 226
  and Stoke Newington 158 *contd*

Devonshire House MM *contd*
  women's 354
  Whitechapel burial ground 344–45
Devonshire Square 168
Devonshire, Earl & Countess of 167
Dewsbery (Dewsbury), William xvii, 66, 159
diaries: Friend in Essex 393
diet: *see* food and drink
Dillworth, William 188, 388
Dillwyn [surname] 388
Dillwyn, George 388
Dillwyn, Lewis 147
Dillwyn, William 271n, 380n, 381, 388
Dimsdale, family 150
discipline (*see also* advices; condemnation, papers of; disorderly conduct; disownments; plainness)
  in business meetings 73–74, 382
  development of 41–59
  lowness 263, 280, 306, 316, 325, 382
  meetings for discipline (*see also* business meetings; monthly meetings; quarterly meetings; Six Weeks Meeting; Two Weeks Meeting): 179–80, 186–91, 204–06, 227, 252–57, 287–89, 305–07; ministers' mtgs not 81–82; privacy, legal decision 84; worship at 74
  revision (1861) xvi
  revival of (late 18th century) xx, xvii, 188, 248, 289; John Fothergill and 259, 393; QM report 381–88; YM committee 235, 326
  Six Weeks Meeting and 118, 124–26
  workhouse 364
discontinued meetings, QM to advise 100
dishonesty *see* fraud; honesty,
disinterments 222, 236, 329, 331
disorderly conduct (incl. delinquency, disorderly "conversation" and "walkers"; *see also* condemnation, papers of; discipline; disownments) 88, 116, 172, 188–89, 201, 228–29, 230–32
  at business meetings 74
  Six Weeks Meeting and 118, 122–24
  women 180n
disorderly marriages 47–48, **89**, 121, 124, 128, 212, 228
disorderly preachers 120, 203
disownment (incl. exclusion from meetings; *see also* condemnation, papers of; discipline) 77, 187, 188, 228, 235, 317

condemnation, paper of, preceding 187, 231, 288
G. Fox and 57
individuals: T.F. Ball xxix, Hannah Barnard 83n; Elias Bockett 80; Alexander Galloway 369n; William Gibson jun 80; Hannah Lightfoot 255; James Jackson 203; Elizabeth Nicholls 190; James Sargent 191
and marriage 123, 212, 256
Morning Meeting and 81–82
Six Weeks Meeting and 97, 100, 106, 118–19, 122–24, 256
statistics xxvi, 123
testimonies of denial 97, 100, 106, 190–91, 288
disputes (*see also* debate)
  between Friends 43, 50, 87, 120, 233, 313
  between meetings xxx; Bull & Mouth–Women's 121; Croydon–Wandsworth 325; Peel with others 208
Dissenters: *see* Nonconformists
distillers
  Elias Bockett 80
  neighbour of workhouse 373
distraint of goods ("distress") *see* sufferings
disturbance of meetings
  arrival of corpses 207
  crowd/rude people 136, 178, 202, 215
  noise from street 78, 195
  by preachers 273
  protection by city marshal 133
  precautions against 194, 202
  by soldiers 152–54, 173, 202, 216, 217
ditches, Tottenham 303
Ditchside: MM boundaries 197
Dixon, Simon xxii, xxxi
Doctors' Commons
  court: procs against Richard Claridge 200
  neighbourhood: Gerrard Roberts 36, 336
documents: *see* manuscripts; records
Docwra, Anne 281n
Dodman, Dennis, tenant of Wheeler St 165
Dolphin Inn, Bishopsgate 146, 168, 170, 174
Dog Row: MM boundary 171
Dolston (Dalston): MM boundary 171
domestic staff: *see* caretakers; doorkeepers; housekeeper (Isl. Rd School); servants
donations: *see* funds (collections; contributions)
Donne, William 255

430

doorkeepers (caretakers) 161, 206, 300, 351
  Thomas Ball, Devonshire House xxvii
doorkeepers ("solid Friends") for Yearly
  Meeting 78, 120, 178
Dorking 316, 317
Downer, Anne (later, Whitehead) 19, 174,
  182, 266, 281n, 344
Downes, Sarah 182
drainage: Tottenham 303; workhouse 373
Draper, Stephen, gaoler 232
drawbridge: MM boundary 171
dress (*see also* clothing; plainness) 76–77,
  117, 393
  in burial 237–38
  G. Fox and 57
  Dr John Fothergill's 260
  illustrations showing **xii, 25, 54, 55, 79**
  G. Latey, effect on as tailor 250
  at marriages 254
  QM report (1761) 382, 383–84
  white (Joseph Rule) 359
  wigs 77, 117, 372n
  women's riding hoods 227
Dring, Robert and Simon 19, 24, 36
  Robert's maid 20
drink (*see also* beer; brewers; distillers; food
    and drink; innkeepers; temperance)
  ale for elderly people 375n
  W. Beck & T.F. Ball and xxv
  beer and wine at meetings 233, 322
  for ministers 206, 257–58, 321
  excessive 47, 116, 123, 124, 230, 317, 383
  at marriages 128
  moderation 260
  wine trade xxiv, xxv, 145n, 336
drowsiness: *see* sleeping in meeting
drunkenness *see* drink
Dry, Elizabeth 301, 344
Dublin Yearly Meeting, Hannah Barnard certificate from 82
Dudley, Howard, lithograph of Peckham **225**
dunghill, Whitechapel: MM boundary 171
Durham, early monthly meeting 44
Dutch at Nore, as sign 39
Dymond, Edith and Henry 380

Eagles (Eccles), Solomon 142, 276
Ealing, conference of three MMs at 290
earnings: *see* remuneration
East Ham (Ham) 276
East India Company 178, 271

East Smithfield: MM boundaries 171
Eastcott, Dorothy 277
Eastern England: ministers in
  Elizabeth Morton 294
  G. Whitehead 174
eating: *see* food and drink
Eccles (Eagles), Solomon xviii, 142, 276
Eccles, Anne 276
ecclesiastical courts 290
Eccleston, John 177, 178
Eccleston, Theodore 80, 131, 177, 178, 180
Eddy, J.T. 149
Eden St, Kingston 313
Edge, John 84
Edler, John 315
Edmonton 200, 162n, 295
education: *see* schools
Edwards, William 167
elderly people (*see also* almshouses; widows)
  house at Whitechapel burial ground 335
  Plaistow Home for Ancient Friends 375
  at workhouse 362, 364, 368–69, 370, 372,
    373, 375n; leave Islington Rd 378;
    Friends' School to support via SWM 379
elders ("ancient Friends" other than aged
    poor; *see also* discipline; ministers, overseers) [*table after* 78], 115, 200, 256,
    294n, 395
  Baptist 13
  early meeting at Swarthmoor 44
  early usage 53
  lack of 210, 257, 306
  at marriages 128,
  Morning Meeting 143, 336, 338, 339, 341
  and overseers 79, 386
election and free grace 14, 15
elections to Parliament (q.v.) 341
Elin "not owned" (woman at Wheeler St)
  165
Eliot, Frances 324
Eliot, John 200, 324, 332
Eliot, Mary 324
Elliott [surname], on SWM 107
Elliott, Admiral, sells Ham House 260
Ellis, Josiah 196
Ellwood, Ann Mercy 370
Ellwood, Thomas
  on E. Burrough 22, 38, 136
  and G. Fox *Journal* 342
  and Jordans, 355, 358, 359
  on J. Nayler 29   *contd*

431

Ellwood, Thomas *contd*
  on Peningtons 356
  and John Perrot 45
Elson, John 36, 192, 193, 196, 198–200, 222
Elson, Mary 92, 129, 193, 194, 198–200, 347n
  and Peel chest of books 207
  legacy to workhouse 365
Emden, sufferings in 131
emigration (*see also* certificates) 119, 301, 396
employment (*see also* apprentices; occupations; remuneration; workhouse) 42, 72
Enfield (Endfield) 301–02
  Elizabeth Dry's 344
  G. Fox in 295
  Widow French 72
  William Shewen removes to 235
  and Tottenham 302, 303
Enfield MM 71, 96, 296, 305,
  including Flamstead End 298
  and Stoke Newington 212,
  Waltham and Epping join 274, 297
Episcopalians: *see* Church of England 281n
Epistles
  of Caution on marriage etc 253
  G. Fox's: *see* Fox, George
  reading of 203, 227
  Ann Whitehead and Mary Elson 347
  Yearly Meeting: distribution 172; recd 341
Epping 295, 297–298, 344
  originally with Barking MM 274,
  Waltham, alternation with 297, 305
  women Fds 307
Erwood, Gabriel 233
Esher 314, 315–16, **316**, 317
  Baptists use meeting house 328
Essex
  diary by Friend in 393
  William Mead's library to mtgs in 279
  parts near Middlesex 295
Essex Quarterly Meeting 71, 274, 297
Established Church: *see* Church of England
Estaugh, John 235
Europe: John Bellers' proposals 362
evangelical Quakerism xvi–xvii, xviii, 83
  William Beck's xxv
Evenden, Doreen xxii
evening meetings: *see* times of meetings
Ewer St (*see also* Southwark) 219–21, 222
Ewer, James 219
Exchequer, fines not received by 83–84
excise, query on 55

exclusion from mtgs *see also* disownment 119
exhumations 222, 236, 329, 331
expenses: *see* finance

F., J., gone to America 340
Fair St: Mary Webb's (*see also* Southwark) 215, 216
Fairman, Mary 227,
Fairman, Robert 227, 233
Falcon (*see also* Castle and Falcon) 127
Falcon, Upper Ground 215
false measures 231
falsehood: *see* honesty
families, visiting of 201, 204, 289
Family of Love 40n
Farant, Ann and John 229
farmers: Barking 274; Croydon 324
Farnborough, Mariabella 200
Farrand, Banks 158
Farrand, John 280
Fell [surname] 389
Fell, Margaret, later Fox 155, 331
Fell, Sarah marries William Mead 278
Fell, [Thomas], Judge 18
fences, Southwark 218, 222
Fenchurch St, The Ship: William Mead 177
Fenstanton, Hunts 15
Fern Hall, Barking 278
Field, John, schoolmaster 143, 360
Field Lane, house owned by Peel 210
Fielder, Ann 311, 318
Fielder, John 311, 312, 314, 318
Fielder, Mary later Latey 318
Fifth Monarchy Men 34, 61, 137
finance (meetings'): *see also* funds; horses, payment for; quota; remuneration; rents
  accounts 103, 232, 350, 352; SWM, 107, 114, 130–31; Westminster 252, 257
  Croydon MM 325; Devonshire House MM; 183; Gracechurch St meeting house costs 150; ministers expenses 126; Peel, QM aid to 206, 210; Plaistow Women's Meeting (for burials) 277
  Six Weeks Meeting and Mtg of Twelve (*see also* quota) 73, 91, 94, 95, 100, 112; disputes before SWM 121
  taxes (MMs and SWM) 101, 101, 102, 106, 112
Wanstead, proceeds of sale 275
Westminster meeting house costs 243–44
Westminster MM 252, 257

Finch, John 284, 294
Finch, Thomas 294
fines: *see* sufferings
Finsbury 329
Finsbury Circus
　William Beck x, xxiv
　and Square, built 151
fires (conflagrations)
　commission on 245
　fire engines, Southwark 234
　Gracechurch St 134, 147, 161, 337
　Great 135, 141, 145, 152, 167, 245, 336; as sign 39
　Limehouse 101
　relief after 101, 183
　Savoy (1669) 245,
　Wapping and Shadwell (1682) 101, 271–72n
fires (heating): chimneys 169, 318–19; workhouse 365, 368, 369n
First-Day Schools 166, 395
Fish St Hill: MM boundary 171
Fisher, Martha 246, 257, 344
Fisher, Samuel 216, 330
Fishmongers' Company 146, 147, 149
Flamstead End 298
Flanders: conscription to 272
flax spinning 317, 376, 377
Fleet Prison, rooms rented in 132
Fleet St: Hanging Sword Court 72
Fleet St: MM boundaries 197, 249
Fleetwood, family 249
Fleming, Daniel, Blackman St 37, 215
Fletcher, Isaac 381, 388
Fleur-de-Luce, sign of: Gerrard Roberts 145n
floods, relief after 183
flying meeting: General MM 290
Folkestone: Robert Howard from 331
food and drink (*see also* drink; temperance)
　Dr John Fothergill's moderation 260
　at funerals, expenses 277
　at marriages, excessive 117, 254
　after meetings 291, 321–22, 327, 357
　sparing before worship 204
　workhouse 363n, 366–368, 369n, 371, 373
Fookes, George 200
Forbes, Christiana 323
Ford, Philip 113, 120
Ford(s) Green, nr Winchmore Hill 290, 296
foreigners, relief for 131
forms (benches): *see* seating
Forster, Josiah 307

Forster, William xxix, 307
Fortnightly Meeting: *see* Two Weeks Meeting
fortnightly meetings: *see* times of meetings
Fossick, Samuel: Gracechurch St premises 161
Foster, Dame Blandina 332
Foster, James 158
Foster, Joseph Talwin 161, 170
Foster, Mary 92
Foster, Sir Reginald, bart 332
Foster, Robert 381, 388
Foster, Thomas 83, 389
Fothergill, Ann 244, 256
Fothergill, Dr John 259–61, 393
　Gracechurch St 146, 150
　and Six Weeks Meeting 106, 109, 110
　and Westminster 244, 250, 256, 259
　and workhouse 372
Fothergill, Samuel xvii, 188, 341, 381, 388
Fowler family 150
Fowler [surname] 389
Fowler, Henry 177
Fox, Christopher 373n
Fox, George
　advices and discipline 47–52, 76, 95, 122, 124, 130, 292
　in America 64n
　William Beck on xxvi, xxx
　and Bible xvii, 147, 296
　and conscience 57
　correspondence (*see also* Epistles *below*): from Josiah Coale 228n; from J. Nayler 321n; from John Sands 282n; ms letter (1684) 290
　and Oliver Cromwell 31–32
　death and funeral xxx, 154–57, 330
　and William Dewsbury 159
　and Elizabeth Dry 301
　at Enfield 295, 301
　Epistles (vol.2 of *Works*; *see also* To all that would know...) 52, 318; William Penn on 58; Preface 39, 53; references (1698 ed.): "p.6 etc" ["Concerning the first spreading of the truth"] 261n, 347, 349; "p.13" [Ep.14 "A Word from the Lord to Friends"] 26; "p.107" [Ep.137 "For Francis Howgill and Edward Burrough"] 27; "p.192" [Ep.222 "A General Epistle to be read in all the Christian Meetings in the World"] 28; "p.284" and "p.290" [Ep.264 "An additional extract from other　　*contd*

433

Fox, George: Epistles *contd*
of G.F.'s epistles"] 57, 71n; p.317
[Ep.283 "To Friends in Bristol in time of suffering"] 64; "p.333" [Ep.301 "To all the women's meetings"] 28; "p.341" [Ep.308 "My dear Friends in England..."] 53; "p.555" [Ep.418 "To the Six Weeks Meeting in London"] 92
at Ford(s) Green 290, 296
at Gooses (Harold Hill) 278, 295
"Friends' Fellowship must be in the Spirit" 47–52
at Gracechurch St 152; death 154
grave 331
at Guttershedge (Hendon) 308
healing 347
and F. Howgill 21
Journal: editing and publication 342; Preface by William Penn (refs 1765 ed.) 28, 40n, 58; references (1694 ed.): early visit to London (1644) 18n; early organisation (c.1660) 68n, 87; organisation and discipline (1666–68) 44, 70, 88, 228, 229; later years 94–95, 155, 278, 295–96, 308, 318
at Kingston 155, 318
later years in London 155
Macaulay on xiv
on marriage 47–48, 50, 128, 129, 229
and membership 57
opposition to 58
and organisation of Society of Friends 44, 59, 87, 393; Box Meeting 147, 261n, 348–49; "gospel order" 47, 49; Meeting of Twelve 113; monthly meetings 46, 70, 204, 290–91; Morning Meeting 336, 341, 342; Quarterly meeting 70, 71n; representative meetings 95; Six Weeks meeting 70, 91, 92n, 94–98; Women's Two Weeks Meeting 346–50
pastoral letters (*see also* Epistles) 52
at Peel MM 204
and plainness 57
and the poor 129; fraudulent paupers 130
preaching 25, 126
Primer 292, 342n
and prisons: Scarborough 44, 88; kind gaolers 232
Saint's Heavenly and Spiritual Worship, The 318
and schools 132, 360

at South Mimms 299
and sufferings 64n
threshing meetings (public) 26–27
To All that would Know the Kingdom of Heaven (distrib. by Isabel Buttery) 19, 20
at Tottenham 302
Uxbridge 282n, 290
and Valiant Sixty 44, 174
at Wheeler Street 165n
G. Whitehead as successor 176
worship, time of 125–25
Fox, Margaret, previously Fell 155, 331
Fox, William Edward, Ratcliff watercolour **276**
Frame, Anne 200
France, calamity in (1721): solemn mtgs 234
Franklin, Dr. [Benjamin] 259
fraud (cheating, embezzlement) xxvii, 50, 123, 130, 191, 231
Freame, John Osgood 301
Freame, Joseph 300
Frederickstadt, meeting house at 239
Freehold Estates Company 149
freeholds 170, 192–93, 330, 332, 359
Freeman, Mary 235
French Prophets 253
French (Widow, Enfield) 72
frequency of meetings: *see* times of meetings
Fretwell, Ralph 342
Friend, The xxix–xxx
"Friends Fellowship must be in the Spirit" (G. Fox) 47–52
Friends' Institute xxvi, xxvii, 148n, **170**
William Beck lecture ix
Friends' School (Clerkenwell/Islington Rd/Croydon: *see also* workhouse) 75, 194, 327, 361–80
Fry, Elizabeth 150, 275, 278, 389, 393
Fryer, Charles 380
Fryer, Elizabeth 277
Fuller (an infamous fellow) 330
funds (*see also* finance; legacies; poor relief; property; rents): apprentices 374; Box/Women's Two Weeks Mtg 345, 347, 348, 351, 352; building maintenance 234, 300; Devonshire House MM 183, 189; Peel MM 206, 210; poor's stock 104, 120, 291; Quarterly Meeting 72, 75; Six Weeks Meeting 97, 100, 107–108; workhouse 371, 372
borrowing, by SWM/Twelve 101, 102
briefs, charitable 183, 203   *contd*

funds *contd*
  collections: Box Meeting (*see also* women's) 352; boxes, for collections 317, 350–351; Croydon 327; Dev. Ho. 172, 183; General MM 290–91; Hendon 309; Horslydown 234; Ireland, for relief of English sufferings 297; Kingston 317; Longford 283, 292; Mtg of Twelve, to order 96–97; Peel 203; Ratcliff, for loss in fire 271; Six Weeks Mtg 100, 101, 102, 103, 108; for Friends abroad 130; Southwark 227; Staines 284; Uxbridge 285, 286; Westminster 257; women's meetings 350, 351; Women's Two-Weeks meeting 347, 353; workhouse, subscription 366
  contributions and subscriptions: Cobham 315; Croydon–Wandsworth dispute 319; Horslydown meeting house 226, Longford MM 289; MM subscription lists 105; SWM quota 100, 102–03, 107–12, 184, 208, 210; Tottenham enlargement 303; Westminster MM 252; Winchmore Hill 300; workhouse 366, 367, 371, 372, 374
  debts: Barking 280; Devonshire House MM 184; Longford MM deficit 289; Six Weeks Meeting 102, 103, 104, 107, 208–09; Westminster 257
  investments, SWM 100, 103, 108, 112
  loans: to poor, written off 206; Six Weeks Meeting 100, 101; by Women's Two-Weeks Meeting 350
funerals (*see also* burial grounds)
  bidders 129, 206
  coaches at 78, 157
  costs and fees 129, 180, 232–33, 277
  of disowned people 119, 231
  extravagance 117, 154
  Gracechurch St 154, 156–57
  individuals: Mary Elson 199; John Fothergill 260; G. Fox 156–57, 330; W. Gibson sen 79, 154; Joseph Rule 359
  Peel and Westminster 207–08
  punctuality 270
  Six Weeks Meeting advice 118
furniture (*see also* galleries; seating): costly 117; Mary Elson's legacy 199

Gadshill, Kent: pretended robbery 191
galleries (*see also* seating)
  architectural galleries: Devonshire House 168, 170; Gracechurch St 148; Horslydown 218 ; Little Almonry 242; Old Park, Southwark 219, 221; Peel 195; Ratcliff 268, for children 269; women and 74, 125
  ministers' and elders' galleries 126, 340; Bull & Mouth 80; Devonshire House 169; Gracechurch St 264; Holloway 264; Kingston 313; New Park, Southwark 227, 255; Peel 193–94, 203; Ratcliff 268; for women 193–94, 227, 344
Galloway, Alexander 369n
games and gaming 123, 254, 383
  G. Fox on 47
  ninepins 230–31
gaolers: Joseph Green 163; Stephen Draper 232
gardeners: Robert Walburton 212
gardens 151
  John Fothergill's arboretum 260
Gatehouse Prison, G. Latey in 251
Gatton, Surrey 317
Gay, Claude 147, 250
General Committee on discipline (YM) 235
general meetings
  Baptist 13
  early period 47–52, 69, 71n
  of ministering Friends 338
  monthly meetings (quarterly MMs) 186; Kingston 314; West Middlesex joint 290
  for worship 69n
George & Vulture, Tottenham: school at 307
George III
  and Hannah Lightfoot q.v.: account of xix
  and Savoy tenure 246
George Inn, Uxbridge 285
George Yard, Lombard St 80, 342n
George's Court (nr Hicks's Hall): Richard Claridge 200
German, relief for 131
Germany
  Theodore Eccleston in 178,
  Emden, sufferings in 131
  Frederickstadt, meeting house 239
  Holstein, sufferings in 130, 131
Gesope [Jessop?], Thomas 230
gestures (*see also* plainness) 77, 78
Gibson, William, jun 79–80
Gibson, William, sen 79, 154
Gilby, Joseph 293
Giles (St Giles) poor relief district, Westminster MM 257

girls (*see also* children)
  John Row legacy for education 185n
  schools: Ann Barclay's 361; Shacklewell 360
  at workhouse 367–368
Glaisyer, Joseph 359
Gloucester mtg house by Samuel Daukes 284
gloves, giving at births 117
Godalming, 316, 317, 326
Goddard, Anne, later Whitehead 175
Godfrey, Lawford 225
going naked as a sign 142
Gold, J., house at White Hart Court 152
gold, wearing of 77
Golden Lane, Katherine Cage Court 191
Goldie, Mark xxii
Goodson, John, surgeon 130
Goodwin, James 272
Gooses, house in Essex 155, 278, 279, 295
Gopsill, John 225
gospel order (*see also* discipline) 47, 49
Goswell Road 374
Gouldney, Henry 155, 156
Gouldney, John 152
Gove, Richard 293
Gracechurch Street (Gracious St, Gratia St)
  MM boundary 171
  Penn and Mead preach in 153, 154
Gracechurch St meeting (White Hart Court)
  55, 105, 144–57, **156**, 161, 336, 353
  acquired 142
  "battle for" xxii, 153–54
  carriages 151
  William Dewsbury at 159
  fire 134, 147, 161, 337
  funerals 154–57, 330
  marriages at [*table after* 88]
  Peter the Great at 239
  "retired" meeting 125
  sale of 264
  and Stoke Newington xxiv
  Yearly Meeting at 170
Gracechurch St MM (*see also* Bull & Mouth MM) 89, 110, 144–61
  Devonshire House MM, union with 148, 152, 172n, 189
  ministers and elders [*table after* 78]
  and Peel MM (Stoke Newington) 157
  records lost xxiii, 147, 337
  schools 361
  Six Weeks Meeting 107, 110, 111
  women's meeting 354

Gracious St: *see* Gracechurch St
grand juries 214
grass, burial grounds 277; sheep 333, 335
Gratia St: *see* Gracechurch St
gravediggers/gravemakers (*see also* burial grounds): 129, 333; Holmes, Michael 335
Gravel Lane, passage from Devonshire Square 168
graves: *see* burial grounds; funerals
Gray, Abraham, legacy to SWM 109n
grazing 333, 335, 364
Great Almonry (*see also* Little Almonry) 241
Great Eastern Railway Co: purchase Quaker St premises 166
Great Fire 135, 141, 145, 152, 167, 245, 336
  as sign 39
"Great Indignity" as sign 39
Great Plague 39, 141, 152, 176, 356
  burials 330, 332
Great Storm (1703) xx, 165, 274
Great Tower (Savoy) 245
Green Walk, Southwark 221
Green, Joseph, gaoler 163
Greenwell (Grenwel), Anne 174
Greenwich, Nicholas Bond's 223, 240
Greig, William, lease of Bunhill land 334
Grellet, Stephen 261
Greyhound, Croydon 327
Griffin, Edward: school at Longford 292
grocers: G. Whitehead 174
Groom, Samuel 272
Grove, The (Peningtons' home) 356, 359
Grubb [surname] 390
Grubb, Sarah 147
Guildford 316, 317
Guildhall, procession of Alexander I to 265
Gurnel, Jonathan 287
Gurney family 150
Gurney [surname] 388, 389
Gurney, Samuel 275, 278, 380
Guttershedge (Hendon) 308, 344
Gwillim, Thomas, preaching in Uxbridge 282

haberdashers: Mann, Edward 296,
Hacker, Colonel 26
Hackleton, Thomas 37, 215, 219
Hackney (Gilbert Sikes) 37
Haddock, Robert 239
Hagen, Gilbert 225
Hagen, Jacob 106, 372
Haile(s), Colonel 219, 220, 221

hair
  hairstyles, in burial 238
  loss of, excusing wigs 77
Hale, Judge 245
Halsey, Edward 287
Halsey, Mary, legacy to SWM 110n
Ham House, Upton 260
Ham, transferred to Plaistow 276
Hamm, Thomas xiv
Hammersmith 36, 101, 248, 261–64, **261**, 347n
  and Brentford 286
  Claude Gay at 250
Hammersmith MM 71, 96, 261–64
  General Monthly Meeting 290,
  Hendon MM, proposal to join with 309
  union with Westminster MM 249
Hampson, Widow: Bull & Mouth 144
Hampstead, Fifth Monarchists at 137
Hampton Court, G. Fox meets Oliver
  Cromwell 32, 311
Hanbury, family 150, 151, 184
Hanbury, Osgood, marriage 89
handicraftsmen 183, 249
Hanging Sword Court 72
Hanover St (Long Acre) 247
Hanwell Lunatic Asylum (architect of) 58
Hanworth 291
Harding, David 278, 280
Harding, John, cheat 130
Harman, family 150
Harman, Philip 185, 225
Harold (Harold's) Hill (or Wood) 274, 278–279, 280
Harris, family 150, 158
Harris, Edward 158
Harris, Richard 313
Harris, Tim xxii
Harrison of Chester, architect 158
Hart upon Hope (field), Deptford 223
Hart, Nicholas [Stephen ?] 251
Hart, Stephen (New Palace Yard) 36, 240,
Hart, Thomas, schoolmaster 247, 248, 301
Hartrick, A.S., drawing of Peel **210**
Harwood, Philip, in Newgate 138
Hasgood, Andrew 318
hats
  beauish 77
  hat honour xxvi, 5, 138, 265, 268
  and worship 45, 49, **156**, 228
Hatch, Elizabeth 162n
Havering-atte-Bower 278, 295

Hawkins, Richard 250, 251, 258, 332, 363n
Hayes, Alice 302, 307
Hayly, (Hayes), Widow 308, 344
Hayward, E. D. 236
Hayward, John (Haward) 372
headborough (city functionary) 198
Heale, Daniel and Deborah 285
Heale, Joseph 285, 293
Heale, Richard, physician 293
healing: G. Fox 347
hearses (*see also* funerals) 117, 157
heating: *see* fires
Heemskerk, Egbert van, pictures of Quaker
  meetings **25**, 344
Helmet, The (Samuel Vasses' house) 36, 347
Hemming's Row: *see* Westminster
Hendon (Guttershedge) 308, 344
Hendon MM 71, 96, 304, 308–10
  and Brentford 286,
  General Monthly Meeting 290,
Hermitage: Ratcliff poor district bdy 273
Hermitage Bridge: MM boundary 171
Hermitage Field 375
Hertford, William Weston of 185n
Hertfordshire 295; QM 298, 305
Hewlett, John 81–82
Hezekiah: "Nehushtan" (2 Kings 18:4) 331
Hickman, John 299
Hicksites xvi
Hicks's Hall, St John's St
  Richard Claridge's house near 200
  Middlesex Sessions 203n, 212
hierarchy of mtgs: *see* Society of Friends
High Church government 34, 35
highwaymen xxvi
Hill, Judith 256
Hilton Gang (informers) xxii
Hinde, Luke 342n
Hine, W.F. (Baptist) 328
history xiii–xxxii
  disregard for 355
  William Sewel 45n, 159, 178
Hitchcock, Tim xxiii
Hitchin: mtg house by Samuel Daukes 284
Hoare family 150,
Hoare, Samuel jun 300
Hoddesdon: MM boundary 295
Hodges, Samuel, butcher 299
Hodgkin, Dr [Thomas] 237
Hog Land: MM boundary 171
Hogell, Robert 229

Hogesdon (Hoxton): MM boundary 171
Holborn: MM boundaries 197, 249
Holborn Viaduct Commissioners 210
Holden, Francis 318
Hole, John 248
Hole-in-the-Wall (Long Acre) 247–48
Holford, Mary (poor relief) 206
holidays (*see also* times and seasons) 76, 312
    school 375n
Holland 129n
    John Bringhurst moves to 342n
    Theodore Eccleston in 178
    Joseph Heale visits 293
    sufferings in 130, 131
Holloway 148, 264, **264**
    transferred to Westminster MM 210,
Holloway Land: MM boundary 171
Holmes, Benjamin 286
Holmes, Michael and son John 335
Holmes, Thomas 20
Holstein, sufferings in 130, 131
Holy Cross, Waltham (*see also* Waltham) 296
holy days: *see* holidays; times and seasons
Homerton (Hummerton): MM boundaries 171
honesty
    disownments for falsehood 190, 191
    G. Fox on dishonesty 47
    in trade 231
    QM report (1761) 384
Honour, Elizabeth 200
Hookes, Ellis 125, 235, 339, 340
    and E. Burrough's works 28n
    records of sufferings 51, 153,
    salary 113,
    and Six Weeks Meeting 70, 114, 124
hop trade 222
Hope Court, Wentworth St 233
Hope Schools for All 334
Hope, John 165
Hope, The (between Chiswick and Hammersmith) 262
Horle, Craig xxii
Horn [surname] (two women) 389
Horne, Benjamin 372
Horne, Hannah De 201n
horses
    Book of Common Prayer tied to 281n
    for ministers 100, 126–27, 339, 364
    payment for: Mtg of Twelve 113; MMs 208, 317, 322–23; SWM 105, 106, 208

    stabling and grazing 100, 126–27, 335, 356, 364
    usein persecution 139, 251
Horslydown (*see also* Southwark) 216–19, 226, 292
    as Cambrian Chapel **220**
    fire engine 234
    joined with Park 226
    marriages at [*table after* 88]
    origins: Widow Webb's 37, 215, 216, 343 ["Jebb", *sic*]
Horslydown MM: *see* Southwark MM
Horton, William 231
Hoskins, James 81, 250
hospital, workhouse as 366
Hospital (New), Shoreditch: MM boundary 171
hospitality, among Friends 150
Houndsditch 168, 170, 174, 183, 184
Hounslow 315
House of Commons: *see* Parliament
House of Correction 266
House of Detention 163n, 363
housekeeper, Islington Road School 378
houses
    built (*see also* almshouses; tenements) 335
    meetings in: *see* meetings, private
    "rich adorning" (*see also* plainness) 117
How, Sarah, legacy to SWM 109n
Howard, John 259
Howard, Luke 150, 331n, 380n. 389
Howard, Robert 331n, 376
Howarth [surname] 390
Howe (preacher) 7
Howgill, Francis 20–28, 63, 134, 215, 266, 342n, 346
Howker, Dr 228
Hoxton (Hogesdon): MM boundary 171
Hoyland, Charles x, xxix
Hubard, Stephen 318
Hubbersty, Stephen 308
Hubbert, Ann 200
Hubbert, Samuel 329n
Hubberthorne, Richard 20, 32, 33, 35, 38, 139n, 330
    and Women's Two Weeks Meeting 346
Huddleston, John 298
Hudson, John 286
Hudson, Thomas 220–221, 232
Hunger Hill, Bucks 358
Hunt, John 200, 209

Hunter, Robert 317
Hunton, Thomas 158
Huntingdonshire 15, 101
husbandmen: Jordan, William 308,
Hustler, Christiana, Irish minister 181
Hutcheson, Robert 200
Hutchinson, Lady 6
Hutton, Richard (*see also* workhouse, steward) xxiii

Illustrated London News, picture of Women's Yearly Meeting **354**
immigrants ("strangers"), relief for 131, 349
immorality: *see* disorderly conduct; disorderly marriages
imprisonment: *see* prisoners, prisons
inaudible speech, at marriages 181–82
inconsistency, disownments for 123
Independents 8–17, 68n, 140
   James Jackson 203
   Daniel Neal xiv
"Indignity, Great" as sign 39
industrial work (*see also* occupations) 90
infirm: *see* sick
informers 4, 65, 68n, 84, 174, 202–203
   Hilton Gang xxii
Inman, Joseph and Sarah 191
innkeepers 127; Gabriel Erwood 233
inns (public houses: *see also* drink)
   authors' attitude to xxv
   committees held in 233
   frequenting of 383
   Beehive, The (Wanstead) 275; British Workman (temperance pub) xxv; Castle and Falcon 127; Cock Inn 127; Dolphin Inn, Bishopsgate 146, 168, 170, 174; Falcon 127; Falcon (Upper Ground) 215; Greyhound (Croydon) 327; Platter, The 127; Ram, The (Wandsworth) 322; Rose and Crown (Wandsworth) 322; Ship Inn (Southwark) 127; Ship, The (Fenchurch St) 177; Two Brewers (Bermondsey) 215; White Lion (Croydon) 327
inquest on John Sparsfield 173
Inspection Committee, workhouse 372
inspection of meeting houses 100, 106
Institute: *see* Bedford Inst.; Friends' Inst.
insurance 147, 303
   lack of, for fire and flood 183
interrupting 73
Interval Friends 180, 256

investments: *see* funds
Ireland
   T.F. Ball in xxvii
   ministers to/from 82, 181, 338
   relief of English sufferings 292, 297,
Isleworth (Brentford) 286–87
Islington 329, 380
   MM boundaries 197
Islington Road School/workhouse (St John's Road) 375–79
   accommodation of elderly people 375
   Clerkenwell, removal from 374
   committee 377
   Croydon, removal to 327,
   engraving xix, **378**
Ivy Lane 138

Jackson, James, disorderly preaching 203
Jacob Street (Widow Webb's q.v.: *see also* Southwark) 37
Jamaica 121, 231, 292
James House (St James's) 36
James II, King 65, 220, 252, 337
   G. Whitehead and 176–77
Janson family 150
Janson, Edward 376
Janson, Frederick 158
Janson, William 380n
Jebb [*sic*], Widow: *see* Webb, Mary
Jeffreys, John, schoolmaster 242
Jennings, Isaac: Dev. Ho. tenant 169
Jennings, John 194, 200, 209
Jersey: Claude Gay of 147
Jessop (Gesope) 230
Jesus, J. Nayler's appearance as 29–30
jokes, made by William Gibson jun 80
Jones, Rufus xiv, xxi
Jones, Thomas 216, 218
Jordan, William, legacies 308, 309
Jordans **355**, 355–59; "iconic" xxi
journalists: T.F. Ball xxix
journeymen, members at Peel 201
judges: *see* justices
juries (*see also* legal system) 62–63, 67, 173
   grand 214
   Penn–Mead trial 153
justices (judges, magistrates; *see also* legal system) 30–31, 46, 251, 267, 319
   books given to 113
   Sir Richard Brown 138, 175
   burial cost 277   *contd*

justices *contd*
  Chief Baron 84
  dishonest 198
  G. Latey, friend of 240–41
  Hale, Judge 245
  powers 62–63
  workhouse lease from 368

K., Mary, rambling in Suffolk 340
Katherine Cage Court, Golden Lane 191
Keane, Mary (Keene) 250, 255
Keith, George 120, 360
Kelvedon, Essex: Joseph Dell of 294
Kemp, Mary 277
Kendal [surname] 389
Kendall, John, *Catechism* 378
Kennedy, Thomas xvi, xxxi
Kensington 389; road to, MM boundary 249
Kent, John 182
Kent, William 165
King, Thomas 275, 278
King Court, Lombard Street: recording clerk's office 133
King St (Long Acre) 247
King's Arms [Longford area], wrestling 288
King's Bench prison marshal 232
King's Head, Pudding Lane 233
kings: *see* Charles II, James II, William III, George III
Kingston, G. Fox's son-in-law at 155
Kingston meeting 311–15, **316**, 317
  frequency of meetings 316,
  meeting in street 318
  ministers sent to 321n
Kingston MM 283, 311–28,
  ministers and elders [*table after* 78]
  and Quarterly Meeting 76
  and Six Weeks Meeting 110, 111, 112
  union with Croydon and Wandsworth 320 326, 327
Kitching, John 177
Kits End 299
Kitto, F. Bowyer xxx
Knight [surname] 388
Knightsbridge: MM boundary 249
knitting, at workhouse 368
Knockall's Alley, Long Acre 247
Kuweidt, John 322

labouring Friends: *see* ministers
Lacey, Thomas 84

Lamb, John 328
Lamb, Mary 200
Lambeth Marsh 37, 215
Lancashire
  early monthly meeting 44
  William Gibson in 79
Landers, John xxii
Landes, Jordan xxiii
landmarks, Uxbridge property 285
Lane family 359
Langley Park, Bucks 291
languages, in schools 132, 361
Larkes, James 303
Latey, Gilbert 250–251
  and Box Meeting 346, 348
  and Charles II 220, 250–251
  on Croydon 323
  on Greenwich 223
  on Hammersmith 262
  on Kingston 311; married there 318; buried 312
  at Pall Mall meeting 240–41
  Pietists, to visit 131
  private meetings 36
  at Savoy 246, 252
  Six Weeks Meeting 92, 168
  on Wheeler St xix
Latey, Mary 251, 318
Latin, teaching 131, 132
laundry
  washerwomen, Bunhill burial gd 333
  washing machine, Islington Rd 376
law: *see* Acts of Parliament; justices; legal system
law Latin and court hand, at school 132
Lay, Benjamin 81
Lea Bridge: boundary, Tottenham MM 295
lead coffins 236–238, 270
Leake, George, undertaker 236
leases
  costs, Mtg of Twelve 113
  drafting 121
  locations: Bull & Mouth 143–44; Devonshire House 167, 168, 170; Epping 297; Gracechurch St (White Hart Court) 146, 147, 149; Holloway 264, 264; Horslydown 218; Little Almonry 242–243; Long Acre 247, 248; Longford 283; Peel 193, 195; Savoy 245, 246; Sarah Sawyer's house 196; Southwark 222; Staines 285;   *contd*

leases: locations *contd*
 Waltham Abbey 296; Wandsworth 318; Wapping 270; Westminster (Peter's Court) 244; Wheeler St 164, 165, 166; workhouse (Clerkenwell) 368, 374; (Islington Rd) 374, 379
leather-dryers: use of Bunhill burial gd 333
lectures: William Beck ix; William Tanner 59
legacies: *see also* funds; wills
 Bunhill: for upkeep 333n; Westminster MM land 332
 Devonshire House MM 185n, 189
 individuals: Jacob Agar 109n; Margaret Bell, 185n; Devereux Bowley 374n; Samuel Brewster 374; Mariabella Briggin[s] 210; Thomas Broadbank 110n; Peter Cockfield 109n; Anthony Crosfield 372; Eliot family, Croydon 324; Mary Elson 199, 365; Richard Fielder 314; Abraham Gray 109n; Mary Halsey 110n; Richard Harris 313; Richard Hawkins 258, 332; Sarah How 109n; William Jordan 308, 309; Joseph Lum 109; William and Sarah Mead(e) 279; John Miers 109n; Daniel Mildred 109; Anthony Neatby 110n; John Paris 109n; Hannah Plumstead 110n; Robert Plumstead 185n; Row, John 110n, 185n; John and Sarah Sherwin 109n; John Smith 333n; Joseph Smith 110n; Thomas Smith 109n; Anthony Sterry 110n; Mary Sterry 110n, 328; Richard Sterry 109n; Thomas Talwin 109n, 185n, 374; Cornelius Taylor 374; John Warner 374n; William Weston 185n; George Whitehead 177; Mary Yoakley 233
 for poor 120, 121
 and Quarterly Meeting area 75, 110
 Six Weeks Meeting and 96, 103, 119–120
 to SWM fund 108, 109
 to workhouse 367, 371
legal system: *see also* Acts of Parliament; courts; deeds; distraint; fines; juries; justices; leases; prisons; sufferings; wills
 history xxii
 laws affecting Friends 31, 35, 60–68
 legal costs of property 113
 legal drafting (Thomas Lewis) 121
 legal questions, QM deciding 79
 legal sanction for Friends marriages 181
 legal status of Quaker business mtgs 84

litigation between Friends 120; by William Weston's heir 185n
Penn–Mead trial 153
legislation: *see* Acts of Parliament; Parliament
Leighton and Upperside MM (Bucks) 356
length of meetings (*see also* times of meetings): proposal for two-day QM 76
Leominster, Presbyterians at 68n
Letchworth, Robert 200
Letchworth, Thomas 177
Letters (ed Abram Rawlinson Barclay) 25, 67, 70, 134, 136, 156
Lettsom, Dr. [John Coakley] 150, 259
Levellers 15
Lewis, Thomas 121
Leytonstone: meeting at almshouses 276
liberal (Hicksite) Quakerism xvi
libraries (*see also* books; literature; manuscripts; records)
 Friends House xvi, xxvii, xxv–xxvi, xxxiii
 Friends Institute 148n
 Gracechurch St 148
 Guildhall Library xxxiii
 William Mead(e)'s library 279
 Peel 207
 Westminster 251, 258–61
Lidbetter, Hubert: picture collection xxxiii
 Esher 316; Hammersmith 261; Holloway 264; Plaistow 277, 281; Staines 286, 294; Stoke Newington 157; Uxbridge 287; Wandsworth 317; Westminster 265; Winchmore Hill 300
Light within 17
Lightfoot, Hannah 255; account of xix
lighting (street): Cavendish Court 169; Little Almonry 249
Lilburne, John 330
Lilley, Ruth 314
Lilsworth 314
Limehouse, fire at 101
Limekilns: The Hope (between Chiswick and Hammersmith) 36, 262
Lincoln's Inn: MM boundary 249
Lindoe, John 381, 388
linendrapers: Mead(e), William 177
Lister [surname] 388
Lister, Elizabeth (later Beck) 151n
Lister, John 147, 158, 159, 161n
Lister, Joseph xxiv
Lister, Joseph Jackson xxiv
lists, membership 172, 350

literature (books, "papers" and "writings"; *see also* Fox, George; libraries)
  adverse 41, 42, 113; Francis Bugg 177
  bibliography 397–418; Joseph Smith, 259, 362n; John Whiting 258–59
  distribution 19; abroad 120
  in meetings 292, 321
  Morning Meeting 113, 337, 338, 341, 342
  not approved 79, 83, 119
  for the poor 386
  publishing (incl. printers and booksellers) xxii, 133, 145
  for young people 292; and servants 253
litigation: *see* legal system
Little Almonry (meeting) 241–43, 244, 248
  barred by justices 251
Little Almonry (street), poorly lit 249
Little St Thomas Apostle 145n
Littlefield 314
Livery Companies: *see* City
Lloyd family 150, 151
Lloyd, Sampson jun 381, 388
loans: *see* funds
Lodge, John, Amsterdam 131
Lombard St 151, 154; George Yard 80, 342n; recording clerk's office 133
London: description (c.1654) 3–7; history xxi, xxii, xxiii, xxix
London or City Meeting: *see* Bull & Mouth
London and Middlesex Quarterly Meeting: *see* Quarterly Meeting
London Bridge: MM boundaries 171
London Metropolitan Archives xxxiii
"London Quaker, The": engraving **79**
Londoners, character of 22–23
Long Acre (Hole in the Wall) 247–248
Long Lane, Bermondsey 222, 223, 236
Longditch, Westminster 241
Longford 101, 283, 287
Longford MM 282–94, **286**, 361
  account of sufferings xviii
  Barking meeting house, contribution 275
  ministers and elders [*table after* 78]
  and Quarterly Meeting 75, 76
  records 287
  and SWM 110, 111, 112,
  union with Westminster MM 249
looter, at Gracechurch St fire 161
Lord Mayor (Sir Richard Brown) 37, 137, 138–39, 142
  G. Whitehead fined by 153

Lord's supper (sacrament) 14, 340
lottery 340
Loveday, Henry 277, 280
Lower Redcross St (Burial Ground; *see also* Southwark, Park) 236
Lucas, William 391n
Ludgate: MM boundaries 197
Lum, Joseph, legacy to SWM 109
Lunatic Asylum, Hanwell 158
lunatics: *see* mental illness
lying-in (*see also* midwives) Box Meeting 345
Lynes, Elizabeth 294
Lyons, Sarah 313

Macaulay, Thomas Babington xiv, 224
madness: *see* mental illness
magistrates: *see* justices; legal system
Mags, Prudence 230
Maitland's *History of London* 33–34, 168, 176
majority voting: workhouse committee 364
Malcolm, James Peller [erroneous ref] xix, 376
Maldon, Essex 84
Manchester Difficulty xxxi
Mander, Alice 277
Mann, Edward, haberdasher 296, 297
manners (*see also* hat honour; plainness) 77–78, 393–94
Mansell, Ann 323
manuscripts (*see also* Barclay, A.R.; records)
  annotated *London Friends' Meetings* xxv
  illustrations xv, xvii, xx, xxviii, 78, 89, 334
  letter about Emperor Alexander [Richard Low Beck] 265
  lost in fire 147
  for publication 341, 342
  Southwark MSS (Walter Miers) 235
maps and plans
  Bull & Mouth **24**
  London (17th century) **3**; (1863) **2**; (present-day) **ii**
  Tottenham burial ground **301**
maritime trades (Ratcliff) 271
Mark Lane 391
Markes, Nathaniel 120
markets 317, 325
marriage (*including* weddings)
  business at meetings: monthly meetings 46, 181–2 186, 290, 292–93, 351; Quarterly Mtg 384; SWM 118, 128–29; Two-Weeks Mtg 89, 346, 353 *contd*

marriage *contd*
  celebration 117, 129, 375n
  clearness for 81, 119, 323
  conduct of 254, 267, 341
  disorderly 88, 121, 129, 191, 228, 288
  fees 180
  George Fox and 47–8, 50, 128, 129, 229
  to non-Quaker 79, 253, 256; Act (1860) xvi
  by priest 48, 119, 123, 124, 230, 253, 255
  records and certificates 48, 71n, 87, 323, 341, 353
  statistics xxvi, [*table after* 88]
Marriott, Ruth 200
Marshal, City: payment to 133
marshal, King's Bench prison 232
Marshman, Berry 244
Marshman, James 255
Marshfield, Thames Ditton 314
martyrdom (*see also* sufferings) 140n, 374n
  E. Burrough and F. Howgill 23
  John Sparsfield 173
Marygold Stairs: David Barrow's 215
Marylebone: MM boundary 249
Master (title, Islington Rd School) 377
Masterman, family 150, 151, 359
mathematics (arithmetic) in schools 361, 377
Matson, Hester 261
Matthews, Sarah 36, 250, 343
Mayor: *see* Lord Mayor
Mead(e), William xxiii, 131, 177, 180, 275
  G. Fox with 295
  money 278–79
  Penn–Mead trial xix, 153–54
  Six Weeks Meeting 92, 120, 168
Mead, Sir Nathaniel 279
Meade, Sarah 275, 277, 278, 279
mechanics (Ratcliff) 271
medicine
  John Bellers' proposals 362
  physicians: John Fothergill 150; Richard Heale 293; Thomas Hodgkin 237; John Coakley Lettsom 150; Robert Pope 294
  at workhouse 372
meeting: usage 269
meeting of ancient Friends: *see* Morning Mtg
meeting houses (buildings): *see also* meetings, *below*
  built or rented: Barking 274–75, 286; Brentford 287; Bull & Mouth 24, 134–44; Croydon 324; Deptford 223–24; Devonshire House 160–70; Enfield 301; Epping 297–98; Esher 315; Flamstead End 298; Gracechurch St (White Hart Court) 142, 144–57; Hammersmith 262–64; Hendon 308; Holloway 148, 244; Horslydown (Southwark) 217–19; Kingston 312–15; Little Almonry (Westminster) 241–43; Long Acre 247–48; Longford 283; Mill Hill 308–310; New Park (Southwark) 221–23; Old Park (Southwark) 219–21; Peckham 224–25; Peel 192–95; Peter's Court or Hemming's Row (Westminster) 243–44; Plaistow 276–77; Ratcliff 267–69; Savoy 244–47; South Mimms 299; Stoke Newington 148, 157–58, 211–13; Tottenham 302–04; Uxbridge 285–86; Waltham Abbey 296–97; Wandsworth 318–19; Wapping 269–70; Wheeler St 162–66; Winchmore Hill 299–301; Woolwich 224
  query on 54
  Six Weeks Meeting and 91; finance 96, 101, 103; inspection and repairs 100, 106, 107; rents xxv, 113
Meeting for Sufferings
  Algiers captives 131
  Devonshire House building 170,
  and literature 362, 338
  and Six Weeks Meeting/Twelve 97, 99, 101, 102, 120
Meeting of Twelve 101, 112–14, 143, 196, 211, 302
  and ministers 126
  and poor 130
  and Six Weeks Meeting 94–97, 100, 103
Meeting, Six Weeks: *see* Six Weeks Meeting
Meeting, Two-Weeks: *see* Two Weeks Meeting; *see also* women
meetings (*see also* elders; ministers; monthly meetings; Society of Friends, organisation of; times of meetings)
  administrative structure (*see also* Fox, George; discipline) xvi, 40
  Baptist 13
  for discipline: *see* discipline
  general 41, 69
  laws against (*see also* Acts of Parliament; legal system) 60–68
  monthly: *see* monthly meetings
  meetings opened and closed, QM responsibility 71, 100   *contd*

443

meetings *contd*
  private (in houses): 24, 119; "appointed" (Longford MM) 291; "retired" 27, 32, 125, 226, 272, 278; suppressed by Devonshire House MM 179; women 343
  private meetings, City/London locations (1654, Southwark) **3**, 215; (1662 list) **3**, 36–37; others 162, 196, 221, 240, 247, 266–67. Country: Enfield MM 301; Esher 315; Greenwich (Nicholas Bond) 223; Kingston (Fielders) 311; Kit's End 299; Longford MM 291; Mill Hill (Samuel Rodgers) 309; Staines (Patience Ashfield) 284; Tottenham 302; Uxbridge (William Winch) 282
  public and private distinct 24, 26, 32
  public: Esher 316 ; threshing 24, 27, 32, 136, 240; women "too prominent" 340
  Quarterly Meeting concern for 76
  quarterly: *see* quarterly meetings
  registration 65
  in street 165n, 173, 202, 251 268
  women's: *see* women
  for worship 2, 178–79, 202–03, 226–27, 248–49; Algiers captives 131; Advices, reading of 327–28; and discipline 78, 124–26; list of (1662) 36–37; seating of: *see* seating; sleeping in 117, 125, 204
membership (*see also* certificates; disownment; residence; settlement; statistics)
  definitions 56, 182, 189, 205
  G. Fox and 57
  lists xxv, 123, 172, 291
  and poor relief 208
  and residence 78, 121, 321
  statistics 172, 201, 331
men
  dress 77, 117
  men's meetings: 52, 180; and marriages 47; Kingston MM 314; Meeting of Twelve 95; Quarterly Meeting 74; Two Weeks Meeting 85, 86
  ministers: in gallery 169, 344; Morning Meeting 124, 143n, 336, 338; and pastoral care 43, 345–46
  and women; meeting jointly 92–93, 180, 235, 252, 386; separate seating 125
mental illness 80, 130, 228
  and depictions of J. Nayler xvii–xviii
Mercer's Company 264
Mercer's Rd, Holloway 264

merchant tailors: Oakley, John 162
merchants and traders (*see also* occupations) 150, 183, 271, 249
messengers, Baptist ministry 13
Messer [surname] 388
Messer, Josiah 265
Metropolitan Board of Works 222
Michael Yoakley's Almshouses 158, 182–3
Middlesex meetings: *see also* country Friends' School admissions 378
  North Middx and Herts border (*see also* Enfield; South Mimms) 295, 305
  and Quarterly Meeting (q.v.) 72, 306
  and Six Weeks Meeting 96
  West Middlesex, see Longford MM
Middlesex Sessions 212
midwives xxii
  Lyons, Sarah 313
Miers, John, legacy to SWM 109n
Miers, Walter 183, 221, 235
Mildred family 359
Mildred, Daniel 107, 177; legacy to SWM 109
Mildred, Rebecca 286
Mildred Court 389
Mile End (Green) 37, 266–67, 334
  Ratcliff poor district boundary 273
militia (volunteer defence corps; *see also* soldiers) 151, 169, 272, 288, 385
Mill Hill 304, 308–10
Million Bank Yard (Gracechurch St) 145
Mills, Benjamin, weaver 166
Milton, John, cottage at Chalfont 356
Mimms Green (*see also* South Mimms) 299
Minchard, Lieutenant 173
ministers (ancient Friends; public Friends; *see also* elders)
  Baptist 12–13, 14
  deceased, reporting 54, 293; burial at Bunhill 334
  Independent 11
  galleries, seating etc 169, 193–94, 247, 268
  horses (q.v.) 100, 126–27, 339, 364
  individuals named 177–78, 199–200, 225, 250–51, 293–94, 328
  Ireland, from 181
  lack of 210, 257
  Morning Mtg (q.v.) 69, 85, 143n, 336–42
  in organisation 41, 81, 86, 87, 124
  pastoral care 345–46
  recording of 339; opposition to 81
  Quarterly Meeting of 76, 79   *contd*

ministers *contd*
  and Six Weeks Meeting 96, 99, 118
  statistics [*table after* 78]
  travelling: 291, 293–94, 356, 395; abroad 341; American 393; MMs and 102
  unacceptable (*see also* ministry) 339–40
  visiting 215, 227n, 319, 338, 339; country meetings 212, 213, 280, 309, 321, 326n
  wine or ale for 206, 257–58, 321
  Yearly Meeting 53, 82, 356
ministry
  active (evangelical) xvii
  unacceptable 80, 115, 179, 182, 203, 294n
Minories: collections 183; MM boundary 171
minute books: *see* records
miracles, Hannah Barnard's reservations 82
missions xxv
  early Quaker zeal xvii, 395
  Esher 316
  mission halls 334, 335
Mitcham 37, 323–24
Moline [surname] on SWM 107
Moline, Sparks 376, 389
Mollesson, Gilbert (Mollyson) 200, 207, 239
money (*see also* banking; bankruptcy; finance; funds; remuneration; wealth)
  currency 121, 182, 230, 234
  disputes between Friends about 87
  gifts at marriages and burials 129
Monk, George, General 240
Montagu, Basil 66n
monthly meetings: *see also* clerks; discipline; records
  appeals 79
  attendance 58, 209, 254, 353
  autonomy 53, 56, 111
  boundaries 120, 121, 151, 170–71, 197, 249
  establishment 41, 44, 70, 85, 352; not covering City at first 88
  finance and property 101, 102, 111
  G. Fox and 46–47, 82, 88, 92; funeral 157
  General Monthly Meeting (Longford, Hendon and Hammersmith) 290
  interval Friends 180, 256
  London & Middlesex area: *see* Barking MM; Bull & Mouth MM; Devonshire House MM; Croydon MM; Deptford MM; Enfield MM; Gracechurch St MM; Hammersmith MM; Hendon MM; Kingston MM; Longford MM; Peel MM; Ratcliff MM; Southwark MM; Tottenham MM; Waltham Abbey MM; Wandsworth MM; Westminster MM
  loose talk about MM business 227
  and Meeting of Twelve 113
  membership 205
  Morning Meeting and 336, 342
  nature x
  outside London: Coggeshall MM 84; early MMs in north 44; Leighton and Upperside MM (Bucks) 356
  pastoral visiting (*see also* poor) 118
  poor 104, 129, 130, 131–32, 177, 347
  and Quarterly Mtg 73, 76, 100, 351, 381
  quarterly monthly meetings 186, 205, 227, 252–53, 280, 292
  queries 51, 56
  schools 131–32, 361, 378
  and Six Weeks Meeting 91, 94, 97, 99, 104, 111; quota 102, 103, 107, 108, 109
  and workhouse 365, 367, 368, 370, 373
  Yearly Meeting collections 350, 351
monthly meetings for worship: *see* times of meetings for worship
Moore, Rosemary xxi
Moorfields 26, 151; Simon Dring's 36
  MM boundaries 171, 197
  Three Needle Alley 191
Moorgate (Moorfields) 19, 36
  MM boundaries 197
mop-making, workhouse 367, 371, 373
Morning Meeting (*see also* elders; literature; ministers) 125, 336–42, 348
  and discipline 81–82
  origin 69, 85, 143n
  publications 113, 342, 362; ceasing role 338, 341
  and Six Weeks Meeting 124, 126
  Westminster 256–57
morning meetings: *see* times of meetings
Mortimer, Elizabeth 277
Mortlake, Theodore Eccleston's death 178
Morton, Elizabeth, later Dell 294
Morton, John Latimer, schoolmaster 294n
Morton, Michael 255
Morton, Thomas, of Barnsley 294n
mourning (*see also* funerals; plainness) 72, 77, 117
mowing (burial grounds: *see also* sheep) 277
mulberries, Mary Scott's 263
Mulberry Garden, The (Clerkenwell) 373
mysticism 395–96

445

Nags Head Court (White Hart Court) 146
naked as a sign: Solomon Eccles xviii, 142, 276
names, unusual 40n
Nayler (Naylor), James 17, 29–30, 45
  G. Fox, letter to 321n
  historical accounts xvii–xviii
Neal (Neale), Daniel *History of Puritans* 140n
Neatby, Anthony, legacy to SWM 110n
Neave, Moses 291
needlework, in schools 361, 377
"Nehushtan" (2 Kings 18:4) 331
Netherwood, John, innkeeper 127
New Gravel Lane: Ratcliff poor district boundary 272–73
New Hospital, Shoreditch: MM boundary 171
New Palace Yard, Stephen Hart's 36, 240
New Park: *see* Southwark
New Prison 163
New Southwark St, construction of 222
Newgate Gaol 38, 137, 173
  Besse's description 202
  E. Burrough's death 86, 139
  G. Whitehead in 175
Newington Butts (Southwark) 215
Newington Green (near Stoke Newington, q.v.): MM boundaries 197
Newman Henry S., drawings **171, 260**
Newman, Modesty 340
Newport, Earl of 249
Newport, Rhode Island 81
Nicholls, Elizabeth, disownment 190
Nichols, John (Nickolls) 259
night, meetings at: *see* times of meetings
Nightingale Lane: MM boundary 171
ninepins, in prison 230–31
noise: *see* disturbance
nominations: *see* appointments
Nonconformists (Dissenters) xviii, 6–7, 8–17, 34, 37, 137–38, 140
  Hammersmith 264
  history xiv
  Plague, courage during 176
  Proclamation of General Indulgence 337
  schools 200, 374n
  in Southwark 214
non-Quakers
  marriage to: *see* marriage
  receiving poor relief 233
Norbiton Common 314
Norbiton Street, Kingston 312

North London Railway (Broad St site) 329
North of England
  early MMs 44
  ministry in 80, 293
  "Valiant Sixty" from 20, 174
Northampton, fire at 101
Northcott, John (Northcote) 283, 287
Northumberland, early monthly meeting 44
Norton, Thomas 235
Norwich 20
nudity: *see* naked as a sign
numbers: *see* statistics

Oakley (Okeley), John 36, 162, 172, 299
oakum at workhouse 364
oaths xxiii, 61, 65, 118, 123, 198, 362
occupations and trades (pursued by Friends)
  of bridegrooms (table) 90
  and ministry 13, 395
  other refs: accountants xxvii; alchemy 225; apprentice teachers 360, 370, 380; architects xxiv. 158, 284, 375, 376; banking 149, 150, 278, 300n, 307; bidders to funerals 129, 233; boarding house keepers xxvii; books, printing and binding 133; booksellers 145; brewers (*see also* Brewers' Company) 166, 262; builders 219; businessmen (*see also* business) 204, 326; butchers 299; caretakers (doorkeepers) 161, 277, 300, 351; carpenters 192, 193, 194, 224; chandlers 225, 229; cheesemongers 161; chemists xxiv, 150; clerks 100, 106; combmakers 225; constables (q.v.) 288; coopers 137, 145a, 231, 336; corn trade 222; craftsmen 321; distillers 80, 373; doctors, *see* physicians; farmers 324; flax spinning 317, 376, 377; gardeners 212; gravediggers 335; grocers 174; haberdashers 296; hop trade 222; husbandmen 308; innkeepers 127, 233; journalists xxix; knitting 368; linendrapers 177; maritime trades 271; mechanics 271; merchant tailors 150, 183, 249, 271; midwives xxii, 313; mop-making (workhouse) 367, 371, 372; oakum (workhouse) 364; opticians xxiv; oranges, selling 230; physicians 150, 237, 293, 294, 372; pinmakers 292; priests become Quakers 200, 203; printers 133, 321, 342n; publishers xxx, 145; ropemakers 269; *contd*

occupations and trades *contd*
  sackmaking (workhouse) 375n; sailors 271; schoolmasters/mistresses: *see* schools; scientists xxiv, 150; servants, *see main entry*; sewing (workhouse) 368, 369–70; instructor 370; shipwrights 271; shoemakers 182, 267, 373; silk manufacturers 189; silk winding (workhouse) 364; smiths 230; soldiers become Friends 19, 266; spinning 130, 317, 364, 367, 369, 376; stationers 161; steward (workhouse) 366, 367n369n, 375n, 377; surgeons 130, 372; surveyor (Six Weeks Meeting) 236; tailors (*see also* merchant) 191, 250–51, (workhouse) 373; tinplate workers 331n; tradesmen/women 175, 249; undertakers 236; washerwomen 333; weavers 165, 166, 183; workhouse trades 364, 366
Ogilby (topographer) 168
Okeley (Oakley), John 36, 162, 172, 299
Old Bailey 38n, 175
Old Bedlam: MM boundary 171
Old Brentford 286
Old Ford: MM boundary 171
Old Park: *see* Southwark
Old Street 329, 331
Oldenburg, Duchess of 265
older people: *see* elderly
optics: Joseph Jackson Lister; Richard and Joseph Beck xxiv
oranges, woman selling 230
organisation: *see* Society of Friends, organisation of
orphans and fatherless; *see also* widows 48, 101, 115, 118, 121, 348
Osgood family 150, 151
Osgood, John 145
Osgood, Joseph 300
Otter, John 267, 276
outdoor meetings: *see* meetings in street
outward conformity 77
Overend, John 380n
overseers xxvii, 29, 226
  development of 180, 256, 293
  and elders 79
  family visiting 20
  lack of 289, 306, 326
  and revival of discipline 235, 384, 386
Owen, Richard 72
Oxford, Earl of 262

Pace, Mary 235
Pace, Thomas 158
Padley, John 225
Padley, Thomas 235
Pagitt, Ephraim *Heresiography* 8
Paile, Robert 220
Paine, Thomas: bones 391
Palace Yard, New 36,
Palatines, poor 183
Pall Mall (Elizabeth Trott's) 36, 240–41, 343
papers of condemnation: *see* condemnation
Papists: *see* Catholics
pardon, royal (Charles II) 176
Paris, John, legacy to SWM 109n
parish xviii, xxii; relief 130, 293, 349
Park Lane, Croydon 324
Park St, Stoke Newington 158
Parker, Alexander 32, 67, 92, 267, 331
Park, Old and New: *see* Southwark
Parliament: *see also* Acts of
  books given to 113
  E. Burrough 37, 139
  and Charles II 64, 65
  elections 341
  J. Nayler 30
  petition 33
  G. Whitehead 36, 175
particular meetings (*see also* meetings) 71n
Partridge, Benjamin 177
Partridge, Richard 107, 177
pastoral letters, G. Fox q.v. 52
pasture: *see* grazing
Patin, the smith 230
Payne, John 301
peace testimony: *see also* militia; war 288, 385
Pearson, Anthony 32
Peckham 224–25, **225**, 226
  · suburban migration to 157, 222
Peckrill, Isaac 225
Peel 36, 101, 110, 192–95, **210**
  marriages at [*table after* 88]
  worship 201–04; and workhouse/school 366, 377
Peel MM 71, 88, 192–213
  and burials 332, 333
  condemnations book **89**
  and Dev. Ho. MM 121, 172n, 189
  and Gracechurch St MM 157
  and Hendon MM 308, 309–10
  ministers and elders [*table after* 78]
  poor relief 105   *contd*

447

Peel MM *contd*
   and SWM 99, 102, 104, 107, 110, 111, 121; secession 105
   and Westminster MM 249, 264
   women's meeting 354
Pembroke, Earl of 249
penal laws (*see also* Acts of Parliament; sufferings) 60–68
Penington family 355, 356
Penington, John 359
Penn, William,
   and G. Fox 28, 40n, 53, 58, 155; at funeral 155, 330
   grave at Jordans 355, 358
   and James II (Old Park mtg house) 220
   Macaulay on xiv
   Penn-Mead trial xix, 153, 154
   property 276, 359
   and relief 131
   Wheeler St, arrested at 163, 165n
Penn, William (grandson), marriage 323,
Pennsylvania 81, 131, 193, 293, 301
penny lottery, minister engaged in 340
Penny family 359
Penrose, James Doyle xxi
pensioners (boarders, workhouse) 365, 369n
Pentecost: *see* Whitsuntide
Pepys, Samuel at New Palace Yard 240
Perrin, J. E., Baptist 328
Perrot, John 45, 88
personalities: influence of 393
persecutions: *see* sufferings
Peter the Great, of Russia xiv, 223–24, 239
Peter's Court: *see* Westminster
Peters, Elinor 328
Peters, Kate xxii
Petty France: MM boundary 171
Philadelphia (*see also* Pennsylvania) 81, 301
Phillips [surname] 388, 389, 390
Phillips, Richard 261, 265
physicians: *see* medicine
Piccadilly poor relief district, Westminster MM 257
Pickering (uncle of G. Fox) 18n
Pickworth, Henry 342
Pierce, Joseph Jun. 324
Pietists, relief for 131
pigs: hog-yard drainage, workhouse 373
pillory: *see* sufferings
Pim [surname] 388
Pim, Abigail 200

Pim, John 200
Pindar ("Pinner") of Wakefield: MM boundaries 197
pinmakers: Griffin, Edward 292
Pitt, Andrew 200
Pitt, William 235
plague pits 329
Plague, Great 39, 141, 152, 176, 356
   burials 330, 332
plainness: *see also* discipline; hat honour; manners
   and children, query on 54, 56
   discipline revision (1861) xvi
   dress: 76, 382, 383–84, 393; effect on G. Latey as tailor 250
   G. Fox and forms 57
   at funerals 117, 154
   at marriages 254
   QM and 77, 382, 383–84
   scriptural basis 12
   speech (incl. "thou") 5, 76, 382, 383–84, 393; workhouse boys 366
Plaise, manor court 276
Plaistow 151, 273, 276–278, **277**, **281**
   and Barking MM 274, 281
Plaistow Home for Ancient Friends 375
Plashet 389
Platter, The (inn) 127
playhouses 78
pleasures, G. Fox on 47
Plesaunce, Elizabeth, Peel freehold 192, 193
Plumstead, Hannah, legacy to SWM 110n
Plumstead, Robert (Plumpsted), legacy 185n
poems
   "Country Quaker, The" 390
   "Recollections of London" 388–91
Pollard's Trust 103
poor (relief etc)
   apprenticeships 97, 98
   Box Meeting (q.v.: *see also* women) 261n, 344–48
   John Bellers on 362
   E. Burrough 43, 87,
   casual: *see* Six Weeks Meeting
   disputes about 208, 319
   elderly 379
   G. Fox on 98, 347, 348,
   funds 104, 291, 313; legacies 120, 121, G. Whitehead 177; Mary Elson 199
   housing (*see also* almshouses) 101, 221, 233, 333, 335   *contd*

poor *contd*
  missions 273, 395
  monthly (and general) meetings 49, 102, 111, 112: Croydon 319, 325, 327; Devonshire House 182–83, 184; General MM 290–291; Kingston 313, 317; Longford 293; Peel 206, 208, 209; Southwark 221, 232–33; Westminster districts 257-58
  parish relief 130, 293, 349
  poor's stock: *see* funds
  prisoners 51
  Quarterly Meeting 98
  query on 55
  schools 131–32, 379
  settlement 130
  SWM 103, 104, 113, 118, 129–31, 379
    casual 94, 100, 105, 106, 129, 131
  visiting 272, 386
  women (poor) 221, 246
  women's mtgs 180n; Plaistow 277; Two Weeks 349; *see also* Box Meeting
  workhouse 363–74
Pope, John Perrot's mission to 45
Pope, Margaret 284, 294
Pope, Dr Robert xxvi, 294
Popish Plot (*see also* Catholics) 64
population: *see* statistics
Post, Jacob 200, 372
postern gate, Petty France: MM boundary 171
Potter, John 219
Pratt, Sarah 228
Prayer, Book of Common 281n
prayer (*see also* hats; standing)
  and Conventicle Acts 63
preaching xxx, 32n, 63, 136
  clergy at Gracechurch St 153–54
  disorderly 120, 203, 273, 288
  nonconformist 7, 12,
  separatist 115, 121
  in street 268, 282
  on tubs 344
  unapproved 306
premises: *see* meeting houses
Presbyterians 8–17, 68n, 74n
  and Conventicle Acts 140
  Sir Richard Brown former 138,
pressed men 288
Pretender (Young), city defences against 169
Price [surname] 389
Price, Jacob M. xxiii
prices, food (*see also* food and drink) 371

pride, Quarterly Meeting paper on 77
priests
  former: R. Claridge 200; J. Jackson 203
  at Gracechurch St 153–154
  marriage before 48, 230, 255
  Quakers disturbing 281n
  Vicar of Tottenham 200
Primer, G. Fox's 292, 342n
printers 133; William Bradford, John Bringhurst, Giles Calvert, Andrew Sowle 342n
prisons (*see also* legal system; sufferings) 33, 39, 62, 64, 137, 138, 231
  deaths in 54, 330
  locations: Algiers, captives in 130, 131, 178; Appleby Castle, F. Howgill's death 21; Bridewell 20, 138, 142, 267; Compter, The 232; Fleet 132; Gatehouse 251; House of Correction 266; House of Detention 163n, 363; King's Bench 232; Kingston 312; Montagu, Basil, on 66n; New Prison 163; Newgate 37–38; Queen's Bench 200; Scarborough Castle, G. Fox in 44, 48; Tower of London (q.v.) 267; Warwick 66n; White Lion 216
  reform 394
  statistics 65, 201, 267
prisoners: (*see also* legal system; sufferings) captives in Algiers 130, 131, 178; John Bringhurst, printer 342n; Anne Downer 266; John Elson 198; G. Fox, Scarborough 44, 88; G. Latey 251; Peel Fds 201, 202 Southwark Fds 216, 228n; Wheeler St Fds 163; G. Whitehead 175
  release under royal pardon 176
  relief 51, 113 132, 163, 232; Women's Two-Weeks Meeting 347, 349
  report on sufferings 54
privacy: discipline, meetings for (q.v.) 84
private meetings: *see* meetings, private
Proclamations, Charles II 34, 37, 137, 138
  Proclamation of General Indulgence 337
promiscuity, G. Fox on 49
property: *see also* funds; meeting houses
  MMs and 111; London and country, in QM 75; Peel, division 210
  poor relief recipients 233
  SWM business 91, 94, 96
  Wheeler St, ownership of 164
prophecy 16, 27, 340
Prophets, French 253
protection by City Marshal 133

Pryor, John 148
public baths: Dr John Fothergill 260
public celebrations: QM report (1761) 385
public Friends: *see* ministers
public houses: *see* inns
public and private meetings: *see* meetings
publication history (*London Friends' Meetings*) xxix–xxxii
publications: *see* literature; Morning Meeting; printers
publishers (*see also* literature) Isaac Sowle, Tace [Sowle] Raylton 145
Pudding Lane (King's Head) 233
Pugin, A.C., picture of Westminster **265**
punctuality (*see also* times of meetings) 78, 194, 320, 382
  in business dealings 384
  funerals 270
  at marriages 254
punishment, at school 375n
Puritans 10
Pyot, Edward 35, 139n

"Quaker answer" 62–63
"Quakers meeting": Egbert van Heemskerk pictures **25**, 344
Quaker Street (formerly Westbury St) 36, 162, 165, 166, 300
"Quakers Synod, The" **54**
quarterly collection, SWM: *see* quota
Quarterly Meeting: *term used here, as usually in the book, for* London & Middlesex Quarterly Meeting, *or the London QM, and the Middlesex QM (more generally, see* quarterly meetings*)* 69–84, 88, 356
  appeals: individuals 79-80; 83; Peel vs SWM 105
  apprenticeships 97, 98
  arrangements 73–75; Devonshire House 143, 170; at Jordans 356; worship 350
  boundaries: Barking MM transferred from Essex QM 274; Herts–North Middx area 305; Kingston MM transferred from Surrey QM 311, 314
  country and town: "London" and "Middx" QMs 72, 75, 111, 306; workhouse, country children at 372
  discipline 76-79; 381–88; advices 115, 118; "interval Friends" 179–180; on marriages 181–82; on plainness **78**
  queries 186, 187–188n, 248; on women's meetings 353
  funds 104, 110, 206, 351; debt 374; workhouse 366
  meetings/meeting houses: 204 (evening meetings); Brentford 286–287; Enfield 301; Harold Hill 278; Longford 283; Mill Hill 309; Sarah Sawyer's 196; Stoke Newington meeting 157; Tottenham 302; Tottenham/Stoke Newington 303; Uxbridge 286; Wapping 270; Winchmore Hill 300; Wanstead 275
  monthly meetings 252, 381; Barking 280; Devonshire House 186, 187–88n; General MM in W. Middx 290; Longford MM 282; Peel 105, 206, 210; Peel and Hendon 308, 310; Ratcliff and Barking MM union 273; Westminster 248
  of Ministers and Elders 79, 338
  records 56, 70, 105; paper on plainness **78**; wills (Mtg of Twelve) 96
  schools 360, 361, 373, 378, 380
  Six Weeks Meeting 95, 99–100, 105-06, 121; as cash committee 91, 107; fund, 108; Peel vs SWM 105, 209
  Two Weeks Mtg, dissolution of 89
  women's meetings 254, 256, 353
  workhouse 364, 366, 370, 371, 372, 373
quarterly meetings (*see also* Essex QM, Herts QM, Surrey QM) 41, 51, 53, 55–57, 124, 254
  John Bellers pamphlet recommended 362
  women's 354
quarterly monthly meetings (*see also* general meetings; monthly meetings): Barking 280; Devonshire House 186; Peel 205; Longford 292; Southwark 227; Westminster 252–53
Queen's Bench, Richard Claridge 200
Queries (*see also* advices; discipline) 54
  answering of 55–57, 179, 205, 341, 387; Croydon, not answered 326; Devonshire House 186, 187–188n; Peel 210; Westminster 252, 256
  at Morning Meeting 338
  from YM (1755) 382
quietness (*see also* disturbance; silence)
  Clerkenwell inmates at Peel 194
quota, Six Weeks Mtg ("quarterly collection") 100, 102–03, 107–12, 184, 208, 210
  alternatives to 75
  change to system 111–12

450

race, T.F. Ball on xxvii
railways 166, 327, 329, 356
Ram, Wandsworth 322
Ranters 15, 25, 40n, 392; behaviour similar to 141, 229; and hats 49
Ratcliff 37, 267–270, **276**
  Joseph Besse's death 201n
  meeting house 110; soldiers demolish 163
  marriages at [*table after* 88]
  "retired" meeting 125
Ratcliff MM 71, 88, 266–273
  ministers and elders [*table after* 78]
  schools 361
  and Six Weeks Meeting 99, 102, 105, 107, 110, 111
  women's meeting 354
Ratcliff and Barking MMs, union 273, 280–81; Ratcliff & Barking MM 83, 112
Raw [surname] (Row?) 388
Raylton, Tace {Sowle}, bookseller / publisher 145
Reading 2
Reay, Barry xix
"Recollections of London" (poem) 388–91
recording clerk 70, 97, 84, 321; Benjamin Bealing 84; Ellis Hookes 70; Richard Richardson 131, 360
  office ("The Chamber") 133
recording of ministers: *see* ministers
record-keeping: Joseph Besse at Peel 201
records and registers (incl documents; manuscripts; minutes; "papers", "writings"; *see also* recording clerk)
  Baptist 15
  Box Meeting 350, 351, 352
  care of 133; "not forthcoming", Longford MM 289
  courts xxii
  G. Fox's advices in 52n
  illustrations of **xv**, **xvii**, **xx**, **xxviii**, **78**, **89**, **301**, **334**
  lost in fire 147
  Ministering Friends, Books of 339
  monthly meeting minutes etc (*see also* Somerset House, below): Devonshire House xx, xxviii; Gracechurch St 134; General MM 291; Hendon 309; Kingston 314; Longford; 287; Peel 89, 204; Ratcliff 271; Southwark 46, 228, 232; Westminster 252
  Morning Meeting 337
  poor relief 98, 182
  Quarterly Meeting 56, 70, 78,105
  register of apprenticeships 98
  registers of births, marriages and burials xxii, 71, 97, 100–01; burials at Bunhill 331, 332; Croydon 326; E. Burrough on 43, 87; G. Fox on 51, surrendered to Registrar General 280, 305
  registers, parish: Chalfont St Giles 359
  registration of meeting places 65, 196, 298, 211–12
  research in ix–xi
  Six Weeks Meeting 91, 92, 94
  at Somerset House [now National Archives, Kew]: Barking MM 279–80; Enfield/Tottenham 305; Waltham Abbey MM 305
  sufferings 55–56, 65
  title deeds 96, 192, 195
  Two Weeks Meeting 85, 89
  wills (Mtg of Twelve) 96
  Women's Two-Weeks 350, 351
  workhouse 363
  Yearly Meeting 337
Reigate 316, 317
registers: *see* records and registers
re-interments, Southwark 236
rejoicing, disturbances from 133
relief: *see* fires; floods; parish; poor; sufferings
religious liberty (*see also* toleration) 394
removals: *see* certificates; membership; residence; settlement
remuneration: Bedford Institute (T.F. Ball) xxviii; Devonshire House 180; Peel (Joseph Besse) 201, 206; recording clerk (Ellis Hookes) 113; Six Weeks Meeting clerk 100, SWM rent collector (W. Beck) xxv; servants' wages 208; workhouse, earnings at 365
rents
  payments 112, 149, 211
  receipts xxv, 100, 106
  relief for poor 113, 129, 182
repairs: *see also* meeting houses 101, 102, 106, 107, 112; Devonshire House 169–70; Peel 194; Wheeler St 164
representative (select) mtgs 58, 95, 205, 252
  Meeting of Twelve 94, 112–13
  Quarterly Meeting 71n, 100, 325
  Six Weeks Meeting 99, 102, 111, 112
  Yearly Meeting 53, 72, 120, 124
republicanism, at Restoration 137

residence: *see also* certificates; membership; settlement
  and boundaries 121, 171
  country/suburban residence 72, 183; Barking 78, 280; and burials 334; Croydon 326, 327; Gracechurch St, away from xxiv; Peckham 222, 226; Peel, away from 201; Staines and Uxbridge 289; Stoke Newington xxiv, 148, 151, 157, 189; Tottenham/Enfield area 295; Wandsworth 321; Winchmore Hill 300
  in meeting houses 164
  and poor 185
resignations (*see also* disownments; membership) xxvi, 123
Restoration xxii, 136–37, 249
resurrection, Quakers said to deny 25
"retired" meetings: *see* meetings, private
revival of discipline: *see* discipline
Revolution (1688) 220
Reynardson family 307
Reynolds, Foster 327
Reynolds, Joseph 327
Reynolds, William F 380n
Rhode Island 81
Ribble, nr South Mimms 299
Richardson, Ann (poor relief) 206
Richardson, Elizabeth 293
Richardson, Richard, schoolmaster and recording clerk 131, 132, 294, 333, 360, 380n
Rickmansworth, William Penn's house 359
Ridgway, Martha, Irish minister 181
Ridley, Nicholas; wife in Bridewell 138
Roake, Mary 293
Roberts, Gerrard
  early meetings 36, 346
  G. Fox stays with 346, 347
  Gracechurch St 145–46, 152
  Morning Meeting 69, 85, 126, 143n, 336
  Southwark 235,
Robinson, Sir John xix, 34, 37, 163–64, 266, 268
Rogers, Samuel 309
Rome, John Perrot's mission to 45
Romford 279, 280
ropemakers: Bushel, Marmaduke 269
Rose and Crown, Wandsworth 322
Rose and Rainbow Court: *see* Sawyer, Sarah
Rose, Aquila 80–81
Rosemary Lane: MM boundary 171

Roubiliac, Louis François, studio 244
Rouse, John 226
Routh, Martha 389
Routh, Zachary 225
Row, John, silk manufacturer 177, 189, 388
  legacies 110n, 185n
rowing: young men on Thames 254
Rowlandson, Thomas: Westminster **265**
Rowntree, John Stephenson xvi
Royal Briefs 183
Rudd, Sarah 294
rude people/boys, disturbance
  to meetings 136; Devonshire House 178; Peel 202; Ratcliff 268; Southwark 218, 222; Waltham Abbey 296; Walworth 215; Westminster 248; Wheeler St 178
  to Thomas Hart's school 248
Rudyard, Thomas 92, 132
Rule Joseph 359
rules: *see* discipline; settlement; workhouse
Russell family, Jordans puchased from 359
Russell, Joseph 294
Russia: Alexander I 261, 265; Peter the Great 223–224, 239
Ryan, cheesemonger (Gracechurch St) 161
Ryan, Michele Denise xxiii

Sabbath observance 14, 20, 30
Sabbath school, Westminster 244
sack-making, at workhouse 375n
sacrament (Lord's supper) 14, 340
sailors (Ratcliff) 271
St Giles (Giles) poor relief district, Westminster MM 257
St George's Place, Holloway 264
St James's (James House) 36, 241
St John's Lane (Peel) 195
St John's Road (Islington Road) 374
St John's St (Peel) 192, 195, **210**
St John's St: Hicks's Hall 203
St Martin's Lane 243
St Martin's le Grand (Bull & Mouth) 135
St Olave's, lease of Horslydown from Church of England 218
St Paul's Cathedral, women pour blood 141
St Paul's Churchyard, arrest for preaching 20
St Thomas Apostle 36; Little 145n
Sale, H.W., photographs **157**, **286**, **287**, **294**, **316**, **317**
Salisbury, Earl of, estate in Westminster 243
Sally [Salé or Sla, N. Africa], captives in 131

452

Salter, Thomas, master, Islington Road School 378
Saltpetre Bank: MM boundary 171
salvation xvii
Sanderson family 150
Sanderson, John 158, 389
Sands, John 282n
Sands' plan of Bull & Mouth (1717) **24**
Sandwich (Sandy's) Court 168
Sargent, James, tailor of Moorfields 191
satire against Friends 80–81
Savery, William 393
savings bank: Priscilla Wakefield's 307
Savoy 36, 244–247, 248
  library at 258
  marriages at [*table after* 88]
  Sir William and Lady Sawkell 262
  seized/barred 220, 251, 252
  Jane Woodcock and Martha Fisher's 344
  William Woodcock's 240
Sawyer, Sarah 36, 196–7, 200, 343, 351, 353
Scarborough Castle, G. Fox's imprisonment 88
Scattergood, Thomas 271
Schnebbelie, etching of Jordans **355**
Schoolhouse Lane, Ratcliff 267
schools (incl educational principles) 180n, 187, 360–61, 394
  John Bellers' proposals 362
  curriculum 132, 361, 377, 378
  plainness 77
  punishmentl 375n
  queries on 54, 55
  schoolmasters 395, 367n; named: T.F. Ball xxvii; Joseph Besse 201; Edward F. Brady 380; Richard Claridge 200, 302, 307, 360; Henry Dymond 380; John Field 360; Charles Fryer 380; George Whitehead 174; Edward Griffin 292; Thomas Hart 247,248; John Jeffreys 242; John Field 143; George Keith 360; John Latimer Morton 294n; Joseph Pierce, jun. 324; Richard Richardson 131–132, 360; Thomas Salter 378; Richard Scoryer 221, 323, 360; John Sharp 380; Christopher Taylor 360; William Tomlinson 132; John Wall 361; John Withers 377
  schoolmistresses, named: Trafford, Rachael 328; Elizabeth Brady 380; Edith Dymond 380; workhouse 367, 368, 370
  schools (specific) Ackworth 259; Ann Barclay's (girls) 361; Barking 360; Bull & Mouth 143, 360; Bunhill (British School) 334; Croydon 324, 327, 379–80; Devonshire House 81, 131–32, 187, 361; Friends' School (Clerkenwell/Islington Rd/Croydon) 75, 194, 327, 361–80; Gracechurch St 361; Horslydown 361; Islington Road 327, 375–79; Long Acre 247, 248; Longford 292; Park, Southwark 221; Ratcliff 361; Sabbath school, Westminster 244; Shacklewell (girls) 132, 360; Southwark (Horslydown, Park) 221, 361; Theobalds 360; Tottenham 200, 302, 303, 307, 360, 361; Waltham 297, 360; Wandsworth 294n, 323, 360; Westminster 242, 244, 247; workhouse (*see also* Friends School) 75, 194, 361–74
  times 76, 376
  Six Weeks Meeting and 118, 131–32
  teacher training 323, 360, 370, 380
  William Weston bequest 185n
science: John Bellers' proposals 362
scientists: Richard Low Beck xxiv; William Allen 150; Luke Howard 150; Joseph Lister xxiv; Joseph Jackson Lister xxiv
Scoryer, Richard: school at Wandsworth 221, 323, 360; continued 294n
Scotland: Elizabeth Richardson visits 293
Scott, Mary 263
Scripture: *see* Bible
seating (benches/forms): *see also* galleries, standing 169, 219, 224, 291, 298
  arrangement 125, 172, 193–94
  for children 269
  design 264
  for meeting in street 173, 318
  not used at first; *see also* standing 135
  Peter the Great's bench 223
  removed by soldiers 217, 219, 268
  without backs 178, 313
Second-Day Morning Meeting: *see* Morning Meeting
sects 8–17
Sedbergh, F. Howgill in 21
Seebohn, Benjamin 149
Seekers 40n, 178
seizure of goods: *see* distraint
select meetings: *see* representative meetings
Separatists 115, 121
sermon, William Dewsbery's last 159

servants
- Bibles, provision of 84
- caretakers/cleaning 206, 277
- doorkeepers 161, 206, 300, 351; Thomas Ball, Devonshire House xxvii
- employment 48, 87, 351, 366, 368n; deserting service 119; dismissed on becoming Quakers 42
- housekeeper, Islington Road School 378
- at meetings 201, 204; quarterly monthly meetings, to edify 186, 227, 253, 280
- named: Thomas Ball xxvii; husband of Sarah Blackbury 262; Ellinor Cart 182; Elizabeth Carter 206
- plainness, query on 56
- removal certificates 384
- wages 105, 208
- workhouse: staff 375n; placement 366, 368n

settlement, rules of (*see also* membership; poor; residence) 79, 123, 130, 185, 208
Sewel, William 45n, 159, 178
sewing at workhouse 367, 368, 369–70
sewing instructor: Ellwood, Ann Mercy 370
Shacklewell: girls' school 132, 360
Shacklewell: MM boundaries 171,
Shad, Gabriel, informer 198
Shadwell, fire (1682) 101, 271
Shapton, Abraham: Wanstead 275
Sharp, John 380
Sharples, Isaac, at Gracechurch St **156**
shattering of sects 8, 15
Shaw's wife 225
Shear Lane: MM boundary 197, 249
sheep and cattle, at burial grounds 333, 335
sheriffs 152, 176
Sherlow, William, Interval Friend 180
Sherwin, John and Sarah, legacy to SWM 109n
Shewen, Ann 301
Shewen, William of Bermondsey 37, 215, 226
  move to Enfield 235
Shillitoe, Thomas 304, 307
Ship Inn, Southwark 127
Ship Yard, Tottenham 307
Ship, The, Fenchurch St: William Mead 177
ships, deaths and overcrowding 121, 330
shipwrights (Ratcliff) 271
shoemakers: "a poor" 182; John Otter 267
shoemaking, at workhouse 373
shops, holidays: *see* times and seasons
Shoreditch: collections in 183, 184
  MM boundaries 171

shutters for women's room, Jordans 357
sick, care for 346, 348, 349, 365
  infirm poor, at workhouse 368n
signs and portents 39, 141, 202
  naked as a sign (S. Eccles) xviii, 142, 276
  signal judgments on persecutors 54
Sikes, Gilbert (Gobert) of Hackney 37
silence: in worship (q.v.) 20, 32, 247, 319
Silesian widow, relief for 131
silk manufacturers: Peter Bedford 189; John Row 189
silk winding, at workhouse 364
Simms, John 182
simplicity: *see* plainness
Simpson, William 173, 268, 282
Sims, Dilwyn 388
Sion College 74n
sitting: *see* seating
Six Weeks Meeting (*see also* discipline; disownment; Quarterly Meeting) 70, 73, 91–133
  and burial grounds 236, **301**, 333, 334
  funds: Devonshire House contributions 183–84; quota 100, 102–03, 107–12, 184, 208, 210; rents xxv; school income to SWM 379 ; workhouse, lack of 372
  history x, xxiii
  locations: at Brewers Hall 143; at Gracechurch St 144
  and meeting houses (q.v.): Barking 275; Devonshire House 168; Epping 297; Gracechurch St 145–46; Hammersmith 262; Holloway 264; Horslydown 218; Long Acre 247; Peckham 224; Peel 194, 195; Plaistow 276, 277; Ratcliff 269; South Mimms 299; Southwark Old Park 220; Stoke Newington 158, 211; Tottenham 302, burial ground plan 301; Wanstead 275; Wheeler St xx, 166 Winchmore Hill 300
  meetings: Devonshire House, popularity 178; Deptford MM 223; Mill Hill 309; Longford MM subsidy to 289; Peel, dispute 208–09; Peel and Hendon 308; Ratcliff secession 273; Westminster, ministers 257
  members and staff: Thomas Ball, doorkeeper's duties xxvii; William Beck (rent collector / surveyor) xxv; Ellin Claipoole 31n; Gerrard Roberts 145–46

contd

Six Weeks Meeting *contd*
  Plaistow Home for Ancient Friends 375
  records **xx**, **301**, 337
  school, income to SWM 379
  workhouse 364, 365, 369n, 372
Skeats, Herbert *History* xiv, 140
skeletons (*see also* burial grounds) 236
Skelton, John 200
slander 50
slavery: campaign against 394; John Otter sent to Virginia as slave 267
sleeping arrangements, workhouse 364
sleeping in meeting 78, 117, 125, 204, 382
small meetings, alternating 304–05
Smee, Sylvia: Devonshire House etching **167**
Smith [surname] 388
Smith, Frederick 376,
Smith, Isaac 300
Smith, John, legacy for Bunhill upkeep 333n
Smith, Joseph (fd of T. Scattergood) 271n
Smith, Joseph, legacy to SWM 110n
Smith, Joseph (bibliographer) xiv, 259, 362n
Smith, Richard 327
Smith, Thomas, legacy to SWM 109n
smiths: "old Patin" 230
smoking: *see* tobacco
Snail, Tower St: Humphery Bach/Bates 36
Society of Friends, organisation of (*see also* business meetings; discipline; Fox, George; monthly meetings; quarterly meetings; Six Weeks Meeting; Two Weeks Meeting) xvi, 40 106–07
soldiers (train-bands, troops: *see also* arms; militia; peace testimony)
  abuse by, New Palace Yard 240
  become Friends: Amor Stoddart 19, 266
  Sir Richard Brown's 35, 139
  conscription (James Goodwin) 272
  Cromwell's 12
  destruction of Ratcliff by 163
  disrupt meetings: Bull & Mouth 139; Gracechurch St 152–54; Hammersmith 262; Peel 202; Ratcliff 268; Southwark (Horslydown) 216–17, (Old Park) 219–20; Wheeler St 173;
  and Fifth Monarchists 137
  quartered in meeting houses: Devonshire House169–170; Savoy 252; Southwark (Old Park) 219–21
  Peter the Great's (Frederickstadt) 239
  take over Peel 198

Somerset 59
Somerset House, records [now at National Archives] 279–80, 305
South Mimms (Mimms) 299, 304, 305, 309
South Sea Bubble 184
Southwark, meetings 37, 215; fire engines kept 234; marriages at [*table after* 88];"retired" 125, 226; weekday 226
  Horslydown 216–19, 226, 292; as Cambrian Chapel **220**; joined with Park 226; origins: (Widow Webb's) 37, 215, 216, 343 ["Jebb", *sic*]
  Park, Old (Ewer St) 219–21; building fund (SWM) 101, 107; origins 215
  Park, New (Worcester St or Redcross St) **220**, **221**, 221–23; burial ground 220, 221–22, 225, 236–38; sale of 222, 226
Southwark (or Horslydown) MM 71, 214–39
  boundary 71
  and Deptford MM 223
  disorderly walkers 88
  ministers and elders [*table after* 78]
  records 46, 217; MSS 235
  schools 361
  Six Weeks Mtg 99, 102, 104, 107, 110, 111
  women's mtg (not held) 353
  and workhouse 371
Southwark: Nonconformists 214; Ship Inn 127
Sowle, Andrew 342n
Sowle, Isaac 145
Sowle, Tace [Sowle] Raylton 145
Spaniard, relief for 131
Sparsfield, John 173
speaking: *see also* business meetings; discipline; ministry; speech 73–74, 98, 364
  at marriages 181–82
  women's 340
speculation, financial 78
speech, plainness 76–77, 382, 393
spinning: by poor and children 130, 317, 364, 367, 369, 376
Spirit (Holy) 15, 28
  and conservative Quakerism xvii
  at YM xxi
spirituality, history of xxxi
Spitalfields (Westbury St/Quaker St, Wheeler St) 36, 162, 163, 189
  Bedford Institute (q.v.) xvii
  collections in 183, 184
sports: 383; ninepins in prison 230–31; rowing 254; wrestling 26, 288

St: *alphabetised as* Saint
stables: *see* horses
Stacey [surname] 388, 390
Stacey, George sen. 200
Stacey, Mary 200
staff, workhouse/Islington Rd School (*see also* servants) 371, 372, 377–78
Staines 103, 284, **286**, 287, 289, **294**
  Dr Pope of 294
Staines MM, SWM representative 96
Stampers, Francis 165n
standing at meetings 73, 178, 193–94
  in prayer **xxvi**
  on stools 247
stationer's shop, Gracechurch St 161
statistics (*see also* membership; records and registers; tables) 32, 172, 249, 291
  attendance 201, 324
  burials 331
  elderly and children, workhouse 372
  marriages and disownments xxvi, 123
  membership 172, 201
  ministers and elders [*table after* 78]
  population xix, xxii, 32n
  sufferings xxii, 65, 267
Steel, Jonathan 327
steeple-houses: *see also* Church of England 281n; Anne Downer and 266,
Steevens, Mary 294
Stepney 26, 37, 266
  Ratcliff poor district boundary 273
Sterry family 150, 189
Sterry [surname] (two women) 389
Sterry, Anthony: legacy to SWM 110n
Sterry, Mary: legacy to SWM 110n, 328
Sterry, Richard: legacy to SWM 109n
Stevenson, Daniel 235
steward, workhouse: *see* workhouse
Stoakes, John 182
stocks (punishment): *see* sufferings
Stodart, Anne, on SWM 92
Stoddart, Amor [or Amos, *sic*] 19, 216, 266, 301, 332
Stodder, John, carpenter 193, 194
Stoke Newington (Newington) xxiii 148, 151, 152, 189, 389
  Beck family xxiv; William Beck and xxvi
  first meeting 211–13, **211**
  MM boundaries 197
  second meeting 157–59, **157**
  and Tottenham 302–3

Stokes, J, bidder to burials 206
Stone Bridge, Whitechapel Rd: MM boundary 171
stones, memorial: *see* burial grounds
stoning at Mitcham 324
stools, standing on 247
Storer, J. & H.S. engraving of Islington Road Schools **378**
Storm, Great (1703) 165, 274
Story, Thomas 40n, 58, 177, 239, 394
  on William Gibson 80
  satirised by James Hoskins 81
Stott, Widow [Mary] 360
Stoughton, John xiv
Strand: *see also* Savoy 245, 246, 249, 250, 258n
  Westminster MM poor relief district 257
  Worcester House 36, 223, 240, 249
Stratford 150, 275
Streatham, Cambs 14
street lighting: Cavendish Court 169; Little Almonry 249
street, meetings held in 165n, 173, 202, 251, 268
Strellett, John 327
strict observance (*see also* discipline) 77
Stringfellow, John 72
Stuart, Will 231
Sturge, family 150
Sturge, Clement Y., Ratcliff photo 276
Sturge, Samuel 235
Sturgess, Thomas 230
Styles, William 231
subscriptions (*see also* funds, contributions):
  for *London Friends' Meetings* xi, xxx–xxxi
substitutes (*see also* militia) 385
suburban residence: *see* residence
suburbs, poor in (Peel MM area) 208
sufferings (arrests; distraint; fines; persecutions): *see also* Acts of Parliament; courts; disturbance; justices; legal system; martyrdom; meetings; prisons; rude people; soldiers; tithes
  xviii, 392
  Charles II's reign 37–39, 62–65, 152
  Cromwell and 30, 31, 60
  distraint of goods (or "distress") 64, 153, 174, 198, 202, 263, 300
  G. Fox and 95
  fines, for meeting 35, 62–64,153, 216, 272, 299, 319; for refusing oath 198; unrecovered by Exchequer 83–84   *contd*

sufferings *contd*
   individuals (*see also* prisoners) John
      Bringhurst 342n; Isabel Buttery 343;
      John and Mary Elson 198
   James II and 337
   locations: Bull & Mouth 137–42; Croydon
      324; Devonshire House 173–74;
      Gracechurch St 153–54; Ham (Essex)
      276; Hammersmith 262; Horslydown
      216, 217; Kingston 311–12; Longford
      MM 292; Mile End Green 266–67; Peel
      200, 202–203; Ratcliff 268, 272; South
      Mimms 299; Waltham Abbey 296;
      Wandsworth 319; Westminster 251;
      Wheeler St 163; Winchmore Hill 300
   Meeting for *see* Meeting for Sufferings
   and ministry 395
   Parliament and 33, 65
   pillory and stocks 267, 342n
   records of **xv**, 43, 51, 56, 71n, 87, 97, 134;
      Joseph Besse's volumes 201; reports to
      Yearly Meeting from QMs 54
   relief for 130–31, 296, 347, 349
   statistics xxii
   transportation (banishment) 61, 62, 140,
      267, 330
   violence in 217, 251, 324
Suffolk, Mary K. rambling in 340
superstitious practices 228; alchemy 225
surgeons: John Goodson 130
   at workhouse 372
Surrey 311; G. Whitehead in 176
Surrey QM 317
   attempted unions of Croydon, Kingston,
      Wandsworth MMs 314, 319, 320
   Kingston MM transferred from 76
   and local meetings 316, 321–22, 326, 327;
      Croydon–Wandsworth dispute 319, 325
surveyor, Six Weeks Meeting xxv, xxix, 236
Swan Alley 35n
Swarthmoor: establishment of MMs 44
   G. Fox at 337
Swarthmore MSS 282n
Swift, Anne 293
Swift, Edward 283

tables: Disownment and Resignations 123;
   Marriages (bridegrooms) 90; Marriages
   (meetings) [*after* 88]; Ministers & Elders
   [*after* 78]
Taillor, Margaret 277

tailors: G. Latey 250–251; James Sargent, of
   Moorfields 191
   merchant tailors: John Oakley 162
   workhouse, tailoring at 373
Talbot, Thomas 288
talebearing 50, 382
talk, loose, about MM business 227
Tallack, William xiv, xv, xviii, 189
Talwin, Thomas 170, 172, 177, 374
   legacies 185n, 109n
tankard and salver, expenses at Peel 206
Tanner [surname] (woman) 225
Tanner, John 284
Tate's Place, Barking 274
Taylor, Adam xiv
taxes (*see also* excise, query on)
   MMs and SWM 101, 101, 102, 106, 112
   Gerrard Roberts for White Hart Court 146
Taylor, Christopher 132, 301, 360
Taylor, Cornelius 374
Taylor, John 151n
Taylor, Joseph 151n
Taylor (Taillor), Margaret 277
Taylor, Mary, widow 169
Taylor, Thomas 301
teaching: *see* schools
teeth 236
temperance: *see also* drink xxv, 260, 383, 384,
   394
Temple: MM boundaries 197, 249
tenants in meeting houses 164, 169, 242,
   243, 313, 318
tenements (*see also* almshouses)
   Bunhill 206, 333
   Horslydown 218
   Long Acre 247–48
   Old Park, Southwark 220
tents, meetings in 162
testimonies of denial: *see* disownments
testimonies to ministers deceased, at YM
   293, 294
Thames 202; MM boundaries 171, 197, 249;
   young men rowing on 254
Thames Ditton 314
thatch: Winchmore Hill 300
Theobalds (Tibbalds): ministers sent 321n
   school 360
Theydon Garnon 297
Thomas Apostles (St Thomas): Gerrard
   Roberts' 36
Thompson, George 250

"thou", use of (*see also* plainness) 5
Three Needle Alley, Moorfields 191
"Three Sarahs" 36
threshing (large public) meetings (*see also* meetings, public) 24–27, 32, 136, 240
Tibbalds: *see* Theobalds
Tidman, E. 226
times and seasons 355
  anniversaries/centenaries xx, 355
  holy days 76, 312; Whitsun xxi, 70, 355
  public rejoicing/fasts 385
  Sabbath observance 14, 20, 30
  school holidays 375n
  shops 312, 385
times of meetings (*see also* meetings; punctuality)
  meetings for business/discipline: Box Meeting 344 (and Women's Two Weeks) 351; Croydon MM 326; Devonshire House 181; Longford, on First Days 289; Morning Meeting 338, 340, 341; Peel MM 203, 205; QM 75, (two-day proposal) 76, (annually, Jordans) 355; Six Weeks Meeting 93, 104; Two Weeks Meeting 46; Westminster MM 252; Women's Two Weeks 351; Yearly Meeting, at Whitsuntide xxi, 70, 355
  times of meetings for worship – frequency: appointed meetings, Longford MM 291; QM report (1761) 382; smaller meetings less often, advantages 304–05; South Mimms 3/yr 299; Surrey (range of mtgs) 316; workhouse 346, 366
  fortnightly and other patterns: Brentford 287; Enfield 301; Harold('s) Hill 278; Staines, variable 284; Winchmore Hill 300; (alternating) Epping / Waltham Abbey 297; Mill Hill / Winchmore Hill / Mimms 309; Stoke Newington/ Tottenham 211, 302, 303
  quarterly: general meetings 50 (*see also* quarterly monthly meetings)
  weekly (where significant): Croydon 327, Esher 315; Tottenham 212
times of meetings for worship – hour of day: G. Fox on 124–25; QM and 71, (1761 report) 382, 385; Wandsworth various 320; within Westminster MM 248; Westminster Quarterly Monthly Meeting 253
  afternoon meetings 125: Croydon 324; Dev. Ho. 179; Dorking 316; Peel 203, 204; Ratcliff 272; Stoke Newington 213;Wanstead 275; Westminster 248, 254
  evening meetings: Devonshire House 179; Gracechurch St 148; Kingston 317; Peel 204; Southwark Park 226–27; Tottenham 303; Wapping 270
  night meetings (private, suppressed) 179
  week-day meetings: attendance encouraged 79, 125; Brentford 3rd days 287; Capel, monthly 316; Croydon 316, 324; Devonshire House 179; Dorking 316; Epping 297; Gracechurch St weekday evening 148; Hammersmith 263; Peel 204, (MM held after) 205; Ratcliff 271; Savoy 248; Southwark Park and Horslydown 226; Stoke Newington 158; Uxbridge 282n; Wandsworth 316; Wapping 270; Westminster 254, 271; Wheeler St 166, 179; workhouse 364
Tindall, family 150
tin-plate workers: Howard, Robert 331n,
tithes:(*see also* Church of England; sufferings) 31, 61, 136, 312, 319
  G. Fox on 51
  payment of 123, 288
  QM query on 55, 56, 383
  relief 178
title deeds 96, 192, 195
tobacco: smoking at workhouse 368, 369n
  at Surrey QM 322
toleration xviii, 152, 395
  James II and 65
  Toleration Act (1689; *see also* registering of meeting places) 65, 84, 178, 298
tombs: *see* burial grounds
Tomlinson, William, schoolmaster 132
Tooley Street: Compter prison 232
Tottenham 295, **301**, 302–304, 305
  burial ground: T.F. Ball xxix; plan **301**
  Richard Claridge at 200, 360
  and Stoke Newington 211, 212
Tottenham MM: *see also* Enfield MM 274, 295–307
  and Barking mtg house 275
  London and Middlesex QMs, union 75
  ministers and elders [*table after* 78]
  and schools 361, 379
  and Six Weeks Meeting 110, 111, 112
  and Uxbridge mtg house 286,
Tower Hamlets jurisdiction 266
Tower Hill 125, 183, 184; MM boundary 171

Tower of London: imprisonment in 267
  Sir J. Robinson governor 34, 37, 163, 266
Tower Street 36
Tower, Great (Savoy) 245
Townsend, Whitechapel: MM boundary 171
Townsend, Alice 277
Townsend, Deborah 200
Townsend, Elizabeth 200
Townsend, John 200
trade (*see also* occupations) 150, 175, 249;
  honesty in 384; inappropriate 76
Trafford, Rachael 328
train-bands: *see* soldiers
transport
  railways 166, 327, 329, 356
  stages 151
transportation (banishment): *see* sufferings
travelling ministers: *see* ministers
Travers, Rebecca 92, 128, 129, 324 351
treasurers (*see also* finance; funds)
  Southwark MM 232
trees 285, 334
Trefford, Rachel 129, 268
troops: *see* soldiers
Trott, Elizabeth 36, 240, 241, 251, 343
Truman & Co, brewers: Wheeler St 166
trusts
  Devonshire House 177, 185n
  and Meeting of Twelve 96
  QM and wills (q.v.) 71
  Yoakley's almshouses 182–83
Tsar: *see* Alexander I; Peter the Great
tub preachers **25**, 344
Tuke family 390
Tuke, Samuel: Hanwell Lunatic Asylum 158
Turner, Judge 63
Turnstile Alley: MM boundary 249
Twelve, Meeting of: *see* Meeting of Twelve
Two Brewers, Southwark 215
Two Weeks Meeting 70, 85–91, 143, 193–94, 353
  becomes Bull & Mouth MM 46, 91, 92
  E. Burrough and 42, 44, 346
  at Devonshire House 169
  Men's Two Weeks 351, 353
  stock 351, 352
  Women's 351, 353, 370, 373
  young men's pastimes 254

undertakers: George Leake 236
Unitarian views, disownment for 83

United Monthly Meeting of Kingston,
  Wandsworth and Croydon 314
Upper Ground: Thomas Hackleton's 215
Upperside, Leighton and, MM (Bucks) 356
Upton: Ham House 260
Uxbridge 282, 285–86, 287, **287,** 289, 290
  on route to Jordans 355
Uxbridge Fair, displaces Longford MM 289,
Uxbridge MM (*see also* Longford MM) 71

"Valiant Sixty" 44
Vandewall, family (Van de wall / Vandewald) 184, 358
Vandewall, Daniel 372
Vasse(s) (Vaux), Samuel 36, 347, 349
Vaston, James 177, 185n
Vaughan, [Robert Alfred] 395
Vaughton, John 131, 250, 253, 330
Venner, Thomas: Fifth Monarchist 34–35n, 137
ventilation: Ratcliff 269
vermin: workhouse children 373
Vincent, Lady 315
violence (*see also* sufferings)
  against women 230, 251
Virginia, transportation to 267
visitation of MMs, QM report (1761) 381
visiting ministers: *see* ministers
visits: by overseers 384, 386; to widows etc 118
volunteer defence corps: *see* militia
voting at business meetings (workhouse) 364

wages, for clerks (SWM) 100
Waite, Daniel 247
Wakefield, Priscilla 307
Walburton, Robert 212
Waldenfield, Samuel 120, 307
Wales 20; early monthly meeting 44
Walker, Adam, meeting in house of 215
Walker, Benjamin 235
Wall, John 81, 361
Walls, City: MM boundary 171
Waltham (Holy) Cross 296
Waltham Abbey 296–97, 305, 307
  with Barking MM, formerly 274
  boys' school 360
  G. Fox 295, 296
  and Tottenham 302
Waltham MM; from Essex QM, united with Enfield 297

Walthamstow 297
Walton on Thames 315
Walworth 37, 215
Wandsworth 178, 316, **317**, 318–25
　schools 221, 294n, 360, 374
　Surrey QM 317
Wandsworth MM 314, 318–25, 326–27
Wanstead 274, 275–276, 297
Wapping: 105, 269
　fire (1682) 101, 271
　marriages at, [*table after* 88]
war (*see also* militia; peace testimony) disownments for 123; threat of 151
Warboys (Hunts) 15
Warner, John 226, 372, 374n
Warner, Robert 380n
Warner, Simeon 225, 372
Warwick gaol, description (1815) 66n
washerwomen: use of Bunhill burial gd 333
washing, Islington Road School 376
washing machine, Islington Road School 376
water supply 4
Watling Street: Robert Dring's 19, 36
Watson, Jane, Irish minister 181
Watts, George 133, 331
wealth 390
　and Devonshire House MM 172
　Gracechurch St 150
weavers 183
　Dodman, Dennis 165;
　Mills, Benjamin 166
Webb, Maria, *Fells of Swarthmore* xiv, 331
Webb, Mary (Widow) 37, 215, 216, 343
　["Jebb", *sic*]
weddings: *see* marriage
Welch, William, SWM clerk 94
Wellclose: MM boundary 171
　Ratcliff poor district boundary 273
Wentworth St (Hope Court) 233
Wesley, John 394
Wesleyan Chapel, former (Holloway) 264
Wesleyans, Esher 328
West Ham (Westham, Ham) 276
West [surname] 107, 389, 390
West, J. Walter xxi
Westbury St (later Quaker St) 36, 162, 165, 166, 300
Westminster Abbey, Little Almonry lease from 242–43
　threshing mtg near 240,
Westminster (*see also* Savoy) 36

Little Almonry 241–43, 244, 248, barred by justices 251
New Palace Yard (Nicholas Bond) 223
Peter's Court, or Hemming's Row 243–44, 259; Alexander I 261, 265; Benjamin Bangs 268n; and Holloway building 264; James Hoskins of 81; marriages at [*table after* 88]; mtg arrangements 248, 271; Two Weeks rough minute books at 89
Westminster poor relief district 257
Westminster MM 71, 88, 185–86, 240–265
　boundaries 201, 210, 226, 249
　Bunhill, land at 332
　funerals at Peel 207–208
　Longford MM, union 282, 289
　ministers and elders [*table after* 78], 294n
　Six Weeks Meeting: disputes with 105, 121; quota 102, 104, 107, 110, 111, 112; representatives 99, 107, 111, 121
　no schools (1758) 361
　no women's meeting (1755) 354
Westmorland, early monthly meeting 44
Weston [surname] 107
Weston Common 314
Weston, William 177; bequest 185n
Westwood, William 177
Weybridge 315
Wheeler Street 71, 162–66, 169, 179
　disturbances at xix, 178
　falls down xx, 166
　marriages at [*table after* 88]
　John Okeley's house 300
Wheeler Street MM (later Devonshire House MM) 88, 99, 179
　boundaries 171
Wheeler, Granville: freehold, Wheeler St 166
white, wearing of (Joseph Rule) 359
White, Elinor 313
White, Winifred xxiii
White Hart Court *see* Gracechurch Street
White Lion, Croydon 327
White Lion Prison, Samuel Fisher dies in 216
Whitechapel 175, 230, 347
　burial ground 334–35, **335**
　MM boundaries 171
Whitecross Street 36, 250
　burial ground entrance 333
Whitehead, Ann(e) (former Downer) 19, 92, 129, 199, 266, 344, 347n, 352
Whitehead, George xxiii, xxvi, 80, 141, 174–77, 188, 351　　　　　*contd*

460

Whitehead, George *contd*
  on G. Fox 52, 330; funeral of 156
  Gracechurch St, preacher 153
  and informers xxii
  on G. Latey 251
  Mill Hill 309
  Norwich 20
  at Parliament 36, 139n
  Pietists, relief for 131
  and QM advice against speculation 78
  Six Weeks Meeting 92
  soldiers at mtg houses 217, 219, 220, 252
  Wheeler St 165n
Whitehead, Thomas 200
Whitehorse St (Whithorse St): Ratcliff poor district boundary 272
Whitfield, George 394
Whithouse, John "a madman" 228
Whiting, John 258, 259
Whitrow, Joan, books not approved 119
Whitsuntide, for Yearly Meeting xxi, 70, 355
widows: *see also* orphans
  accommodation: *see also* almshouses 169, 193, 246
  G. Fox on 348
  monthly meetingss to visit 118
  relief 129, 182, 349
  remarriage 48,
  Six Weeks Meeting and 100, 101, 115
wifebeating 230
Wigham, Hannah, Irish minister 181
wigs: 77, 117
  at workhouse 372n
Wilkin(s), Henry 381, 388
Wilkinson, John 58, 261, 265, 389
Wilkinson, Thomas 388
Willet, Joseph 225
William III: toleration 178, 220, 392
  unusual suffering under 272
Willis, Mary 253
wills (*see also* legacies; records)
  advice on 119–20, 312n
  intestacy, G. Fox on 48
  Mtg of Twelve to keep 96, 100
  QM, recorded by 71
  William Weston's, disputed 185n
Willson, J.J., drawing of Yearly Meeting (1860) **xii**
Wilson, Isaac 381, 388
Winch, William 282
Winchmore Hill 162n, 260, 295, 296, 299, **300**

frequency 305,
  and Mill Hill 309
  and Tottenham 303
Windmill Hill: MM boundaries 197
windows: improved ventilation, Ratcliff 269
wine: *see* drink
wine-coopers: Roberts, Gerrard 145n, 336,
wine trade: Becks xxiv, xxv
Wise, Thomas, jun x
Withers, Ann and John 200, 377
Withers, Ellen Hayes, later Ball xxvii
women: *see also* midwives; widows
  blood poured by, at St Paul's 141
  Box Meeting 144, 147, 196, 206, 261n, 344–48; G. Whitehead legacy 177; and Women's Two-Weeks Mtg 348–49, 351
  Devonshire House Women's Mtg Ho 172
  dress 77, 117, 227
  education and schools 132, 180n, 323, 360, 361
  joint meetings with men 252, 386
  Jordans, women's room 357
  Kingston burial ground, upkeep 313
  meetings xxiii, 44, 88, 125, 248, 353
  ministers and elders 227, 338, 340, 341, 344
  galleries 193–94, 169, 227
  Monthly Meetings 121, 382, 387; Croydon 327; Devonshire House 180; Peel 205–06; Plaistow 277–78; Southwark **221**, 235n; Tottenham 307; Wandsworth 319–20; Westminster 254, 256
  and poor relief 43, 87, 257
  poor women: *see also* Box Meeting; widows 221
  Quarterly Meetings 74, 354
  seating 125, 193–4
  Six Weeks Meeting 92
  speaking 340
  violence against 230, 251
  "Women's Meeting, The" 121, 129
  Women's Two-Weeks Meeting 206, 345, 346, 348–49, 351, 370, 373
  Yearly Meeting 353, **354**
Wood Street, fight in 35
Wood, family 150
Woodcock, Jane 245–246, 257, 343
Woodcock, William 36, 240, 244–45, 249
Woodford 276
Woodward, Jacob, legacy to SWM 109n
wool trade 222

Walthamstow 297
Walton on Thames 315
Walworth 37, 215
Wandsworth 178, 316, **317**, 318–25
  schools 221, 294n, 360, 374
  Surrey QM 317
Wandsworth MM 314, 318–25, 326–27
Wanstead 274, 275–276, 297
Wapping: 105, 269
  fire (1682) 101, 271
  marriages at, [*table after* 88]
war (*see also* militia; peace testimony) disownments for 123; threat of 151
Warboys (Hunts) 15
Warner, John 226, 372, 374n
Warner, Robert 380n
Warner, Simeon 225, 372
Warwick gaol, description (1815) 66n
washerwomen: use of Bunhill burial gd 333
washing, Islington Road School 376
washing machine, Islington Road School 376
water supply 4
Watling Street: Robert Dring's 19, 36
Watson, Jane, Irish minister 181
Watts, George 133, 331
wealth 390
  and Devonshire House MM 172
  Gracechurch St 150
weavers 183
  Dodman, Dennis 165;
  Mills, Benjamin 166
Webb, Maria, *Fells of Swarthmore* xiv, 331
Webb, Mary (Widow) 37, 215, 216, 343 ["Jebb", *sic*]
weddings: *see* marriage
Welch, William, SWM clerk 94
Wellclose: MM boundary 171
  Ratcliff poor district boundary 273
Wentworth St (Hope Court) 233
Wesley, John 394
Wesleyan Chapel, former (Holloway) 264
Wesleyans, Esher 328
West Ham (Westham, Ham) 276
West [surname] 107, 389, 390
West, J. Walter xxi
Westbury St (later Quaker St) 36, 162, 165, 166, 300
Westminster Abbey, Little Almonry lease from 242–43
  threshing mtg near 240,
Westminster (*see also* Savoy) 36

Little Almonry 241–43, 244, 248, barred by justices 251
New Palace Yard (Nicholas Bond) 223
Peter's Court, or Hemming's Row 243–44, 259; Alexander I 261, 265; Benjamin Bangs 268n; and Holloway building 264; James Hoskins of 81; marriages at [*table after* 88]; mtg arrangements 248, 271; Two Weeks rough minute books at 89
Westminster poor relief district 257
Westminster MM 71, 88, 185–86, 240–265
  boundaries 201, 210, 226, 249
  Bunhill, land at 332
  funerals at Peel 207–208
  Longford MM, union 282, 289
  ministers and elders [*table after* 78], 294n
  Six Weeks Meeting: disputes with 105, 121; quota 102, 104, 107, 110, 111, 112; representatives 99, 107, 111, 121
  no schools (1758) 361
  no women's meeting (1755) 354
Westmorland, early monthly meeting 44
Weston [surname] 107
Weston Common 314
Weston, William 177; bequest 185n
Westwood, William 177
Weybridge 315
Wheeler Street 71, 162–66, 169, 179
  disturbances at xix, 178
  falls down xx, 166
  marriages at [*table after* 88]
  John Okeley's house 300
Wheeler Street MM (later Devonshire House MM) 88, 99, 179
  boundaries 171
Wheeler, Granville: freehold, Wheeler St 166
white, wearing of (Joseph Rule) 359
White, Elinor 313
White, Winifred xxiii
White Hart Court *see* Gracechurch Street
White Lion, Croydon 327
White Lion Prison, Samuel Fisher dies in 216
Whitechapel 175, 230, 347
  burial ground 334–35, **335**
  MM boundaries 171
Whitecross Street 36, 250
  burial ground entrance 333
Whitehead, Ann(e) (former Downer) 19, 92, 129, 199, 266, 344, 347n, 352
Whitehead, George xxiii, xxvi, 80, 141, 174–77, 188, 351 *contd*

Whitehead, George *contd*
  on G. Fox 52, 330; funeral of 156
  Gracechurch St, preacher 153
  and informers xxii
  on G. Latey 251
  Mill Hill 309
  Norwich 20
  at Parliament 36, 139n
  Pietists, relief for 131
  and QM advice against speculation 78
  Six Weeks Meeting 92
  soldiers at mtg houses 217, 219, 220, 252
  Wheeler St 165n
Whitehead, Thomas 200
Whitehorse St (Whithorse St): Ratcliff poor district boundary 272
Whitfield, George 394
Whithouse, John "a madman" 228
Whiting, John 258, 259
Whitrow, Joan, books not approved 119
Whitsuntide, for Yearly Meeting xxi, 70, 355
widows: *see also* orphans
  accommodation: *see also* almshouses 169, 193, 246
  G. Fox on 348
  monthly meetingss to visit 118
  relief 129, 182, 349
  remarriage 48,
  Six Weeks Meeting and 100, 101, 115
wifebeating 230
Wigham, Hannah, Irish minister 181
wigs: 77, 117
  at workhouse 372n
Wilkin(s), Henry 381, 388
Wilkinson, John 58, 261, 265, 389
Wilkinson, Thomas 388
Willet, Joseph 225
William III: toleration 178, 220, 392
  unusual suffering under 272
Willis, Mary 253
wills (*see also* legacies; records)
  advice on 119–20, 312n
  intestacy, G. Fox on 48
  Mtg of Twelve to keep 96, 100
  QM, recorded by 71
  William Weston's, disputed 185n
Willson, J.J., drawing of Yearly Meeting (1860) **xii**
Wilson, Isaac 381, 388
Winch, William 282
Winchmore Hill 162n, 260, 295, 296, 299, **300**

frequency 305,
and Mill Hill 309
and Tottenham 303
Windmill Hill: MM boundaries 197
windows: improved ventilation, Ratcliff 269
wine: *see* drink
wine-coopers: Roberts, Gerrard 145n, 336,
wine trade: Becks xxiv, xxv
Wise, Thomas, jun x
Withers, Ann and John 200, 377
Withers, Ellen Hayes, later Ball xxvii
women: *see also* midwives; widows
  blood poured by, at St Paul's 141
  Box Meeting 144, 147, 196, 206, 261n, 344–48; G. Whitehead legacy 177; and Women's Two-Weeks Mtg 348–49, 351
  Devonshire House Women's Mtg Ho 172
  dress 77, 117, 227
  education and schools 132, 180n, 323, 360, 361
  joint meetings with men 252, 386
  Jordans, women's room 357
  Kingston burial ground, upkeep 313
  meetings xxiii, 44, 88, 125, 248, 353
  ministers and elders 227, 338, 340, 341, 344
  galleries 193–94, 169, 227
  Monthly Meetings 121, 382, 387; Croydon 327; Devonshire House 180; Peel 205–06; Plaistow 277–78; Southwark **221**, 235n; Tottenham 307; Wandsworth 319–20; Westminster 254, 256
  and poor relief 43, 87, 257
  poor women: *see also* Box Meeting; widows 221
  Quarterly Meetings 74, 354
  seating 125, 193-4
  Six Weeks Meeting 92
  speaking 340
  violence against 230, 251
  "Women's Meeting, The" 121, 129
  Women's Two-Weeks Meeting 206, 345, 346, 348–49, 351, 370, 373
  Yearly Meeting 353, **354**
Wood Street, fight in 35
Wood, family 150
Woodcock, Jane 245–246, 257, 343
Woodcock, William 36, 240, 244–45, 249
Woodford 276
Woodward, Jacob, legacy to SWM 109n
wool trade 222

wool-carding, at workhouse 373
Wooldridge, Humphrey 200
woollen, burials in 118
Woolley, Mary 92
Woolwich 224
Worcester House, Strand 36, 223, 240, 249
Worcester St, Southwark 36, 221–2
Wordsworth, William, T. Wilkinson and 390
workhouse, Clerkenwell (*see also* schools) 75, 107, 130, 184, 361–75
  ministers' horses at 127, 364
  rules 365
  Six Weeks Meeting and 107
  steward xxiii, 366–67n, 369n, 375n; restyled master 377
  G. Whitehead legacy 177
  worship at Peel 194
workhouse, Little Almonry next to 241
workhouse, Stoke Newington premises 213
worship (*see also* meetings, for worship) 2
  accounts of, to Morning Meeting 338
  at meetings for business/discipline 74, 252, 340
  Quarterly MM 186
Wren, Sir Christopher 217
wrestling 288; E. Burrough preaching at 26
Wright, Joseph, purchases Wanstead 275
Wright, Nathaniel 255
writings: *see* literature, manuscripts, records
Wyeth, Joseph 80
Wyld, William 299

Yanworth (Cumberland), T. Wilkinson of 388
Yard Room, Barking 278
Yates, Benjamin 196, 207
Yates, G., engravings of Horslydown and New Park **220, 221**
Yates, Sarah 36, 196, 343
Yeames, Frederick xiii
Yeardley, John 159
Yearly Meeting **xii**, xiv, xxxi
  appeals to: Hannah Barnard 83; Elias Bockett 80; Thomas Foster 83; John Hewlett 82; George Keith 120
  collections at 350, 351
  development of 41, 53, 70, 91–92
  William Dewsbury at 159
  and discipline: (YM 1751) 188; (YM 1755) 248, 382–84; (YM 1760) 57, 235, 259, 381
  doorkeepers 78
  Epistles 83, 172

  G. Fox and 59, 295
  Herts QM and Enfield MM 298
  location for 146, 170
  ministers: deceased 293; Ministers and Elders, YM of 82, 338, 341; travelling 356
  and Morning Meeting 113, 338, 341
  QM and 56–57, 72, 79, 188n, 298
  queries at 54–57
  records 337
  representatives 55, 58, 120, 124
  schoolmasters at 360
  Settlement, Rules of (1737) 123, 208
  Six Weeks Meeting and 91, 120
  Surrey QM (q.v.), union of MMs in 320, 326
  Uxbridge meeting house 285
  Whitsuntide xxi, 70, 355
  and women's meetings 180n, 353–54
  Women's YM 354
yeomen 258, 274, 359
Yoakley, Mary 233
Yoakley, Michael 177
  almshouses 158, 182–183, 233
Yoakley, Thomas 92, 267, 270
Yonge, Ralph 230
York, Duke of (*see also* James II) 241
Yorkshire: early monthly meeting 44
  Friends from 21–23, 29, 158, 159
young people: *see also* children
  arrested 267
  carrying coffins 118
  cohabiting 128
  education 360–380
  instruction 227, 291–92, 382–3, 384
  at meeting 125, 148, 276
  at MM/QM 125, 186, 227, 252–3, 386–7
  second generation Quakers 122
Young Pretender, city defences against 169

Zach, Thomas 114
Zachary, family 359

www.ingramcontent.com/pod-product-compliance
Lightning Source LLC
Chambersburg PA
CBHW031700230426
43668CB00006B/57